*Time to Declare: Second Innings*

# Time to Declare

## Second Innings

David Owen

POLITICO'S

*Time to Declare* first published by Michael Joseph 1991

*Balkan Odyssey* first published by Victor Gollancz 1995

*The Hubris Syndrome* first published by Politico's Publishing 2007

*In Sickness and in Power* first published by Methuen Publishing 2008

This revised abridgement published 2009 by
Politico's Publishing, an imprint of
Methuen Publishing Ltd
8 Artillery Row
London
SW1P 1RZ

10 9 8 7 6 5 4 3 2 1

A CIP catalogue record for this book is available from the British Library.

ISBN 978-1-84275-236-4

Set in Bembo by SX Composing DTP, Rayleigh, Essex

Printed in the UK by CPI William Clowes Beccles NR34 7TL

# Contents

# Acknowledgements

My first thanks are to Jonathan Wadman, who has taken on the task of condensing and editing four books: *Time to Declare*, published by Michael Joseph in 1991; *Balkan Odyssey*, published by Victor Gollancz in 1995; *The Hubris Syndrome*, published by Politico's in 2007; and *In Sickness and in Power*, published by Methuen in 2008, the last two of which were edited by Jonathan. He has made the final decisions about what should be deleted and what retained. Apart from saving me from that difficult task I felt it was better to have a person from a younger generation to make the hard decisions about what was relevant from the past for the future. He has undertaken this task with tremendous enthusiasm and considerable skill and has ensured that this book reflects my thinking on political issues right up to July 2009. I am extremely grateful to him.

Each of the four books had their own acknowledgements and I do not intend to reproduce them here. But to those who helped me I hope they will feel that this edition brings back to life their work with a new and added relevance.

To Debs.
*Id est semper idem, amor.*

# 1

# Physician and politician

My great-grandfather knew Lloyd George. Alderman William
Llewellyn was chairman of Glamorgan County Council and chairman of the Bridgend bench of magistrates. A staunch Liberal, he was
a moving spirit in first the Mid-Glamorgan then the Ogmore
Divisional Liberal and Labour Party, of which he also became
chairman. To this day it is difficult for English people to understand
the high levels of support for the Labour Party among the
professional middle classes in Wales. This, I suspect, flows at least in
part from the bonds forged early in the last century between the
then strong Liberal Party and the newly emerging Labour Party.
More than once my great-grandfather was approached with a view
to representing the division in Parliament but he always declined. He
apparently disliked Asquith but liked Lloyd George. He was a leading
member of the Calvinistic Methodists and a deacon of the church at
Ogmore Vale. He had started life as a grocer and provision merchant
in Ogmore, having moved there from Llantrisant. Over the years The
Gwalia, as his shop was called, grew until it was described as 'a mecca
of the valley and neighbourhood'. But the old original shop was
retained. Today, that hundred-year-old building, painstakingly
dismantled and transported brick by brick, has been rebuilt at St
Fagans National History Museum in Cardiff. My great-grandfather
lived a prosperous life with a chauffeur-driven Daimler, a large house
and servants. When he died in 1923 at the age of seventy-three he
left an estate of £44,240 gross value, which in present day values is
over £1½ million.

Alderman Llewellyn had seven sons and one daughter. My
grandfather, who I always called Gear, was his second son, christened
George. He was a most remarkable man. He had been blind ever
since, as a boy of twelve, a pocket knife with which he had been

playing slipped out of his hands and cut one of his eyes. He lost the sight of that eye and in spite of all the care and skill with which he was treated, the other eye became infected and total blindness followed. His father searched high and low, and eventually found the only place in the country where blind students were prepared for university – at Powyke near Worcester. There, as far as possible, he lived the life of a normal schoolboy, playing cricket with a bell inside the ball so that the boys, though blind, could hit it and even catch it in the field. He became expert in Braille and took a degree at Cambridge, followed by a doctorate in Dublin. The Bible in Braille occupied a whole wall in his library. I can almost smell them now, those big volumes with their thick brown pages balanced on his knee. Aged six, I would sit on the arm of the chair while he passed his delicate fingers lightly over the raised dots and read out one of his favourite passages.

Gear taught me to read, often from editorials in *The Times*, listening carefully as I attempted to pronounce the difficult words and, when necessary, spelling them out. In the winter and spring of 1945 we walked together down from his rectory in Llandow, in the Vale of Glamorgan, to church, where he would read morning service and I would go to the village school. Living in Llandow I started to learn Welsh, and Gear, who spoke Welsh fluently and listened to the news on the radio in Welsh, would help me. It was an enchanting period. In church he conducted the whole service himself, reading the lessons as well as preaching, and people were amazed to find he could read with such ease and rapidity. He was also a good musician, playing the piano with some skill. He had for many years coached mature students for university and one of these, a local miner, went on to become the Bishop of Bath and Wells. I still feel Gear's influence on me. Rarely have I taken any important decision in my life before asking myself what he might have done in the same circumstances.

Gear's elder brother, Tom, took over the family business, eventually leaving it in his will to the longest-serving employees. Mr Tom, as he was called, was described by someone who worked there as a short rotund man, with a beaming face, very blustery of speech, like a character from Dickens. I met him once as a small boy and can only remember his vast tummy, his cheerfulness and swollen legs. His brother Dill, who developed tuberculosis and was unable to follow a profession, also worked for their father. Among the other brothers, David became a solicitor in Bridgend, William a mining engineer and Beve a doctor in public health. The only daughter, Elizabeth, married a clergyman.

The brother whose career most closely paralleled my own was Edgar. He was a family doctor in Splott, which is an area of Cardiff then dominated by the steel works. He was a great character and adored by his patients. After the war he became infuriated by the politicians on the city council and so decided to join his wife, who was already a Ratepayer councillor. He was elected in 1951. A photograph of him electioneering in a pony and trap, bedecked in a massive rosette, shows the first combination of doctor-politician in the family's history. His wife Jenny, who had first stood and won as a Ratepayer in 1946, was a strikingly good-looking woman and a considerable character. She was the first person in eighteen years to beat the Labour candidate in her ward. She stood again in 1949 and won and then lost her seat three years later. The wish to be an independent in local government and to stand against party politics was later mirrored by my mother and, some will say, by me too.

My mother, Molly, was half Welsh. She was born in 1910 in Gilfach Goch and died aged ninety in Plymouth. While Gear was wholly Welsh her mother, Elizabeth Phillipe, was Irish. Granny Llew's family name was Sealy, from County Cork. Her mother had eloped with a wandering German-Swiss minstrel, apparently a great charmer called Phillipe. He had been at a Jesuit school, preparing for the priesthood, but had broken away in his late teens and joined a touring German band.

My father, John Owen, was born in 1907 in Glyneath and died aged eighty-seven in Plymouth. He was the eldest son of a Merchant Navy captain whose family was in shipping in Penarth, and who had tragically died in an accident on his ship during the First World War, when my father was still very young. Because of my own love of the sea I have always wanted to know more about him. He used to fascinate my father and his brother with stories from all over the world. One story was of navigating his ship through the Magellan Straits when the relevant charts had been lost, no mean feat of navigation. My father went to Brecon College and then to Cardiff

University, to start his medical studies, followed by St Mary's Hospital, London.

I did not know my father's mother, always called Granny O, anywhere near as well as Granny Llew, I think probably because she never got on very well with my mother. Her father, my paternal great-grandfather, Dr Morris, had been a noted and fiery Welsh Congregationalist minister. He spent some time 'hot gospelling' in Plymouth in the state of Pennsylvania in the USA.

Members of my family describe themselves as 'of the blood' and, as my family tree shows, my blood is three-quarters Welsh with a little Irish and German-Swiss to liven it up. I was born into this passionate Celtic family on 2 July 1938. Appeasement was at its height that summer and two months after my birth, the Prime Minister, Neville Chamberlain, returned from Munich claiming 'peace in our time'. My mother used to refer contemptuously to Chamberlain waving 'that silly bit of paper'. Father had come down to live in Plympton to start in medical practice a year before my parents married in December 1934. My sister Susan continues to live near Plymouth, in Newton Noss, a fishing village on the river Yealm. So I am both a West Countryman and a Welshman.

Neither of my parents before the war was in the slightest bit political. Yet perhaps because Plymouth's social life was dominated by the Royal Navy families who were their friends, they did not approve of the activities of Nancy Astor, then the MP for Plymouth Sutton and a key figure in the Cliveden set. This was named after her country house, where she and her friends planned the appeasement of Adolf Hitler. My father had gone into the Territorial Army in 1936, as much for the social life as anything else. By 1938, when I was born in Plympton, my parents were waiting for a war that seemed inevitable. My mother recalls an almost forced gaiety as they milked the last few months, sensing that their pleasant way of life was going to end.

Plympton was then a small town, five miles from Plymouth's city centre. A few miles to the north lay the edge of Dartmoor, and a few miles to the south the Devon coast and the river Yealm. The old saying that 'Plympton was a borough town when Plymouth was a furry down' is literally true. Long before Plymouth existed, Plympton had a priory, dating from Saxon times, and a castle which was one of the seats of the Redvers, Earls of Devon. Plympton was the main port in the area, and records of cargoes of slate exist from the year 1178. But the silting of the river Plym from the tin streaming valleys on Dartmoor meant that the Laira estuary and the creek up to Plympton became progressively shallower. Sutton Pool and the fishing village of Sutton at the mouth of the Plym became a more attractive port. Plympton was so worried about losing its maritime trade to Plymouth that it insisted on being made a stannary town along with three other Devon towns, Tavistock, Ashburton and Chagford. The growth of the port of Plymouth, however, could not be stopped. By 1334 Sutton was paying more to the Crown than all the Cornish ports put together. Plymouth finally won its independence and its self-government with the granting of a borough charter in 1439.

The war was a much more traumatic experience for my father than he ever admitted and the memory of being evacuated by ship from France, the shelling, the burnt-out tanks and all the horror of the desert war in north Africa haunted him throughout his life. When the war ended he was a lieutenant-colonel, commanding a convalescent hospital in Rome. Mother had not seen him for three years when he was eventually demobbed in Taunton in October 1945. Immediately afterwards they came with my sister to take me out from school for the weekend. I walked up to a strange man with a moustache, shook him by the hand and he said, 'What's your name?'

'Owen, sir.'

'In that case, I'm your father.'

At the age of seven I could not recognise my own father.

Looking back on the war, my mother was amazed that she never doubted for one moment that we would win. When I began to read the history of those years, and realised the grave risk of invasion, I was staggered that people like my mother were not more frightened and that their fear was not transmitted to us children. I can never remember having nightmares about the war, and that is a remarkable testimony to the way the bombing and news of casualties was handled by those around me. We were bombed in Newport and then lived near Abergavenny, my mother having returned to work in the Welsh valleys in the school dentistry service.

Friends in Plymouth kept us very aware of the devastation of the city. In two intense raids on 20 and 21 March 1941 and in five fearful attacks in April a rain of destruction fell on the city with thousands of high-explosive bombs and tens of thousands of incendiaries. The devastation by blast and fire meant that Plymouth was the worst-blitzed city in the country. Our house was not affected, but when we returned in 1945 not a single part of the city, industrial, business or residential, had escaped the bombing. The city council bravely decided to plan for a new city actually during the war and they asked the town planner Patrick Abercrombie to draw up plans so that building could start immediately peace came. The rebuilding of Plymouth is an abiding childhood memory. Each year the ruins shrank and buildings grew. There were endless road diversions and a sense of a city being reconstructed out of the ashes. That experience gave me a fellow feeling for other cities bombed in Europe. In particular it explains why I always identified with the city of Berlin.

In the general election of 1945 Plymouth voted in three new Labour members of Parliament. The ousted Devonport MP was Leslie Hore-Belisha of Belisha Beacon fame. He held the seat first as a Liberal then as a National Liberal. In the 1935 election, as a member of the National Coalition, he had argued that, in the name of true Liberalism, Liberals should vote against Isaac Foot in the Bodmin constituency. Isaac Foot was a prominent West Country Liberal. He was a leading solicitor in the city, a Methodist lay preacher, a bibliophile and a world authority on Oliver Cromwell. He had been an MP for only a few years. No one in the West Country was neutral about Isaac Foot nor, indeed, about the entire Foot family. You loved them or you hated them. After being defeated, a furious Isaac Foot hired Devonport Guildhall and staged a full-scale denunciation of Hore-Belisha's political record, which just goes to show that hell hath no fury like a Foot scorned, something I too was to experience.

In 1940 Hore-Belisha resigned from the wartime Cabinet after losing the confidence of the Army chiefs. In 1945 he was defending Devonport as a National Independent, having become virtually a Conservative. It was fate that he should lose, by just over 2,000 votes, to Michael Foot, Isaac's son. He had been the member of Parliament from 1923 to 1945, the longest-serving MP in Devonport's history until I surpassed his record in 1988.

It was not until I began to research my family background that I realised that Lloyd George had cast a long shadow over all my family's political attitudes. Far from coming from a non-political family as I used to claim, I now recognise that there was considerable family involvement in local politics. Moreover, the family has had a surprisingly large number of clerics and doctors, which has probably had its influence as well. Winston Churchill, speaking in March 1945 in the House of Commons on Lloyd George's death and on the eve of his own great victory, said that when historians surveyed the first quarter of the twentieth century they would see how far the history of Britain, in peace and in war, had been moulded by the life of this one man. Undoubtedly he was the greatest single political influence on my maternal great-grandfather and also my grandfather Gear.

This political tradition did not involve only my mother's side of the family. It was also present in my father's. Two of his relatives were Lord Mayors of Cardiff – Sir Illtyd Thomas, who was his grandmother's first cousin, and Alderman Lewis, his great-great-grandfather, who held the office in the 1880s. After the war my father was approached by the local Plympton Labour Party to stand as a candidate for the rural district council. It must have become known that he had asked my mother to vote Labour by proxy for him in the 1945 election while he was still serving in the RAMC in Italy. The approach from the Labour Party was written up in the local newspaper and infuriated my godfather, Dr Ball, who believed it would harm their joint practice. So, in deference to his partners, my father told the Labour Party that his politics were still 'fluid'. This did not stop the local Constitutional Club demanding that he should resign immediately from being vice-president; he had been blissfully unaware that this was a Conservative organisation, believing it to be a drinking club. Somewhat bruised by this encounter with party politics he never took any further interest, voting for all the parties at different times. But he always joked that no member of our family 'ever votes Tory without a stiff drink before and after'. He became chairman of Plympton St Maurice Parish Council as an Independent and would walk annually around the borders of the parish 'beating the bounds', dressed up in robes with mace bearers and having all the paraphernalia of a truly 'rotten borough'. They would deliberate in Plympton St Maurice's lovely town hall, surrounded by portraits painted by Plympton's most distinguished MP, the artist Sir Joshua Reynolds.

My father also took me to my first political meeting in February 1950. It was half term and my grandfather Gear was staying with us. All three of us went off to the Exmouth Hall, Devonport to hear Aneurin Bevan, the then Minister of Health, speak in support of Michael Foot. The meeting was packed. Well over a thousand people were present, some in a large overflow meeting downstairs and several hundred standing outside in the rain and wind. The meeting started with everyone singing the first verse of 'Land of my Fathers'. I was allowed to squeeze to the front. I watched spellbound as Bevan spoke for eighty-five minutes without a script, freely quoting figures to strengthen his argument and weaken his opponents. If I read his words reported in the local newspaper, I can recapture his oratory with his Welsh accent, a slight stutter and long pauses between sentences.

Asked how he thought he was going to get the vote of the middle classes when he called them 'lower than vermin', Aneurin Bevan replied, 'For heaven's sake, don't continually parade around the country sentences maliciously selected from their context in public speeches.' Asked what the socialists were going to do to prevent communism spreading, he said, 'Communists are weakest in Britain where socialists are the strongest,' adding that 'the communists are stronger in France and Italy, where the socialists are not in power'. For a young eleven-year-old this was a heady experience and my grandfather had no doubt that we had listened to the future Prime Minister. It also meant that when later locked in controversy with Michael Foot I was able to claim that I had known him man and boy. That same night Winston Churchill spoke in the Forum cinema, Devonport in support of his son, Randolph Churchill. Plymouth politics retained their rumbustious reputation.

In 1957 my mother became a Devon county councillor as a genuine Independent. I canvassed for her on the slogan 'Keep politics out of local government'. She was never defeated, serving for over seventeen years and becoming an alderman. When Plymouth took over Plympton as a result of Richard Crossman's controversial local government boundary changes, my mother led the 'Hands off Plympton' campaign while I, as a Plymouth MP, supported the takeover. My mother never let me forget it! Like her grandfather, she became chairman of the bench of magistrates.

It is hard to describe the effect of this small, feminine, well-dressed, combative, tenacious person on any committee on which she sat. She had her admirers and her detractors, since few felt neutral about her activities. Yet the mentally handicapped in Devon and beyond benefited immensely from her being their champion, whether as vice-chairman of the health committee on Devon County Council or on the Plymouth Hospital management committee. When my sister and I were at home in the school holidays, a typical breakfast would start with Mother saying, 'The plan now is . . .' She would then outline exactly what we would do and not a moment would be wasted. She would lay out our programme for the day in minute detail, whether it was to go swimming on the moor or the sea, to play badminton or perhaps to go Scottish dancing. At the same time, she would be stimulating an argument over breakfast on ways in which Devon could introduce comprehensive education, hotly defending the ending of the eleven-plus examinations and proposing radical reforms of schools, for social services and health centres for family doctors. It was an invigorating environment in which to grow up.

I used to think my going into politics was an accident, and often said so. Now I believe it was a more natural development than I realised.

My father found getting back to civilian medical practice difficult. He was used to ordering his patients around and some Plymptonians in those early years did not take kindly to being treated as if they were in the Army. There was constant friction with my godfather in the practice and the joy of the pre-war partnership was never recaptured. As with so many other couples, it was also a strain after all the absent years for my parents to pick up as if the war had not happened. They had to grow back together.

When I was a medical student I would go on night calls with my father. It was through these late-night car trips up on Dartmoor that we consolidated our relationship, which because of his absence in the war had taken time to develop. Our love flowered slowly. I probably did not discover the full delight of his personality and humour until I was over twenty-one and studying at St Thomas'

Hospital. In later years his patients still loved him and long after he retired they would stop me in the street and ask about him, saying, 'He would listen to you, not like doctors do these days.' His practice extended down to Laira, including quite a large part of the Plymouth Sutton constituency which I initially represented in 1966. I still attribute my small majority of only 747 in the 1970 election to patients of my father voting for him through voting for me.

Given these strong family connections with local politics, medicine, religion and the sea, my own interests are perhaps less surprising. My roots are in the Welsh radical political tradition. It was always considered perfectly natural by my family that when I did start to commit myself politically it would not be to the Conservative Party.

In July 1956, eighteen and no longer a schoolboy, I was doing a holiday job while waiting to go to Cambridge University. My employer was Costain, the construction firm, and the project a new sewage works near my home. Starting at 6 a.m. and often doing overtime in the evenings and on Saturdays, I earned good money. Then, suddenly, Colonel Nasser seized the Suez Canal. The Prime Minister, Sir Anthony Eden, said that Nasser could not be allowed 'to have his thumb on our windpipe'. That was mild language compared with what I was hearing as we dug trenches for the sewer pipes. Most of my fellow workers had done their National Service and some had served in the Second World War. They were adamant from the start that the Egyptians should not be allowed to get away with it. Prior to Suez the only subject of conversation was sex. Suddenly that was swept away. We were all military strategists and the question that dominated was when to go in and retake the Suez Canal.

Whenever the *Daily Mirror* or the *Daily Herald* had any reports of Labour MPs objecting to Britain using force against the Egyptians my workmates went wild. Castigating the newspaper, expressing their disagreement with Labour in abrasive terms, soon they saw even Hugh Gaitskell, Labour's leader, as a backslider. Not for them sensible warnings that while force could not be excluded if it was used it should be consistent with the Charter of the United Nations. For them it was clear cut. The 'Gippos' had hit us, so we should hit them.

This was a political eye opener for me. It was not simple jingoism. What they were expressing was their gut understanding that sometimes force has to be met by force. It left me with an understanding of some of the basic attitudes of millions of Labour voters. I disagreed with them because I did not see that national-isation of the Suez Canal Company was an invasion, it was more a confiscation. Nevertheless, Suez taught me one vital political lesson – never automatically to follow the assumptions of the small group that tends to dominate Labour and Liberal Party thinking on defence and foreign affairs. These people are afraid of exercising military power and have been for decades. Yet they do not speak for public opinion in Britain. There are more people prepared to match force with force than is often apparent. The average person does believe that for a deterrent to be of any value, one has to be prepared to use it, and they expect their politicians to be able to stand up for British interests even in the age of imperial decline. Suez brought home to me, and it was reinforced at the time of the Falklands War, that there is a robustness about the British people's character which is often underestimated by the liberal intelligentsia or what some now call the chattering classes.

Some Labour leaders have always understood this robust nature. Hugh Dalton during the 1930s stood out with Winston Churchill over appeasement. Clement Attlee and Ernest Bevin in the immediate aftermath of the Second World War, despite the yearning for peace, did not ignore the ominous build-up of Stalin's power and influence. They took the decision for Britain to manufacture its own atomic bomb when our wartime nuclear co-operation with the US was suddenly shut off. Hugh Gaitskell, Harold Wilson and Jim Callaghan during the Cold War stood firm on the need at times to threaten the use of force.

Labour's ambivalence to military power has hinged on the attitudes of key trade union leaders. When Ernest Bevin told the pacifist Labour leader George Lansbury to stop hawking his conscience around the conference hall before the Second World War, he was speaking as a leader of the Transport and General Workers' Union (TGWU) who was in touch with the feelings of his members. When Frank Cousins attacked Hugh Gaitskell and campaigned to ban the bomb, he won the party conference vote, but by 1961 lost because he was out of touch with people like those on the building site with me. When Jack Jones spoke as leader of the TGWU for unilateral nuclear disarmament against Harold Wilson and James Callaghan he was unrepresentative, and both leaders were prepared to stand up to him and as a consequence he lost too. Ron Todd, his successor, was able to win with his block vote at the party conferences between 1980 and 1988 only because Michael Foot and then Neil Kinnock were paid-up members of CND. When Neil Kinnock decided to shift and endorse Trident in 1989, he had no major difficulty in changing conference policy, for the average Labour supporter had never agreed with it. The Conservatives always thrive if Labour give them the political ammunition they want to depict Labour as soft on defence. Sensibly, Labour leaders such as Tony Blair and Gordon Brown never gave them that chance.

It always made my blood boil when the Conservative Party had the brass neck to hold political meetings with the Union Jack draped over the table, as if it had a monopoly on patriotism. It irritated me to see Prime Minister Margaret Thatcher, rather than the Queen, take the salute at the march past outside the Guildhall after the Falklands War. The great wartime Prime Ministers, Lloyd George and Churchill, would never have taken the salute at such a parade. They understood that that role was the monarch's on behalf of the whole nation. It was the correct decision for John Major to invite the Queen to take the salute after the first Gulf War. The Conservatives have often tried to monopolise patriotism at election time, particularly in the naval dockyard constituencies, which were bastions of working-class Toryism. When canvassing for Labour votes in Plymouth, I often put my foot in the door when it was being slammed in my face on a council estate by a dockyard worker saying, 'We're true blue here,' or 'I'm for Queen and Country.' Their vote was almost certainly lost but I still felt the need to challenge face to face their belief that Labour and later the SDP were any less patriotic than the Conservatives. The Conservative argument that Labour could not be trusted with the defence of our nation always stuck in my gullet when I was a member of the Labour Party. Sadly, like many others, from 1981 to 1989 I too was not able to trust Labour on defence and I was glad not to have to defend them from within during this period. From 1992 under John Smith I began to trust Labour on defence again but, as described later, Tony Blair lost my trust and that of millions of others over his incompetent and disingenuous handling of the war in Iraq of 2003.

The Suez Canal in 1956 did not just run through Lady Eden's drawing room in 10 Downing Street, it ran also through my parents' sitting room. My sister Susan was due to marry Garth Mumford, a lieutenant in the Royal Navy, and the invitations had already been sent out. He was serving as an engineer on the aircraft carrier HMS *Theseus* and the whole ship's company was put on full alert to sail for the Mediterranean. The wedding was cancelled and then suddenly reinstated when he was given three days' surprise leave. They were married in our local church in Plympton St Maurice and the village came out to see the bride, who walked from the church the hundred yards to our home, Castlehayes, where we had a marquee in the garden. Then on 4 August the *Theseus* set sail from Portsmouth for Cyprus with men of the 16th Parachute Brigade on board. Our family was like the family of every other serviceman with an impending war and worried about Garth's safety.

All through those summer months the Suez crisis was on everyone's lips. My parents, particularly my mother, were against Eden and for Gaitskell. The *Observer* was strongly critical of the government and provided me with most of my facts and counter-arguments on the building site. Whether sitting eating a snack, leaning on our shovels or waiting to lay concrete we argued over the rights and wrongs of using force. I backed Hugh Gaitskell though I did not know him. In particular I liked his emphasis on the need to retain the support of President Eisenhower. That just seemed common sense. Going it alone was nostalgic nonsense. I knew very little then about the political and military ins and outs of the Suez crisis. But the Conservative Party and most of the press seemed to many of my generation to be still living in an imperial age that had passed. Nasser never struck me as even remotely like Hitler or Mussolini. For Britain to act only with France and for them both to act clandestinely with Israel seemed risky and wrong. At the time Hugh Gaitskell's enemies succeeded in giving the impression that he had copped out, initially supporting Eden's policy of using force and then changing his mind under pressure from Labour MPs. Looking back now at what he said, the criticism hardly seems justified. But in the House of Commons it is so often the impression that counts.

The actual words are never as important as the feel which the words leave.

Memories of the Suez debacle were to influence me strongly on two future occasions. I became convinced that Selwyn Lloyd, the Foreign Secretary, was lying to the House of Commons when challenged over the involvement of Israel. We now know that he and Eden systematically deceived Parliament. They were not the first to mislead Parliament, nor will they be the last, but their deception was on a massive scale. As a consequence, in January 1971 I was one of the fifty-five MPs who voted against Selwyn Lloyd becoming the Speaker of the House of Commons. I felt that no one with his record of deceit should be placed in that particular position. I have to admit that he turned out to be an excellent Speaker but that did not make me regret my vote.

I was also influenced by the anger and contempt that servicemen like my brother-in-law felt when being asked to go to war against a background of bitter party infighting in the House of Commons. Because of that experience I tried very hard to contribute to all-party agreement on the Argentine invasion of the Falklands, on Iraq's invasion of Kuwait, on NATO's war with Serbia over Kosovo and after 9/11 on attacking Afghanistan and the need to topple Saddam Hussein. Waging war is too serious and too dangerous to be conducted against a background of a political battle in Westminster.

The Suez affair rumbled on through the summer. In September with my parents and newly married sister, I drove to Cambridge to start as a freshman at Sidney Sussex College. Within a few weeks of term starting, the British, French and Israeli forces went into Suez, at the very moment that Hungary was being raped by the Russians. Anatomy and physiology studies were set aside and like many other Cambridge undergraduates I plunged into the frenzy of political debate. I attended frequent demonstrations and protests against government foreign policy. We were furious over the sheer ineptitude of the Conservative government, let alone the folly of their military action. I felt disgust at our inability to do anything to help Hungary as it rose up in revolt against Soviet occupation, though for a while, with the release of Cardinal Mindszenty, it looked as if the Hungarians would succeed. In Cambridge we agonised long into the night about whether we should go to

Hungary as our counterparts had done in another part of Europe during the Spanish Civil War. Circumstances were very different this time but nevertheless some went even though it was pretty clear that they would have difficulty in getting into Hungary. I regretted not going, even if it had meant the frustration of waiting on the Austrian border.

Then on 5 November before dawn, while the US was putting on pressure for an Anglo-French and Israeli withdrawal from Egypt, 1,000 tanks of the Red Army attacked the Hungarian forces in Budapest. The West watched, impotent. The Hungarian people overturned trams to use as barricades, the young fought with Molotov cocktails. But the Russians used heavy shells, their tanks fired at the barricades, and the deeply repressive side of Soviet communism was there for all to see. We listened to the sound of Radio Budapest. I have never forgotten the last words when it was silenced: 'Help Hungary . . . Help . . . Help . . . Help . . .' My generation of students were as influenced by this as the generation a decade later were affected by Vietnam.

What happened in Hungary left me fiercely hostile to Soviet communism. From that moment I never ceased to oppose its practice and ideology. My feelings were reinforced by the Soviet suppression of the Prague uprising in the spring of 1968. Initially it all appeared hopeful with Alexander Dubček, the Czech Prime Minister, appearing to be in control. I was Navy Minister at the moment Czechoslovakia was invaded. Again I felt the frustration that we in the West were not prepared to respond more vigorously. Logic told me it would be foolish to attempt to use force, but I believed there should have been serious sanctions. Then, over the invasion of Afghanistan in 1979, the West should have instituted tough sanctions. I supported our athletes not attending the Moscow Olympics but the collective will did not exist in Europe. Most of my big political battles inside and outside the Labour Party were destined to be about how the Western democracies could defeat – through NATO, the European Community and the UN – the ideology of Soviet communism. The seed of my defiance was sown in Cambridge as I watched Hungary go under.

Surprisingly, despite these highly political events in 1956 and the response they evoked in me, I did not become involved in party politics at Cambridge. I never joined any political party. I went along to the Cambridge Union and took a life membership for ten pounds but the one debate I attended put me off. I disliked, and still do, the mannered style of both the Oxford and Cambridge Union debates and have only rarely accepted invitations to debate, preferring to speak and answer questions. During my three years at Cambridge, if one excludes a number of comments about apartheid in South Africa, there are only two political references in my notebooks and they refer to my horror of nuclear weapons. The first was a reference to a NATO conference, asking whether we were right to use A-bombs as the ultimate deterrent, saying no one would be fool enough to start a war and how easily a small strife could work into a world cataclysm. The second was a reference to a letter which I had written to *The Times*, though it was not published, arguing that though the nuclear bomb was a deterrent it was nevertheless morally evil to believe that one could use it.

The underlying morality of nuclear deterrence has always fascinated me. I was persuaded by the speeches of Hugh Gaitskell in 1961 that the West needed nuclear weapons for military deterrence, and by Harold Wilson and Denis Healey in 1965 that Britain should continue to build Polaris. Far from finding that the closer I came to influencing nuclear policy, the more hardened I became, I found the nearer, the more I worried. After Hiroshima the nuclear genie was out of the bottle. But I have spent a lot of my life trying to put it back in and after the Cold War was over I began increasingly to believe we might be able to do so. To use any weapon of mass destruction, chemical, biological or nuclear, is to cross a threshold of immorality far higher than that involved in conventional war. How to ensure that nuclear weapons are never actually used, while being prepared to threaten credibly to use them, is a deep moral dilemma. For there to be any morality to deterrence there has to be a subtle and determined strategy underpinning it which fosters public horror at any nuclear release and yet does not undermine the credibility of threatening release. Continued public debate on the morality of nuclear deterrence is essential in order to buttress the politicians in their reluctance ever to authorise the military to use nuclear weapons. Despite this moral questioning, I never felt the remotest temptation to join CND or any of the student peace movements. They seemed to me even then to be escaping rather than confronting these dilemmas. In government as Navy Minister and as Foreign Secretary I found nuclear deterrence a major preoccupation. I spent the 1980s as a member of the Palme Commission on Defence and Disarmament and championed the concept which produced 'common security'. This had a profound influence on Mikhail Gorbachev. I also served in the 1990s on the Carnegie Commission on the Prevention of Deadly Conflict. In 2009 I published *Nuclear Papers*, an argument for not replacing the Trident ballistic missile submarines but choosing a less sophisticated and less costly alternative using cruise missiles with nuclear warheads on existing submarines.

The closest I came to finding a political forum in Cambridge was Great St Mary's Church, where the vicar was Mervyn Stockwood. That November he preached a whole sermon on the politics of Suez and reading it now brings back the sense of outrage. Mervyn Stockwood was a priest who saw that Christianity could thrive on controversy. For nineteen years before coming to Cambridge he had been in Bristol, first as curate, and then vicar, of St Matthew's, Moorfields. He had also been a Bristol City Labour councillor. He was a socialist who managed to be a close friend of both Stafford Cripps and Walter Monckton when they were respectively Labour and Conservative members of Parliament for Bristol. Coming to Great St Mary's in 1955, he had been determined to make Christianity relevant and he succeeded beyond anyone's expect-ations. Queues of undergraduates would form outside the church before a service. Inside, even without a famous preacher, the pews were packed. In part this was a tribute to Mervyn Stockwood's electric personality and his ability to generate controversy but there must have been at the same time a religious revival among under-graduates. In church matters he was often surprisingly conservative, also very high church; far too high for my liking. His flamboyant personality made him far fonder than I of ritual and ceremony.

In November 1958 Mervyn was asked by the Prime Minister, Harold Macmillan, to become Bishop of Southwark. Explaining to us in a sermon why he had agreed to go to Southwark, he laid stress on the virtue of the apostolic succession. Then, typically, to lighten the congregation's gloom, he told us about the Somerset farmer who, when visiting the Vatican, was shown some hens which were said to be in direct succession to the cock which crew when St Peter denied our Lord. The farmer, being of a practical turn of mind, made one comment: 'Be they good layers?' So Mervyn joked that he was more interested in apostolic success than in apostolic succession. No shrinking violet, he enjoyed being the 'red' bishop. He had always refused to wear a dog collar, and made much of wearing a tie. On becoming a bishop he used to wear a deep red–purple cassock which struck my father's brother, who was then a prebendary of St Paul's Cathedral, as the height of ostentation. He used to regale me with how the then Bishop of London, seeing Mervyn at a party in this garb, sidled up and said, 'Ah, Mervyn, incognito I presume.'

Mervyn Stockwood attracted such criticism. Of course he was a showman, but he was also a devout private man and a man of prayer. He certainly had a profound influence on my life.

My anatomy book, which I still have on my shelves, had been written by Solly Zuckerman when he was professor of anatomy at Birmingham University. Ten years later, when I was Navy Minister, we came to know each other because of his involvement with Polaris. Then ten years after that he became my adviser on nuclear disarmament in the Foreign Office while he was working in the Cabinet Office and I greatly valued his friendship. It was an unusual appointment but Solly's whole career had been an extraordinary one, helped by being on Admiral Mountbatten's staff as scientific adviser during the war. Few have wielded so much influence in Whitehall over so long a period, irrespective of the political complexion of the government. He always believed in nuclear deterrence but was a fervent critic of battlefield nuclear weapons and was the man behind Earl Mountbatten's often quoted speech to the Stockholm International Peace Research Institute, SIPRI, in 1979 when he said, 'Wars cannot be fought with nuclear weapons.' His career is an example of how the trained mind can turn to other disciplines with considerable effect. By his own engaging personality he saved Britain billions of pounds. For without his friendship with the prickly Admiral Rickover of the US Navy we would never have had Polaris and then the Trident agreement, which allowed us access to US missile technology at knock-down prices. In Britain we do not use academics in government to anywhere near the same extent as in the United States and we miss the rigour of the good mind and the freshness they can bring to the stale atmosphere of government.

Studying the history and philosophy of science as part of my tripos examination helped extend my mind beyond medicine. I also became a regular attender at F. R. Leavis's lectures on English literature. He was a renowned lecturer – categorical, uncompromising – and fed my interest in the writings of D. H. Lawrence, in particular his novel *The Rainbow*. He also opened up for me the poems of T. S. Eliot. He could castigate Eliot for being so disparaging of Lawrence and yet in the same breath extol his merits as a poet and critic. The Humanist Society meetings were fascinating too, the most valuable part being at the end when its elderly president, E. M. Forster, would give a short but precise synopsis of what had been discussed. My exploration of humanism was undertaken deliberately to offset the predominance of Christianity hitherto. My religious views were already beginning to change. The certainties of my faith were becoming a little frayed at the edges and I found myself questioning more of the Church's teaching. That questioning has continued to the present day, but I remain a communicant.

At Sidney Sussex, whose main claim to fame is that Oliver Cromwell was one of its students, I read and greatly enjoyed C. V. Wedgwood's short life of Cromwell. It was a trick of fate that my wife became her literary agent and actively stimulated Dame Veronica's publisher to bring out a new edition of that very same volume. The Cromwellian Society, which a group of us revived, was dedicated to good food. The society justified using Cromwell's name on the grounds that the Great Protector was a formidable trencherman. To this day I have never been able to find out whether or not this is true. The Owen family claim a link to Cromwell through the Williams family on my grandmother's side. Plymouth was a Cromwellian city and Freedom Fields marks the place where the citizens held out against the Crown. I believe this radicalism of the then Plymothians explains in part why, for twenty years, I was the only Labour or Social Democrat MP in the south-west peninsula from Bristol downwards. As if to demonstrate my Cromwellian streak, I put his portrait up in the Foreign Secretary's room, but not surprisingly my successor, Lord Carrington, took it down.

I had the chance to go on an expedition to Afghanistan in the summer of 1959, after graduating from Cambridge and before starting at St Thomas'. It was too great an adventure to miss. We drove in a Land Rover, which was christened the 'Bugger', through Yugoslavia, Bulgaria, Turkey, Iran, Afghanistan, Pakistan and India, and the spiritual experience of the trip wound itself into my life. I threw myself into the mysticism of Asia and was left with a longstanding interest in the Muslim, Buddhist and Hindu faiths.

The prime purpose of our trip had emerged before I joined through discussion with experts on Afghanistan in Cambridge: it was to visit the Minaret de Jham, in a remote mountain valley in the centre of Afghanistan. The minaret, which marked the site of Firuzkoh, the capital of the Ghorid Empire, had only been discovered the year before by a French archaeologist and many experts wanted more photographs. It was amazing that such a beautiful minaret in such perfect condition should have remained undiscovered all those years.

Sir Mortimer Wheeler, whose famous archaeological career had been mainly in the Indian subcontinent, then lived in Cambridge and he had, after questioning me closely, agreed to sponsor our expedition. We also needed a scientific purpose, to encourage commercial sponsorship. The physiology department agreed that one of my companions, Jan Fischer, also a medical student, and I should investigate diurnal rhythm – the clock in one's own body which controls not just sleeping and waking but most bodily functions and is affected by jet lag. The uniquely wide temperature difference in Afghanistan, very cold at night and very hot during the day, was known to affect people's diurnal rhythm. We had to collect and measure the volume of all our urine in large measuring cylinders. We had to note the volume, the time and the outside temperature. This routine two or three times a day provided us all with endless amusement, but I doubt if the science of diurnal rhythm was much advanced.

In Tehran I had my first stormy encounter with the British Diplomatic Service. It was not to be my last. We found our embassy totally useless in helping us to obtain permission to drive into the centre of Afghanistan. No doubt they were fed up with young people driving through without the proper entry permits. But when we went with Jan to the Swiss embassy we were given a first-class helpful service. Even though only he in our party was Swiss, they made us welcome, took infinite trouble over our visas and helped us find out about Andrew Gerry, who had contracted typhoid and whom we had had to leave behind at Erzurum in Turkey to recover. He eventually caught up with us in Kabul.

Sleeping in the Afghani tents, sharing the tribe's food as they wandered, I began to understand and respect the Islamic faith. As they grazed their animals on the parched mountain ranges at over 10,000 feet, I was witnessing a way of life unchanged down the centuries. They were generous and welcoming, killing and cooking a sheep when we arrived unexpectedly, sometimes after the sun had fallen at their camp site. Then as we left I would look back on the camps, refreshed by an insight into a new life. Women were unveiled and respected. The Afghanis elected their own leader, in one case a tall handsome bearded figure with a natural authority. Listening to him talk with the Koran open on his lap, even though I could not understand what he was saying, I sensed respect for religious laws that had been handed down and were still genuinely revered. One night when our interpreter had explained that two of us were becoming doctors we were taken to see a woman who was having difficulty delivering her baby. It was pretty clear that her pelvis was too small for the child's head. We could do nothing and knew that without a Caesarean operation, both would die. It was a harsh world up there in the mountains, but it was magical.

After Afghanistan we drove into Pakistan via the Khyber Pass and India. The expedition lasted over four months and we never once slept in a hotel, though we relented to the extent of taking a bath in a hotel in Delhi. We lived alongside very poor people in a way that I would never do again. Countries which had previously been names on a map came alive.

India was very different. Visiting Benares I smelt the fecundity of the Hindu faith. In the temples I saw its joyous eroticism in the explicit carvings. I watched as the bodies from the funeral pyre were slid into the bubbling, surging river Ganges and, far from being repelled, I felt that this religion had a message about the sanctity of all forms of life.

We drove back into Iran from Pakistan via Dr Holland's missionary eye hospital in Quetta. One could not but be impressed by the dedication of Dr Holland and his fellow missionaries but I was shocked to see Muslims being converted to Christianity merely by the miracle of having their cataracts removed. They came in blind and they left seeing. Not surprisingly, in that atmosphere of prayer, some were converted. They then faced, as Christians, the penalty of becoming outcasts when they returned to their villages. I could not see any Christian virtue in this. What right did we Christians have so blatantly to interfere with a Muslim community? By now my own religious faith bore little relation to the Church of England or for that matter to the simpler, and to me preferable, Church of Wales. I felt that there was a far wider spiritual horizon than that which could be covered by the teachings of any one church. I became and have remained a convinced ecumenicist.

Two years later, in 1961, I went to Zurich to stay with Jan. I had been given leave of absence to study psychiatry there and it turned out to be a wonderful time to think and read. Jan was working at the Burgholzli Psychiatric Clinic, where Carl Jung had started his work, and I stayed with him in his flat in the old part of the city. Enthralled by Jung's writing during the week, we climbed together in the Swiss Alps at the weekend. As I wrestled with the analyst's approach to patients, I found comfort in Freud's description of the goal of psychoanalysis as being 'to substitute for neurotic misery ordinary human unhappiness'.

Early the following year I drove over to Berlin in my car. For the first time I saw this city for which I had felt an early affinity. The Movietone News film of the Berlin Airlift in 1947 was my first international political memory, and Berlin, divided, became a symbolic city for me. Later, in June 1963, when President Kennedy had gone to Berlin and made his famous '*Ich bin ein Berliner*' speech, I had felt that emotional attachment deepen. Over the years, I travelled to Berlin many times as a politician, and accompanied the Queen there as part of her official visit in 1978. So when the Berlin Wall came crashing down in 1989 I relived those memories and, like many other people around the world, my heart lifted.

There was a palpable tension in Berlin during those early months of 1962. The obscene wall had not yet been built but we waited interminably at passport control before crossing over at Checkpoint Charlie into East Berlin. It was my first visit to a communist country. Its drabness, the smell of its petrol and its poverty left an indelible impression. In light snow we crossed East Germany to Prague. Arriving in the dark, we drove in a flurry of snow up the cobbled, winding streets to the castle. Hearing the noise of the wheels echoing from the walls and seeing the snowflakes in the headlights, I felt as if I were travelling in a horse-drawn carriage. Next morning I found that Prague, no longer with its snow-white covering, was besmirched by the tell-tale signs of Soviet communism. But there was an underlying beauty to the city that not even a massive statue of Stalin could blight. I knew that this city would some day be free. It took twenty-seven years.

I started at St Thomas' Hospital in October 1959. It was an eye opener to be living an inner-city life for the first time. The poverty I found in Lambeth around the hospital shocked me, for I had lived so far a very sheltered, relatively prosperous southern life. I will never forget helping a district nurse to deliver a baby in a home with my backside outside the windowsill, the bedroom being too small for it to be anywhere else. At that stage the farthest north I had ever been in Britain was Cambridge. Bad housing, far worse than anything I had seen in Plymouth or Cambridge, was commonplace and Rachmanism, the exploitation of property, was being exposed. These bad social conditions helped me make up my mind to join the Labour Party, which I had voted for in the general election, and to take more interest in politics.

I joined the Labour Party in Vauxhall in 1960 after some months' delay because the office was always closed whenever I went to join up. I attended meetings organised by the mainly Bevanite Victory for Socialism Group, but also joined the Fabian Society and was becoming more and more interested in Hugh Gaitskell's rethinking of the Labour Party's principles.

I remember clearly hearing Gaitskell decry the fact that there were too many 'armchair socialists' and in 1960 I heard extracts from a speech on the radio which appears to be one he made in Nottingham in February. He was justifying his belief that Clause IV in the Labour Party constitution, which talked of 'common ownership of the means of production, distribution and exchange', should be changed. He emphasised that what was wrong with Clause IV was the vague threat that it carried to all private property and he described it as meaningless phrases and mere theology. I had not hitherto realised that he was not against public enterprise and very much in favour of co-operative ownership. From that day on he was the British politician in whom I placed the greatest trust. His arguments and intellectual authority persuaded me that my earlier attitudes to both nationalisation and unilateral nuclear disarmament had not been properly thought through. By the time he gave the famous speech when he promised to 'fight and fight again to save the party we love' in 1960, I was a fervent admirer. But it was from afar. I never met him personally or even saw him speak, other than on television, yet he demonstrated to me that one could retain one's integrity in politics and that a politician could stick with the policies he believed in through thick and thin. I have little doubt that it was because he was the leader that I put my name forward for selection as a parliamentary candidate in 1962.

When facing some of the more difficult choices of my career, I have asked myself how Hugh Gaitskell would have handled a similar situation. That he loved the Labour Party there is no doubt and perhaps there could never have been circumstances in which he would have left it. Yet his biographer concludes that he had felt in 1960 that he should, and would have to, resign the leadership if the conference went against him again in 1961 on unilateral nuclear disarmament. Fortunately they did not and he succeeded in having the earlier decision reversed.

I relished the opportunity in 1985 to give the Gaitskell Memorial Lecture at Nottingham University on ownership. I said then:

> This does not mean that Hugh Gaitskell, who would have been nearly seventy-five when the SDP was formed, would have left the Labour Party. I do not personally believe he would have done so, if for no other reason than, had he lived, I suspect the need for a creation of the SDP would never have existed.

St Thomas' is an unusually beautiful hospital. Situated on the south bank of the Thames, it looks out across the river to the Houses of Parliament. The old building had the high ceilings and long wards that Florence Nightingale designed. They were light and airy and, if a little noisy, at least not smelly. The horror was the new buildings. Two attempts at a new design, both half built, are a monument to the scandalous way in which the NHS managed its capital building programme for decades after the war, building in fits and starts.

To have lived under the shadow of Big Ben for years before I entered the House of Commons gives a strange feeling of continuity to my life. Working late at night in the hospital when the lights of London were out, I used to look over the river and see the Commons sitting late, all ablaze. Later I looked back from the terrace in front of Parliament into the wards of the hospital. In those early years I never contemplated becoming an MP.

St Thomas' Medical School was a stimulating place. It has never been afraid of taking on older students or people with an unconventional background and has an inner sense of superiority: the saying is 'You can tell a Thomas' man anywhere but you cannot tell him anything!' I was not an idle student but nor was I the most active. I remember soon after I qualified my neighbour in the doctors' dining room, who had been at Oxford and was only three months ahead of me as a medical student at St Thomas', asking me what hospital I had trained at. He was not joking. Clearly my attendance had been neither sufficiently frequent nor sufficiently marked to make any impact on him.

My great interest was not the operating theatre but the dramatic theatre. It has been a long tradition of theatreland to give free tickets to nurses in the London teaching hospitals. Nurses had the first call on the tickets but any that were left over were available for medical students. For three years there was hardly a show in London that I did not see. Then the Royal Court Theatre became my favourite haunt. It was the time when John Osborne and Arnold Wesker were putting on their plays and it was a lively and stimulating theatre. One evening after attending the Royal Court I wandered out around the back of the theatre and found a little bistro in Bourne Street. I peered in through the window, opened the door and was immediately asked, in a none-too-civil tone by a woman of indeterminate age dressed all in black, who I was and what I was doing coming to her restaurant. Somewhat taken aback, I said I was a medical student looking for a cheap supper. Whereupon, to my amazement, she suddenly embraced me and announced to everyone present that she loved medical students. She sat me down in front of a plateful of goulash which looked awful but tasted magnificent. That was my introduction to Elizabeth Furse. I loved her all her life. I ate more of her meals than anyone's other than my wife's or mother's and had more arguments about politics in her presence than in the House of Commons.

My houseboat, *Amanda*, which I bought for £600, was moored alongside Chelsea Embankment. It had the fashionable address of 106 Cheyne Walk, Chelsea. She had been a ship's lifeboat, hanging in the davits. Although she was only 30 feet long there was room for a bed in the bow of the boat, where there was no headroom at all. Then a small cabin with a central ladder coming out onto the deck through a hatchway. A small bath and a chemical closet were on one side and a minute kitchen with a Calor gas cooker and water heater. There was room for a desk and a spare bunk bed. In the stern was a glass-walled sitting room, which was the only place where I could stand upright. There was a telephone and mains electricity. The water tank on the deck was filled every day and my rent was thirty shillings a week (one shilling a foot) paid to the Chelsea Yacht and Boat Company. It was an idyllic life. Next door to me there was a large converted Thames barge on which there were four girls. They were part of the Bluebell dancing team. We were like brother and sisters, never getting involved in each other's relationships but flitting in and out of our boats, going to the cinema or the theatre together if anyone was free. The contrast with hospital life could hardly have been more marked. On my boat I lived a relaxed bohemian life. Dorothy Tutin, the actress, had a boat a few hundred yards from mine which gave us some notoriety, but in those days the houseboats had not yet become fashionable and it was a cheap place to live. We had our own community, presided over by the old night watchman who guarded the gangway. He knew exactly who was seeing whom, when and where, and was a marvellous source of gossip and intrigue.

The other part of my non-medical life was politics. I was helping to draft a Young Fabian pamphlet on the pharmaceutical industry. It was because someone heard me speak at a Fabian school in 1961 on the drug industry that I was asked early in 1962 to speak on the subject in Devon to a Labour Party women's conference. Following this meeting some of the women attending from the Torrington Constituency Labour Party suggested my name for their selection of prospective parliamentary candidates. So in a small way my parliamentary career started in the same week as my becoming a newly qualified doctor.

No threshold I have crossed in my life has been as dramatic as that between medical student and doctor. A life of relative irresponsibility suddenly had to become responsible. I was now treating patients on my own and their lives depended on what I did. Decisions had sometimes to be taken very quickly. Often there was no time for consulting anyone else, only to make the diagnosis and to start treatment. My six years of training was under the real test.

In those days, medical students were not given as much to do clinically before qualifying as they are today. There was no gradual transition. I walked into the small Royal Waterloo Hospital on Waterloo Bridge in the morning and by lunchtime the house physician I had replaced had left. I was now responsible for the male and female medical wards, two small wards with skin patients and the children's ward.

The atmosphere of a busy hospital ward then had a rhythm to it which pulsed through twenty-four hours a day. As a doctor I was on call night and day with only every other weekend off. Now the hours are reduced and young doctors no longer experience the natural cycle of a particular patient's illness. When a death came it cast a pall for a few hours but the open wards encouraged patients to worry about others and a camaraderie developed: offputting to some, supportive for others. The ward sister's personality imprinted itself on the nurses and through them on the patients. The doctors were not as important as they thought. The people who cleaned the floors and did the domestic chores contributed to the patients' lives in a way far more satisfying way than just working in an office. In St Thomas' a legacy of Florence Nightingale meant that the school of nursing, named after her, insisted on prayers taking place each evening when the night and day staff changed over. To see the nurses and sister in their striking headgear kneeling around the central table with all the main lights off, lit only by a table lamp, evoked a sense of vocation which was a crucially important part of the nursing profession's tradition. It is very different today. There is little point in looking back with nostalgia, but we have nevertheless lost something intangible, a continuity of care.

I remember on my first day eating lunch in the little doctors' dining room with a contemporary who had just started as house surgeon to the hospital when the telephone rang. It was the emergency bed service asking if I had a spare medical bed. Blind panic tempted me to say we were full but I knew that this moment had to be faced. So before accepting the patient I asked as much detail as was decent about the ambulanceman's description of his symptoms. I then rushed off to the privacy of my ground-floor bedroom, where I tried to match the description I had been given with a differential diagnosis in the house physician's 'bible'. This book was literally to become a life saver during the next few days. Slim enough to be carried in the pockets of my long white coat, it was an instant reference point.

No doctor forgets his first few cases. They are indelibly imprinted on the mind because of the fear which surrounds the diagnosis and treatment. The psychological trauma of being out of one's depth is always frightening, devastatingly so in times that one has sole responsibility, however good the training. The magic of medicine is built around this very special relationship of doctor to patient. Nurses can assist, even other doctors can help, but the decision as to what to do can frequently only be taken by one person, for neither medicine nor surgery is easy to practise collectively. It is individuals who practise the art and science of medicine and that, for many doctors, is its strength and fascination. I have never ceased to love medicine and have often longed to return to it. A sign that medicine is still there in the back of my mind is that in anxiety dreams, still coming in my seventies, although less frequently, I can wake in a sweat, having dreamt that I have failed my medical examinations. Sometimes the anxiety is all the worse for dreaming that I am actually practising while still unqualified. Freud explained anxiety dreams as being a mechanism for reassurance, pointing out that invariably if the dream involves something like examinations, the dreamer already knows the result, and the particular exam has been passed. But the fact that it keeps recurring is also likely to be a subconscious wish to be successful.

Only a week into working at the Royal Waterloo, I had a letter from the South-West Regional Labour Party asking if I would be prepared to have my name put forward for the shortlist to choose a prospective

Labour candidate for the Torrington constituency. I am amazed that I said yes. I was assured that if I was chosen it would not make major demands on my time and that as long as I visited one weekend a month that was all that would be needed until the election campaign, when I should take three weeks off work. I had always been very troubled by the way in which my medical student friends, on becoming doctors, lost all interest in life outside the hospital. They appeared to be medical vegetables and I was loath to see this happen to me. Anyhow I did not expect to win the selection contest. Another factor was that Elizabeth Furse had a charming thatched cottage near the village of Dolton, in the heart of the Torrington constituency. I could plan on taking one of two weekends off a month to drive down to north Devon, leaving at midnight on Friday and returning in the early hours of Monday morning. To commit one of my two weekends was not an impossible burden when I knew that I was going to a beautiful part of Devon, the northern edge of Dartmoor on the river Torridge. Knowing too that I would have somewhere to stay and bring girlfriends was crucial. Although travelling down would take time, it would be a real break from hospital when I got there. The advantage would be that I would be forced to read newspapers and to keep up with current affairs. Nevertheless, my decision to accept nomination was a pretty extra-ordinary one since most junior doctors find little time for anything else during this hectic period in their lives.

I decided not to tell anyone in the hospital of my candidacy. I was intent on a serious medical career and I felt that if the consultants knew that I was involved in politics they would not consider I was really committed to medicine. A few weeks later, on a fine sunny Saturday morning in August, I drove down to Bideford for the selection conference in my Morris Minor convertible. I still have the long speech which I had written out for my selection conference while stopping at a couple of roadside cafés. It was my first party political speech. Hitherto, whenever I had spoken to Fabian Society meetings it had been about the drugs industry or social services. Even I could not have actually delivered to the selection committee all of the detail about what should be our negotiating position to enter the EEC, though I suspect I sent some of them to sleep. But reading the text of my speech now, it is clear that it follows in all major respects the approach of Hugh Gaitskell, then the party leader.

It started with a short section about how I saw the aims of the Labour Party:

> to form a society where there are no social classes, where there is equal opportunity for everyone to achieve the level that their varying talents and application will allow, where there is a high degree of economic equality, full employment and a rising level of productivity, a democracy in all spheres of society due to a general spirit of co-operation between its members. Yet even as I say these words, I realise how much there is still to be done and since we believe that such changes must come through parliamentary democracy, they will of necessity come gradually, step by step, and we must persuade our fellow citizens that our ends are just and that the means we choose are right.

A few sniping attacks on the 'pitiful sight' of Harold Macmillan sacking a third of his Cabinet and at Lord Home for obstructing the UN was all that it contained of party politics. Indeed I said that I felt 'strongly that politics is more than mud-slinging and popular rhetoric. The task of the Labour Party is to make people think and realise for themselves the cost of a society founded on an ill-gotten and insecure affluence.' After only a short section in the speech on social problems it went on:

> Yet because I believe that the issue of the Common Market is more important than anything in our history for the last fifty years, I feel I cannot and will not shirk examining the main factors that confront us ... If it were to be a liberal, outward-looking institution, imbued with vigour and enterprise, I would welcome it – but should it be a tight, parochially exclusive European bloc, I would distrust it and actively do all in my power to stop our entry.

Enumerating the difficulties, I nevertheless took a rather more optimistic line than Gaitskell: 'I believe that with care these difficulties are surmountable. We cannot cling to the past forever – we must accept that only by putting aside some of our most treasured nationalistic traditions will any real form of international government come about.'

There were two other people on the shortlist and after the delegates had heard all three of us, they voted. Much to my surprise they chose me to fight the seat.

The sitting MP was Percy Browne, who had won it back for the Conservatives in the 1959 general election from the Liberal, Mark Bonham Carter. Mark Bonham Carter had won the by-election in March 1958 with a majority of only 219, polling 13,408 votes. His Conservative opponent in the by-election was Anthony Royle, who later became MP for Richmond. Though Royle was a charming person, it was not hard to depict him as a city slicker, using the constituency as a convenience en route to Parliament, and he was the wrong choice for that constituency. Yet even though Mark Bonham Carter increased his vote to 15,018 in the 1959 general election it was not enough for him to keep his seat. Percy Browne was a very popular local farmer and steeplechase jockey who had taken part in the Grand National, and something of a local hero. He polled 17,283 votes and Ray Dobson, who was the Labour candidate and later became MP for Bristol North East, managed 5,633 votes.

My candidature, not surprisingly, provoked no national publicity so no one in St Thomas' realised what I was doing. A general election was expected in the autumn of 1963 at the earliest. Later that afternoon I drove down to Plymouth and told my parents what had happened. Much to my surprise it was my mother who was violently opposed to what I had done: 'You're a bloody fool!' She feared that I had ruined a promising medical career. Yet my father, whom I had expected to be opposed, was wholly in favour. Amused rather than annoyed he wisely judged that as long as I continued to work hard and the consultants did not discover for some months they would not hold it against me. He proved to be correct. Eventually the story leaked out in the hospital but by the time it did everyone could see it made not the slightest difference to my ability to work very long hours. As the election drew near it was surprising how many consultants drew me aside and told me they were going to vote Labour. There was no doubt that Labour was starting to appeal to the middle class again as it had in 1945.

A fortnight after my selection I drove down to north Devon for my first public engagement, a garden fête organised by the local Labour Party. I was asked if I would judge the baby show. This was my first major political mistake. I thought that all one did was to choose the baby with the most attractive face. What an error. Judging a baby show is an accomplished skill, in which weight, length, hair and colour are as carefully assessed as by a racehorse owner at a yearling sale. When, after a cursory glance, I announced the winner, uproar followed from angry mothers who felt that they had been cheated. I must have lost at least fifty votes that afternoon.

My first political speech in public as the adopted prospective candidate was slightly more successful. It was on the European Community. The report in the local newspaper gives some clues as to why this issue was to become so central to my whole political career:

> Dr David Owen said that in the Common Market issue the country was facing one of its most important decisions. The question was fundamental to everything we had or held dear. We must all realise that entry into the Common Market would be something irrevocable – it was not something one joined and got out of, but something one entered and had to stay in. It was not just an economic Common Market but fundamentally political with its motives including some form of federation or supra-national authority. The Labour Party had been accused of sitting on the fence about the issue. He, personally, thought Mr Gaitskell's recent TV statement on the Common Market most statesman-like and would be the line upon which the Labour Party would make up its mind when they knew more. There were such questions as whether British agriculture was going to be safeguarded, whether the people of this country would be able to control their country, whether it was possible to carry out a socialist programme and for a socialist government to carry out any legislation they might wish. He believed that socialism was international and the EEC might well be a step towards international government. While it might be very foolish to cling to nationalistic ideals he thought it would be equally foolish to take the Liberal view that we should just go into the Common Market which he thought 'just juvenile'. Referring to nationalisation, Dr Owen said they did not believe that everything should be nationalised. They believed in free enterprise but they also believed that the government should be able to control basic things.

From that day to this, my political career has been dominated by the question of British membership of the European Community. I have twice resigned with it as the most important issue: firstly in 1972, with Roy Jenkins, from being a junior defence spokesman for the Labour Party, and then in 1980 from the shadow Cabinet when Michael Foot was elected leader. But I have never been at any stage a federalist, or a believer in a United States of Europe. On 21 September 1962 I watched Hugh Gaitskell reply on television to Prime Minister Harold Macmillan's broadcast of the night before. He asked if Macmillan wanted to enter a European federation. If so it 'means the end of Britain as an independent nation; we become no more than "Texas" or "California" in the United States of Europe. It means the end of a thousand years of history; it means the end of the Commonwealth to become just a province of Europe.' I liked Gaitskell's warning against a federalist Europe and broadly accepted his line of questioning the terms of entry in my own speeches but I also definitely wanted us to join the European Community, though I saw no reason why it should be inevitable that it became a single European state.

I was so busy in hospital that I did not attend the Labour Party conference on 3 October, when Gaitskell made his detailed assessment of the case for entry. I did not realise how much his speech was interpreted by his friends as coming down against it. Later, Charlie Pannell, a fellow Leeds MP with Gaitskell, told me how his wife Dora had said, 'Charlie, all the wrong people are cheering.' I am afraid that if I had been there I too would have cheered. George Brown, the deputy leader of the party, had to wind up the debate and many say he managed brilliantly in very difficult circumstances to put the case for entry, which Hugh Gaitskell's speech had brushed aside. The part of Gaitskell's speech which I childishly relished was his rubbishing of my Liberal opponent in Torrington.

Gaitskell recalled that at the Liberal Party conference the idea of our going into a European federation was greeted with wild enthusiasm by all the delegates. 'They are a little young, I think. I am all for youth but I like it to be sensible as well. After the conference a desperate attempt was made by Mr Bonham Carter to show that of course they were not committed to federation at all. Well, I prefer to go by what Mr Grimond says.' Gaitskell then quoted Grimond that if you are going to 'control the running of Europe democratically, you've got to move towards some form of federalism and if anyone says different to that they are really misleading the public', and then exclaimed, 'That is one in the eye to Mr Bonham Carter!'

It was more than one in the eye for I frequently thereafter quoted Gaitskell's speech in the constituency against Mark Bonham Carter. It probably did more for my morale than for my tally of votes – this sort of party political badinage is of no real interest except to party activists. It warms the immediate, not the wider, audience. Fighting this marginal seat, Bonham Carter must have thought that the Liberal commitment to federalism was a vote loser. Jo Grimond, by contrast, then leader of the Liberal Party, was more cavalier, a quality that made him one of our most engaging politicians and won him admiration throughout his career. I have always felt that it is good for politics that the federalist cause should have a political party ready to push its case and the Liberal Party has been broadly federalist ever since. I was never a federalist then, nor am I now, and it was to be one of the reasons why, twenty-five years later, I did not want the SDP to merge with the Liberal Party.

My six months at the Royal Waterloo were enriched by having Brendan Devlin as the surgical registrar. His irreverence blew through the corridors with a freshness and vigour that some found enervating and others intensely irritating. I revelled in it. Even then he was a brilliant surgeon and he went on to build an impressive career in the north-east, masterminding the extremely important confidential enquiry reports into post-operative deaths from his unit in the Royal College of Surgeons. Operating with him at weekends, I learnt enough general surgery from him to confirm that I was not made to be a surgeon. The reason that surgeons are not called 'Doctor' but 'Mister' is that they were originally barbers. In the olden days the man who shaved you and cut your hair would also be the person to amputate your leg. I wanted to be a doctor only from the neck up. I was becoming more and more interested in the brain and not so much in what lay below. I then thought of an ingenious wheeze. I would apply to do the eye houseman's post at St Thomas' for my compulsory six-month house surgeon's job. Very wisely, the

General Medical Council has now closed this loophole and insists that a young doctor's pre-registration surgical job must include general surgery. Fortunately, Hugh Wallace, the dermatologist whose ward I was looking after, was a close friend of Harold Ridley, the senior eye surgeon at St Thomas'. He strongly backed my application and I was accepted.

Harold Ridley was world famous for his operation to insert a lens actually into the eye to replace the opaque lens removed in a cataract operation. He was small, dapper and a Conservative. It is to his credit that he took me on knowing I was a prospective Labour candidate. During the six months I worked for him in the main hospital we got on extraordinarily well. There was far more humour and fun to him than many people realised. He was extremely conscientious and if one did anything for any of his private patients he insisted on paying very generously. Like most people who worked for him I became very attached to him. He was when very old belatedly given a knighthood in the 2000 New Year Honours list, a recognition he had long deserved.

Gradually I was allowed to do more routine operating, which I enjoyed. Unlike general surgery, there is no smell, virtually no blood and it requires considerable precision. Before I finished I was doing simple cataract operations on my own. Few patients are more grateful than those who have their eyesight restored or improved. When I was campaigning in the European election in 1984 in a Milton Keynes shopping centre an old man came charging across to greet me, saying to the accompanying crowd, 'This is the man who saved my eyesight.' He then proceeded to tell the television cameras, journalists and well-wishers how I had done a brilliant operation on his eyes. This gratitude was heartening but in fact removing a mature cataract in most cases is relatively simple and the lens pops out, rather like shelling a pea. Sadly the footage was as far as I know never shown on television.

I was assisting Harold Ridley in the operating theatre one day when he asked whether I had thought about applying for the neurology house physician's post when my job with him ended. I expressed surprise that I might be even considered, for it was the plum job in the hospital, desired by everyone who had just finished their compulsory pre-registration year. He said that if I wanted to apply he would strongly recommend me. I was appointed and it proved to be fascinating. It meant that I stood in for the children's house physician on alternate weekends so I could reinforce what I had already learnt about paediatrics.

One night when I was on duty in St Thomas' Hospital, an extraordinary coincidence took place. I was asked by a friend to look after one of his patients who had been admitted that day, very seriously ill. He mentioned the patient was a Conservative MP and had a nasty thrombosis in his lungs. When I went to see the patient he was asleep with his face turned away from me. I picked up his wrist to take his pulse and literally gasped when I read his name tag. The man lying in front of me was Percy Browne, the MP for Torrington. I urgently telephoned a friend and got him out of bed moaning and groaning to take over responsibility. Having this particular MP dead on my hands would have been very embarrassing. Fortunately Percy Browne survived and I used to drop in and chat to him as he recovered. Like most people I became captivated by his charm and I was very glad when he stood down on health grounds since I never had to campaign against him. He told me the story of the then professor of medicine, Sharpy-Schafer, who on being shown his electro-cardiograph and being told that he was an MP said, 'This is a by-election heart.'

In the summer of 1963 I visited Torrington and attended the annual general meeting of Torrington Labour Party. The Conservative candidate for the next election, in Percy Browne's place, was Peter Mills, a West Country farmer, active in the church and prominent on a local TV programme, *Faith for Life*. It was possible that we could have had an autumn election but because of John Profumo's involvement with Christine Keeler and his resignation in June, it looked more likely to be in 1964.

The Torrington constituency party president was Dr C. G. Jones, who was a very popular general practitioner in Okehampton. With the almost feudal nature of north Devon politics he gave the party a badge of respectability and made it easier for the more timid Labour supporters to declare themselves. The chairman of the party was Fred Dennis, a stalwart of the NUR, who worked in the Meldon quarry, then under threat of closure, which produced the ballast laid between sleepers on railway tracks all over the country. My agent was Len Mullholland, who lived in Bideford, over the water on the Barnstaple side of the river Torridge. His whole life was bound up with the Labour Party. Without his efforts over many years, the Torrington Labour Party would never have been anywhere near as strong. These and people like Nora Gee in Okehampton and George Allan, the man who delivered all the post in Chagford, made the atmosphere of the local Labour Party. They were genuine people with nothing to gain from being associated with the Labour Party and not infrequently something to lose. They took me into their homes, their wives mothered me, fed me and treated me as one of their own.

It was during the two years as their prospective candidate that I began to understand why Hugh Gaitskell had felt able to say he would fight for the party we 'love'. It is hard for those who take a cynical view of politics and the role of party to understand the emotional attachment that can easily develop. I have never believed that one should elevate party loyalty beyond reasonable limits, and obviously not beyond loyalty to the vital interests of one's country, but I too grew to love the atmosphere of the Torrington Labour Party. These people saw the Labour Party as a vehicle for helping to create a more generous, fair and just society. There was no envy or malice in their aspirations; their politics came from generous hearts. For them, fairness or a more equitable society was to evolve not out of confiscation but from persuasion. Many of them were devout Methodists and they saw their political activity as an extension of their chapel-going. Many such people are still in the Labour Party and even when I clashed with Labour and left to form the SDP I tried always to remember it.

I then left Torrington and St Thomas' far behind, flying off for a holiday in Greece. Before I left London I had agreed, in Elizabeth's bistro, to meet a diplomat, Martin Morland, whom I barely knew, in order to travel by car to Mount Athos. At the stroke of three, he drove up alongside the café in Athens where we had agreed to meet. After a long drive north we took a boat to Mount Athos. No female is allowed on the peninsula, which is governed by the Greek Orthodox monks in numerous monasteries. You have to have a special permit to visit but the experience is a profound one. Walking from monastery to monastery along paths softened by pine needles you catch breathtaking views of the sea. The monasteries themselves were then in bad repair, their former wealth having been long dissipated. In my hand I had Robert Byron's book *The Station*, written when he was twenty-two, full of the spirit of Byzantium and describing 'the Holy Mountain Athos, station of a faith where all the years have stopped'. The monks offer their hospitality free to their visitors though one is expected to give a donation. It was all very frugal, sleeping on hard beds and eating very simple fare; it was an unforgettable experience. I repeated it with my son Gareth in 1998, and the condition of the monasteries had by then been much improved. Martin and I then drove south to Athens and took a boat to Hydra, where I had been in 1960 with my first love. I was fancy free at the time and ripe to fall in love, which I promptly did, with Martin's beautiful cousin, Tessa Fraser. These friendships lasted. I am godfather to Martin's daughter and Tessa is godmother to my eldest son, Tristan.

On my return, my heavy workload as the neurology house physician left little time for politics, though I continued to visit Torrington once a month. During the autumn the political conference season was particularly dramatic. Labour was doing well in the opinion polls, Harold Wilson having spelt out the main theme of modernisation for the forthcoming election and striking a chord in a very receptive country. The Conservative conference was both dramatic and bruising. Since the start of the year, with General de Gaulle's veto of Britain's attempt to get into the Common Market, Prime Minister Harold Macmillan's 'Supermac' image had begun to crack. He wrote in his diary at that time, 'All our policies at home and abroad are in ruins.' Despite Macmillan's declaration that he was not going to be brought down 'by a couple of tarts', the Profumo affair further tarnished the party. There was a feeling that after twelve years of the Conservatives it was time for a change.

Macmillan told the Cabinet of his decision to stay on and fight the next election while in some pain in the morning, and that afternoon his surgeon advised him to have a prostatectomy. Harold Macmillan might never have actually resigned if Sir John Richardson, his physician, had been there from the outset. The surgeon, Macmillan thought, had advised a three- to four-month period off work, whereas Sir John was adamant that after six weeks he would be fit and well. Unfortunately Sir John, who had known Macmillan since the war in north Africa, was away on holiday. Such are the vagaries of life. Sir John, who taught me as a medical student at St Thomas', believed strongly that he could have prevented the resignation and he was not given to exaggeration. Had he done so, Harold Wilson might never have won the 1964 election against Macmillan. Becoming Prime Minister always owes more to accident than design.

On 18 October it was announced from King Edward VII's Hospital for Officers that Macmillan had seen the Queen and tendered his resignation. The Queen then sent for Lord Home, who resigned his earldom to become Sir Alec Douglas-Home. He proved to be a more formidable opponent than most of us in the Labour Party were ready to accept at the time. Given Labour's then large poll lead and political memories of the Tory Party conference, dominated by the power struggle between Lord Hailsham, Rab Butler and Reginald Maudling, it was amazing that the Conservatives came so close to winning the election in 1964, particularly since Iain Macleod, the most brilliant of the up-and-coming Cabinet ministers, and Enoch Powell refused even to serve under Douglas-Home.

At the time, the very welcome upshot of Macmillan's resignation for me was that an election was now unlikely until the autumn of 1964 and I could concentrate on medicine. I was still learning much about how best to handle patients. A woman who was well known in the communications world came into the hospital with a suspected brain tumour. She was much older than she looked, always beautifully dressed, charming and sophisticated. She managed the indignity of having her head shaved for the operation with great panache and wore an excellent wig afterwards. Most of her glamorous visitors had no idea how serious her operation had been – her brain tumour was unfortunately found to be far advanced and there was no case even for radiotherapy. Initially it was felt better to tell her that we thought the tumour would turn out to be benign. Gradually as the days went by she persisted in her demand to be told the true diagnosis. Her consultant, Dr Reginald Kelly, was a wise man and sensed that she did not really wish to know the whole truth. He kept delaying telling her. I talked to her a lot in the evenings and was becoming almost too fond of her as a person, anxious that we were not being truthful with her. On a number of occasions I said that we ought to reveal the diagnosis. Eventually Reggie Kelly suggested that I should tell her. I told her one evening and she was very brave, seeming to take it extremely well. Next morning in the ward I was surprised to find she was not in her bed. I asked the ward sister where she was. The sister said, 'What do you mean? She's there, in her normal bed.' We walked back and I saw the truth. She had removed her wig, abandoned her make-up, the scar on her scalp was visible and she looked thirty years older. She died a few days later. She had simply given up the will to live and I felt deeply responsible. It was an object lesson. Despite the fashionable enthusiasm for doctors always to tell every patient their diagnosis, there are still some cases where it is better to let people live in hope.

Around that time the same message of caution was reinforced for me in dealing with another patient. This man was a doctor and he came in under a consultant who had been a great friend of his as a medical student. He was a very buoyant personality and was talking all the time about how he knew he had cancer and that his friend had told him that he would let him know the diagnosis as soon as the pathology reports were back. He did indeed have cancer and his consultant told me he thought in view of their friendship it would be better if he saw him alone and gave him the results. Next day I went in to see him and he made no mention at all of the tests and rather oddly talked about everything else but his own medical condition. When the consultant came round I asked him whether he had given the diagnosis since it appeared that he still did not know. He assured me he had. Soon it became obvious that this patient, though an intelligent doctor, was determined to block out the conversation he had had and the diagnosis he had been given. He proceeded to lead his life for the next few months with absolutely no regard whatever to the diagnosis. He divorced his wife, married again and never told anyone until he came into hospital to die. It was a bizarre incident but once again it showed that there are no rules of general application in medicine. Everyone is an individual and each case has to be judged on its own merit.

When my six months ended in January 1964 I went to the National

Heart Hospital to do cardiology as a preparation for my higher examination for membership of the Royal College of Physicians. Sadly Dr Elkington, the senior neurologist at St Thomas', was ill. I was asked if I would help out and do a locum as neurology registrar. It was a wonderful opportunity and I jumped at it, even though it would mean having little time to study for my membership. After a few months, a permanent vacancy for the post of neurology and psychiatric registrar came up, and I was fortunate to be chosen.

That spring, Jim Callaghan, the shadow Chancellor of the Exchequer, came to Exeter. It was the first time we had met and a photograph of us together appeared in the local press, which was a help. He was very friendly but if anyone had said that thirteen years later he would make me his Foreign Secretary we would both have been dumbfounded.

The general election was called for September 1964. I simply took three weeks' unpaid leave from the hospital for the campaign and drove down to Bideford and tried to rent a flat. The estate agents were clearly frightened of having any property linked with Labour and so we eventually took one in my mother's name. It was a completely amateur campaign; we had very few people in the constituency who owned cars and it was so far flung that it was difficult to canvass. The main enjoyment was having three and sometimes four village meetings a night. A very close girlfriend and her sister came down to help and we all enjoyed ourselves and were seen to do so. We had hardly any money, barely enough to cover the cost of printing an election address, but fortunately Courage beer decided to launch a national campaign with big posters saying VOTE FOR COURAGE. My supporters decided to take advantage of this and fly-posted all over the constituency with a large 'Owen', so that it read VOTE OWEN FOR COURAGE. All we could hope for was to avoid losing our deposit. No Labour MP came near the constituency throughout the campaign. My only visiting speaker was a Labour peer who was a great expert in inland waterways and who came to speak in the little seaport of Appledore.

Mark Bonham Carter made few inroads into the Conservative vote during the campaign. My election message to the constituency had at least a certain brutal frankness to it and it showed I had little time for the Liberals:

The party of our dreams is usually far removed from the party of reality. Possibly the most unpleasant feature of politics is the inherent compromise that it demands from each of us. Yet, if we are not to end up with a party for each individual voter, we all know that we have to come to terms with this situation. Politics, with its overall concern with power, poses the question at each election, which party is to govern? Minority groups and small parties like the Liberals who, because of their gradual decline, no longer appear as a party that can possibly govern, serve merely to confuse the issue. They may provide a comfortable alternative to the dissatisfied voter who shirks compromise, but they do not represent a serious alternative.

The Liberals believed that they would win back Torrington in the 1964 general election. It was clear to everyone that as the Labour candidate the only question for me was whether I could save my deposit. It was a seat for a one-off, light-hearted candidature or for a candidate out to earn his spurs towards being selected later for a safe seat. Mark Bonham Carter was Asquith's grandson and the son of Lady Violet Bonham Carter. He was almost as unsuitable a candidate for this rural constituency as Anthony Royle. In a cattle market surrounded by rubicund West Country-men he stood out, wan and ill at ease. He had about him the cultivated effortless superiority that marks out many of those who pass through Balliol College, Oxford. 'Life', the old joke goes, 'is one Balliol man after another', and there were not many Balliol men among Liberal voters in Torrington. The more I saw of him at close quarters, the more I was put off by his political manner. His attractive wife was a considerable asset but his mother a dubious one. On polling day Lady Violet insisted on entering all the polling stations. Electoral law clearly says that this is only allowed if you are the candidate or the candidate's agent. The Torrington Labour Party, already fed up with her 'Lady Bountiful' act, complained to the returning officer but, despite that, and much to our fury, she continued on her way, saying she had done this at every election since her father was Prime Minister. Mark Bonham Carter's commitment to the European Community, which he had vigorously championed in the House of Commons following his by-election success, began to wilt in the constituency as he tried to win over the Devon dairy farmers, who were in those days firmly against going into the Common Market. It was the first of many reminders of how Liberal candidates try to win votes by saying different things to different people. Admittedly this candidate did it with considerably more style and elegance than normal. But he played the same game and earned more scepticism than votes from the farmers, who are notoriously hard headed.

Mark Bonham Carter told me years afterwards at Roy Jenkins's house in East Hendred that he believed that my intervention had robbed him of the seat. This was nonsense for I increased the Labour vote by less than 200. Once he had lost the seat in 1959, he no longer had the advantage of incumbency. To have a chance of recovering the seat in 1964 would have required him to go and live in the constituency and nurse it day by day, which is what Peter Mills was doing. Even so he would have had great difficulty in winning. At the count, when my pile of votes passed the point at which the deposit was saved, a cheer went up from the Labour Party, generously supported by the Conservatives. This was not based on the old two-party conspiracy against the Liberals: both Labour and Conservative Party workers agreed that the Liberals had fought the dirtiest campaign.

The final result was:

| Peter Mills | Conservative | 16,899 |
| Mark Bonham Carter | Liberal | 14,831 |
| David Owen | Labour | 5,867 |

I returned to London, quite happy to switch right out of politics and to concentrate on medicine. I was now living in a stylish black-floored, white-walled basement flat in Chesham Street, Belgravia, having sold *Amanda* for a thousand pounds. I later heard that *Amanda* had sunk in the middle of the night, holed below the waterline after settling on a milk bottle. At the hospital I was now combining what I had always wanted to do, psychiatry with neurology, and working for Dr William Sargant. He was a giant both physically, a second row rugby forward who played for St Mary's Hospital, and clinically, a dominating personality with the therapeutic courage of a lion, author of a bestselling book on brainwashing called *Battle for the Mind*. That generation of psychiatrists who worked at the Maudsley Hospital transformed British psychiatry. They pioneered the unlocking of all doors and the treating of psychiatric patients in all respects like patients in medical wards of general hospitals. Before the war psychotherapy and psychoanalytical treatments had done nothing to cut the size of the large remote Victorian psychiatric hospitals. People were protected in hospital wards rather than treated. The most many psychiatrists could hope to do was to shield them against the three Ss: starvation, sleeplessness and suicide. Even after the war patients were still virtually imprisoned with wards locked and, in all too many cases, patients neglected. The transformation of their life during the 1950s was a social revolution. Psychiatric patients began to be treated with physical methods like electro-convulsive therapy (ECT) and the special anti-depressant drugs began to appear.

William Sargant was a human dynamo. Controversial, committed, he was the sort of person of whom legends are made. He was adamant that no doors should be locked and no windows barred. He believed that patients should be trusted and treated in general wards even if suicidal. He was confident that with a combination of drugs and electric shock therapy even seriously ill psychiatric patients could be safely treated in general hospitals. What was more important, he practised what he preached.

Sargant delighted in being the bête noire of the psychoanalysts. The previous psychiatrist at St Thomas' was a Freudian who, with Dr Ernest Jones, led the British psychoanalytic movement. Sargant claimed that he used to tell students during the war, much to their amusement, that they did not fear Zeppelins or bombs as such; their alarm was due to the accident of these being also phallic symbols which aroused subconscious homosexual libido and other fears. While Sargant was seen as the hammer of the analysts, he actually believed that they had something to contribute to neurotic patients. But he was adamant in his belief that analysis provided absolutely nothing of clinical value for patients suffering from psychoses.

The massive and all-redeeming feature of the man was his optimism. He had a passionate commitment to lifting his patients' depression. He was able to understand that those who were depressed were in many senses far more ill than people with cancer or in severe pain. In part this was because he himself had become depressed in 1934 when he had first developed tuberculosis as a young doctor and had then begun to lose interest in his medical research work. He would punch home to students how dreadful it was to be depressed by reminding them how rare it was for patients suffering from intractable pain to commit suicide. By contrast the sheer horror of feeling depressed drives many to suicide. Sargant claimed that he was entitled to take some risks with the treatment of a depressed patient in the same way that a surgeon takes risks with his patients. When side effects were discovered for such successful drugs as chlorpromazine hydrochloride, commonly called Largactil, used in the treatment of schizophrenia, or the then newly discovered monoamine oxidase inhibitors used for anxiety depression, Sargant would not only refuse to stop dispensing them but he would defend the side effects by reference to the number of patients who were expected to die just by virtue of having an anaesthetic. He would also argue that the fact that you did not know how a drug worked should not preclude one from using it if it alleviated symptoms. After all, he would say, clinicians used quinine for years in the treatment of malaria without the slightest idea how it was acting in the patient's body.

The widespread use of electro-convulsive therapy in St Thomas' alarmed people. Yet I saw too many patients respond dramatically to ECT to harbour many doubts about its efficacy in carefully selected patients suffering psychotic rather than neurotic symptoms. I remember a professor I treated through three episodes of depression. He came down with depression every year at exactly the same time and had done so for a decade. The early signs were a disturbed sleep rhythm and lethargy and within a few weeks he became classically depressed, slowed up, indecisive, weeping involuntarily and quite unable to teach his students. Each year he resisted ECT until in desperation he accepted our advice and agreed to have it. After three treatments his depression would lift and he would be dramatically better. I remember too how women who had become depressed after childbirth responded to ECT with as few as one or two treatments. Such cases are a medical emergency, since these women can become so distressed that they kill their newborn child as well as themselves.

I was reminded how controversial all this treatment was when some years later I was having lunch in Soho with Anthony Howard, then editor of the *New Statesman,* and a doctor friend of his. Talking as one might among doctors I used the shorthand description for ECT and said that if my wife ever got depressed after childbirth 'I wouldn't hesitate to plug her into the mains'. A few months later he used that quote in a profile and, ever since, it has kept recurring without any linkage to post-puerperal depression. So I simply became the man who would not hesitate to plug his wife into the mains!

The good diagnostician picks up the minutiae which others ignore. I once interviewed a policeman for over an hour and at the end of it pronounced him quite sane. Sargant diagnosed him as a paranoid schizophrenic within five minutes purely on the strength of an unguarded admission that he would leave Scotland Yard well after midnight to walk home and then do the return journey in the very early morning. I thought when he first said this that it was bizarre behaviour but nothing more. Sargant had the wit to look at the distance between his home address and Scotland Yard and calculate that each walk would take him over one and a half hours. When he put it to the policeman that this meant walking three hours every day in addition to his long hours at the Yard, he admitted it without blinking an eyelid. Normal people do not behave like this but even so for Sargant to certify him, much to the anger of senior officers in the Metropolitan Police who thought he was sane, was a big risk. The vindication came many months later when the policeman, by then in a psychiatric hospital, developed florid schizophrenia.

Another doctor working in St Thomas' was H. J. Shorvon, who during the war had developed with Sargant the technique of abreaction. He allowed me to treat one of his old patients who had first come with a totally paralysed arm, having been strafed by German fighter planes in the water off the beaches of Dunkirk. If left untreated for more than a few weeks the arm would become completely paralysed. The treatment was to inject him with sodium amytal so that he would become drowsy and then help him to re-enact the traumatic experience of Dunkirk. When his tension was relieved, his arm would immediately start to function normally. The key to the treatment was for him to act out, as he became relaxed, his wartime experience. This meant I would have to help by generating the same atmosphere, shouting urgently, 'The bombs are dropping! There's the splash of the bomb! The boat's sinking! You've got to get off! Swim to the lifeboat! The plane's coming in to attack! The tracer bullets are coming towards you!' As I did this he would gradually react until, the moment when the excitement and tension had come back, he would suddenly virtually drown in front of one. His throat would gurgle. He would cough, splutter and retch and one could almost hear the water in his mouth and lungs. Then as quickly as it had come, it would all stop. He would go to sleep for an hour or more and then walk out of the hospital with his arm swinging normally.

We did not use this abreaction technique a lot but once it led to a medical emergency. A young woman was referred to Shorvon for a second opinion by a dermatologist. She was thought to be suffering from a rare peripheral vascular disease. Her nails and the tips of her fingers had been literally rotting for a couple of years and no treatment had alleviated it. The question was whether there was any underlying psychopathology. Under abreaction Shorvon, without much difficulty, got her to reveal that she had been putting her fingers every day into phenol. This was her way of drawing attention to herself and to her underlying mental anxiety. He decided that this revelation was too dramatic for her to wake up and face so soon. So she was given continuous sleeping drugs for a week and then gradually brought around, by which time the skin on her fingers was beginning to heal. She was then treated with a mixture of psychotherapy and anti-depressants.

Not surprisingly in this fascinating atmosphere of positive psychiatry, I decided that I would not become a consultant neuro-logist but aim to be a professor of psychiatry. Before doing so I needed an academic research background and so after two years as the neurology and psychiatric registrar, I left to take up a research fellowship on the medical unit of St Thomas'.

I had by then also embarked on a more serious attempt to become an MP in Plymouth, although I was still loath to admit it to myself. Early in 1965 I had been asked if I would allow my name to be put forward for the constituency of Plymouth Sutton by Alderman Fred Stott, who was a much respected Labour member of the social services committee and a justice of the peace with my mother. Dr

John Dunwoody, who had nearly won for Labour in 1964, had decided not to contest it again, preferring to wait for a safe constituency. His readiness to leave that seat helped to lull me into a false sense of its being impossible to win. I felt he would not be leaving it if he thought it could be won and therefore it was not likely to return me to Parliament and so disrupt my medical career.

I well remember the day on which I decided to let my name be placed on the shortlist for this constituency. It was a sunny day and we were waiting for a case conference due to start in the sitting room on Ward 5 of the Royal Waterloo Hospital. Sargant burst into the room, demanding to know where the ward sister was. He was clearly enraged. It transpired that the sister in charge, finding that many of her nurses were burning their stiff white aprons on the electric fires when turning around in the patient's small rooms, had arranged for grilles to be put over the electric bars. Sargant saw this as symbolic of going back to the bad old days of locked wards and treating psychiatric patients like imbeciles. Eventually the sister managed to persuade him that nothing like this was intended, nor could fairly be construed. Even so he continued to act like a spoilt child. In a flash forward I saw myself in Sargant's position in thirty years' time, behaving in exactly the same way. Medicine then appeared to me to offer only a constricted vision and politics a much broader canvas. Over the years as I have watched eminent politicians and physicians, that superficial judgement has certainly not been borne out. Both are capable of behaving childishly, often with remarkable pettiness, and Sargant's tirade on Ward 5 has been mirrored often enough, even in my presence, by Cabinet ministers. But at the time it was an incident that overcame my hesitation and helped me to continue in politics. That night I wrote to the Constituency Labour Party accepting nomination.

A few weeks later I attended the selection conference, having been placed on the shortlist. The strongest challenge came from an extremely attractive candidate, Betty Boothroyd. She spoke far better than I, as many of the general management committee teasingly reminded me over the years, but I was the local boy, known to some of them when fighting Torrington. A few of the delegates were patients of my father's or knew my mother and no doubt they gave me the benefit of the doubt. Betty Boothroyd later became MP for

West Bromwich West and a highly successful Speaker, the first woman to hold the post.

British politics is unusual in having so many MPs who have not been born or bred in their constituency. In America such politicians are called carpet-baggers and are only very rarely chosen. The fact that I am a Plymothian was a considerable help in holding my seat against the tide of public opinion in 1970, 1974, 1979 and 1983. It meant that visiting my constituency was going home. As I stepped off the train at Plymouth station I smelt the sea and felt instantly different. It was as if I had gained an extra lung. I had also been shortlisted for a selection conference, on the day before the Plymouth selection, for the Falmouth & Camborne seat. This was an existing Labour seat, where Frank Hayman was due to retire. I had, however, driven down there a few weeks before and concluded that it was not the best constituency for me. The extra 70 miles made the journey from London too far. Also, looking around and assessing the constituency, I did not believe it was as safe in reality as it looked on paper. When I withdrew my name, Sara Barker, the then Labour national agent, horrified on being told that I had withdrawn in order to take my chance on being selected for Plymouth Sutton, shrieked down the phone, so that everyone in the neurology clinic where I was working heard every word, that my decision was incomprehensible. Her attitude reinforced my feeling that Plymouth Sutton was not winnable and right up until the last week of the general election campaign I believed that I was still heading for a medical not a political career. I had compromised with Sara Barker to the extent that I agreed to go down to Falmouth for the selection conference and to tell them then why I was withdrawing before they voted. This ensured no adverse press speculation. As things turned out Falmouth was not as safe as people thought and while John Dunwoody won the seat in 1966 he lost in 1970, as did his wife Gwyneth in Exeter. I was left thereafter as the only Labour MP in England west of Bristol.

On the medical unit I carried forward the work which I had already begun with my colleague David Marsden. Our first paper, published in December 1965 in the *Lancet*, was entitled 'The Effect of Adrenergic Beta Blockade on Parkinsonian Tremor'. David Marsden went on to have a very successful career in neuro-pharmacology, being the professor of neurology at the National Hospital for Nervous Diseases, Queen's Square, London, until he died in 1999. We wrote together, and with others, five main papers over the next two years, some while I was an MP. David Marsden was undoubtedly the brains behind our research while I provided some of the drive. He taught me the discipline of scientific method. Politics has helped corrupt that discipline of forming judgements on facts but I have avoided making some major political errors by insisting on obtaining the facts first. I have also tried to ensure I learnt by trying to conduct a post mortem on decisions taken that have gone wrong. The sheer indiscipline of political decision-making still sometimes shocks me. Hunch, panic, prejudice are all major determinants and this will continue while we retain an adversarial parliamentary and legal system on which a peculiarly ideological media industry thrives, but more of this later.

Despite enjoying research, politics was destined eventually to push out medicine, though not without a struggle. Having won the seat in Plymouth in the 1966 general election with a majority of 5,222 over the Conservative incumbent, I turned up at St Thomas' Hospital on the Monday morning after the election, determined to continue as a doctor while an MP. In the hospital everyone thought my being an MP was a great joke. Fortunately the professor of medicine, Bill Cranston, and Reggie Kelly were delighted that I wished to continue to do research and both felt it would be a great waste if I gave up medicine entirely. So for the next two years I tried to be both a doctor and a politician. Foolishly I did not sit for the third-part viva of my membership examination for the Royal College of Physicians. Very few things have given me more pleasure than being made many years later a fellow of the Royal College.

In my passport I went on calling myself a medical practitioner until I became Foreign Secretary, when my passport 'to allow the bearer to pass freely without let or hindrance' was issued by myself to myself. In the 1980s, it seemed wiser to stop the pretence and to call myself a politician. But by then it was too late to drop the courtesy title of Doctor, even if I had wanted to, which I had not. The general public are often surprised to find PhDs calling themselves Doctor, and they still say to me, 'You're a proper doctor.' They often still call me Doctor rather than Lord, and if, as I hope, we soon start to elect members of the Second Chamber, perhaps I will revert to being called Doctor.

In 1967 the Labour government's prices and incomes policy dictated wage restraint for everyone and I became rather guilty about continuing to take a part-time salary from the St Thomas' Endowment Fund while also being paid as an MP. I decided to work on the medical unit unpaid. This was an error because while I was being paid I felt an obligation to attend the hospital but once that sense of obligation was removed, the demands of the House of Commons began to take precedence. Nevertheless, until the moment I became Minister for the Navy in July 1968, when I was no longer allowed to continue as a doctor, medicine came first and politics second in my heart. This ordering of my priorities was helped by Kenneth Robinson, the then Minister of Health, appointing me as a governor of Charing Cross Hospital. This was an investment for me for I began to learn about the difficulty of administering the National Health Service, which proved invaluable when I became Minister of Health in 1974. At that stage we were planning the new hospital in Fulham and the move from the Strand, opposite Charing Cross railway station. It would be helpful if more MPs were appointed to public bodies and gained practical experience of administering the public sector as some already do for payment in the private sector. There is now a ministerial reluctance to make such appointments and, as a result, the debates in Parliament on the NHS and other public services risk getting out of touch with the realities within these services.

In one other way medicine and politics came together. There was in those days no doctor employed in the Palace of Westminster and the medical MPs were expected to cope with any emergencies. The police sensibly called the doctors with the most knowledge first. In my early years I was near the top of their list. As the years passed they wisely dropped me to the bottom. Diagnosing and examining these medical emergencies was not easy as the facilities in the early days were pretty dreadful, just a small box of a room with a couch. This has now improved. If certain of the diagnosis I would send them off to St Thomas', confident that when I met my colleagues next day in the hospital they would not be able to rib me. If unsure of the diagnosis I sent them to the Westminster Hospital so as to avoid my friends in St Thomas' smiling at my expense.

On one occasion an elderly Conservative MP appeared to have had an acute heart attack. But there was something odd about his case and because of this I sent him to the Westminster Hospital. My doubts were raised because I had felt his femoral arteries for a normal pulsation and had not been able to detect any pulse. If absent, it meant that he had had a coarctation of the aorta. This is when the wall of the artery splits and blood flows in, compressing the inner wall so that virtually no blood passes through. This split can spread up to involve the coronary arteries. So I wrote in the referral letter, '?Heart attack? Coarctation of the aorta.'

I was later told by the consultant, in a generous letter of thanks, that the MP was in hospital for a few days not responding to treatment; the consultant asked the young house physician who had referred the patient and was told, laughingly, an MP who was a doctor. When the consultant asked what the MP doctor had diagnosed, he was told, with even louder laughter, coarctation. The consultant then leant over and felt for a femoral pulse and, finding none ordered an immediate X-ray. A few hours later the MP was operated on successfully for a coarctation. I have dined out on that story, suitably garnished, for years.

Another problem occurred when I was asked to see an MP who had collapsed in the chamber. I arranged for the MP to be taken and put on the couch in the medical emergency room. After a while I left, asking the policeman to look in from time to time and promising to return in half an hour. I came back at intervals over the next few hours. By this time the young policeman was so concerned at this comatose MP being left in the room that he called the police superintendent. On my return they were both there and asked politely if I did not think it wise to call an ambulance and arrange for the MP to be admitted to hospital. I said no and continued periodic visits for another few hours, by which time the MP was ready to leave to go home. I am not sure the young policeman ever realised the diagnosis. The MP was, quite simply, drunk.

The early 1960s were a heady time in politics and British life. Satire was the medium, two fingers to the politicians was the message. It was exemplified by the show *Beyond the Fringe*, the magazine *Private Eye* and the television series *That Was the Week that Was*. All guyed politicians and a typical jibe was David Frost's summing up of the general election between Sir Alec Douglas-Home and Harold Wilson as a battle between Dull Alec and Smart Alec. Michael Shank's *The Stagnant Society* hit a raw nerve. Anthony Sampson's *The Anatomy of Britain* and a series of Penguin Specials, asking what was wrong with Britain, pointed to the answer: 'the Establishment'. What the Establishment was was harder to define. We, who were on the outside, felt those who were on the inside were the reason for our decline. Where we went wrong was to believe that it would be enough to change the players. We underestimated the extent to which the new Labour arrivals were going to be absorbed by the old Conservative hands. Soon they would ape their habits and their prejudices, become obsessed about editorial opinion in top people's newspapers and fall for all the flummery surrounding 'the Palace' – even become members of the same all-male clubs.

I was part of the medical establishment at St Thomas' Hospital. Politicians and other eminent people came in fairly frequently as patients, and this helped me to see different facets of the Establishment and to look sceptically at its values. Yet at that stage I did not look sceptically at Harold Wilson. I was staggered that as many as 103 Labour MPs had voted for George Brown to be leader of the Labour Party in 1963. It seemed amazing to me that Harold Wilson should have won with only 144 votes. Within a few months of entering the House of Commons, I was to find out why sound, sensible MPs had voted for George despite their anxieties about his personality and his weakness for alcohol. They simply did not trust Harold Wilson. But to me, Harold Wilson's 'white heat of the technological revolution' seemed to match the needs of the country. He appeared classless, modern and, with a statistician's mind, able to reverse the 'brain drain' and understand the scientific needs of the country. To my generation Britain was still languishing in nostalgia, looking back to 1940, to the Battle of Britain when we stood alone.

I first met Harold Wilson at Plymouth railway station, twelve days before the March 1966 general election. Traditionally Prime Ministers are welcomed by the stationmaster. Harold Wilson stepped off the train in his famous Gannex coat, pipe puffing, accompanied by Mary, his wife. I was just part of the group, along with other West Country candidates, when suddenly his aide sought me out, no doubt because I was the candidate for the most marginal seat. I went up to Harold Wilson to shake hands but before I knew what was happening, he took me by the arm and propelled me forward to walk alongside him towards the television cameras at the end of the platform. The all-important television pictures that night were of me talking animatedly to the Prime Minister as if we were intimate friends. It was brilliant politics and the first of many incidents that demonstrated his recognition of Marshall McLuhan's gospel that 'the medium is the message'.

The press handout and the closed, ticket-only political meeting of the twenty-first century are killing off some of the magic of the hustings but it was still there in the 1960s. In Chatham in 1964, Wilson had rhetorically asked, 'Why do I speak about the Navy?' and a heckler had shouted back, 'Because you're in Chatham.' He had given a rollicking speech in the 1964 election in the Forum cinema in Devonport, which I went to as the candidate for Torrington. Ridiculing the overstaffed Navy, he reverted to being the statistician. 'We have 101 ships in commission. We have of course plenty of admirals – eighty-five. Our admiral:warship co-efficient is 0.851.' His audience loved it, it was our Harold the 'Cheeky Chappy'.

I admired what Wilson had said in 1964 to the Scottish Labour Party at Rothesay: 'The Labour Party is a moral crusade or it is nothing. We shall not suffer this party, on which the hopes of millions depend, to become either a soulless bureaucracy or a vote-dealing Tammany Hall.' I laughed when at Bellevue in Manchester in 1963 after Lord Home had succeeded Harold Macmillan as leader of the Conservative Party, he derided the Tories as the party of privilege: 'The selection had been through the machinery of an autocratic cabal. I am worried to know how a scion of an effete establishment can understand the scientific revolution. After half a century of democratic advance the whole process has ground to a halt with a 14th Earl.' Sir Alec Douglas-Home had the good humour to reply that one could say that Harold was the 14th Mr Wilson. Wilson was a political Walter Mitty and I was to discover those fourteen Mr Wilsons in the years to come.

It is very easy in retrospect to downplay the way in which Harold Wilson dominated British politics in the 1960s. The *Economist* was correct when it entitled an editorial during the 1966 election 'The issue is Wilson'. To someone like myself, outside the inner workings of either Parliament or the Labour Party, Wilson was something of a miracle worker and even a hero.

In Plymouth that afternoon Harold Wilson was for me, and many others, after the death of Hugh Gaitskell simply the best leader the Labour Party and the country could possibly have. Before he spoke to that enthusiastic meeting of party workers from all over the West Country in Plymouth Guildhall, I made a eulogising introductory speech. I can still hear myself quoting President Kennedy: 'We are not here to curse the darkness, but to light a candle that can lead us from the darkness into a safe and sane future. Prime Minister, you have lit that candle, may it always burn – welcome to Plymouth.' Even allowing for politician's rhetoric, I did in a way believe it.

My attitudes had been influenced by reading *The Making of the Prime Minister* by Anthony Howard and Richard West, a breathless and somewhat euphoric account of what had led up to the hair's-breadth victory in 1964. Modelled on Theodore White's 1960 classic, *The Making of the President*, it suggested parallels with Kennedy. It was why I had used the Kennedy quotation in my welcoming speech and this image had been reinforced by Wilson's own attempt to mirror JFK's 'first hundred days'. Since those days, apart from his skilful handling of the Cuban missile crisis, I have become more and more disenchanted with President Kennedy's actual record both as a politician and as a person. He now seems more style than substance. In those early days too I thought the gritty Yorkshire pipe-smoking Harold Wilson was like my favourite US President, peppery old Harry Truman, who really did give them hell. But I was soon to realise that Wilson had none of the Truman decisiveness.

Nevertheless it was a heady day for a young candidate to have the Prime Minister coming down to help in one's campaign. It was naïve of me given that Sutton was a highly marginal seat but I did not realise, or perhaps did not want to realise, that I was likely to get into Parliament. I was still deeply ambivalent about whether I wanted to forsake medicine for politics and only Peter Shore's parting remark at the station, 'See you at Westminster', made me recognise that this might be about to happen. When I almost automatically said, 'You're joking,' it became very apparent that he meant every word of it.

Peter Shore was right; the general public watching the seventeen months of the 1964–6 government, starting with a majority of only five and a horrendous balance of payments deficit, estimated at £800 million, did feel that the problems had been handled with great skill and were ready to renew Wilson's mandate. I now know that most of the key economic decisions taken in this period were wrong and I have become very wary of repeating a period of minority government, as in 1974, in 2010 unless there is a fixed-term mechanism for such a parliament to risk unpopular decisions.

In the 1960s Britain was part of the post-war Bretton Woods system of fixed exchange rates. While devaluation was possible, it was frowned on, particularly by the Americans, since sterling was a reserve currency. If devaluation was to have been avoided then government spending should have been ruthlessly cut back in 1964. Since manifesto commitments and thirteen years of accumulated good intentions in opposition made this virtually impossible, Labour should have devalued. Reggie Maudling, the outgoing Conservative Chancellor, would almost certainly have done so. Harold Wilson's own resistance to devaluation perhaps stemmed from his experience in 1949 when Hugh Gaitskell had championed devaluation. Moreover, his strange deference to President Johnson meant that we were left defending an unrealistic parity for far too long and we also maintained a level of defence spending greatly in excess of any other European country long after it was clear we could not afford to do so.

The actual 1966 general election campaign in Plymouth was surprisingly uneventful. Despite its potential for damage, defence never became a major political issue in the constituency. The cancellation of the aircraft carrier-building programme did not have the expected local effect that I had feared the month before, when Christopher Mayhew had resigned as Minister for the Navy. Mayhew was in favour of drastic defence cuts, but argued that there must also be cuts in commitments to match. He did not see how we could maintain a world role in the 1970s, including a presence east of Suez, with an entirely arbitrary defence cost ceiling which had forced the exclusion of new carriers. He was proven to be right. Denis Healey's resistance to cutting our world commitments only staved off the inevitable.

On election day I was carried to a surprisingly large victory on the coat tails of one person – Harold Wilson. There was a large swing to Labour and John and Gwyneth Dunwoody won Falmouth & Camborne and Exeter respectively. We had not had three Labour MPs in the West Country since the 1945 Labour landslide. The Labour government had an overall majority of seventy-five.

On the Sunday after the election I drove back to London to my house in Limehouse, 78 Narrow Street, on the Thames. It was still virtually a building site. I had bought it for £3,000 the year before and I was slowly doing it up using odd-job men and doing a lot myself. The roof was leaking and only one room was habitable, where I had to eat and sleep. My plan had been to rebuild the house around me but this would now have to change. As long as I could keep working at both St Thomas' and Parliament I felt I would have enough money to have builders in and increase my mortgage. The next day I turned up at St Thomas' Hospital determined to show that nothing had happened that would stop me continuing as a doctor. I was greeted with a mixture of amazement and humour but even the most Tory of consultants seemed genuinely pleased.

When the 1966 parliament assembled I walked over the bridge to take the oath of allegiance and started to find my way around the maze that is the Palace of Westminster. I suppose I ought to have felt very proud or very humble but I am afraid my memories are more mundane. The hardest thing was to discover where the lavatories were; as if to demonstrate its club-like nature, all the doors are unmarked. I was not eligible for even a desk, let alone a room. All I had was a locker for my papers, not even as large as a golf locker in a club room. The policemen became for me, as for all MPs, guides, guardians and friends and gradually I settled in and got used to the Palace of Westminster as a place of work.

On that first day there was a note on the message board to ring Gerry Reynolds, the MP for Islington North, in the Ministry of Defence. Gerry had come down to speak for me in the election and we had got on extremely well. His private secretary said that the minister wanted me to come over and have a cup of tea. After being directed to where the ministry was, such was my ignorance of Whitehall, and passing through security, I found myself admitted to a large sitting room dominated by a picture of Kitchener. It was almost like looking at the famous poster 'Your country needs you'. Gerry asked me if I would become his parliamentary private secretary. A PPS, I was told, is the minister's eyes and ears in the House of Commons, where civil servants could not go. The disadvantage was that I would not be able to speak on defence matters because I could not be seen to be critical of the ministry. Silence seemed to me to present great problems in view of the fact that the Royal Navy dockyard in Devonport was by far the largest employer in the city. But Gerry explained that I would be able to claim to have the minister's ear and that becoming a PPS would be considered by the press to be an unusually rapid promotion. I accepted without really knowing what I was letting myself in for. It was, as it turned out, an excellent decision and we became good friends, our friendship ending only with Gerry's tragically early death in 1969.

It was Gerry who proposed my name for the 1963 Club, a dining club for people who were closely identified with Hugh Gaitskell. At my first dinner the conversation kept referring to 'CDS', and eventually I asked my next door neighbour Jack Diamond, who had also come down to speak for me in the general election, what the initials meant. He was amazed to discover that I had not been involved in the Campaign for Democratic Socialism, which Bill Rodgers, who was also a member of the club, had brilliantly master-minded. The campaign had been a crucial element in swinging the votes in the 1961 conference to defeat the unilateralist nuclear defence motion which had been passed the previous year. Members of the 1963 Club included Tony Crosland, Roy Jenkins, Dick Taverne, Chris Mayhew, Woodrow Wyatt and Dick Mabon. David Marquand joined with me and though he was also a new MP he had had a long association with the CDS and knew most of the other members of the club.

Thus within months of becoming a member of Parliament, I was pitched into the inner circle of people who, at their mildest, were highly suspicious of Harold Wilson and, at their strongest, loathed his guts. I was totally ignorant of all the tensions and bitterness of the past, much of which stemmed from the Bevanite period and was reinforced in 1960 when Wilson had challenged Gaitskell for the leadership. Slowly as I read more about the Bevan–Gaitskell clash and talked to people who were involved in the controversies, I began to understand why Harold Wilson was not quite the knight in shining armour that I had allowed myself to believe in. I also became aware of the inner tensions within the 1963 Club. While Roy Jenkins, Jack Diamond and Gerry Reynolds had staunchly supported George Brown in the leadership election, Tony Crosland had supported Jim Callaghan. Even during our dinners one could sense the intense competition between Roy Jenkins and Tony Crosland. The two were longstanding friends since before the war at Oxford. Tony had become close to Roy's parents while a student. Both had been in the Army during the war. Roy had become an MP first, in 1948, and pursued his interest in biography by writing a book on Clement Attlee, for whom his father, Arthur Jenkins, had been PPS. Tony had come into the House of Commons in 1950. His main interest was economics and in 1956, when he was out of the House of Commons, he had written *The Future of Socialism*, a book which had a profound influence on me and many of my generation.

The dinners themselves and the friendships that were opened up were a revelation. For a young backbencher, listening as we went round the table, each contributing to the discussion, it was fascinating, particularly hearing Tony and Roy talk, often indiscreetly, about what was going on in Cabinet. It is impossible to exaggerate how ignorant and innocent I was about so much of the internal politics of the Labour Party.

My routine working day was to go to St Thomas' and work in the medical unit laboratory from nine in the morning through lunch until Prime Minister's Questions at 3.15 p.m. or the opening of interesting debates. If I was on a committee sitting in the morning, I would have lunch at a big table seating seven in the Labour end of the Members' Dining Room. Anyone would sit there – Charlie Pannell, the Leeds MP, and Bob Mellish from Bermondsey, were regulars full of earthy common sense; Jim Callaghan and on occasions Harold Wilson might join us. There was always a friendly atmosphere and I learnt much about politics round that table. When the SDP was formed and we were no longer welcome, I missed the camaraderie and the House became a much lonelier place.

I began quickly to learn about parliamentary procedure, as Gerry Reynolds was guiding legislation on the Territorial Army through the House of Commons and I had to be on the committee with him while the bill was examined line by line. My actual responsibilities as

PPS were, however, pretty minimal. I had to see that Gerry was paired but that presented little problem since his Tory pair never wanted to vote if there was the slightest chance of avoiding being in the House.

On 16 May I made my maiden speech, on the second reading of the Industrial Development Bill. I cannot recall being very nervous but I had written out large chunks of my speech. It was certainly not a great oratorical occasion. I referred to the radical spirit which had run through Plymouth for generations, how the city had welcomed the Reform Act with peals of bells, and paid tribute to a family which had added lustre to that radical tradition:

> Isaac Foot fought Sutton on many occasions. He brought up his family within the Division Bell and we on this side of the House are grateful for the contribution which three members of his family have made to this party, from Michael, who represented Devonport with fiery independence, to Hugh for his international contributions to this country, and to Dingle for his legalistic skill. But one brother remains in Plymouth and serves the city, and for this, too, the citizens are grateful. I hope, in the years to come, in some measure to represent a radical tradition in this House.

Michael Foot, who had come in to listen to my speech, sent me a generous note of congratulations which finished with 'Up Argyle!' As the years passed, support for Plymouth Argyle Football Club was one of the few issues on which we were in total agreement.

Around this time the seamen's strike started. This showdown with the National Union of Seamen caused some strain in my relations with the small Plymouth branch since I supported the government line and the declaration of a state of emergency. Wilson's allegations that the strike committee was under communist influence, led by 'a tightly knit group of politically motivated men', heightened the drama and his words inflamed the left outside as well as inside the Labour Party. The strike ended on 1 July, but since that was also the day the Steel Nationalisation Bill was published, international confidence was not restored. When Frank Cousins then resigned as Minister of Technology in order to fight the imposition of an incomes policy, international bankers, or as Labour preferred to call them 'the gnomes of Zurich', began to get restless. On 13 July I was present in the House of Commons when Wilson foolishly announced that steps were about to be taken to reduce demand at home and cut back spending overseas. Far from reassuring world opinion, this was construed as meaning that a devaluation was imminent. A dramatic run on the pound developed. By now in Parliament I and other new Labour MPs were beginning to realise that the government we had been voted in to support was facing a real crisis.

For the first time the Cabinet actually discussed devaluation. George Brown argued the case in favour and was supported by Roy Jenkins and Tony Crosland. They stressed that, with demand down, if the pound was devalued, the British economy would have the chance of breaking out of the stop–go cycle with improved export orders. George Brown also mentioned that Georges Pompidou, the French Prime Minister, had said the devaluation was a necessary prerequisite if Britain was to enter the Common Market. Harold Wilson was still adamantly opposed to devaluation and at one time said if George wanted to resign on the issue, that was fine by him. Wilson invoked the Anglo-American alliance, saying that devaluation would bring trouble to the dollar and threaten the whole monetary system. He was supported by Denis Healey and Michael Stewart. Jim Callaghan wobbled. My notebook has Peter Jay claiming that on 11 July Jim Callaghan told George Brown that he too wished to devalue and that he said it again on the Sunday while the Prime Minister was in Moscow, though he was then dissuaded by Wilson. The respective memoirs of the key participants, Harold, Jim and George, throw surprisingly little light on what exactly happened over those few days. The chaos inside the government machine was, however, pretty clear to see, especially when Treasury officials initially announced that cigarettes were going up by fivepence, then had to apologise, saying that was on yesterday's list. The fifty pound travel allowance was fixed by Jim Callaghan after inspecting a sample of travel brochures. It was not too surprising that, even to its supporters, the government looked incompetent and indecisive.

I watched all this unfold with horror and I listened in a state of shock in the House on 20 July as Harold Wilson announced a deflationary package which clearly amounted to a massive stop to the economy. We were back in the very stop–go cycle which I, along with all other Labour MPs, had attacked the Conservatives for inflicting on the country.

A six-month standstill on wages and dividends was to be followed by another period of restraint and a twelve-month price freeze. Iain Macleod summed it all up when he said later of those July measures:

> The truth about this Parliament is that it died three months after the last general election, when it was clear that they were elected on a false prospectus. And four years is a terrible time to wait for a burial service, while the corpse lies cold in the lobbies of Westminster.

Iain Macleod was the most attractive senior Conservative politician facing me across the chamber. I was not put off by the quip that 'he was too clever by half'. I already respected him for what I knew of his tenure as Minister of Health and also as Secretary of State for the Colonies. Tough on the trade unions, as he showed over the London bus strike, and a believer in incentives, he was liberal in outlook and extremely principled over race. But what I discovered, watching him as shadow Chancellor, was that he had a genuine interest and concern for unemployment and in particular shared my interest in child poverty. I worked with him on a new charity called Crisis at Christmas, addressing a candlelit vigil off the back of a lorry one evening at Hyde Park. It was strangely disconcerting to discover this degree of commitment and concern in a Conservative, who was no closet egalitarian. He would have been an effective, possibly the most outstanding, post-war Chancellor, had he not died in 1970, within a month of achieving the office. He was superbly well equipped, both in parliamentary skill and intellectual grasp, to master the Treasury as it has never been mastered in my time in Parliament. Nigel Lawson was the Chancellor intellectually able to dominate the Treasury. Roy Jenkins was the best Chancellor in the House of Commons but conventional in policy. The only Chancellor to leave behind a strong and thriving economic legacy was, strangely enough, Geoffrey Howe. Perhaps history will be kinder to his record than his contemporaries, who could never forgive him for 3½ million unemployed, a million of which many felt was unnecessarily imposed.

The night after Wilson's statement in the House of Commons, every Labour MP seemed to be pacing the corridors or sitting in the tea room. Ministers who had never talked to me before suddenly stopped for a chat in the corridor. 'Has George resigned?' 'Anything on the tapes?' The whole cliff-hanging episode was a farce, with George Brown's resignation announced by the BBC and then contradicted. A year later George Brown admitted to David Marquand and me that he wished he had gone then. With hindsight he speculated that if he had, things might have been very different. I wonder whether they would. He claimed that he had been influenced to stay by the 100 backbench MPs, who had signed a round robin urging him to stay. I rather doubt this view, though obviously as an emotional man he would have been affected by this sign of broad-based support. The presence of Bert Bowden, the chief whip, at the late-night 10 Downing Street meeting was crucial, for Bert was as straight a politician as one could find, a decent, honourable man who tapped directly into George's own sense of loyalty to the party. His appeal not to resign, which from Harold Wilson's mouth had had little effect, worked. Eventually George, helped or hindered by Harold's brandy and with Bert beside him, announced emotionally on the pavement outside No. 10 that he was staying.

The tolerance of the public to 'Brother George' throughout this period owed a lot to his being seen as a character with much the same vices and weaknesses as most of us recognise in ourselves or someone close to us. But the Nonconformist voters in the Celtic fringe were not as amused and he was never very popular in my constituency. George's opposition to the July measures embarrassed the left for they thought they had a monopoly of conscience. That night I saw for the first time the old relics of the back-handed infighting that went on at the height of the Bevanite crisis. But it was not just the conventional left who poured out the filth on George; other people were going around with the whips, eroding his position. There were dark hints about 'things which we can't say but if you only knew'. If these were just a reference to George's drinking habits, there can have been no MP who was not well aware of his weakness. Even after one glass of sherry he could appear tight.

Indeed, George Brown did not even need alcohol to appear

drunk, as a story told to me by one of his detectives well illustrates. His Special Branch protection team had driven him back to the Foreign Secretary's house in Carlton Gardens and George had jumped out of the car and told them not to wait since he knew his wife Sophie was in the flat. George, in high spirits, proceeded to play 'God Save the Queen' on the door bell. Sophie, thinking he had had too much to drink again, refused over the intercom to open the door. The detectives, disappearing down the street, fortunately looked back and saw George out in the road, gesticulating wildly. They backed the car up and George explained what had happened. He then asked his detective to speak to his wife on the intercom which he did, assuring Sophie Brown that he had been with George all day and that he had not had a drop of alcohol. So Sophie agreed to open the door and the detectives drove off. If even his own wife could not tell whether George was drunk or not, it was far harder for us. The truth was that George's normal ebullience and manic mood swings were exacerbated but not always triggered by alcohol.

It was inevitable that George Brown would have to leave the Department of Economic Affairs after the July 1966 deflation but the decision to appoint him Foreign Secretary was highly significant, for it meant that Wilson was ready to join the Common Market. George's longstanding enthusiasm for membership ensured that the balance of opinion in the Cabinet would shift decisively in favour of applying to join. Supported by Roy Jenkins, Tony Crosland and Ray Gunter, George Brown proceeded to push toward the Common Market with gusto. In doing so, he made light of the very serious reservations which the French had about Britain's membership. In May 1967 the House of Commons debated the issue and the government had a majority of 426 for what George Brown called 'a clear, clean and uncluttered application'. In view of the equivalent vote in 1971, when sixty-nine of us Labour MPs voted with the Conservative government, it is worth noting that few Labour MPs thought it disreputable then, in 1967, to be accompanied into the division lobby by most Conservative MPs.

However, a few days later, General de Gaulle described the obstacles to British entry as 'formidable' and asserted that Britain had to undertake a 'deep economic and political transformation' before membership would be possible, even though, he said, there had 'never been any question of a veto'. Wilson described the French position as 'Yes, but'. It was clear to most of us that the French 'but' had not been overcome. Yet George Brown had chalked up a major achievement – the Labour Party, after five years of deep scepticism about the Common Market, was now formally committed to join. Somewhat naïvely I believed that the matter was now resolved and that the arguments in the party over the principle of entry would never recur. How wrong I was.

The Common Market represented a real issue within the Labour Party because membership carried with it an explicit, not just implicit, acceptance of the market economy. I never had any hang-ups about accepting a market economy. Competition meant in most cases more choice and from an early stage I wanted membership of the EEC. It just seemed the natural state of affairs for me. For those on the left in the Labour Party who did not accept the need for competition, profits and the dominance of the market economy, the EEC did represent a threat to implementing their form of socialism. This fight over accepting market economics had to be faced up to and those like Wilson who tried to avoid or circumvent the fight in the 1960s and again in the 1970s laid the foundation for the far more divisive fight in the 1980s. In 1971, sixty-nine of us Labour MPs chose the market economy as well as the European Community. Labour rejection of the European Community in 1980 became the trigger for the creation of the SDP, and my emphasis on the social market as leader from 1983 was our contribution to Margaret Thatcher's market-dominated counter-revolution.

Harold Wilson's character is too complex to allow simple analysis. I have never been able to write or speak about him without checking myself halfway through, to toughen my criticism if I have been speaking favourably of him or to soften what I have been saying if I have been critical. The pendulum of opinion about him from political commentators as well as that of the public has swung wildly, both while he was actively engaged in politics and even when in retirement.

Historians will take some time to put Harold Wilson's contri-bution to British politics in the 1960s and 1970s in its proper perspective, but I believe he will be judged better by historians than by his contemporaries. He was, though I only attended Cabinet sub-committees under him, a good chairman of committees. His period of dominance in the Cabinet lasted for less than two years. After July 1966 he was only *primus inter pares* and at times not even that. He had cronies but he did not pack his Cabinet with them, keeping them to his kitchen Cabinet. A virtue, frequently under-estimated, was his courage and at times he could show an insouciance bordering on recklessness when his policies were under attack. He went right to the cliff edge over trade union reform and only abandoned the white paper 'In Place of Strife' when he had been disowned by the entire Cabinet, with only Barbara Castle staying loyal. He refused to put our armed forces into Vietnam despite the pleading of President Lyndon Johnson. After what happened in Iraq under Tony Blair this looks wise. Wilson sensed Johnson's personality would have no regard to our views and only wanted the visual effect of a Scottish piper in a kilt! Wilson never-theless fought against the Labour left, who wanted him to attack American policy over Vietnam.

Wilson suffered badly from the politician's illness – press paranoia. But he was also paranoid about his colleagues. Admittedly sometimes this had some justification, for all the senior politicians around him were manoeuvring for advantage and he never had a major figure totally loyal to him. Everyone exhibits some traits of paranoia but for Wilson this characteristic became ever more overt. It debilitated his judgement and his performance. At one time he seemed obsessed about being bugged in No. 10 and his relationship with the Secret Service was a touchy and difficult one. Some say that the suspicious side of his nature was fed by Marcia Williams, his political secretary, who later became Lady Falkender. That she fought to prevent Wilson being taken over by the Civil Service is in no doubt. In my few dealings with her, I always found her a highly political, kind and efficient person and in a sense she was right to be concerned about the effect of the Civil Service on Wilson. He had been a civil servant during the war and was an instinctive bureaucrat. She sensed that unless the Labour Party view was championed by someone very close to him, its interests would go by default. It will, however, be on winning the 1975 referendum on remaining in the European Community that Harold Wilson's reputation will recover most ground.

Personally I have cause to be grateful for he promoted me three times in his governments and without this I would never have had the political good fortune to become Foreign Secretary under Jim

Callaghan. Yet he drove me close to despair about the practice of politics, perhaps because I was young and he promised so much and appeared to have achieved so little. My despair was far greater with Tony Blair.

Whereas Harold Wilson was paranoid, George Brown was deeply emotional. Yet George Brown's instincts as a politician made me forgive his vices as a minister. I am glad, however, that I never worked for him. In the Foreign Office even his exceptional private secretaries, normally people who support the most controversial holder of the office, could not abide him. Stories involving George at the Foreign Office abound, most of them considerably garnished and some apocryphal. One such story was that at a reception abroad, when George was slightly less than sober, the band started to play some music and he approached a guest wearing a beautiful purple dress and requested the pleasure of a dance. He received a polite but firm refusal. He persisted. 'No,' said his intended partner, 'for two reasons: the first is that this is the national anthem. The second is that I am the Archbishop of Montevideo!'

Iain Macleod, at the Conservative Party conference, said, 'There is a National Society for Not Being Beastly to George Brown, and I pay my dues like anyone else. And now that he is Foreign Secretary, I only hope [pause] I only hope!' He was not the only one. George Brown could be a bully and a braggart. But he also had a sharp intellect with a mind that had the capacity to cut through waffle and focus on the core of a problem. He had a deep affection for Britain and the courage to speak his mind. He showed this when he said 'May God forgive you' to Bulganin and Khrushchev on their visit to London as they were talking cant while being entertained by the Labour Party in the House of Commons. His instinctively decent values owed a lot to his Christian beliefs and when the history of Britain's membership of the European Community can be properly assessed there will have to be a special place for his passionate advocacy. His eventual resignation as Foreign Secretary in humiliating circumstances was sad but by then inevitable. In fairness, Harold Wilson showed more patience over George's conduct than was probably wise for maintaining the respect of the public in his government. But it was a measure of George's following in the Labour Party that he could not easily be sacked and had to be allowed to destroy himself politically.

George Brown remained an interesting person. He came to see me in 1978 before going to Iran in an attempt to influence the Shah and his analysis of the situation was clear and concise. He was financially helped in those later years by the textile industrialist Sir David Alliance in an act of unselfish generosity. Lunches with George Brown at the RAC towards the end of his life, when he supported the SDP, were always interesting. He was, in the words of Lord Willis in his funeral address, 'a steam engine of a man'.

In those difficult times when economics dominated politics and financial stringency limited Parliament's initiatives, one of the things a young Labour MP like me could do was to support enthusiastically legislation for social reforms that cost little but could have a considerable beneficial effect for individuals. Two private member's bills, one legislating on abortion and the other on homosexuality, were particularly worthwhile and though they were later to be glibly dismissed as contributing to a so-called 'permissive society', they were in fact long overdue.

The Child Poverty Action Group was another area in which I was involved and I had instituted a separate debate on child poverty just before the Christmas recess in 1966. I have always believed that the mother needs a direct payment for help in bringing up children and I campaigned for generous child benefit through all my years in the House of Commons. It was an important plank of SDP social policy. It gave me great pleasure when John Major's government in 1991 reversed Conservative policy under Margaret Thatcher and agreed to inflation-proof child benefit. I was initially delighted by Gordon Brown's tax credit scheme and the ending of the incentive for a low-paid man with a large family to stay on benefit; sadly it has not been part of a much bolder move, which we advocated in the SDP, of bringing the tax and benefit systems together.

All this activity on social questions which were not popular with everyone led to a trenchant exchange in my constituency general management committee. An older engine driver and stalwart in ASLEF got up after hearing my parliamentary report and said, 'David, I accept that you're all in favour of abortion and that you support family allowances for unmarried mothers but I do draw the line at buggery.' He was rather upset when the entire committee burst into uncontrollable laughter. They were decent, tolerant people in my constituency Labour Party and they never tried to inhibit me from exercising my judgement on such questions even if on occasions they felt the backlash in Plymouth pubs or even the Labour Club.

The widespread disillusionment that stemmed from the July 1966 deflationary measures was debilitating for the entire Labour Party. It haunted us as candidates still in the 1970 general election and contributed to our defeat. It could never be, for us young idealists, 'glad confident morning again'. The general public knew we had adopted wholesale the very economic measures that we ourselves had helped them to identify as Tory. Labour could not avoid paying a heavy electoral price. Worse, a few of us young iconoclastic MPs knew the measures were doomed to fail from the start. By the time the forced devaluation of the pound came in November 1967 we were part of a demoralised parliamentary party where Harold Wilson was derided privately by both the left and the right wings of the party.

It was not easy for an MP like me, with no economic expertise, to advocate devaluation prior to its happening in 1967. When we did, we were charged with irresponsibility for selling the pound short or were accused of being out-of-touch middle-class academics. We devaluationists on the right formed informally what we called the 'Snakes and Alligators', a very loose grouping with MPs such as Eric Heffer and others on the left. It was also the time when I began to build important friendships with three MPs: David Marquand, John Mackintosh and Jack Ashley.

My political guru was Tony Crosland, who used to say that he was completely excluded from any true economic discussion, and that it was just Jim and Harold fixing things between them. Tony was Jim Callaghan's choice to succeed him as Chancellor and he was bitterly disappointed when Wilson chose Roy Jenkins instead. To some extent one has to restrict discussion on as sensitive a subject as devaluation but it became unmentionable. For Wilson defence of the pound was a symbol of patriotic fervour. To advocate devaluation was to him the equivalent of hauling down the flag.

All this time I was closer to Tony Crosland and saw more of him than I did of Roy Jenkins. One reason was that I found he was more interested in discussing serious policies. He, like Roy, gossiped but his gossip was funnier and mostly about the Labour Party, whereas Roy's gossip was more about personalities and life outside politics – interesting, but not as relevant. Both were very ambitious. Tony was jealous of Roy and vice versa. Their friendship had not been helped when Roy had let everyone know that he had turned down Wilson's offer to go to Education before Tony took the job on. Tony was a better choice for Education, not because Roy's children were going through private schooling – after all, so were Harold Wilson's – but because he was more interested in education. Both in practice would have followed education policies pretty similar to Edward Boyle, the former Conservative Education Minister. Tony refused to impose comprehensive schooling, adopting an evolutionary approach to its introduction.

In June 1967 Tony had asked David Marquand and me to his room to help him write a speech about an alternative economic strategy and I found Shirley Williams there as well. It was the first real conversation we had ever been involved in together. She had come into the House of Commons in 1964 and our paths had never crossed. She made a lively contribution and the issue we were discussing was whether to go on preaching the hitherto accepted wisdom, namely that direct taxes were fairer than indirect taxes. For the first time I began to explore whether value added tax might be a more acceptable way of raising revenue and since then have steadily moved towards wanting an expenditure tax, which would encourage saving and not reduce the incentive to earn more.

David Marquand, John Mackintosh and I wrote a fifteen-page pamphlet which was published by *Socialist Commentary*, to coincide with that year's party conference. We called it *Change Gear* and, for ambitious backbenchers, the pamphlet represented a considerable risk, being a comprehensive rebuttal of most of government policy.

By the autumn of 1967 the government had at long last accepted that we could not continue with military bases east of Suez. General de Gaulle was delaying the whole question of opening negotiations over British membership of the Common Market. Sterling was weak and the government was still resisting the devaluation which we had all three publicly advocated. In our pamphlet we tried to stress positive new policies and directions. We committed ourselves to value added tax as part of joining the Common Market; higher social expenditure but with selectivity in social services through negative income tax and some charging; positive discrimination on race; devolution for Scotland and Wales, regional government in England; and the televising of Parliament. The pamphlet was featured in the *Observer* and generated a fair amount of press comment as it seemed to help fill a widely perceived intellectual vacuum.

On Saturday 18 November at 9.30 in the evening, devaluation was announced and the new sterling exchange rate against the dollar was set at $2.40 to the pound. The bank rate went to 8 per cent. Harold Wilson then went on television and made probably the biggest political mistake of his life when trying to explain what devaluation meant. 'It does not, of course, mean that the pound here in Britain, in your pocket or purse or in your bank, has been devalued.' It was left to Lord Cromer, the former governor of the Bank of England, who intensely disliked Wilson, to say that the Prime Minister was talking nonsense and that the pound in the pocket as well as in savings had been reduced by two shillings and tenpence. The Conservative Party never allowed Wilson to forget his words. There was a very angry debate in the House of Commons and Wilson, in his opening speech, sounded to me like a ferret in a sack. John Boyd-Carpenter, from the Tory benches, said what I privately thought, 'When he is in a corner with a thoroughly bad case he lashes out with personally offensive references, wholly irrelevant historical allusions and does everything to distract attention from the main issue.' Summing up, Jim Callaghan made a more sombre and dignified speech and few of us doubted when he sat down that it would not be long before he ceased to be Chancellor. Because of this he was not given a hard time: the House has a sense of these occasions. In fact he had sent a letter of resignation to Wilson before devaluation was announced and had agreed to stay on for only a few days.

Eleven days after devaluation Jim Callaghan swapped places with Roy Jenkins, Jim becoming Home Secretary and Roy Chancellor of the Exchequer. It was the correct decision to have a new Chancellor and probably to choose Roy rather than Tony Crosland. The government lacked authority and credibility and only a new Chancellor could restore confidence. Wilson was himself totally discredited and the government was still having a terrible press. By then the initial misplaced euphoria among many Labour MPs had been replaced by the realisation that we were going to be very lucky, despite our massive majority, to win the next election. Dick Crossman wrote in his diary on 31 December 1967, 'This government has failed more abysmally than any government since 1931.' At that time Dick was going through one of his loyalist phases and rallying round Harold Wilson, so his private judgement was all the more interesting.

After devaluation, public expenditure had to be further cut. The strength of Roy Jenkins's opposition as the new Chancellor to the defence commitments and foreign exchange spending in the Far East and the Persian Gulf only became apparent in the January 1968 Cabinet meetings on public expenditure. In December 1967, just before the Christmas recess, I went with David Marquand to Roy Jenkins's room at the Treasury to discuss the impending cuts in public expenditure which we had all been warned to expect as a consequence of devaluation. My own knowledge of Roy was, at that time, limited – friendly, but certainly not intimate – the result of the odd conversation in the Smoking Room and his presence at the monthly 1963 Club dinners. David Marquand knew Roy far better than I, going back through their involvement in the CDS – when I was a busy medical student. It was David who, no doubt, felt most at ease during our conversation. Roy revealed to us in that meeting that he was determined to achieve the cancellation of the F-111 aircraft, which he clearly saw not only as too expensive, but also as a symbol of the worldwide defence strategy and of the east-of-Suez presence and commitment that he wanted to reverse.

It was also interesting that, although the EEC 1967 application had already been rejected by de Gaulle in his 27 November press conference, for Roy Europe was still our prime area of national interest. Listening to him talking, remarkably frankly, about the short-term expenditure cuts, one sensed a much deeper philo-sophical approach, for he started by analysing the long-term objectives and then putting together the individual expenditure savings, within the long-term framework. It was an approach which the government hitherto had so singularly lacked. Yet he was perhaps too cautious for my liking – he did not have, like Tony Crosland, a passionate and overriding commitment to redistributing income and opportunities more widely. But looking back I have little doubt that

Roy's attitude to public expenditure was correct and if Tony had been Chancellor he would have had to reduce his enthusiasm for public spending.

In February 1968, Labour MPs were faced with a searing emotional issue as to what to do about the Kenyan Asians, who, fearing that their livelihood was threatened by a programme of 'Africanisation', were coming in increasing numbers into Britain. For some time, between 6,000 and 7,000 immigrants a year had come in from Kenya, mainly but not exclusively Asians. But this number had rapidly increased in the latter part of 1967. By January 1968 the number arriving was eight times that of January of the previous year, and almost all were Asians.

Under the 1963 Kenya Independence Act, holders of British passports had the right to return to the United Kingdom at any time, an escape hole designed by Duncan Sandys, the minister responsible, to encourage white settlers to stay in Kenya. It was felt that giving them the safeguard of being able to come back to Britain would be a stabilising factor at independence but it could not exclude Indians without introducing flagrant discrimination. Now the Duncan Sandys promise was being taken up but by blacks, not whites. It was argued that Britain was entitled to slow the flow of immigration while not putting an absolute stop to it. This argument soon led us into the absurd situation of legislating to stem the flow of immigration that had been stimulated by fear of that very legislation. Press comment, built up by Enoch Powell, had already fanned the flames of racial prejudice.

In October 1967 in a speech at Deal, chosen to coincide with the Tory conference at Brighton, Powell had called for the so-called 'legal loophole' which allowed the immigration of Asians from Kenya to be stopped. In Walsall on 9 February 1968 he talked about 'a problem which at the present rate will, by the end of the century, be similar in magnitude to that in the United States now'. Night after night television pictures of Kenyan Asians arriving at airports created an atmosphere of panic. Jim Callaghan, who had inherited the build-up in the numbers from Roy Jenkins, then brought forward the Commonwealth Immigrants Bill, which had already been prepared by the Home Office in case of such an emergency. It was given its second reading on 27 February and its committee stages were rushed through the House of Commons in two days with the co-operation of the Conservative opposition.

That Duncan Sandys, the man responsible for the original legislation, should have allowed himself to join Enoch Powell in his campaign was disgraceful. It was Iain Macleod, a former Colonial Secretary, who challenged him trenchantly in a *Spectator* article: 'Your Kenya Constitution is devastatingly clear. So is Hansard. So are all the statutes. And so therefore is my position. I gave my word. I meant to give it. I wish to keep it.' Despite Macleod's position, the Conservative opposition under Ted Heath decided to support the Labour government's legislation. Later, when Powell spoke in Birmingham in April, saying, 'Like the Roman, I see the river Tiber flowing with much blood,' Heath removed him from the shadow Cabinet. This was to Heath's immense credit because public opinion was wholly with Powell and many Conservative activists saw him as the saviour of the nation. Heath thought the whole tone of the speech was incompatible with the Conservative Party's attitude to race relations and demonstrated to me for the first time the decisiveness and principle which I later learnt to respect.

I agonised as to how to vote. Too often we just voted like sheep, the House dividing ritually along purely party lines. On this bill I felt I would take my own decision; it was undoubtedly racial in character but perhaps it had to be racial since it was dealing with deep-seated racial prejudice in Britain. Many of my closest friends were split on the question. John Mackintosh was determined to vote against it. David Marquand in the end abstained. I vacillated hour by hour yet was never tempted to abstain as in my view that would have been a cop-out. I forced myself to ask what would happen if the immigration continued, as it undoubtedly would, at these levels for a few more months. What would happen in the areas of highest immigration? The answer, it seemed to me, was violence, for the tension in these areas was mounting. It would put an intolerable strain on race relations. This was a vote with a straight choice. Continuing with no controls or legislating to slow the rate of immigration. Principle dictated continuing, prudence indicated slowing. I was determined not to let those MPs in government do my dirty work for me. If after due consideration my reasoned view was that emergency action was necessary, then the bill deserved to be supported.

I listened to every word of the debate and found myself being moved by speakers on both sides of the argument. In winding up the debate David Ennals tried to defend the legislation, claiming that it was not racial, an offensive claim in my view. I felt that, by admitting what we all knew, that Britain was riddled with racial prejudice, we could get on top of prejudice and root it out. But only if we accepted the charge of institutionalised racialism could we improve race relations in those urban centres where Asian immigrants were concentrated. As ten o'clock approached, so did decision time. With a heavy heart I voted for the bill.

I indulged in much soul-searching on whether or not my decision had been a good one. It was to the credit of Iain Macleod, at the cost of some strain in his relations with the shadow Cabinet, that he voted against, with Liberal and some Labour MPs. He was joined by a few Conservatives, among whom were three from the West Country: Dame Joan Vickers (Plymouth Devonport), Michael Heseltine (Tavistock) and John Nott (St Ives). This all added to my distress and made me question my own claim to be a radical. I left for America, still arguing with myself and pondering the deeper issues involved and feeling less proud to be an MP than at any time since I had entered Parliament. But that vote illustrates what being a Member of Parliament is about – exercising one's judgement. My vote could have gone either way. In the end I'd tried to imagine being Home Secretary and voted as I thought was in the national interest.

# 2

# Marriage, Navy Minister and opposition

I flew into New York for my first visit to the United States of America on Leap Year Day 1968 and went that night to the English Speaking Union for a welcoming reception. I was tired after all the heart-searching over my vote to support the Kenyan Asian legislation but buoyed up by the vibrancy of New York.

The reception seemed like any other cocktail party. Then out of the corner of my eye I saw John Pardoe, in those days the Liberal MP for North Cornwall, talking animatedly to the most beautiful girl in the room. She had long, dark, wavy hair, long legs and a splendid figure. I strolled over to join them and as we all talked I became more and more captivated. She had a flashing smile, but it was her effervescence that was so unusual. I knew the party would not last long and I could feel the jet lag catching up on me. So I acted far more boldly than I would normally do and I asked her whether she would show me New York. She hesitated, said she could not do the next day but what about Saturday.

I had two free days in front of me before I was due to fly down to Washington on the Sunday. I kicked around New York seeing various tourist sites, all the time looking forward to meeting this stranger of whom I knew little more than that she worked in the Time Life Building for a French publisher whose name I could barely pronounce, let alone spell.

To meet a new girlfriend is always exciting. To meet one in a different continent, yet with a common language, multiplies the excitement. Everything needs explaining, every minute is precious, hours spent sleeping are stolen hours. We filled every moment with ourselves and the city became just a backdrop. We described our different lives, families, friends. Night turned to day and still we talked. At that time she barely knew what an MP was. She had also inherited from her father no great love of the British; she thought them stuck up and cold. She had apparently said some years before that she would never marry a politician, a doctor or an Englishman. My first task was to explain that the Welsh are not English and that a Celt is a very different animal to her idea of a typical Briton, much more passionate and emotional. We soon discovered a shared love of singing. Unlike any of my other girlfriends, it was music which made her fly. Poetry, books, art all mattered to her but music was an essential part of her life.

On Sunday, after less than twenty-four hours together, I had to leave to fly down with the others on the delegation to Washington. I had no idea whether I would be able to return. We were due to be in Maryland the following weekend so I vowed, without the slightest idea how I would manage it, that somehow I would get back. I decided that the best reason I could give to Betsey Brown, our lively and shrewd hostess for the trip, was that I had been invited to look around one of the hospitals there.

I arrived back in New York that Friday evening. Next morning we hired a car and drove out to St James, Long Island, on another clear crisp day. Apparently her parents were quite used to her bringing people home at next to no notice. I had no idea of what sort of house we were going to or even what sort of people to expect but as we drove through the hideous suburbia I started to imagine the house. Nothing that I saw in those 70 miles prepared me for it. A sign at the entrance to the driveway said 'By the Harbor' and through the trees there was a long, graceful, white, wooden clapboard house with one high spruce on its left and surrounded by woods. Charging around the drive in front of the house were two dogs which leapt up to welcome Debbie as we opened the car door.

I was introduced to her father, Kyrill Schabert, and Mickey, her lively, attractive stepmother. Barely had I seen the inside of the house before, in borrowed old clothes, I was outside helping to cut down and trim back an old apple tree with a power saw. Then Debbie and I went for a long walk by Long Island Sound. We felt the rush of air on our faces from the wild geese flying past, so near that I felt I could touch them. On my return I found the inside of the house as enchanting as the outside with roaring wood fires in both the dining room and the study, which was lined with books. It was a house that had a lived-in elegance. Everywhere there was good, mostly European, taste. Kyrill's father and grandfather had been German and Mickey's family were from Hungary. The pure American blood in Debbie came from her mother, Mary Smith, who died when Debbie was seven but remains a continued presence in her life. Everyone who knew her mother says they are uncannily similar and share the same gaiety and *joie de vivre*.

Sunday morning came all too quickly. Debbie dropped me at John F. Kennedy airport, from where I was to fly to New Hampshire. We had been together for just two short periods, in total a little less than four days. I promised to try and fly back but it was not going to be easy. We were due to fly the following Friday to London from Boston and we expected an important vote and a three-line whip in Parliament on the Monday we were back.

The New Hampshire primary was in its final stages. It proved to be fascinating. Senator Gene McCarthy was pushing ahead fast every day against all the other Democratic presidential candidates. Running on a Vietnam peace ticket, Gene McCarthy was an intellectual but had captured the imagination in this mainly rural state. Bobby Kennedy had not yet declared that he was a presidential candidate. Voting was due while we were there on Tuesday 12 March. By then most of my colleagues and certainly Betsey realised I had seen a little more in New York than a hospital.

On Wednesday we and the rest of America were sent reeling. In the Democratic primary Senator McCarthy secured some 42.5 per cent of the vote. President Lyndon Johnson's name was not theoretically on the ballot but as a write-in candidate, he received only 49.5 per cent. It was a sharp rebuff for the President's Vietnam policy. Bobby Kennedy, to no one's surprise, announced his candidacy four days later, and soon afterwards President Johnson announced his intention not to run for a further term. Whether or not he was influenced to stand down by the New Hampshire primary, we will never know. A complex man behind the folksy image over Vietnam, his motivation full of self-doubt defied analysis. For me he was never the hate figure of the left's chant, 'Hey, hey, LBJ, how many kids did you kill today?' It was rare for a Southerner to champion civil rights as he did, unusual to be a Roosevelt New

Dealer in Congress. He had an extraordinarily good legislative record on trying to grapple with poverty and racial discrimination. History should be kinder to him than the generations who still blame him for Vietnam. I, like most people, had agonised over the conduct of the Vietnam War and by 1968 I was finding it harder and harder to justify. Debbie was against the war and had wanted McCarthy to do well.

On Friday in Boston I finally decided to say to hell with the whips in London and fly to New York. I flew down with Betsey Brown, who cracked up laughing when Debbie and I turned up at the same dinner party. That Saturday in New York Debbie and I went to a party where we met Sandy Cortesi, who had been at school with Debbie, and his wife Lale, who was then nearly nine months pregnant. We all agreed to have dinner the following night. Sandy was to become my closest friend and godfather to my second son, Gareth. On Monday 18 March I flew back to London, too late to vote, but that could not have mattered less to me. I was head over heels in love despite the fact that we had seen each other in total for less than seven days.

George Brown had resigned on the morning I arrived back in London. Like almost all resignations it was the accumulation of events, not just the event itself. He had been particularly upset ever since the decision, taken as part of the expenditure cuts, to go back on raising the school-leaving age from fifteen to sixteen. For George, who had left school without any chance of going to university, this was an emotional issue and he had found it very hard to accept. Roy Jenkins argued this was vitally necessary as part of his overall package. I had felt that the psychological effect of imposing prescription charges would be enough, but Roy was Chancellor and I felt strongly we had to back his judgement.

On 2 July, my thirtieth birthday, I had been dining in the House of Commons with Robert Maclennan, then the Labour MP for Caithness & Sutherland. The main topic we were discussing was how to get rid of Harold Wilson when a message was brought to me by one of the badge holders, who circulate all around the House of Commons, asking me to go over to 10 Downing Street immediately to see the Prime Minister. In a letter to Debbie I wrote:

This evening I was called to No. 10 Downing Street by the Prime Minister and asked to be the Minister for the Royal Navy and to join the government. My full title, as from the Queen accepting the appointment, will be Parliamentary Under-Secretary to the Ministry of Defence for the Royal Navy. It means a bigger salary, an official car and some work which I can get my teeth into.

It does, however, involve me in this government. I thought as deeply as I could if I should serve but everyone I spoke to was insistent that I should, even though my view of the Prime Minister has not changed. It's part of the political game that you operate inside. I know all this. I know my friends would have taken the job if offered. I know that to refuse would have been jejune and revealed a disdain for politics. But I really did question whether I should have done it. Of course the Prime Minister knows what I feel – he knows that I'm potentially dangerous on the back benches so he has in effect bought me off – all this is true and it worries me that I have allowed myself in effect to be a pawn on his cynical chess board but for all this it offers me a real job, a position in which I can really try to influence events and to start on the ladder of political office.

Being offered the job by Harold Wilson was all the more incredible since I had spoken sharp words to him two months before in a lift in the House of Commons. I had asked him to stop his staff briefing the press against Brian Walden, John Mackintosh, David Marquand and myself. Afterwards I expected that I had completely burnt my boats. What an unpredictable man Harold Wilson was.

On 22 August Soviet troops invaded Czechoslovakia. Alexander Dubček and other liberal communist leaders were herded into a troop carrier, driven off and deprived of all power. The Prague Spring was crushed by Russian tanks, and the Brezhnev doctrine, that the USSR had the right and the will to use force to stop any country in eastern Europe from breaking out towards the West, was brutally established. The most bizarre feature of what happened as far as I was personally concerned was the discovery of how bad was NATO intelligence. That evening, before I left the Ministry of Defence, I was reading highly classified reports which said there would be no invasion. I was then woken up to be told that the Russians were invading. There was nothing NATO could do. Indeed, nothing was what NATO had already decided to do. Nevertheless, I felt almost as bad about our inactivity as I had about

Hungary in 1956. I had now learnt an important word, *realpolitik*, the acceptance of reality. I was often to use it in the future. I never felt comfortable over letting the Soviet Union go unchallenged in its so-called spheres of influence. Gradually in the 1970s, through the human rights campaigns, we began to develop a more principled and active foreign policy towards the USSR. Still at this time the conventional wisdom was that the West had no alternative but to take such repression on the chin and virtually to turn the other cheek.

In June Debbie had telephoned to say she was coming over for a summer holiday and on the evening of 27 August she walked through customs in a colourful jungle print dress. I knew now that everything was going to be all right. Our seven days together had not been a dream. All the anguished writing and physical frustration of the last five months just disappeared in a wave of certainty. We had two days together in London before flying across the Channel from Lydd with my Volkswagen Beetle and setting off happily for the south of France. On our way back we drove through the Dordogne, staying near Cahors in a very expensive castle hotel. We decided we could only afford to have a little for dinner but that it should be of the very best. So we ordered champagne and a plateful of truffles. The waiter raised his eyebrows but served a memorable meal, made all the more so by a thunderstorm which put out all the lights and left us to eat by candlelight amidst flashes of lightning. By now we knew we were both deeply in love; the only unspoken question was whether we were going to marry.

We flew back to Lydd and I rang up my sister Susan to see if we could visit her in Bromley. Not only was her husband, Garth, home but my mother and father were staying with them. I wanted Debbie to meet my parents just as I had been able to meet hers, and we all had dinner together. It was clear that both my parents were enchanted with Debbie. Afterwards they told me they were surprised we did not tell them we were getting engaged that evening.

I telephoned her at St James in October and asked her to marry me. She said one word – 'Sure'. We planned to get married in America over Christmas, hopefully with my family. My parents had never before been to America, they had never met Debbie's parents, they had never spent Christmas outside our own family since 1945. It was nevertheless an amazingly happy and tension-free Christmas and wedding. Any worries the two families might have had were greatly helped by my father getting deliciously tight on the first evening. He discovered that an American dry Martini has a lot more gin and very little Martini.

We had married having seen each other for only twenty-four days. We had met in one continent and were now to live in another.

To enter the government on one's thirtieth birthday would be a thrilling enough experience in any junior ministerial post. But to have overall responsibility for the Royal Navy was the best job I could possibly have been offered. I have never doubted the need for relatively strong armed forces. I believe that laws not underwritten by force are ignored or circumvented. My father as a doctor and my uncle as a clergyman had both served in the Army during the Second World War. Moreover it is hard to be born and bred in Plymouth without having a special place in one's heart for the Navy. I would have joined the Royal Navy as a cadet at Dartmouth if the thirteen-year-old entry had been retained. So here I was, at a time when I might have been a mere lieutenant, Gilbert and Sullivan's 'ruler of the Queen's Navee'. It was a daunting task, though my post was nowhere near as powerful or as grand as that of the First Lord of the Admiralty. That historic post, held twice by Winston Churchill, had been abolished in 1964, the holder having ceased to be a member of the Cabinet in 1940. Gradually the role of Minister of State for the Navy was eroded too as the power of the Secretary of State for Defence grew, until only a mere parliamentary under-secretary was responsible for the Navy. In the reorganisation of 1984 all three of the single services lost even this junior minister. The Admiralty Board, however, still existed, as did the Admiralty Board Room. Thanks to the restoration work after it was bombed in 1941, the first time I sat in the chair of a board meeting I was looking on a scene which differed little from that which my predecessors saw as they drew up orders to the fleet before the Battle of Trafalgar. The dial operated by a vane on the roof told the admirals which way the wind was blowing in Whitehall, but as one of the admirals said to me, 'Your job is to tell us which way the political wind is blowing and then we can bear off to take account of it.' That was as good a job description as I would or could get.

There were 100,000 officers, ratings and Royal Marines in naval service when I was appointed and 226 ships, excluding survey vessels and depot and supply ships, though only 166 of these were operational. In a supplementary statement on defence, presented to Parliament in the month that I joined the ministry, it was announced that the plan was to withdraw British forces from bases in the Persian Gulf and in South East Asia by the end of 1971. For the next two years, therefore, I was heavily involved in the withdrawal from east of Suez. I visited the Navy and the Royal Marines in Singapore and was amazed to find that the naval dockyard buildings and equipment covered a vast area. Though we were acting against the government of Singapore's wishes, in fact our withdrawal was the stimulus which helped create the dynamic market economy which has since transformed Singapore. In preparing to close down the Royal Navy base in Bahrain there was more heart-searching. At a minimal cost that base enabled us to offer some stability to countries which needed a few more years to settle in as independent states. But unfortunately we had moved forces from Aden to the Gulf instead of taking them home, and in doing so had given our military deployment in the Gulf a higher political profile. So it had been decided to remove all our service bases.

Cynics within the Labour Party were predicting that my promotion was Harold Wilson's way of making one of his critics live with the consequences of glibly advocating defence cuts. The more charitable explanation of his motives, and the one to which I subscribed, was that he realised the only way my marginal seat could be held was if its own MP was seen to protect its interests. Nevertheless, it was in some sense poetic justice that a rebellious backbencher, who had argued for devaluation, defence cuts and withdrawal east of Suez, should now defend and implement that policy at home and abroad.

The British military presence in the Far East had been one of the few disputed features of what had been a largely bipartisan defence policy since 1940. Some of us who were against such an extensive deployment in the Far East could nevertheless see the virtues of having a permanent, stabilising military presence. But with our chronic balance of payments deficit, the high cost of these commitments in foreign exchange meant that we could no longer support them. Also our military forces were insufficiently strong to match our commitments and the continued presence of a military force outside Europe was no guarantee of effective action. We felt we should concentrate on developing the ability to deploy quickly and to sustain logistically a credible fighting force from Europe.

When Denis Healey took office in 1964 as Defence Secretary, the Ministry of Defence was heavily committed to confrontation with Indonesia. It can be argued that this inhibited him and the incoming Labour government from taking a strategic decision to reduce overseas military commitments. The mistake was not to realign British foreign and defence policy immediately after the 1966 general election victory. Then the new Indonesian government was discussing with Malaysia the possibility of ending confrontation. The opposition to doing this came from President Johnson and his Secretary of State, Dean Rusk, who saw any British withdrawal as undermining the American position in Vietnam and leaving the US vulnerably exposed as the only foreign power with overseas bases in the Far East. Harold Wilson deferred to Washington but he was also personally very susceptible in those days to Lee Kuan Yew's arguments against withdrawal.

The Americans strongly resented our withdrawal, particularly from the Persian Gulf. Dean Rusk had told George Brown, 'For God's sake act like Britain,' and that our opting out of our responsibilities was the end of an era; he sensed, he said, 'the acrid aroma of a *fait accompli*'. Australia and New Zealand were also upset; Malaysia and Singapore felt let down. Service morale in Britain probably sank lower than at any time since the abortive invasion in 1956 of Suez.

In 1972 I wrote a book called *The Politics of Defence*, in which I argued that, if a firm decision to withdraw had been made in the summer of 1966 at the latest, millions of pounds would have been saved, the absurdity of transferring troops from Aden to expensive new barracks in the small Gulf states would have been avoided and the re-equipment programme for the services could have been logically developed to support primary British defence interests within western Europe. Also a major realignment of British foreign and defence policy would have been given an overall coherence and logic which would have shown it to be the historic and long overdue decision that it essentially was. In the event, the historic perspective was completely lost, the decision was seen by the world and presented inside Britain by a Conservative opposition as an undignified scuttle, a panic reaction to financial pressures and an example of incompetent and ill-considered government.

Denis Healey was my boss for two years and a very stimulating one to have. Though he can change his opinion with ease, he often does so because of another characteristic, loyalty. Of all the senior politicians I have known, Denis was by far the most loyal to decisions he did not like, to colleagues he served or who served him, to Labour Party policy he disliked and above all to his wife Edna and his family. This quality of his, more than any other, means that I have always measured Denis by a stringent but more generous yardstick than I use for any other politician. He also has great style. I can hear him, as if it were yesterday, getting up from a dinner at Admiralty House and announcing with a chuckle that he was off 'to vote for the people against privilege'. It was not just a joke. There was always a hint of 'Denis the Menace' against privilege, and justly so. For all his faults he is a big man and I have been lucky to learn from him; even more, he in his nineties and I in my seventies, to know him and Edna as friends.

When I took office the First Sea Lord was Admiral Sir Varyl Begg GCB DSO DSC, an admiral with salt both in his ears and on his tongue. He adored the Navy and once he saw that I loved it too we got on well. But he did not suffer fools gladly and on my first day he told me straight out that he was still recovering from the shock of having a thirty-year-old put in charge. He was shortly to retire, having taken the Navy through the trauma of the aircraft carrier cancellation following the resignation of the then First Sea Lord, Sir Richard Luce. He had extracted one significant concession from Denis Healey, that three new cruisers should fill the gap left by the aircraft carriers. Apart from providing excellent command and control facilities, no one really knew what would be the maritime role of these large surface ships.

The new First Sea Lord, Sir Michael le Fanu, was a completely different character. He was red headed, red blooded and particularly incensed about the loss of the carriers. Amid much publicity he flew 8,000 miles to Singapore as a navigator in a Buccaneer within days of taking office. Then irreverently called 'Lee Fan Yew' or the

'Chinese Admiral', he called on Lee Kuan Yew, the Prime Minister of Singapore. Totally devoid of pomposity and the friendliest of men, he had a fund of funny rather schoolboyish stories, usually at his own expense. He was loved by almost everyone who knew him in the Navy. Stories about him abounded. Once, when he was commander in chief of the Middle East, charged with withdrawing from Aden, he was on an airfield dressed in plain khaki uniform and unself-consciously started to help an airman unload an aircraft. The airman, not seeing the four stars on his shirt and sensing after a while that he was slowing down, said, 'Come on, Ginge, get a bloody move on!' When Mike le Fanu was asked what he did then, he replied, 'Exactly what I was told to, I got a move on.'

When the Second Sea Lord, Admiral Sir Frank Twiss, persuaded all of us on the Admiralty Board to get rid of the naval tot, Mike le Fanu realised its political sensitivity and did everything to show that this was a naval decision, earning another nickname, 'Dry Ginger' – later the title of a breezy book about him by Richard Baker. The rum ration was the equivalent of 4½ pub measures. After the bosun at the wheel had had his midday tot he would have failed a breathalyser test. The Admiralty Board feared a backlash and at one meeting we solemnly talked about the risk of mutiny. A doggerel going around the lower deck at the time went like this:

> Jack's always done his duty
> To country and to throne,
> And all he asks in fairness
> Is: leave his tot alone.

We softened the blow by allowing spirits in the petty officers' mess for the first time and extra beer for the ratings was also given at my suggestion. I had to defend the decision to abolish the tot in a debate in the House of Commons in January 1970. I announced £2.7 million for a Sailors' Fund so that all the rum savings went back in improved leisure facilities. In those days the annual Navy estimates debate was quite an occasion and it mattered to the Navy what was said. Sadly, over the years, its importance has declined, as have the number of MPs who have served in the Navy.

With Mike le Fanu I embarked on one of the more delicate

Whitehall operations that I was involved in. He was determined to retain naval air power in one form or another despite not being able to build new aircraft carriers. He had already, largely to boost morale, taken and passed a helicopter pilot's course. He knew that the Royal Air Force, having won the inter-service battle over the carriers, was watching the Navy very carefully. He was determined to move with stealth. His surprising first decision was to take me into his confidence. This must have been difficult since he could not be sure which way I would go on the issue and whether or not I would tell Denis Healey. I was flattered to be trusted but also I had never been party to the earlier decision to cancel the carriers and privately had considerable reservations about its wisdom. If we could retain air power at minimal cost, this would be very attractive and I felt at liberty to authorise the Navy to explore this new option entirely on a single-service basis. Denis Healey would have to agree any eventual decision but meanwhile there was no point in putting a navy cat among the light blue pigeons.

The first step, at the existing design stage of the new cruiser, was to move the command and control centre from midships to the side. Our justification was that we needed the space for the large Sea King helicopters necessary for the agreed anti-submarine warfare capability. Then the number of helicopters necessary for 24-hour cover was increased and so the deck enlarged. Mike le Fanu was adamant that it should not be rechristened a mini-carrier and that we should stick to calling it a cruiser, albeit a through-deck cruiser. He also knew, because he had very close links with the US Navy, that the US Marines were very interested in our Harrier jump jet. After a suitable interval I was asked to authorise the flying of a Harrier on and off the helicopter deck of the existing cruiser, HMS *Blake*. I feared that this would trigger off press comment about the return of the aircraft carriers, so I briefed the head of the Royal Naval Press Office to angle all the publicity towards export sales of the Harrier to the Americans and to keep clear of any implications for the Royal Navy. Gradually, as it became clear that the US Navy was likely to buy Harriers, it was possible to discuss having special Sea Harriers designed to be embarked on naval vessels, and to make provision for a few as part of the mix with helicopters on the through-deck cruisers. The problem then was who should fly the Harrier.

I suggested to Mike le Fanu that the Navy should propose that these Harriers be flown by RAF pilots. He saw the virtue of this immediately and, despite some criticism from the Fleet Air Arm that we were selling out, we got it agreed within the ministry that the Harriers should not be permanently based at sea and that the Navy should stick to flying helicopters. Soon Mike le Fanu's readiness to play along was justified: as he had predicted, RAF pilots lost any initial enthusiasm for going to sea. Some found themselves sick in rough weather and others disliked living aboard ship. After a while it became generally accepted, along with the fact that the through-deck cruiser was really a mini-carrier, that the Fleet Air Arm should fly naval Harriers.

One of the last decisions that Denis Healey took before we left office in 1970 was to approve HMS *Invincible* as the first of that particular class of ship. It was a fateful decision. When Argentina invaded the Falklands in 1982, the then First Sea Lord, Admiral Leach, who had been captain of naval plans in my time, knew very well that he had indigenous air power available both on the old carrier HMS *Hermes* and the new mini-carrier, *Invincible*. It is widely acknowledged that Leach personally made the crucial difference, with his strong recommendation to Margaret Thatcher when they met in the House of Commons on the night of the invasion that a task force should be sent to repossess the islands. I have no doubt that without the Harrier jets the task force would have had far greater difficulty in defeating the Argentines. Indeed without them it might well have been impossible. To me one surprising feature of the Falklands engagement was how vulnerable our ships were to incoming missiles. This weakness had been well known in the Ministry of Defence when I was there and I thought we had instigated provision for new anti-missile defences years before. I only discovered during the Falklands War that these had been cancelled in the 1970s because of financial constraints. We were very lucky not to lose even more ships.

A fascinating part of my job was dealing with the Polaris nuclear deterrent programme. The four submarines were not yet complete and we were still building up the operational base in Faslane. The whole programme was on a very tight schedule so that the transfer of the deterrent role would coincide with the phasing out of the ageing V-bomber force.

I have pondered long and hard the case for Britain keeping a nuclear deterrent which we can threaten to use independently. With an American wife and all three of my children with dual citizenship, I have profound respect for the United States. But I believe Clem Attlee and Ernest Bevin were right in 1946 that Britain should make her own atom bomb. I will never forget that the US only had troops on the ground in the 1914–18 War by its closing stages; that, even with the most powerful President in their history, Franklin Roosevelt, they did not come into the Second World War until America had been attacked by the Japanese at Pearl Harbor; that, despite making available all our nuclear know-how and scientists for the A-bomb programme, the US Congress turned around imme-diately after the war and tried to freeze the UK out of any further nuclear co-operation and that President Harry Truman went along with their decision. I do not wish my country to be wholly dependent on the reaction of a US President if we are ever threatened by nuclear blackmail. Our possession of nuclear weapons, as for the French, also ensures that no US President can ignore our views on major security questions, nor those of western Europe. These facts are sufficient to convince me that it is a crucial national interest to maintain a minimum independent nuclear deterrent, until we can be sure that all nuclear weapons are on a firm negotiating track to be eliminated.

I travelled to Florida for a test firing of a Polaris missile by HMS *Renown*. I boarded the ship in the early morning and we sailed for the missile firing range, returning the same night. The actual firing was remarkable: only a slight judder in the ship confirmed that the missile had been launched. Later the result was radioed back to us showing, over hundreds of miles, pinpoint accuracy. The whole Polaris programme and then that of Trident has been a remarkable testimony not just to the relationship between the United States and the United Kingdom, but also to the warm friendship that exists between the two navies. Britain has had a fantastic bargain, being able to purchase sophisticated hardware without paying anything near the full research and development costs. The question for the twenty-first century, with the Cold War over, is whether we can manage with a less costly deterrent. I believe we can.

I developed a keen interest as Navy Minister in submarine warfare and, after studying the analysis of the relative vulnerabilities, I became convinced that in an age of satellite photography old-fashioned naval terms like 'over-the-horizon deployment' were out of date. It seemed that the shrouding quality of the sea meant that we should put the balance of the Navy underwater. I argued for submarines at the expense of the surface fleet. In this service atmosphere I also began to study leadership, reading about Lord Nelson. It surprised me to find that the man who understood Nelson's greatest quality was General de Gaulle, who would often quote Admiral Fisher's comments on Admiral Jellicoe after the Battle of Jutland: 'He has all Nelson's qualities but one: he doesn't know how to disobey.'

General de Gaulle had fascinated me since I was eighteen. I watched in May 1968, the 'month of the barricades', when France was shaken and brought to a virtual standstill with rioting students and two million workers out on strike, how President de Gaulle had vacillated and then secretly sought and been assured of the support of the armed forces, whereupon he clamped down. François Mitterrand, the leader of the left, attacked him for provoking a civil war and said, after de Gaulle's broadcast, 'The voice we have just heard is the voice of dictatorship.' At the end of June, de Gaulle won a resounding victory in a general election, in the process ensuring that the Communists were blamed, as *Le Monde* put it, for 'barricades they did not put up and for strike pickets they did not command'. But by April 1969, at the age of seventy-eight, having only achieved a 47 per cent 'Yes' vote on a constitutional referendum to reorganise regional government, he resigned. It was hubris that led him to make the referendum in effect a vote of confidence, which brought about his own dramatic fall from power. Yet by threatening to resign if he did not win the referendum, he invited his own downfall. That he would use such a tactic could have been predicted from reading his own views on leadership, published when he was only a young colonel. In *The Edge of the Sword*, originally published in France in 1932, he reveals views which he followed throughout his life:

This passion for self-reliance is obviously accompanied by some roughness of method. The man of character incorporates in his own

person the severity inherent in his effort. This is felt by his subor-
dinates and at times they groan under it. In any event, a leader of this
quality is inevitably aloof, for there can be no authority without
prestige, nor prestige unless he keeps his distance.

Appropriately this formidable leader was toppled by the people
speaking directly to him in a referendum, for it had been successive
referenda which had given him the authority he needed to defeat
the colonels in Algeria, to replace the constitution of the Fourth
Republic, and to revive the fortunes of France.

His successor as President, Georges Pompidou, lifted the veto on
British entry. Yet de Gaulle's legacy remains: he showed that the
much-needed renovation of Europe would only be accomplished by
retaining the vitality and drive that stems from the nation state. A
Europe that denigrates or downplays nationhood will in my view
never achieve its full potential. De Gaulle's vision of a 'Europe des
patries' goes with the grain of European history. The federalist vision
of another eminent Frenchman, Jean Monnet, of a United States of
Europe not only goes against the grain of our history but is a
bureaucrat's dream.

I strongly supported the Labour government's decision to open
negotiations for entry to the European Community just before the
calling of the general election. There was little party political
difference on the issue. Each party had its small but vocal group of
anti-Marketeers but it was reasonable to expect a successful outcome
to the negotiations and when Edward Heath, in a speech in Paris,
talked of the whole-hearted consent of the British people, most
people assumed that this was already present.

An issue close to my heart, which ran on right up to the 1970
election, was what to do with the Royal Navy dockyards. In 1968
we had four fully operating, in Rosyth, Chatham, Portsmouth and
Plymouth. Rosyth dockyard was inviolable as we were building it up
in order to refit Polaris submarines. Chatham dockyard had just had
millions of pounds spent on it to refit the new hunter-killer nuclear-
powered submarines. Portsmouth and Plymouth had as yet no
nuclear refitting facilities and were confined to refitting surface ships
and diesel submarines. It was obvious to me that if Devonport
dockyard was going to survive it had to move into nuclear

submarine refitting. Fortunately Devonport had far more berthage space than Chatham for surface ships and far better and quicker access to the Atlantic. Yet even so, the best short-term financial choice for the Navy was to close Devonport dockyard. This appalling prospect dawned on me in my first few weeks in office and I realised I was facing an acute political challenge. I did not see how I could be the minister who closed down by far the largest industrial employer in the city of Plymouth, for at that stage the general manager's department of Devonport dockyard employed 18,000 people. So within a few months of taking office I was looking down the barrel of a political gun, loaded and aimed at my head. If we had to close Devonport, resignation might have helped me in Plymouth but it would have been an admission to my parliamentary colleagues that I was not prepared to let the national good override my fear of losing my marginal seat. I decided that I would tough it out. I would fight my corner for Plymouth but only on its intrinsic merits. I felt that if it once looked as if I put my constituency interests before the best interest of the Navy, my influence within the Ministry of Defence would be immediately marginalised.

Fortunately for me the chief of Fleet Support, Vice-Admiral Turner, showed remarkable understanding of the political difficulties I faced. He was also very worried about the difficulty of retaining skilled workers at Chatham when there was so much competition for labour from local industry. In Devonport, where unemployment levels were high, retention of skilled people was much easier. Soon it was the naval staff who wanted Plymouth developed as a nuclear refitting base. But they also wanted all four dockyards to be retained with the largest cutback in the labour force being concentrated in Devonport. They preferred no cutbacks in Portsmouth because there were so many other naval installations nearby and because so many of them had their own houses there. I, however, wanted Portsmouth to take its share of the cutback in dockyard numbers, in part to reduce the number of jobs lost in Plymouth. Gerry Reynolds, as Minister of Defence for Administration, knew that financial savings only come from strategic cuts and he was adamant in wanting one dockyard to close completely. If we closed Chatham, the political problem was that we would have to spend a lot more capital on building alternative nuclear refitting facilities in Plymouth as well as explaining away Christopher Mayhew's earlier decision to build Chatham up.

After a lot of infighting, it was time for a decision which could only come from Denis Healey. Fortunately he accepted the package which we had hammered out. Chatham was to close completely, Devonport was to be extensively modernised with a new nuclear refitting base and three new covered slips for refitting Leander frigates. Portsmouth was to lose some of its labour force. Devonport was eventually to lose 5,000 jobs over a period of years. My task was to convince everyone that the £75 million modernisation of the dockyard guaranteed its future and that the job losses were a necessary and unavoidable evil. Fortunately the dockyard unions were very understanding. They knew that at one stage Devonport had been very near to being closed and were well aware of all the fighting I had done on their behalf. Nevertheless, the announcement, coming at the start of 1970, ensured that the future job losses risked becoming a major issue at the general election even though we hoped to achieve them all by natural wastage. It was unusual for any minister to face an issue of such magnitude intimately involving his own constituency. I had had to balance any number of different interests: the Treasury need for savings, the Navy's need for greater dockyard efficiency and the needs of my own constituents for jobs and spending power within the city. Fortunately the outcome was far better than I could ever have hoped when I first started to grapple with it eighteen months earlier.

Quite apart from strategic decisions about the dockyards, I was also heavily involved in the struggle to make them more efficient, something which has eluded everyone who has tried since Samuel Pepys. I was directly responsible for 45,800 industrial civil servants with very different needs from the much larger number of non-industrial civil servants. I chaired the Whitley Council and was closely involved with trade union leaders. It was very educative and meant that far from being solely involved in naval matters, I was dealing with domestic industrial issues.

When Barbara Castle, the Employment Minister, embarked on preparing her white paper 'In Place of Strife', I was involved, not because of attending Cabinet sub-committees, for that was normally done by the more senior ministers in the department, but because the Navy Department was the largest industrial employer within government. In its own right the department was part of the consultation process within and outside government. My trade union contacts through the Whitley machinery also ensured that I was hearing the views of the trade unions directly. Until this time I had given very little thought to the place of the trade union movement in British society, or the underlying philosophical issues surrounding industrial relations. As a backbencher I had merely noted the Donovan report, published in March 1968. Creating a royal commission was one of Harold Wilson's characteristic ways of resolving pressing problems. This one, appointed in April 1965, when the government barely had a majority, was a committee deliberately chosen to produce a consensus, not provoke a crisis. I did not feel strongly either way about the commission's recommendations and the 145,000-word report, lengthy like most royal commission reports and covering all aspects of the trade unions' and employers' associations, seemed destined to gather dust.

It was A. P. Herbert, speaking in the House of Commons with the candour and independence of a man elected by Oxford graduates under the old system of university seats, who wisely said, 'A royal commission is generally appointed not so much for digging up the truth, as for digging it in: and a government department appointing a royal commission is like a dog burying a bone, except that a dog does eventually return to the bone.' As Peter Jenkins wrote in *The Battle of Downing Street*, after more than three years the dog returned to the bone, and the dog was called Barbara Castle.

The Donovan report went down like a lead balloon with the press and the general public. This was not surprising given the recent spate of industrial action. Strikes had become commonplace and they were widely felt to be damaging our export performance and giving Britain a reputation as an unreliable supplier. George Woodcock, the TUC general secretary, bizarrely having been made one of the commissioners, was rightly judged to have pulled the wool over the eyes of the chairman, Lord Donovan, himself a former Labour member of Parliament. Harold Wilson had no doubt, like many other people, that it was still necessary to 'do something about the unions'. Barbara Castle was never a legislative laggard and responded to the challenge. Not for her some minor legislative adjustment! What she wanted was far more ambitious, a wholly new philosophy of industrial relations. She succeeded, for the white paper, published on 18 January 1969, was a major document of state, whatever one thought of its contents.

Despite ministerial opposition, Wilson pushed the white paper through Cabinet. From then on, members of the government were bound to support it at least in public. I believed that the proposals were broadly correct and initially it seemed as if the generally favourable press would carry a somewhat reluctant group of trade union MPs along with the reforms. Yet it became clear to me, even in Plymouth with no history of militant trade unionism, that there was trouble ahead. On 26 March, the NEC of the Labour Party rejected 'In Place of Strife', with Jim Callaghan once again voting against Barbara Castle. For all his protestations of innocence, Jim Callaghan was daring Wilson to sack him. He had now become, in Peter Jenkins's words, 'the Keeper of the Cloth Cap'.

I did not know Jim Callaghan well. I was not, however, as instinctively hostile to him personally as many of the other young professional Labour MPs. Some close to Roy Jenkins had privately and semi-publicly pilloried Jim over the Kenyan Asians. But I felt that Roy had been lucky to escape from the Home Office in time and that it was bad luck on Jim that he had inherited this particular poisoned chalice on taking office. My occasional meetings with Peter Jay gave me insight into Jim's thinking on some issues and I disliked patronising talk about his populism. It seemed instinctive and not false to me. Populism is a strange political characteristic, it can be as much a vice as a virtue. Tony Crosland nurturing his own image as friend of the Grimsby fishermen and supporter of Grimsby Town Football Club had its amusing side but I understood his feelings for they were genuine. The fishermen around the Barbican in Plymouth, although in those days much fewer in number than the Grimsby fishermen, were also full of character, adding something to my constituency as well. Having watched Plymouth Argyle from the terraces ever since I was a small boy, I could also identify with Crosland's enthusiasm for football. What I disliked intensely was people pretending to be what they were not. As a medical student, working on building sites, well before becoming a politician, I sensed that no people were quicker at detecting a phoney than the British working class. They far prefer people to be what they are. To relate to popular feeling is a political strength. What is self-defeating is to be seen to be at the beck and call of public opinion.

Now Jim Callaghan had an issue on which to campaign. At the end of 1967 Jim's political career had looked as if it were destined to decline. Devaluation had been a severe blow to his self-esteem. Yet now with his self-confidence recovered he skilfully began to use his power base as Home Secretary to considerable effect. He had a natural public persona rather like Dixon of Dock Green, the police-man everyone could trust. He was helped in this by the knowledge he had gained when, for years in opposition, he had been spokesman for the Police Federation. He instinctively targeted trade unionist opinion, with which he felt comfortable and had known well since he started as assistant secretary of the Inland Revenue Staff Federation. Jim Callaghan's political weakness at that time was not just his record as Chancellor but that he appeared to have too many chips on his shoulder. He could be very edgy, but disguised this with a breezy bonhomie. He resented the bitter criticism that had come his way over the Kenyan Asians and, as someone who had loved and known Africa from the time he had shadowed the Colonial Office, he could never understand why President Kenyatta virtually escaped criticism for first depriving Kenyan-born Asians of their livelihoods and then expelling them. Fortunately, towards the end of 1968 the Kenyan government did slow and then essentially end the withdrawal of Asians' work permits. This meant that the UK voucher system did not have the dire effects that were once feared. But the politician in Jim knew that he had to defuse the slur of racialism and in June 1968 he introduced legislation to create the Race Relations Board. He peremptorily threw out Barbara Wootton's well-argued report arguing that legislation on the drug cannabis should be relaxed. But as if to balance that tough action he identified with the Home Office's role of responsibility for children. It was he who set up, on Leo Abse's prompting, the committee to look into reform of the law of adoption, which I was a few years later to take up for my private member's legislation. Soon he had established a distinctive image: hard on immigration but soft on race relations, hard on drugs but soft on children, hard on gaming but soft on bingo.

Jim Callaghan had made a formidable political recovery and it even meant that his name began to be tentatively floated as a candidate to oust Harold Wilson. In the House of Commons tea room, where some older Labour MPs virtually used to live, Jim always retained a following. It was these people who saw, early on, that Barbara's trade union reform package was going to end in tears. At one stage, John Mackintosh went to see Jim to ask if he was willing to stand for the leadership to replace Harold. George Lawson, an older, centrist figure and Scottish whip, then went with the same request. Callaghan told them both that he did not think there was a solid body of opinion in the party in favour of a change of leadership. On a later occasion Denis Healey sent Alan Lee Williams, his parliamentary private secretary, to see if Jim would support him making a move for the leadership. Jim told Alan bluntly 'No' and added that he did not believe that Denis would ever make a move. When he was asked why he came to that conclusion he said, not without justification, that if Denis had been serious he would have come himself, rather than sending a boy to do a man's job. These refusals did not stem from any love of Harold Wilson or lack of ambition. Jim simply calculated correctly that after devaluation, despite his wise handling of the situation in Northern Ireland, he was never in a sufficiently strong position to challenge Wilson himself. He judged too that all the emissaries wanted him to do was to open up a contest and then they would vote for someone else, most frequently Roy Jenkins. He could not have been unaware that Roy rarely missed an opportunity in private to put him down, nor that at one stage, with Barbara Castle, Roy had wanted Harold Wilson to sack him. Woodrow Wyatt, a good friend of Roy's and slightly of mine, not a man to shrink from either controversy or publicity, called for Jim to be sacked and so he deserved to be. For he was now in open rebellion against the Cabinet majority on trade union reforms. Attlee would have demanded loyalty or promptly had his resignation. But Wilson was no Attlee. He always disliked sacking people and was chronically indecisive. At that time in particular he lacked the self-confidence to act and so used the Wilsonian device of briefing the press that he had reprimanded Callaghan in Cabinet when in fact he had done nothing of the sort.

Jim's and Roy's rivalry was fed by mutual dislike. It was well concealed, but the combustible contempt lay not far below the surface. Roy thought Jim was unintelligent and philistine. Jim thought Roy arrogant and effete.

The Cabinet was now beginning to turn in on itself and we junior ministers began to hedge our bets on 'In Place of Strife', by leaving it for Barbara Castle to champion. Wilson looked weak, the government divided. It was in this debilitated state that the Cabinet drifted towards a commitment to legislate. On 15 April 1969, making his second Budget statement, Roy Jenkins first won cheers on the Labour side by announcing that there would be no renewal of the powers under the 1968 Prices and Incomes Act but then stimulated the Conservative benches to cheer when he announced that there would be immediate legislation on 'In Place of Strife'. In his years as Chancellor it was one of Roy's few political mistakes to ally himself to a sinking ship and then abandon it.

At the fateful Cabinet meeting on 17 June an intervention right at the start by Bob Mellish smashed any hope of carrying the legislation. 'Prime Minister, before you consult your colleagues of the Cabinet, I feel you and they should hear what your chief whip has to say.' He told them bluntly that there was not a hope of the measure being carried in the House of Commons, that the party would not stand for it and that the penal clauses had to go. As Peter Jenkins describes it in his book, 'The scene now resembled the interruption of the preacher in the dockyard church when, in the words of the old seaman's song, "up jumped Jack, in the third row back" and mouthed some dreadful obscenity.' Then, as one colleague put it later, 'Roy slid elegantly onto the fence'. Once that happened Harold Wilson knew that the desertion was complete. He was being told to settle with the TUC General Council on the best terms available. Now Wilson showed the one quality that no one could deny him – guts. He refused to be browbeaten by the Cabinet and was adamant that he would not be instructed as to what to say when he met the General Council next morning. That evening the buzz I was picking up in the tea room of the House of Commons was that Harold and Barbara were totally isolated. Even so the defiant message from No. 10 was, 'The little man's not going to go.' Barbara Castle went to bed thinking that this might be her last day as a Cabinet minister and that tomorrow there might be another tenant in No. 10.

Next morning a cocky Harold Wilson weaved and ducked with the General Council but they knew they had him on the ropes. Over lunch, Barbara Castle and he decided that they had to deal. They would grasp the lifebelt that had been thrown to them by Vic Feather, the TUC general secretary. The Bridlington declaration of 1939 had always been much loved by the trade union movement. It is the voluntary code preventing unions from poaching members. So Harold Wilson announced, after the lunch interval, that he was ready to enter into negotiations over 'a solemn and binding undertaking' which the TUC must accept as having the same standing as the Bridlington declaration. This provoked the wisecrack from a civil servant in the Department of Employment about Solomon Binding being a character out of George Eliot. It was agreed the TUC would place an obligation on trade unions 'to take energetic steps to obtain an immediate resumption of work', where they, the TUC, thought strike action unreasonable.

Harold Wilson went on television that night to explain the government's climbdown. He was followed the next evening by Edward Heath, who said of Wilson, 'He knows, you know, the world knows after last Wednesday, that although they may still wear the trappings of office, the power resides elsewhere.' Who could have guessed that within five years Edward Heath would suffer an even greater humiliation at the hands of the trade unions in 10 Downing Street? For those of us watching this miserable spectacle from within the government there were many lessons, not least of which was that reform of the trade union movement, once started by the government, had to be followed through, for no vested interest could be seen to defeat a democratic government without damaging that government and the country.

What I, and I suspect many others, did not sufficiently realise then was that it was not Harold Wilson's nerve that had cracked but the Cabinet's. Wilson had gone to the limit. Indeed, in fairness, he had gone well beyond most Prime Ministers' limits. He was like a man hanging over a cliff edge who had had to be pulled back up to safety. I took the view that Harold and Barbara should never have got us into this mess in the first place. But that was too easy a conclusion. The truth was more unpalatable for moderates like me. It was we, the supposedly hard men on the right, who had lost our nerve. First and foremost of those who had backed off was Roy Jenkins. It is impossible to know what would have happened if he had stuck with

Harold and Barbara and defied the Cabinet. In retrospect, that is what he should have done, for if that Labour government had stood up to the trade unions and been seen to win, Labour would have won in 1970. Roy Jenkins would within a year or so have succeeded Harold Wilson as Prime Minister. Wilson, to his credit, knew this. In a bitter exchange with Hugh Scanlon, then president of the AEU, at Chequers in June he showed that he understood the penalty of backing down. Scanlon said, 'Prime Minister, we don't want you to become another Ramsay MacDonald.' To which Wilson replied, 'I have no intention of becoming another Ramsay MacDonald. Nor do I intend to be another Dubček. Get your tanks off my lawn, Hughie!' The tanks stayed on the lawn until Arthur Scargill's defeat by Margaret Thatcher in 1985.

At that time I had no inkling that the Cabinet was likely to fold. I was defending the forthcoming legislation in my own constituency and slowly winning the argument. It was not until after the general election that I became fully aware of the true story. In the interval I had done what many other MPs on the right tended perhaps too often to do – blamed Harold Wilson. I had made him the scapegoat and had depicted him as the softie on the trade unions, when in truth he was the hard man. The whole incident only demonstrates yet again the complex personality of Harold Wilson, both the man and the politician.

Given the political traumas of the four years of government, it is amazing that, when Harold Wilson announced on 18 May that a general election was going to be held on 18 June 1970, it was possible for me to believe that Labour would win the election. On 12 May a Gallup poll had actually shown Labour 7½ per cent ahead of the Conservatives. Even as late as December 1969, the Conservatives had looked comfortably ahead. But the local election results in May and the opinion polls all indicated that the Conservative lead had melted like spring snow.

The reason for the polls changing was Roy Jenkins's Budget, delivered on 14 April. It was variously described as honest, dull, not a bribing Budget, and, by the *Financial Times*, as a political non-event. Nevertheless, Labour found itself ahead in the opinion polls for the first time since 1967. After the general election conventional wisdom held that Roy's third Budget was too responsible and had lost us the election. Yet it justly concentrated on taking two million people out of paying any tax at all. The judgement of most people, even on the left, in May or early June, was that Roy's integrity was an electoral asset. The mistake was to go for an early election and that was Harold Wilson's decision. The press was carefully massaged so as to make a June election acceptable and by the time it was announced most Labour MPs, including myself, were in favour of going. In retrospect it was a foolish decision and people remembered the bad years. I do not believe that the electorate switched around during the campaign because England lost to Germany in the World Cup in Mexico or because the trade figures showed a freak deficit because of the purchase of two jumbo jets. The electorate needed more time.

I did not realise until very late the extent to which the electorate had not been taken in by the government's recent successes with the economy. On the Thursday a week before polling day Roy Jenkins came to my house after speaking on my behalf and the sole topic of conversation over dinner was what jobs he and I would have in the new government! I began to be uneasy towards polling day but put that down to nerves. It was not until I was driving in to my count in Plymouth Guildhall and heard on the car radio that Gwyneth Dunwoody had lost her seat in Exeter that I realised I was in trouble. The pundits were predicting that, on the national swing, I would lose in Plymouth Sutton. The Conservatives very nearly made a clean sweep of all the constituencies in Devon and Cornwall. I held on in Plymouth Sutton by 747 votes, but John Dunwoody lost Falmouth & Camborne, showing that I had made the correct choice in 1965 and that Sutton was a safer seat than Falmouth. Jeremy Thorpe kept his leadership of a decimated Liberal Party by a mere 369 votes in North Devon and John Pardoe held North Cornwall by 630 votes. Edward Heath had vanquished his critics to become Prime Minister with a deceptively effective campaign that appeared to peak at exactly the right moment. Only one poll had predicted a Conservative victory and that only at the last moment, in the London *Evening Standard*. On the Sunday before the election the weighted average of five national opinion polls showed Labour having a 6.4 per cent lead.

Waiting anxiously for my result during the count in Plymouth Guildhall, I felt convinced that I had lost and a strange calm came over me as I thought through my next step. As I went round talking to friends and supporters, scrutinising the count, there was no sadness to be leaving Parliament. It had been an amazing experience and I had no regrets. But there was no sense of shock that it was over. I would ring the Maudsley Hospital, which specialised in psychiatry, next morning and see if I could be accepted as a registrar. It would mean having to catch up by taking the final part of my membership and by working for a diploma in psychological medicine but I felt a keen sense of anticipation and even joy at the prospect of returning to medicine.

My agent, Alf Sweetland, was with the returning officer counting all the bundles and it was impossible to tell who was ahead. He was not allowed to tell me the result but suddenly he looked at me. He then deliberately turned around and put his thumb up behind his back. I had won. There was no elation; if anything, I was rather disappointed. I was still an MP but it was pretty clear by then, from the results already in, that Labour was going out of government. Mounting the platform with Debbie to hear the official result I galvanised myself into believing that we had won a great victory in Plymouth. We had and yet it all felt very hollow. My idealistic beliefs in what a Labour government could do had made my victory four years before a thrilling one. Now those ideals lay shattered. The new Conservative government had a working majority with 330 MPs to Labour's 287 and the Liberals' 6. They could expect to run for the full five years if they needed to. My anxiety was what to do to keep myself busy. I knew the House of Commons by itself would not fill my working day. I wondered about trying to become a clinical assistant in the Department of Psychiatry at St Thomas'.

Then, that weekend, Sandy Cortesi rang from America, first to commiserate over our losing the election but also to ask if I would be interested in becoming chairman of Decision Technology International as there was likely to be a vacancy very shortly. Sandy had talked a lot about Decision Technology on his visits from the US. It was a fast-growing computer-based consultancy, with its head office in Boston and another office in New York. The presiding genius was Arnold Amstutz from the Massachusetts Institute of Technology. He had designed a computer model of the New York stock market. He had also designed a model of the US pharmaceutical industry as a marketing tool. In Europe the company had a contract with Rolls-Royce to build a computer model to mirror the production line of the RB-211 aero engine.

Decision Technology had also developed a sophisticated method of measuring political views through studies of attitude and awareness. They had worked with Robert Kennedy and a number of other politicians. Sandy's offer provided a unique opportunity to learn about business. All too conscious that I had not had experience of private industry or of the workings of the marketplace, a weakness I shared with most Labour MPs, the chairmanship of Decision Technology offered me an opportunity to learn about management and the ethos of the private sector. It would also make a very useful addition to our family income. I also felt it would be easier to combine politics with business than with medicine. So I accepted and for two years it gave me a valuable insight into a different world.

The first political issue was an internal one – the deputy leadership of the Labour Party. Despite a vigorous campaign, George Brown had lost his seat, which had been adversely affected by boundary changes.

The deputy leadership of the Labour Party has never been considered an important position. It was created for Herbert Morrison and only Michael Foot succeeded in using it as a stepping stone to the leadership of the party. Nevertheless, the holder is automatically a member of the National Executive Committee of the Labour Party and the NEC, in opposition, becomes a powerful body.

Somewhat to my surprise I was asked to a meeting in Dick Taverne's London flat to decide whether or not Roy Jenkins should stand. Prior to this, though aware they went on, I had not been involved in any of the meetings which were attended only by committed Jenkins supporters. In retrospect I suppose it was from this moment that I became classified as a Jenkinsite. Yet my political heart remained with Tony Crosland. I did not make a wholehearted commitment to Roy as the future leader of the Labour Party until the summer of 1971, when it became clear to me that Tony Crosland was not prepared to recognise that Britain's entry into the European Community was a major issue. Susan Crosland has since revealed that Tony was discovered to have high blood pressure soon after the election and that may have contributed to a political lassitude not easy to distinguish from Tony's natural and rather attractive laid-back manner. He still worked very hard in the 1970 parliament, particularly on local government questions, but some of his vivacity had gone.

At the Taverne meeting the general conviction was that at some point Roy should run for the leadership. George Thomson and Bill Rodgers were the most militant, arguing strongly that Roy should stand for the deputy leadership, even if Jim Callaghan stood. In fact it was pretty clear by then that he preferred to remain treasurer of the party, which carried an automatic seat on the NEC and had the virtue of being the only office elected by all sections of the annual conference. At the other end of the spectrum, David Marquand, and I to a lesser extent, questioned whether it was wise to be bound to Harold Wilson by becoming his deputy. Eventually Roy agreed to stand but not without clearly warning us all that for him the European Community was a central political issue and if the party was to oppose entry it would be no good any of us invoking party loyalty or the fact that he was deputy leader. We should know that now, he said, rather than finding it out later.

On 8 July the parliamentary party gave Roy an overall majority with 133 votes. Michael Foot got sixty-seven votes and Fred Peart forty-eight. The vote sent a warning, which pro-Marketeers underestimated at the time, in the form of the large number of anti-EEC moderates voting for Peart. Michael Foot had yet to widen his support beyond the traditional left but Peart's vote meant there was now a body of MPs whose hostility to the European Community would be likely to determine who in the parliamentary leadership had their support. George Thomson was made shadow Defence Minister and, intriguingly, Harold Lever was party spokesman on Common Market matters with Denis Healey shadow Foreign Minister. This line-up gave Harold Wilson tactical control of a pro-European policy. I was a junior Defence spokesman.

In Parliament it rapidly became clear that Europe would dominate. The incoming Conservative government took up the negotiating stance that we had already been preparing over the last six months and the speech which Anthony Barber eventually gave at the opening of the EEC negotiations in Brussels was very little different from the draft approved during the election campaign by George Thomson. He was to have been the Labour government's negotiator, had we won. The negotiations began but public opinion was still against entry, with only 22 per cent positively in favour. So keeping bipartisan agreement, which was not the natural state of affairs in Parliament, was in the government's interest.

Yet for a time it did seem as though, on Europe, the consensus would hold. At the Labour Party conference, Harold Wilson's speech made a reference to Europe which was fairly unexceptional, though, as usual, it was capable of being interpreted in a number of different ways. Apart from a narrow vote at conference in favour of the NEC's cautious resolution on the EEC – a majority of only 95,000 – there was little real evidence to justify the sceptics who predicted that Wilson would eventually reject the EEC.

The next few months passed pretty quietly on the European side. Denis Healey was convinced with his usual certitude that the French would once again reject British entry. Parliament listened restlessly to the rather drab reports from Geoffrey Rippon, who had replaced Anthony Barber as chief negotiator. Only Peter Shore had staked his career on the issue, refusing the offer of a relatively minor frontbench appointment and going to the back benches, where he was rapidly taking over from Douglas Jay as the official anti-Market spokesman.

It seemed to me, and I expect to many others, that there was nothing much to be worried about: superficially, it appeared that, to Harold Wilson and most of the influential members of the shadow Cabinet, the commitment to entry was irrevocable and that everything, as before, would depend on France.

Soon things began to change. In the early months of 1971, it became increasingly obvious that the high unemployment figures, the government's total inability to restrain prices and their determined commitment not to intervene in industry were making them very unpopular. It also affected the whole issue of entering the EEC. A new factor too was Jim Callaghan's attitude. Ever sensitive to any change of feeling in the party, he was starting to tell his friends that he was less and less convinced of the case for British entry into the EEC. The manner in which by nudge and wink Jim began to indicate his impending change was reminiscent of the way he handled his disapproval in 1969 of the proposed legislation envisaged in 'In Place of Strife'. The shift was initially almost imperceptible, never anything one could actually seize upon to criticise, always leaving enough room to swing back to support entry if the climate changed. But unlike in 1969 there was no prime ministerial patronage to check his movement and that of others like him away from the official line.

It is hardly surprising that the agreement over Europe felt the strain of polarised politics as economic growth slowed, output fell and unemployment rose. It can be argued with some justice that the only difference between Thatcher's and Heath's early years in No. 10 is that when confronted with high unemployment her nerve held and his did not. The Heath U-turn came with the one-clause bill to rescue Rolls-Royce, followed by an interventionist Industry Act in 1972. Then came the statutory income policy of 1972 and 1973, which marked the big U-turn, distorting the market economy and raising the question about whether it was compatible with Conservative philosophy. However, for the first few years, Heath out-Thatchered Thatcher. His style came from his days as a colonel in the war: peremptory, prickly, authoritarian; but it was also accompanied by a basic decency, a rigid incorruptibility, although you had to look for it buried under an offputting veneer of executive efficiency. So from the Labour side in those days there was very little respect, indeed there was considerable animosity towards Heath.

As the government's reputation fell, Labour leaders found it increasingly difficult to agree with them on anything and the European Community became another issue for instant opposition. Yet it was the Labour Party which was to damage itself on this issue from 1971 to 1987. The true story of the formation of the SDP begins here in early 1971, over policy towards the European Community.

On the night of 19 January 1971, when a running three-line whip kept a large number of MPs in the House of Commons, a straight anti-EEC motion was touted around and received 119 signatures from Labour MPs. This eventually rose to 132. It was a formidable achievement. From that moment on, there could be justified doubt as to whether there was a genuine majority for British entry to the EEC among the Parliamentary Labour Party. In this climate, in March, John Roper, David Marquand, Bob Maclennan and I left the House of Commons for a quick dinner in an Italian restaurant before voting at 10 p.m. I proposed a suggestion for a counter-attack. A parliamentary motion was out of the question for we could not match John Silkin's numbers for his anti-Common Market motion. We needed, in contrast, to demonstrate both the quality of the support for entry in the PLP and the extent of support that still existed in the shadow Cabinet. My suggestion for a European declaration, signed by prominent socialists in the ten countries which would, hopefully, make up the new Europe, was accepted as a way of obtaining a commitment from some of the people whose open support was now vital. None of us had any illusions about the logistical difficulty of producing such a statement in such a short time.

We first sounded out Roy Jenkins, who was cautiously enthusiastic. Denis Healey was a much more difficult problem. He had reached the same conclusion as Hugh Gaitskell in 1962, coming down marginally against Britain's entry on the terms likely to be available. He admired Scandinavian socialism, and later admitted that he overestimated the Commonwealth's potential to influence world affairs. Denis had supported Douglas Jay in the Cabinet in opposing a second application for membership in 1966 but had, without too much unhappiness, gone along with the majority decision. It was decided that Roy Hattersley and I should approach him, for we had worked with him in the Ministry of Defence and had considerable respect for him. However, only a few days before, Denis had made a speech which left some wondering whether he too was not starting to change. We were ready to have a stand-up row. Dealing with Denis Healey is quite different from dealing with most politicians: he respects straight talk. In the event, we did not need to say anything – Denis seemed to know that this was not like most meetings. As often, when nervous, he hid it by talking in a joke Yorkshire dialect. 'Well, lads, what can I do for you?' was his opening gambit. We showed him the declaration and, to our surprise, he signed immediately and promised to discuss it with Willy Brandt, the former German Chancellor, whom he was due to see at Königswinter. This was important since it was obvious from the start that Willy Brandt's signature would be crucial in obtaining the support of other Europeans. In fact, Roy Jenkins had already written to him and told him that David Marquand and Bob Maclennan would discuss the wording of the declaration with him in Bonn, since they too were going to Königswinter.

With most of the key European figures either having agreed to sign or already being approached, we met on Thursday 6 May, in Roy Hattersley's house in Gayfere Street. All through the weekend people were contacted, telegrams sent to European capitals. The end response was remarkable. On Monday morning it was apparent that we might even reach 100, although I was adamant that we should not take topping-up signatures from the Lords. We decided to put the advertisement only in the *Guardian* and ten minutes before the 2 p.m. deadline on Monday 10 May, we had the 100 signatures.

The statement in the *Guardian*, after various redrafts and problems with the translated meaning, said:

> We, the undersigned Parliamentarians, are convinced that the causes of social democracy, world peace and economic advance in both developed and developing countries would be strengthened by the addition of the United Kingdom, Norway, Denmark and Ireland to the European Economic Community.

Since the wording was fairly bland, it was vital that no one of substance should sign and then later announce their opposition to entry on the basis that it was not incompatible with signing the declaration. The greatest danger of this, we thought, could come from either Tony Benn, who was at that stage nominally a supporter of entry, or from Jim Callaghan. Roy felt that both should have the opportunity of signing the declaration. It would be hard, he felt, to justify their exclusion before the other members of the shadow Cabinet, since they were supposed to be in favour of entry. Harold Wilson had been informed of the proposed declaration some time before by Roy and had also been told that Willy Brandt would be asked to sign. We quite deliberately did not ask Harold Wilson to sign, though it was always understood that if he had wished to we would have been delighted. In public Harold's position was that he thought it inappropriate to sign but he raised no objections to the declaration.

So I spoke to Tony Benn with the express hope of not obtaining his signature. It proved an easy task. He clearly had no intention of signing, making it plain that his opposition was not to entry but to the manner in which the decision was being made. He seemed genuinely shocked that I could believe that we could go in without calling an election or a referendum.

Jim Callaghan was a much more formidable proposition and I was uneasy in having to tackle him. Over the years I had developed a wary regard for him. Unlike so many of the other people close to Roy, I could not help but like him and it was perhaps because of this that I was delegated to approach him. I waited until late on the Sunday. I wanted to make him a totally genuine offer to sign but to resist any argument for delay. I had difficulty in contacting Jim and eventually had to ring Peter Jay, who first rang his father-in-law to see if I could be given his number on the farm. When I got through we both fenced hard: Jim was trying to find out who else had signed in the shadow Cabinet, which I was quite happy to reveal, but he was also arguing for a delay, presumably so that it could be discussed at the Wednesday shadow Cabinet. He told me he would not be in London on the Monday but I pleaded newspaper deadlines and international co-ordination problems and this eventually led Jim to say that if the machinery was already in motion and could not be stopped, he would have to accept that the declaration must go ahead. We then agreed a formula: he would say that he had been approached but refused to sign on the grounds that it was better for the shadow Cabinet members to stay outside such an initiative. He had not, in consequence, been given the wording of the declaration, which meant that he had no view on it.

I had no complaints. It meant Jim could not brief the press to say the statement was innocuous and the sort of statement he would be usually quite happy to sign. To have him downplaying the whole initiative would have been very damaging. It was now also too late for him to brief the press for the Monday editions.

The *Guardian* declaration had a major impact, steeling the ranks of the pro-Marketeers inside the PLP and raising the morale of our supporters outside Parliament. For all this, the harsh fact was now becoming clear: the party outside was moving relentlessly against entry and Harold Wilson's position on the fence was looking very lopsided. In conversation with middle-of-the-road Labour MPs one could sense that many were preparing for a retreat from any previous commitment to entry, claiming that the EEC was not that important and that we should really be concentrating on housing, education and health.

The shift was also becoming apparent to the press, not least to

David Watt, political editor of the *Financial Times*, who, with his wife Susan, had become close friends of ours. David knew the Labour Party inside out from his time as Common Market correspondent on the old *Daily Herald*. He was getting more and more concerned that the Labour Party was about to switch away from its support for entry. On 7 May he wrote in the *Financial Times* that

> if the leader of the Labour Party starts at this late stage to discover a sudden burning indignation on behalf of the Caribbean sugar producers, Scottish fishermen and New Zealand farmers, many of us will be quietly sick, but quite a lot of the Parliamentary Labour Party may find it convincing.

Many of us were soon to be sick. The Heath–Pompidou breakthrough meeting took place on 20–21 May 1971 and it was now clear that France was going to accept Britain as a member of the Community. Just four days later, the pro-Marketeers were dealt a major blow. Jim Callaghan made his devastating 'Language of Chaucer' speech at a by-election meeting for Bob Mitchell in Southampton. Bob later became an SDP MP but he was a rarity, being against the European Community but firmly on the right of the party. While paying lip service to the ongoing negotiations, Jim did not even attempt to disguise his belief that the Labour Party should reject entry. He defined terms of entry that were not remotely negotiable and he knew it. Picking up on a *Panorama* interview when President Pompidou had referred to French as the language of Europe, Jim played shamelessly to the gallery. 'Millions of people in Britain', he declared, 'have been surprised to hear that the language of Chaucer, Shakespeare and Milton must in future be regarded as an American import from which we must protect ourselves if we are to build a new Europe.' Whatever one's views of the European Union in the twenty-first century, it is a fact that English has become the most important working language.

However, Jim's speech could not simply be dismissed as the small change of an internal party battle. In a perceptive passage he anticipated the controversy of the 1990s over whether a single currency meant a federalist Europe:

I understand there is to be a confederation of member states whose ministers will retain full powers of decision. That is to say, they can disagree with decisions taken by other countries and so can prevent action by the EEC countries. This is a contradictory position for, if there is to be a successful economic and monetary union, then member states will have to subordinate their own fiscal, taxation and monetary policies to a central governing body.

This was a direct reply to Edward Heath, who had said decisions would have to be taken unanimously with a veto retained. By exposing that a unified economic and monetary policy meant a big step towards a United States of Europe, Jim also drew attention to the way Heath, throughout this period, sold entry to the British public as joining a Community of nation states. I never realised that Edward Heath was hiding his own federalist opinions at every stage of the negotiations as well as during the passage of the legislation. He was not the only one. I only later discovered that Roy Jenkins was a closet federalist.

The dubious tactic of the federalists since the 1960s has been to deny they wanted a single executive European President, a European Cabinet or an authoritative European Parliament but to quietly push in this direction over a whole series of small decisions. In this sense the anti-Europeans were right in the early 1970s – there was a secret agenda. Yet many of the pro-Europeans were, like me, deeply suspicious of a federalist Europe. An uneasy truce was reached amongst the pro-Europeans in British politics to postpone serious discussions on this question until Britain was firmly embedded within the European Community. It is revealing that the federalist debate in Britain only surfaced from 1988 onwards, the moment when it was clear that Labour's internal battle against membership was perhaps finally over.

It is quite extraordinary that Jim Callaghan's autobiography, *Time and Chance*, has no account of his '*Non merci beaucoup*' speech in Southampton. The impact of the speech on Harold Wilson and its effect within the Labour Party was tremendous. I have no doubt that if Jim Callaghan had supported entry in 1971, as he had as Chancellor when it was debated in 1967 and as Home Secretary when Labour formally applied in 1970, then Harold Wilson would not have come out against the terms of the negotiations. For Harold did not need to understand French to know what Jim was up to. He had already had reported to him Jim's reputed comment to a journalist not willing to go to Southampton, 'Well, if you want to hear the next leader of the Labour Party, you'd better arrange to be there.' As he had done with 'In Place of Strife', Jim was putting himself at the vanguard of mainstream Labour Party opinion. If Harold Wilson wanted to stay true to the application for member-ship which he had launched, he was going to have to fight Jim Callaghan once again and with no certainty as to the outcome. And if Wilson had any doubts as to which way the wind was blowing, the conduct of two other members of the shadow Cabinet, Denis Healey and Tony Crosland, would have convinced him.

No sooner had we celebrated Denis's support than a few weeks later he began stressing entry terms that were not negotiable. The Healey tank had turned, only to bulldoze off in the opposite direction at the same speed. It was as cynical a piece of politics as I have ever seen. Tony Crosland's 'apostasy', as it was woundingly described by the *Sunday Times*, leaked out from the general management committee in his Grimsby constituency on the same day as Denis Healey's *volte-face* was complete. For Tony, we were told, membership of the European Community was not that important, perhaps seventh in his list of priorities. There was no way in which Tony could make this argument sound convincing. He had been a longstanding supporter of entry into the European Community, and he had been upset by Hugh Gaitskell's anti-Community stance in 1962. How could he behave like this? Undoubtedly he was influenced by jealousy of Roy Jenkins, who was ahead of him in the leadership stakes and by the fact that many who supported Roy had acted with monumental insensitivity towards Tony. None of us had done nearly enough to keep Roy and Tony working together. We had lined ourselves up in separate camps as if preparing for war.

I kick myself for not having learnt that lesson of the need to nurse bruised egos in my dealings with the three other members of the Gang of Four after our 1983 election defeat. Too often it is lack of communication as well as ambitions and animosities which determine people's political positions.

Not surprisingly, as David Watt had foreseen, Harold Wilson

discovered New Zealand farmers at the Labour Party's special conference in Central Hall, Westminster. Eleven days later the National Executive of the Labour Party voted by sixteen votes to six to invite the Parliamentary Labour Party to unite wholeheartedly in voting against the government's policy over the European Community.

The clash of personality can never be divorced from politics. It of course occurs in all walks of life but is peculiarly heightened by the cockpit of politics that is the House of Commons. Wilson was naturally determined to hold onto the leadership. Callaghan, Jenkins, Crosland and Healey were all fighting in their various ways to become leader. The clash of personality had debilitated the Wilson government of 1964–70 and was now haunting Labour in opposition. Superficially the discord between Roy Jenkins and Tony Crosland was the least defensible. Longtime personal friends, they were supposed to agree on most political issues. Although Tony was a far more ideological politician than Roy, both were fiercely ambitious and deeply emotional, though they desperately tried to hide these characteristics both from themselves as well as from their friends. Roy gave the impression to some of not giving a damn about the Labour Party, seeing the issue only in terms of editorials in the *Times*, and of being also unduly obsessed about his own personal position; whereas Tony appeared to elevate the Labour Party, particularly in Grimsby, to a position where its interests came well before those of the country. He was also never as uninterested as he pretended to be in jockeying for position as a potential leader of the Labour Party. Tony's problem was that Roy was thought to have a far better chance of winning the leadership. It was becoming very hard to be a friend of both men.

Over the weekend of 19–20 June I saw a lot of Willie Whitelaw, then Leader of the House, since we were both at an Anglo-American parliamentarians' conference at Ditchley Park in Oxfordshire. He made it clear that he was arguing in the Cabinet for a free vote and he insisted the door was not shut on a free vote, though he conceded it was unlikely. The wording used by Heath in the House had been deliberately chosen to leave open the possibility of having a free vote in the autumn. Whitelaw was adamant that, after the vote in principle, the government would have to be responsible for the subsequent legislation but he attached great importance to the achievement of a substantial pro-entry vote in principle in October and clearly felt that if there was a free vote many more Labour MPs would feel it possible to vote for entry than if they had to flout a three-line whip. In retrospect, there can be no doubt that, if Whitelaw had been able to convince the Cabinet in July to support a free vote, it would have been very difficult for the Labour Party to have insisted on a three-line whip. Unfortunately he failed and the Cabinet made the major tactical blunder of holding out until forced to concede a free vote in October, by which time Labour were heading for a three-line whip.

The widely used argument was that it was necessary to hold the prospect of a three-line whip over Conservative MPs during the summer so that Conservative Associations could pressurise their anti-Market MPs. But the numbers who would have been so pressured were very small, probably ten MPs at most. The real reason was that Edward Heath believed he could carry the vote relying only on Conservative votes and attached great importance to doing so. Over the summer, the momentum therefore built up for a Labour three-line whip against entry. Our resolve to support entry was undiminished. About fifty of the Labour pro-Marketeers met under Bill Rodgers's chairmanship just before the summer recess. At that meeting, it was made clear that there were sixty-plus who were committed to vote for entry, even against the expected conference decision, and against a three-line whip. This did a lot to strengthen people's morale and I went away for the summer feeling I had made a commitment before close colleagues and that there could now be no turning back. Nor did I want to. Not for the first or last time in my political career I was rejecting Disraeli's dictum 'damn your principles and stick to your party'.

It was remarkable how firm our group's resolve proved to be. Instead of the summer months showing a steady slipping in support, the group's strength actually increased. By conference we were certain of at least sixty-five votes in favour and throughout October Bill Rodgers's figures were far more accurate, as events proved, than the underestimates made by the official opposition whips. Although it was not widely discussed, Roy Jenkins's intention to vote for entry, finally confirmed in October in answer to pleas from the left to abstain, was never in doubt.

Before the Brighton conference I had to face a selection conference for the new Devonport constituency. I was determined that there should be no misunderstanding and so I told the general management committee that within weeks I had every intention of voting for the principle of entry contained in the government white paper. I was the single candidate under the then rules since I was the sitting MP for parts of the new constituency and I only had to get 50 per cent of the votes. I did this easily, but there was some dissent so the chairman asked if the meeting would agree, for press purposes, to take another vote in order to make it unanimous. To her credit, one of the delegates who was passionately anti-Common Market objected to this procedure. But then a few weeks later she refused to condemn my vote.

The six-day debate to approve the government's decision of principle to join the European Community on the basis of the arrangements which had been negotiated was the most important debate in my time in the House of Commons. More than 200 MPs were trying to catch the Speaker's eye and it was called 'the Great Debate'. John Mackintosh spoke at 6.30 a.m. and even at that unearthly hour it was a lucid demolition of the nineteenth-century concept of sovereignty. I had earlier challenged Michael Foot on this point, controversially intervening in his speech to say:

> Before my Honourable Friend gets carried away by his own rhetoric, on the important point of principle which he rightly raised on the issue of sovereignty, how does he square the fact that membership of the United Nations also carries with it some secession of sovereignty, and membership of any treaty or any organisation involves sharing, compromise and, if he likes, haggling?

Earlier that day Geoffrey Rippon quoted President Pompidou's explanation about sovereignty and the treaty in a press conference held on 21 January 1971 and it remains the best description I have heard of the realities of Community membership:

> How will the Council of Ministers be able to take its decision? I ask everybody and in particular our partners to consider how coalition governments work. When everybody is of the same opinion all goes

well. If that is not the case, there is a majority and a minority. At that point either the minority considers the question is not vital and yields, or thinks the contrary and breaks the coalition. It is plain that, in our construction of Europe, one cannot break without everything collapsing. I therefore conclude that important decisions can only be taken on the basis of unanimous agreement and that what is at issue here is political reality rather than juridical rule. If one ignores that reality everything would be destroyed.

There is no possible interpretation of President Pompidou's words or the fact that they were quoted by our chief negotiator in that debate which gives any evidence for the argument that we were joining up for a United States of Europe committed to ever greater integration and that Britain would have no right to veto such a development.

The debate grew tense towards the end. When the division was called I, along with sixty-eight other Labour MPs, voted to support entry into the Common Market and twenty, including Tony Crosland, abstained. There was a majority of 112 for the principle of entry into the European Community. Had every Labour MP and all the Conservative rebels voted against, Britain would not have become a member of the European Community. It was the best parliamentary vote that I have ever cast and I have no regrets whatever for voting as I did. Had I known how cravenly New Labour in their pro-Europeanism would pursue the path of integration after the 2005 election and drop their commitment to a referendum on the EU constitution, I would never have wanted them to win that election and I would have opposed them, as I did for Labour's anti-Europeanism in 1983 and 1987.

What I did regret in 1972, and bitterly, was thereafter voting against the legislation necessary to ensure that entry was enshrined in British law. Now that the white paper on the principle was passed, we faced months of votes on the mechanics, each bit of which was essential to entry. The truth is that we allowed ourselves to drift into a messy compromise over how to vote. A rather bogus logic was developed to justify our behaviour, namely that it was not the job of an opposition to carry government legislation. I never really accepted this and believed that voting against would be very embarrassing. This was one reason why I had shown interest earlier in abstaining on the white paper for I felt we could hold to that and abstain throughout the legislation.

The pro-Marketeers entered the new year fearful, in many cases, of being undermined in their constituencies. On 19 January 1972 Harold Wilson unceremoniously sacked Bill Rodgers from his position as a second-tier spokesman on the opposition front bench. This was a direct challenge to Roy Jenkins for Bill had acted as chief of staff of the pro-Market campaign and was known to be very close to Roy. But, cleverly, Wilson did reappoint Dick Taverne. It was a neatly judged knifing of Roy Jenkins, diminishing him without provoking him.

On the night of 17 February, on the second reading of the European Communities Bill, I cast the worst vote I ever cast in Parliament and the one of which I am most ashamed. It was the first of the votes to put in place the necessary mechanisms for entry. I felt physically sick, passing through what I knew to be the wrong division lobby and voting against the bill. That night I was closer to leaving Parliament than at any other time. I had had dinner in the House with Roy and we had all drunk rather too much, trying to hide our feelings. It was a very emotional occasion. All the indications were that the government would have a fairly comfortable majority of a little under twenty. As 10 p.m. came nearer it became obvious that it might be close. I talked to Austen Albu, who was uncertain what he would do, and also to the veteran Labour MP George Strauss, who was upset that most of us intended to vote against the second reading and felt strongly that we should abstain. Roy decided not to wait for the result and went up to his room. Voting against the bill had been a desperately difficult decision for him personally: he really felt it might be better to resign. Like us all, however, he buoyed himself up with the false belief that this would be the last hurdle.

The division result was announced to a tense House and the majority of only eight was shattering news. We had boosted our party but nearly broken the bill. There was a snarling, vicious scene as the Labour benches erupted, with Jimmy Hamilton and others rounding on the Liberals, who had quite reasonably voted for entry. I left and walked up with Roy Hattersley to Roy Jenkins's room in a gloomy mood.

The next few weeks were, in many respects, one of our worst periods. The pro-Market forces were in disarray, guilt was the dominant emotion – most people felt deeply distressed at how near we had come to seeing our entry to the Community rejected. Once again, the anguish had to be faced over what was more important – Britain going into the Common Market or splitting the Labour Party. The anti-Market forces – both Tory and Labour – had scented blood. The successful alliance between Enoch Powell and Michael Foot, which had forced the shelving of the House of Lords Reform Bill, might succeed once again. The legislation on the European Bill was now clearly threatened and there would be tremendous pressure for frequent three-line whips.

Partly to break out of this frustrating downward spiral, Roy Jenkins had agreed some months before to embark on a course of speeches. Debbie helped Roy with the publishing arrangements for *What Matters Now* and he generously gave her a Persian rug as thanks. We still have it in our sitting room and it serves to remind us both of a happy time when Roy and Jennifer Jenkins were our friends. A number of us put a great deal of time and effort into these speeches. David Marquand contributed most to the writing, often while staying for the weekend at Buttermere, our house in Wiltshire, and he included a reference to 'breaking the mould', a concept later taken up by the SDP. The ideas came from a large number of people whom we consulted. Roy, of course, provided his own distinctive gloss but at times I wondered whether he was focusing sufficiently on the radical nature of many of the suggestions. They were put to him and were easily accepted but when he had the opportunity to put some of them into action in government, particularly on poverty and the inner cities, Roy singularly failed to champion them. As chairman of the home affairs Cabinet sub-committee between 1974 and 1976 Roy could have instigated a radical programme, even though we were then in a very difficult financial situation, but he showed precious little interest in pushing forward the ideas established in his own programme. More than any other single thing, this eroded my commitment to him as a future leader.

The intention behind the speeches was straightforward and political. It was to be the 'Unauthorised Programme'. Just as Joseph Chamberlain, another Birmingham MP, had used this vehicle in 1885 to stamp his own distinctive mark on British politics, we hoped it would provide a rallying point for people who wanted to see Roy Jenkins succeed Harold Wilson as leader of the Labour Party.

So when the first speech on poverty was delivered to the Worsley Labour Party on Saturday 11 March, not surprisingly it was marked by Sunday newspaper headlines: 'JENKINS OPENS HIS BID TO OUST WILSON'; 'JENKINS OPENS HIS BID FOR LABOUR LEADERSHIP'; 'JENKINS'S BID FOR THE TOP'. The next day I was sitting out in the spring sun in Buttermere, extremely pleased by what had been achieved, and listening to *The World This Weekend*. I heard Gordon Clough ask Roy, 'A bid to oust Mr Wilson? How do you react to those headlines?' Roy replied, 'Well, I react by regarding them as a totally distorting picture . . . I rather resent it when the whole press reacts to this as though it is a personal issue, which it is not, and tries to create a great leadership crisis which does not exist.' It was the first time that Roy Jenkins the politician totally exasperated me. If he was going to take this line, I believed he should not have gone on the programme. It was certainly not necessary to deny he was challenging for the leadership in terms which came close to those we laugh at in *Yes, Minister*.

I had thought that Roy accepted that we were embarking on an outright challenge to Wilson and all that his style of leadership implied. Yet here he was, having demonstrated his readiness to strike, showing his disinclination to wound. It reflected many things, not least Roy's ambivalence towards Wilson. I understood this because it was something I had shared but by then I had no doubts whatever about Wilson's leadership. I wanted him out and would have preferred any of the likely alternatives – Roy, Jim or Denis. Roy of course had only one preference – to replace Wilson himself. Roy was always unsure as to whether he could use Wilson as the ladder to No. 10 or whether he had to destroy Wilson to achieve it. Whereas he would be scathing about Jim Callaghan, he was then not as vicious about Wilson. He despised Denis Healey's twists and turns and was uneasy dealing with Tony Crosland but to Wilson there was a sense of indebtedness. However, this was not the time to be paralysed by ambivalence and for the first time I developed a deep anxiety about whether Roy, despite his ambition, had the stomach for an open fight to achieve it, or whether he would always prefer the indirect, less overt feline approach.

Whatever he said on the radio, one of the effects of Roy's speech was that Harold Wilson believed that he was now after his job. Although this was not a new feeling, the intensity with which Wilson felt it was. Not even in 1969 had Wilson looked so vulnerable, for now in opposition he had very little patronage. He must have been only too well aware of how damaging his somersault over the European Community a few months earlier had been to what was left of his reputation. Yet he saw the situation very differently from us. He felt resentful that he had been left to wade around in the shit, as he put it, while Roy and others like me could ignore the responsibility for party unity and bask in the glow of a favourable press which called us men of integrity. From then on Wilson seemed determined to face down the Jenkins challenge.

On 15 March the shadow Cabinet met for the first discussion on the referendum. Tony Benn had been campaigning for some time in favour of a referendum but the issue now was specific – whether or not to support a Tory backbencher's amendment to the European Communities Bill that supported a referendum. In the shadow Cabinet there were only four votes in favour of the amendment and on this first occasion Harold Wilson spoke against. Then fate intervened. The very next day President Pompidou announced that there would be a referendum in France on the question of enlarging the Community. It was purely a constitutional ratification procedure in France, though having the advantage of splitting the Socialists from the Communists, but in Britain its effect on the Labour Party was dramatic for it gave Wilson the opportunity to use the issue to isolate Jenkins. The referendum issue was brought by Tony Benn to Labour's NEC on 22 March and they voted in favour by thirteen votes to eleven, with Wilson, Jenkins and Callaghan not attending. This was even though at the previous Brighton conference the NEC had called successfully for the defeat of a similar referendum motion. Then on 24 March, Edward Heath announced a plan for occasional referenda in Northern Ireland on the issue of union with the South and the momentum for a European referendum was now building up, so much so that when the shadow Cabinet met on 29 March the pending referendum amendment vote in the House of Commons was on the agenda yet again. This time Harold Wilson spoke early, advocating support for the referendum amendment. Neither Willie

Ross nor Denis Healey, who had previously been against, attended and, in the case of Ross at least, Wilson's influence was felt to be at work. Usually loyal to Wilson, Ross was passionately anti-referendum, believing that the Scottish Nationalists would use it to force through separatism or even the devolution which he opposed. So, by eight votes to six, the shadow Cabinet reversed its position and recommended the Labour Party to vote with Enoch Powell in favour of a consultative referendum.

After the decision had been taken Tony Crosland said that he hoped nobody would take the issue as one of principle. Roy deliberately made no comment. He was determined not to start yet another period of press speculation about his voting intentions and about a possible resignation. He had learned his lesson from the too-wide and extensive consultation that took place over the second reading.

Next morning, when I met Roy in his room with David Marquand, John Roper and Bob Maclennan to discuss a speech he was due to deliver, he took a telephone call from Harold Lever. It was clear from listening to Roy's half of the conversation that Harold now believed that resignation was inevitable and essential. Roy had previously talked to George Thomson and George had apparently made it clear that he felt he personally had no other option than to resign, that in speeches up and down the country he had deeply committed himself against a referendum. Roy remained enigmatic, giving no real indication of his feelings, except that it was a serious situation and he wanted a week to think things over. He then asked me to drive down to the country with him.

In the car Roy explained he was fed up with the constant lobbying: every shadow Cabinet was a battle, as was every meeting of the NEC. He had just lost the battle to ensure that Gwyn Morgan, the assistant general secretary, would take over the general secretaryship of the Labour Party from Sir Harry Nicholas. John Cartwright, who was on the NEC and voted albeit without much enthusiasm for Gwyn, believed that the last-minute switching of votes was influenced by the controversy building up over the European Community. The whole European issue had been one long emotional struggle. In addition the scars of our vote on the second reading had gone pretty deep and the press reaction and speculation over Roy's critical speech in Lancashire had stiffened support for

Harold Wilson. That controversy too had been more than he had reckoned with, so his guard was down while Wilson's was up.

It is easy to forget the exhaustion and emotional strain of politics. One thing I had learnt over the previous few months was that Roy Jenkins was as emotional as every Celt and to vote against the second reading was for him as for me one of the hardest things we had ever done in politics.

Discussing the situation, I was certain of one thing, that in the end Roy would make his own decision and would not be easily persuaded to stay his hand. I remembered how, some months back in the Reform Club at lunch, he had said that the decisions he most regretted taking in his life were those where he had been most cautious. Looking ahead, we were already worried about the forthcoming vote on Clause 2, which was the core of the bill, for to lose that clause would be to lose the legislation. If Wilson and the shadow Cabinet could reverse their decision on the referendum with such apparent disregard for everything that had been said before, it was only a matter of time before they could engineer another crisis to embarrass us.

The *Times*'s editorial on Harold Wilson – 'What can one say of such a man, save that he should never be Prime Minister again' – must have hurt for he always took press criticism, from whatever source, far more seriously than it merited. Sensitive, embittered and lonely, his paranoid feelings about the press only intensified by criticism, to Wilson the story was very different. He was the martyr, the man who had put party unity before his own personal position. Roy had allowed his personal commitment to come before party unity; only he, Harold, had withstood, as he described it, the 'mud, filthy mud' that was being thrown.

It is hard, even now, not to feel real sympathy for Wilson in his European predicament, now also facing his deputy leader's challenge on the very basis of the party's social philosophy. Roy's Lancashire speech on the new challenge of injustice was, we all knew, a fervent attack on Wilson's values, leadership and standing. Previously Wilson had never seen Roy Jenkins as a rival because he lacked a base in the party. Callaghan was always the real danger. Perhaps after the Lancashire speech Wilson had now decided to ignore the short-term cost to his own credibility and would force his deputy leader to severe humiliation and compromise so that his image would be tarnished. This was typical of the restless insouciance which often characterised Wilson's approach. Wilson must have recognised that this could mean Roy's resignation but he might have thought that Roy would swallow even this.

One further aspect of our conversation, which I had recorded in my notebook, in the light of subsequent events had particular significance. When I, for the first time, raised the whole question of us perhaps being forced into a new political party, Roy said that, if one was a Chartist, one would take the view that this was highly possible but it was clear that it had no attraction whatever for him – his roots were then still too deep in the Labour Party.

Roy was under no illusion at all that resignation would damage his chances of becoming leader. I only wanted one promise – that he would fight back for a number of years. I got my assurance with the wry comment that this was not a commitment for a decade. It was clear that Roy intended to fight – he would not go off and write, to the exclusion of politics, or take some financially lucrative appointment in the City. Unlike Jim Callaghan, he remarked, he was not intending to become a director of an Italian bank.

Having put my point vigorously about the need for him to still attend Prime Minister's Questions and party meetings, I told Roy that whatever decision he made on resignation, whether I agreed with it or not, I too would resign. I felt that he needed to have the certain knowledge that some of us would come with him. In these situations we had to retain a basic cohesion and loyalty and, though I still felt unsure which was the right course and indeed went on putting the case for accepting a referendum and against resignation, over the last year I had developed enough confidence in his judgement to make his decision my decision.

Over that Easter weekend Tony and Susan Crosland came to stay at Buttermere for the night. It was a delightful visit. We only had a short talk about politics. It was clear that Tony could see no reason why the referendum vote should pose any substantial difficulty. He had voted against but there it was, they had lost in the shadow Cabinet. The situation was awful, yes, but there was nothing anyone could, or should, do. The only time I think I shook Tony's argument at all was when I reminded him of his own attitude to unilateralism in 1961. There must, I asked, be some issues on which one has to fight. The referendum might not be the issue, but the compromises were increasing. He was off to Japan in a few days so I warned him that the referendum could turn out to be a major turning point, although I felt I could not tell him that I thought Roy was about to resign. We left the issue thereafter for it was pointless to argue further, our basic positions were so different. Tony had convinced himself that the EEC was a minor issue; starting from such a premise, any discussion of resignation, conscience or principle was bound to be meaningless.

His was a breathtaking position – intellectually impudent as well as suspect. It flew in the face of all the conventional wisdoms. There was scarcely any significant figure, left, right or centre, in the EEC controversy who thought entry a minor issue. However, the attraction of the position for anyone not wanting a fight within the Labour Party, yet wanting to remain consistent, was immense.

I was determined that we should not be open to the charge of failing to look at all the options rationally and objectively. I drafted a memo, which Debbie typed up on Thursday morning, and showed it to Bob Maclennan as we drove down to East Hendred for lunch. The memo started from three basic assumptions: that the PLP would support a consultative referendum before ratification, despite any opposition we might put up at the party meeting; that less than half of the eighty-nine pro-European voters or abstainers would consider abstention even if Roy and the other members of the shadow Cabinet resigned; and finally that the Labour Party conference in October would support the commitment for any incoming Labour government to have a referendum on whether or not Britain should stay within the EEC. If these assumptions were correct, by far the most important was that relating to the likely position of the party at the next election. To vote now against a referendum, quite apart from any short-term problems, would make for immense difficulties over the general election manifesto. It would, in my opinion, make it impossible for Roy to become leader this side of the general election, and the continued existence of the commitment would make it difficult for Roy to challenge to be leader in the early years following an election defeat. Given that the pressures for a commitment to come out of the EEC were now pretty strong, the only way of holding off such a commitment would be to compromise on the referendum. Therefore to vote against a referendum could well start a process whereby a group of us would have no options other than to reverse our earlier position or not to stand at the next election.

Once we arrived at his home for lunch, Roy's argument became clear: he was convinced that to have a referendum would destroy the party. He kept reiterating that the central activity of constituency parties was to get Labour supporters to the polls to put their crosses on a ballot paper on polling day. Whatever might be said at the start, as the campaign progressed, a referendum would become identified with a general election in party workers' minds. He said, with immense passion, that he was convinced that, whatever people's intentions at the start of the campaign, before the end he and others would inevitably run a very substantial risk of being expelled from the party. To the argument that we would have to have a written undertaking that pro-Marketeers would be free to campaign, he forcefully reminded us of other similar pledges on Europe. What about what the party had already said over the referendum? Though he was well controlled, I could detect very considerable emotion – he was stretched like taut elastic. He did not believe a word that Wilson now said. Certainly the catalogue of lies, half-truths and twists and turns was a depressing background against which to travel down a new referendum road, particularly one dependent on assurances from Harold Wilson.

I left Roy's late that Thursday afternoon, totally convinced that he was going to resign. My memo and views on referenda notwith-standing, I was determined not to leave him alone and isolated: not only did he need a few people to resign with him but I had also felt throughout a sufficient doubt about the referendum to be content to accept his judgement. On the drive back, however, Bob Maclennan was still adamantly against resignation and he asked if I minded him showing my memo to George Thomson. Bob had been George's parliamentary private secretary when we were in govern-ment and was very close to him. I had no fear that it would go any further. George, it turned out, was unconvinced and did a great deal to persuade Bob to resign.

The day after the East Hendred lunch, Roy Hattersley rang and spoke to Debbie: it appeared to her that he had spoken to Jennifer

Jenkins on the telephone and was aware of everything, including my
memo. He asked me to drop by for a chat, which I did, on Friday
evening on my way down to Wiltshire. Debbie was waiting in the
car with Tristan, so I was in a hurry. Mistakenly, I gave a copy of my
memo to Roy Hattersley. He was extremely enthusiastic, so much so
that I even found myself forced to argue against it, stressing the
problems of being able to actually support entry in any referendum.
I think he really wanted Roy Jenkins to vote for a referendum but
for the rest of us to ensure that the referendum was lost by sufficient
abstentions. Yet it was not clear whether he was prepared to abstain
himself and I told him of Bill Rodgers's view that, without some
form of leadership, it was hard to see that we would get enough
abstentions. He knew that George Thomson and Harold Lever
wanted to resign and that it was impossible for Roy Jenkins to stay
while they went. In sum, I was not certain whether Roy Hattersley
was ready to resign. But he did say as I left that he was an animal who
hunted in a pack and that we would both have to resign if Roy
Jenkins did. The one thing he felt very strongly about was that, since
we were both reluctant to see Roy Jenkins resign, we should not let
him know our intention to resign in advance. I said I could not
threaten Roy Jenkins like this. He had always known that I would
go if he did and anyhow I had already told him that I would resign.
I could not, I said, use this as an indirect bargaining chip. It was,
anyhow, a pretty worthless one: Roy Jenkins was going to make this
decision on his own.

  Roy Hattersley asked if he could keep my memorandum, with
the intention of showing it to John Harris, his main aide when it
came to dealing with the press, on his arrival from America. Some
sixth sense made me reluctant to part with it but I did. I felt slightly
that in giving it to him I was moving behind Roy Jenkins's back for
I knew in my heart that Roy Jenkins was now going to resign. Roy
Hattersley claimed to know of the existence of a first draft of
Roy Jenkins's resignation letter, though I was not sure whether he
had seen it.

  I left Roy Hattersley's house tired and rather depressed. I told
Debbie that we would both be resigning together with very much
the same doubts, anxieties and beliefs. She flatly refused to believe
that Roy Hattersley would resign. I shared Roy Hattersley's dislike

of resignation as a tactic in most circumstances in politics; the arguments for holding one's ground and fighting from within are usually overwhelming. However, this situation was quite different. Apart from other considerations, the referendum vote in the House of Commons promised to be the closest yet. There was a real possibility of a far larger number of Tory rebel votes or abstentions than hitherto and the morale of the pro-Marketeers was being progressively undermined. The pressure being put on pro-Market members in the constituencies was also mounting – not only was Dick Taverne in deep trouble but Edward Lyons was being seriously threatened in his new Leeds constituency and others like Pat Duffy were feeling pressure too. The climate could not have been worse to attempt to rally a mass abstention and Bill Rodgers felt this would be particularly difficult if all the shadow Cabinet pro-Marketeers voted for the referendum. I greatly valued Bill Rodgers's judgement, but decided to conduct a straw poll of my own and its conclusion was very similar. The will to fight was disappearing.

That evening at Buttermere, Roy Jenkins rang to ask Debbie and me over for lunch the next day. Bob McNamara and some others were coming and he wanted, I suspected, to tell me his decision. It was a lovely spring day. I talked to McNamara about the Cuban missile crisis and it was clear that he still considered control of nuclear weapons to be, with population control, the most urgent issue facing mankind. He was fascinating about the Nassau meeting in 1962, confirming that it was Macmillan's powers of persuasion with Kennedy over Polaris which were the key factor. Throughout lunch, the conversation never touched on the Common Market or the referendum and it was as though we were unconscious of the slow-burning fuse that was relentlessly moving towards detonation. Then, once we had eaten, Roy and I went into his study for a private chat and he showed me a handwritten draft of his resignation letter to Wilson. It came as no surprise, although after Roy Hattersley's remark I had been expecting it to be a typed letter, since, when he had claimed to have seen the letter, he implied that Roy's secretary had typed it out. Perhaps he had made the whole thing up to sound me out and to see if I knew of the existence of a resignation letter. I made a few detailed suggestions but the letter was very clear and the only point over which I was very strong was the need to say that Roy did not wish his other friends to resign as well. This seemed to me to be important in terms of party unity and to prevent ill feeling between those who wanted to resign and those who wished to remain. As we left, Roy and Bob McNamara were going for a walk on the Downs and I knew nothing would change his mind.

On Monday after lunch I was sitting in the House of Commons library when Roy Hattersley came in. He said that Roy Jenkins had put his resignation letter in and that it would be public later in the afternoon. Though he still regretted the resignation and talked wistfully of my alternative proposal, he did nothing to indicate he was not intending, personally, to resign. He was clearly overwrought but seemed to be facing the inevitable. Suddenly, our conversation was interrupted by one of the staff of the Whips' Office coming in to say that Harold Wilson wished to see him immediately. He got up straightaway, almost as if he had been expecting the call. It seemed to me rather odd that he should be summoned so soon but I assumed that Harold Wilson would try and persuade him not to resign.

In the course of winding up my speech in the debate, I hinted at my intention to resign. It seemed that there might be some advantage in indicating this to my friends and it might also serve to prevent any blandishments aimed at persuading me to stay on. It had to be a veiled reference because I wanted to tell Harold Wilson personally first but if, as had been agreed, we were not resigning until Wednesday there seemed to be no harm in stiffening the resolve of others. It would undoubtedly have strengthened the position of the three in the shadow Cabinet if they had been accompanied by more influential ex-ministers than me, like Shirley Williams and Roy Hattersley, but anyone who resigned was taking an immense risk with their career. Since I knew Shirley was not going to resign, it seemed not unreasonable for Roy Hattersley to stay and far better to keep his goodwill. He was very dejected and clearly upset by his internal conflict and I felt rather sorry for him. I had a quick chat with Dick Taverne, who had no doubts about resigning, and we confirmed that we would resign together but agreed to wait until Wednesday.

Now Roy Hattersley became the prime target for Harold Wilson's wooing. He was, apart from John Harris, supposedly Roy Jenkins's closest confidant and principal adviser. On the same Monday afternoon that he had talked to Hattersley, Harold Wilson saw Selwyn Lloyd, the Speaker of the House, on other business and confided that he was not unduly worried. Roy Jenkins would go off and write biographies, he said, and he had, in effect, bought off the most ambitious of his lieutenants in Roy Hattersley, which would stop a large number of consequential resignations. I presumed that Roy Hattersley had been offered the Defence post earlier that Monday afternoon.

On Tuesday evening I had a message that Wilson wished to see me. It was a civilised and friendly conversation. I thanked him genuinely for his kindness in the past and for giving me the opportunity to serve in his government. I told him that what most concerned me was that, irrespective of his own wishes, there was beginning to be a real risk that, with the shift against entry to the EEC gathering momentum in the PLP, even if we won an election he might not be able to keep Britain in the EEC and that a referendum commitment would take the decision out of his hands.

Harold Wilson obviously knew of the memorandum I had sent to Roy Jenkins arguing the case against resigning, and this embarrassed me. He went so far as to talk about the contents of what he described as a detailed letter. I left furious at what I thought could only have been the divulging of my memorandum by either Bob Maclennan or Roy Hattersley. I was quickly able to eliminate Bob from suspicion as I spoke to him immediately afterwards. He was rather upset; he had decided not to resign and was embarrassed and uncertain about his position, having had a drink in the Harcourt Room with George Thomson. He confirmed that Harold had already had the memo and had specifically mentioned its existence. Bob had told him, quite reasonably, once he knew that Wilson was aware of its existence, that he had strongly supported my arguments.

Leaving Bob, I then issued a short statement to the Press Association saying that I had resigned but would be issuing no further statement or resignation letter. This was Denis Healey's advice, to say no more than that my reasons were the same as those of Roy Jenkins and that I had no wish to exacerbate the situation. Roy Hattersley, it was announced, would now take over from George Thomson as shadow Minister of Defence, though since he was not elected he could not formally be a member of the shadow Cabinet. Had he not resigned and not accepted preferment, he would have been only doing the same as Shirley Williams, Tom Bradley, Alex Lyon, Denis Howell, Ivor Richard and, at that stage, Bob Maclennan. However, actually filling dead men's shoes when you were as closely involved with them as Roy Hattersley had been caused considerable offence and looked disreputable. He then published a pompous and self-seeking letter which reaffirmed his support for the European Community in a blatant attempt to mollify his friends. Since he later boasted that Harold Wilson had encouraged him to write it and virtually helped draft it, it was a transparently synthetic gesture.

Roy Hattersley's behaviour throughout had been that of tortured ambition. I could not help feeling how much stronger he would have been if, while deciding not to resign, he had refused Harold's offer, letting it be known that he had refused George Thomson's post. If he had done this he would certainly have been elected to the shadow Cabinet next time round in his own right. As it was he had put himself at Harold Wilson's mercy and Harold excluded him from his real Cabinet in 1974; Roy only came into the Cabinet in 1976 at the invitation of Jim Callaghan.

There is rarely an objectively right time to resign. The politically right time is usually seen as a tactical resignation which is damaging because it reeks of opportunism. A delayed resignation damages because it attracts the stigma of weakness and indecision. History itself can be a poor judge of political resignation, for each has its unique character, risks, opportunities, pressures and frustrations. They all coalesce at the time, so that the whole can only be seen as the expression of a multitude of factors. In the end, most individuals do what they feel they have to do and damn the consequences.

Our resignation did not end the battle over EEC entry. It is Edward Heath to whom most of the credit must go for first negotiating entry and then having the nerve to take the legislation through Parliament. He had to contend with a serious, open and long-running revolt among his own members, and listen to endless jibes from Enoch Powell and others that he had failed to get the full-hearted consent of the British people. Yet he never wavered and his position in history will be assured by this singular act of statesmanship.

The commitment to introduce a referendum became, as I had predicted in my memorandum, a settled commitment for the

Labour Party at the next election. Personally, never having had much problem with the concept, I was quite content to fight an election promising a referendum but it remained a difficulty for Roy Jenkins as he had wound himself up into a rather pedantic posture over the referendum as an undesirable constitutional innovation. It is true that they had often been used by fascist governments and tended to be a mechanism for preserving the status quo but they also have the potential to let public opinion express itself outside the straitjacket of party allegiance. The 1975 referendum on the European Community was a success and I have argued since 1982 that it should be the mechanism for introducing proportional representation. Referenda were successfully used in Scotland and Wales for devolved government in 1997. One was promised by all parties in the 1997 election before any British government would accept the euro and again by Labour on the EU constitution in 2005.

There were many casualties within the Labour Party in 1972 from the European Community debacle. In personal terms the one I most regretted was my alienation from Tony Crosland. After Roy had resigned I argued within our group that we should vote for Tony as deputy leader, but this was viewed with the utmost horror. I had voted for Tony in the shadow Cabinet elections after the white paper vote, as had Bill Rodgers, but even then others had withheld their vote on the basis that Tony had behaved badly and ought to be punished. This time, however, Bill was adamantly against voting for Tony, not wanting him to profit at Roy's expense. I was in a minority of one so when Tony Crosland rang me and asked if I would vote for him I was very embarrassed. I told him there was a debate going on but like a fool I promised that I would let him know when I had decided. Even more foolishly I kept that promise and wrote to him, trying to justify my supporting his opponent, Ted Short. Instead of just saying that I felt bound by group solidarity I tried to produce some specious arguments which I did not believe as to why Ted Short would be a better deputy leader. The letter had a stench about it and deserved to be treated with contempt. Our relationship only came close to recovering a few months before Tony's death in February 1977.

On 9 January 1972, for the first time since 1926, the National Union of Mineworkers called an official strike nationwide. It was clear that miners' wages had fallen quite dramatically against their counterparts in skilled manual work. I had great sympathy at that time for the miners. Though I believed an MP should always advocate negotiation and very rarely, if ever, endorse strike action, on this occasion I did feel that they had been sorely provoked. Politically, it was a remarkable period. On 22 January 1973 Edward Heath signed the treaty to make the UK a member of the European Community. As he went into the Egmont Palace to sign, he was splattered with ink by a woman demonstrating not against Europe but, of all things, against the redevelopment of Covent Garden. Unemployment was rising over the million mark and in the middle of February came some nine-hour electricity blackouts and industry was placed on a three-day week.

One of the new developments was the spontaneous emergence of the flying picket, with miners taking to the road instead of staying in their isolated villages. This had a personal impact. One morning, coming out of my house in Limehouse, I saw that a picket had been established outside the Stepney coal-fired power station, only 100 yards away. The pickets looked pretty cold, with only a Dormobile van for protection, and I asked them if they would like a hot drink. I went back in to tell Debbie, and she brewed them a cup of tea. I asked them if they would like to use our lavatory and telephone while they were picketing, and they were grateful. When I returned that evening, I found most of the miners in our house and that Debbie, in her open American way and fearing that their van would be too cold for them, had invited them not only to use our kitchen but to sleep the night. They were delightful company. Having driven down from Nottinghamshire, and finding nothing to do, they had chosen to go to this power station, which was not even generating electricity. By pure chance their picket proved to be very effective, because inside was stored the fuel which lit up the furnaces for many other power stations in the south of England. During all this time we had twelve miners staying in our house in Narrow Street. Four men used to sleep in shifts on the floor in our spare bedroom and they all shared our kitchen and bathroom. They were incredibly neat and tidy, immensely considerate and, given the smallness of our house, for we had not yet expanded next door, remarkably unobtrusive. That is, apart from the smell of fry-ups drifting up from the kitchen into our bedroom in the middle of the night when the night shift came back from picket duty. After a fortnight the Nottingham miners were replaced by miners from Kent who were different in character, but equally engaging. When the Nottingham miners left they called Debbie down to the garage and their spokesman proceeded to make a short speech, finally bringing a bunch of flowers out from behind his back and presenting a Dinky toy to Tristan. For her it was a very moving occasion which she has never forgotten. Eventually the miners' case went to an independent tribunal chaired by Lord Wilberforce and their stance was vindicated with a 17 per cent pay award.

Twelve years later, in 1984, at Buxton in Derbyshire a miner appeared outside the SDP conference claiming to have been one of those who stayed with us, and got some mileage out of this with the press. But the miners' strike in 1984–5 had none of the validity or the dignity of the 1972 dispute. Large intimidating pickets were by then developing into a grave threat to the nation. The NUM leaders of 1972, Joe Gormley and Lawrence Daly, were very different from Arthur Scargill and Peter Heathfield both in ideology and in behaviour. I felt my support for the Conservative government over the strike in 1984–5 was as justified as my refusal to support them in 1972.

When she was Secretary of State for Education, I had my first meeting with Margaret Thatcher. A medical friend had come to dinner with her and when she bumped into me in the division lobby she asked if I would go down to the Harcourt Room and have a drink. Debbie was waiting for me in the Family Room, so she came as well. It was a revealing occasion, for as the conversation developed Margaret Thatcher's best and worst qualities were on display: consideration for a constituent and the wish to get to the bottom of a problem coupled with a total inability to comprehend that depression affects adolescents. To her it appeared more a matter of what used to be called 'lack of moral fibre'. She turned to Debbie to say that she had never been able to understand how any seventeen-year-old could be depressed. Debbie listened aghast. Eventually, as we were walking away from the table, Margaret Thatcher turned to me and said, with Debbie two feet away, 'Is your wife always so quiet?' Anyone who knows Debbie will realise how unusual was her silence.

She was simply amazed at Mrs Thatcher's sheer insensitivity. But Margaret Thatcher has never been able to understand the non-achievers or how society, whose existence she came close to denying, has a public responsibility to help shoulder some of their burdens.

In early 1973 I made extensive visits to both Israel and Egypt. After Israel had allowed former Vice-President Nixon to visit without any official notice being taken of him, only to find him becoming President, it developed a sophisticated system for spotting visitors who might have influence in the future. Though I was only a backbench MP, every door was opened for me and I met all the significant leaders, tramped over the Golan Heights, visited Gaza and got a real feel for the security problems on the ground. In Egypt too I had no difficulty in seeing all the key people, in particular General Shazli, the commander of the Egyptian forces. I came away convinced there was going to be another war with Israel. I also developed detailed ideas for the demilitarisation of Sinai and spoke about them in a foreign affairs debate in the House of Commons in June 1973. Predictably, war did follow. On 6 October, as Israel celebrated Yom Kippur, the Day of Atonement, Egyptian forces stormed across the Suez Canal. I was appalled when the Foreign Secretary, Lord Home, and the Prime Minister, Edward Heath, refused to supply, during the actual fighting, shells for the Centurion tanks that Israel had bought from us. I considered it then, and still do, the most cynical act of British foreign policy since Suez. It showed not just the Arab influence within the Foreign Office but a total lack of principle in standing by one's commitments from two politicians whom I had hitherto respected. For the first time I began to wonder whether Alec Douglas-Home had shaken off the attitudes towards appeasement he had held as parliamentary private secretary to Neville Chamberlain. British influence with Israel only started to recover after Prime Minister Begin's visit to the UK in 1977. Israeli politicians on the left as well as the right were confirmed in the distrust which had developed when we were in control of Palestine. It was a craven act which had everything to do with the threat of being cut off from Arab oil and for which I felt then and still today real anger.

Meanwhile, my political life in Westminster was not very happy. Dick Taverne's position in Lincoln, where the constituency party had asked him to stand down, was particularly distressing for us all, even more so for Roy and Bill since Dick was a close friend of theirs. I did not know Dick well but felt, as they did, that we ought to do more to help and yet it was impossible to do so unless we were ready to be expelled from the Labour Party. It was nonsense to say, as some Labour MPs did, that Dick Taverne deserved to be in trouble in Lincoln. A myth was propagated that he was a bad constituency member whereas in fact an ORC poll in October 1972 showed that 82 per cent of his constituents thought he was a good MP and only 2 per cent a bad one. The truth was that he was the victim of a particularly dedicated group of left-wing activists, ably led by Leo Beckett, now the husband of Margaret Beckett, the MP for Derby South and former Labour Cabinet minister.

The deselection of Dick Taverne in Lincoln was a foretaste of things to come and he quite rightly decided not to take it lying down. He resigned in October after the 1972 party conference, having held off the announcement for a few months to reduce the pressure on Roy and other friends. It was not in the interests of the Labour Party to have the by-election quickly when they knew Dick was determined to fight. So they delayed moving the writ until February, which, under a parliamentary convention, it is their right to do. The by-election was not therefore held until 1 March 1973. This highly dubious delaying tactic was one of the reasons why, when the SDP was formed, Labour MPs who joined were not keen to force by-elections in their constituencies. Delay can give a massive advantage to the party defending the seat. At that time agreement between the Conservative and Labour whips allowed the party whose MP had resigned to fix the by-election date, keeping the former MP in limbo for five or six months without pay or influence. Now a by-election has to be held within three months. It was to Dick Taverne's credit that he pressed on, standing as Democratic Labour and campaigning to win. If any of us had gone to campaign for him we would have been instantly thrown out under the rules of the Labour Party. So the opening meeting of his campaign was addressed not by fellow MPs but by my old friend Mervyn Stockwood, still Bishop of Southwark, and by Bernard Levin, the columnist on the *Times*. In the event Dick Taverne had a spectacular victory with a majority of 13,000, gaining 58 per cent of the vote to Labour's 23 per cent and the Conservatives' 18 per cent. Although he managed to hold onto the seat again in the February 1974 election, he lost it the following October – to Margaret Beckett.

Should the pro-Europe, moderate Labour MPs have split from the Labour Party and fought with Dick Taverne then? Should we have created the SDP when we rebelled over Europe in 1971 rather than in 1981? I have no doubt that it would not have been possible to do so. We all of us had to go through the traumas that lay ahead and also feel within ourselves that we had fought our corner before most of us would have dreamt of leaving the Labour Party. Even so, leaving Labour in 1981 was hard enough. Without that ten-year struggle behind us very few, if any, would have come to the SDP. Another criticism is that we did not fight vigorously enough within the Labour Party during that ten-year interval. In our defence, it is hard to fight the left if the party leader is not interested in doing so. This was the decade of what I called in 1980 'fudge and mudge'. Neither Harold Wilson nor Jim Callaghan felt it prudent openly to confront the left in the 1970s. Each in his different way formed a partnership with Michael Foot to head off the left rather than face them down. All the while the balance of power was shifting. The full extent of the shift in the Labour Party was masked while we were in government from 1974 to 1979 and it only became obvious to those outside in 1980, when the left forced changes to the party's constitution. Then we really saw how the left had come to dominate the constituencies and could use deselection to intimidate Labour MPs. We on the inside knew it was happening and never really mobilised the centre ground when we were in government, in part because many of us were too busy as ministers, in part because we had grown used to the protection of the trade union block vote, fixed up mainly by the leader and helped by the use of patronage.

To have split off in 1971 would also have been to break on a single, albeit major, issue of policy, the European Community. By 1981 there were several major issues of policy: the European Community, nuclear deterrence, nationalisation, as well as a major constitutional issue with the trade union-dominated electoral college. Indeed, by 1981, the Labour position on Europe had become even less defensible than in 1971. For by then the European Community had been given a massive endorsement in the 1975 referendum. In 1980 Labour indefensibly committed themselves to come out of the Community without even another referendum. It was on that policy that they fought the 1983 general election. It was inconceivable, after all I had gone through in 1971–2 to get Britain into the Community and, as Foreign Secretary, to keep us in, that I could have stood as a Labour MP in 1983 on their manifesto.

Uncomfortable though it was, I think Dick Taverne had to fight Lincoln without the help of his friends in the Labour Party. It would have been quixotic for Roy Jenkins to have spoken on his platform in Lincoln and, though it deeply upset Roy to have to stand on the sidelines, I do not believe he should have felt guilty about this decision. At this time in 1973, unfortunately, Lincoln appeared to depress Roy rather than to energise him. He became even more convinced that Labour would lose the next election and indeed began to make his wish that this would happen all too obvious. Such a position was an untenable indulgence for a senior politician: he could not operate effectively within a political party while, even temporarily, wanting its defeat.

In 1973 and in 1974, on the eve of the election, we had a number of group discussions about what would happen if Labour won. Almost everyone present believed that Roy should insist on being Chancellor of the Exchequer if he was to serve in the government. Some even believed that he should bargain for this with Wilson before finally deciding whether to stand for the shadow Cabinet in the autumn. What I think frustrated a number of us was Roy's reluctance even to contemplate negotiating for the Chancellorship. His reasoning was that he needed Wilson's full support if he was to have authority within the party to do the job properly.

A few of us returned to this argument at Bob Maclennan's house on the eve of the February 1974 election but Roy was still very reluctant to bid for the Chancellorship. He argued that the effect of the oil shock was such that he would have to be as draconian a Chancellor as he had been in 1967 and that, while then he had had the full support of Wilson, he would not be able to operate successfully if he imposed himself on Wilson. There was more than a grain of truth in his arguments but the real anxiety was his defeatist mood.

The cause of the February 1974 general election was the struggle that Edward Heath's government was having with the second miners' strike. On this occasion I was not as sympathetic to the miners' case. Having rolled the government over in 1972, they were coming back for more and if they won again with the strike weapon it would augur ill for parliamentary democracy.

When Heath called the election I thought the Conservatives would win and I was facing the fight of my life in Devonport. We now had three constituencies in Plymouth. The new Devonport had been carved out of my own Sutton seat and Dame Joan Vickers's old Devonport and there was a new Drake constituency. We were fighting each other as sitting MPs. Dame Joan was a formidable adversary. Statuesque, looking far younger than her age, with blue hair and a long and devoted record as the member for Devonport, she presented a very strong challenge. As the campaign built up I sensed that people were voting against Heath's government even if they were not voting positively for a Labour government. Jeremy Thorpe conducted a very effective campaign on the basis that neither Heath nor Wilson could unite the country and the Liberal vote soared to 6,059,519, which was 19.3 per cent of votes in the UK. The result of all these factors was that Labour squeezed home but without a real working majority. Our Plymouth campaign was summed up in a letter from my hard-working constituency secretary, Barbara Furzeman: 'It was worth every foot-weary, rain-sodden inch of the way.' Despite the traditional Labour Party fear that their voters would stay away in the rain, we won but the margin was a mere 437 votes. Still, I had won the seat back for Labour for it was Dame Joan Vickers who had defeated Michael Foot, the sitting MP, in 1955, and then beaten him again in 1959, after which he had gone to Ebbw Vale to take over Aneurin Bevan's seat. I was thrilled for many reasons but first because I could go on representing Plymouth in Parliament.

Next day it was clear that Edward Heath, who only had 297 MPs against Labour's 301, would try and stay on with the help of the fourteen Liberal MPs. He asked Jeremy Thorpe to come to No. 10 and in his eagerness Jeremy made, I thought, a tactical mistake. He would have been well advised to say that, though he was ready to come and talk to the Prime Minister, he could only do so on the basis that the Liberal Party was ready to contribute to a government of national unity. He then should have consulted a few prominent centrist figures before going in to see Edward Heath, strengthening his negotiating hand in the process. Instead he got ensnared in problems with his activists, who disliked Heath and had no experience of the problems of government. The Liberals had not been involved in government since the wartime coalition and, before that, for just one year since Lloyd George's 1922 resignation. After the Conservative election victory in 1951, Winston Churchill had asked the Liberal leader, Clement Davies, to serve in his Cabinet on a personal basis but he had refused. Most of Jeremy Thorpe's colleagues appeared to be basically against any arrangement with the Conservatives, let alone Heath. Heath offered Thorpe a Cabinet position and a Speaker's conference on electoral reform. Even with Liberal support, the Conservatives would have been short of an overall majority. But the potential for a bargain of mutual advantage existed as Heath was ready to offer the Nationalists Scottish and Welsh assemblies. The Liberal Party failed to seize their opportunity, but on the spin of the electoral roulette wheel, another opportunity will no doubt arise. It might even come at the next election, due before June 2010.

Harold Wilson meanwhile had decided to sit tight and wait. The Sunday following the election, Roy and Jennifer Jenkins came over to Buttermere for lunch. We first gossiped about the election and Heath's tactics in trying to stay on and then went for a long walk on the ridge overlooking the Kennet valley. Roy told me that he had spoken to Harold Wilson and had gained the impression that Wilson might want him to be Chancellor. Roy's earlier desire to be Wilson's positive choice and not forced on him looked as if it might be fulfilled.

The shadow Cabinet met on Monday while the whole nation was watching the comings and goings at No. 10. It began to look more and more likely that Harold Wilson would be called to form a new government. That evening, after Edward Heath had resigned, a group of us met with Roy for dinner. Everyone was tired and there was a great sense of let-down when Roy said he had been told by Wilson that he would not be Chancellor but Home Secretary.

I do not recall Roy mentioning that evening that Wilson had also offered him the task, as Home Secretary, of co-ordinating policy towards Northern Ireland. My notebook says he told me when we talked in the Home Office two days later. Anyhow, it transpired that he could have made his own choice for a Northern Ireland Minister and he could have insisted on whoever it was being in the Cabinet, working to him as Home Secretary, rather as the Chief Secretary to the Treasury works to the Chancellor and, as Roy had insisted in 1968, should be in the Cabinet. If Roy had accepted, his obvious choice to go to Northern Ireland would have been Bill Rodgers. Bill would have been extremely good in that testing post, particularly since he would have had to face the backlash against the Sunningdale agreement from the Protestant Ulster Defence Force. More importantly, Roy himself would have had the authority and the nerve to insist that when these self-styled Protestant loyalists went on strike they were faced down.

If Roy had taken the additional responsibility for Northern Ireland, I am convinced that the Sunningdale agreement and its breakthrough power-sharing executive would not have been overthrown. Bill Rodgers would have had his position in the party greatly strengthened and Roy would have been in the centre of British politics as Home Secretary, not on the fringe during the crucial years before Wilson's resignation. It was not to be. During that depressing dinner, without exactly knowing why, I felt that Roy, and by association all of us in that room, had been outmanoeuvred yet again by Harold Wilson. It was a dismal start to a Labour government and as yet I did not know whether I would even be part of that government.

# 3

# In government again: Health Minister and Foreign Secretary

On Monday 4 March Edward Heath resigned and Harold Wilson was summoned to the Palace. It was the shabbiest victory I have ever taken part in: we were back in government by courtesy of the National Union of Mineworkers. We gave the face workers their full claim and strike action ceased. Edward Heath's folly was in calling an election on the issue of 'who governs the country'. It seemed pathetic for a Prime Minister to be calling into question his own authority. Heath should have told the country that there was no alternative to paying the miners, but that before a general election in the summer he would put before them specific proposals to ensure that the trade unions would not again hold the country to ransom. He would then have trounced Labour.

For Harold Wilson the victory was neither shabby nor depressing. For him, it was one of those rare occasions when the humiliation of previous defeat is avenged and victory is especially sweet. He would have been less than human if he had not felt some satisfaction seeing the press photographs of Edward Heath's famous piano leaving No. 10.

The Cabinet met on Tuesday at 5 p.m. and it was clear that the junior ministerial appointments would not be announced that night. I waited with no great anticipation of office. I was so disillusioned with Harold Wilson that I did not even care very much. Ministerial office was not the be-all and end-all so I did not hang around at the end of a telephone waiting for a call from Downing Street.

Barbara Castle had been told on the first night that she would be Secretary of State for Health and Social Services and that she would have Brian O'Malley as Minister for Pensions. Elizabeth Shore, Peter Shore's wife, a medical doctor in the department, suggested my name to Barbara for the Health side. Barbara then proposed to Harold on the telephone that I should be appointed. Harold's reply was, 'I like the idea. Let me think about it.'

On Wednesday morning I went to No. 10 and Harold offered me the job of Parliamentary Under-Secretary of Health. In retrospect I am amazed that I quibbled and said I did not believe the job could be done effectively without the more senior status of minister of state, if I or anyone else was to deal effectively with the doctors in the dispute over pay beds that undoubtedly lay ahead. Harold was somewhat taken aback and obviously anxious to get on with compiling his list of junior ministers, rather than wrangle with a young pup who ought to have been grateful for the bone thrown to him. He suggested that I should mull it over and talk to Barbara Castle but just as I was walking out he promised that if I accepted I would have responsibility as under-secretary for introducing the children's legislation that I had put forward as a private member. He knew well that this would more than tempt me.

Barbara had gathered from Harold that my acceptance was a little dicey so she rang me up and suggested that I come round to the Elephant and Castle. Although I did not know it at the time, she had already had to persuade Brian O'Malley that he could not be made a full Minister for Pensions. The last thing she wanted to hear me say was that I did not think it was worth my while to come merely as a parliamentary secretary. I explained that unless I had greater authority over the pay beds controversy the doctors would be appealing over my head to her all the time. Also, it meant I had not advanced in seniority since I was last in government. She totally agreed about my needing more authority to deal with the doctors and she promised to try to persuade Harold to make me a minister of state soon, which she did.

In the main being a doctor was an advantage rather than a hindrance. At that time only one other medical doctor, Lord Addison, had been Minister of Health. Many of the issues faced by the minister have a large scientific content and to be trained in that discipline means that the complexities are easier to unravel. On the other hand, there is the temptation as a doctor to ride hobby horses and follow prejudices. Also, the social workers might have been more suspicious of a doctor if I had not already shown my interest in reforming the law affecting children; they were eagerly awaiting new legislation on adoption which I hoped to bring forward into law by 1975. Generally speaking, the practice that ministers exercise judgement in areas in which they are not experts is worth maintaining. However, in the climate of early 1974, it was a bonus to have as the minister responsible for the NHS someone who knew its inner workings. Inflation was heading towards 27 per cent, the NHS was facing a fundamental administrative upheaval and the medical profession was militant and determined to overthrow the government's manifesto commitment over pay beds.

There were any number of specific instances where it helped to be a doctor. Twice, the Chief Medical Officer of Health, Dr Yellowlees, asked for assistance to keep the World Health Organization's smallpox eradication campaign on course. The WHO campaign had started in 1969, when there were ten million smallpox cases worldwide. On one occasion we were asked for an extra £1 million and on another for £½ million. The need was desperate but Dr Yellowlees had been quite unable to find these sums within his own budget. As a doctor I needed no convincing that tracking down those last few cases of smallpox, mainly in the Horn of Africa, was a critical health priority. I rode roughshod over the departmental objections and just told them to find the money. With this push they easily found the cash and, with contributions from a few other major countries, the programme continued and was brought to a successful conclusion. The last naturally occurring case was in Somalia in 1977. Now even the need for a smallpox vaccination has vanished. It is almost incredible to think that that vital WHO programme could ever have been in danger because of financial trouble. Yet WHO could, if it had the money, mobilise resources to eradicate malaria and some other world killers like bilharzia, a worm found in rivers and reservoirs. If only a fraction of the money invested in modern drugs were put into such preventive health programmes the health of the world would be transformed. If only a UN secretary general had the standing and the authority to mobilise all the special UN agencies for a few targeted programmes, the sum of human happiness could be greatly enhanced. Meanwhile, the UN and the special agencies often pull against each other and there is no firm ordering of priorities.

My medical background also helped in dealing with two controversial issues: cigarette-smoking and abortion. Both were subjects that Barbara Castle wanted to have little to do with. Since she smoked like a chimney she knew that it would be humbug for her to lead an anti-smoking campaign and yet she could see that this was the biggest health hazard that we faced. She supported me to the hilt in my determination to control the tobacco industry. The voluntary agreements we made became progressively tougher but I felt that tobacco products should come under the 1968 Medicines Act, a very sophisticated piece of legislation capable of protecting the legitimate needs of industry while balancing independent scientific advice on the danger of certain products to an individual's health. After a bitter inter-departmental battle, I won acceptance in government for legislation to designate tobacco as a product to be controlled under the act. Unfortunately, when I went off to the Foreign Office, the tobacco industry mobilised its supporters among the MPs and they used their considerable influence over the legislation programme to ensure that it was postponed indefinitely.

On abortion Barbara Castle was atypically extremely nervous of public opinion. She apparently felt that a controversy over abortion had lost her in the past a number of votes with Catholics in her Blackburn constituency. Anyhow, whatever the reason, in the main she preferred me to handle it. She did, however, throw her whole political weight in the Parliamentary Labour Party against the setting up of another select committee to examine the Abortion Act. We had been forced to concede a select committee in 1974 but we were confident we had the votes to resist its re-establishment. Abortion was an issue on which I found it a help openly to use my medical knowledge when handling public and parliamentary debate and to defuse controversy.

The headlines in the London *Evening Standard* when we took office were all about London becoming the abortion capital of the world. The growth and abuse taking place in private clinics was shocking, threatening the more liberal abortion law that I had supported as a backbencher in 1967. At the committee stage of this bill tougher powers to regulate private clinics were urged on David Steel, the sponsor of the 1967 bill, but he had resisted, probably on government advice. Now I was told by the departmental lawyers that we needed fresh primary legislation in order to clamp down. I was anxious about introducing any new legislation, for the mood of the

House of Commons in the middle of 1974 was very different from the reformist mood in 1966 when Labour had a large majority. I judged that any new legislation risked the imposition of restrictive amendments to the actual grounds on which an abortion could be authorised. I decided therefore to try to use existing legislation, though I might be taken to court for going beyond the powers those laws gave me. We presented regulations to the House of Commons to enable us to clamp down on this private abortion racket. I told our lawyers that, if challenged, I would be ready to go to court and defend my decision since it was so clearly in the public interest for us to act. Even legislation to fix the number of weeks beyond which no abortion could take place could have had a restrictive amendment attached to it. So I deliberately delayed this legislation as well. The time limit was next fixed and passed in government legislation during a free vote on embryo research fifteen years later.

In the Department of Health the task which took up much of my time was supervising the legislation to reform the adoption laws. It was a most unusual situation, with me bringing all the volunteers who had helped me as a backbencher to work together with the departmental officials. Instead of being prickly, the officials welcomed this outside involvement and as a result we built on and improved my private member's bill. Our problem was the innate conservatism of the Home Office but Alex Lyon, who was a junior minister there, was a great help and did his best to swing opinion round, particularly over the new concept of guardianship. I found the Lord Chancellor's Department surprisingly progressive in comparison to the Home Office. I could also always rely on Leo Abse, an influential Labour MP who had been the most important single influence behind the adoption reform movement, to put a little pressure on in the correct places. He was generous with his advice, having steered through more controversial legislation than any other MP.

My main concern was to ensure that we had the balance right between the natural parents and the child. The British Association of Social Workers helped to ensure this by going out on a limb for the rights of the natural parent and this concentrated people's attention on a substantive issue. The Directors of Social Services were a wiser group and they did much to reorientate the social work profession to ensure that it took greater account of the child's interest than hitherto. I was always vexed over giving an eighteen-year-old the right to see their adoption certificate, thus making it easier to trace their natural parents. The right already existed in Scotland. It was not technically the retrospective legislation that its critics alleged it to be but it came too close to being retrospective for my comfort, besides raising deep ethical questions. I agonised for those parents who would live in fear of unpleasant emotional encounters. In practice the counselling safeguard we introduced worked well and there have been very few distressing cases. There have, however, been many happy reunions and many more adoptees, satisfied just to know the names of their natural parents, have taken the matter no further. The legislation has adapted to changing attitudes and it did provide the framework for a living law, with the reporting-back and research procedures that I had always wanted. It represents the most constructive legislative contribution I have made to British politics but it could never have been done without the help of many hundreds of people.

At the same time as we were making satisfying progress here, we became entangled in a controversy that was to have a much less desirable outcome. In the summer of 1974 Sir Philip Rogers, the permanent secretary, came to see Barbara Castle and myself to discuss privately our controversial manifesto commitment to phase pay beds out of NHS hospitals. Sir Philip deployed a strong case against our taking any action. He warned us that, in the best interests of the NHS, we should avoid a confrontation with the doctors on this issue. Rather movingly, he insisted that if the secretary of state, having heard him out, came to a different conclusion then that would be the last that she heard of it and everyone in the department would carry out her policy faithfully and to the best of their abilities. Barbara handled him very well, thanked him for his courtesy and his memo and then concisely and clearly put the counter-arguments for phasing out. For my part, I made it clear that I agreed completely with her judgement.

Sir Philip kept his promise and from then on defended our decisions and refused to let the British Medical Association get away with the attempt to present officials as not being fully behind our policy. It was a fine example of the best of the Civil Service tradition of serving governments irrespective of party. The Civil Service must, however, be able to warn ministers of the pitfalls and perhaps we would have been wiser to drop our policy. But it would have been very hard, almost impossible to do. Eventually, after a protracted struggle, we forced pay bed legislation onto the statute book, only for it to be removed by the incoming Conservative government. The fight left a damaging legacy, for many consultants never again gave the NHS the long hours of extra unpaid effort which they had willingly given before.

The pay bed dispute today is just a vignette of history, a symbol of how very different attitudes were in the 1970s. But then we were in the last throes of the corporatist state. Leaders of the trade unions and the BMA expected to bargain directly with ministers. It was the era of beer and sandwiches at No. 10, which ended with the Winter of Discontent in 1979 and with the defeat of the Labour government. The union pressures were strong. In any case, to Barbara Castle, phasing out pay beds for the NHS was a sacred mission. It was the means whereby she would redress the historic error of her hero, Aneurin Bevan. In her mythology he had been simply led astray when he agreed to keep pay beds, whereas in truth it was part of his historic compromise with the consultants and had smoothed the path for the original legislation. He recognised it was the consultants' price and it allowed him to say, with contempt, 'I stuffed their mouths with gold.'

To Barbara Castle personally the manifesto commitment itself was compromise enough. Left to her own devices, I always felt she would have legislated without a qualm for a total ban on private practice. The doctors also sensed this and, however much she said that she was only committed to phasing out pay beds and was not proposing the abolition of private medicine, they detected an ulterior motive. The BMA strategy was to present pay beds as merely the thin end of the wedge: that we were abolishing private medicine through the back door by phasing out pay beds so fast and they could not build private facilities outside the NHS. Just when I was beginning to convince the profession that she was not opposed to private medicine outside the NHS, she insisted on legislating for licensing arrangements to control the building of new private health facilities. Logically, there was a good case for such controls but politically it was madness to propose them at that time, for it fed

BMA propaganda and it was the touch paper that the BMA leaders used to ignite the profession. The BMA always wanted to fight on the fundamental principle of their right to practise privately. If the BMA were allowed to get away with fighting on this ground, I knew they would be able to rely on the support of the many thousands of doctors who, like myself, had never charged a patient in their life and never had any intention of doing so. So most of my battles with Barbara over licensing were to try to win back those doctors who believed in working full time for the NHS but who nevertheless prized the independence of the profession. No politician who has ever had to deal with the BMA has escaped unscathed. It was David Lloyd George who said on 11 June 1911 in Birmingham:

> I had two hours' discussion with the medical men themselves the other day. I do not think there has been anything like it since the days when Daniel went into the lions' den . . . but I can assure you they treated me with the same civility as the lions treated my illustrious predecessor . . . except these lions knew their anatomy.

In July 1974 the pay beds issue, which was festering beneath the surface, was suddenly splashed across the headlines of every popular newspaper. It provided an incident which starkly illustrated the state of corporatist Britain. 'Granny', 'Ma' or 'Mrs' Brookestone, depending on which paper you read, was leading a strike action against pay beds on the private fifteenth floor of Charing Cross Hospital. She was demanding that the privileges of the private patients should be shared with NHS patients so as to shorten waiting lists. Until this was conceded she and her colleagues were prepared to withhold basic domestic services to private patients. At one stage it looked as if a compromise between the local consultants and the local hospital administrators would solve the strike but then the BMA intervened to stiffen the consultants' line, refusing to let their members moderate the right to fill the predetermined number of private beds. Before we knew where we were, Barbara Castle and I were negotiating directly with the BMA and the general secretaries of NUPE and COHSE on this one local dispute.

The negotiations had their funny moments. One was late at night when we needed to locate Albert Spanswick, the leader of COHSE.

He was traced to a caravan site and came on the telephone to speak to Barbara Castle. She was explaining in her usual animated way the intricacies of the agreement, whereby the private floor was to become a mixed ward, and found Albert, to her disappointment, uninterested in the detail and only too happy to agree. What she did not realise was that he had been hauled out of bed and had walked in his pyjamas in the pouring rain across the camp site to take her call in a public telephone box.

After we had won round the union bosses someone had to undertake the task of convincing Mrs Brookestone and her colleagues who had brought on the whole action. In those days it seemed quite natural for Barbara and me to talk to the local strike leaders together with the local consultants to explain the complicated arrangements agreed with their national leader. When private patients were treated in special units elsewhere in the hospital the equivalent number of beds on the private floor would be occupied by NHS patients. In her diary, Barbara Castle captures Mrs Brookestone's reaction very well, 'All we have got is one for one,' she complained. 'Yes, Brooky,' explained one of the consultants – now free from the shadow of the BMA to renew his normal friendly relations with Ma B. and her staff – 'but you know that the private floor is always underoccupied. In future these beds will not be kept empty. When we move a private patient to a specialised unit, as we do frequently, we will move an NHS patient immediately into the empty bed.' The issue was resolved, but what a farce. We should never have been involved in this local dispute. But there was very little alternative, given the militant mood of NUPE and their wish to force the pace, fearing that Labour would lose the election which everyone knew could not be postponed for much longer.

On 11 October 1974 Labour won the general election but with an overall majority of only three. Labour had 319 MPs and the Conservatives 276. The Liberal vote slumped but they had only one less MP. I again fought Dame Joan Vickers in Devonport but this time I had a majority of over 2,000 and I felt fairly confident of victory throughout my campaign. I was greatly helped by the extensive favourable publicity for the Children's Bill. Nevertheless it was a government that postponed every difficult and unpopular measure, simply biding its time until it could become popular enough to win again. It prompted me to begin to contemplate having fixed terms and, when there was not a proper working majority, forcing political parties to come together for a few years in an inter-party agreement or formal coalition to govern in the national interest. All we did was postpone the necessary economic measures until after the European referendum in 1975.

Harold Wilson's resignation took place at a special Cabinet meeting on the morning of 16 March 1976. It came as no surprise to me because Roy Jenkins had told me when walking after lunch at Buttermere in early January that Wilson was going to resign. Roy did not tell me then who had tipped him off but it later emerged that it was Arnold Goodman, acting on Harold Wilson's instructions. I discussed with Roy in January what we should do to organise support within the Parliamentary Labour Party over the next few months, yet I felt he was listless and not even enthused about the prospect of standing. He said that he could not tell any of his friends and I was surprised that he had told me. Jim Callaghan subsequently revealed that he was also told at about the same time by Harold Lever and it was confirmed to him directly by Harold Wilson after his sixtieth birthday party on 11 March.

There are many murky rumours surrounding Wilson's surprising resignation in 1976. Some of them were perhaps fed by the people involved in the misinformation and denigration that did undoubtedly stem from MI5 in the early 1970s in relation to Northern Ireland. I was also named in this campaign, as was Merlyn Rees. Whether my label as a subversive was due to my support, back in 1966, for the human rights movement in Northern Ireland I do not know. I had come across sloppy MI5 labelling once before, when I was Navy Minister. Jim Callaghan was then Home Secretary and he told me over lunch in the Members' Dining Room how an ashen-faced civil servant had arrived in his room to say that a traitor had been unmasked and that it was a Labour MP, David Owen. Jim's reaction was one of disbelief. When they checked back with MI5 they found it was the Labour MP Will Owen, not me, who was under suspicion. Will Owen was in fact acquitted at the Central Criminal Court in May 1970 of passing state secrets to Czechoslovakia.

The explanation I favour for Harold Wilson's resignation is that he had some health problem in the early 1970s and that he had promised his wife, Mary, when it was discovered, that he would not stay long if he won the election. Whether or not this was true, Wilson knew that a round of public cuts was inevitable and, understandably after the success of the referendum on the EEC, he could not face having to preside over yet another dismal period of IMF-induced expenditure constraint and internal party strife. What we also now know is that Wilson was having difficulty with his memory, which had been photographic, and that he later developed severe Alzheimer's disease. Whether this was a very early sign of the mental deterioration to come is debatable; maybe we will develop bio-chemical tests which indicate the early build-up of amyloid deposits in the brain or other tests, but so far they still elude the medical profession.

Three weeks later, at the age of sixty-four, Jim Callaghan became Prime Minister. I never for one moment believed that Roy would beat Jim and I suspect nor did Roy. I tried, as did others, to whip up some enthusiasm for Roy among Labour MPs but he just did not have the basic support. Most of his potential voters had sensed some years before that his moment was past and they had switched allegiance. In the main their votes had gone to Jim Callaghan, with a few going to Denis Healey. Once the result of the first ballot was known, Roy was determined to withdraw. Tony Crosland, who was bottom of the poll, automatically dropped out. There was no need for Roy to do so but he had lost any stomach he might once have had for the contest. I felt disinclined even to try to persuade him to keep his name on the ballot. I was then rung up by Denis asking for my vote and I promised that I would vote for him on the second ballot, though I could see he had no chance of beating Jim. Barbara Castle reports in her *Diaries* that she tried to persuade me to vote for Michael Foot in the final ballot. She did so but, if I gave her the impression that there was any hope of my voting for Michael, that was purely tactical. But I cannot say I was a great enthusiast for Jim Callaghan.

Roy Jenkins was not surprised to lose but he was hurt when Jim Callaghan kept him at the Home Office, making it plain he was not prepared to risk the uneasy truce in the party over the European

Community by appointing Roy Foreign Secretary. Jim judged that Tony Crosland would arouse less suspicion. It was also a matter of personality; Jim liked Tony and disapproved of Roy. I suspect too that, knowing from his own time as Foreign Secretary that they would be thrust into constant contact, he thought that it would be more enjoyable travelling with Tony Crosland. Roy, who had already been sounded out by Harold Wilson over whether he would like to be president of the European Commission, later went to see Jim Callaghan and he agreed to nominate him as president. Since both Valéry Giscard d'Estaing and Helmut Schmidt had indicated they would like Roy to take the job, there was little doubt the post would be his.

I had told Roy after a meal at East Hendred that I thought he should accept the presidency. It was not, as some people later alleged during our leadership contest in 1982, done brutally or in an unkindly way. We discussed the options in a warm and affectionate mood. There was no sense of pushing him out of British politics and my advice was in line with a decision he had already virtually made in his own mind. I felt that if he stayed his frustration level would rise and I feared conflict with Jim and resignation in a fit of pique. Roy made it clear he would stay active and not rule out coming back to the House of Commons, though I was very sceptical of that ever happening.

One of Jim's first acts as Prime Minister was to sack Barbara Castle, with whom he had never got on. It was a sad end to a distinguished career. Politics is a brutal business and it would have been kinder for Jim to have let her carry through the pay beds compromise legislation and relieve her of office in the summer. But he must have felt a need to put his own stamp on the government and Barbara was very much a part of Harold's era.

I admired Barbara Castle. She was a lady of quality and one of our great women politicians. She had the ability to be the first woman Prime Minister had the Labour Party not then been so deeply chauvinistic. Harold Wilson had wanted to give her serious economic responsibilities in 1968 but this was blocked by Roy Jenkins as Chancellor of the Exchequer, who did not want a repeat of the divided responsibility for economic questions which had haunted Labour from 1964 to 1966 with Jim Callaghan at the Treasury and

George Brown at the Department of Economic Affairs. She was an excellent Minister for Overseas Development and an innovative Minister of Transport. The main thrust of her proposals as Secretary of State for Employment, 'In Place of Strife', were correctly judged and her courage in standing by them was exemplary. Even six years later, though past her prime, as Secretary of State for Health and Social Security she had the ability to grasp the core of any problem. She had a formidable intellect and instinctive judgement which, in government, usually triumphed over ideology. Only in opposition did she revert to being a rather typical left-wing member of the National Executive Committee, where ideology governed intellect. She could also abandon her prejudices. I remember, for example, persuading her to go to the Play Group Movement's annual meeting. Begrudgingly she agreed but was dismissive of my claim that they were a splendidly irreverent and radical force in society. She came back enthused and started to lecture me about their merits and how we should help. Typical Barbara!

Above all she had tremendous fighting spirit, which permeated everything. One of her favourite and true sayings was that politics is all about guts. From the outside she appeared as tough as nails but there was a softer streak which one saw when she talked about or involved her husband, Ted. I increasingly felt that this streak should have been more visible but if it had been she might not have survived in the still depressingly male-dominated world of politics. She survived on her sheer toughness. One night she fell and hurt her leg quite badly but insisted on staying and voting into the early hours of the morning. After I had helped her home and into her flat, with Jack Straw, then her young political adviser, the last thing she said was that she had to write her diary before going to bed. Most of us would have gone to bed and written it when we woke up. But then the great value of her *Diaries* is that they were despatches written from the battlefield. They lack objectivity but they convey immediacy.

Barbara was feminine and proud of it. Sometimes in our all-night negotiating sessions, when I was exhausted and longing for sleep, I would look across at her, immaculate, not a hair out of place, her stockings smooth, her skirt uncrumpled, and would be amazed that I was looking at a woman of sixty-five. She seemed more like someone in her late forties. Of course she could be impossible at times. She simply had to toughen up any negotiating position she was presented with: so much so in fact that sometimes I used deliberately to propose something slightly weaker than I wanted in the full knowledge that she would strengthen it. We would then achieve a position which was at least negotiable. However, she was always open to argument and I knew that if my case was strong I could usually convince her. Most of her criticisms of me in her *Diaries* have some substance and are perceptive.

Barbara Castle had many of the characteristics which later came to be associated with Margaret Thatcher. Interestingly, she respected Margaret Thatcher from the moment she was chosen as leader of the Conservative Party in February 1975. Her diary entries make this clear and they tally with my recollection of what she was saying at the time.

I wonder whether Margaret Thatcher ever had reciprocal views about Barbara. Not many people believed in 1975 that she would be a threat to Labour. Barbara sensed it immediately and I remember being surprised at that assessment. It showed that her political antennae were well tuned to the voters of middle England, even if her own political stance was anathema to them. She understood people, even when she disagreed with them.

In September 1976 the Prime Minister rang to ask if I would go to the Foreign and Commonwealth Office as Tony Crosland's deputy in place of Roy Hattersley, who was going into the Cabinet. I was delighted, though I should have liked to go into the Cabinet myself. I managed to mention this in passing to Jim Callaghan and he said that after I had widened my experience he would certainly not rule it out. He emphasised that my task was to prepare for and carry through our six-month presidency of the Community and he implied he would consider another move up for me after July 1977. Meanwhile, since for much of the time I would be putting the British case in the Council of Foreign Ministers, I would have a responsible position.

I left the DHSS at the best time. Health expenditure had increased every year. Barbara had fought the department's corner with the Chief Secretary of the Treasury, Joel Barnett, very effectively – probably too effectively for the good of the economy. Health spending was now 6 per cent of GDP, having increased by a full 1 per cent over the last two years – the biggest step-like increase in the history of the NHS. Sadly, the weakness of our economy meant that it was not capable of being sustained and in relative terms health spending slipped back over the remaining years of the Labour government. But I enjoyed myself and it had been perhaps the most fulfilling 2½ years of my life.

The Secretary of State for India's oval office is a small but beautifully proportioned room with a striking curved window looking out over St James's Park. On the south-west side of the room are two doorways, designed to allow visiting Indian princes of equal rank to enter the room simultaneously so that neither lost face. There is also an exquisite domed ceiling. It was in the midst of this splendour that, as minister of state in the Foreign Office, I now found myself authorising or querying expenditure often of only a few thousand pounds. In the Ministry of Health, in my ugly glass box overlooking the railway line at the Elephant and Castle, I rarely saw any spending proposal that was not expressed in millions. The Diplomatic Service employed 6,000 people; the Department of Health was responsible for over a million. The contrast was immense. Now every day I was dropped off at the Foreign Office entrance by the statue of Clive of India and I almost felt as if the Empire were still with us. Nor for my generation, who can still remember school maps with the British Empire coloured pink and covering a quarter of the globe, is it a totally remote concept. Our childhood reading – whether old copies of *Chums*, *Boy's Own* or books and poems – was often rooted in Empire. Perhaps that gave me too nostalgic a view of our imperial past without an appreciation of the offsetting realities of having lived through the harshness and the problems of exercising power across such vast and diverse cultures.

My main task was to brief myself thoroughly on the European Community. As I did, it dawned on me that the UK really did have a lousy deal. The Common Agricultural Policy, which we had always known worked against our interests, was out of control – big surpluses were building up in milk products, olive oil and wine and costs were soaring. It was also clear that in a few years' time the UK budgetary contribution would rise so much that we were quite likely to find ourselves the nation making the largest contribution.

We also had to cope with a fishing policy which had been cobbled up by the original six members on the eve of the Community's expansion and which could hardly have been more unhelpful to UK fishing interests. On top of this we had Iceland drastically limiting our fishing rights. In those early weeks I was almost driven to conclude that Harold Wilson had been right after all in 1971 and that the terms had been unacceptable. Certainly they were far more adverse than I had ever realised and it was clear that we would face a grinding, acrimonious debate to recoup lost ground. Yet talking to Foreign Office officials, with some notable exceptions, I found the senior diplomats so dismissive, even light-hearted, about these realities that I soon despaired of being able to develop a tough nego-tiating stance which we would stick to.

It is a feature of life that sects within a faith often have greater difficulty in working together harmoniously than they have in their relationship with non-believers. So it was over Europe. The Foreign Office and I clashed, sometimes fairly violently, because we all believed in Europe. It was not a matter of indifference to them or to me, Europe was high on both of our lists of priorities. Trouble arose because we differed over what sort of European Community the UK had joined in 1973 and what its future shape should be. I believed the Community should be a union of independent nations; many diplomats believed it had to develop into a single state. The Foreign Office generally kept coming back to the intentions of the founding fathers. No one can deny that they wanted an eventual European state, but that ignores what people and countries have wished since General de Gaulle won his battle for the recognition of a veto with the Luxembourg compromise. Moreover, Edward Heath specifically disavowed a federalist intention at the time of British entry. To argue later that a United States of Europe is what Britain signed up for is retrospectively to change the interpretation of the kind of Community we entered.

Yet I was only minister of state; policy questions were determined ultimately by Tony Crosland. When I took over from him I was immensely grateful, however, for the detailed knowledge I had acquired earlier. I vowed then to shift the whole emphasis of the Foreign Office to a more self-confident, assertive stance towards the Community.

The biggest source of friction I had to contend with at the Foreign Office was a relatively small number of senior diplomats who had got used to having a campaigning role over the European Community and had built up strong links with journalists sympathetic to Europe. Over the years they had been given more political licence by Conservative and Labour politicians than is proper for officials. In the process some of them had become zealots for the European Community and all its works and were none too keen to accept political control. In particular, they found it hard to understand that my determination to spill a little blood on the diplomatic carpets of Europe from time to time was not playing to anti-European sentiment but stemmed from the belief that having a sticking point and being prepared to stand one's ground on occasions was necessary to protect British interests. They also did not comprehend that my distaste and disdain for moves designed to pave the way for the Euro-federalists' dream, the United States of Europe, was all of a piece with my longstanding and strong commitment to Britain playing a full part in the European Community. The principal pro-European politicians with whom they were in contact, such as Edward Heath, Roy Jenkins and Jo Grimond, were federalists and when I joined the Foreign Office they too easily assumed, due to my resignation with Roy, that I would be too.

The Foreign Office had also developed a passionate commitment to the Arab cause as well as to the European Community. Why there is this marked Arab identification among British diplomats is the subject of much speculation. Some see it as a phenomenon similar to the fascination that Arabia held for T. E. Lawrence, others to a basic British anti-Semitism. The Foreign Office explanation is that there is only one Israel and many Arab countries and therefore many more diplomats serve in Arab countries and learn to empathise with the Arabs and their support for the Palestinian cause. The other factor is that over the years oil has been a vital British interest, first because we had none of our own and then because we needed to co-operate as we became through the North Sea a significant oil producer.

By contrast, many British politicians have always admired Israel's democracy and the courage of its people. They have developed strong links with Israeli politicians. It was Israel that was the issue on which

Ernest Bevin, when Foreign Secretary, had the most trouble with the Labour Party. Though Bevin was a great Foreign Secretary, it was widely felt that his attitude to the Palestinian problem was far too pro-Arab and quite unduly influenced by the Foreign Office. Sir Alec Douglas-Home and Edward Heath have been the Prime Ministers most critical of Israel; Winston Churchill, Harold Wilson, Margaret Thatcher and Tony Blair its most deeply committed friends.

The main anxiety people have about the Foreign Office stems from its reputation as the home of appeasers. This began with its pre-war involvement in, and support for, Chamberlain's appeasement policy, which culminated in Munich. Post-war, the Foreign Office had a shadowy role – shared with most of our leading politicians – over whether or when to join the European Community. It was not alone, however, in being slow to anticipate the development of European unity. Politicians of the calibre of Attlee and Bevin, Churchill and Eden, saw European unity as a purely continental matter, desirable for those countries but not a matter to trouble ourselves with. The Foreign Office was vigorous in its internal opposition to Eden's ill-fated Suez venture, taking the lead from its Arabists, and on this occasion was proved right. Foreign Office diplomats also had a good record in supporting the free spirits in eastern Europe and were always in favour of the eventual reunification of Germany. So the Foreign Office's record of being proved correct on foreign policy questions is a mixed one. As to its tendency to split the difference, that is part of the art of diplomacy. Any lack of backbone in the operation of foreign policy is a reflection on the personalities involved, the Foreign Secretary in particular, rather than the Foreign Office itself. If the Foreign Secretary is weak, the official view predominates and that too reflects personality, especially that of the permanent under-secretary. With the new generation of senior diplomats in the 1990s the tendency towards appeasement began to fade. This helped John Major's determination in the Treaty of Maastricht to have an opt-out from the euro and the Social Chapter. But it was there in the Foreign Office from the 1920s to the 1980s and at times became the predominant mood. I hope it never returns. What was more worrying, and in some respects related, was the downgrading of Foreign Office views and the advice of the Foreign Secretary, which started under Margaret Thatcher and developed massively and with disastrous results under Tony Blair in the early part of the twenty-first century.

When Jim Callaghan became Prime Minister in April 1976 he knew that before many months had passed he would have to persuade his colleagues to submit to financial constraints dictated by the International Monetary Fund. In his autobiography Jim recalls that the day after taking office on 5 April he met with the governor of the Bank of England, Gordon Richardson, and writes that it was uncannily like stepping back twelve years and listening, as the new Chancellor of the Exchequer, to the then governor, Lord Cromer. The message was about the weakness of sterling, the fact that the United States was gloomy about its future and that the borrowing requirement was too high, threatening to crowd out much-needed private investment.

My attitude to Jim Callaghan became much more positive at the Labour Party conference at Blackpool while listening to his speech on 28 September. I felt that, for the first time since Roy Jenkins opened his Budget in 1968, someone in the Labour Party leadership was really grappling honestly with the economic situation facing the country. That speech is renowned for the words widely attributed to Peter Jay:

> We used to think that you could spend your way out of recession and increase employment by cutting taxes and boosting government spending. I tell you in all candour that that option no longer exists, and that in so far as it ever did exist, it only worked on each occasion since the war by injecting a bigger dose of inflation into the economy, followed by a higher level of unemployment as the next step. Higher inflation followed by higher unemployment. We have just escaped from the highest rate of inflation this country has known; we have not yet escaped from the consequences: high unemployment. That is the history of the last twenty years.

It was a brave speech. The conference audience recognised it as such and, in the main, responded warmly to its frankness. The next day, from the Imperial Hotel in Blackpool, Jim Callaghan rang President Ford to warn him that we would need a stand-by loan from the International Monetary Fund and a safety net for sterling.

From then on, the more I saw of him as Prime Minister the more I admired Jim Callaghan. He was an example of someone who grew in office. Having achieved his ambition he relaxed more and lost his personal chippiness and wholly unwarranted sense of inferiority. Though he never went to university, he had a good mind and considerable experience and his leadership qualities now came to the fore. Members of the Cabinet began to trust each other and the Downing Street press office stopped denigrating Cabinet colleagues. The one exception was Tony Benn, whom Jim could never understand, though he tried hard. Ministers were supported even when they had made mistakes. An atmosphere of genuine trust started to emanate from No. 10. It was a wonderful change from Wilson's paranoia and was a formidable transformation. So it was that 'Honest Jim' became the public image and fortunately it had real substance to back it up.

Watching the IMF discussions from the sidelines convinced me that modern Cabinet government becomes almost impossible unless the four most senior Cabinet ministers resolve any differences before they come to full Cabinet. It becomes very difficult to handle Cabinet discussion, let alone Cabinet cohesion, if the Chancellor of the Exchequer, the Foreign Secretary or the Home Secretary disagree openly in Cabinet with the Prime Minister. It is incumbent on them to discuss issues thoroughly, to try very hard to agree, and to only go to Cabinet to fight their corner as a last resort. In the end Tony Crosland put his loyalty to Jim first. He was experienced enough to know that the Cabinet could not reject Jim Callaghan's advice once he had declared his support for the Chancellor of the Exchequer.

That experience also convinced me that the relaxed attitude to public expenditure favoured by those of us close to Tony Crosland needed to be considerably revised. 'Sound money' could be scoffed at but without it inflation eroded the social purposes of public expenditure. Ever since 1976 I have been far more cautious about expanding public spending and far more resistant to accepting inflation as the price of growth. Denis Healey had learnt that lesson and started monetary targets and monetary discipline in his last few years as Chancellor of the Exchequer, with my full support. It is a myth fostered by the Labour Party in opposition that monetarism started with Margaret Thatcher but it became a hallmark of her success. Fiscal indiscipline sadly came back after the 2001 general election under Tony Blair and Gordon Brown.

On Sunday 13 February, Tony Crosland had a stroke at his country home in Adderbury, Oxford. I was called up by Ewen Fergusson, Tony Crosland's private secretary, and told that Tony was ill, and from his tone and brief description I could sense that it was serious, for Tony was partly paralysed. I was shocked, even though I had guessed for some time, travelling with him in Europe, that Tony was not well. In 1971 he had been diagnosed as having high blood pressure and that is one of the commonest causes of strokes. His lifestyle, the long hours, good food, little exercise, alcohol and cigars could not have helped.

It was hard to accept that a life so full should now be ebbing away. Only a few weeks before he, Susan, Debbie and I had had lunch together in the kitchen of their house in Lansdowne Road. Susan had cooked an excellent meal. Tony and I had drunk too much and Tony had gossiped deliciously and flippantly about the diplomats we knew, all in a haze of cigar smoke. We had driven back together for a meeting at the Foreign Office and I had gone to my room to pick up my papers. By the time I arrived Tony had started the meeting and he had looked up ferociously and berated me for being late. The officials seemed rather stunned. Only Ewen Fergusson was grinning broadly, knowing that we had had lunch together.

Tony loved to tease. He particularly enjoyed teasing the European press. On one of the last occasions I was with him we had been up most of the night negotiating once again in Brussels over fish. Tony had been in the chair as president of the Council of Foreign Ministers and I had argued the British case. The council started at 10 a.m. on Tuesday and finished at 5 a.m. on Wednesday. After the council – as dawn broke – Tony had to brief the press. He was in hilarious form and we all laughed our way through the complex fish quotas we had been discussing and which he, as the MP for Grimsby, was the only one fully to understand. We then flew back to Northolt military airport so that we could all be back in the Foreign Office for a normal working day on the Wednesday. The strain of such a lifestyle was bound to tell.

When I returned to London on that Sunday evening, I had a telephone call from Jim Callaghan. He asked about Tony's condition and I told him that from what little I knew it sounded as if he had had a stroke, with a blood clot on the brain, rather than just an arterial spasm. He questioned me about how much work Tony had been doing and if I had noticed whether or not he had been ill. He then asked me to look after the department and not to hesitate to let him know if there were any problems. So, on Monday morning, I went to my own room in the Foreign Office and prepared to look at areas of policy in which I had not been previously involved. I was quickly thrown in at the deep end. Ewen Fergusson came in to tell me that there was an important meeting on Rhodesia that afternoon and he felt that I should chair it. After some thought about exactly what was appropriate, we decided to hold it in Tony's room since we could not fit everyone into mine. We agreed that I would continue to work from my own room for the rest of the time.

I had not been involved in policy over Rhodesia at any time before for it was handled mainly by Tony Crosland as secretary of state. The ill-fated Geneva conference had been Tony's initiative to build on Henry Kissinger's proposals for a council of state, half white and half black. The objective of the conference was to thrash out arrangements for an interim government which would eventually lead to black majority rule in Rhodesia. In September 1976 Ian Smith had for the first time publicly conceded 'majority rule' in two years but, far from being a change of heart, this just served as a platform for his own delaying tactics. Smith attended the conference in Geneva merely to agree the nuts and bolts of Kissinger's council of state. The black Rhodesian leaders, however, were in the main totally opposed to a council of state. The Geneva conference was adjourned in December 1976 after seven weeks of unsuccessful and largely acrimonious negotiation.

It was a difficult week for everyone. Tony was dying and the department was on hold. I took only those decisions that could not be postponed. On Wednesday 16 February I received a message to say that I was to attend the Cabinet on Thursday morning and that, rather surprisingly, the Prime Minister wanted me to feel free to speak on subjects other than foreign affairs. Before the meeting started, Jim asked me what I was going to speak on in Cabinet under the foreign affairs item. I had thought it had been arranged between our two private secretaries that there was nothing to report but Jim

Callaghan mentioned subjects which he thought I should raise. In retrospect it is clear that he wanted me to speak at the Cabinet meeting because he had already decided to make me Foreign Secretary.

On Saturday 19 February, having been unconscious for some days, Tony Crosland died, with Susan and his two stepdaughters at his bedside. Like so many people in the country I was deeply saddened. We had been friends, never very close, but in recent months getting closer. I admired his razor-sharp mind and his debonair style. I was enchanted by his gaiety, when he allowed it to break through, for it danced like rays of sunlight, banishing the other impression of cynicism and world-weariness.

On Monday 21 February Prince Saud (the Saudi Foreign Minister, who still retains that position), the Prime Minister and I had lunch in the small dining room which links the big dining room and the reception rooms on the first floor of No. 10. Jim made no mention of who was to succeed Tony, though his mind must have been on this as well as his forthcoming tribute to Tony in the House. But he did keep joking about how young Prince Saud was, at only thirty-six. Later, down at the House, Jim gave a moving tribute to Tony Crosland, wistfully saying that he was 'gifted beyond the reach of many of us'. The House was full and there was an overwhelming mood of sorrow for someone who had been such an attractive member of the House – good looking, arrogant, rude and yet intellectually honest and fundamentally decent. The manner of his dying and the daily medical bulletins had moved the House more than Tony had ever done in his lifetime for he was never a great speaker. Yet everyone felt that something had gone from the chamber of the Commons. There was a massive intellectual gap, and also, of course, an immediate political gap. Tony had undoubtedly seen himself succeeding Jim Callaghan as leader in a few years' time and so his death was also that of a lost leader.

I walked back to the Foreign Office wondering what Jim Callaghan would do and how it would affect me. There had been much speculation in the newspapers but it was all rather diffuse. A *Times* editorial had hinted at an interim arrangement where I might be asked to continue to run the Foreign Office until the Budget, which was not far off, and then Jim would move Denis across to be

Foreign Secretary and appoint someone else as Chancellor of the Exchequer, bringing me into the Cabinet in a junior post. This was certainly the summit of my hopes. Denis Healey was definitely the favourite to succeed, with Edmund Dell taking over from him. Some suggested Shirley Williams for the Foreign Office and a few Roy Hattersley. No one suggested me.

When I arrived back in the Foreign Office my Private Secretary told me that 10 Downing Street had been on the telephone. Would I go and see the Prime Minister in his room in the House? I found Jim Callaghan sitting alone. He asked me to sit down and said simply, 'David, I am going to make you Foreign Secretary.' I was stunned. Jim said in his autobiography that I went as white as a sheet. It took me a few seconds to reply and then he said that this was not going to be a temporary appointment. He had discussed the situation with Denis Healey and Denis really did not quite know what he wanted to do. So, as Jim put it, he had decided the issue for him – he would stay at the Treasury. He would be telling the press that I was not a stop-gap appointment and that I should look on it as if I were going to remain Foreign Secretary for a reasonable period of time. The one warning he gave me was that if the good of the government made a change necessary, by which I took him to mean if Denis Healey ran into serious political unpopularity as Chancellor of the Exchequer, then I could be moved to make room for him. But otherwise I could expect to stay until the election. The one thing over which he went out of his way to reassure me was that he was not promoting me to this seniority in Cabinet only to demote me in a few months' time. I left promising not to tell anyone until it was announced at six o'clock.

I drove home to tell Debbie by myself. It would be the last time for 2¼ years that I would be alone in a car: tomorrow Detective Superintendent Alan Dickinson would come. He was the most senior member of Tony's Scotland Yard protection team and a cultured, modest and delightful person. It would be hard to find anyone more considerate, discreet and pleasant. But it is difficult to exaggerate the effect on one's personal freedom of being constantly accompanied, always having to think of the impact on the detectives of any change of plan. I enjoy my own company, finding strength in solitary reflection and peace in being alone. To have that curtailed was the single most unattractive feature of my new job.

Debbie and I quickly decided not to move to the Foreign Secretary's flat at the top of Carlton Gardens and instead to go on living in our own home. We also decided that Debbie would continue with her literary agency. The telephone rang pretty incessantly as we watched reaction on the television news bulletins. Our number was in the directory and, despite some very unpleasant anonymous calls, of which 'nigger lover' was the most printable, we have never gone ex-directory. The hardest task that night was to persuade the journalists and photographers assembled outside the door in Narrow Street to go home. At one time I even had to restrain Debbie from putting the dustbins out for that would have provided them with an unusual photocall. Eventually at about eleven o'clock they cleared away, bribed by our agreeing to a photocall next morning with the boys.

Arriving for the first time as Foreign Secretary at the Ambassador's Entrance of the Foreign Office, which overlooks Horse Guards Parade, on that Tuesday morning, 22 February 1977, I felt a tinge of awe. I had already worked there for nearly six months. But today I was accompanied by a Special Branch detective and was now referred to by diplomats as Secretary of State. Every telegram that went out from the Foreign Office would have 'Owen' at the bottom and a selection from the large number of those telegrams would come to me every day wherever I was in the world to provide a briefing system of immense value. Even something as simple as getting in the lift to my private office was a reminder of the history that lay behind my new post. It still travelled at the slow pace demanded by Ernie Bevin's doctors when he developed his heart condition.

My office too was full of history. The secretary of state's room is the loveliest office in the whole of Whitehall, with its big windows looking out west to St James's Park and north across Horse Guards Parade. It is huge; difficult to envisage as a working office. I used to imagine it with three double-decker buses parked in a row. That is a slight exaggeration, but gives some indication of its size. Yet, particularly at night, it has a warmth and intimacy that evoked Sir Edward Grey in 1914 watching the lamps going out all over Europe. My desk faced the mantelpiece, above which hung a portrait of Palmerston, brought in by George Brown to replace one of George III. In those early days, with the government about to lose its majority in the House of Commons, I thought I might stay in office for an even shorter time than Patrick Gordon Walker. Only when I had been there for a decent interval did I feel confident enough to remove Palmerston and replace him with a painting of General Jung Bahdour Koowar Ranajee, who was Prime Minister and commander in chief of Nepal at the age of thirty-two. Tony Benn was very sniffy about this picture, saying that at least Lord Palmerston was a British Foreign Secretary. The Ranajee picture, in its size and colour, matches the room's green and gold ceiling and walls, brown curtains and chairs but I took Tony's point and I later balanced this image of Empire by introducing a portrait of Oliver Cromwell. Lord Carrington perhaps not surprisingly took that one down. But interestingly Ranajee still looked down on the Foreign Secretary's desk, a reminder of distant shores and broader responsibilities, until Robin Cook removed him.

When the Israeli Prime Minister Menachem Begin came over to London later in 1977 he asked if he could see my room because it was where the Balfour declaration was signed in 1917. This declaration was the first authoritative pledge to create a homeland for the Jews. As Begin walked in a hush fell and I sensed it was like a shrine for him. He was deeply moved and was obviously praying. Feeling I should mark the occasion, I took from the shelves a leather-bound volume of Hansard. I chose it carefully to include the speech I had made in 1973 on the demilitarisation of Sinai, hoping it might concentrate his mind. He appeared thrilled by the gift; I gathered later from his son that he treasured the book thereafter and that none of his family had ever been able to disillusion him when he claimed it had been in the room when the Balfour declaration had been signed! The Foreign Office were not so pleased as they were never able to replace it. The particular skilled bookbinder had died and, for some years, whenever I returned after I had ceased to be Foreign Secretary, I would notice the gap in the bookcase with a smile.

The outer office was where four people worked. The principal private secretary, Ewen Fergusson, had served Jim Callaghan as well as Tony Crosland. His physique was that of a big, burly, Scottish international rugby forward, but it disguised a delicate mover within the Whitehall machine. He got on extremely well with everyone but that too was deceptive – he was shrewd, holding firm opinions which he carefully hid in order to generate a climate of bonhomie. He was a wise counsellor and later became ambassador to South Africa and France. George Walden succeeded Ewen in 1978. George was robust with the department, believing that his prime duty was to serve the Foreign Secretary and he did that loyally, flowering under Peter Carrington. He went on to become a Conservative MP.

Two younger diplomats acted as assistant private secretaries. For most of my time they were Kieran Prendergast, independent and tough minded, and from 1997 to 2005 under-secretary to Kofi Annan at the UN; and Stephen Wall, imaginative, immensely thorough and hard-working, who served John Major in No. 10, was our permanent representative to the EU from 1995 to 2000, and then returned to Downing Street to be directly responsible to Tony Blair for Europe. At the desk as people came in through the door of the private office sat Maggie Turner, disciplined and an extremely competent keeper of the Foreign Secretary's diary. One of the first things I had to do was to persuade her to stay. She was an attractive home civil servant of twenty-five who had been Tony Crosland's diary secretary in the Department of the Environment. He had created a huge kerfuffle in the Diplomatic Service by demanding that she should come with him to the Foreign Office. Now she agreed to remain and since she had by then earned the respect and affection of everyone who worked with her, it was not difficult to arrange. She proved vital, since a Foreign Secretary, more than most, depends on someone who can juggle the diary to fit in the demands of the Foreign Office at home and abroad, the Cabinet Office, Parliament, and, in my case, Plymouth, family and friends. Foreign statesmen were flying in and out of London with increasing frequency, often giving no notice, or else they were cancelling without warning. It was impossible to fit in all the requests. She was able to say no firmly but without ruffling too many feathers, soothe bruised feelings and settle the debris I too often left in my wake. After losing the general election, I managed to persuade her to come out of the Civil Service and run my political office, which, as Maggie Smart since her marriage and with two children, she does with consummate skill from an electronic office in Berkhamsted to this day. Throughout my period as secretary of state, these people in my private office were a delight and a tonic. Everyone worked with dedication and immense skill. It became a powerhouse, full of zest, from which I was determined to get to grips with the Foreign Office. We were an irreverent guerrilla force. At times I was too tough on the Foreign Office but the pace had to be fast and my reactions were at times too furious.

The private secretary in the Foreign Office has an internal authority I have not found anywhere else in Whitehall. He – there has never yet been a woman – acts as the hinge for two crucial relationships: that between the Foreign Secretary and the Prime Minister, and that between the Foreign Secretary and the head of the Diplomatic Service. Of the two, the link across the road to No. 10 is by far the more important and sometimes preserving it means that the Foreign Secretary is wise to differ from the collective wisdom of the Diplomatic Service. An example of this came some months later when Jim Callaghan sent a note over from his private secretary to mine asking what the Foreign Secretary thought of inviting the new Israeli Prime Minister, Menachem Begin, for an official visit. The Prime Minister, I later discovered, remarked at the time, 'Now we will discover who is in charge of the Foreign Office.' He knew the bias towards the Arab viewpoint. As he had guessed, the reaction was to advise me to say no and to explain as my justification that public opinion in Britain would not welcome a visit from the former leader of Irgun, the organisation thought to be responsible for the blowing up of the King David Hotel in 1946. The diplomats knew I would overrule such advice and I wrote back to say I thought he should be invited.

Soon after my appointment, Jim mentioned informally that Harold Wilson had said when he retired that he would loyally support Jim's government even if he thought it was wrong, with one exception. The exception was Israel. I knew, therefore, that I had to watch this issue carefully. Fortunately, once President Sadat flew to Jerusalem in November 1977, we were into a highly positive round of diplomacy leading up to the Camp David agreement and the Egyptian–Israeli Treaty. Prime Minister Begin had to cancel his visit to Britain because of Sadat's visit but he was so keen to come that he reinstated it for early December, even announcing the date before we had agreed it. This almost accidentally put us in a more influential role than any other European country and both Begin and Sadat tended to call in on us in London en route to or from the United States. Prior to this, despite George Brown's sponsorship of the famous Resolution 242 in the UN Security Council in 1967, Britain had not had much involvement in the peace process, mainly because we had progressively lost influence where it counted, in Jerusalem. I was the first Foreign Secretary to visit Israel and Margaret Thatcher the first Prime Minister.

Relations between Jim Callaghan and me, and between No. 10 and the Foreign Office, were exceptionally good for 2¼ years. Indeed we barely had a hiccup. When I was appointed I hardly knew Jim at all and the good initial relationship owed much to Ewen Fergusson. It helped that Ewen, having worked for Jim, knew how his mind worked and could anticipate his reactions. My relationship was also helped by Jim's ability to drop hints about his inner thinking. He did this particularly on plane or car trips when there were no officials present for, apart from those officials who worked close to him, he was suspicious of Whitehall. I was amazed how Jim consciously chose not to interfere, once actually going to the lengths of ringing me up to apologise for fixing up a meeting with President Kaunda in Kano by telephone without being able to consult me first.

For years I had chafed at Britain's relative economic decline and I never accepted that we had to resign ourselves to its continuance, nor that it meant that we had to give in continuously when we negotiated in Europe. In my first Commons speech as Foreign Secretary I deliberately struck an expansive note, saying that it was time to stop selling ourselves short, that we needed more self-confidence, more national buoyancy, that we were in danger of exaggerating our weaknesses and underplaying our potential. The battle over Europe within the Foreign Office began very soon after I took office since it was high time that we developed a strategy to cut farm prices and challenge the growing percentage of the Community budget taken by the Common Agricultural Policy. In the spring of 1977, John Silkin and I agreed to aim for a zero farm price rise by the spring of 1979. Inflation generally was so high that farm prices could only be taken down in three steps. The Commission, under Roy Jenkins, supported this strategy. They were surprised and even annoyed when the Conservative government abandoned this sensible stance in the early summer of 1979 and left the Commission in the lurch supporting a zero farm price settlement.

In 1977 the Euro-diplomats were still in the first flush of post-referendum euphoria and were very reluctant to sound warnings about the manifest unfairness of the British budgetary contribution. It was all too easy for them to dismiss even serious criticism as being anti-European because too many in the Labour Cabinet were still at heart against the Community. But these diplomats had become far too protective of their own handiwork. Criticism of the terms of their negotiations was, for some, a personal slight. It would have been much wiser if we had had a new team of diplomats to deal with the European Community after entry, people with no hang-ups from the past, people who understood that the compromises which were legitimate for getting into the European Community might have to be disowned and renegotiated once in. Some of the Euro-diplomats found it easy to explain my stance as deriving from a wish to curry favour with the left in order to win more votes and get elected to the Labour Party NEC. A quite prominent diplomat told me much later that it was only when he saw me, out of office, in 1980, fight within the Labour Party for the European Community that he understood what I had been working for inside the Foreign Office. When Margaret Thatcher became Prime Minister, those same diplomats began to realise that standing up for one's interests in the European Community was not just part of an internal Labour Party battle. The climate in the press changed too and the budgetary consequences of entry were more clearly seen as unfair to the UK, so that it became more widely accepted that we had to fight for the terms to be changed.

I tried to build on the Foreign Office's planning staff by creating my own policy section within the private office. It was made up of a variety of experts. One was Michael Stewart, working part time while still teaching economics at University College, London. Michael Stewart had originally had the much more challenging task of advising Tony Crosland, who really knew about economics. He agreed to stay on in the less satisfying role of educating me in economics. As a result I felt more confident participating in domestic Cabinet economic discussions and in the mysteries of international economics. His expertise was also very helpful when the Prime

Minister invited me to the seminars he chaired on monetary and exchange rate policy. This was not a formal Cabinet sub-committee. Attended by Gordon Richardson, the governor of the Bank of England, it was a vehicle for the Prime Minister to involve himself in what had hitherto been the sole preserve of the Chancellor of the Exchequer. It was generous of Jim Callaghan to invite me along, and I suspect it was to educate me as much as anything.

Paul Lever, a bright, iconoclastic diplomat, dealt with security questions, particularly the nuclear deterrent and arms control. He later succeeded Kieran Prendergast in my private office and went on to become ambassador to Germany. What was important was that Paul appeared to have a good relationship with the head of the Defence Department, David Gillmore, an astute, determined person, later the permanent under-secretary in charge of the Diplomatic Service in 1992, when I became the EU negotiator in the former Yugoslavia.

David Stephen was my political adviser; these advisers, a relatively new feature then, were paid as civil servants but given a special dispensation to be involved in party politics. David was involved in all aspects of my activity. He had worked for the International Department of the Labour Party and as secretary of the Runnymede Trust. A Spanish speaker, he had strong links with the human rights movements in Latin America, and the Latin American Department to their credit used his knowledge to the full. He visited Ovamboland in Namibia, to report on the SWAPO guerrilla campaign, and Maputo. Later he had a distinguished career at the UN.

The Foreign Office is staffed by dedicated and often brilliant people and I am dubious about whether it retains an appeasing identity. As far as there is one it stems from the fact that the culture of diplomacy elevates splitting the difference to an art form. Also 'going native', which means empathising with the country within which one is living, is inevitable. Before 1997 much could be learnt about the conduct of foreign policy by watching the relationship between the Treasury and the Foreign Office as they battled for dominance in the co-ordination of Britain's European Union negotiating stance. The Foreign Office's skills ought to have made it pre-eminent, but if its key officials were thought to lack backbone then the Treasury became more powerful with ministers. The

Treasury was less hierarchical, more irreverent and readier to fight Britain's corner but it did not always know when it is better to bend, wiser to settle. All this changed after New Labour's first election victory, when Tony Blair conceded to Gordon Brown in the Treasury a dominating role in the domestic field and started to take for himself into No. 10 many of the powers hitherto exercised by the Foreign Secretary and the Defence Secretary. This process was formalised after the 2001 election.

My own style as Foreign Secretary was not above reproach and at times I left myself open to justified criticism for I was too brash and abrasive. It is easy to make excuses – the pace I set myself was taxing, even given my relative youth. But my impatience was too often on display and a little more time should have been spent on mollifying bruised egos. Wiser, older, I would now handle myself differently. Set against this, as the years have passed so have the exuberance and the irrepressibility of youth. Issues I tackled then I would probably shirk now. Age softens and whether the advantages of that outweigh the disadvantages is not easy to determine. Suffice to say, I was not a paragon of virtue and the critics of my style had some fair points.

I was and remain a blue-water diplomatist. I want our reach to go out from Europe across the oceans of the world. I believe we should have some presence in virtually every country represented in the UN, however small. We should not be ashamed of having one-person missions operating with a telephone, a laptop computer and a small safe, with none of the paraphernalia of a full-blown embassy. Wide coverage is a responsibility that comes with being a permanent member of the Security Council, a status that is a fortuitous consequence of our history but one which we should retain and defend with vigour. There is a reluctance among some to shoulder this worldwide responsibility. It is seen as an embarrassing relic of Empire to be abandoned rather than as an opportunity to be exploited. It would be folly for Britain to acquiesce and allow its own and France's seats on the Security Council to become European Union seats rotating with whoever has the presidency. It is worrying that Javier Solana, the EU high representative for the Common Foreign and Security Policy (CFSP), suggested EU representation without any consultation with the member countries' Foreign Ministers. The wording negotiated for the Treaty of Lisbon on this crucial area was always far too mealy mouthed for me. Words matter in international treaties; opaque language only portends trouble later. We have in the UK conceded far too much already in the language that governs the CFSP and we ignore at our peril the craftily worded compromises of those who want a single foreign and security policy.

It has been a happy tradition that as far as possible foreign policy is conducted in Britain on a bipartisan basis, though this was put under great strain in the aftermath of the invasion of Iraq in 2003 and Tony Blair's refusal to honour his 2005 manifesto commitment to a referendum on the proposed EU constitution. The Foreign Secretary is never refused a pair for voting and this eases the burden of travel considerably. Apart from the European Community, the post-war issues which had most tested cross-party co-operation were Suez and Rhodesia. I was always going to come under severe attack from the Conservative right wing on Rhodesia, particularly since Margaret Thatcher sympathised with their views. She knew very little then about Africa and her main adviser seemed to be Laurens van der Post, who, when I met him at her request, was rightly concerned about the Shona/Ndebele tribal divide in Rhodesia. Margaret Thatcher, however, unwisely committed herself to Bishop Abel Muzorewa and gave a pre-election commitment to support the internal settlement, which undoubtedly hindered our diplomacy. When she won the election she found it was the first promise she was unable to fulfil.

While Iran, the Falklands, the Middle East and nuclear weapons would all later play their part, the immediate issues seemed clear – Rhodesia and Europe. On European questions I was already well briefed. But on Rhodesia I needed to think out the fundamentals.

Henry Kissinger's belated involvement in southern Africa taught me that US power was crucial. But if the US was to be involved there had to be close partnership and a working relationship with British diplomats. American diplomats had not had the experience in Africa that we had built up over the years and there was room for a lot of misunderstanding if we acted separately. In any case, the new Carter administration was already far more actively engaged over South Africa and apartheid than the Ford administration, so Washington needed to be sounded out by our officials quickly to see if we could work more closely together on Rhodesia.

The critical question was how to persuade and pressurise South Africa. We needed the classic combination of stick and carrot. There was no doubt that the South Africans were able to deliver a settlement at any time but they had to be convinced it was in their interests. For them, a dependent white-dominated buffer state of Rhodesia had its advantages. We had to persuade them of the disadvantages, raise the price of their support and increase the incentive to co-operate. The previous strategy of playing both ends, South Africa and black Africa, against the middle, Rhodesia and Namibia, had diminished British influence in Africa and in the world. White minority governments in Mozambique and Angola had collapsed with the fall of the Portuguese Empire. Britain looked, and indeed was, a paper tiger over Rhodesia. It was obvious that sanctions against South Africa had to be progressively invoked, something which Britain had shrunk from doing under Labour as well as Conservative governments. That did not mean comprehensive all-out economic sanctions but it did mean a readiness to squeeze its economy.

Over Namibia and Rhodesia, and South Africa itself, there was a choice to make and I was determined we would make it. Majority rule, and soon, was where both principle and interest now lay. The white minority groups were not viable and they were playing for time at a heavy price in lives and in human misery. Eventually, even in South Africa, blacks would gain the vote. I believed Britain's trading interests, as well as our political interests, lay in ensuring that we were not identified with sustaining racial discrimination or minority rule. This meant abandoning neutrality and being partisan in our determination to have fair elections. It meant that we would no longer, because of our history, our culture or racial prejudice, act as apologists for the minority governments in Rhodesia, Namibia and South Africa, which held power by exploitation and violence. I was not advocating a starry-eyed policy divorced from self-interest. On the contrary, I believed that Britain had to curb and put its large financial interests in South Africa at risk in the medium term in order to be able to secure them in the long term.

Politically we would now have to hold back from promoting settlements involving a qualified franchise and we would have to refuse to identify ourselves with any internal solutions. We had to understand that the black leaders and their supporters who came from Rhodesia and Namibia were fighting outside the countries because there was no hope of gaining their freedom by staying and living under white domination. Many were principled people, active Christians, forced to become liberation fighters. For others, their Marxism was secondary to their nationalism. We could not supply them with arms, for this would disqualify us from any diplomatic influence in South Africa, but we would champion negotiations and fair elections in order to minimise the influence of the communist countries who were supplying the freedom fighters with arms. A hard core of the guerrilla fighters were not committed to the ballot box at all. We had a role here too. We had to restore faith in democracy and support those black politicians who were democrats. Some, like Denis Healey, argued that all we could realistically do was to wait until the freedom fighters won. That was far too fatalistic. It would also have been a politically impossible position to adopt in the House of Commons or in the UN. It would have encouraged those who wanted to impose their rule by force of arms and we would have been seen as ignoring the ballot box.

Britain, whether we liked it or not, was held responsible internationally for Ian Smith's UDI. We had to have an active diplomatic role. Some in the Cabinet disliked any active Rhodesian policy for the domestic political risks due to family links, and militarily due to the danger of being sucked in. Jim Callaghan had warned me in our first conversation after my appointment that a majority in the Cabinet was opposed to any commitment of British military forces in Rhodesia. Even then my mind was turning on how to involve the United Nations.

I wanted to turn the earlier strategy upside down. Instead of attempting to establish an all-party interim government and then taking eighteen months to produce a constitution, we with the US would produce a draft constitution by the summer and hold an all-party constitutional conference to discuss it. Since the collapse of the Sunningdale arrangement in Northern Ireland, I was deeply suspicious of trying anything which smacked of power-sharing. Power-sharing was based upon an idealistic interpretation of how political men and women behave. Like it or not, the whole basis of democratic politics is the clash of different views and different ideologies. Compromise, not consensus, is the dynamic of politics. Trying to put everyone together in government was political engineering on a grand scale. Essentially unstable anywhere, in Rhodesia it was totally unworkable. The weakness of Geneva was that we had tried to put together the newly developed Patriotic Front of Joshua Nkomo and Robert Mugabe, itself divided, with Bishop Muzorewa, the Reverend Ndabaningi Sithole and the Smith regime, and hoped to weld them together into a team of ministers under the benign chairmanship of a resident commissioner. It was asking too much to expect them to work together in government while producing not only a constitution but also plans for holding elections which they would all then contest. Even if we had been able to reach nominal agreement, it would have broken down within a few months. The four main factions would have been jockeying for power, attempting to rig both the elections and the constitution in their favour. Even without the experience of Geneva, it seemed too optimistic to believe that such a combination could work. Subsequent events at the Lancaster House conference in 1980 only confirmed that judgement. The Patriotic Front immediately split and Mugabe and Nkomo fought each other for power. Lancaster House also confirmed that dealing with the constitution first was the right strategy since, when that conference started in 1979, they had been discussing virtually the same constitution for two years. Our Anglo-American plans proved a good investment and the old saying about the need to 'palaver' in Africa meant that our two-year diplomatic effort was not in vain.

Whatever my own priorities, world events had a habit of blowing us off course. When I was working on Rhodesia, problems would blow up in Tehran or in Buenos Aires; when I was grappling with budget problems in Brussels, I would have to fly to the other end of the world to fulfil a longstanding engagement. Being Foreign Secretary is not a job that allows for neat and ordered tackling of problems. If I ever doubted this, my first Cabinet meeting showed why. I was keen to inform my colleagues of progress on Rhodesia, where talks between the US and ourselves had begun. In the end, however, the discussion turned to Idi Amin.

Cabinet always has on its agenda a separate and early item on foreign affairs, and the Foreign Secretary normally makes an oral report. This is a useful convention allowing Cabinet to be kept informed without the formality of detailed papers. It was the time to encourage early discussion in areas of foreign policy which were likely to become controversial. I reported that our soundings in the Commonwealth had shown that we were a long way from being able to mobilise a majority to oppose Uganda's General Amin attending the London conference of Commonwealth heads of government. This issue was to plague us over the next few months. The black Commonwealth, led by Nigeria, was suspicious of our motives for wanting Amin excluded, blithely ignoring the monstrous nature of the human rights abuses he was perpetrating in Uganda. Days before the Commonwealth conference, I was told by Merlyn Rees in the middle of the Lord Mayor of London's lunch that he had just been informed that Amin had flown into Dublin. We had agreed we would have to mobilise the police to hold his plane while it was refuelled and then insist that it fly off. If he just flew into Heathrow we had already decided that we would not let him off his plane. Fortunately it all turned out to be a false alarm; Amin never came. But the issue did not go away. Later he was ousted by Tanzanian armed intervention, and we aided Julius Nyerere in the attempt. I will never be sure whether it was wise to do so. The price we extracted from Nyerere for our material support was the promise that a mild, decent former children's doctor should be President rather than Milton Obote. Unfortunately the doctor did not have the necessary authority. The end result was that Obote returned to the presidency, Uganda was riven again and human rights were trampled. Although not quite as bad as Amin's, Obote's rule was still a disaster. At the start of the twenty-first century Uganda still remains a problem, albeit somewhat overshadowed by events in the Democratic Republic of Congo and the dire state of Kenya, despite the eventual stepping down of President Moi.

My most immediate political problem was how to handle the British presidency of the European Community and the related issue of direct elections for the European Parliament. This was the first time since we had entered the Community that the UK had held the chair and it was an opportunity to try and nudge the development of the Community in directions which we favoured. Today, directly electing members to the European Parliament seems logical but in

1977 it was a controversial issue within the Labour Party. It was seen by Michael Foot as a challenge to the authority of the House of Commons and was threatening to split the party.

We had an enjoyable and good-natured special Cabinet meeting on a Friday to discuss direct elections. It was not so much a decision-making meeting as an attempt to harmonise the diverse opinions. Hitherto our representation at the European Parliament had come from existing MPs and peers and, purely in terms of British interests, this was working rather well. It provided a valuable link between the two parliaments and was educating MPs about continental politics. Some on the left, like the young John Prescott, were developing as European socialists and becoming adept at handling the politics of the European Parliament. Most ministers, including me, would have preferred this indirect representation to continue, but eventually I and others managed to convince the majority of the Cabinet that this was not an achievable option, that the other eight member states were determined to have the Europe-wide elections provided for in the Treaty of Rome and there was no way that we could block this. I had not realised until then quite how vehemently Michael Foot was opposed to the whole concept of a European Parliament. He believed that it would gradually challenge the Westminster Parliament since all parliaments fight to expand their power base. Michael had a romantic attachment to the Westminster Parliament. He saw its power as stemming only from debate on the floor of the Commons. He opposed select committees and reform of the Lords. All he wanted was the cut and thrust of debate. His Cornish blood made him ready to take up the mantle of Trelawney, except that it was the English Channel rather than the river Tamar which was to be his frontier. He was deaf to the argument that the Treaty of Rome made legislation for a directly elected assembly imperative. Tony Benn too was opposed to any direct election, on the not unreasonable grounds of its potential for stimulating a move towards Euro-federalism. The Cabinet was clearly heading for major trouble. Merlyn Rees feared problems in the House too, worrying that any legislation might suffer the same fate on the floor of the House as Dick Crossman's attempt to reform the House of Lords. I was more sanguine and thought that the Conservative pro-Marketeers would see the legislation onto the statute book in the end.

Without great enthusiasm, the Cabinet turned to the voting mechanism for the elections. I proposed the regional list system of proportional representation and was surprised that it was given a good hearing. A clear majority preferred it to first-past-the-post voting for Europe. It was an important moment. Already, proportional representation had been introduced into the UK for the Northern Ireland Assembly by Edward Heath and for their three seats in the European Parliament it was the only way to ensure minority representation. This discussion was the first time that a Cabinet had been minded to introduce a proper system of proportional voting for an election in all parts of the UK. Even Tony Benn seemed to be concerned about the dangers a Conservative landslide in European elections would present to a Labour government at Westminster. As practical politicians, the Cabinet majority sensed, in view of the specific commitment in the Treaty of Rome, that early legislation and a proportional voting system was the best of all the unappealing courses open to us.

I wanted France to be the first country I visited as Foreign Secretary. I love travelling in France. I share the ambivalence of many British people towards France and the French, but affection easily outweighs suspicion. In my bones politically I know that on the big issues, when the chips are really down, the French, of all the European Community countries, are the most likely to react like the British and be there with us in times of crisis. This was shown by President Mitterrand in 1982 over the Falklands, and I will go to my grave believing that President Chirac would not have split with us as deeply over Iraq if he had been handled better and if Tony Blair had not pushed so unrealistically for a second Security Council resolution in 2003. France and the UK are destined to be linked together and yet separate. The incipient tension in our relationship has more constructive than destructive aspects. I wanted then, and want to this day, improved Anglo-French relations. But it is a strange feature of French policy since Mitterrand that they seem far too relaxed about ever greater integration within the EU, and the comparative ease with which President Sarkozy pushed aside the French people's vote in 2004 against the EU constitution may betoken a readiness to bury the concept behind the Luxembourg compromise and allow majority voting to triumph over the perceived vital national interest of a member state. Yet somehow I can never see France accepting that override if it affected her vital national interests.

To stay in the grandeur of the British embassy in Paris is a delightful experience at any time but in the first flush of my promotion to Foreign Secretary it was something very special. The French Foreign Minister, Louis de Guiringaud, had laid on at no notice a large, sumptuous dinner party at the Quai d'Orsay. I was not expecting to speak but when he rose to propose a toast it became clear that his speech was going to need more than a cursory response. The fertile mind of our ambassador, Sir Nicholas Henderson, came to the rescue, and he frequently passed menu cards along to me with excellent suggestions as to what I should say. The end result was a far better speech than it would have been if I had carefully prepared it.

In handling the tensions that lay ahead between myself and the Euro-federalists I was adamant that I would not be party to any gossip about how awful the Callaghan government was, and with Roy Jenkins, by then president of the Commission, coming on Saturday I also had to be wary of any attempt by Nico Henderson to develop between Roy, a close friend of Nico's, and me as Foreign Secretary anything that could even remotely be seen as a hostile axis to Jim Callaghan. Admittedly I had not been a great proponent of Jim Callaghan in the past. However, I genuinely thought that in his initial period as Prime Minister he had shown himself to be a far better leader and more trustworthy politician than ever he had been before. I certainly now owed him my loyalty and unless that loyalty proved to be misplaced he would have it in full measure. Also, I believed strongly that Roy Jenkins could not be a good president unless he managed to distance himself from Britain and removed any suspicion in Brussels of bias. We had different roles to play and by the very nature of these different roles we would inevitably clash from time to time, for British interests and the wider good of the European Community could not invariably coincide.

European Union membership is a continuous negotiation. If you have an interest to protect, particularly as majority voting becomes more frequent, you need allies and you have to find them among those who also have an interest to uphold, not always the same interests as your own. We, like every other EU country, have to assemble coalitions, sometimes quite brazenly scratching their backs if they will scratch ours. Also, since we, like every other EU nation, still have in the last analysis a somewhat tenuous veto power, it must be seen that, selectively and very occasionally, we are prepared to use it if vital interests in foreign and defence policy are involved. In one sense the veto is a deterrent in developing the CFSP, more powerful for rarely being used. The Labour Party throughout the 1980s could not make up its mind whether to support or to criticise Mrs Thatcher for being tough towards the Community. What was important was that many Foreign Office Euro-diplomats slowly adapted to the Thatcher style. Where Margaret Thatcher came unstuck was in pushing too hard on all issues and in not varying her tone. She became too strident and demanding for the strength of her own European negotiating stance. But, nevertheless, her hard line from No. 10 was often essential. The tragedy of New Labour was that they came into government in 1997 with all the zeal of their new-found conversion to EU membership and seemed never to want to use a veto again in the EU, going to absurd lengths to avoid being in a minority of one.

In 1977 Roy Jenkins and I were both having to adjust to a potentially fraught relationship. He had been my mentor and now I, as president of the Council of Foreign Ministers for the next few months, though not actually his master, was the mouthpiece of European Community ministers. It was bound to be difficult for him as a new president of the Commission and vastly more experienced than I to have me holding the very office which only some months back Callaghan had denied him. I have no major complaints about how Roy handled our relationship throughout the next 2¼ years. Various bits of gossip would come back to me about what he was saying but, apart from minor irritation, I cannot say I objected to his odd put-downs, most of which are faithfully recorded in his book *European Diary*. My workload was so great that I did not have the time or inclination to get excited about petty jealousies. Slowly, however, our friendship ebbed away. It was not long before he was being referred to by the nickname which first surfaced in Brussels, '*Le Roi Jean Quinze*', both at home and in my private office. For the most part it was good-natured ribbing. Over the so-called battle of 'Jenkins's seat' at the London economic summit I was far more supportive of Roy than I think he ever realised. It really does matter where the president is placed in the hierarchy of the EU and whether he is treated as a head of government or as a mere Foreign Secretary. Fighting for position is an occupational hazard of becoming president of the Commission. Jacques Delors threatened to turn the office of president into a real power position, gaining the ultimate accolade, a *Sun* headline: 'UP YOURS DELORS'. Sadly for Roy he was unable to turn the presidency into the influential position that he had hoped for and this manifested itself in periodic frustration.

An added difficulty was the seething contempt in which Roy held Jim Callaghan and the deep suspicion that underlay Jim's reaction to Roy. Gradually this improved, particularly as Jim became ever more European. As they grew older and less competitive they started, in the middle 1980s, even in private, to speak more warmly about each other. Ultimately they sparred with the warmth of old punch-drunk pugilists working out in the verbal gymnasium provided by the House of Lords for politicians no longer in the House of Commons.

President Valéry Giscard d'Estaing, himself fond of position, had spotted the Jenkins weakness for pomp and recognition and began to play Roy like a fish on a line. A photocall confined initially to heads of government would, at Giscard's rather imperious invitation, be widened to include the president of the Commission. Roy, lurking in the background, would then join the group, but Giscard would only put him on the end of the row or at the back. It was all absurd but while some people would have taken it as a source of amusement, for Roy it was torture. Leaving Roy fretting on the sidelines or pleasing him by meeting him at the front door or providing a guard of honour became a sort of game for the Elysée Palace. European Union protocol is pretty tedious and the French President was forever standing on his own dignity, even with as good a friend as Helmut Schmidt. On one occasion when Germany was the host for a European Council, Schmidt decided he had had enough of Giscard always arriving last because he was a head of state. So they both circled the driveway in their cars until Giscard cracked.

Helmut Schmidt was the European politician I most admired. He seemed to me the archetypal Social Democrat – market orientated on economic questions, resolute on defence, socially aware and with an understanding and sympathy for trade unionism. When he talked of social partnership it had real meaning. He was never sucked in by any of the interest groups that play in the foothills of politics. He represented the strength and solidity of his home town, that great seaport, Hamburg. He also knew how to make a deal. Once in Buckingham Palace he and I settled a three-year formula for ending the Anglo-German financial offset arrangement which covered the cost of our forces in BAOR. Hans-Dietrich Genscher, as Foreign Minister, would not commit himself, whereas Helmut with no hauteur healed what was a running sore literally on the back of an envelope, which I kept for years but unfortunately now seem to have lost.

In fairness to Roy, the fight to ensure that he was represented at the economic summit in London was a matter of some substance. As host, Jim was bound to want to conduct his own show without having Roy in his shadow. Why Giscard, who had previously pressed Roy to become president in the first place, was now so anxious to keep the Commission outside and in its place was beyond rational explanation. The Benelux countries were determined that the president of the Commission should come to the summit to represent them. Eventually it was agreed that the president should attend for those parts of the discussion that dealt with trade. The Americans thought we Europeans were crazy with these petty arguments. Giscard even refused to attend the opening dinner at No. 10 because Roy was going to be present. Thankfully, today the president of the Commission attends throughout economic summits and the whole absurdity has been put to rest.

My private advice to Jim had been to let Giscard argue the case and take the political flak. I suspect Roy was being told by Crispin Tickell, the Foreign Office diplomat on attachment to him as chef de cabinet, that I was refusing to sign the letter to the Prime Minister supporting Roy's presence at the London summit which the department was pressing me to send. What he did not know was that I had already discussed the issue frequently with Jim Callaghan and was jollying him along to accept the inevitable. The last thing Jim needed was a formal letter from me. This was a typical example of the constant flow of gossip among private secretaries which sometimes inflames relations instead of smoothing them. One such piece of Foreign Office gossip arose from an incident that took place on my appointment. Roy's office had sent a routine formal telegram of congratulations. On receiving it, and not realising that Roy had had nothing to do with its wording, I cursed loudly about its pomposity. Doubtless my expletives were not deleted in transmission from my private secretary to his chef de cabinet. For me, it was only a transient irritation of no consequence whatever. But passed on in this way it obviously nagged at Roy and he mentioned it to me years later. Of such small molehills are mountains made. I suspect our friendship, founded as it was on inequality of position, could never have been sustained on the basis of any equality of position which only pointed up the differences in our personalities. No doubt I should have tried harder with Roy and for a short period at the turn of the year in 1980 we did grow closer and almost became friends again. But that ended only a few months later in the autumn of 1981.

On the early evening of 9 March the Prime Minister and I flew out on Concorde to Washington to meet President Carter. Audrey Callaghan was on the plane, as was Debbie. Concorde had been taken as part of a promotion campaign since we were still locked in the battle to achieve landing rights in New York. Jim was the first European head of government to visit President Carter. In part this was because he was the president of the European Council but it was also because, as a dyed-in-the-wool Atlanticist, he wanted to establish his own special relationship with the new President. It was a thrill to fly Concorde and for Debbie it was going home. She had voted for Jimmy Carter and to visit her capital city in such style was exciting.

Before leaving, Jim Callaghan had agreed that I should put to President Carter the idea of a constitutional conference for Rhodesia. The conference would be based on discussing a specific constitution which our two countries would present jointly after consultation with all the parties vying for power in an independent Zimbabwe. On the trip we talked about some of the details and I got a fascinating first glimpse of the small political mafia that surrounded Jim. Bernard Donoughue, the head of the Policy Unit, was a sensitive operator who paced round the Whitehall jungle like a political leopard. He coupled highly manipulative skills with a good academic mind. Tom McCaffrey, the press secretary, was solid and sensible, older than the others and had Jim's total trust. Unassuming and friendly, he had considerable newspaper management skills. When he had come over from the Home Office with Jim to run the Foreign Office News Department, a post zealously guarded by the diplomats, he had been viewed with the utmost suspicion but his sheer professionalism won through. Then there was Tom McNally, Jim's political adviser, who had been international secretary to the Labour Party and also with him in the Foreign Office. He had a gritty guile, became a Labour MP and then joined the SDP and became for a time close to me. Later he joined the Liberal Democrats, becoming their leader in the House of Lords. Finally, there was Roger Stott, Jim's parliamentary private secretary, a young mainstream MP with his ear close to the ground. I sensed that Jim would not be diverted too far from domestic politics with them around, and since that is where the votes were, this was reassuring. Whenever I travelled with the Prime Minister I was always struck by the way he surrounded himself with these four and never allowed the pomp and circumstance of foreign travel to supplant the nitty-gritty of party politics at home. Jim was a domestic Prime Minister and this was one of the reasons why he chose to interfere so little in foreign policy. The home front, he knew, was where the next general election would be won or lost. It was therefore all the harsher that, coming back from a heads of government meeting in Guadeloupe in January 1979 he was saddled at the start of the Winter of Discontent with the headline, which he never uttered, 'CRISIS? WHAT CRISIS?'

We went into the first session with President Carter next morning after brief welcoming speeches but without the traditional speeches on the White House lawn since this was one of the trappings banished by Carter at the outset of his administration. The nineteen-gun salute for the Prime Minister had also been cancelled for fear of provoking a besieged gunman in City Hall two blocks away.

The President and the Prime Minister went off to the Oval Office and I was left in the Cabinet Room with Secretary of State Cyrus Vance, whom I had never met before. We soon developed a close working partnership but also a sustained personal friendship which continued through the 1980s on the Palme commission and as joint negotiators in the former Yugoslavia, he for the UN and I for the EU. Our first discussion was on Rhodesia. In less than fifteen minutes, helped by a prior meeting between officials, we had agreed the outline of a joint approach. When the President and the Prime Minister came back I summarised what had been discussed and it was quickly endorsed by President Carter. In this brisk fashion, the Anglo-American initiative on Rhodesia began.

The only difference during the trip between Jim and me arose when he talked to the British press about this initiative. He tried to downplay US involvement over Rhodesia and talk up the extent of British control. However, I did not want it thought that Britain was in the driving seat, with a little American help. I wanted it seen that we were sharing the driving and that the initiative would carry all the clout of American diplomacy. In this way I hoped it would be impossible for Ian Smith or the South Africans to divide and rule. Picking Britain off and isolating us was a tactic that had been used to considerable effect in the past. I eventually managed to counteract his presentation.

Another reason for my anxiety to bind in the Americans was the way Mr Smith had been able, over the years, to exploit domestic divisions in Britain. I calculated that some Conservative critics would now hesitate before backing Smith by, for instance, opposing the renewal of sanctions, since they would not want to put themselves against the US. For some on the right support for Rhodesian UDI had become the vehicle for expressing racial prejudice. The Tory right also enjoyed the Salisbury connection and they would not hesitate to block, if they could, the tougher line I intended to take with Smith. Given the small Labour majority, the Cabinet's proven reluctance to risk any military involvement and our weakened economic position, we could not take even these people on alone. For me to attempt to settle Rhodesia on our own would be to risk another abject failure. With American strength and power I had a renewed opportunity. I kept saying publicly that I had no *amour propre*, that Africa needed American strength and American commitment. The British attempt to keep responsibility for Rhodesia to ourselves had always been a mistake and the outcome of Wilson's posturing on HMS *Fearless* and HMS *Tiger* only revealed our weakness.

On that first day Cy Vance understood completely why I wanted his support and he never wavered throughout the whole exercise. Once, while walking up the stairs of State House in Dar es Salaam to see President Nyerere, he told me he did not agree with me over retaining the Rhodesian police force in the transition but that he would back me nonetheless, which he proceeded to do with the utmost conviction. With friends like that one can do business. Another advantage of our joint initiative was that it had a new momentum. Andrew Young, a young black politician, had been appointed as the US ambassador to the United Nations. He was a civil rights activist, had been a close associate of Martin Luther King and was a long-time political associate of Jimmy Carter in Atlanta, Georgia, the state of which Carter had been governor. Andy Young was able to enthuse Third World countries in a way I never could. The price of his participation was more than a little unevenness in negotiations and some unconventional diplomacy but it was a price worth paying, even if I did once say with regard to Palestine that he 'shot from the lip'.

Another significant policy development stemmed from a discussion I had with Jim one evening before Carter's ceremonial dinner in the White House. Jim could see that the proliferation of nuclear weapons was of massive concern to Carter and that we would have to develop our policies quickly to match his. It was decided, with Sir John Hunt, secretary to the Cabinet, to form a special Cabinet sub-committee on nuclear non-proliferation which I would chair. Jim was obviously pleased to discover that this was an area in which I was not only interested but reasonably well informed thanks to my periodic lunches with Solly Zuckerman.

The White House dinner was an enjoyable occasion. When Jim spoke he said that he was shy about talking about the special relationship but since the President had mentioned it earlier he felt it did describe with accuracy the ease and common feelings we had for each other. He quoted Shakespeare on friendship, 'Grapple them to thy heart with hoops of steel', and gave the President some worsted fabric with the almost imperceptible repeat of the letters JC, forming a silver silk pinstripe, which he had already had made up for himself into a suit. We ate roast beef and an American tenor sang the Welsh hymn 'All Through the Night'. As farmers and fellow Baptists the two got on very well together.

In my more detailed conversations with Cy Vance in the State Department the vexed question of sanctions against South Africa kept recurring. Both of us were in no doubt that any initiative on Rhodesia and Namibia was doomed unless we were able to bring pressure on South Africa. I had sensed before that one of the levers which the Americans had used during Henry Kissinger's time was the Shah of Iran, who was the main supplier of oil to South Africa. That was now confirmed. We agreed to do all we could discreetly to mobilise this pressure again in support of our Anglo-American initiative.

In the UN Andy Young was much seized by the prospect of bringing, under the UN Charter, mandatory sanctions against South Africa. This meant declaring that, because of apartheid, a threat to peace existed, in or around South Africa. In the early months of the new administration there was a great deal of unreality about what was said on this subject. Andy Young was playing to the Third World gallery in the UN, while Cy Vance was encountering powerful resistance over sanctions in Congress and from some sections of American business interests and this countered the support the US was getting in the UN.

I had a similar problem over South Africa for I had to cope with a Labour Cabinet which included a powerful group of ministers who were against any trade or economic sanctions because they would reduce exports, as well as a Whitehall machine which was adamantly opposed. I had first to overcome the traditional bureaucratic argument about the slippery slope and it took me some time before I made any headway. My first task was to make Cabinet colleagues and Whitehall officials aware that the Americans were already definitely heading towards some sanctions and, if we were not to slip down towards total sanctions, we had at the very least to keep the US State Department alongside. To say that Britain would use its veto against economic sanctions on its own was unrealistic. Even in the unlikely event that a Cabinet majority agreed to a lone veto, they would never agree to continue it once they had felt the worldwide hostility that would break around us. However, it would be a completely different and far more acceptable proposition to use our veto at the same time as the US. So the key Cabinet sub-committee had to be persuaded to bend at least to the extent of having some sanctions considered as an option. The Foreign Office

had to be persuaded too. Within Whitehall it was virtually a forbidden subject and to outwit the Whitehall consensus I had to first
win the battle within the Foreign Office. I was not to find it easy and
I needed Cy Vance. He was in tune with the Congressional realities
and ready to curb Andy Young's exuberance, so we slowly began to
develop a coherent joint policy over sanctions.

On 17 March the Cabinet met and Jim Callaghan reported on
our trip to Washington and to Ottawa. I felt on top of the world. My
office was a hive of activity and everywhere I looked there were
important, challenging things to be done. My anxiety was whether
or not Labour would be in office long enough to achieve any of
them. That night in the debate on public expenditure, the government faced almost certain defeat. To avoid a vote the whips used the
tactical device of moving the adjournment of the House and then
abstaining when a division was forced by the Scottish Nationalists. It
was a pretty disreputable exercise and Margaret Thatcher, as Leader
of the Opposition, was within her rights to demand an early debate
on a motion of no confidence. It was by no means certain we would
win it. There were then 311 Labour MPs, 280 Conservatives, 13
Liberals, 11 Scottish Nationalists, 8 Ulster Unionists, 3 Welsh
Nationalists, 2 Scottish Labour Party, 1 SDLP, 1 Independent Ulster
Unionist, 1 Independent Irish Republican and 1 Vanguard Unionist
Progressive Party. The Labour government, if ever faced by a
combination of all the other parties, would lose the vote by ten.

The debate was arranged for Wednesday 23 March and that
weekend the press was full of speculation about discussions between
the leader of the Liberal Party, David Steel, and Michael Foot, on
behalf of the government. Yet while this was winning all the
attention a vital hard-nosed deal was being stitched up between
Michael Foot and Enoch Powell, now an Ulster Unionist. They were
old friends, their friendship rooted in their mutual love of Parliament
and their unrealistic interpretation of parliamentary sovereignty.
They had combined frequently in the past to fight European
Community legislation and reform of the House of Lords. They
trusted each other and understood how parliamentary deals are
made. In addition, the Ulster Unionist MPs had long felt aggrieved
by their underrepresentation in the Commons. Since this was a fair
complaint, a decision to bring their constituency numbers in line

with the average constituency in Britain was a fairly simple conces-sion. After the weekend, the Prime Minister saw Jim Molyneaux, the leader of the Ulster Unionists, with Enoch Powell and Michael Foot, and promised an all-party conference under the chairmanship of Mr Speaker to examine the case for an increase in the number of Northern Ireland seats. There was no formal agreement but the understandings reached were sufficient for three Ulster Unionists to abstain. Thus was born the informal Labour–Unionist pact, which lasted until 1979. It was commented on much less than the formal Lib–Lab pact, both at the time and subsequently. Yet I believe that it was a more stable relationship and was at least as important in the survival of the Labour government.

All eyes were on the probability of the Liberals doing a deal with Labour. Pacts between political parties can take many forms. To retain power you can swap political influence for MPs' votes, to gain power you need the most MPs and that is best done by standing down candidates in key seats. With rare exceptions since 1918 both the Liberal and Labour Parties have fought shy of standing candi-dates down. The Conservatives, far more ruthless about winning and retaining power, have never shown the same restraint over either type of pact. Lord Salisbury was prepared to make a pre-election pact by standing down for Liberal Unionists under Joseph Chamberlain and Stanley Baldwin was ready to participate in a National Government under Ramsay MacDonald. Winston Churchill was always ready to work with his former Liberal colleagues. After the Second World War, Conservatives readily absorbed Liberals into the Conservative Party. But they also had an electoral pact with the Liberals in 1951 and 1955 involving four seats in Bolton and Huddersfield. Until Edward Heath, they were more than willing, despite occasional differences of policy, to link up with Ulster politicians. The SDP was ready to work in the Alliance with the Liberals but most SDP MPs would have been ready to consider a pact with the Conservatives or Labour if policy were agreed.

Looking to the next general election, which must be held by June 2010, it may be that the Liberal Democrats will decide to say publicly that they will talk to whichever party after the election has the most MPs. David Cameron and Nick Clegg had already begun to co-operate on some issues in 2008 and 2009, mainly on civil liberty issues, but there was still a lot of suspicion. Much of the suspicion related to past events, whether between the Liberals and Labour or between the Liberals and the Conservatives.

By a quirk of history, my great-grandfather was, because of a by-election in the constituency of Mid-Glamorgan, in which he lived, deeply involved with the first Lib–Lab pact, which had been agreed in 1903 between Herbert Gladstone and Ramsay MacDonald. After the 1906 election there were twenty-four Lib–Lab MPs, mainly miners from Wales, who could only be distinguished from Labour MPs by their taking of the Liberal whip. When the executive of the South Wales Miners' Federation recommended that Vernon Hartshorn, the miners' agent for the Maesteg area, should fight the parliamentary by-election in Mid-Glamorgan in 1910 for Labour, they were choosing an able and articulate critic of the then Lib–Lab pact. The Liberal chief whip, who had been involved in negotiating the memorandum with Labour, had already promised the seat to Vernon Hartshorn. But the local Liberal Association felt betrayed and in the teeth of strong opposition from the Parliamentary Liberal Party they fought and beat Labour. My great-grandfather, Alderman Llewellyn, was the honorary treasurer of the association. The Conservatives failed to contest as their candidate was away on a yacht cruise. No Liberal MP, however, came down to help in the local Liberal campaign and great damage was done to the concept of Lib-Labism, not just in Wales but in the country at large. The Conservatives began to profit from battles between Liberal and Labour candidates and virtually all Liberal–Labour co-operation had ceased by the time of the Coupon election in 1918. Lloyd George had had three Conservatives in his War Cabinet, formed in 1916, but his split with Asquith weakened the Liberals and the support of Conservative MPs was withheld in 1922. Churchill, previously a Liberal, brought Archibald Sinclair into his War Cabinet in May 1940 and was always ready to work with the Liberal Party.

On Monday 21 March, David Steel came to see the Prime Minister for a preliminary meeting. It went well and on Tuesday Michael Foot, David Steel and his Liberal colleague, John Pardoe, were in almost constant touch. Jim Callaghan also twice met with David Steel and eventually very late that night an agreement was reached between the two of them.

The Cabinet was called for noon. It was a momentous meeting. We all knew that, unless Jim had been successful in his discussions, we were going to lose the vote of confidence that night. The agreement was circulated and I read the document carefully; it seemed to me that apart from what I saw as the window-dressing of joint consultation, the key section of the agreement related to proportional representation. But I later realised that this perspective was wrong. For David Steel, it was the joint consultation which was the essence of the agreement and that was Jim Callaghan's understanding too. I suppose David Steel thought consultation would develop into more than the fig leaf that it became. But by emphasising this side of the agreement he let slip a golden opportunity to make progress on proportional representation.

The section of the agreement relating to proportional representation was incredibly weak. When Jim explained exactly what he had agreed, I was astonished that the Liberals had not been able to extract a firm government commitment to vote for proportional representation for the European Parliament. The Liberals knew that a majority of the Cabinet had already accepted that proportional representation should be in the legislation since I had personally told Jeremy Thorpe that this was the case. If they had dug their toes in and refused a pact without Labour officially supporting proportional representation for the European elections, Jim would have had to persuade the Cabinet to accept this. In my judgement the majority of the Cabinet, including Michael Foot, would have accepted this as a necessary price. I doubt if even Tony Benn would have resigned: he had stomached many more indigestible items than this over his years in Cabinet. The MPs from Northern Ireland, where there was already proportional representation, could not have objected, nor would the Scottish Nationalists.

I was doubly amazed at the agreement that David Steel had signed because I knew well that Liberals still resented the way that Labour had exploited earlier Lib–Lab pacts. People like John Pardoe were determined that the Liberals should not be taken for a ride again. They wanted something concrete and a government commitment to support proportional representation for Europe fitted the bill. So what happened? John Pardoe was clearly under the impression that he and David Steel had agreed on their sticking point – 'No proportional representation, no pact.' Yet, whatever David Steel's intention, when he met Jim late that night his resolve weakened. He allowed himself to be persuaded that Jim could not deliver a firm Cabinet commitment to proportional representation but that he personally would support it in a free vote, and so David signed up for the watered-down version that was presented to us in Cabinet. The Liberal MPs were then trapped, unable to disown the pact without disowning their leader and leaving the party in disarray.

David Steel in his defence relies on that private assurance from Jim Callaghan. This was, of course, true but it was never going to be enough to swing the issue. For proportional representation to win the day there would have had to be a whip on all Labour MPs and only a few voting against it. The Liberals had lost a chance to change the voting system.

The Liberals had had a better opportunity during the 1916–17 Speaker's conference presided over by James Lowther and set up with the support of Asquith. That conference recommended proportional representation in rural areas unanimously and the alternative vote in the boroughs by eleven votes to eight. The House of Commons then rejected proportional representation and by a majority of one supported the alternative vote, whereby voters go 1, 2, 3, 4 and so on down the ballot paper showing a preference for the candidates in a single constituency. The Lords then reinstated proportional representation and rejected the alternative vote. Lloyd George, by then Prime Minister, disliked the idea of proportional representation because he saw it as a challenge to the two-party system, then made up of Conservatives and Liberals. As the historian Lord Blake said of the Liberals who had voted against proportional representation, 'The party has been kicking its collective self ever since. And Britain has bumbled along to this day with what is virtually a unicameral sovereign legislature elected on the first-past-the-post system – the least fair, most arbitrary and least democratic of all methods of election in the democratic world.'

A lot will depend on whether the Conservative Party obtains an overall working majority at the general election of 2009 or 2010; if it does, proportional representation will remain dead for some more years. If the Conservatives were to be the largest party but without an overall majority, the Liberal Democrats could legitimately argue for a fixed term to the parliament, within which, before the next election, a referendum on proportional representation would have to be held and, if the vote was for change, legislation enacted for that forthcoming election. The Liberal Democrats could not legitimately keep Labour, if no longer the largest party, in power after 2009/2010 in any deal to legislate for proportional representation without a referendum, given that Labour promised such a referendum in their 1997 manifesto and then never acted on the commitment. The time when proportional representation could be introduced by a political deal between the parties is over. Referenda now are too well established in the UK as necessary prior to constitutional change.

It was a dramatic moment as we went round the Cabinet table, each saying whether they supported the Lib–Lab pact. I could see no point in making a long contribution so I just said, 'I support the agreement.' My main surprise was the opposition of Bruce Millan on the grounds that it would gravely damage the party. In my eyes he had always been a staunch Callaghanite and indeed Jim looked amazed. It showed the depth of scepticism towards any form of pact-making. The opposition of Peter Shore was predictable for he was implacably opposed to direct elections. Stan Orme and Tony Benn's opposition was along the traditional left-wing exclusive view that any association with any other party was always wrong. But then I was even more surprised when Albert Booth and John Silkin supported the agreement. So the Cabinet, by twenty votes to four, were in favour of the Lib–Lab pact. The Prime Minister made it clear that he would expect all members of the Cabinet to be in the Division Lobby to vote in effect for the agreement that night.

In a packed House, Mrs Thatcher's motion of no confidence was rejected by 322 votes to 298. If the Liberals had voted against us we might just have been able to persuade more Ulster Unionists to abstain. If we had not, the government would have lost by two votes. A general election would then have been held which we would have lost. I would have been in my post for thirty-two days, the shortest time of any British Foreign Secretary. I would have accomplished nothing, for all I had done so far was lay the foundations, and I would have been very lucky to hold Devonport.

★

The time of pussyfooting around over Rhodesia's independence was past. I was determined to bring UDI to an end and ensure majority rule for Zimbabwe. With the government's future now assured well into 1978, I had the necessary political authority for a trip to Africa. In the run-up to my visit, which took place in April 1977, I tried to consult as wide a range of opinion as I could. Over lunch at No. 10 with Jim Callaghan and the President of Senegal, I tried to enlist the President's help as he was influential in French-speaking Africa. That same evening I took the issue to the Parliamentary Labour Party and found them in good heart. They clearly liked the activist stance that I was taking over Rhodesia. Yet it was interesting how warmly a number of influential MPs spoke of Bishop Muzorewa: the important role he had played in mobilising opinion inside Rhodesia to convince the Pearce commission that Lord Home's initiative in the early 1970s did not carry majority support had made him many friends. I also managed to use an EEC Council of Ministers meeting in Luxembourg to lobby support for our policy among Foreign Ministers, under the mantle of what was then called Political Co-operation. One of the most interesting meetings I had was one I requested with Lord Goodman, Harold Wilson's lawyer, with whom I had worked on the pay beds issue. He had had many meetings with Ian Smith and gave me excellent advice on how to handle him. He had no doubt that Smith was a frequent stranger to the truth but the more he had his back against the wall, the more he twisted and turned. He suggested that I should propose starting off with a completely new sheet at a meeting with only the two of us present.

Given the Lib–Lab pact, a meeting with Jeremy Thorpe was an obligation, but it was also a pleasure for he was knowledgeable about Africa. Over the years, he had developed strong links with Kenneth Kaunda and on Rhodesia he warned me that the Tory right wing were just waiting for an opportunity to put a motion of censure down on me personally. Like some of my Labour colleagues he stressed the importance of Muzorewa, whom I was due to see next day. When I did, try as I might, I found it hard to believe that Muzorewa was likely to emerge as a key figure. He was doing a lot of lecturing on the Methodist circuit in the United States and seemed pretty out of touch with the younger, radical nationalists who were becoming more and more influential inside as well as outside Rhodesia.

Perhaps the most important meeting before my trip was with Cy Vance, who came through London and met with the Prime Minister and myself. Next day we had extensive discussions on a range of issues and co-ordinated what I would say on my African trip. We agreed that in Cape Town I should raise our deep anxieties about an internal settlement for Namibia which excluded nationalist leaders fighting for independence outside the country. We also decided we would both try to persuade the Shah to support our Namibian and Rhodesian initiatives. We hoped for a private threat from the Shah that he would stop supplying oil to South Africa if the UN viewpoint on Namibia were ignored.

Before flying out I had a meeting with Joshua Nkomo. He was the oldest of the nationalist leaders, a vast man with a laugh that rumbled around his large belly; friendly, earthy but shrewd. There was little doubt that he would come to a constitutional conference but he held his negotiating hand close to his chest, as one would have expected from such a veteran negotiator. Like an elephant, he had a long memory but despite his bulk moved with care and precision.

During the flight the press corps were eager to have a conference, which I conducted in the aisle. The question on the lips of every reporter was 'Are you going to Rhodesia?' All I would say at that time was that if I thought it would help I would consider it. My intention was to see Mr Smith in South Africa first and only then decide whether to go into Rhodesia, although in my own mind I was certain that I would go. No Labour Cabinet minister had visited Rhodesia since UDI in 1965, though Alec Douglas-Home, when Foreign Secretary, had gone there in 1971. When Jim Callaghan was Foreign Secretary, he had visited six African countries, including South Africa, but he had not felt it right to go to Rhodesia. He had been uneasy about me going but had agreed to the strategy.

My purpose in Africa was to win acceptance to opening discussions about a constitution for an independent Zimbabwe – to get the South Africans to put pressure on Smith and persuade the frontline Presidents to put pressure on the Patriotic Front of Nkomo and Mugabe. The first port of call was Tanzania and Debbie and I arrived at Dar es Salaam having slept well on the plane. I met Robert Mugabe there for the first time. He was like a coiled spring, tense and very prickly and also somewhat withdrawn. He was quite convinced that the conflict could only be settled by 'a bitter and bloody war', which could be 'resolved only on the battlefield'. I countered his line by telling the press that our American-backed proposals could bring majority rule to Rhodesia through 'the ballot rather than the gun', but it was painfully apparent that, after Geneva, Mugabe had lost any faith he might ever have had in diplomacy. 'The struggle might be protracted, bitter and bloody, but this is the price Zimbabweans should be prepared to pay,' he told reporters. 'Dr Owen has failed to convince us that Britain is in a position to effect the transfer of power to the people of Zimbabwe.' At that stage, it was impossible to convince him that he should talk to Mr Smith. When I raised the question of an amnesty for crimes committed since UDI he was not just adamantly opposed but outraged that the idea should even be contemplated. He and I were to return to this issue time and time again but he was implacable about the need for retribution, which made his speech of reconciliation after his ballot victory in 1980 even more remarkable.

And so we flew on to Cape Town, where we stayed with the ambassador, Sir David Scott, a seasoned, sage adviser and one on whom I relied a great deal over the years ahead. There I met Mr Smith for the first time. Because he was the head of an illegal government I never referred to him as 'Prime Minister' and relations were always formal and stiff, in keeping with his own manner. As I had planned, we went for a walk in the garden before we all sat down for the formal meeting. I suggested that he and I should open a new page and try to develop trust by talking frankly together. I would far prefer that he was rude to me directly than that he misled me behind my back. He professed to be quite unaware that I was actually intending to visit Rhodesia. Only when he realised that I really was planning to come did his mood change and we quickly agreed certain safeguards and who he would release from prison so I could see them. His problem now, he explained, was that his people were expecting him to be angry with me and to persuade me to come to Rhodesia. I said I had no objection if he wanted to make that case when the meeting started and I would listen and then concede gracefully. This is exactly what we did. So realistically did he perform that even my private secretary thought that Smith had been pretty bloody to me and was amazed when I told him that we had pre-arranged the whole thing.

What was surprising was that Smith welcomed American participation in a constitutional conference, perhaps because he was obsessed about the growth of communist influence in southern Africa and felt that America too would be disturbed by this development, perhaps because he thought that, as with Henry Kissinger's initiative, he could play off the US officials against the British. So it was announced that evening that we were changing our plans and I would fly to Rhodesia after having visited Lusaka.

Two days later I met President Kenneth Kaunda and there was none of the animosity which I had previously feared. Kenneth was emotional and friendly, yet if one had to sum up the atmosphere of our meeting in one word, it would be sceptical. He had been let down too often by Britain in his own struggle for independence during the colonial days to be totally trusting. Since UDI, he had had to watch Zambia, a newly independent country, bleed because of Britain's inability to suppress a revolt against the Crown. Unspoken was the thought that if a black government had declared UDI in Rhodesia, British military might would have crushed the revolt within days. Sadly, he was quite right: Britain's failure to act had had everything to do with its being a white revolt and the reluctance to put our armed forces in was because it meant confronting our 'kith and kin'. In 1965, with only a narrow majority and an election pending, Labour did not have the self-confidence to act. He wondered whether we now had the self-confidence to uphold the principles underpinning the Anglo-American initiative. President Kaunda's courtesy and affection for Britain always remained; his attitude was more of sorrow than of anger. He wanted to believe that I would succeed but he doubted I would. One question on which he privately wanted reassurance was whether the Prime Minister was backing me because he had picked up some scurrilous press speculation that Jim was distancing himself from the Rhodesian problem. I was able to reassure him that Jim Callaghan was fully supportive and that we would have an independent investigation of alleged sanctions-busting by BP and Shell in the 1960s under the last Labour government. It later became obvious that that government had condoned the oil companies' illegal actions.

I flew next morning into Salisbury in an RAF plane to a colony in rebellion against the Crown. Determined to distance ourselves from the illegal regime, we did not even use their official car. I stepped instead into a Rolls-Royce that had been driven up from South Africa. We stayed only thirty-seven hours, during which I met dozens of different delegations, called again on Mr Smith, went on television for a half-hour interview, managed to visit a tribal trust land and even to drink the local beer. Surprisingly the visit turned out to be a considerable success. I always spoke about the inevitability of a transfer of power. Mr Smith replied with demands for entrenched clauses in the constitution, a qualified franchise, an impartial judiciary and safeguards for white pensions, investment, land rights and the maintenance of the forces of law and order. At this stage we were still talking about the widest possible franchise, and I made it clear to him that I saw great difficulties in limiting the franchise, favouring one person, one vote.

I arrived back in London to find a mood of optimism. The press reports of my tour had been extensive and almost universally favourable. Jim Callaghan in particular was very pleased. He wrote to say it had been one of the best weeks for his government and said much the same in Cabinet. I had no specific agreement to show but the atmosphere was transformed, Geneva was now behind us and the Anglo-American initiative firmly launched. A momentum for dialogue and negotiation had been created which, though it would slow down very considerably, just about carried through to the Lancaster House conference convened by Lord Carrington in the winter of 1979.

The situation in Rhodesia deteriorated progressively in almost every regard. The level of violence in the war between the guerrilla fighters and the Rhodesian armed forces increased. With each incident I was dragged down to the House of Commons to make statements of sympathy. What it demonstrated was the necessity of having, as part of our plan, measures to keep all the different forces from fighting each other while any elections took place. I was becoming 'Dr Death' in *Private Eye*.

I had already been rebuffed by the Cabinet, as Jim Callaghan had warned me I might, over my wish to have a Commonwealth force to go into Rhodesia to supervise a ceasefire and monitor the elections. My preference for a Commonwealth force rather than one provided by the United Nations stemmed from my desire to maximise British influence and minimise the risk of a Soviet veto, which would be ever present if we brought in the UN. Denis Healey, having been involved in the decisions not to use force at the beginning of the crisis in 1965, was adamant that we should not be sucked in now. His opposition to a Commonwealth peacekeeping force was decisive in a Cabinet already reluctant to commit British forces and only too keen to be swayed towards the UN. Denis's argument played on the fear that, with a Commonwealth force, we could not avoid making a sizeable British military contribution which would have to expand if the security situation worsened and other Commonwealth contributions were shown to be inadequate. In Cabinet, my main supporter for a Commonwealth force was Michael Foot but the unlikely combination of Denis Healey, Roy Mason and Tony Benn sank such a force in favour of the second-best option of a UN force.

That the Labour Cabinet feared the responsibilities inherent in a Commonwealth force was yet another sign of the party's then chronic incapacity to understand the exercise of power. It is to Lord Carrington's credit that he convinced Margaret Thatcher and the Conservative government, as part of the Lancaster House settlement, to restore a fully fledged British governor and to support him with a Commonwealth force containing a strong British element.

The Anglo-American plan was then agreed by our two governments. First, there would have to be a ceasefire; only then and by agreement would Britain assume responsibility for governing Rhodesia. During a period of no longer than six months there would be free and fair elections on the basis of one person, one vote. All executive and legislative powers would be vested in the resident commissioner, who would also be commander in chief of both the Rhodesian armed forces and the forces of the Patriotic Front. A United Nations force, under its own command, would supervise the ceasefire and assist in maintaining security.

The next task was to get the approval of the United Nations Security Council for UN involvement and authorisation for the secretary general, Kurt Waldheim, to appoint the Indian lieutenant-general Prem Chand, whom he had chosen as his representative in discussions with Lord Carver, who had agreed to become resident commissioner. This was only done after extensive haggling in New York, where I spoke directly to Andrei Gromyko to avoid a Soviet veto. In the end they and the Chinese settled for an abstention. With the white paper detailing the constitution, agreement to the UN force and Lord Carver and Prem Chand all in place, we and the Americans had a firm, principled and credible plan which was able to withstand a constant battering, from all sides, over the next two years.

By the spring of 1978 I had become convinced that Robert Mugabe was a zealot and a fanatic, espousing Maoist communism while secretly attending mass in Maputo. His Jesuit upbringing meant he was fatefully conflicted and in my judgement not the best person to become the first elected leader of a new independent Zimbabwe. With the Zambian and Nigerian governments in the lead I privately conducted months of secret diplomacy with Joshua Nkomo to try and have him installed for an interim period as Prime Minister of Zimbabwe, supported by the Rhodesian military, with Ian Smith stepping down. All this was revealed in 2009 following the release of documents under the thirty-year rule. The initiative came unstuck in the late summer of 1978.

The best decision I made in my entire time as Foreign Secretary was not to convene a Lancaster House conference in November 1978. Everything was ready. The actual conference arrangements had all been thought through. The draft constitution was even printed. For the first time for years, Smith wanted to come to a conference, in itself grounds for suspicion. Both Jim Callaghan and President Carter were under growing domestic pressure to endorse a conference. I was too, I admit, sorely tempted, for the Conservative opposition strategy, revealed in a two-day debate on Rhodesia, was to paint me as the obstacle to a conference and to urge Jim Callaghan to chair it. So I knew that if I agreed to call a conference I would simultaneously outflank the Conservatives and put myself centre stage. The world's attention would be on London, and the gambler in me was eager to act.

At that most vulnerable moment Sir Anthony Duff, who oversaw African policy in the Foreign Office, asked to see me with Lord Carver. I had come to have profound respect for the judgement of both Duff and Carver. They had one simple message: 'You, Secretary of State, have always said that you would not convene a conference until you were reasonably sure that it would succeed. You know, and we know, that a conference now will fail.' Sadly, I knew in my heart that what they were saying was true. Rarely for me, I just listened and offered very few comments, except to say I would think about it. When they had gone I looked out through the windows into the November evening over St James's Park. I knew what I had to do, I had to kill off an early conference.

Once I had accepted this hard fact, it did not prove too hard to achieve. With Duff's support, I could carry Whitehall, and the way out with the public and the politicians lay in Jim Callaghan's wish to appoint a politician to report back to him about the feasibility of a conference. I thought it would be possible to defuse the issue by convincing that person and others that there was no choice but to be patient. The key was the person Jim chose: a wise one could only report one way. I went over to No. 10 to discuss possible candidates with Jim Callaghan. I urged him to appoint Cledwyn Hughes, who had political sensitivity in abundance and also the experience of being Commonwealth Secretary. Fortunately, Jim agreed. From that day on, I never doubted that Cledwyn would find against an early conference. What is more important, he did so in a way that carried conviction across party lines in the House of Commons. On 30 November Carver ceased to be the resident commissioner designate. I went with him to No. 10 and Jim thanked him for all he had done. All of us were aware that a settlement in Rhodesia would have to wait until the general election, even though I never admitted that this was what we were doing. Essentially, even from September 1977 to May 1979, I was waiting for the power struggle within Rhodesia to reach deadlock.

I had always hoped that Peter Carrington would succeed me if the Conservatives won the election, for he understood Africa better than any of their senior politicians. He had used his non-executive directorship of Rio Tinto Zinc to keep himself well informed about Africa and whenever I had briefed him confidentially I had found him totally realistic. Flying back together on the plane from Jomo Kenyatta's funeral, we had talked very frankly. At one stage when we were looking for a secretary general for NATO to replace Joseph Luns, who was outstaying his welcome, I approached him, with the agreement of Cy Vance, to see if he would accept the job. He asked for time to go away and, as he put it, 'consult his mistress'. He came back and politely refused; and when I said, 'That means you have been offered my job,' his eyes had a tell-tale twinkle. So when the election was lost and I heard that he was going to take my place, I was delighted but not surprised.

Lord Carrington deserved all his success, first at the Commonwealth conference in Lusaka, and then at the Lancaster House conference which followed. Field Marshal Lord Carver wrote in his autobiography, *Out of Step*, that one of the principal differences between Carrington's Lancaster House settlement and my Anglo-American proposals was that he made no attempt to disband or disarm any of the military forces on either side until after the elections, when a new government came to power. It was a gamble that paid off, helped by an overwhelming victory for Mugabe and much wise handling of the pre- and post-election period by Lord Soames, the interim governor. Mugabe presided over a remarkable initial reconciliation, but I was right about his character flaws: within six months he had made an agreement for the North Koreans to train a separate army brigade, the 5th Brigade, which a few years later repressed and massacred the Ndebele in Mashonaland. He sidelined Nkomo and pursued a course of becoming a dictator, resulting in the eventual economic destruction of Zimbabwe.

In Cabinet in May Jim announced that with extreme reluctance he would agree to the Cabinet having a free vote on the bill on direct elections for the European Parliament which he wanted to present to Parliament after Whitsun. Normally the rule of collective responsibility means that all members of the government vote as one body. I, having written privately to Jim saying that he had no option but to concede to Michael Foot on this issue, supported his decision; though it would be difficult in Europe I thought I could persuade my colleagues on the Council of Foreign Ministers that the legislation for direct elections would pass and that we were not back-sliding. Michael Foot, ever one for a historical parallel, reminded the Cabinet that Lloyd George and Asquith had voted in different lobbies on the Conciliation Bill. No doubt Michael, with his Ebbw Vale constituency, related to Lloyd George, but a less Asquithian figure than Jim Callaghan, an abstemious Baptist, it would be hard to find. Jim then made it clear to those who were against the bill that he hoped they would abstain.

A free vote had, of course, already been conceded in the context of the Lib–Lab pact on the method of electing MEPs. To his credit, Michael did not personally make use of this concession, even though it was available to him. When the legislation on direct elections came up he, like other Cabinet dissenters, abstained on the vote of overall principle in second reading on 24 November, but voted with Jim Callaghan in favour of proportional representation on 13 December. I am sure that this was more through personal loyalty to Jim than any belief in proportional representation. He would have known that first-past-the-post was going to be chosen by the House so he could feel safe in solidarity with Jim. Perhaps, having been party to the negotiations with the Liberals, he also felt it would ease future relations with them if he voted for proportional representation. It is hard to estimate how many more of the Cabinet would have voted against the Lib–Lab pact itself if they had thought they would have to vote for proportional representation as part of the bargain. Only fourteen of the Cabinet voted for proportional representation to elect the MEPs. Tony Benn voted against and the rest abstained.

Our presidency of the European Community ended with the European Council in London on 29–30 June 1977. Nothing much happened. Valéry Giscard d'Estaing, aided and abetted by Helmut Schmidt, expressed his antagonism once more to Jimmy Carter on civil nuclear power and Jim defended the US President stoutly. I cannot say that our presidency was a great success, but nor was it the disaster it sometimes looked as if it might have been. Given the continuing divisions on Europe within the Cabinet, most ministers had co-operated fairly well and many had enjoyed chairing their specialised councils. While some of the animosity against the Community in the Labour Party was abating, we were far from having a committed, coherent line. I strongly welcomed Jim Callaghan's decision to have a special Cabinet meeting on our European position at the end of July. He asked me to ensure that the papers were written by me and not the Foreign Office. I decided to involve his staff, particularly his political adviser, Tom McNally, in the preparation of the papers for I knew the department's draft contribution would be bland and likely to go down badly with those colleagues who wanted to feel that there were some political objectives underpinning our strategy.

On Thursday 28 July I went to a lunch which Harry Walston, a prosperous farmer and Labour peer, had fixed up in his Albany flat. It was the first time the Jenkinsites had met since I had become Foreign Secretary and I thought I would look a bit of a prima donna if I did not turn up. It was a good thing that I did for Bill Rodgers had clearly briefed Roy Jenkins about the Cabinet papers. Roy launched into characteristically oblique and coded criticism of people who were backsliding on Europe, without mentioning who he was attacking. Essentially he objected to favouring enlargement because it would lead to a loosening and slowing of the momentum towards union. I had no objection to being criticised, but he was in danger of forgetting that, as president of the Commission, he represented a different interest. So I pointed out that Roy's interests were not from now on necessarily always going to be identical with British interests. I also argued the anti-federalist case and it did no harm to have the issues aired. The group was not wholly on Roy's side and there was a new petulance in his attitude which not everyone liked. Roy knew perfectly well that the pure milk of Euro-federalism could not possibly be imbibed, either by the Labour Party or by the British electorate. Yet he was already showing that being away in Brussels somewhat dulls one's political reflexes at home, and in any case he no longer had to worry about inner Labour Party arguments.

I thought little more of the meeting until I was telephoned by David Watt; he told me that he wanted to write in his *Financial Times* column next day about the forthcoming Cabinet meeting. He gave me the impression that he knew exactly what was in my Cabinet papers and he put it to me that it was being said by my supposed friends that I was chickening out of my commitment to the European Community. This was such a travesty of what I had written that I overreacted and rebutted my critics point by point, in the process revealing practically everything in the Cabinet papers. Though a great friend, David was also a skilled journalist and beguiled me into blowing the gaff. I had just experienced Denis Healey's leaking to Peter Jenkins of the *Guardian* that I had been overturned by the Cabinet over a Commonwealth peacekeeping

force for Rhodesia, so I was a bit touchy. Next morning I arrived in
the Foreign Office to find my private secretary, Ewen Fergusson,
ominously formal. 'The Prime Minister, Secretary of State, is very
annoyed.' 'Why the hell is he annoyed?' I said. Ewen produced the
*Financial Times* with David Watt's article; a quick reading showed that
he had given a very good précis of the papers I had put to Cabinet
and the criticisms of some of my pro-Market Cabinet colleagues. I
went over to see Jim at No. 10, trying to appear relaxed but inwardly
feeling like an errant schoolboy. He was in his 'honest copper' role,
adopting a 'What's all this 'ere?' tone. I thought the best thing to do
was to be totally honest. I apologised for the article, said it was all my
fault and explained how frustration had led me to say too much. Jim
was rather nonplussed to find a Cabinet minister actually admitting
responsibility for a press story. He was sympathetic to the position
that I had been put in but he was also angry and talked about
cancelling the Cabinet meeting. Tony Benn, in his *Diaries 1977–80*
(pages 201–6), describes what then happened as one of the most
remarkable Cabinets he had ever attended and, give or take a little,
his is an excellent account.

The passion aroused over the years by Britain's membership of the
European Community stemmed from an incipient tension over
federalism. The question of federalism had been raised in 1962 by
Gaitskell. It had been there in the background through the 1970–71
negotiations, but Edward Heath had denied any federalist intention
at every stage. It was argued by those anti the EEC in the referendum
but the public saw the question in simple terms: whether to stay in
or come out.

It is not surprising that the EU is in 2009 still a divisive issue for
people in the UK. A significant number, in my view correctly, want to
retain the essentials of our nationhood and will fight to do so.
Sovereignty is not an absolute but a matter of degree. As I had said in
my own speech to Parliament at the time of entry on 26 October 1971,
it is 'foolish to try to sell the concept of the EEC and not admit that
this means giving up some sovereignty. Of course it does, and I believe
it rightly does. I believe this is one of the central appeals of it.' The skill
is to voluntarily surrender and pool such sovereignty as is necessary to
maintain the coherence of the EU, but to still retain in 2009 the sinews
of nationhood. As the European Union strives for greater unity, the

wise politicians will know what are the essentials of nationhood that must not be eroded. It was de Gaulle who in the Luxembourg compromise developed the ultimate safeguard of a nation's vital interests once invoked acting in effect as a veto. It was later upheld by François Mitterrand's government in the French National Assembly prior to ratification of the Maastricht Treaty in 1992. It cannot be invoked lightly or often, but that it is still there will concentrate minds and help negotiations after the election due before June 2010.

The outcome of our all-day Cabinet meeting was that, despite the passions aroused, we now had an official government policy which was firmly pro-European, anti-federalist and committed to enlargement of the Community to include Greece, Portugal and Spain. It was Jim's and my task to sell that package first to the Labour Party at the autumn conference and then to the country.

The emotional key to unlock the left's suspicion and hostility to the Community was Spain. To Jack Jones, then the powerful leader of the TGWU, Spain was the symbol of international socialism. As a young man, he had fought in the Civil War against Franco. If I could use Spanish entry to swing his heart and that of Michael Foot, the Labour conference could be won. On 5 September I flew with Debbie to Madrid as part of my strategy for demonstrating the Labour government's commitment to early Spanish entry. The three key people who ensured that Spain moved from fascism under Franco to democracy within the European Community were the Prime Minister, Adolfo Suárez, the Socialist Leader of the Opposition and later Prime Minister, Felipe González, and King Juan Carlos. Each in his own way was impressive. They all represented a younger generation, but the person who played the crucial role was Suárez. Of all the heads of government I met during my time as Foreign Secretary, he was the one personality without whom one felt the government would collapse. In this case that meant the transition to democracy would not succeed. For those early years of transition he exercised iron will and determination. Without his inside knowledge of the old Franco regime he would not have been able to bridge the massive gap between those whose instincts and attitudes had been shaped by decades of fascism and the new generation of young, idealistic, democratic Europeans. He had established a friendship with Felipe González and he spoke openly to me about how they both realised that the Socialist Party's time was coming but that it must not come too early. When Suárez resigned as Prime Minister in circumstances which have never been fully explained, exhausted and frustrated, it fell to the King to bridge the gap. He alone held the loyalty of the armed forces and stopped a military takeover. Only when that military threat was averted could Felipe González speak and act for the new generation of Spaniards, irrespective of their political inclinations. But this was for the future. In 1977 the issue was simple. Should the UK help Spain to enter the EEC and brush aside the pessimistic prophecies of economic gloom from France and within the Commission, where Spain was still seen as a millstone round the neck of the Community? The answer was 'yes', and we were a crucial help.

There were dire predictions from many quarters about the weakness of the Spanish economy, its protectionist nature and the domination of the state-owned industries. Very few people anticipated the remarkable speed with which the Spanish economy adjusted within the European Community. The British Labour government and the German Social Democratic–Liberal coalition government strongly supported entry for political reasons. We accepted that there would be economic problems but felt that without the buttressing of Community membership the ever present risk of a military coup would almost certainly be realised. Unlike NATO, which, in my view wrongly, never made membership or its continuation dependent on being a demo-cracy (for example, allowing Greece to remain a member while under military rule between 1967 and 1974), the Treaty of Rome is quite clear: no country can remain a member of the European Community if it has abandoned democracy. I urged Felipe González to use Socialist International to mobilise opinion in favour of Spain's entry and arranged for him to come to London, as Leader of the Opposition in Spain, on an official visit.

At a Foreign Affairs Council meeting in Brussels on 20 September we firmed up on Spanish entry. The French feared the effect of Spanish agriculture on their southern voters, but in 1977 Giscard d'Estaing was very keen that Greece should join, and eventually that was the deal: all three – Greece, Portugal and Spain – or none, though the French were given one concession, that Greece could come in earlier.

At that time, my attention was constantly switching from Europe to Africa. I left that council meeting in Brussels early to fly back for a memorial service for Steve Biko, the young South African leader of the Black Consciousness Movement. I had admired what he had been saying and writing in South Africa and wanted to demonstrate that his death was not going to be ignored by the Western democracies. My gesture was appreciated, and talking to people afterwards, most of those in St Paul's crypt were amazed at my presence. It was the worldwide sense of outrage at the way Biko had been battered to death in a prison cell that led to the UN Security Council passing a mandatory arms embargo against South Africa in November 1977 on the basis that apartheid represented a threat to peace.

The Labour Party conference started on Monday 3 October in Brighton. For the first time, I was standing for a place on the Constituency Section of the National Executive of the Labour Party. The result was announced as usual on the Tuesday morning. I polled 176,000 votes, which was more than I had expected. Jack Ashley just managed to get on as the seventh member with 287,000 votes and I was very pleased for him. Dennis Skinner was the runner-up, followed by Neil Kinnock, Peter Shore and then me. Jim Callaghan, in the speech that followed, spoke bluntly to the conference about the need to cut inflation, which was still running at 16 per cent. 'Please don't support us with general expressions of good will and kind words, and then undermine us through unjustified wage increases or price increases – either back us or sack us.' We had to a considerable extent defused the debate on the Common Market by issuing a letter from Jim Callaghan to the National Executive on the eve of the conference. I had sweated blood with Tom McNally and others in helping Jim to draft this letter, which followed up the all-day Cabinet meeting. The letter was firm in rejecting any possibility of British withdrawal from the Community. It also warned the party about the damage that was being done to Britain's position by constant speculation as to our basic commitment. Roy Jenkins, predictably, did not like the emphasis on a loose Community coming with enlargement and the limiting of the powers of the European Parliament. But he was far less critical than when I had first embarked on trying to defuse the issue of our membership within the party.

It was left to Michael Foot to sum up the debate and divert attention from the hostile NEC document on the merits of which Tony Benn had regaled the Cabinet. Michael, a veteran of the Bevanite clash with Gaitskell, nevertheless evoked memories of Hugh Gaitskell's speech to the conference in 1962 against a federalist Community. He also helpfully laid particular stress on the Community as a vehicle for continuing negotiations on the matters which Jim Callaghan's letter had placed on the agenda. The strategy of emphasising enlargement worked, for, he said, 'I do not see how I, as an international socialist, or this movement, as an international movement, could say that we were going to slam the door in the faces of our comrades from Greece and Portugal and Spain.' This was the most forthcoming statement about British membership that I have ever known Michael Foot to make. The main interest on foreign affairs surrounded Rhodesia; I spoke in the debate on southern Africa and the conference was broadly content with the policy I was pursuing.

On the Saturday morning I flew to the Belgian 'Schloss Gymnich' weekend at Villiers-le-Temple, where I was asked to report on the Labour Party conference. Because of my relief at having emerged unscathed from my internal battle, I was probably too complacent about the effect of the Callaghan letter on other Foreign Ministers. What sounded all right in Brighton was less attractive in Belgium for, deliberately, it contained little of the Euro-speak which they all used about union and unity. Although Hans-Dietrich Genscher was a little critical in our meeting, he gave a far more hostile briefing to the press before leaving us early that Saturday evening. On Sunday morning I had to sort out the controversy he had left behind with the British press and also answer questions about Reg Prentice, who had decided to join the Conservative Party.

I talked about Reg to Roy Jenkins, who was at the meeting, for he knew him better than I and had actually spoken for Reg with Shirley Williams at a riotous meeting in Newham Town Hall in September 1975. Prentice had had a miserable life with his left-wing dominated local party and one could well understand why he had decided to leave. It was, however, one of the first signs of the importance Margaret Thatcher would give to attracting converts to the Conservative Party. The Labour Party never understood that this was a clever strategy, diminishing Labour in the eyes of the electorate. They only compounded the effect by accusing people like Reg Prentice of being traitors. Margaret Thatcher's wooing in opposition of Labour supporters like Paul Johnson, a former editor of the *New Statesman*, and Hugh Thomas, the young historian who had written a brilliant book on the Spanish Civil War, began to set an intellectual climate in which the exciting ideas were felt to be coming from the right. She also persuaded Woodrow Wyatt, the former Labour MP, of her worth, which had a considerable dividend in his journalism for the *News of the World* and the *Times* and his contacts on the left. It was subtle politics, while being fiercely party political, to appear open intellectually to ideas from a broader base.

That Sunday afternoon, 9 October, I left Bierset in Belgium and flew direct to Moscow. I arrived not really knowing what sort of reception to expect. Anglo-Russian relations had not been warm for some time. The freeze had started when Sir Alec Douglas-Home had expelled ninety Soviet diplomats and officials in September 1971. At a meeting with Andrei Gromyko in New York a fortnight earlier he had decided not to veto in the Security Council our resolution over Rhodesia and this was perhaps a sign that they wanted to thaw our relationship. Gromyko was at the foot of the steps to greet me and from that moment it became clear that the Russians were laying down the red carpet. Driving into Moscow, he pointed out the tank memorial marking the point that the German Panzer divisions had reached, a timely reminder of why Soviet military chiefs overinsured. When Gromyko and I signed the Anglo-Soviet Agreement on the Prevention of an Accidental Outbreak of Nuclear War, not only did President Brezhnev turn up but all the senior military figures and a number of other Politburo members. This was their way of indicating that they wanted improved relations. The treaty itself was of no great significance, the US and France already having signed something similar. What the Russians wanted was to convince us that their anxieties about Jimmy Carter's attitude to the Strategic Arms Limitation Talks (SALT) were genuine. They had carefully noted Jim Callaghan's developing friendship with Jimmy Carter and now they wanted us to use our influence.

Soviet–US relations were bad that autumn, the main source of tension between the two superpowers being SALT. In the spring of 1977 Cy Vance had gone to Moscow to put a new approach to Gromyko for the SALT II negotiations, which were the follow-up to SALT I, signed by Nixon and Brezhnev in 1972. Jimmy Carter wanted 'deep cuts' in the number of strategic weapons. It was a proposal somewhat similar to that which Mikhail Gorbachev tried on President Reagan at Reykjavik in October 1986. But in 1977 the old guard, who then dominated the Politburo in Moscow, were appalled. They thought that Carter was out to trick them and was going back on the Vladivostok agreement, made with President Ford. Cy Vance had sensed that the Russian bureaucracy would not like this proposition and had won from Jimmy Carter the right, if it was turned down, to put forward an alternative approach. Unfortunately, by the time Cy put forward this alternative, Gromyko had just switched off and refused to do anything for the next few months other than rubbish the deep cuts proposal as a 'cheap and shady manoeuvre'.

I found Gromyko readier than hitherto to accept that Jimmy Carter's intentions towards arms control were at least genuine but he was still perplexed about the emphasis that was being given to human rights. I was in a cleft stick. All my instincts sympathised with Carter's wish to elevate human rights and I was not afraid of embarrassing the Soviet Union. But I also wanted, as did Vance, substantive progress on arms control. Up to a point, we could aspire to both. But even though there was no explicit linkage, implicitly we did face choices. If forced to choose, I was more concerned then about the troubling build-up of nuclear weapons. We in Britain also, for the first time, were represented directly in the negotiations for a comprehensive test ban treaty and we wanted progress in this area as well. Our main fear was nuclear proliferation, particularly in Pakistan and South Africa. Much of my visit was spent in trying to assess the tolerances on these issues and trying to weigh up how hard we could push in one area without adversely affecting others. My personal problem was that I was much more hostile to Soviet communism than Jim Callaghan and the mainstream of Labour Party thinking. The Soviet military's attempt to starve Berlin in 1947, to suppress the Hungarians' bid for freedom in 1956 and to snuff out the Dubček reforms in Czechoslovakia in 1968 were ever present memories for me. The Union of Soviet Socialist Republics, once described as 'a lie in every word', was an empire put together by violence and held together by terror. Reagan was not wrong when he called it an 'evil empire'. It might have been imprudent, but it was accurate. I can see no redeeming features in Leninism or Stalinism. The world has rightly never forgotten Nazi crimes and the evil of the Holocaust, but I had for a long time been amazed at the way the world ignored Soviet communism's record of mass murder and bloody suppression of ethnic minorities. Now under Brezhnev, the Soviet economy was stagnant and its totalitarian party corrupt. I had to deal with these people within the diplomatic niceties but I despised and distrusted them. I never doubted that both Brezhnev and Gromyko would not hesitate to suppress or invade another country in their sphere of influence, so when the invasion of Afghanistan came in 1979, it was no surprise. Why Carter was so shocked I could never understand. The Russians were afraid of Islamic fundamentalism with so many Muslims within their empire; their influence in Afghanistan was longstanding and they were not prepared to stand by while it was overturned, as had happened to the West with the toppling of the Shah earlier in 1979.

On human rights Gromyko was as dour as usual, resenting our intervention in what he considered to be internal Soviet affairs. He listened to my representations on Sakharov and others and promised to look at the list of people we wanted them to release so they could travel to the West, but he left me under no doubt that any concessions would be made from pure cynicism, merely as a device for improving British press comment and public attitudes to the USSR. To entertain our delegations, Gromyko and his wife gave an informal supper party followed by Russian folk singing. It turned out to be a lively and enjoyable evening, with Gromyko totally relaxed and joining in the songs. The inscrutable mask was allowed to drop and I saw a different facet to his personality. But that he was ready to acquiesce in brutal suppression I never doubted.

The word 'détente' had been strongly criticised by the right wing in America in the latter days of President Ford's period in office and the hawks were beginning to criticise President Carter for identifying with détente. In 1989 the world saw that détente had, over twenty-five years, contributed to a more stable and safer East–West relationship. What President Carter was trying to do in championing human rights twelve years earlier was immensely important. We had to rescue the seventh principle of the Helsinki Final Act, which pledged the thirty-five signatory states to uphold human rights and fundamental freedoms and which the Russians were trying to bury. Our task over the next few decades was to move that commitment from an aspiration in some countries to a reality. In the case of the Soviet Union, since it had never even been an aspiration but a cynical commitment undertaken with no intention of fulfilment, we had to devise a political strategy which would provide incentives for the Soviets to implement reforms and disincentives if they continued abusing human rights. In the first speech I made as Foreign Secretary, I said that Britain would take its stand on human rights in every corner of the globe but we would not discriminate and we would apply the same standards and judgements to communist countries as we did to Chile, Uganda and South Africa. I warned that in many areas we were dealing with entrenched attitudes which, in the nature of things, would not change overnight, but that the Final Act was already seen as an inspiration and a point of reference, and I drew attention to the signatories of Charter 77 in Czechoslovakia.

In retrospect, the push on human rights from the Western democracies which started in 1977 was a critical influence on Václav Havel's ability to mobilise the peaceful protest in Czechoslovakia which won the country its freedom. The fall of the Berlin Wall in 1989 became, like 1848, the Springtime of Nations. It could not have occurred so quickly had there not been a past history of patriotism, pluralism and market economies. But nor could it have occurred if the Western democracies had accepted the Soviet interpretation of the Helsinki Final Act. A series of review conferences and a whole range of protests and sanctions had forced the Soviet Union to realise that it did not have *carte blanche* to ignore human rights.

Nothing in my period as Foreign Secretary gave me as much intellectual satisfaction as trying to develop this strategy for achieving greater individual freedom. Of course there were numerous inconsistencies in the British and Western approaches, and the closet supporters of Soviet communism would always seize upon them. They would use our support for the Shah, our readiness to talk to the Argentines or our trade with South Africa as a way of devaluing our criticism of Brezhnev. After the invasion of Afghanistan, when the Third World turned against the Soviet Union, even members of the Politburo began to recognise that they could not ignore criticism.

We were picking up straws in the wind that Yury Andropov, head of the KGB, was aware that Soviet propaganda was becoming less effective as more countries began to see that the Soviet Empire was in decline. Perestroika and glasnost did not arrive with Gorbachev – they were first introduced when Andropov became General Secretary – and they had a firm base in the realpolitik of the KGB. This should never be forgotten in interpreting the history of the 1980s. The decision to retrench to the boundaries of the USSR, to pull out of Afghanistan and pull back from eastern Europe was KGB-led and owed nothing to respect for democracy. Yet still in the twenty-first century, with Soviet communism dead, some people react negatively to anyone with KGB connections. This is too simplistic: often these people were reformers and in many cases, relatively speaking, still are.

The insistent demands of the Western democracies on individual cases were in the 1970s starting to have an impact. Gromyko might look at the ceiling every time I mentioned Andrei Sakharov and try to pretend he was not listening, but, provided we gauged the tolerances correctly, we could push them a little further at each stage. In 1978 I published a book called *Human Rights*, an unusual event for a Foreign Secretary given that every word had to be cleared by the various government departments. It stimulated some debate. At times the language used and the attitudes struck by ourselves and the United States differed, and the French and the Germans too had their own style and understandably made different estimates of what was and was not tolerable. This was quite helpful in that the Soviet Union had to respond in different ways and could not portray it simply as Western propaganda. Inevitably, when arms control negotiations were at crucial stages, human rights pressures were reduced. But by encouraging the development of human rights pressures from non-governmental organisations and individuals, I hoped that the pressure from public opinion would be maintained on the Soviet Union even when governments might be relaxing theirs. It began to be accepted that governments could not always act at the same tempo and intensity as individuals or pressure groups. But if they co-operated each could reinforce the other. It became fashionable during Reagan's presidency to denigrate President Carter, but for raising the profile of human rights and for being ready to risk the ire of the Soviet Union in their defence, the world owes Carter an immeasurable debt.

At the European Council meeting in Copenhagen on 7 April 1978, Helmut Schmidt developed his ideas for a new monetary system for Europe. This did not come as a total surprise. But what did surprise Jim Callaghan and the Treasury official who had come to Denmark specifically for this issue was the boldness of the actual proposals. We in Britain had been tending to explain what was happening in terms of window-dressing to the existing 'snake in the tunnel' currency arrangement so as to make it easier for France to join. It soon became clear that Schmidt's scheme was capable of developing into more than just a Deutschmark zone. While Jim Callaghan wanted currency stability, he was more worried about the dollar and felt that concentrating on the European currencies was too narrow a focus. Also he claimed that in Schmidt's system a strong Deutschmark would pull sterling up and do political damage to the British economy in the run-up to an election. When, next morning, Helmut Schmidt, Valéry Giscard d'Estaing and Jim Callaghan met for breakfast it was clear that France was going to join and Jim reserved the British position. Talking to him over that weekend, I inferred that he was not prepared to risk the row in the Labour Party that would undoubtedly come if we were to join the European Monetary System (EMS) before the election.

At the Bremen European Summit on 6 July the EMS was moved further forward and I began to feel that Jim Callaghan was becoming much more ambivalent about the consequences of not joining the scheme. He still felt that the internal Labour Party politics made joining inadvisable, but I sensed that, with the Bonn summit imminent, he knew he would not be in a strong position to argue for worldwide currency stability while dragging his feet on the European proposals. Moreover, the Americans seemed increasingly favourable to the EMS. In fact, at the Bonn G7 summit Carter sounded less enthusiastic than we had anticipated. Eventually agreement on a co-ordinated package was reached, with Helmut Schmidt conceding a higher target for German growth than at one time looked likely. We will never know whether this economic programme could have achieved its objectives because it was dealt a massive blow by the oil price rise in early 1979. I suspected that Jim's emphasis at the summit on global economic management tended to exaggerate the capacity of governments to deliver, and that what was needed was much more month-to-month co-operation between finance ministers and their national banks. As in London the year before, the Bonn summit was mainly important for the opportunity to ease some of the tensions between Helmut Schmidt and Jimmy Carter.

All this time British officials were involved in discussions about the development of the EMS, even though Jim had made it clear to Helmut Schmidt and Valéry Giscard d'Estaing that he was not going to join. It was assumed initially that we would have nothing to do with the system but a paper was put up to me suggesting that Britain should join the EMS but not the Exchange Rate Mechanism (ERM). In effect that meant standing aside from the fundamental element, a commitment to keep one's currency from fluctuating beyond certain bands. I was mulling over this possibility when Jim Callaghan passed a note across the Cabinet table during our meeting on Thursday 21 September to ask if I would have lunch with him at the Athenaeum. Prime Ministers are automatically given membership of this club, though Jim hardly ever used it. We were due to fly out to Kano in Nigeria next day to meet President Kaunda and we used the lunch, accompanied by Ken Stowe, Jim's principal private secretary, to think through our strategy for what promised to be an emotional and rather difficult meeting. We feared Kenneth Kaunda was about to purchase Soviet air defences to stop the Rhodesian Air Force violating Zambian air space and putting their troops in to hit targets in Lusaka. This humiliation had already been inflicted and the President was determined to prevent it happening again.

After lunch, Jim decided to walk back through St James's Park and he motioned to Ken to hang back so that we could talk privately. He then brought up the issue of the EMS. He was concerned about a speech which Denis Healey had made the day before in Canada which appeared to argue that we should join the ERM. Denis was soon due to speak to the IMF in Washington. Jim reiterated his view that the party would not wear entry to the ERM and that it would have to wait until after the election. I suggested the possibility of joining the EMS but not the ERM. Jim pondered this for a moment and then asked me what I thought Denis's attitude would be. I thought Denis, in view of what he had said in Canada, could be persuaded, and Jim suggested that I get my Foreign Office officials to square the Treasury officials. We felt that we could perhaps then sell this somewhat ingenious approach to the party. Later Denis agreed and Jim managed to push the distinction between joining the EMS, but standing aside from the ERM, through the Cabinet in early November. He cleverly did this by first getting everyone to accept that we wanted a zone of monetary stability, then that we should commit ourselves to helping to achieve this, but that we should not accept any obligations restricting our own freedom to manage the sterling exchange rate as we thought fit. I was doubtful whether all the Cabinet members really understood what we were actually going to do, and suspected that Jim had squared Peter Shore earlier. It was the ERM which was the element in the EMS which Peter was most adamantly opposed to and he certainly knew exactly what was happening for he was always vigilant and well informed on any aspect of policy involving the Community. I do not believe, given the political climate at the end of 1978, that we could have gone any closer to being a full member of the EMS, and that it was an achievement to come as far as we did. This separation of the issues, with joining the currency kept distinct from joining in with economic co-ordination, was pursued by John Major over the Maastricht Treaty in 1991.

The Parliamentary Labour Party was very uneasy about the EMS issue. Well over 100 backbench Labour MPs signed an early day motion against it and at a meeting of the PLP there was an attempt to restrict Jim's freedom to sign up for any arrangement; he had to insist vigorously on the government's right to settle during the give-and-take of a Community negotiation. The Irish government, meanwhile, had cleverly winkled extra financial support out of Germany and France as their price for signing up for full EMS membership at the EEC summit in early December. Prior to the Paris summit, a green paper was published on EMS which the

Labour Party NEC predictably attacked. We signed the EMS agreement in Paris and Giscard d'Estaing presented all the signatories with the first minted ECUs. Eventually Parliament agreed that we would be associated with the development of the European Currency Unit and we made up our national share of gold deposits and committed dollar reserves. This ensured that the ECU had sufficient backing from all nine countries. The great advantage of this compromise was that the necessary procedural hurdles were passed by the Labour government for full membership at a later date. When, under a Conservative government, Britain belatedly joined the ERM in October 1990, no new authority was required and entry was fixed up quickly and conveniently over the weekend. We were to come out of the ERM even more quickly on Black Wednesday, 16 September 1992.

In 1978 nuclear strategic issues began to haunt European politics and cause tense relations with the United States, which remained until the IMF Treaty was negotiated in 1986. In 1977 Helmut Schmidt, in a speech to the International Institute for Strategic Studies in London, drew attention to the build-up of the Soviet SS-20s and argued for the need to maintain a Euro-strategic nuclear balance. Hitherto the conventional wisdom, which I supported, had been that the strategic balance was maintained globally and we had no need to reach a balance only within the European region. In March 1978, the French Foreign Minister expressed my own sentiments about Schmidt's speech when he said that to endorse the concept of a Euro-strategic nuclear balance was the 'equivalent to recognising that the central, strategic forces of the US do not protect western Europe'. Even so, we in Britain, France and the US realised that the very fact that Germany, and particularly Schmidt, a former Defence Minister, felt so anxious about the Soviet build-up of SS-20s meant that it would be necessary to look at the whole question of modernising existing nuclear weapons in Europe. But for me the strength of the case for modernising was not primarily to match Soviet SS-20s but to join the US global deterrent firmly to Europe. It was in this mood that most of the European countries in NATO had supported the idea of the enhanced radiation weapon or neutron bomb. Some unfortunate publicity had portrayed in very simplistic terms the neutron bomb as killing people but not damaging buildings. This not surprisingly provoked an emotive public debate. While CND took it up in the UK, their protests were containable. But in Germany Helmut Schmidt began to come under considerable pressure from some Social Democrat MPs in his party who pressed him to refuse to deploy the neutron bomb on German territory. Schmidt, assured by the US Defence Secretary that it was essential, fought and won a battle with his own party in support of the neutron bomb. Only then did he discover that Jimmy Carter had serious reservations. In early 1978, which had been declared UN Disarmament Year, Carter, on finding that the Soviet Union was seizing on the neutron bomb as a tool for its propaganda, sensed that the Soviets were likely to win that propaganda battle. Once he was briefed that NATO was itself divided he began to backtrack. The British Ministry of Defence was all in favour of the neutron bomb, though I was not. Cy Vance, like me, had gone along with the military. In my case it was because I had more important battles ahead of me over British nuclear strategy. With Jim Callaghan supporting Fred Mulley, I judged it wiser to acquiesce since my doubts stemmed from a more fundamental and longstanding questioning about the wisdom of deploying any tactical nuclear weapons, particularly nuclear artillery. I had long believed that short-range weapons were both dangerous and unnecessary and should be the first weapon system to be negotiated away. They were dangerous on many grounds but particularly because they could be overrun in a border dispute and commanders were then faced by the 'lose or use' dilemma. They were unnecessary because, with the pinpoint accuracy of the modern strategic nuclear missile, and with the new technology for cruise, one could plan to fire into the European theatre from submarines, aircraft or land bases without having nuclear weapons stationed near the East–West frontier. Cy Vance had told me that he wanted the neutron bomb like 'a hole in the head'. But the sudden manner of Carter's cancellation upset Vance as well as Schmidt and the Europeans. It raised very large questions about the reliability of an American President. Helmut Schmidt was still angry and exasperated by Carter's cancellation at the time of the Bonn summit. The two men were utterly incompatible and unfortunately were to remain so until Carter's four-year presidency came to an end. Fortunately over the last twenty years all these battlefield nuclear weapons have been removed from Europe and that is an achievement for multilateral disarmament.

In order to try and avoid any further confusion, Zbig Brzezinski was sent round Europe in the late summer to sound out Jim Callaghan, Helmut Schmidt and Valéry Giscard d'Estaing on whether they would meet with Jimmy Carter early in 1979. This was agreed and a meeting was held that January in Guadeloupe, mainly for the four to talk privately about nuclear questions. This meeting brought to a head our own discussion on the continuation of the British independent nuclear deterrent.

The political problem that we faced over nuclear deterrence lay at the heart of the Callaghan government. Michael Foot did not believe in nuclear deterrence and, as an original Aldermaston marcher and CND activist, was not prepared to be involved. He sat on the defence and overseas policy committee of the Cabinet but it never handled specific nuclear questions. These had been handled ever since 1974, first under Wilson and then under Callaghan, by a small and special grouping of ministers. In my time it was a group of four – the Prime Minister, the Foreign Secretary, the Chancellor of the Exchequer and the Defence Minister.

The Labour Cabinet had agreed after the second general election in 1974 to update Polaris. But like all nuclear matters it was slipped through the Labour Party, avoiding discussion because to do so would risk a row. The hardening and modernising programme for the Polaris warhead under the secret codename Antelope was first examined when I was Navy Minister in 1969. Expenditure was authorised under the codename Chevaline by Edward Heath near the end of his government. In 1977 I became involved again after the scandalous escalation in the cost of the Chevaline project. This had quadrupled and the four of us met to consider cancelling. We decided not to cancel but for very mixed reasons. Jim Callaghan believed it was militarily necessary to improve the warhead. Fred Mulley believed he had to keep the chiefs of staff happy and, since they believed it was necessary despite the ABM Treaty, he went along with it in spite of his doubts. Denis Healey initially argued for cancellation. But he wanted to be Foreign Secretary and to align himself with Jim, if we won the new election. So, even though he disliked the cost and thought it militarily unnecessary, he acquiesced.

I believed it was not militarily necessary after the ABM Treaty but, since we had spent three-quarters of the total cost, I feared cancellation would leak out and this would raise military questions capable of destroying the political effectiveness of Polaris as a deterrent without an improved warhead. Since nuclear deterrence is as much psychological and political as military, I therefore favoured continuing with Chevaline.

But I also believed in 1977 that the cost escalation on the nuclear warhead was a warning to us that we had not got the financial weight to continue with a highly sophisticated nuclear deterrent, since in any new missile system that we bought from the United States, we would still have to rely on Aldermaston to manufacture and develop its nuclear warhead. They could do this for a simple system, but increasing sophistication of the new generation of Trident warheads would present us with similar problems to those we had encountered over Chevaline. I began to feel we were playing out of our league and that we needed to look at a cut-price deterrent.

The four of us examined in considerable depth the difficult question of what to do about replacing Polaris. I fought to explore the option of the cruise missile as a cheaper minimum deterrent. The Ministry of Defence were strongly against this, wanting the best available, irrespective of cost, which was undoubtedly Trident. I had to develop the arguments initially inside my own private office policy unit. When the paper the four of us had commissioned from officials eventually arrived I was, however, ready and tabled instantly a long, detailed and very different paper stressing the value of cruise as a less sophisticated option. Typically, we were called to the meeting in the latter part of 1978 to discuss the officials' long-delayed paper at only a few days' notice. But to everyone's surprise my detailed alternative options paper was presented simultaneously. As a result the four of us explored the Tomahawk cruise missile, a very new concept, with information which Peter Jay had sent from Washington. I had appointed Peter ambassador after securing the agreement of Jim, his father-in-law. The Ministry of Defence made every effort to dismiss cruise missiles even as an option and to boost the case for Trident and for continuing with an inter-continental ballistic missile system. I never had any doubt that Trident was a highly effective super-sophisticated system and that it was necessary for the US to go ahead with it. The unanswered question for me was whether a cheaper more flexible missile system existed, a weapons system which needed an unsophisticated and therefore cheaper nuclear warhead.

The four of us never doubted that we wanted Polaris replaced and that Britain should retain its independent nuclear deterrent. Yet none of us ever felt able to go out and argue the case positively to the parliamentary party, let alone the party in the country. All we did to justify nuclear deterrence was done in the context of maintaining Polaris and the need for NATO to have modern US nuclear weapons. If Jim Callaghan had won the next election he would have argued for Trident. In my judgement, Michael Foot's self-imposed exclusion from even discussing these issues during our whole period in government made him unfit ever to be Prime Minister. I could understand his attitude while it looked as if he acknowledged that, because of his unilateralist ideas, he could never seek to be Prime Minister. Only when he decided to put himself forward as leader of the Labour Party in 1980 did I make my decision not to serve under him. During the 1983 general election in a speech in Bristol, I declared that, for this reason, he was totally unfit to hold the office of Prime Minister. In 2009 Liverpool University Press published all of my documents in a book called *Nuclear Papers* under the thirty-year rule. I used them to argue the case against Tony Blair's decision, taken in 2007 as part of his legacy initiative, to replace Trident with another expensive ballistic missile system.

It was at a meeting on nuclear questions on 12 December 1978 that, almost by accident, we had to decide whether to make the vote at the end of that day's debate, on an inflationary pay award at Ford (see below), an issue of confidence. I recall the incident in some detail because it is a vignette of how that Labour government, without sufficient votes, constantly had to cobble together a majority. It was a daily part of the government's life which I rarely saw at close quarters. With the benefit of hindsight, I have no doubt that this was the moment that the Labour Party lost the 1979 general election, although Roy Hattersley among others had forgotten all the details when I reminded him nearly thirty years later. Many people believe that the election was lost when Jim Callaghan announced to the Cabinet on Thursday 7 September that he was not going to call one. I told Jim before this decision that, though I thought any election then would be close, I did not think we would win. With my marginal Devonport constituency, I was far from confident of victory that September. I detected considerable reservations about the performance of the Labour government in the minds of my electors. Of course, if we had had an election in the autumn of 1978, Labour would not have lost by anywhere near as large a margin as in May 1979, but Prime Ministers hold elections to win. I still do not believe we would have won that October.

There were undoubted risks in facing the winter without the Lib–Lab pact, which had ended in the summer. Yet the Liberals, by bailing out at that stage, felt few of the benefits of their pact with us. They thought with one bound they would be free, but they did not escape responsibility for the Winter of Discontent in the public mind, however unjustifiably. We knew that the Ulster Unionists would stay with us at least until the legislation for the extra MPs in Northern Ireland had taken effect, and that the Scottish Nationalists would want the devolution referendum planned for early 1979 to go ahead.

By December the political situation was becoming dominated by pay policy questions. The Ford Motor Company, which had been profitable in 1978, had been ready at least to take account of the government's pay guideline, ill-advisedly set by Jim in a very personal decision, at the unrealistically low level of 5 per cent. However, having resisted a nine-week strike, they decided to settle with a massive pay increase of 17 per cent. Our pay policy, though predominantly voluntary, had been underpinned by some mild sanctions, one of which was that private firms which ignored the government's pay guidelines were told that they could not expect to have any government orders for their products. The Cabinet decided that Ford could not be an exception. A debate on the Ford sanctions was then forced by the Conservatives, and thirty members of the Tribune Group of left-wing Labour MPs tabled an amendment expressing their opposition to any form of incomes policy. Though this amendment was not called, the Conservative opposition's amendment was; it demanded the abandonment of any sanctions against companies which broke the pay guidelines. It was obvious that the government could well lose if there were any Labour abstentions, since the Liberals and the Scottish Nationalists were going to vote with the Conservatives. Jim Callaghan along with Michael Foot had already urged the Tribune Group not to abstain on the Conservative motion. Michael Foot, as Leader of the House, and Michael Cocks, the chief whip, asked to see Jim urgently that morning, having just met with the Tribune Group again. Jim decided to call them into our meeting and to open the discussion up as to our next move.

Denis Healey argued that some of the Tribune MPs threatening to abstain would think more than twice if we declared the vote to be one of confidence, in effect threatening them with a general election. Michael Foot was strongly against such a gamble, knowing that it would lead to a general election if we lost the confidence vote. He preferred to lose that night without declaring it a matter of confidence and then have a no-confidence debate next day, when the Scottish Nationalists would support us. Michael Cocks explained that eighteen of our members were away in Luxembourg, Cledwyn Hughes was in Lagos and Arthur Irvine was ill. We realised that if we lost, having made it a vote of confidence, we would have to hold a general election in January on the old register and have a break in canvassing over the Christmas period. This did not worry me and to be standing firm against inflation seemed an ideal battleground. It would be Conservatives and Liberals who had voted for inflation and letting Ford off the hook. Clearly fed up and moving towards making it a motion of confidence, Jim decided to adjourn and meet again at 12.45 p.m. to hear a further report from the whips. In the meantime, I would try to contact Cledwyn in Lagos to see if he could fly back in time to vote.

At 12.45 p.m. Michael Cocks reported that there was a marginal chance of winning if we made it a vote of confidence. There appeared to be some uncertainty as to the exact whereabouts of the delegation to the European Parliament, which raised a fundamental doubt about the whips' assessment that we could win. I had not been able to get hold of Cledwyn. Michael Foot had sounded out Enoch Powell and though there was no chance of the Irish voting with us, some might conveniently be away. Denis and Jim still seemed keen to make it a vote of confidence. They felt if we won that we could hold the sanctions policy afterwards. I doubted this but said very little and Fred Mulley was also quiet.

My main anxiety was to keep Jim in a mood which would not, as we used to joke, 'send him off to the farm'. If we had an early election, it was vital for him to be in a confident mood, happy that he had decided to provoke the left and not feeling that he had been pushed into an election against his will. We agreed to meet at three o'clock in Jim's room in the House as he and Fred Mulley had a lunch fixed with the chiefs of staff. I had lunch with Harry Walston and to my surprise found that he was against Ford being penalised by sanctions. This shook me a little and he was also wholly relaxed about the consequences of our losing the vote that night but restoring the position next day. I felt perhaps we were exaggerating the significance of the Ford decision and that fewer people would care than I had hitherto thought if Ford got away without penalty. So when Denis argued strongly after lunch that sanctions would crumble and our anti-inflation policy would be in ruins if we did not win the vote, I was too complacent. Fred Mulley had told me that he had advised Jim to 'stick with Michael'. I wanted a decision which was Jim's, one that he could live with when he shaved next morning. I was convinced it was no use foisting anything on him. We were then told that the delegation of MPs were in Brussels, but five minutes later we heard they were in Luxembourg. This was the last straw as far as I was concerned for I felt that if we made it a vote of confidence we were likely to have our people anywhere rather than in the Division Lobby. Roy Hattersley, who was opening for us in the debate, and Joel Barnett were called in. Roy strongly backed Denis while Joel also agreed to a vote of confidence, but only if we could guarantee that we could win it. Then Jim moved decisively to support Michael's argument not to make it an issue of confidence. I guessed, however, he was hoping in this way to put strong psychological pressure on Michael to deliver the Tribunites.

So the die was cast. We would not make it a vote of confidence. We would probably lose and we would call a vote of confidence next day. We did lose, by two votes, 285 to 283. Enough Tribunites had abstained, as we predicted, to lose us the vote. That night the government tabled a motion of confidence which was debated next day. We had a majority of ten, with the Scottish Nationalists voting for us. Yet we had lost the ability to threaten anyone with sanctions. As it turned out, Denis Healey and Roy Hattersley were shown to have been correct. Sanctions were like a finger in a dyke; once removed the whole edifice of restraint collapsed. Before we knew where we were the Winter of Discontent descended on us, dooming us to lose the general election.

I believe if we had made the Ford sanctions debate a vote of confidence we would have won, for enough Tribunites would have folded under such pressure and not abstained. Even if we had lost, I believe we would have won a general election in January. Even more important, if we had not lost the Ford vote Jim Callaghan's morale would have been much higher. He would have confronted any trouble that winter with more confidence and we might even have won a September 1979 general election. But politics is full of 'ifs'.

The government was beginning to look tired and was running out of steam. We were facing an increasingly confident Margaret Thatcher and a Conservative Party which had rediscovered the will to win. I had by chance witnessed this one particular incident but Jim, Michael and Denis had been facing similar issues since 1974. The whole process of maintaining a majority in the House of Commons and beating back inflation was beginning to wear them out.

The toppling of the Shah by Ayatollah Khomeini at the head of the Iranian Revolution in early 1979 was, predictably, a geopolitical disaster. The power of Iran in the region was within months dissipated and destroyed. If the revolution had not occurred, there would have been no invasion of Afghanistan by the USSR in late 1979, no Iran–Iraq War from 1980 to 1987, no Iraqi invasion of Kuwait in 1990, and no second Iraq War in 2003. Death would not have claimed a million or more Muslims on the battlefield. The wave of Islamic fundamentalism would not have gathered such destructive force or led to such severe abuses of human rights, abuses which in retrospect make the Shah's rule look less unattractive and even the loathsome SAVAK not as odious. Nor would there have been US troops in Saudi Arabia, the issue which inflamed Osama bin Laden and helped precipitate the decision to create al-Qaeda and led to the two aircraft crashing into the Twin Towers in New York on 11 September 2001.

I have often pondered the events surrounding the Shah's fall. Immediately after the revolution in 1979, I arranged for the Foreign Office to conduct a detailed post mortem on where mistakes might have been made. In fact that report came to my successor Lord Carrington. It is always hard to admit error, but it is my considered belief that in 1978 the Western democracies had it in their power to influence events inside Iran so that the revolution could have been averted. It would almost certainly have meant the Shah retiring on bogus health grounds (at that time we did not know he was already suffering from a blood cancer), with a regency instituted until he could be succeeded by his son Reza, though without imperial powers. In this way I believe that Iran could have been guided towards becoming a democratic state with a constitutional monarch, rather along the lines of the transition in Spain from Franco's dictatorship to monarchy and democracy. I take part of the blame myself for not, as Foreign Secretary, acting with sufficient foresight or being successful enough in mobilising the Western countries to provide a firmer policy towards getting the Shah out of Iran in the late summer of 1978.

The most frequent criticism of the West during this time is that we failed to anticipate the revolution. I am not convinced that this is fair. We agonised constantly about whether or not the Shah's regime could survive. 'Is the Emperor Fully Clothed?' was the title of a despatch sent from our embassy in Tehran in August 1977. The real criticism is not of our anticipation skills but of our handling of the Shah. We failed to remember how weak he was before he took on the airs of an autocrat. We were far too deferential before his charade of leadership while he vacillated month by month. We failed to infuse him with the decisiveness and ruthlessness which were necessary not just for his survival but for his country's rejection of an Islamic revolution.

The Iran with which I had to deal as Foreign Secretary was a very different country from the one through which I had travelled extensively in 1959 on the way to and from Afghanistan. By 1977 it was almost unrecognisable, with hugely increased wealth, power and sophistication. Iran was by then producing nearly 12 per cent of the world's oil and some 16 per cent of Britain's. British Petroleum obtained between 40 and 45 per cent of its total oil supplies from Iran. With its vast oil revenues Iran was a major purchaser. Britain sold Iran about £200 million worth of industrial goods, motor cars and military equipment a year. We had recently sold them 750 Chieftain tanks and some 250 Scorpions. The UK was Iran's fourth largest supplier after the US, Japan and West Germany. France also had extensive interests and the European Community took about 13 per cent of its oil supply from Iran. After the rapid financial and political collapse of Iran following the revolution, the rule of Khomeini and the Iran–Iraq War, it is easy to forget how economically important Iran was under the Shah. Politically too; for by the 1970s Iran totally dominated the Gulf region.

At the start of 1974 the Shah was the single most important influence in the Middle East. Ever more vain and imperious, he was nevertheless shrewd. Broadly, his instincts were compatible with the interests of the Western democracies, so we encouraged him. Iran was a member of the defence organisation CENTO along with, initially, Iraq, Pakistan, Turkey, the UK and the US. The Shah was also a strong supporter of the free flow of trade within the Gulf. Yet he was very conscious of having a 1,000-mile border with the USSR and always maintained a private channel to Moscow. For us in Britain, Iran's historic significance was that it lay between Russia and the warm-water ports, between the USSR and India. Even in the 1970s we felt we had interests in the Indian sub-continent though, apart from sentiment, they were not easy to define. Good relations with the Shah were correctly judged to be an essential part of British foreign policy and much retrospective nonsense has been written about whether Britain should ever have supported the Shah. Economically, by the mid 1970s the Shah's favour was important to us, for we desperately needed to be able to offset the oil price shock by selling an increased proportion of our industrial output to Iran.

There was, however, an ambivalence about Anglo-Iranian relations. Britain, after 150 years of influence and, some would say, gross interference in Iran's internal affairs, was the subject of much suspicion within Iran. Almost every person one met there was ready to ascribe almost magical powers to the British Secret Service. The CIA and the Israeli intelligence service, Mossad, both powerfully represented in Iran, were treated by Persians as being of far inferior quality. The Shah had become obsessive about the hidden hand of Britain, attributing to us a role and an influence which we ourselves were never able to live up to. The Iranians were also in part flattered by, in part suspicious of the number of British diplomats over the years who had a profound knowledge of and love for Persian history, literature and culture. So in fact the MI6 presence had been deliberately run down.

Even before the late 1970s, our ambassadors had always been watching for signs of instability. Back in the 1960s our embassy in Tehran was reporting that the collapse of the regime might or might not be imminent; they worried about an old-fashioned society being invaded by new ideas and how the superimposition of industrial-isation was destroying the traditional way of life. One of the most astute ambassadors who ever served in Tehran, Sir Denis Wright, drew attention to the genuine dilemma that faced the Shah. If he was to carry his reforms through he needed to tighten his political grip on the country. The trouble with this, as history has so often shown, is that genuine reformist leaders who take undemocratic powers turn into reactionary dictators. The Shah was never an enlightened democrat but he was a genuine moderniser, though his autocratic style hid a neurotic and indecisive personality.

The Shah's liberalisation policy virtually coincided with my period as secretary of state. It was initiated in 1977, a reaction to the global interest in human rights then. While it certainly suited my mood and that of the incoming Carter administration, it was not dictated by us. The apologists for the Shah never cease to blame Carter for his downfall. But in fairness, just as Carter's stress on human rights was a reaction to trends of opinion already apparent in the world, so the Shah too was reacting. Iran's prisons were opened up for inspection by the International Red Cross. The public were admitted, for the first time since 1972, to the trials of political prisoners and some political prisoners were released. There is no evidence that the Shah made these decisions because of US or UK pressure. I talked to him about the concerns of Amnesty International when in Tehran and he responded, but he knew that if his son were to succeed him in a mood of peace and harmony then the popularity of the monarchy had to be safeguarded.

The Shah was aware of the organised opposition and he did try to identify ways of curbing its influence. The entrenched opposition comprised those who took as their symbol Ayatollah Khomeini, first exiled in Turkey, then in Iraq, and latterly living on the outskirts of Paris, but it could also be seen round the old National Front politicians like Shahpour Bakhtiar and Mehdi Bazargan. The largest element of opposition and the least organised was the city dwellers, who grew restless as inflation rose. Everyone knew that the Great Civilisation was coming apart at the seams, and this was emphasised by a series of power cuts demonstrating how dismally the planners had failed in making provision for power. Nevertheless, given the Shah's apparent readiness to address some of their concerns, there was no reason why urban dissatisfaction could not have been contained with more anticipation and flexibility.

Unrest grew throughout Iran during 1978 and it was during that summer that the Western democracies had the opportunity to rethink a strategy to bind Iran to the West. It was obvious by then that the Shah was vulnerable, perched on an unstable edifice. Too many people had direct access to him. There was no Cabinet to sift information and determine priorities. One young Foreign Office analyst likened the structure to a series of parallel columns with each pillar representing an independent interest, be it SAVAK, the Prime Minister, the supreme commanding officer or the central bank. All reported direct to the Shah. It was just about manageable in normal times but an impossible structure to operate in a crisis, particularly if there was indecision at the head.

Martial law was declared in Isfahan in August and the Shah promised further liberalisation, saying that elections for a new parliament due in June 1979 would be totally free and that bills would be presented to the National Assembly providing for free expression and assembly. The trouble was that no one believed it would be done.

On 22 October a television interview I had recorded with Brian Walden a week before was transmitted. It was an object lesson about allowing an interview to be put in the can for later transmission. During that week the Shah's position had deteriorated and I would probably have toned down my comments. Brian, a friend who had been a fellow Labour MP, had come to Buttermere to do a general interview and it was only after this, relaxing over coffee in the kitchen, that I expressed my surprise that the new great cause of the far left was the support of Khomeini and all he stood for in terms of turning the clock back. Brian asked me if I would put this on tape and I foolishly agreed. I argued in the interview that this was a situation where Britain could not hedge its bets, that one did not back off when one's friends were under attack and that, against the regional background, it would not be in our interests for the Shah to be deposed. I added that human rights in Iran would not be increased if Britain supported the fanatical Muslim element. It was a bravura performance and the deterioration in human rights after the revolution showed its predictions to be correct in almost every particular but, to say the least, it was imprudent. It exacerbated feeling in the Labour Party and made Jim Callaghan even more hesitant about supporting the Shah.

The Labour Party NEC sent a deputation to see me on 9 November about Iran. The deputation included Neil Kinnock. It was the first time we had really talked and he was reasonable, realistic and flattering. I was well known and admired, he said, as a proponent of human rights so they wanted to know why I had adopted my present position on Iran. In reply I emphasised that I remained unhappy about the human rights record but urged them to accept that if I were to make public what we were saying in private our influence would plummet to zero. Neil Kinnock thought that the Shah as an absolute monarch could concede more, that we should toughen up on arms sales and cancel the Queen's visit. He acknowledged Iran's strategic importance and saw the alternatives now available as either a hawkish reactionary Muslim government or an essentially unstable military regime, both of which would alarm the Soviet Union and be bad for relations with the West.

By late December the situation was hopeless. I held an office meeting on 20 December and said that

> the Shah has not yet tried conducting a severe crackdown and that might well be the last and only option. It would be very unpleasant politically for Britain if he did crack down but it might work in Iran, where, given the absence of an alternative and the threat of chaos, there could be a greater acceptance of the ruthless exercise of power that we in the West could not easily imagine, let alone support.

I reaffirmed that I did not feel that I had been misled about Iran. We had been grossly overcommitted economically but this had been a deliberate attempt to offset the oil price rise. I thought that we would get the worst of all possible worlds if we shifted policies now, but added that henceforward, 'we are not to advocate or be thought to be advocating solutions, nor should we become involved in advising the Shah or others about what they should do'. Despite this decision not to advocate solutions, on 29 December I was cabled with a draft telegram suggesting some advice to Cy Vance. The Foreign Office wanted me to argue with Cy Vance against a military clampdown. I refused to send the telegram. I had decided that the causes and the cures for the present crisis lay in Iran. It was no longer for us in the West to intervene either way. As I had said with emphasis, at the earlier office meeting, in a confusing situation we should follow the old naval maxim 'In a fog, slow right down but don't change course'.

On 16 January 1979 the Shah left Tehran, flying first to see President Sadat in Egypt and then on to Morocco. The CIA tried to establish a deal with Khomeini while also bringing in General Heyser, the deputy Supreme Allied Commander in Europe. The street battles from 9 to 11 February scuppered any CIA hopes of a deal with Khomeini, who returned to Tehran on 11 February. The streets filled with masses of people and the once proud Iranian army simply collapsed. I recognised the new regime from the Royal Yacht in the Gulf, while the Queen was visiting Saudi Arabia.

Revolutionary committees were established all over the country. Anyone associated with the Shah's regime was dragged off to prison. The new Prime Minister, Mehdi Bazargan, was powerless to intervene. Summary trials were held and people publicly executed. The former Prime Minister, Amir-Abbas Hoveyda, was tried, sentenced to death and, in a matter of minutes, shot in the prison cell. *Paris Match* published a picture of his body with three revolutionaries, one of whom, full of smiles, was carrying a machine gun; alongside it was a photograph of one of the Shah's family swimming in the Bahamas.

In the middle of March, Cy Vance made what he called 'one of the most distasteful recommendations I have ever had to make to the President', namely that the Shah should not come to the United

States. With a similar sense of shame I had sent a note to Jim Callaghan that the Shah – who never formally applied to come – should be politely turned away. There was no honour in my decision, just the cold calculation of national interest. I had stuck to the Shah far longer than was good for my own position in domestic politics, but even so I felt it to be a despicable act to turn him away, given Britain's long history of offering political asylum. It was depressing that all but a few MPs now turned completely against the Shah. It was as if they were blind, on both Labour and Conservative benches, to what was bound to happen in Iran under the Ayatollah. On 20 February I made a statement recognising the new government. Unwisely, given the mood of the House, I said that I was prepared for our record of support for the Shah 'to be justified by history'. That was met with mirth and the cutting jibe from the Conservative MP, Sir Peter Tapsell, that 'history may have other things on its mind'. Yet the old adage 'He who laughs last laughs longest' was borne out. Soon the criticism was not for defending the Shah but for letting him fall. Thirty years later, on 19 June 2009 Ayatollah Ali Khameni denounced Britain as the 'most evil' of Iran's enemies as street protests grew over fraudulent elections. The Opposition candidate Hossein Moussavi was leading a Koranic revolution 'commanding right and forbidding wrong'.

In early January 1979, with Soviet strategic missile forces building and more and more intermediate SS-20 missiles being targeted on western Europe, it was urgent for the West to be seen to be responding with firmness and retaining its unity. The dismay and confusion over the neutron bomb had to be put behind us. Jim Callaghan, President Carter, Helmut Schmidt and President Giscard d'Estaing held a meeting in Guadeloupe. For the first time, and with my full agreement, Jim formally raised with Carter the question of replacing Polaris with Trident. He was assured that Carter could see no objection to transferring this technology to the United Kingdom. There are many people in the Labour Party who have accused Jim Callaghan of defying the Labour Party's manifesto commitment, which was not to replace Polaris. There is no truth in this allegation. He never committed a future Labour government but he also prudently never allowed the delay in calling the election to interfere with the timetable for necessary decisions about Polaris's replacement. Encouraged by the secretary to the Cabinet, Sir John Hunt, and myself, Jim used his friendship with Jimmy Carter over Trident in much the same way that Harold Macmillan had used his personal relationship with President Kennedy over Polaris. This meant that when Margaret Thatcher came into office she found awaiting her a minute written that very day by Jim Callaghan authorising her to see all his contacts and correspondence with President Carter on the future of the nuclear deterrent. He also made available to her the comprehensive report by officials, received in December, on the various options we had commissioned and discussed for continuing Britain's independent nuclear deterrent. That was honourable conduct, not repaid by the Conservative government's conduct in making public the Chevaline programme for apparent domestic political advantage.

President Carter had made it clear at Guadeloupe that he would only agree to fund the Pershing 1 missile replacement and ground-launched cruise missiles if he could be sure that the European nations would agree to them being deployed on their territory later. Then Helmut Schmidt developed the argument that Germany could not take cruise missiles alone and that at least one other European nation would have to accept cruise missiles on its territory, hence the UK's later acceptance of some missiles. Carter replied to the three European heads of government that he would discuss with Leonid Brezhnev the build-up of the Soviet SS-20s and that he would open negotiations about these, as well as American nuclear forces already in Europe, but that the negotiations would have to be predicated on the fact that some of the US systems were going to be modernised and that he was not going to accept a ban on modernisation during the negotiations.

A study had been initiated in NATO much earlier, and made public at the time, to look at five options: modernising Pershing 1; building a new intermediate ground-launched missile; deploying cruise missiles at sea, or in the air, or on the land. The eventual decision to go for land-based missiles was emerging as part of NATO's collective decision-making during the spring of 1979. No final decision was taken during the period of the Labour government but the planning assumption at official level seemed to be moving towards land-based missiles, mainly because it was felt that sea-basing did not have as much potential for binding the US global deterrent into Europe. I favoured sea-basing because it was far less provocative in terms of public opinion and also avoided the 'use or lose' risk of forward deployment.

I was only a bystander in the Cabinet during the Winter of Discontent, for I was not a member of the Civil Contingency Unit, which was meeting constantly at ministerial level as well as at official level. My only input was that I could not accept the arguments against declaring a state of emergency. Clearly this was what Jim wanted, and indeed at Cabinet on 18 January I thought that it had been agreed. I did intervene to say that it was psychologically necessary, for the public expected it and simply did not understand the technical arguments that all the powers necessary to use troops and commandeer ambulances already existed. Jim's authority inside the government was by this time greatly reduced, and John Silkin with his TGWU links was able to block the declaration of a state of emergency. That day our third child, Lucy, was born.

On Thursday 1 February the health service unions and the local authority unions were on strike, and Jim was well aware that indiscipline and what I described as thuggery were threatening the government. He sadly felt unable to do what I think he knew he should, namely go on television and demonstrate that he had had enough. At this stage we were not even able to bury the dead and ambulances were failing to pick up patients. If Jim had expressed his disgust on television it could have been very powerful. Most people in the country knew of his gut sympathy with the trade union movement, so if ever he placed the whole authority of his office on the line and denounced the strikers I had little doubt that their action could be made ineffective. Jim admitted, rather poignantly at one stage, that there was not a single night when he did not consider going on television but then asked himself if anything would be different next day. I felt he underestimated his own personal authority and the strength of the office he held. It was a very distressing time for me in Cabinet. Because I was slightly distanced from the day-to-day handling of events, I saw perhaps more clearly that we were witnessing the terminal stages of the government. In a strange way, Jim knew it too. I felt that he had resigned himself to electoral defeat and only had one objective, the perfectly honourable one of keeping the Labour Party together. He, like so many of his generation, was haunted by the mythology that surrounded the figure of Ramsay MacDonald, and dreaded the thought of breaking the Labour Party. Like the captain of a ship that had lost its mast and whose crew were injured, he just wanted to get his vessel to port without sinking. It was difficult to isolate our domestic position from our standing in international affairs. In Rhodesia the situation was still not ripe for a negotiated settlement, but if we had held a Lancaster House conference that winter the perception of a government losing its authority at home would have had an impact in the conference as it would only have confirmed Ian Smith's wish to hang on in the hope of being able to manipulate a new Conservative government. Foreign policy, to be effective, needs the clout of a government that is looking assured and confident at home.

On 1 March, St David's Day, the referenda on devolution were held in Scotland and Wales. It was the moment when the fate of the government was sealed, and in many respects deservedly so. I was a longstanding supporter of devolution but it had been adopted by Labour not out of conviction but out of expediency. Regrettably, many people within the party did not truly believe in it. Devolution was a political reaction to the appeal of the Nationalists. The refusal even to consider proportional representation seriously for the Scottish Parliament, which could have kept the Lib–Lab pact going at no great price, left many convinced devolutionists fearing that, in some future political circumstances, the Scottish Nationalists might hold an overall majority. In Wales, devolution was rejected by four to one. In Scotland, though there was a small majority in favour, it did not jump the 40 per cent hurdle specified under the Devolution Act. The government now had to table repeal orders and it was clear that we could not ask loyal MPs in the north-east who had disliked devolution all along to vote down the order for Scotland.

On 28 March the Scottish National Party tabled a motion of censure and the Conservative Party gave it their support. We could have squeezed through by promising a gas pipeline to Northern Ireland, but Jim Callaghan drew the line at this. He did, however, accept the speeding up of the promised legislation to give compensation to state quarrymen suffering from lung disease and this ensured the votes of the Welsh Nationalists. Gerry Fitt, from the SDLP, who objected to the increased number of MPs in Northern Ireland, abstained. He had been wooed assiduously by Airey Neave, the Conservative spokesman on Northern Ireland, tragically to be blown up by the IRA a few days later. We went down by 311 votes to 310, the first time since 1924 that a motion of no confidence in the government of the day had been lost. As I passed Jim's room behind the Speaker's chair after the vote, he called me in. 'Will you be all right in Devonport?' he asked anxiously. Considerate to the last, Jim was nevertheless not speaking like a man confident of victory at the polls. If he was worried about Devonport, he felt we were heading for defeat. At Cabinet next morning we all felt it was sensible to coincide the general election with voting for the council elections on 3 May. Then Jim went to the Palace to ask the Queen to dissolve Parliament.

On Tuesday 3 April, with Debbie, I went to Windsor Castle for dinner and to spend the night as a guest of the Queen. It was a delightful evening. Jim and Audrey Callaghan, unexpectedly, were also present, which made it very special for both of us and it was a time to thank him for all his support during my time as Foreign Secretary. The Queen ensured that elections were the last thing any of us thought about, and after dinner the Queen's librarian showed each of us an item of special historic interest to us personally – for me it was the anatomical drawings of Leonardo da Vinci. Next morning Debbie and I walked through Windsor Park before returning to London when Parliament was formally dissolved.

On the Friday we had an eight-hour joint meeting of the Cabinet with the NEC for the final drafting of the manifesto. I successfully opposed the anti-Marketeers, making a commitment to repeal Section 2(1) of the 1972 European Communities Act by which Community instruments take effect directly as law in the member states. They knew, and they were right, that a change in the direct applicability would put us in breach of our treaty obligations and on a collision course with our European partners. By contrast, making ministers accountable to the House of Commons prior to forming any commitment in the Council of Ministers is a perfectly reasonable element of democratic accountability, though it is wise to preserve some degree of flexibility for ministers in negotiating. I was also very worried about the wording over a replacement for Polaris. I was sent a note before the meeting to say that Fred Mulley wanted the nuclear section to read:

Since 1974 we have renounced any intention of moving towards the production of a new generation of nuclear weapons or to a successor to the Polaris nuclear force *which will remain effective into the 1990s; we still believe this may be the best course for Britain*. But many great issues affecting our allies and the world are involved, and we believe there must be a full and informed debate about them, and a balanced appraisal of all the relevant considerations, including cost and arms control factors as well as our security interest and our contributions to NATO, before Parliament makes a final decision in a few years' time.

I supported Fred Mulley, but the all-important italicised words disappeared in the various drafting sessions, to be replaced by 'We reiterate our belief that this is the best course for Britain.' That flatly contradicted the view that we did need to replace Polaris, expressed by the four of us involved in nuclear decisions. To this day I have never understood why Jim acquiesced. I think he was just too weary to have another row. Instead he wasted valuable ammunition shooting down the proposed abolition of the Lords, a trivial issue by comparison, when all that was really likely was not abolition but the election of a second chamber.

During the election campaign in Plymouth I realised for the first time how unpopular the left wing of the Labour Party, and particularly Tony Benn, had become. Though I had been scrupulous in keeping my advice bureaux, my hectic schedule and particularly foreign travel meant that I was more out of touch with the grassroots opinion in the constituency than I would have liked. Whereas the left had always been tolerated in the Labour Party, I found that many traditional Labour voters, particularly those working in the dockyard, now saw and described them as communists. They did not mince their words about them either. The Winter of Discontent had brought out a new mood of personal bitterness in politics.

A distinctive feature was the racial backlash, which I felt for the first time in Plymouth. People from Rhodesia canvassing for the Conservatives heightened press interest. A nasty, vicious card which had a letter from another Dr Owen claiming I was responsible for a terrorist attack in Rhodesia with a picture of a woman dead, and probably having been raped, with her dead child by her side, was pushed through the door of every council house in my constituency. It was despicable and I felt its effect on the doorstep. The *Sun* ran a centre-page spread on 'Dr Smug' and on that day of all days copies of the *Daily Mirror* missed the train to Plymouth. Distributing my own leaflets at 6 a.m. at the dockyard gate, I felt as if every single person took a copy of the *Sun*. Debbie was more relaxed, saying no one would read its highly personalised attacks, but they would like the photographs. Sure enough, in telephone calls to the office, if the article was mentioned, it was only to say, 'Lovely picture of David in the *Sun* today.' Newspapers are not as powerful in swinging votes as politicians think.

In Plymouth, and when I travelled to speak elsewhere in the country, I never, throughout the campaign, believed that a Labour government would be returned. We started 13 per cent behind in the opinion polls and, though slowly improving, the gap never went below 2 per cent and realistically never looked as though it was below 4 per cent. The Winter of Discontent hung over us like a dark cloud and justly. Unlike 1970, when I had completely misjudged the public mood, this time I felt it was against us from the beginning to the end and at times I was certain of losing in Devonport. But despite the very adverse swing against Labour in the south-west, I managed to hold onto my seat by 1,001 votes.

When I woke up late on Friday morning, though the election was lost, results were still coming in and I was still Her Majesty's Principal Secretary of State for Foreign and Commonwealth Affairs. Then I saw on television the outgoing Prime Minister, Jim Callaghan, driving to Buckingham Palace to see the Queen. I rang the Foreign Office and sent a farewell message to every embassy in the world to thank them for all their past service. It was to be the last of hundreds of thousands of telegrams to end with the name 'Owen'. I was no longer a minister of the Crown. No further telegrams would come from around the world for decision at all times of the day and night. No more despatch boxes, no Cabinet papers, no intelligence reports. The scrambler telephone could be taken away and personal protection was needed no longer. I suggested to the detectives that they should go back to London and thanked them for all their kindness, patience and courtesy. They had, after all, been ready to risk their lives for mine, and during the election an IRA scare involving me had meant for the first time a team of six detectives, with some staying overnight.

I climbed into my car and, for the first time for nearly 2½ years, drove alone through the streets of Devonport, with neither a detective beside me nor a police car following. I sang at the top of my voice; strangely, my predominant feeling was one of freedom – freedom to be alone, freedom to decide what to do with the rest of the day, freedom to be with my family. I planned a bicycle ride with my boys, just us three. Gradually, as the hours passed, other emotions crowded in, including regret at so much unfinished business. As I listened to the news on the radio, there was a feeling of detachment now that the events unfolding were outside one's influence or control. I felt sadness at leaving people who had become friends – private secretaries, detectives, drivers, diplomats. The telephone rang as I watched the *Nine o'Clock News*. It was Cy Vance, the US Secretary of State – the first of many Foreign Ministers ringing or writing as old friends. As I put the receiver down I felt tears come to my eyes for he had been a true friend. The world of modern diplomacy is tough and exacting; there is a tremendous amount of travelling, but it is not impersonal. I had forged close friendships, built up through hours of working closely together, whether in New York, Africa or Brussels.

One thing remained constant: I was still the MP for Devonport, and this was the post I valued most of all. The telephone rang as if to reinforce this. It was a constituency problem, a young mother separated from her husband and wanting to find a flat so that she could bring her children out of temporary care. The day that had started in the early hours with the count going on in the Guildhall ended with my parents, wife and children sitting around the fire at the family home in Plymouth. A whole new life of opposition now opened up. Despite the disappointment of losing a Labour government, I comforted myself with thinking how different it would have been if I had lost Devonport. That would have left an unfillable gap. I would have felt empty, bruised and battered.

Defeat had come as no surprise to Jim Callaghan, for the realistic defeatist mood which I had detected the night we lost the censure vote was there throughout the campaign. His senior policy adviser,

Bernard Donoughue, recalls near to polling day encouraging Jim with poll figures showing that Labour might just squeak through. Jim turned to him and said quietly:

> I should not be too sure. You know there are times, perhaps once every thirty years, when there is a sea change in politics. It then does not matter what you say or what you do. There is a shift in what the public wants and what it approves of. I suspect there is now such a sea change – and it is for Mrs Thatcher.

That sea change in the public mood came back to sweep Tony Blair and New Labour into office eighteen years later in 1997. The question in 2009, in the wake of the international and British economic crises and the sense of a return of sleaze, was whether another sea change would after twelve years benefit the Conservative Party. But I fear that the mood of disillusionment has become much deeper than it was in 1979 or 1997. There is today, as I write in June 2009, a very different atmosphere: we face both an economic and a political crisis.

# 4

# Leaving Labour and creating the SDP

'Where there is discord may we bring harmony . . . Where there is despair may we bring hope.' With these words of St Francis of Assisi, Margaret Thatcher stepped across the threshold of 10 Downing Street on Friday 4 May 1979. Despite having been personally well behind Jim Callaghan in all the polls, she had just won a stunning victory. A seven per cent swing to the Conservatives had given them 339 MPs, Labour only 269, the Liberals 11, the Ulster parties 12 and the Nationalists 4. With an overall majority of forty-three, she had that most precious asset, a secure parliamentary majority, something which Jim Callaghan never achieved. It was soon apparent that she intended to use it to start a decade of radicalism that would shake the innate conservatism of this country to its foundations.

That weekend I talked on the telephone to Peter Jay, who had done a good job as our ambassador in Washington. As he was about to speak to Jim, I said I hoped Jim would resign immediately. I could see no advantage in his hanging on as leader of the party in opposition; he had done his best but he would be blamed for defeat. If he went now, he could go with dignity and hand over quickly to Denis Healey. Peter promised to pass on my views and I did not attempt to intrude any further. Yet, a few days later, when the old Cabinet met in the suite of rooms allocated to the Leader of the Opposition, it was clear that Jim intended to stay on as leader. Michael Foot proposed, later that morning, that Jim should be re-elected leader by the Parliamentary Labour Party, and he hoped that it would be unanimous. No one dissented.

The next day, Tony Benn announced that he was not going to stand for the shadow Cabinet. I thought his decision wise. Throughout my time in the Cabinet, he had been totally out of sympathy with his colleagues and his relationship with Jim was tetchy. He was correct to choose the freedom of the back benches. Rather selfishly, I also thought that it would make it easier for me to get elected to the shadow Cabinet. However, Tony's decision also had a significant drawback. The left would now have a redoubtable activist as its leader. Tony, unfettered and in opposition, would be far more formidable than he had ever been in government and his position on the NEC and his appeal in the constituencies gave him a growing power base. Tony's critics were mistaken about him. He was not mad, nor was he a simple militant purist ideologue. He was a deeply ambitious politician whose ambition was harnessed to a superficial intellect and a total lack of proportion.

The following Wednesday the PLP met and we started a messy post mortem on Labour's defeat. It was tense at times but it was not bitter and Jim, winding up the debate, tried to rally the PLP, urging it to look forward and give leadership to the party in the country, quoting an old Chinese proverb, 'A fish rots from the head'. This was far too simplistic an analysis. The Labour Party was suffering from two interlocking problems. The first was at the top of the party and it was intellectual. The Keynesian revolution had run out of intellectual steam – instead of maintaining full employment, it had produced high unemployment and inflation at the same time. It also offered no response to increasingly flexible patterns of production, to demands for lower taxation and individuals' aspiration for higher material standards as well as greater freedom, let alone to the crisis of confidence in British industry. The Labour left moved into this intellectual gap by accepting the analysis of decline, aggressively argued by the Conservative right as well, but putting the blame on insufficiently strong government intervention and proposing this time to take control of the commanding heights of the economy. Their recipe was more state socialism, not less. There was no adequate response to the Labour left from the centre or right of the Labour Party. Exhausted after years in government and intellectually demoralised, they were content to fight a defensive battle. The second and associated problem was an organisational one affecting the body of the party. As the trade unions continued the revolt against the party leadership that had started with the winter of strikes, the centre retreated and started to compromise itself out of existence. Organisations like the Militant Tendency had spread their tentacles and built up their strength in the constituencies. There was little resistance as first the key office-holding positions in the constituencies changed hands and then the very nature of the constituency general management committees was altered to reflect activist priorities; the politics of minority interests began to flourish.

Any counter-attack would depend on the capacity to develop new ideas as well as provide organisational support. The Campaign for Labour Victory (CLV) had been formed in February 1977 as a grassroots organisation to complement the Manifesto Group inside the parliamentary party. Of the Cabinet ministers, Bill Rodgers had been the main force behind it. I had supported the CLV, but now I started to give it more time and energy. It had many problems associated with lack of money but it was also insufficiently geared to winning the battle of ideas.

No sooner was the general election over than it was time to fight the first direct elections for the European Parliament. This provided the Labour left with an opportunity, which they seized, to shift the policy of the party, with the NEC controlling the Euro-manifesto. There was little enthusiasm within Labour for the elections and the Conservatives, with their morale high, grabbed their opportunity to score a second victory. Polling took place on Thursday 7 June and counting, Europe-wide, took place on the Sunday. I spoke in different parts of the country, but it was an apathetic campaign. On Monday 4 June in Bradford and in Halifax I claimed that the Labour Party was the most 'unequivocally non-federalist of all the parties fighting in the election'. That was not without justification since the Conservatives had yet to discover their identity on Europe under Margaret Thatcher and were still Heathite. I added, however, that 'in arguing against the supranational federal Europe it is not necessary to pour scorn on the noble idea which it incorporates'.

The following day, between two speaking engagements in Derbyshire, I spent a few hours alone in the Peak District walking along a railway line transformed into one of the most sensational walks in England. I have often returned but have never quite recaptured the beauty of that day or the peace it gave me for reflection. It was there that I decided that, be my political life long or short, henceforth I was going to be true to myself and not repeat the miserable experience of our last time in opposition, from 1970 to 1974, when I had compromised so much that I had begun to loathe politics and despise myself.

It is hard to understand if you do not come from the West Country, with its strong Nonconformist tradition and respect for the Liberal Party, the traumatic effect of Jeremy Thorpe's trial at the Old Bailey in the middle of May. Saturation coverage of the committal proceedings in Minehead during the previous December and now the whole saga coming out again ensured that it was a long-drawn-out embarrassment for the Liberal Party. The revelations about unsavoury financial dealings within the party over many years were particularly unpleasant. And it was not just Jeremy Thorpe – also involved as a key witness was Peter Bessell, who had been a Liberal MP in the West Country, representing Bodmin from 1964 to 1970. The effect on West Country Liberalism was considerable. The protracted trial made a dreadful background to the Liberal Party campaign for the European elections and, not surprisingly, they did very badly.

The European campaign moved my thinking a little further on electoral reform, which I had advocated in Cabinet in 1977. I was now openly campaigning for proportional representation for the European Assembly. However, I was not happy with the list system and I was still not ready to concede the case for proportional representation for Westminster, even though my experience in Europe as Foreign Secretary meant that I had no fear of coalition government. In answering letters, I said that the difference between the two elections was that we faced immense distortion in the European elections because of the small number of very big constituencies, while in the general election there were eight times as many constituencies, allowing a much better chance of getting a more accurate spread of opinion. I did not have a closed mind on the need for electoral reform at Westminster, but at that time I did not believe that the disadvantages of the current system were sufficient to justify a change. Broadly speaking, I believed our system for MPs, with coalitions within the existing parties rather than coalition between them, had served us reasonably well. In the European elections, where there was no legislative or executive authority at stake, the need for a decisive voice was not so marked. I also believed that the case for proportional representation was particularly strong for Scottish and

Welsh assemblies, if and when they were established, and that once the European parliamentary elections had been conducted under PR it would be possible to make a judgement about whether there was any need for a change at Westminster.

Two days after the Euro-election result, Sir Geoffrey Howe presented his first Budget. Despite his having said on 21 April in a general election press release, 'We have absolutely no intention of doubling VAT,' and Margaret Thatcher's saying on 23 April at a Conservative press conference, 'We have no intention of doubling VAT,' VAT was raised from 8 per cent to 15 per cent. No wonder people despair of finding honesty in politics, but it was, apart from misleading the electorate, a wise choice. It brought in substantial revenues and gave the government the necessary cushioning to make progressive cuts in income tax thereafter.

In mid-June the results of the shadow Cabinet elections were announced. Denis Healey topped the poll, but with John Silkin and Peter Shore, committed anti-Marketeers, coming second and third respectively, it was not hard to see trouble looming on that front. Peter Shore had not been on the slate of either the Tribune Group or the centre-right and, as the only candidate elected without being on a slate, he had done particularly well. I was elected, coming tenth with Roy Mason and John Smith below me. When I saw Jim Callaghan after the result it came as no surprise that I was not going to shadow Foreign Affairs. I was quite happy that he offered me Energy since it would involve me in economic questions while keeping a foothold in international affairs. In addition, with Jim's help, I was appointed to the TUC–Labour Party liaison committee, a good way to meet members of the TUC General Council. It was a body which Jim hoped, in opposition, would become as important as the NEC, if not more so.

Revealingly, when Jim spoke to me about the Foreign Affairs portfolio, he made it clear that the reason he wanted to appoint Peter Shore to shadow Foreign Affairs was because he wanted the parliamentary party to have a choice in the leadership election and Peter needed international experience if the party was going to see him as a credible challenger. In this way, although he was at pains to point out that he had no preference, he showed his own doubts about Denis as leader. He said that he thought that Michael Foot would not want to be leader and he seemed to be building Peter up to take Michael's place as leader of the centre-left. His doubts about Denis were not new to me; I had picked them up on a number of occasions in the past. I also knew Jim liked Peter and recognised in him his own robust patriotism. It had been noticeable in the Cabinet how much Jim bothered to ensure that he carried Peter's support and now he was giving him a chance to shine.

In fact, as it turned out, it was another promotion that in the long run determined the leadership of the party. Neil Kinnock, who had failed to get on the shadow Cabinet, was made shadow Education spokesman. Previously Jim had offered him a junior ministerial post which he had refused, but now it was sensible to give his career a boost and to try and detach him from the left, particularly since he had been elected to the NEC for the first time in 1978. It was also a way for Jim to keep Michael Foot happy, for he had always been a strong supporter of Neil Kinnock.

The scene was set for a battle for control of the Labour Party. On Wednesday 11 July the parliamentary party met to discuss changes to the Labour Party constitution, which had already been published and were known as the Benn–Heffer proposals. Tony Benn introduced them, and as so often with him, they ranged from the deadly serious to the trivial, with no real connecting strand other than to rub Jim's nose in the dirt. The most serious was the proposal to change Clause V so as to give the NEC the final say on the election manifesto, ending the veto of the Cabinet or shadow Cabinet. Benn and Heffer also wanted all staff, including personal aides and research assistants, to be employed by the party organisation, an indirect attack on the leader of the parliamentary party and members of the shadow Cabinet. The left's resentment, not widely shared, was over the way in which the PLP was developing independently of the party in the country, and controlling parliamentary assistants was one way of reining back this independence. It was also proposed that the shadow Cabinet and principal spokespersons should be elected by the PLP, this time a direct attack on the patronage of the leader of the party. Jim should probably have scoffed at it and treated much of it with derision. Instead, he seemed defensive and a little rattled. Tony Benn had drawn blood and while some of the detail was eventually shelved by a decision to establish a commission of enquiry, there was no doubt that at the annual conference he was going to be able to mount a pretty strong offensive.

At a joint meeting of the shadow Cabinet and the NEC on 26 July, I concentrated on opposing any changes in the way the manifesto was drawn up. This was, I believed, the central issue. I accepted only that there was a strong case to re-establish greater trust in the party since in the past we had suffered from a vicious circle whereby conference resolutions that were passed had been ignored, thus provoking the conference to pass even more unrealistic resolutions which were then further ignored, and so a pattern of irresponsibility had become built into conference resolution-making. The Benn changes would only deepen the existing mistrust.

In September the CLV issued a statement billed by the press as being in the name of Roy Hattersley, Roy Mason, Bill Rodgers, David Owen and Shirley Williams, all of us CLV supporters. It declared that Jim Callaghan had the backing of 'the mainstream of Labour supporters in the firm stand he is taking against constitutional changes that would turn the Labour Party into a narrow, sectarian and intolerant organisation'.

When the Labour conference met, the motion for the election of the party leader by an electoral college was lost and I hoped this would be the last we heard of it. Mandatory reselection of members, once in every parliament, was, however, carried. Ultimate control of the manifesto, it was decided, should now lie with the NEC. The delicate balance of power between the parliamentary party, elected by the country as a whole, and the party activists in the NEC and the Labour Party conference was under serious threat. Even though all these issues would be covered by the commission of inquiry and would therefore come back to the next annual conference, few of us had any doubt that Tony Benn was masterminding a fundamental change in the balance of the party, a historic shift from elected representatives to non-elected party caucuses.

The general backbiting against Jim Callaghan personally among Labour activists on the left was becoming very nasty, and on 9 November, speaking at Ted Rowlands's Merthyr Tydfil Constituency Labour Party annual dinner, I declared that I was proud to have been a member of Jim Callaghan's Cabinet and was not prepared to see him used as a scapegoat for our defeat. Not only was he our greatest electoral asset, I did not believe that the 1979 manifesto had lost us any votes in this constituency or in my own.

On 18 November, Hugo Young, writing in the *Sunday Times*, previewed the BBC Dimbleby Lecture, which Roy Jenkins was due to give the following Thursday. It started rather unkindly, saying that most people would have forgotten who Roy Jenkins was, since for three years he had been in Europe 'jetting from capital to capital as the pseudo-equal, or more often the impotent servant, of a Prime Ministers' club he never managed to join'. Predicting that within a year the Labour Party would be in the hands of the two least trusted groups in the whole of public life, the Bennite left or the trade union leadership, he asked whether Roy Jenkins on his return from Europe would simply join the natural beneficiaries of political extremism, the Liberal Party. 'It would surely be a quixotic and futile thing for an ambitious man to do.' He concluded that, since Roy himself was scarcely a popular figure to compare with Shirley Williams, if he 'is to make any headway he is going to have to find the moment, to put it simply, when Mr Rodgers can be persuaded that the future of Britain is more important than the sensibilities of a few party worthies in Stockton on Tees [Bill Rodgers's constituency]'. By emphasising the role of Bill, Hugo Young was stressing the need to win over the traditional Labour Party in the north-east, a haven of moderation.

Some have tried to pretend that the Dimbleby Lecture was the first and critical move that led inevitably to the founding of the SDP. Roy's lecture was undoubtedly for some an important milestone, but in my view it was neither the first nor the most critical. It was of nowhere near the same political significance as, for example, the 28 October 1971 vote of the sixty-nine Labour MPs who defied a three-line whip to support entry to the European Community, or the decision of the Parliamentary Labour Party to elect Michael Foot as its leader in November 1980. The main thrust of the lecture was an elegant and convincing case for proportional representation and coalition government. Never before had it been championed by such a senior political figure or taken to such a mass audience on prime time television; and Roy got a large number of letters, overwhelmingly supportive, which increased his enthusiasm for realignment.

For someone in my position trying, with others, to mobilise the Manifesto Group of MPs in Parliament and the CLV in the country to fight a desperate battle inside the Labour Party, Roy's speech was a diversion from the task in hand. Roy was out of British politics and was bound to see things differently. I made my view clear the next day, speaking at the South-West Staffordshire Constituency Labour Party dinner on Friday 23 November. 'The centre of the Labour Party must now stand firm. We will not be tempted by siren voices from outside, from those who have given up the fight from within.' I stressed that I was not prepared to admit defeat, to accept that within two years we could not turn our party once more into a strong electoral force capable of ousting Mrs Thatcher and regaining power as a broad-based party with appeal across the classes and the divisions of British society. I also said that new parties did not carry instant solutions and that proportional representation did not of itself guarantee political stability. But equally the Labour Party must recognise that if we were to continue to resist proportional representation then this was only credible and tolerable if the Labour Party itself represented a coalition which mirrored the broad spread of views of Labour voters. I stressed that if we narrowed our coalition within the party then we would forfeit the support of many millions of people who currently voted Labour, and proportional representation would become irresistible.

The things that Roy was saying were not, however, lost on me or on others like Bill Rodgers. When on 27 November at a joint meeting of the NEC and the shadow Cabinet, I once more spoke passionately against giving the NEC ultimate control of the manifesto. I warned that there was a political vacuum which could easily be filled by the Liberals if the Labour Party tore itself apart over constitutional changes. That Saturday, Bill spoke in Abertillery in even more outspoken terms, in effect giving the Labour Party one year to put its house in order and predicting that if it did not it would split.

Over the next year, the views of those of us who were to form the SDP repeatedly diverged, came together, or crossed on this crucial question of fighting inside the party or leaving it. At this stage, I was more firmly fighting from within the Labour Party than Bill or Shirley Williams. According to Roy's European diary, while Bill was listening to the Dimbleby Lecture he claimed he had had a vision of himself sitting in the headquarters of the new party with his sleeves rolled up, actually organising things. Even so, Roy records that when he had lunch with both of them on the day of Bill's Abertillery speech, they were anxious – Shirley perhaps a little more than Bill – to tell him that it was always possible, though not likely, that things would go sufficiently well in the Labour Party to make them want to stay. Roy thought then that Bill had reached the watershed, whereas Shirley had not. For my part, I was nowhere near the watershed and there was a lot of fight still in me. The irony was that it would be Shirley and Bill, in the latter part of 1980, who would be the ones who looked closest to backtracking and staying with Labour.

At the end of November the European Council in Dublin Castle had the British budgetary question on the agenda and Margaret Thatcher demanded 'her money' back. After the initial honeymoon with all things European, and having in the summer foolishly lifted the British veto on a zero farm price settlement, she found that she had no bargaining power and instead behaved, as one of the participants patronisingly observed, like 'the grocer's daughter'. From a nation of shopkeepers, what did one expect? Britain and the European Community were on a collision course and Margaret Thatcher was riding a populist issue with the reckless abandon that was to become all too familiar. The politics of Europe were once again set to divide Britain and not just the Labour Party. My position remained as it always had been, strongly pro-Europe but strongly against federalism, and I believed that the budgetary mechanism had to be altered in favour of the UK.

The political situation inside the Labour Party steadily got worse. On 13 December Francis Pym announced to the House of Commons that the government was accepting the deployment of 160 cruise missiles in Britain, initially at Greenham Common and then at Molesworth. Bill Rodgers replied from the front bench for the Labour Party and managed to avoid outright opposition to the deployment decision, concentrating more on the absence of parliamentary debate. But the Labour left now had a defence issue to get their teeth into and the policy debate was about to become as divisive as the internal constitutional debate.

The parliamentary party discussed the cruise missile decision on 16 January 1980 and, even though the decision was overshadowed by the Soviet invasion of Afghanistan, we knew there was enough dissent within the party to indicate that trouble lay ahead. Sure enough, it surfaced again at the joint meeting of the shadow Cabinet with the NEC on 30 January. Tony Benn's intervention, sloganising future policy to 'No cruise, no Pershing and no successor to Polaris', showed that he was determined to widen the attack from constitutional questions to the most divisive issue within the party, defence. The policy reversals and constitutional changes were undoubtedly depressing. But far worse was the way that decent, moderate people seemed to have gone into hiding. It was as if the party were in a collective funk and everyone was looking for the nearest hole in which they could bury themselves for a few years in the hope that the nightmare of the left in control of the party would somehow pass without their having to do anything to prevent it. There seemed to be so little fight left, let alone the energy to embark on the rethink of fundamentals so desperately needed.

The *Times* commissioned a poll in mid-January showing that on the issue of a new centre party, the public was as split as its potential leaders. A clear majority of people favoured the formation of a new party in the centre, but rather ominously there was no consensus on its component parts. There was a strong desire to avoid a split in the Labour Party but a deep unease about the working of the political system, significantly greater among Labour and Liberal voters. At the time the poll was taken Labour was still ahead with 42 per cent, the Conservatives had 39 per cent, the Liberals 16 per cent and the Nationalists 2 per cent. What emerged was that a centre party which consisted only of a breakaway group of moderate and right-wing Labour candidates would succeed only in splitting the Labour vote without having any real chance of winning power. It was thought that the effect would be to give Britain two Liberal-sized parties in the centre. If a centre party was formed, David Steel emerged as the clear favourite to be its leader, with Edward Heath second, Shirley Williams third and Roy Jenkins fourth, with less than half the support of David Steel. Bill Rodgers, the only other candidate mentioned, had barely any support.

In early February, the parliamentary party witnessed a small vignette of the future when Neil Kinnock, speaking as shadow Education Minister, gave the first sign that he might split off from his hitherto firm identification with the far left. In a fit of righteousness he refused to commit the party to repealing the Education Bill, and while he was prepared to say we would end the assisted places scheme, he was not prepared to pledge the reinstitution of school meals and free milk. This caused outrage on the left and Neil tried to speak again, forgetting the old adage, 'When in a hole, stop digging.' It was, nevertheless, a sign that he was coming to grips with the realities of public expenditure, and starting to speak as though he might one day be in government. I was pleased by his speech and did not enjoy seeing him attacked, though many on the left and the right were bitter at what he said and delighted to embarrass him. However, eight years and two election defeats were needed before Neil Kinnock was prepared to fully abandon the left-wing policies that he had espoused since his youth.

On 4 March 1980 Robert Mugabe won the election in Zimbabwe with an overall majority and Margaret Thatcher's government had its first major success – albeit achieved as a result of their first U-turn. By one of those tricks of fate, because Peter Shore, who was by then shadow Foreign Minister, was out of the country watching the elections, Jim Callaghan asked me, though shadow Energy spokesman, to respond to the announcement in the House of Commons giving the details of Mugabe's victory. For the Conservative right wing it was a shattering result: even the government had been confident that Mugabe's ZANU would not win outright and an Nkomo-led coalition would be the outcome. As I rose to speak in reply there was a strange stillness in the House. Those Conservative MPs who had lambasted me month after month for insisting that the Patriotic Front, and in particular Robert Mugabe, whom they loathed, had to be a party to any settlement, were strangely silent. I decided not to utter a word of self-justification and instead to lavish praise upon the government. Robert Mugabe's outright victory was a vindication of much that I had done as Foreign Secretary in opposing the internal agreement and I did not need to spell it out, for everyone in the House of Commons that day knew the score.

I will always treasure Elizabeth Longford's report of the Queen's views:

On Zimbabwe Independence Day a high official said to her, 'What a superb job Lord Carrington has done.'

'Yes, indeed. But we mustn't forget that it was David Owen who put it all in train.'

The official knew this was true and admired her all the more for recognising it.

Only in Africa could there have been such a reconciliation as Robert Mugabe started as Prime Minister in 1980. He asked General Walls to stay on, citing the fact that he had tried to kill him as justification for now asking him to protect his life. The head of Rhodesian intelligence also stayed on to serve Mugabe. But, as I have already described, Mugabe, a zealot and a fanatic, was bent on building up his own power base. In October 1980, only six months after independence, Mugabe secretly signed an agreement with North Korea to train a new 5th Brigade, composed almost entirely of Shona-speaking former guerrillas which used indiscriminate force, with beatings, arson and mass murder in January 1983 against the Matabele people. Sadly Mugabe's government did not embrace the market economy, and when Nelson Mandela was released in 1990 it was the new South Africa that became the economic lead country in southern Africa, and Zimbabwe began to slip behind, with the Shona becoming ever more assertive and Mugabe, by now President, ever more dictatorial. By 2009 Mugabe was still in charge at the age of eighty-five and the official inflation rate reached astronomical heights. South Africa eventually brokered a sort of coalition between ZANU-PF and the opposition Movement for Democratic Change, but no one knew whether it would succeed while Mugabe remained President.

Meanwhile within the Labour Party we did not succeed in the CLV in igniting any sustained flame of resistance. We had no large financial resources and only limited union backing, and we had to contend with apathy and the increasing fear of deselection. It might have been a reflection on our own personalities or the way we were campaigning, but it is significant that the Solidarity campaign, which under Roy Hattersley took over from the CLV in the early 1980s, seemed to fare no better. It was only when the trade union leaders stirred themselves, or were stirred by Neil Kinnock, to fight Militant that any real fightback began. Trade unionists found it easier to defeat the Militant Tendency as a separate organisation if they were not encumbered by fighting Militant on policy issues as well. So the trade union leaders who backed the expulsion of militants had a justification of sorts in not shifting party policy until this arguably more damaging long-term threat to the Labour Party was removed. Moderates make bad militants and the CLV did not stop the dismal tide of organisational and political extremism as it lapped at the feet of the Callaghan leadership and threatened to engulf the party. In fairness to the CLV, it needed Jim Callaghan's overt support, not merely covert sympathy.

On 26 March the NEC agreed to a suggestion from Moss Evans of the TGWU that we needed a recall conference to discuss industrial policy. In the event Tony Benn managed to ensure that the policy document presented at the special conference on 31 May, entitled 'Peace, Jobs and Freedom', became the vehicle for a massive shift towards the left's entire policy agenda. The promise to amend the 1972 European Communities Act, for example, talked of 'restoring to the House of Commons the full control of all law-making and tax-gathering powers, now ceded to the European Community', a recipe for leaving. Defence was just as bad – we were now being told that 'the Labour Party opposes the manufacture and deployment of cruise missiles' and was refusing to permit their deployment in Britain by the United States or any other country. When the document was discussed in the shadow Cabinet, Jim Callaghan got rather exasperated when some of us suggested that these commitments were not just difficult to live with, they were impossible to live with and the left's challenge could not simply be ignored. At one stage the NEC even looked as if they might refuse to allow Jim Callaghan, still leader of the party after all, to introduce the document to the conference. The usual moderate blandishments were invoked against not reacting vigorously – the document was not binding on the party, it did not have the status of a manifesto, and if we were low-key now we would be able to retrieve some of the commitments at a later date. I never believed any of this. The situation was deteriorating day by day.

During May 1980, the political atmosphere worsened. By the middle of the month, inflation had risen to 21.8 per cent. Though the Day of Action called by the TUC had not been a great success, it had, nevertheless, mobilised many in the trade union movement who would not normally have protested. The view that the Conservative government was the most reactionary, divisive government in our history was widespread inside the Labour movement. This meant that the climate for the special conference was developing into one of deep hostility to the Conservatives. There was growing intolerance for anyone who could be depicted as in any way supporting policies which could be equated with those of the Conservative government. The constant publicity about the excessive British budgetary contribution to the European Community with headlines like 'Mrs T asks for more' was also arousing all the old, latent hostility to everything stemming from Brussels.

Meanwhile, Tony Benn and the Campaign for Labour Party Democracy had come together with a bizarre grouping of broad left pressure groups – Clause IV, Independent Labour Publications, Institute for Workers Control, Labour Co-ordinating Committee, National Organization of Labour Students, Socialist Campaign for a Labour Victory – all combining to form the Rank and File Mobilising Committee. Each of these groups, to a greater or lesser degree, lived in its own world of purist extremism. One only needed to read a magazine like *London Labour Briefing* to see how remote they were from reality. Headlines like 'The progress of the class struggle in Bromley Ravensbourne' or 'Yes, the international banking crisis is *sexist*' would have been funny if the people who wrote it were not engaged on a serious project to wreck the Labour Party.

The Rank and File Mobilising Committee launched a new publication in June which contained excerpts from a speech by Tony Benn:

> In the heart of parliamentarianism lies the continuation of the Burkeian myth. We've got to deal with that by getting every Labour candidate to sign that he supports the manifesto. Now, that's not an innovation, we did it for the European election. We wouldn't endorse any candidate for the European election until they had signed that they supported the manifesto.

Edmund Burke was a Whig who represented Bristol in Parliament for six years from 1774 to 1780. By now, Tony Benn, as a fellow Bristolian MP, had developed a fetish about challenging everything

Edmund Burke had ever said. But Burke's definition of representative government is as true today as when he first articulated it. It was not as if Burke did not understand the need for party. Long before parties had reached their present dominance, he argued that party government was the best government, for he recognised that MPs needed to unite to promote, by their joint endeavours, the national interest. But Burke also said that an MP as 'your representative owes you not his industry only, but his judgement; and he betrays, instead of serving you, if he sacrifices it to your opinion'. He was quite right. It was becoming ever more obvious that the fight we were embarked on inside the Labour Party was a fight over some of the essential tenets of parliamentary democracy.

Jim Callaghan's speech to the special conference was lacklustre and his words on the European Community and cruise missiles were too carefully crafted to carry conviction or force. He talked about that section of the document 'that seems to point to unilateral action' and went on, 'Whilst I respect those who call for unilateral disarmament, I cannot agree that we should take an insular view of our responsibilities.' This was hardly fighting stuff and I felt the conference was barely listening. I passed Peter Shore and asked him if he was going to speak. To my amazement he said no. I then bumped into Bill Rodgers and found that he too was not intending to speak. He was feeling guilty about it, but Jim had apparently persuaded him that it would be wiser not to. So the shadow Foreign and Defence Ministers were not even going to challenge the conference to stick to the policies we had pursued while in government. I went forward into the hall and sat down next to Denis Healey. I discovered that he intended to speak only on the economy and was not going to touch on foreign affairs. I had already listened to two rabidly unilateralist speeches, both of which were applauded from the platform with exaggerated enthusiasm by Neil Kinnock, so I decided that I would have to speak.

I had not prepared a speech and had no idea when I would be called. I rose at the moment that Lena Jeger, the chairman, called Clive Jenkins and since he spoke in part on energy she must have thought that it would be a good idea to call me as shadow Energy spokesman. So to my surprise I was called after only one other constituency speaker.

I concentrated initially on energy questions and then switched to defence: 'It is no use expecting us to have a place at SALT III if we are going to take decisions on cruise missiles before we have even entered into the negotiations.' This provoked the expected uproar and I went on, 'Oh no, it has to be faced in this country. It is no use expecting your friends and allies to expect you to have a place in those negotiations if you are pre-empting it.' To further cries I added, 'I am telling you as someone who has dealt with those negotiations.' This provoked even louder cries of protest from the floor. 'I will say it to you again. If you think you can enter into arms control negotiations with your hands tied behind your back, with no form of leverage, you are deluding yourself.' Lena Jeger then intervened to call for order: 'The speaker has a right to be heard, comrades. Please be quiet.'

After I had finished speaking, as I returned to my seat I could sense the animosity in some parts of the hall. I wondered whether I should have stayed quiet but my old regional organiser in the south-west patted me on the shoulder and said, 'In fifteen years you'll be very proud of that speech.' The booing did not upset me. It is like boxing, when you barely feel the blows; when speaking you barely hear the boos. I had been heckled enough in the past not to be put off by that – in fact I rather enjoyed it – but it undoubtedly made me more aggressive in response.

It had been a depressing first year out of government. Stripped of the trappings of office, too many of the former Labour Cabinet ministers lacked authority and most were trimming on every issue to accommodate the virulence of the left in Parliament and in their constituencies. I was looking forward to the meeting which I had fixed up with Shirley Williams and Bill Rodgers and little realised that the European Community, which had bitterly divided us three from the Labour Party in 1971–2, was now about to be brought back by the left to actually split the party.

On 5 June 1980 I was stopped by Malcolm Rutherford of the *Financial Times* as I was walking through the underpass to the House of Commons. He told me that the anti-EEC Common Market Safeguards Committee had just issued a statement saying that Labour Party policies and the demands of European Community membership were irreconcilable. The statement, signed by John Silkin, said that they were going to attempt, at the autumn conference, to get the party committed to withdrawing from the European Community with no renegotiation and not even a referendum. It was one more step away from sanity, one that was to precipitate a response that I was almost certain a normally cautious man like John Silkin had not expected.

I left Malcolm Rutherford, went to my office and put out an immediate press release. It argued that millions of Labour Party voters and thousands of Labour Party activists had voted to stay in the EEC and that no more certain recipe for splitting the Labour Party could be imagined than to ask members to choose between their commitment to the party and their belief that it was in the national interest to remain a member of the European Community. I said 'My party or my country' is not a happy choice, but there could be only one answer.

Next morning, I met Shirley Williams and Bill Rodgers in Shirley's flat, where we had our first substantial political discussion since the election. The morning papers had been full of the impending row within the Labour Party over the European Community. We decided to issue a joint statement to catch the Sunday newspapers. Shirley's was the main draft, but we all contributed words and sentences. We declared that for the Labour Party to make a manifesto commitment to leave the European Community in 1983 or 1984 would be 'irresponsible, opportunistic and short sighted', and added that we could have no part in it. We asked, 'Is this decision to be endlessly reopened? Are the old divisions to be stirred up again and again, weakening our national self-confidence and our ability to contribute constructively to economic, energy and social problems?' We ended by saying, 'There are some of us who will not accept a choice between socialism and Europe. We will choose them both.' That was the first indication I had ever given that I could contemplate leaving the Labour Party for a new social democratic party. We resolved to meet over the next few weeks with a view to drafting a much more comprehensive statement covering economic and social questions for we knew that Europe was too narrow a platform. The Gang of Three was born.

The next day our defiance was headline news in the *Sunday Times*. It was an important milestone in the birth of the SDP for it brought together the critical mass needed to attract other Labour MPs. It was also a positive partnership with good humour and give-and-take. We stayed close and pretty cohesive right up until the 1983 general election, when both Bill and Shirley lost their seats.

Our decision to fight together did not imply that any of us was ready to accept Roy Jenkins's dream of a centre party. On Monday 9 June Roy spoke to the Parliamentary Press Gallery, saying that there was no question of his flickering back to British politics, like a moth to a candle, before he finished his presidency of the European Commission on 6 January 1981. However, he talked of an experimental plane, his way of describing the centre party with which the press associated him. Roy's experimental plane was of little interest to me at this time, except that I could see that if he ever took off it would have profound consequences for our fight within the Labour Party. I believe that Bill and Shirley shared this view. While neither of them told me much about their meetings with Roy Jenkins at this time, in Roy's *European Diary* the impression is given that they were interested in a new party. I recall, however, that in discussions at this time they were still resisting any split and were extremely reluctant to contemplate ever being part of a centre party.

Not surprisingly, the anti-Marketeers hit back at our Gang of Three statement and Peter Shore and John Silkin got involved in the controversy. Jim Callaghan stepped in and called all those in the shadow Cabinet who were arguing in public to a meeting in his room in the House of Commons. He asked us to try and defuse the controversy. Bill and I replied that we could not stay silent: the danger to the European Community was now a very real one, for a resolution demanding withdrawal from the Community had been circulated to constituency parties by the Safeguards Campaign. If we did nothing it would become official Labour Party policy within months. All we could promise, in deference to Jim, was that we would try our best to keep personalities out of the conflict.

Then nemesis struck. The Labour Party commission of enquiry was having a meeting to finalise its report on reforming the party's constitution on the weekend of 14–15 June at the ASTMS training college at Bishop's Stortford. On the Saturday the commission had a major division over the question of mandatory reselection, whereby a constituency, irrespective of whether it was happy with its MP, would have to hold a selection procedure. Even Clive Jenkins had realised that this was a deeply sensitive issue for MPs and had proposed a compromise, stipulating that two-thirds of a constituency party could reject automatic reselection. But Moss Evans voted with the left to defeat this and the full reselection proposal was carried. Jim reacted angrily, saying, 'I can't go back to the PLP with this,' but when he suggested opening MPs' selection to the wider constituency membership, it was pointed out that the PLP had itself rejected this option. The leader of the party was humiliatingly rebuffed.

On the Sunday the conference turned to the question of leadership. Michael Foot proposed continuing the present arrangement with the MPs alone electing the leader. He was only supported by Jim Callaghan and Terry Duffy. It was then that Jim Callaghan was told for the first time by the unions about their concept of an electoral college made up of 50 per cent MPs and 25 per cent trade union representation: 20 per cent for constituency parties and 5 per cent for others, with power to elect the party leader and to control the party manifesto. By the early evening Jim had endorsed it.

I was outraged. It was incomprehensible that Jim Callaghan put his name to such an indefensible proposition. That the leader of the Labour Party and, worse still, when in government the Prime Minister of the country, should be elected by such a body would, I thought, have stuck in his gullet. Why had he not taken the battle to the shadow Cabinet and from there to the parliamentary party? The brutal truth was that fighting would have meant defying the unions and the conference, and this Jim was obviously no longer prepared to attempt. He would have been wiser to have resigned then and there and put all his weight behind Denis Healey to succeed him. No one could blame him for wanting to retire to his farm in Sussex, but many would blame him for putting his authority behind the electoral college.

That Sunday evening, Jim had spoken with Bill Rodgers and tried to square him before the meeting of the shadow Cabinet on the Monday. I was glad he had not attempted to telephone me, for I think we would have had angry words. At the shadow Cabinet, Jim Callaghan and I had our first and only row. I attacked both the concept of the electoral college and the fact that he and Michael had come to us already totally compromised. Jim, who clearly had a guilty conscience over what he had done and was behaving in an unusually furtive way, hit back. He called me a 'political infant', which stimulated Bill to jump to my defence. Suddenly the shadow Cabinet was riven. All of us had served in Cabinet together with good will, often friendship and certainly fundamental respect for Jim Callaghan; that was now jeopardised.

For the first time I really began to wonder whether the Labour Party was now salvageable. I was still not thinking of a centre party but I was questioning my continued membership of Labour. I had tended to agree with Jim Callaghan that 'any party in this country has to rest on organised interests', and that no party could get very far in challenging the two big dominant parties unless it could develop some equivalent organised support. The Liberals lacked such a base and constantly showed their lack of moorings in their indiscipline. The consumer provided a countervailing interest to the producer but so far that had only been mobilised in an apolitical way. But my lack of faith in a new venture no longer shielded me from the reality of what had happened to the old one. I had hitherto argued for continuing the fight within the Labour Party for two to three years more, right up to the general election if necessary. I now despaired. Waiting it out, hoping to turn things round, seemed pointless, for we had suffered a mortal blow at Bishop's Stortford. With this albatross of an electoral college, MPs had lost the last democratic safeguard of being able to mobilise the parliamentary party against the NEC and if need be the Labour Party conference. It was that safeguard which Hugh Gaitskell had used in 1960–61 as the base from which to reverse the conference's unilateralist decision. I wondered whether I would even want to stay in the party beyond the October conference if the electoral college went through. My thoughts were turning once again towards medicine and leaving politics.

I was far from alone in my opposition to the electoral college in the shadow Cabinet, though perhaps mine was expressed with the most vehemence. My opposition was total, and I was so angry with Jim that I felt that if he did not stand down, Denis Healey should challenge him for the leadership. Denis himself was clearly angry but did not know exactly how to get out of the mess we were in without offending Jim. He was loath to do that for he knew Jim could still influence his chances in any leadership election. Roy Hattersley appeared to be strongly opposed, but again seemed to fear offending Jim. Bill Rodgers was appalled, Roy Mason did not like it and nor did Merlyn Rees. Bill, Roy Hattersley and I attended a Manifesto Group meeting of Labour MPs later that day which passed a motion highly critical of the commission's compromise, referring to 'dangerous proposals conjured out of thin air'. The group called upon the commission to go back and produce totally different proposals, fairly pointing out that an electoral college had already been overwhelmingly rejected by the parliamentary party. It said that a college would be 'unworkable and constitutionally unacceptable to those who believe in parliamentary democracy'. In a statement, the Campaign for Labour Victory called the proposals a complete sell-out.

On 15 July 1980 Francis Pym, the Secretary of State for Defence, made an important statement about Britain's strategic nuclear deterrent. He announced that, as the best and most cost-effective way of replacing Polaris, the government had chosen the US Trident submarine-launched ballistic missile system. Bill Rodgers, who replied for the Labour Party, said, 'We believe that the case for buying Trident has not yet been made, and we cannot approve it.' Given the manifesto, he could hardly have said anything else; we were landed with the commitment to oppose Trident. What remained vital was to retain a commitment to a British contribution to NATO's nuclear deterrent – whether that was achieved through cruise missiles deployed on submarines or through air-launched nuclear missiles was nowhere near as important as keeping support for the principle.

As my depression about Labour's attitudes deepened, I increasingly turned to the possibilities and problems of a new party – its origins, its base, its relationship with other parties. These thoughts were uppermost when David Watt and his family came to stay for the weekend at the end of July. David and I went over the new party conundrum in depth. I could speak far more frankly to him than to most others because I completely trusted his discretion. He had talked to Roy Jenkins in Brussels a few months earlier and, while he was pessimistic about the chances of any new party, he had told Roy that he was convinced it could only work if it was based on a Labour Party split. In particular David felt that if Roy were merely intent on joining the Liberals, no breakthrough could ever be achieved. I thus knew Roy's thinking about the Liberals; I also knew that his Liberal friends, like Mark Bonham Carter, would influence him towards the Liberal Party and that in many of his policy attitudes he was already close to the Liberals. Perhaps this should have worried me more but at this stage, at least, Roy was not the politician who interested me. Both David and I agreed that Denis Healey was a far more critical figure than Roy. If only Denis could be persuaded really to fight from within and split only if that failed then we would be in serious business. Reluctantly, however, we both feared that Denis was now so compromised in his attempt to win votes when Jim went, which we were all expecting to be soon, that the chances of persuading him of the necessity to fight now were very slim. The result of this discussion, therefore, was that we were both pessimistic about the chances of any Liberal centre party but felt that we could not rule out a new party of the centre-left and its moment could arrive when some of us might have to split from Labour, regardless of its chances.

Why did I oppose then and continue to oppose Roy's idea of a centre party based on the Liberals? The answer had little to do with feeling myself more 'left wing' than Roy or even with being 'socialist'. Although this word was much bandied about, it shed more heat than light. The truth can only be understood by remembering what Britain was like in 1980. We had suffered decades of economic decline, a series of massive financial crises, a prolonged period of vicious industrial disputes and a collapse of the consensus that underpinned the welfare state. The response of the ruling Establishment during these times had been miserable. There had been a collective failure of will and now, faced with the need to rethink fundamentals, the inclination of the centre was to snipe from the sidelines. This was not confined to politicians – it applied, for example, just as much to the leadership of the Civil Service. In other words the failure of will was a failure of the entire centre.

So I felt that joining a centre party based on the Liberals would be jumping out of the frying pan into the cotton wool. I was determined to remain a redistributionist. I believed that the extremes of left and right could only be defeated by an explicitly radical alternative. Those beliefs I felt could be best expressed by remaining a part of the social democratic, Socialist International world and using continental social democracy as the starting point for a fresh political party in Britain.

For the Gang of Three the main preoccupation now was to draft a more comprehensive policy statement. My diary shows that I had at least five meetings with Bill, Shirley or both prior to the publication of our open letter in the *Guardian* on 1 August. The long letter went through many different drafts with each of us adding and subtracting phrases or words. By the end it was genuinely the property of all three of us. Throughout, the major issue with which we had to grapple was how far we went in implying that we were ready to leave the Labour Party and help create a new party. On 3 July, with a redraft of Bill's initial draft, I wrote to Shirley, 'The hardest question I find to resolve is whether we should explicitly raise again the question of another socialist party. Again on balance I conclude we should, but fairly indirectly, and I think we need to guard against being thought to be "opting out" rather than "fighting on".'

On 1 August our letter duly appeared, prominently positioned in the *Guardian*. The opening sentence read, 'The Labour Party is facing the gravest crisis in its history – graver even than the crisis of 1931.' This was followed by three sections – on the commitment to the mixed economy, the commitment to international socialism and the commitment to representative democracy. However, the sting was in the tail and it was over these words that we had wrestled.

> If the NEC remains committed to pursuing its present course and if, consequently, fears multiply among the people, then support for a centre party will strengthen as disaffected voters move away from Labour. We have already said that we will not support a centre party for it would lack roots and a coherent philosophy. But if the Labour Party abandons its democratic and internationalist principles, the argument may grow for a new democratic socialist party to establish itself as a party of conscience and reform committed to those principles.

David Steel then wrote a letter to the three of us via the *Guardian*, signed 'Yours fraternally'. It only confirmed to me his superficial approach. Its aim was publicity. He had written to Bill and sent copies to Shirley and me. I am not sure that Bill even replied and in as much as we had any view it was one of irritation. For the three of us, rightly or wrongly, the Liberal Party was low on our agenda. There were other priorities. Had we known it was so high on Roy Jenkins's agenda, I am sure that prudence alone would have led us to give the issue more thought at this stage. As it was, all three of us saw the Liberal Party as an issue to be faced after any party was formed and, we hoped, from a position of strength rather than weakness. Our focus was on whether we could create a party which Labour voters could support, replacing the Labour Party by a similar party, though not a replica, or marginalising the Labour Party to its hard unrepresentative left and taking over a substantial part of its voters.

That summer in America I finished writing the manuscript of *Face the Future*, which was due to be published in the new year. As I chronicled Britain's decline, my resolve to try and reverse it with radical changes in our political system increased. Here I was able to talk to American friends about their experience of helping John Anderson. He had campaigned as a third-party candidate for the presidency and their two-party system and first-past-the-post voting had squeezed him dry. I also had time to reflect on the British historical precedents. They were not likely to encourage anyone to split: Ramsay MacDonald's National Government and Oswald Mosley's New Party, the disaffiliation of the Independent Labour Party in 1932, Sir Richard Acland's Common Wealth Party in 1942. All had failed. I returned from America still keen to do battle from within the Labour Party.

Wherever I went I found an extraordinary contrast between people's public and private positions. In private there were any number of Labour MPs and Labour Party members horrified by what was happening and yet in public there were almost none who would fight back. Abroad, fellow socialists were watching with amazement what was happening to the Labour Party, which for many of them had been the model for their social democracy in the immediate post-war period. Surely, I told myself, we could have continental social democracy in Britain. I became more conscious than ever of the contradictions on which British Labourism had been founded, more convinced than ever that Hugh Gaitskell had been right to single out the significance of Clause IV in the constitution after electoral defeat in 1959.

In September, irony of ironies, a few months before I was ready to contemplate leaving the Labour Party, my Devonport constituency became a safe Labour seat. I had been in highly marginal seats for the fourteen years I had been MP, but the Boundary Commissioners now came forward with a proposal to create three Plymouth constituencies, North, East and West. The northern constituency, later called Devonport, bore only a passing resemblance to the original Devonport constituency. But it contained all of the post-war council estates between Dartmoor and the city. It was solid Labour territory and would probably never be won by the Conservatives.

The 1980 Labour Party conference, held at Blackpool, was to prove to be far more disastrous than any of us expected. On Monday 29 September the CLV had a meeting in the Baronial Hall of the Winter Gardens. The Gang of Three all spoke and it was a rousing affair. I said it was time for the compromising to end and the fightback to start, and Shirley warned that there was such a thing as a fascism of the left. That evening in Shirley's room in the Imperial Hotel we heard that Clive Jenkins was confident of swinging the trade union votes to win on an electoral college and on withdrawal from the Community. I heard fellow MPs talk for the first time about leaving the Labour Party without qualifying what they were saying. Ironically many of those who spoke most fervently that night eventually stayed with the party. But that night we all felt doom laden.

Next morning, Tuesday 30 September, the results of the con-stituency section for the NEC showed that my vote had slipped. I had 106,000 votes, Jack Ashley was runner-up and Peter Shore and Roy Hattersley well ahead of me. I was paying the price for the Gang of Three letter. When Jim Callaghan spoke that day he once again made a plea for party unity but there was precious little of it about. Towards the end of his speech he said, 'Nobody here, I think, talks any nonsense about centre parties or the rest of it. It's as dead as a dodo, mere fluff.' It was sad to listen to someone, who over the years had been able to dominate the conference, speak with so little of his former influence or power.

On the Wednesday morning it was my turn. I spoke from the floor against a Clive Jenkins motion urging the Labour Party to include the withdrawal from the European Community as a priority in our next manifesto. My speech attracted applause but it was mixed with cries of dissent, and the withdrawal motion was carried on a card vote by 5,042,000 to 2,097,000. The requisite two-thirds majority was not there to ensure it was in the manifesto but nobody listening to that debate could have had any doubt that Labour would fight the next election on an outright commitment to withdraw and what is more if it won it would take Britain out without a referendum, defying the validity of the one it had offered the British people in 1975.

By the Thursday morning the conference seemed determined to convince the country that it was totally in the grip of the far left by proceeding to vote for unilateral nuclear disarmament. This was despite Bill Rodgers's warning that, if they were to go down a road of the single-handed renunciation of nuclear weapons, Labour would be rejected overwhelmingly by the people whose support they needed for victory.

These blows, coming one upon the other, were shattering and for some of us, decisive. Indeed some of us might have preferred to make our move that day. I certainly think Bill would have been in favour of taking a very significant step away from Labour then. But by the time Bill had spoken to the press after his speech, Shirley was already in full cry at a CLV fringe meeting. We had agreed we would meet before the meeting started to discuss what we would say, but it had not proved possible. It was clear that the electoral college question was going to be referred to a special conference and Shirley said, without consultation, that we would take our battle there. Bill turned to me and said, 'Well, it's nice to know.' It was not Shirley's fault, she had to react, but it showed how these deeply important issues were having to be dealt with rapidly, almost instinctively. Events were moving so fast that we could hardly anticipate them. My mood was very tough indeed when I got up to speak, and the *Guardian* report was correct in saying that I took the whole argument a step further by implying that Jim Callaghan should only stay as leader if he was prepared to join in the fight against the left. 'We are fed up with this fudging and mudging, with mush and slush. We need courage, conviction and hard work ... We cannot turn this party round unless there is much clearer and more decisive leadership.' Some thought the word 'mudging' was there only for euphony, but Eric Partridge's *Dictionary of Slang and Unconventional English* says that it is an old dialect word for 'moving very quietly'.

On Friday morning, 3 October, I worked on a speech which I intended to make on Saturday afternoon at a Labour Party meeting at Blaenau Ffestiniog in north Wales, not exactly a media centre. Mike Thomas came to help me and we decided there and then that we could not defeat the left's call for a wider franchise to elect the leader by advocating that it should be left to MPs. Our best course, and the most principled, would be to exploit the opportunity that conference vote had left us. The party had not been able to agree a specific mechanism for the leader's election. It had only made the commitment to widen the franchise. We had to ensure that one member, one vote became the preferred way of widening the franchise and not the electoral college.

My speech that afternoon was aimed directly at the Bishop's Stortford compromise over an electoral college. I argued that it conceded a principle, and in place of a legitimate, proven, parliamentary procedure offered a mess of pottage. Only on Thursday the voters had seen on their television screens the total shambles surrounding the trade union block vote in Blackpool. Day by day, we had seen in Blackpool why an electoral college, in any of the forms proposed, was not acceptable.

> We cannot have a Prime Minister chosen by block votes that do not accurately reflect the number of their members paying the political levy. We cannot have a Prime Minister chosen by block votes, cast in line with the overall policy of a union whose policy may be determined by a body which includes conservatives, communists and people who do not pay the political levy. We cannot have a Prime Minister chosen by the switching of a block vote where a communist can influence that decision. We cannot have a Prime Minister chosen by the switching of block votes merely because the general secretary of a trade union happens to be absent. We cannot allow the choice of the country's Prime Minister to pass from Parliament to the caucus; to unrepresentative block votes and to unrepresentative delegates.

Driving back to Buttermere late that afternoon over the twisting roads of Snowdonia, I began, really for the first time, to think in detail about what would be necessary to create a new party.

Then on 15 October the inevitable happened. Jim Callaghan formally announced his resignation as Labour Party leader. We were now confronted with a battle on two fronts: we had simultaneously to elect a leader under the old system while trying to get the PLP to reject an electoral college of any kind and support one member, one vote.

All the time that this battle was raging we were grappling with the problem of a new party. On Saturday 19 October Roy and Jennifer Jenkins came over to Buttermere for lunch. Their last visit had been early in 1976, when Roy had told me that Harold Wilson was going to resign, which showed how much we had drifted apart. It was more relaxed than Debbie and I had anticipated but I still could not be sure what sort of party Roy really wanted. During a walk after lunch he told me about his proposed new policy institute, to be an offshoot of the Radical Centre, a small organisation he had already established. I am afraid I concluded that Roy was trying to find a vehicle to make himself Prime Minister and that made me wary. I had just finished reading a book by Dingle Foot which quoted a speech by Lord Randolph Churchill delivered in June 1886 to the electors of Paddington South. He had asked why Mr Gladstone had reserved the Home Rule Bill for his closing days and had concluded it was for one reason only: 'To gratify the imagination of an old man in a hurry.' Though Gladstone was then seventy-seven and Roy was only fifty-nine, it was very obvious that Roy too was an old man in a hurry.

In the shadow Cabinet we decided to go ahead with MPs electing our new leader and the PLP supported us. On 4 November the first ballot results from the leadership election were announced. Denis Healey had 112 votes, Michael Foot 83, John Silkin 38 and Peter Shore 32. It was obvious that Michael could win on the next ballot. On Monday 10 November he duly did so, beating Denis Healey by 139 to 129 votes.

There were press reports that some of the right had deliberately abstained or even voted for Michael Foot in the belief that it was better to bring all the party's problems to a head by electing him, even though they totally disapproved of him. Bill Rodgers and I had taken the precaution of having our voting slips witnessed. Despite the deep doubts we had about Denis Healey by then, we had both voted for him. I do know of two or possibly three right-wing MPs who might have tried that trick of voting for Michael, but they did not change the result. Denis Healey was deluding himself when he said that their few votes were sufficient to explain his defeat. When the Gang of Three had met with him in September before the conference to try to persuade him to risk all by battling on, we had warned him that he was heading for defeat. Although an aggressive campaign would have made defeat by Michael even more likely, it would have left Denis free to challenge him openly a year later and win. As it was, immediately the result was announced, he agreed to serve as Michael's deputy and thereby locked himself into certain defeat at the general election, with Michael still leader.

I have said since that I would not have left the Labour Party if Denis Healey had become the leader. The truth is that I would have stayed and fought alongside him even if he had lost the leadership provided he had shown at least the will to fight. Once Denis accepted the electoral college, as he did during that leadership election, I could see no possibility whatever of shifting the Labour Party back towards sane policies before the next election. The election of Michael Foot was the final straw. I had, after all, watched Michael closely in Plymouth ever since the age of eleven; there were people in the Devonport constituency whom I knew well and who also knew him, and we had many family friends in common. I never disliked him as a person but I deplored his political positions. It was beyond my worst imaginings that he would become leader of the Labour Party. Even in the early 1970s, when he started to poll well in the parliamentary party, it seemed something only for nightmares. Now it was reality. I knew better than most how deep-seated was his antagonism to nuclear deterrence, to serious defence spending and many of the principles on which NATO was founded. His criticism of the economic market basis of the European Community was venomous; his romantic attachment to parliamentary sovereignty and his hostility to any legislation which stemmed from the European Communities Act were passionate. There was no prospect of reversing the shift in Labour Party policy while he was leader or of defeating an electoral college at the special conference in January, and so it proved to be.

I knew that under his leadership I could not remain a member of the shadow Cabinet. The question now was not 'if' I should leave the shadow Cabinet but 'when'. Since I was elected by the PLP and there was the all-important special meeting of the parliamentary party on 13 November in which I hoped to speak, I decided to stay for my elected period but not to put myself up for re-election.

The shadow Cabinet did not take long to distinguish itself under its new leadership by backing a Roy Hattersley motion that accepted an electoral college. It only stipulated that the unions must make sure they consulted their Labour Party supporters who paid the political levy before they cast their vote in the college. Roy Hattersley, who in early November had attacked the block vote, was bent on finding a formula that would ditch us and save his face, even though he knew his motion was unworkable and would be rejected by the NEC and the conference, which it duly was. There is still in 2009 no proper provision for one member, one vote in the trade union section of Labour's electoral college.

At the PLP on 13 November, I was allowed to put the case for one member, one vote which had been spelled out in the shadow Cabinet paper in my name and that of Bill Rodgers. Roy Hattersley advanced his argument on which the shadow Cabinet had devised their ingenious but disreputable hybrid. He claimed it to be a compromise between the administrative practicality of an electoral college and the genuine democracy of one member, one vote. The parliamentary party voted for Roy Hattersley and the shadow Cabinet's electoral college by a very small majority. Of the 268 Labour MPs, barely half attended and the motion was carried by only sixty-eight votes to fifty-nine. The Hattersley compromise had, however, served its purpose. It had divided those in the shadow Cabinet who had originally voted against the electoral college. I warned Roy in the shadow Cabinet that it was really the Kinnock amendment and would one day be used by Neil Kinnock to become leader. Roy Hattersley discovered in 1983 that I was right, and he was deprived of the leadership he coveted.

Shirley and Bill seemed stunned that I intended to leave the shadow Cabinet and they both tried to persuade me to stay. Shirley said that if I were to stand down she would not be able to go ahead with her nomination as a prospective parliamentary candidate in

Stevenage, due to be agreed shortly at a constituency meeting. I argued, though I was not fully convinced, that it was perfectly possible for her to go ahead if she wished and also for Bill to be a member of the shadow Cabinet. We did not have to act in an identical fashion. It was a good-natured argument, but I was not to be shifted. I had always regretted not resigning after the European vote in October 1971 and I was not going to make that mistake again. There was a deeper reason too. I wanted now to be able to talk openly to people about the pros and cons of forming a new party. I did not think it was right to do this while still a member of the shadow Cabinet, nor could I profess loyalty to a leader whose political views were diametrically opposed to my own. Eventually it was agreed that Bill and I would go our separate ways but without any rancour. Shirley said that she would not now agree to be nominated for Stevenage. She warned me, quite rightly as it turned out, that the press would interpret my decision as being a major step towards leaving the Labour Party, however much I tried to explain that I was fighting from within. In retrospect it was a critical meeting. Had Shirley not withdrawn her candidature, maybe the Limehouse Declaration would never have occurred.

I sent my letter off on the Thursday and arranged to see Michael Foot on Friday morning. It was a brief business-like meeting, for he could see my mind was made up, but it was also a sad occasion.

On Saturday 29 November Debbie, the three children (Tristan, Gareth and Lucy) and I drove to East Hendred for a late lunch with Roy and Jennifer Jenkins. It was pleasant occasion but I knew it would be critical. Roy had had his sixtieth birthday a few days earlier; he seemed fit but was getting impatient with what he saw as our prevarication. The rational case for making it a Gang of Four rather than continuing with the Gang of Three was overwhelming. Since I was probably the biggest obstacle to making this transformation, with my scepticism about Roy becoming our leader, it was all the more important that I should take the initiative.

However, I did not feel as though I was acting alone. In a real sense I was speaking as the representative of a number of the other younger MPs who had been talking to me very frankly about the nature of any new party. We were all adamant that it could not be a party created in Roy Jenkins's image. Most of us saw Shirley Williams as the leader and feared that, if Roy joined us, the older MPs likely to split off with us would naturally muster behind him again and vote for him as leader. Moreover, we were in the thick of the battle for one member, one vote to choose the leader of the Labour Party, and there was some anxiety that Roy would want the old system of MPs choosing the leader for any new party.

My first task, therefore, was to get a pledge from Roy that he would accept one member, one vote in a new party. He readily conceded this – all too readily, I now realise. I knew he was serious when he specifically asked if I accepted that he might run for the leadership against Shirley Williams, who, I had already told him, I thought would make the best leader. I said of course he could stand, anyone could, that was the advantage; the members of the party would be free to choose whoever they wished. Debbie was with me at the time and later, when we discussed his reaction in the car, she felt that he had registered that this pledge was crucial to me and other MPs. Since one member, one vote for electing the leader of the Labour Party was at the heart of the then public controversy Roy must have realised it was very important. Just before Christmas he rang me up at Buttermere, somewhat agitated, having heard from various friends of his that I was asserting that I did not think he should ever be the leader. I presumed that he had seen a memo I had sent to Bill and Shirley in early December which was highly critical of his being perceived as the leader right from the start. I then drove over to East Hendred, this being so important, and we settled it, as I thought, once and for all. If a new party were formed, the leader would be elected by one member, one vote, and if Roy won that was perfectly acceptable to me; I joked that I might even vote for him.

All this time we were moving closer and closer to the break with Labour, with many hesitations and fluctuations in mood. On 2 December, for example, Bill urged that the Gang of Three write a letter to members of the CLV to say we were continuing to work together for the interests we all shared and that the fight would continue up to and beyond the special conference on 24 January 1981. I had to write back to him and say that I favoured deleting the words 'and beyond' for by then I was convinced that the special conference must be a threshold. This he accepted. But, despite differences still existing between us, Peter Jenkins rightly based a *Guardian* article in December on the premise that a breakaway from the Labour Party was no longer a mere possibility but had become a distinct probability. He flagged up the special Labour Party conference on 24 January as providing a convenient point of decision if not exactly a deadline. He had obviously spoken to Roy Jenkins, who was declaring that he would act on his own if nothing had been done by Easter. The article also observed that Roy now accepted that any breakaway should be a social democratic party, that he did not expect to return as the leader of any such new party, and that personal ambition was no longer, if it ever had been, his chief motivation. That proved to be sheer disinformation, yet Peter's conclusion, with which I fully concurred, was very sobering:

> The Labour Party is probably in decline and in the course of time there will probably be some kind of realignment in the centre-left. But it could take a long while, perhaps extend over two or three elections; meanwhile, promising careers will be wasted in the wilderness, the Conservatives will probably be kept in power (although not necessarily Mrs Thatcher), and many failures will precede eventual success. Those who set out had better be prepared for a long haul into the unknown.

Despite these warnings, by early December I was ready to cast the die. A year earlier I had written to a friend abroad, saying that I would stay with Labour and fight right up to the election. Now I sat down to explain why I had changed my mind:

> Getting out of the shadow Cabinet was crucial. It means I can with honour think and plan for a social democratic party. I am not yet across the Rubicon but I am rationally calculating the changes necessary and the chances of success. Whatever I decide, I know it will be a gamble. I realise full well in three years I could be without a seat in Parliament – with a busted career – to be truthful I don't mind. I contemplate starting a new life in 1984 with calm and some pleasure.
>
> Why could this succeed? I am not sure it can but what else can? What other way is there and if we do not try how will we ever know? I cannot urge others to be more adventurous, the country to be more

adventurous, if I cling to the system, to the old politics, to the politics of nudge, fudge and mudge. In a strange way, on the Friday after the 1979 election I felt free and devoid of ambition. Fate has given me too much, too early but this means I can at least give back one thing. I can risk all to win all.

The essential is that a new party is not cast in Roy Jenkins's image – he is valuable to us provided he does not lead it. Now, ambition would say let Roy lead it, for that gives me a chance, but that would be to flaw the party before it starts. I have doubts about Shirley on many counts, but she is classless, she is soft, she does have a sense of new politics; so I will use my position to insist on her being given a lead role even within a collective leadership for the launch period. What happens after that depends on the members, for any new party must be one member, one vote.

Can we finance it? Who knows, I don't. I doubt you can ever know until you try. If there were 20,000 who would join and pay £10 a year, that would, with other contributions, probably be sufficient. I write as if I have decided to launch a social democratic party; not quite, but I am very near to trying it. It may be the benefit will never come our way. It may force the Labour Party to have its equivalent of the SPD Bad Godesberg conference.

I will now take three weeks to think. I know I am thought to be impatient, but you know that I rarely act without a lot of thought. I have come to my present position slowly, reluctantly and steadily. It is this inexorableness which makes me feel that the Rubicon will be crossed. They say now is not the time, but when will be? Meanwhile I and others become bitter, Messianic or depressed, believing in nothing passionately, holding on and learning to compromise. Abolish private education, even Shirley is starting down that route. Well, we will say, better than other countries. Perhaps, but why not enjoy life and return to medicine, and that is what I will do.

But all my life I will know there was a time in 1981 when perhaps had we had the courage, the vision; had we been prepared to break out, cut loose, risk all and accept being called traitors, things just might have been different. Britain just might have pulled itself up by its own collective will and common sense if it had just been given the chance. Who knows?

On Friday 5 December I drove up to Leeds with Debbie to be the guest of honour at Denis Healey's constituency Labour Party dinner and dance. Denis and Edna went out of their way to be welcoming and Denis made a very generous speech about me and my period as Foreign Secretary. He had in happier times talked to journalists about my leading the Labour Party eventually. He must have known that anything said that evening could be played back against him by the left if I quit the party, as he by now must have guessed was probable. It was typical that he ignored this danger. The evening represented all that was good in the Labour Party, full of Yorkshire common sense and decent, generous people. Denis was totally at ease in his constituency, which was really one massive council estate. It was this which made him a far more formidable Labour politician than Roy Jenkins or Tony Crosland. In my speech I steered clear of any internal Labour Party politics and that night I wondered again if Labour could be saved from within. Might Denis be persuaded to fight? I also wondered why, given the impending crisis, Denis and I did not lock horns that night. I suspect it was the old bull and the young bull story. He knew he had one fight left in him. I knew I had many. We were bound to fight from now on against each other. Hopefully it would be done with respect.

On Friday 16 January I recorded a *Weekend World* interview with Brian Walden. It went out that Sunday under the title 'The Labour Right: Moment of Truth'. Some of my emotional turmoil overflowed as I said, 'The thing that haunts me, and I think it haunts all socialists, is, if we were to split, would it mean that the centre-left could never be able to form a government in this country?' But the real drama came in the last question. Brian Walden, as a former Labour MP and sympathetic to what we were doing, knew only too well the fury we would encounter were we to leave the Labour Party, so he asked his question in a gentle way – but, typically, inside the velvet glove was an iron fist.

BRIAN WALDEN:
I wonder if I could ask you finally what you'd say to the sort of person who says, 'I understand all that, and there's much that you say, Dr Owen, that I agree with, but, leave the Labour Party? How can you even discuss it, how can you sit there talking about such an emotional

wrench, such an act of treachery, such a destruction of what endless people for many years have fought to build up?' How would you reply to what I would call an old-fashioned Labour loyalist who put that point to you?

DAVID OWEN MP:
Well, I would just ask them, quietly and slowly, to say what, if they used the word 'treachery', is the biggest treachery: to put the Labour Party before your country or your country before the Labour Party?

Up in Grimsby, watching the programme, was the Labour MP Austin Mitchell's agent, a dentist, Paul Genny. He described his reaction on hearing my words. He jumped up in the air, said, 'He is going to do it, he is going to leave,' and dashed out to a friend's house to discuss their next moves, before the programme had even ended. For him and other Labour activists, the charge of treachery was one of the greatest problems. Hearing how it could be turned back on the accuser convinced him that I and others were now heading out of the Labour Party.

He was right. The Gang of Three was becoming the Gang of Four and the new party was being openly discussed. But whatever the impression may have been, it was not a smooth ride. It had already been agreed that the Gang of Three would meet with Roy Jenkins at his house in East Hendred on Sunday 18 January. Unfortunately either Roy or his friends had talked to the *Observer* and on the morning of the meeting I woke to a front-page picture of Roy with a story revealing that we were meeting at East Hendred that Sunday. To me it was just an irritation, another example of an old man in a hurry, but Shirley Williams was outraged. She announced to Roy on the telephone that she was not now prepared to come and so we met at Bill Rodgers' house instead. She had a fair point: the story was slanted to give the impression that we were all being summoned by the king over the water soon to return from Brussels, and that he was in charge of the whole operation. It was not, to put it mildly, a propitious start to the serious drafting of what later became known as the Limehouse Declaration. It was a cynical way of handling publicity, and similar press stories were to become frequent over the next eighteen months. All too often the purpose was clear – to boost Roy at the expense of Shirley.

On Saturday I drove to the Wembley Conference Hall, once again ready to do battle. I went to the floor of the conference to argue a case which I knew, even before I began to speak, was going to be rejected since the trade union block votes had already been pledged. I called for one member, one vote and condemned the electoral college, saying:

> The day this system is used to elect a Prime Minister the whole of the country will be watching the procedures, and then these procedures will be shown to be totally undemocratic. They will be shown to be a totally illegitimate way of electing the Prime Minister of the country.

That system elected Tony Blair leader of the Labour Party in 1994, but only when in opposition, after which some changes were made in the trade union vote to make it appear more democratic. It was also used in the leadership elections for the Welsh Assembly and to choose the Labour candidate for the Mayor of London. Hugo Young in the *Guardian* on 22 February 2000 described the electoral college for London as 'a stitch-up, the block votes were a scandal, the results produced a terribly unimpressive nominee'. Gordon Brown was made Prime Minister without a contest in 2007 and so the system has never been tested in the full public gaze. John Smith and every leader since has known that Labour must introduce a proper one member, one vote system and scrap this TUC-inspired electoral college. Gordon Brown even mentioned his intention to change this when I met him at No. 10 in September 2007, but it remains unfinished business.

We left the conference hall that day utterly disenchanted. I now knew for certain I would have to leave the Labour Party.

On the morning of Sunday 25 January the Gang of Four met at my house in Narrow Street, Limehouse, where I still live. Opposite us in those days was Brightlingsea Buildings, where Clem Attlee lived when he was doing social work in the East End of London. Looking back on the declaration we signed that day, it is hard not to be struck by how orientated it was to the Labour Party. Nevertheless one of the changes from Roy's early draft had been the deletion of 'the party of Attlee or Gaitskell', which shows that, far from him trying to stop our being associated with the Labour Party, Roy wanted to clarify the sort of Labour Party we were ready to identify with. The declaration was not a rallying cry for the new centre party with which Roy had been associated since the Dimbleby Lecture. Indeed we specifically said that we did not believe 'in the politics of an inert centre merely representing the lowest common denominator between two extremes'. Instead we addressed those who had been 'actively and continuously engaged in Labour politics', and some who had been engaged in the past but had given up recently. Although we deliberately made a pitch for people active outside the party political sphere, this was in the main an appeal to those who wanted to resist the drift towards extremism in the Labour Party. There was comment on the absence of a commitment to proportional representation. Interestingly, Roy had never pushed for it to be included. For me the omission was welcome: it did not pre-empt further debate, and it avoided the accusation that this was a statement which could have been issued by the Liberal Party. There would be ample time to make that commitment and none of us doubted that it would come when we wanted to forge an electoral pact with the Liberal Party.

Though the formal launch of the SDP did not take place until 26 March, as far as the Gang of Three was concerned the Rubicon had been crossed – a Social Democratic Party was going to be formed. However, it is now clear to me that, whatever the declaration said, as far as Roy Jenkins was concerned a centre party was going to be formed which would merge with the Liberals. Within five weeks, before the SDP was even formally launched, Roy and his foremost supporters were arguing in the discussion over the interim constitution that people should be allowed to be members of both the SDP and the Liberal Party; even at this stage, it seemed that the SDP was merely to be a transit vehicle. It was as if they wanted a cross between the Salvation Army and the Fabian Society; a move-ment so broad and diffuse that it would become putty in the hands of the Liberal activists, let alone able to withstand the pressures that were bound to be put on us by the old class-based parties. How on earth he thought such a grouping could hold together and prise winnable seats and winnable policies out of the Liberal Party was a mystery. Until it became all too clear that he did not envisage any pressure or leverage being put on the Liberal Party. His whole concept was flatly rejected then, but those who were involved in that short debate could never again entertain any illusions as to Roy's real intentions. Nor did the concept of joint membership ever totally disappear. As the evidence mounted that Roy was so committed to merging with the Liberals, it became ever clearer to me that in honour he should never have signed the Limehouse Declaration to create the Council for Social Democracy in the first place. He had not abandoned his concept of a centre party linked to the Liberals; if we wanted to call ourselves Social Democrats, talk about socialism and even join Socialist International he would go along with that, biding his time until we were out of the Labour Party and had burnt our boats, and then push the Liberal link.

Instinct, which was later backed by hard market-research evidence, indicated that it could only harm our new party if we were too closely identified with the Liberals. But we studiously avoided facing that market research. I had fought the Liberals in the West Country, where they are stronger than in most other parts of the country, for twenty years. I had a pretty good idea of their strengths as well as their weaknesses, whether from fighting Mark Bonham Carter in Torrington or in Devonport Capt. Michael Banks RM (Retd). While Michael Banks was distributing leaflets outside Devonport dockyard gate promising an increase in defence expenditure in the neighbouring constituency of Tavistock, Aza Pinney was stomping the fields in his gumboots promising to reduce defence expenditure. I had lived, only recently, for months with the story of Jeremy Thorpe, Liberal MP for North Devon, splashed across our West Country newspapers, with endless details about the involvement of the former Bodmin Liberal MP Peter Bessell, and of the Liberal Party's financial dealings, which were sleazy to say the least. The 1979 election result in the West Country had been its worst for years. Jeremy Thorpe had lost his seat and sadly, because he was an excellent MP, so had John Pardoe. I had experienced too the Lib–Lab pact and the problems of keeping the Liberal Party to an agreed line. I knew we had to try and work for some form of electoral deal but there was no rush. We had first to build the SDP. Meanwhile Cyril Smith, Liberal MP for Rochdale, was telling people that we ought to be strangled at birth, and that was not a maverick sentiment. David Steel had his problems in containing Liberals who wanted nothing whatever to do with us, but for these and other reasons for the SDP to give the impression that we could not wait to get into bed with the Liberals was the height of political madness. Nevertheless that is what some of the SDP tried to do.

A sad and painful moment came at the end of that exhilarating week. That Friday, I flew down to Plymouth for the Devonport constituency annual general management committee meeting. I told them that I would not be able to stand as a Labour Party candidate at the next election and would not be putting myself forward for reselection. 'I have not', I told them, 'changed my support for the manifesto on which you and I fought the 1979 election and I will conduct myself in Parliament over the years ahead until the next election within the spirit of that manifesto.' I went on BBC TV in the south-west for a late-night interview and found it all very emotional. I was leaving behind friends of fifteen years' standing, people whose help had been invaluable in five close-fought general elections. The pangs of conflicting loyalties were acute and even my few opponents on the left in the constituency were, I think, genuinely upset.

The strains were also showing in Parliament. The Callaghan Cabinet were planning a dinner for Jim and Audrey and, without any warning, Michael Foot wrote to Bill and me returning our cheques and saying we would not be welcome. In the end Edmund Dell joined Shirley, Bill and myself in sending the Callaghans an Ackermann print, and it says a lot for Jim and Audrey that they never used the creation of the SDP as a reason to abandon past friendship. When I visited him at his farm in Sussex a few months before he died in 2005 aged ninety-two Jim pointed out this picture on the wall and tears came to my eyes.

In the House of Commons Michael had set the tone. From then on we passed each other with an occasional nod but never exchanging even pleasantries. There were some MPs who never spoke to me after the Limehouse Declaration. There were a few who never allowed it to make any difference, but with the majority relations were formal. The attacks were not long in coming and for my part I hit back, but initially more in sorrow than in anger.

Michael and I came together once in a pleasant way in the early 1990s, when we were both awarded an honorary degree by the new University of Plymouth.

Handling friends in the Labour Party in Plymouth was perhaps the hardest task. I wrote to one of them in early February, and this first paragraph gives the flavour of how a harrowing situation was handled with mutual respect.

> Many thanks for your letter which you wrote with such sympathy and understanding. It has been a horrible period for me. I hope you will understand why I have been reluctant to involve you all in this decision. I simply do not want to put any of you in a difficult position or in any way try to persuade you to leave the Labour Party. It is different for you in Plymouth as a Labour councillor and for me in my position. There is no hurry to make decisions for you. Unfortunately events are pressing me all the time for rapid decisions.

The secretary of the constituency party, Barbara Furzeman, and the previous chairman, Will Fitzgerald, did join the SDP at once, as did a number of active Labour Party members. What was sad, as is so often the case when ruptures like this occur, was the number of people who drifted away from politics, ceasing to be active in the Labour Party but not joining the SDP either.

On 6 February *Now!* magazine published the results of a constituency poll in Bill Rodgers's and my seats. If there had been a general election next day in Plymouth Devonport and if I had been standing for the Social Democratic Party, I would have gained 55 per cent of the vote; the Conservatives would have come next with 25 per cent, followed by Labour with 16 per cent and the Liberals with 4 per cent. In Stockton, if Bill had been standing, 41 per cent would have voted Social Democrat; Labour would have come next with 28 per cent, then the Conservatives with 22 per cent and the Liberals with 9 per cent. In my own constituency the *Evening Herald* had very early on run a test of opinion which showed that I would win easily. There were two powerful conclusions from these polls. Firstly, if we were to call by-elections there was an extremely good chance that both of us would win and some pollsters thought all twelve MPs would win. Secondly, the Liberal vote was not essential to us, though if we stood as a Social Democrat–Liberal alliance the margin of our victory, not surprisingly, would slightly increase.

Bill Rodgers, however, was adamantly opposed to fighting by-elections. Whether or not he feared losing his own seat I do not know, but on the basis of the *Now!* poll he should have been safe, and had he won in 1981 he would have been much less likely to lose in 1983. His argument was that it would be harder for us to attract some of the MPs less well known in their constituencies if they thought they were going to have to fight a by-election. Also, like me, he was loath to concede any ground to Tony Benn, who was arguing that MPs are not primarily answerable to their constituents, but to a party caucus. Furthermore, the Labour whips would control the date of the by-election after we had resigned, they would order which by-election came first and they would avoid having them on one day. Such was the power of the party machines within Parliament.

These were strong arguments, but there were countervailing ones. The endorsement of the electorate would have given us a more powerful position in the House of Commons and in the country. It would have also sharpened our Social Democratic image immediately and greatly enhanced our authority in dealing with the Liberal Party. Michael Foot constantly asserted that we should all fight by-elections, and I tried to persuade Bill that at least as chairman of the SDP parliamentary committee I should fight one symbolic by-election on behalf of all SDP MPs. In conversation, Bill managed to persuade me that this would be an indulgence and that it would only heighten the constituency pressure on the other eleven to fight as well. Yet I believe we made the wrong decision; we should have fought. It would have demonstrated electoral clout to the Liberals and greatly enhanced the concept of the SDP as a free-standing fourth political party. I am sure too that it would have helped MPs when they came to fight their own seats in the 1983 general election.

A poll in my Devonport constituency conducted between 5 and 8 April for Westward Television showed, like the poll in *Now!* magazine, that I would get 55 per cent of the vote and put Labour second with 21 per cent, the Conservatives on 20 per cent and the Liberals only getting 2 per cent. Yet 79 per cent wanted me to stay on as MP until the general election and only 21 per cent wanted me to resign immediately and hold a by-election.

I had to admit, however, that I was in a very different situation from most people; it was widely felt that I could easily win an early by-election in Devonport. But not everyone else was in that situation. I could have gone on my own ego trip, and very tempting it was for it would have boosted my position in the Gang of Four, but it was not to be, though it continued to worry me. A consequence of this stance – that we were the true protectors of the Labour Party manifesto – was that we were a little too ready to defend some of its elements which we really needed to drop. It pushed us in policy terms further towards being identified with the status quo.

While the Labour Party was tearing itself apart and the SDP was being formed, the government made one of the most significant strategic decisions of its first parliament, one which we can now see helped them to victory both in 1983 and 1987. On 18 February Margaret Thatcher made her second major U-turn, the first being her commitment to recognise the government of Bishop Muzorewa in Rhodesia. In the face of a strike threat from Joe Gormley, the popular miners' president, the government offered more money to keep the coalmines working, but wisely she had begun to build up coal stocks at the power stations in preparation for Arthur Scargill. I had begun to realise that a remarkable feature of Margaret Thatcher's style was her refusal to admit that she ever changed her mind even when it was obvious that she had. She seemed keen to appear more ideological, less pragmatic than the record actually demonstrated. Observing successive Labour Prime Ministers from the opposition benches had clearly made her decide that it was better to be seen as consistently resolute; never to complain, never to explain and never to admit to a U-turn. So much was this her style that whenever I heard her deny that she was turning, I immediately suspected that she was. When she made her famous conference speech in October 1980, 'You turn if you want, the Lady's not for turning', for instance, I wondered if she had already begun to change her economic stance; but in fact she was not changing and Geoffrey Howe's Budget in 1981, in defiance of 364 economists, squeezed demand and paved the way for sustained expansion from 1983–89.

Mrs Thatcher would probably much rather be remembered for her public battles than for her strategic retreats. However, her recognition that coal reserves were insufficient in 1981 and that if a strike were called the government might be beaten was astute and brave. It was probably the wisest political decision of her first period in office, particularly since it was linked to a decision to build up big coal reserves in the power stations and to plan for a predictable confrontation with the incoming president of the NUM, Arthur Scargill, after Joe Gormley retired. Given her temperament it could not have been easy to back off; no doubt she feared cries of 'chicken' and a bad press. But cutting one's losses is a great political skill. Margaret Thatcher was a far more cautious political leader than is often recognised.

The parliamentary committee of the Social Democratic Party was born on Monday 2 March 1981, when twelve Labour members of Parliament resigned the whip and became Social Democrats. I withdrew from all Labour Party organisations, though a little devil meant that I kept my membership of the Socialist Medical Association. They seemed to accept my banker's order and I did not stop it for many years. I was amazed to discover, however, that, though a member of the ASTMS union, I was no longer allowed to attend meetings of its parliamentary committee. This was indefensible since union officials were allowed to attend without being paid-up members of the Labour Party. But Labour policy was to prevent Social Democrats from building relations with the trade union movement. From Labour's point of view, it was logical to try and show that we were not true social democrats by excluding us from union activity.

We were witnessing the start of an aggressive Labour counter-attack. They set out to challenge our socialist, social democratic or left credentials. So links with trade unions were to be denied, links with European socialists were to be undermined and in the House of Commons we were presented at all times as already linked to the Liberals.

The fact that most of our MPs were in very safe Labour seats was bound to be an important influence on what sort of SDP the MPs wished to establish. Most knew that in order to survive they had to win traditional Labour votes. Of all these MPs Mike Thomas was the one who became my closest friend, though I had not known him well before this time. His Newcastle-upon-Tyne East constituency was a solid safe seat with an 18.7 per cent majority. Sponsored by the Co-operative movement, he had been very active in the National Union of Students. When he came into the House of Commons in 1974 he was identified most closely with Shirley Williams and had been Roy Hattersley's parliamentary private secretary when Roy was minister of state in the Foreign Office. He represented the younger generation, those who persuaded the Gang of Four that joining the SDP by credit card was perfectly sensible and efficient, and that we should ignore the jibes of Labour and set a new style. He saw the launch as a marketing opportunity and automatically sought the best professional advice, insisting that we leave behind in the Labour Party all those hang-ups about using the skills of advertising and public relations. But behind all his veneer of modernity and thrusting aggression lay a thoughtful, kind and gentle person, more deeply committed to the values that underpinned the Limehouse Declaration than any of the other people most closely associated with it. Because he fought for the SDP, it was easy to portray him as a hard, ruthless, ambitious politician. That false portrait was hard to shake off. The easiest way to lose such a reputation was of course to back away from confrontation and concede ground to those who denigrate you. That Mike did not choose that course is a tribute to his courage. I can truly say that no one I know gave more of himself to the SDP and, without his readiness to fight for the party, it would have been absorbed into the Liberals and have lost even more independence by 1982.

Did the SDP take the task of attracting Conservatives to our ranks seriously enough? Indeed, was it wise to attract Conservatives towards a social democratic party? This was a major dilemma for me. To widen our appeal I naturally wanted Conservative support, but I knew that in the process we could make it harder for the SDP to build a left-of-centre identity. As a result I was initially rather lukewarm about welcoming Christopher Brocklebank-Fowler and he used to rib me about this in the early months. Helpfully, when he crossed over to us, Christopher's speech stressed the appalling record of the government over unemployment, and on race his stance was well established and principled; so he personally presented no problems. My main priority at that time, however, was to persuade sufficient Labour MPs to join.

Another reason we did not attract more Conservative MPs concerned the nature of the so-called Tory wets. In commenting on my book in early March 1981, Samuel Brittan wrote in the *Financial Times*, 'There is only one plea I would make to the Social Democrats: think several times before seeking soul mates among the Tory "wets".' He argued perceptively that the decentralisers among the Social Democrats should find the Thatcherite distrust of big government less uncongenial than the attitude of the upper-class Tory paternalists and continued, 'A social market economy is much more radical – and in the right sense egalitarian – than anything that has occurred to the Whitelaws, Priors and Carringtons of our political world.' But the social market concept never attracted Roy Jenkins and since he was dominant over economics his views, rooted in the 1960s, carried the day.

The Conservative Party, moreover, like Labour, were counter-attacking to keep their MPs. The Gang of Four were savaged by Margaret Thatcher, of all people, on the grounds that we should have stayed and fought within the Labour Party. How she had the effrontery to argue that case, knowing we would have had to vote for Labour defence policy, shows how desperate the old parties were, and still are, to preserve their duopoly and stamp hard on independents or breakaway movements. Peter Walker, the high priest of the wets, was given the job of holding the wobblers' hands, an astute choice. I also believe that the socially aware Conservatives did gain more influence on policy between the Warrington by-election and the end of the Falklands War. But, since Margaret Thatcher denied any U-turn, only the historians will be able to judge. After the Falklands War the Conservatives did not have to take the SDP challenge very seriously again until 1984 when we won the Portsmouth South by-election, and then we did become a target until 1987.

An early move in identifying the SDP with the left of centre was taken on 2 March. With Roy Jenkins never making the slightest protest, all four of us sent a telegram to the vice-presidents of Socialist International expressing our hope that the SDP would eventually join. In response, at the start of the week in which the SDP was formally launched in March, Ron Hayward, then general secretary of the Labour Party, wrote in pretty intemperate terms to

Socialist International about our desire for affiliation:'I want to make it crystal clear that this would be strongly opposed by the Labour Party which for the reasons I have given would of course be unwilling to belong to an organisation to which such a breakaway group were admitted.'

This question of the Socialist International was important to me and to some of our activists – we even seriously contemplated calling our new party New Labour! But I must admit it soon became irrelevant to many members and most certainly to the public and, in as much as it raised the word 'socialist', was damaging. Shirley and I were too slow to acknowledge that in Britain the word 'socialist' had become indistinguishable from 'Labour' and that few members of the public understood that bureaucratic Fabianism was not all the socialist tradition had to offer, whereas on the Continent the terms 'socialist' and 'social democrat' are virtually interchangeable. There was a certain cussedness about my refusal to reject identification with socialism. I could not and still cannot in 2009 repudiate the great body of socialist thinking and writing about egalitarianism and its linkage to an individual's freedom. The non-Marxist socialist tradition of Christian charity and care is not one that can or should be lost in a crude equation with communism or vulgarising of the socialist viewpoint. British socialists like Robert Owen, William Morris, Professors Tawney and Titmuss and G. D. H. Cole have made a profound contribution to political thought and I will not denigrate their memory by decrying socialism. In retrospect it would have been better simply to have said, 'I am a social democrat full stop,' and adamantly refused to get into any arguments about what socialism was or was not. In my book *Face the Future*, published while I was still nominally a member of the Labour Party, the words 'socialist' and 'social democrat' were interchangeable. When, in the paperback edition, I changed some but by no means all of the references to 'socialist' or 'socialism' to 'social democrat' and 'social democracy' I was taunted by Labour and teased by journalists and also by Denis Healey. I rejoined that we could not expect former Conservatives who were in the SDP to use the word 'socialist'. By November, Roy Jenkins, conveniently forgetting that he was a signatory to the telegram to Socialist International only in March, was saying, 'I don't use the word. I haven't used the word "socialist", or "socialism", for some years past, a substantial number of years past, because I regard it as more obfuscating than clarifying.' He had by then no difficulty in convincing everyone that that was true.

Yet by March 1981 I was still approaching the launch of the SDP with excitement and anticipation. To be a social democrat was a new release, a link with my Labour past but also a springboard for the future. I wanted to take the ethic of redistribution into our new party, but to lose all the trappings of state socialism; to break the institutional links with but not the respect for the trade unions. I wished our SDP would spearhead a counter-revolution to reverse our relative decline, but I had not yet fully realised the extent to which a counter-revolution was already underway with Margaret Thatcher.

The launch of the party on 26 March 1981 was a brilliant success, and the credit goes to Mike Thomas. By giving sole authority to one person we evaded the problems of launching by committee. That morning everything went with a zing: we were out to show that we were a bright, modern, professional party and proud of it. There were 500 journalists when we started at 9.00 a.m. in the Connaught Rooms, and since journalists are not dedicated to early rising, this was itself an achievement. Television crews from all over the world were swarming everywhere and there was an infectious mood of excitement and bustle.

In the House of Commons Hansard noted our presence with an intervention during Prime Minister's Questions:

> MIKE THOMAS
> Far be it from me to intrude on this private quarrel, but will the right honourable Lady ponder on the fact that the emergence of the Social Democratic Party has less to do with her theories of monetarism or the right honourable Gentleman's theories of socialism than with the future of the country?

> PRIME MINISTER
> I recall hearing a comment on the radio this morning about the Social Democratic Party being a new centre party. I heard someone say that such a centre party would be a party with no roots, no principles, no philosophy and no values. That sounded about right, and it was Shirley Williams who said it.

This abrasive exchange demonstrated that launching a party was one thing but sustaining it and building it up to withstand the buffeting of party political warfare was, formidably, quite another.

The three press conferences I attended were inevitably rather sterile affairs, few members of the public being present, but I had a public speaking engagement that evening in Taunton. It had been fixed before the launch date and I decided to keep to it, since another launch press conference was planned for Bristol the following morning. Driving up from Plymouth to the school on the outskirts of Taunton, I envisaged a normal public meeting of around 100 people. As we drew near to the school we noticed a lot of cars. We thought this was a little odd but conjectured that another meeting was being held there. But when we walked into the hall I realised that the launch of the party had triggered off a dramatic political response. It was packed, with well over 800 people present, supposedly the largest political meeting in Taunton since Winston Churchill had spoken there in the 1945 election. The immense enthusiasm was captured by television and supplemented the launch publicity with new, fresh pictures for the evening news bulletins. At that moment, for the first time, I felt that the SDP just might be able to break through the two-party stranglehold that had gripped British politics since the emergence of the Whigs and the Tories.

It is worth recalling what our launch research (five discussion groups with respondents who would consider voting for an alliance of SDP and Liberals at the next general election) said about the SDP versus the Liberals:

> The SDP is also seen as being qualitatively different from the Liberal Party. Policies, once again, are totally irrelevant here. The really salient dimensions on which the SDP and the Liberals are compared are ones on which the SDP is seen as having enormous advantages. The SDP is:
>
> 'New' – as against the rump of a dead party.
>
> 'Risk taking' – as against armchair 'do-gooders' ('They have won their spurs').
>
> 'Experienced' (the SDP members have practical experience of 'real' government).
>
> These are the true criteria and on these counts the SDP is seen as radically different from the Liberals. The Liberal Party vote is at heart

regarded as being a middle-class 'cop out', 'pious', a non-urgent protest vote. More to the point, the Liberals are associated with a particular set of middle-class minority values and lifestyles that are widely disliked and 'discredited'.

In this sense it is highly important that the SDP recognises the basis of its relationship with the Liberal Party – one of considerable bargaining strength – and with 'liberalism', and in a stylistic sense continues to emphasise its basic differences. To suggest too great an identity with the Liberals is likely to limit the appeals of the SDP to an unnecessary degree. By contrast the greatest appeal of the SDP is that it appears to have a real chance of effecting change. The SDP is seen as being a party with some momentum.

The opportunities and the warnings were all encapsulated in that research. The launch was the time in the SDP's history when we were ready to seek out and accept professional advice; when it was considered natural and correct to make decisions against a background of knowledge, not just hunch or instinct.

These were heady days. It was above all immense fun. We were free and unfettered. In any account of the SDP like mine the focus is inevitably on what went wrong, on inner tensions, arguments and personality clashes, but for those of us who lived through the first ten years, it was above all a fascinating experience and, even in retrospect, an extremely worthwhile enterprise. I cannot say I have no regrets; I made errors, took decisions which proved to be wrong and made judgements on people and events which turned out to be false. But that is so of every ten-year segment of my life. To the question 'Do I regret helping create the SDP?', the answer is a resounding 'no'.

By next day it was clear that everything about the launch, including the opening London press conference, had gone extraordinarily well. But I was very worried about one, I think spontaneous, reply by Bill Rodgers to a question on the Liberals which appeared as a new policy statement on the front page of the *Times*. The SDP intended, he said, putting up candidates in about half the 635 seats, apart from Northern Ireland, where they would set up no party organisation. Such plans, he added, would have to be drawn up in consultation with the Liberals. That commitment had never been discussed among the four of us and had far-reaching implications. It implied, right from the start, parity with the Liberals, a massively important decision. What if the SDP was a great success – were we committed to fighting only half the seats? What did parity mean? Any fool could see that to have 317 seats meant nothing. It was which seats you had that mattered. It might be a more realistic and advisable bargain to fight 435 to the Liberals' 200 or vice versa. It was an odd statement to make without any consultation. It was particularly unfortunate since Mike Thomas had presciently prepared extensive briefing notes which we had all studied and agreed before the press conference, in order to cope with just such questions.

The nature of the electoral arrangement with the Liberals was one of the key questions facing the SDP and, with one word, 'parity', Bill Rodgers had pre-empted it. David Steel had been putting constant pressure on us all over this issue, both before and after the Limehouse Declaration. It was perfectly reasonable for him to do so. He was, after all, the leader of the Liberal Party and apart from his own highly developed but perfectly legitimate ambition, his overriding responsibility was to protect the interests of the Liberal Party. He never ceased to champion both and I have no criticism of him. David Steel never made any secret of his wish to build up the Liberal Party so that it could govern the country again. Any Social Democrat who expected him to act differently was gravely underestimating the survival instinct of the Liberal Party and, as we were to see in 1988, their capacity to come back from the most appalling self-inflicted wounds.

On 1 April 1981, a week after the launch, Roy Jenkins, speaking at a Gladstone Club dinner, offered the Liberals a 'partnership of principle'. That meant little in itself but then I read in the newspapers that, at the Königswinter conference that coming weekend, ways towards a formal inter-party agreement were to be pursued between David Steel and Shirley Williams. It was nice to know: again there had been no collective discussion. At Königswinter substantive talks were held without any prior agreement by the steering committee or discussion at the Gang of Four lunches at L'Amico's restaurant, which used to precede the steering committee. The proposals which emerged were reported in considerable detail in the *Guardian*.

All hell broke loose among the SDP MPs. They insisted that both parties should retain their separate identities – there was no idea of a merger; that there must be an arrangement before the next general election; that the Liberals were a loose body and varied in their support in different areas throughout the country; and that there was too much negotiation being conducted in public by the Liberals.

It had been a clear and firm rebuff to all the Gang of Four, and I could not escape responsibility for not having prevented these moves towards the Liberals. For a few weeks this shot across Roy Jenkins's bows meant that we could proceed with the mammoth task of building our own party. But a trend had been set in motion which was to prove impossible to reverse. The press learnt that there had been a row and reported the dissent, but the ferocity of the encounter was toned down; it was not in our interests to repeat the fights we had experienced within the Labour Party. This became the pattern: in our wish to avoid infighting and bickering we presented an outward image of unity. Of course, this is attempted by all political parties, but it served us ill. Issues which should have been thrashed out were hidden under the carpet. This was very much Roy Jenkins's style. Unfortunately it became the house style of the SDP too. Many of our members never realised how strongly and for how long a merger had been pressed within the party and resisted, until in 1987 it all erupted with pent-up ferocity on an unsuspecting public and, in some cases, unsuspecting party members.

I, and many other SDP MPs, had always thought a trial of strength with the Liberals was inevitable. Any electoral pact would entail hard bargaining. The SDP was founded on the understanding that one had to bargain from strength in the international fields of defence and security. I never doubted that we must also bargain from strength in the field of domestic politics. The Liberal Party was bound to fight for its position as the third party and we would have to prove our vote-getting ability first.

My priority from the launch of the party, for the next year at least, was to build up the SDP, its membership, its finances and a core of activists. We already envisaged that our first nationwide electoral test would not come until the May 1982 local government elections. If the SDP could make sensible deals with local Liberals at those elections over a year away, so much the better. But in order to achieve those deals the SDP had to be prepared to put up candidates where Liberals were standing in council elections up and down the country. I envisaged negotiating over parliamentary seats, with one party standing down for the other after the council elections had taken place and we had established the SDP on the ground. By that time we would have developed SDP policy independently and democratically, while of course keeping a weather eye on Liberal Party policy to ensure a sensible measure of compatibility. We would also have established our own one member, one vote democracy and have either chosen or be about to choose our own leader. Meanwhile, I thought, the right strategy was to try to agree an arbitration procedure as to which party would fight which by-elections. Unless we could agree some such procedure with the Liberals, the SDP should fight all by-elections.

The next twelve months were critical. We had to quickly establish our identity and build our party on the ground. Too close an association with the Liberals would gravely damage this. If our potential support had wanted to join the Liberals they would have done so a long time ago. They would not see any point in joining us if we were perceived as moving towards too close an association with the Liberals. In terms of local organisation what would be the point of organising and working for the SDP locally if you already knew or guessed that the Liberals would be fighting your constituency and there would be no SDP candidate? This was a powerful argument for delay – a practical arrangement necessitated by the election system arrived at close to the election would be wholly saleable to our potential members. Gratuitous early embrace was not.

The advantages of early agreement for the Liberals were the mirror image of the disadvantages for us in the SDP. It would enhance their image and give them the credibility they currently did not have. It would protect them from attrition of their membership, many of whom were ready to join the SDP, and attract electoral support, much of which would switch to us; over half, on examination of the current polls, could switch without a second thought. It could also push them over the top in the eighty-one seats in which they ran second, which would give them a majority of the seats won by SDP and Liberal candidates in 1983 or 1984. This would give them the dominant role in Parliament subsequently, gravely undermining our credibility even though we commanded three to five times their electoral support at that time.

To establish the SDP in the country as the third largest party within a year, with the Liberals very clearly the fourth party, was not overambitious. By October 1981 we did achieve this third party position in terms of numbers and political weight in the House of Commons and, on the opinion poll evidence, in the country as well. The SDP was ahead of the Liberal Party in public esteem in every poll. In Gallup polls from March to October, if people were reminded of the existence of the SDP as a separate party we normally had double, sometimes triple, the Liberal Party support.

Our membership was over 50,000 by April and up to 78,000 by the end of 1981, which, given the exaggerated membership claims of the Liberal Party, meant we were probably larger. It could have been more – our membership drive never achieved its full potential partly because of our confused identity. Our financial position was also always considerably stronger than that of the Liberal Party.

Why was such a strategy for building up the SDP not followed that April? Why had we by October 1981 queered our own pitch by forming an alliance and other links with the Liberal Party, and why did we disadvantage ourselves further in terms of seat negotiations? Why had we systematically blurred, diffused and damaged our separate identity as a new party by the autumn of 1982?

The answer was not the Liberal Party. We could have resisted them. Nor was it David Steel, although he was harder to resist when he was acting in cahoots with Roy Jenkins. It was the divisions within our own ranks as to whether the SDP was to be separate from the Liberal Party that destroyed us. I find it impossible to escape the conclusion that Roy Jenkins misled me and some of the other MPs who left the Labour Party in 1981, as well as the members of the SDP in the leadership election in 1982, about his real intentions.

When Roy and I were persuading Shirley Williams to use the term 'realignment' in the Limehouse Declaration it was because that would be a firm indication of our intention to form a new party. We were not using realignment then, however much he subsequently tried to pretend we were, in the way Jo Grimond had sometimes used it, bringing part of the Labour Party together with the Liberals into one party. Nor could Roy pretend that his notion of a centre party from the Dimbleby Lecture had been agreed. It was superseded in later Gang of Four discussions. That was reflected by the rejection of the centrist names for the party he suggested, the Radicals or the

Democrats. The choice of SDP meant that, when we four sent a telegram on 2 March saying we hoped the new party would become a member of Socialist International, we were signalling the launch of a social democratic party within the socialist family. When we launched the SDP on 26 March it was as an independent national fourth political party. If we were to be a catalyst, then it was by continuing with the SDP, for a catalyst by definition is something which does not change itself but brings about changes in others.

The event which gave Roy the opportunity to cast the SDP into an Alliance mould aimed at forging a single party was, quite simply, Warrington, and it came only two months after the launching of the SDP.

At the end of May Sir Thomas Williams, the Labour MP for Warrington, resigned his seat in order to become a judge. We had had some warning of this and I raised the likelihood of the by-election at the SDP steering committee on 27 May, having previously discussed it at a Gang of Four lunch at L'Amico's. There, much to my horror, Shirley expressed extreme reluctance to stand and it was all I could do to stop her closing the option completely there and then. We all agreed that she would be the obvious candidate but as her reluctance became more apparent so Roy's enthusiasm to take on the challenge increased. He was like an old stallion, sniffing the smell of the race course, hoping that if the favourite withdrew he might take her place at the starting line. Shirley agreed to think about it. She then, largely on the advice of Tony King, the professor of politics at Essex University and a close friend, began to back further and further away from fighting Warrington. The word was that she could not afford to be a two-time loser, a reference to her having lost in Stevenage at the last election and implying that she could not win Warrington. Then in the early evening of 3 June we learned of a poll in the *Sun* next day which showed that, if Shirley were the SDP/Liberal candidate in Warrington, 55 per cent in Warrington would vote SDP, 36 per cent Labour and 9 per cent Conservative. Under the headline 'YOU CAN DO IT SHIRL', the *Sun* had a whacking 19 per cent lead for Shirley, with Labour knocked out and the Tories nowhere. Instead of rethinking her position, Shirley pre-empted pressure by rushing out a press release saying that she would not stand.

It was the worst decision Shirley has ever made in politics, and certainly the most damaging single decision for the future of the new SDP. It effectively put paid to Shirley's chances of becoming leader of the SDP and ensured that Roy would be its first leader. I have no doubt that Shirley could have won Warrington, with dramatic consequences for the SDP and for the country. She would have fought a predominantly SDP campaign and we would in consequence have been able to negotiate a far better seat deal with the Liberals than the miserable one we ended up with. Shirley would have been the leader of the SDP and Bill and I would have buttressed her position. There would have been no question but that it was a Social Democratic Party, standing in its own right as one of four parties in British politics. But it was sadly not to be.

The *Sun* poll showed that if Roy Jenkins were the SDP candidate we would lose: Labour would get 46 per cent, just winning the seat from the SDP on 42 per cent, with the Conservatives at 12 per cent. That was very close to the actual outcome, when Roy polled 42.4 per cent of the vote, dramatically reducing the Labour majority from over 10,000 to 1,759. This result nevertheless gave the SDP an immense boost and it was to Roy's credit that he took up the challenge. People were getting used to the unfair press image of him as a bloated bureaucrat from Brussels. In fact he turned out to be, as he always had been, a very effective campaigner and he deservedly won accolades from the press and increased public esteem.

In the midst of the Warrington by-election another one presented itself at Croydon North West, showing once again that, in politics, the unpredictable is normality. At its meeting on 6 July, the steering committee was informed that our area party had agreed to a joint meeting with the Liberals to be held on 24 July with the aim of selecting a joint candidate. Joint selection was the most dangerous device the Liberals had yet designed. I believed that if we conceded joint selection for a single by-election it would establish a precedent which would open up joint selection for all parliamentary seats and gravely undermine our integrity as an independent party. Almost by definition a party which allows members of another party to select its candidate surrenders its independence.

We opposed joint selection and the danger passed for a time but the Croydon problem remained. We all believed that Shirley Williams should fight the seat but it was clear the local Liberals were likely to dig their heels in. We had conceded as part of the agreement over Roy fighting Warrington that the Liberals should have first refusal over the next by-election unless there were special circumstances. By any political standard, with Shirley ready to fight, the Croydon North West by-election was an exceptional circumstance.

Over the next week there was frantic activity. David Steel did try hard to persuade the local Liberals to accept Shirley Williams, even at one moment threatening to come down to Croydon to speak against Bill Pitt, who was the Liberal Party's candidate to fight the seat. It was the first clear demonstration to the general SDP membership of the nature of the Liberal Party and the very considerable autonomy of their local constituency associations. It was not even as if we were dealing with a large, active Liberal Party in Croydon; their numbers were so small that they could all meet in Bill Pitt's front room. He turned out to be a bearded Liberal activist, extremely affable, but a libertarian militant. He had not been christened William Pitt for nothing and the prospect of parliamentary greatness weighed heavily with him. Since he controlled the local party and was able to generate pressure more widely from the Liberal grass roots, the Croydon Liberals were only too happy to refuse to accept Shirley Williams while the local SDP wanted to say no to Bill Pitt. We had a choice – to fight or not to fight – but in truth we barely considered fighting the Liberals.

When joint selection reared its head, both for by-elections and for parliamentary elections, David Steel's view mirrored that of Roy Jenkins – since we were going to merge anyhow, there was no reason for anyone to get agitated about which party fought what seat, how many seats each party fought or whether both parties' members chose the candidate. This was a logical view only if the SDP was never intended to have an independent political life of its own. Since David as a Liberal never intended that it should, who could blame him? Our problem was that Roy shared his view while being a member of the SDP. They both wrapped up their intentions in ringing declarations about the Alliance being a partnership of principle. But since they were both impatient of any fights or arguments about seats, it was inevitable that the Gang of Four would be divided over seat allocations. Before any argument began, David had an automatic ally in Roy, for whom rows over seats were a costly diversion. At that stage for me, and, it must be said, for Bill and Shirley, obtaining winnable seats was the vital element for building up the SDP. But the only way to do this was to be ready to fight. But for Roy to contemplate fighting the Liberals was already considered to be a mortal sin and they soon sensed we were a pushover.

In the event, I suppose Roy would have argued there was no alternative. Whether or not he was duplicitous in helping to found the SDP, why did he become convinced that there was no alternative to amalgamating with the Liberals? He would no doubt have argued that spurning the co-operative relationship offered by the Liberal Party would have meant so many scars from early by-election battles over seats that we could never have built up the SDP. But if the Liberals had fought Roy Jenkins at Warrington, they would have lost their deposit and they would have lost it at Croydon North West too if they had fought Shirley. The very anarchic elements within the Liberal Party which David Steel struggled to contain would of course have relished fighting us at every stage and would not have listened to reason even if we had beaten them convincingly in the early by-elections. But by the Llandudno conference, the Liberal Party would have been in more realistic mood. If we had to wait another year, so what.

Instead, by the time the Liberal assembly was held in Llandudno, commentators were starting to equate our two parties whereas in the spring, we had looked and sounded very different. When Shirley had been invited to speak to the Liberal conference, she wisely referred it to the steering committee. It was all for us keeping our distance and only after some initial reluctance did it eventually agree she could go, and then only if she spoke on the fringe and not in the main conference hall. After Warrington Roy felt under no such constraint.

I was not very surprised therefore to read on my return from a Palme commission meeting in Mexico that the fringe meeting at Llandudno had been turned into a meeting larger than the conference itself or that it had been addressed by Roy Jenkins as well as Shirley Williams, with Jo Grimond and David Steel on the same platform. Why did I go to Mexico for what was not after all a vital drafting meeting of the commission? I think it was because subconsciously I wanted to keep my distance, and already saw I was being sucked into an Alliance with a big 'A' rather than a small 'a' over which I had the profoundest doubts.

A political party needs to innovate, and to strike out on its own with ideas which give it an identity and its followers something to fight for. More than an old party, a new party needs the cutting edge of sharp, even controversial, ideas and the strength of commitment to develop its identity. We needed to feel, like Cromwell's russet-coated captains, 'that we knew what we were fighting for and loved what we knew'. Too much joint activity would lead to an amorphous amalgam, the very 'inert centre' which we had supposedly disavowed in the Limehouse Declaration. The Liberals, with their community politics, had developed an identity which made sense for them. I never decried their pavement politics for, as I used to remind people, tripping up on uneven pavements is one of the commoner reasons for attending casualty departments at local hospitals. But the SDP needed an identity of its own as a serious force for national government and leadership and we could not afford either the time or the energy for too much joint policy activity.

It was always hard to express these views publicly without seeming to want to break up the Alliance. The further the move to amalgamate went, the more difficult it was to oppose joint projects without being seen as a 'splitter'. Nevertheless, in September 1981, I risked controversy and made a speech in Andover endorsing competition between our parties. Coalition politics, I said, did not mean that the partners in the coalition had to agree on every political issue. There should be an open acceptance of competition between the parties while working together, either in opposition or in government. We had to demonstrate a core of agreement on the central issues we would face in government and a readiness to work together for the national good but that did not mean merging or fusing our parties or our policies. It meant respecting our different political identities and distinctive traditions. I argued we would make a great mistake if we interpreted the need to avoid fighting each other in parliamentary and council elections as an injunction to blur our identities. The electorate wanted to see a civilised, friendly, co-operative dialogue between our two parties. It was, I felt, those who were wedded to the old politics who assessed the Alliance against the yardstick of a unified party, or who yearned for authoritarian, hierarchical leadership. They did not understand that coalition politics meant that government decision-making, of necessity, becomes more open because the negotiations are held between, not within, the parties. The compromises become overt unlike those made within Cabinet under the mantle of secrecy and the discipline of a single-party whip.

The problem with those in favour of merger was that they could never understand what made a good coalition partner. If people like me suggested or agreed to some joint policy-making, the next thing was that they wanted all policy-making to be joint. If, in the interests of the Alliance, we tried to downplay differences, the mergerites then pretended that there were no differences.

As the Croydon North West by-election was underway with Bill Pitt standing as the Liberal and SDP Alliance candidate, the Conservative MP for Crosby died. The Gang of Four discussed that by-election with David Steel over a meal, the first we had all had together. We all agreed that Shirley should stand. But, as the SDP travelled to Bradford as part of its 'rolling conference', it began to be clear that the local Liberals were none too happy and we feared a repeat of Croydon with a 'grass roots' revolt. Over breakfast, before Shirley was due to speak, Bill and I discussed the situation with her. It was our unanimous view that Shirley should give a firm indication of her intention to stand. Unjustly she was subsequently attacked in unattributable Liberal and SDP press briefings for having made this pre-emptive decision individually and impulsively in defiance of what had been agreed with David Steel. I was at both meetings and I have no doubt that she was correct to act. If she had teased the conference and the public about her intentions she would have been accused again of dithering.

Behind the scenes both by-elections generated difficulties. But there is no denying their fabulous public success. The Croydon North West by-election was won on 22 October by Bill Pitt with a majority of 3,300 over the Conservative candidate, and a swing of 29 per cent. We all helped, and the local SDP suppressed their doubts about his suitability. It was a formidable achievement given that, even in Croydon, Bill Pitt was nowhere near as well known as Shirley. In Crosby, Shirley campaigned brilliantly, attracting Labour voters on the council estates at the Bootle end of the constituency in a very impressive way. She achieved a swing of 34 per cent. Unfortunately it was a seat which would be immensely hard to win at a general election, particularly with the planned boundary changes, but for the time being it meant that the Gang of Three were united again in Parliament, and her win gave her a tremendous personal boost.

All this time the party was establishing itself while finding it desperately difficult to keep up with events. The seat negotiations presented the trickiest problem, well exemplified by what happened in the West Country. The Liberals were strong here and were happy when the SDP accepted a regional bias in their favour; but they refused to agree that the SDP should be given priority elsewhere, in New Town seats, for example, where there was polling evidence that the SDP were doing better than them.

In terms of realignment it made sense for the SDP and Liberals to widen their joint appeal by appealing to different parts of the electorate. This was the so-called 'Heineken effect', which we knew from polling evidence had the potential to swing votes. But we progressively abandoned that strategy by in effect, in the words of the old song, 'watering the workers' beer' and not enjoining the SDP to go for the Labour vote. As the Liberals showed their inability to trade off a gain in one place for a concession elsewhere, so did the SDP abandon any wish to concentrate on Labour seats. Gradually as the Liberals and SDP began to converge, the SDP tried to get its fair share of the most winnable or 'golden' seats, whatever the local position. Even when the Liberals were running a good second in a seat and we encouraged them to continue building support, with us recouping on the next group of 'silver' seats, we found they fought ruthlessly against our then having a preferential allocation. It was becoming ever more hopeless and only a matter of time before the SDP put its foot down.

Plymouth was a case in point. When we agreed eventually that the Liberals should not be denied all representation and could have one seat, they got very upset when we staked a claim for St Ives and Teignbridge in compensation. Two seats as compensation for one, since the Plymouth seat was in theory highly winnable, seemed fair to us. But in the end we had to settle for the hopeless seat of Honiton rather than Teignbridge.

It was the decentralist, locally orientated Liberals who were demonstrating inflexibility up and down the country. They were political street fighters and despised this claret-swigging SDP that was intent on pinching 'their' seats. Our local people in many cases did have mettle and were prepared to fight, but the steering committee's advice was always to play the negotiations long and cool. What we needed in the SDP leadership was the ability to say after a certain point, 'Well, since there is no agreement, we shall, reluctantly, have to fight.' If we were always going to back off just as things came to the crunch then the SDP negotiating position would never have any backbone.

At least Bill Rodgers did seem to understand this, which, as he was leading the negotiations, was reassuring. Although he kept his cards close to his chest I began to feel towards the end of the year that he realised that we would have to have a showdown. Sure enough, it came. In the *Observer* on 3 January 1982 the front-page headline was 'LIB–SDP TALKS ON SEATS BREAK DOWN'. Bill Rodgers had suspended talks following a collapse in the negotiations over Greenock & Port Glasgow and seats in Derbyshire. When asked whether there was a crisis threatening the Alliance, Bill replied, 'Yes, regrettably there is.' David Steel reiterated Macmillan's notorious phrase about 'a little local difficulty'. David, who had been hotting up the atmosphere the week before by encouraging local Liberals to stand out against 'arrogance and bluster', was quoted as commenting that 'the Liberal Party is not an authoritarian party and the SDP perhaps is'. The word 'perhaps' was a nice touch; rather like a Mafioso greasing a stiletto.

Whether Bill should have gone public in this way I was not sure, but we had to trust each other in our different areas of responsibility and when the press telephoned me I made it clear that I was not prepared to criticise what he had done in any way. However, I sensed from their questions that they had been briefed by Roy Jenkins and his friends in a direction that was highly critical of Bill. On the Monday this started to appear in newspaper comment. That day there was a Gang of Four lunch at Bill's house, though Shirley was unable to come because of a tobogganing accident. I arrived early and reassured Bill that he had my total support. When Roy arrived I saw him, for the first time, express real anger with Bill. It was soon apparent why. Tam Galbraith, the Conservative MP for Glasgow Hillhead and my pair, had died and Bob Maclennan was urging Roy to stand; but the Liberals already had a prospective candidate. Roy was extremely agitated that he might forfeit the chance to fight Hillhead. This could be his last chance to get into Parliament before the leadership election, and here was Bill, his closest colleague in the Gang of Four, gratuitously damaging relations with the Liberals. Within days, over yet another publicised meal in a restaurant, Bill had climbed down and David Steel emerged looking ever more like a choirboy.

At about this time the SDP faced a crucial test of its radicalism. Trade union reform had been the single most important task facing Margaret Thatcher when she took office in 1979, and the reforms she instituted will prove to be her most enduring legacy. It was always clear that this issue would be the one on which the SDP's claim not to be a Mark II Labour Party would be tested. Once Margaret Thatcher had sent Jim Prior off to Northern Ireland and made Norman Tebbit her Secretary of State for Employment, it was inevitable that controversy would follow. Tebbit's speech at the party conference the previous October set the tone: 'My father did not riot. He got on his bike and looked for work.' He is to this day a far more interesting and subtle politician than Michael Foot's crack about being 'a semi-house-trained polecat' implied. He knows that elections are fought and lost among the semi-skilled workers, the C2 voters, and he never had the slightest intention of alienating these people in his approach to trade union reform. What he sensed in his Chingford constituency, on the London–Essex border, in the 1980s and had the self-confidence to capitalise on was the burning resentment of many trade unionists at the conduct of the leaders of their own trade unions and, particularly, the operation of the closed shop. The characteristic, somewhat condescending, view of the liberal intelligentsia – to be found in all parties including the Conservatives – was that reforming the trade unions meant alienating trade unionists. Tebbit knew it was the other way round and that the early 1980s reforms, aimed at increasing the responsibility and accountability of the trade unions, did not go far enough.

Tebbit's 1982 legislation was seen to deal with the closed shop. To oppose it would line up the SDP with all the vested interests of the trade unions, but if we voted for the legislation on the second reading we would be depicted by the Labour Party as anti-trade unionist. In the middle of January I had given a lecture at Leicester University in memory of the former TUC general secretary George Woodcock, where I had emphasised that the SDP valued trade unionism and would never be antagonistic to the concept of workers combining to safeguard their interests. But I was determined that the SDP would not duck Tebbit's challenge. When we discussed how to vote in the parliamentary committee, almost every MP believed that abstaining on the second reading was not a practical course. The overwhelming majority of the committee felt that it was modest legislation, usefully restricting the application of the closed shop, and that, though the scope of the legislation should have been much wider, covering industrial democracy, inner trade union democracy and the political levy, we could not credibly join Labour in voting against it. Bill, Shirley and I agreed that, despite the fact that we were likely to have a split in our vote, with newcomers to the committee, like John Grant and Tom McNally, unable to go along with the majority decision, we should not seek refuge in abstention. Of the twenty-seven SDP MPs in the House of Commons, five voted against the legislation, one abstained but the rest of us voted with the Liberals in favour. The headline in the *Times*, 'ALLIANCE HOLDS TOGETHER IN FIRST CRUCIAL VOTING TEST', was not too bad, but other newspapers focused more damagingly on the split in our party. In truth we were still finding our way over trade union reform. Soon we did begin to hit the right notes, emphasising the need 'to bring the trade unions back to their members' with one member, one vote democracy. The result was that the Conservatives pinched all our ideas, even that very phrase, and put them on the statute book in the 1984 legislation, and by 1988 their legislation concentrated on giving trade union members rights, by then a well-established SDP theme. We supported therefore the 1982, 1984 and 1988 reforms. I was pleased that, as a consequence, the Conservative trade union reforms were seen to be more broadly based and have substantial cross-party support. This was one of the reasons why, when Labour campaigned to 'Kill the Bill' in the hope of placating their militants, they got such a poor response even from trade unionists. When real historians look back over the Thatcher period they will give credit to the SDP for widening the consensus for radical change and ensuring that these changes stuck and were not reversed when Labour eventually returned to government in 1997.

The crucial aspect about the four trade union acts was that they progressed one step at a time in an evolutionary process. Margaret Thatcher had learnt important lessons from Edward Heath's Industrial Relations Act and the TUC's response to it. She also realised that it was not enough to rely on legislation alone. Just as important was to make the trade unions understand that when the government took a stance, it would stick to it, with one exception, already noted, regarding the miners. Thus it withstood the steel strike in 1980, the civil servants' strike in 1981, health workers in 1982, water workers in 1983, miners in 1984–5, teachers in 1985–6 and ambulance workers in 1989–90. During all these strikes ministers deliberately distanced themselves from the negotiations surrounding these disputes. Whereas in the past Conservative ministers had been nearly as ready to intervene as Labour ministers, casting themselves in the role of honest brokers, now ministers were not visibly involved in the negotiations. They were not, however, removed from the battle. They were partisan and political in their comments and stood ready to put the boot into the trade unions whenever they could see a good opportunity. Yet even where the government was the employer, they managed to distance themselves from the actual bargaining process. This approach meant that it was much harder to generate an atmosphere of national crisis around strike action and the average trade unionist came to be far more concerned about maintaining his job than following the call to action by trade union leaders. The SDP was sympathetic to this approach and, in so far as we were able to influence the climate, we unashamedly reinforced the Conservative trade union reform programme. I believe that this was in the national interest and helped to demonstrate that the TUC and Labour Party response was largely ritualistic and contrived.

Then we plunged into the Hillhead campaign. After a *pas de deux* with the local Liberals and the odd pirouette Roy Jenkins was chosen. Everything depended on being able to erode the Labour vote and check the Scottish Nationalists. It turned out to be a dogged and difficult fight. Roy campaigned well but it took time to break down the Glaswegians' suspicions. The journalist Simon Hoggart reported one exchange on the streets during the campaign:

a voter who had been undecided the week before had now made up her mind to support Roy Jenkins. 'Why?' asked the canvasser from the Labour Party. 'Because I have always been against the Common Market,' she said. The astonished party worker then emphasised that Roy Jenkins was a devotee of the EEC – Mr Europe himself. He had even been president of the European Commission. 'Aye,' she replied, 'but he packed it in.' It shows how bizarre the reasons frequently given for supporting a particular candidate are and the reasons for opposing them can be equally bizarre. One SDP candidate, having been called a 'young Turk' on the radio, found that a voter would not support him because she preferred 'an English candidate'.

We started house meetings during the campaign for it soon became clear that the more people saw and heard Roy the better the chance of persuading them to vote for him. He dealt very effectively at a public meeting organised by the Campaign for a Scottish Assembly with the charge that he was not Scottish by meeting it head on:

> I am not a Scotsman [loud ribaldry from the crowd] . . . I am a Welshman, but not a Welsh-speaking Welshman [great roars of outrage, mirth, shouts of 'phoney']. I come in fact from Gwent, where only a small number of people speak Welsh as their first language [more shouts] . . . I have to confess that I don't speak Welsh, but then, how many in this hall speak Gaelic? [Shocked, embarrassed, prolonged silence.]

The opinion polls showed it was going to be a close-run thing but we thought by the last few days that Roy was easing ahead. So it proved. He won by more than 2,000 votes and returned to the House of Commons with a very considerable personal triumph. It would not be more than a few months before the party members would now choose which of the Gang of Four they wished to be their first leader.

During the Hillhead by-election it had been agreed that the leadership election would be brought forward from the autumn to the summer. It was a proposition that was hard to resist. Roy had clearly judged that if he won Hillhead it would be better to have an election quickly while the aura of victory was still around him and he had made it pretty clear that if he lost he had no intention of fighting another by-election. He and his supporters were intent on avoiding a fight with Shirley now that they knew they had lost over the MPs electing the leader and there would be a one member, one vote election. First Bill talked on ITN about keeping the present collective leadership. Then the Jenkinsites began to woo Shirley with the idea of a dual leadership – Roy as party leader, her as president. This two-leader scenario was assiduously run for the next few months and Shirley became progressively more attracted to it. Meanwhile I was fortifying my intention to ensure a challenge to Roy. I was telling friends that if Shirley did not run, I definitely would; but if she decided to stand I might well not. The one thing I was determined to ensure was that the party would be able to choose in a one member, one vote election.

On 30 March Roy Jenkins took his seat in the House of Commons. It had been agreed that I would continue as chairman of the parliamentary committee pending the leadership election, which we began to prepare for. But that day was notable for much more than Roy's arrival. The Falklands crisis was looming. That afternoon there was a statement about South Georgia in which the government admitted that the situation was potentially dangerous and that the question of security in the Falklands area was being reviewed, though they could say nothing in public about their precautionary measures. Three days later, on Friday 2 April, I was due to leave early for Plymouth but, listening to the morning news programmes, I heard that the Argentines were claiming that they were in occupation of the Falkland Islands and that the garrison had surrendered. I cancelled travelling to Plymouth and stayed in the House of Commons, going in at 11.00 a.m. for a statement on the Falkland Islands by the Lord Privy Seal, a senior minister in the Foreign Office. He revealed that there was now a real expectation that an Argentine attack would take place very soon. In my interjection I said I hoped that contingency measures had been taken some weeks earlier to ensure that naval forces were in the area and were capable of intervening if necessary, adding that there should be no question of the House adjourning if there was any possibility of an invasion. At 2.30 p.m. the Leader of the House,

Francis Pym, rose to make another holding statement, promising that there would be an emergency session of Parliament next day, a Saturday, if the situation in the Falklands deteriorated. By this time, MPs on all sides, hearing radio reports of Argentines dancing on the streets of Buenos Aires, were extremely concerned that we had been misled by the earlier statement, and that the government knew that the Falkland Islands had already been invaded. At least the fact that the government was prepared to contemplate coming back on a Saturday demonstrated they understood the seriousness of the situation. Later that night, when the fact of the invasion could no longer be held back, I went on television and strongly supported the immediate despatch of a naval task force, something which we did not know had been under active discussion in the government since Wednesday.

On the Saturday the House assembled at 11.00 a.m. for the most dramatic debate I have ever participated in. I had had a meeting with Bill Rodgers and a few other MPs who had come in early in the room of John Roper, the SDP chief whip. There was never any question but that I would speak in the debate for the SDP. It was a helpful discussion and Bill, though sharing my anxiety about the difficulty of an opposed landing, advised me strongly and wisely against saying anything which would make it hard to repossess the islands. At Prayers the House was packed and the mood sombre. Immediately afterwards the Lord Privy Seal rose to apologise for misleading me and other members in the House the day before. We then had a rather irritating vote on whether the debate should take place for longer than three hours, a fairly typical House of Commons diversion.

But soon the main debate started and the Prime Minister rose to speak: 'The House meets this Saturday to respond to a situation of great gravity. We are here because, for the first time for many years, British sovereign territory has been invaded by a foreign power.' She was clearly shaken. There was none of the self-confident hectoring that we were used to. The speech was nevertheless determined and she said with feeling, 'It is the government's objective to see that the islands are freed from occupation and returned to British administration at the earliest possible moment.' I said to her in my speech that she now had to 'examine ways of restoring the government's authority and ask herself why Britain has been placed in such a humiliating position during the past few days'.

In my speech I outlined the case for a naval blockade: 'There is much to be said for declaring our right to a 200-mile limit round the Falkland Islands. It would be perfectly compatible with international law to declare that no Argentine vessel should appear within that limit and that, if it did, the British Navy would take action.' Winding up the debate, John Nott, the Secretary of State for Defence, made a disastrous, defensive speech, and while dismissing the key question from his own side about why he had not put a hunter-killer submarine on station two weeks earlier, insisted on trying to score a petty point at the expense of Jim Callaghan, who had deployed a submarine and frigates during negotiations in 1977, as if he were still in the Cambridge Union. He said that Jim and I had contradicted each other, Jim having said that Argentina had known about the deployment to the South Atlantic in 1977 and that a diplomatic solution had followed, whereas I had said it had been done in total secrecy. This provoked both Michael Foot and me to intervene and I said, 'If the right honourable Gentleman, the Secretary of State for Defence, has not understood the value to a Foreign Secretary of being able to negotiate in a position of some military influence and strength, he should not be Secretary of State for Defence' – a sentiment which most people in the House that day shared. In fact we did deploy secretly in 1977 because we knew we might have to deploy again. It was a move to ensure we could act if against expectations a surprise invasion had been launched. When John Nott sat down at the end of the debate there were few people in the House who believed that both he and Lord Carrington could stay on. At least one of them, perhaps both, would have to resign.

The House of Commons spoke for the nation that day, reflecting the humiliation that millions felt and a resolve to put this humiliation behind us, to restore our reputation and to retake the islands. Of course there were MPs on all sides who hoped, some none too secretly, that this episode would prove to be the undoing of Margaret Thatcher, while outside the House of Commons commentators representing the liberal intelligentsia affected to yawn at the irrelevance of it all. Over the next few weeks at their London dinner parties the conversation would be full of speculation on how the government would fall if the task force returned with its tail between its legs and General Galtieri's forces still ensconced on the Falkland Islands. But the great majority of MPs and of the British people wanted the government to succeed. In this moment of grave crisis they rightly saw the fortunes of the government and the nation as one.

I never had any doubt that what was at stake was far more than the survival of Margaret Thatcher or of the Conservative Party. It seemed to me that, if Britain were defeated, the peace movement would start to find the public receptive to its demand for swingeing cuts in our defence forces. It was already making considerable progress campaigning against cruise missiles and NATO's strategy of nuclear deterrence. What was the point, its members would argue, in having all these sophisticated weapons if we could not even stand up to General Galtieri? The SDP MPs gave their full-hearted support to the government throughout the Falklands campaign. Of course, they knew that if the government's popularity recovered as a result of retaking the Falkland Islands, there might be adverse political consequences for our young party, but I think, like me, they felt that this was no time for the usual 'hedge your bets' type of opposition which makes it possible to point to trivial qualifications if things go wrong. We stiffened the Liberal Party and held firm in supporting our armed forces, something that was a good deal easier to do once Margaret Thatcher conceded that after the war there would need to be an inquiry into how we had lost the islands in the first place. But her tone on sovereignty became even more entrenched and unrealistic. As I constantly argued, we could *not* use the UN Charter to justify our act of self-defence and then ignore the charter's demands that we negotiate. I did, however, accept that Argentina had to face the fact that there are penalties for going to war. I did not believe then and I do not believe twenty-seven years later that we can do more than share sovereignty or transfer it to the UN at some future date – as a result of Argentine aggression a straight transfer of sovereignty to Argentina is now impossible to foresee. That will mean the retention of our defence capability on the islands for some years ahead and a capacity at times of tension to deploy submarines to the surrounding waters.

As the war developed I spoke frequently both in debates and on statements. The government agreed to brief opposition leaders on Privy Council terms but foolishly Michael Foot refused. Slowly, largely under Denis Healey's influence, Michael Foot's resolve to support the task force began to weaken. The reservations increased and the reluctance actually to use the force that had been deployed deepened. There was nothing one could really put one's finger on but the mood of Labour in the House began to change. Conservative MPs who had been welcoming the interventions from Michael Foot and the Labour front bench started to view them with suspicion, although there was no overt antagonism, and the divisions never approached those which had developed at the time of Suez.

Admiral of the Fleet Sir Terence Lewin was a brilliantly successful chief of the Defence Staff during the Falklands War, first known to me as a naval captain and then a junior admiral when I was Navy Minister, then as First Sea Lord and chief of the Naval Staff when I was Foreign Secretary. On the BBC on 30 January 1983, as he criticised a speech that I had made in the House of Commons about our readiness to open fire in 1977, it sadly became clear that even he had forgotten the terms of the rules of engagement which had been agreed by ministers with the full involvement of the Ministry of Defence. He said:

> I cannot believe that any British government in peacetime would authorise a nuclear submarine, or indeed our ships, to take hostile action, the first hostile action, against another power. No rule of engagement would ever be approved that would allow you to do this and it certainly wasn't approved in 1977.

What Admiral Lewin had forgotten was that ministers had carefully defined what would constitute a hostile action or hostile intent and that ministers did authorise Royal Navy commanders to open fire on Argentine units which displayed hostile intent. Evidence of hostile intent was to include preparing to land military forces on the Falkland Islands or manoeuvring into a position to attack British territory. It is also clear that ministers in 1977 were ready, in the event of a sufficiently serious deterioration in relations between us and the Argentine government, to extend the territorial limit round the islands from 3 to 12 miles and to inform the Argentine government that any of their warships and military aircraft approaching to within 50 miles would be asked to identify itself and state its intention. The Argentines would have been ordered to withdraw beyond 25 miles of the Falkland Islands and, if they had failed to do so, under the doctrine of minimum force they would have been subject to ascending degrees of force, from warning to the discharge of conventional weapons.

Though it was hoped that the commander of the nuclear-powered hunter-killer submarine HMS *Dreadnought* in 1977 would have been under control at all stages of the Commander-in-Chief Fleet, answerable through the chiefs of staff to ministers, it was thought highly desirable that in a deteriorating military situation or where there might be difficulty in communicating with the commanders of the two frigates or of the submarine, they should have very carefully designed political authorisation to act on their own initiative.

It is very clear from what Admiral Lewin said in his broadcast that, besides his doubts about initiating hostile action in 1982, he had another concern relating to the size of the force needed. He said:

> With the degree of Argentine frustration five years further on from 1977, I very much doubt whether the chiefs of staff would have recommended that a force of that small size would have been enough. We would have had to send a much larger force and the situation never really warranted it in those first early days of March 1982.

My reaction to this comment was that if the Argentines' frustration was greater five years on, why had there not been a much earlier and far firmer military response?

It is not every day that Britain is plunged into a war. The Falklands War, once it began, was handled with great skill by Margaret Thatcher and by all our military commanders. I made this very clear in the speech on which Admiral Lewin was commenting. Malcolm Rutherford described that speech in the *Financial Times* on 28 January 1983:

> The most devastating speech came from Dr Owen, who savaged Mrs Thatcher in a manner to which she is plainly unaccustomed. Moreover, he did it from a rational basis of knowledge and experience.

In brief, he said that it was right to respond to Argentine aggression, though there were some qualifications about how the invasion was allowed to take place. It was right in the circumstances even to sink the *Belgrano* – a notably brave statement. But it was wrong to fall back on Fortress Falklands and the 'paramountcy' of the wishes of 1,800 islanders about their future. 'We fought against aggression, not for a flag,' he said. Sometime it would again become necessary to discuss the long-term future of the islands, not only with Argentina but with Latin America.

The sinking of the *Belgrano* was a necessary military operation which effectively trapped the Argentine navy in its ports for the rest of the war. It is unfortunate that this essential military act was to give the government so much grief in the months to come, as small inconsistencies in describing what had happened became large discrepancies. For reasons which I can only assume stemmed from a desire to prevent the Argentines from gaining compensation for the *Belgrano* in international law, a cover-up began. The key mistake was not to reveal everything in the published review some months after the war was over.

In the council elections in May, the Conservative revival got underway; the SDP and Liberals began to suffer. Although the two parties only made an overall gain of ninety-seven seats, in most parts of the country our share of the vote doubled and between us we managed to win a quarter of the vote. Inevitably the SDP lost a large number of councillors who had previously been Labour and were in rock-solid Labour wards. Our bandwagon had clearly slowed down. This was confirmed in the Beaconsfield by-election, which the Liberals fought on 27 May, and in which Labour was represented by Tony Blair, faithfully following all Michael Foot's irresponsible policies! In the Mitcham & Morden by-election on 3 June, Bruce Douglas-Mann lost his seat. Bruce had just joined the SDP from Labour and insisted on a by-election against the wishes of all his new colleagues. It gave the Conservatives a by-election gain, the first time the government of the day had gained a seat in a by-election for more than twenty years. Then, on 14 June, the Argentines surrendered and, from the moment the Union Jack was run up the flagpole at Port Stanley once more, I never doubted that the Conservatives would be re-elected in any general election. At a by-election on 17 June at Coatbridge & Airdrie the fortunes of the Alliance had fallen so far since Hillhead that the unfortunate candidate's deposit was lost. Margaret Thatcher was cock-a-hoop, deservedly enjoying the aura of a successful war leader. It was now for her only a question of waiting for the earliest decent moment at which to call an election without being thought to be exploiting the issue. That did not of course stop her exploiting it.

At this inauspicious electoral moment the SDP leadership contest was finally upon us. Nominations had to be in no later than 12 noon on Friday 11 June and the ballot would be counted on 2 July, my birthday. So, in theory, the leadership election started while the war was on, but in practice it was in abeyance. My nomination was held back because of my hope that Shirley would still decide to stand against Roy. She was abroad and did not finally announce that she would not be a candidate until 18 May. I did not want to confirm my candidacy until I had spoken to her. I offered to stand down if she would prefer a two-horse race, but by then she had made up her mind that she did not want to fight, though she promised to support me. She guessed that she would lose against Roy and that she would easily win the presidency against Bill. In February I had been worried that I would not reach the requisite threshold of MPs to nominate me. By June I had the support of half the twenty-nine SDP MPs.

The newspapers tried to bring out and sharpen the coded disagreements between Roy and me, but I suspect many people had voted before they read any press comment. Should I have acquiesced in the shadow-boxing and in effect allowed myself to be in part an accomplice to Roy's strategy? Should I have challenged the party members outright by telling them we were being merged by stealth? Though the headlines concentrated on personalities – 'ABRASIVE DAVID OR ROUNDED ROY', 'CAN THE DOCTOR WIN WITHOUT A BEDSIDE MANNER?', 'THE GOOD DOCTOR VERSUS ONE OF NATURE'S BANKERS', 'IS DR OWEN'S CUTTING EDGE A SHADE TOO SHARP?' – most of the comment explored the nature of our different approach to the Liberals, but not so obviously as to alert members to the true pressure to merge. The Roy Jenkins sympathisers assiduously sold the line that my election would rupture the Alliance and raised privately or by inference a question mark over whether Roy would continue in politics if he lost. This was a point taken up in the *Scotsman* by James Naughtie, 'An Owen win would certainly threaten to bring Mr Jenkins's political career to a premature close.' An editorial in the *Times*, 'The whisper of the hustings', stressed the SDP's dependence on the Liberals when it argued that I would be a better bet as leader but only of a radical new party and that Roy would be the more comfortable leader.

On the last Sunday of the election campaign my hopes soared when I read the front page of the *Observer*. It showed me leading Roy Jenkins by 47 per cent to 29, but when I studied the detail of the NOP poll it became apparent that the poll was not among SDP members, who were the relevant electorate, but a sample poll of the whole country. In my heart I knew that Roy was going to win but I still dared to hope. The result was announced on my forty-fourth birthday. Out of 68,000 potential voters Roy Jenkins got 26,300 votes and I got 20,900 votes. We had not spilt much political blood but perhaps that was the tragedy of that election. The real issue had been kept in the depths and not allowed to surface.

I do not blame David Steel for masterminding an alliance between the SDP as far as possible on Liberal terms, and later for the takeover of the SDP, because he thought that was in the best interests of the Liberal Party. I believe, however, it was only in their narrow, short-term interest. The broader interest of Liberals was, and still for the Liberal Democrats remains, to build up the number of their MPs and to do everything possible to achieve proportional representation. Apart from the safety and prosperity of the country, proportional representation should be any Liberal leader's central objective, for the first-past-the-post system will always work in favour of the two largest parties. Also the diversity and disaggregation that the Liberal creed of individualism favours will flourish within the coalition politics that accompanies proportional representation. To achieve this there is one task – to enlarge the vote of those who do not wish to support the Labour or Conservative parties and thereby force a change in the voting system to proportional representation. The best way to ensure this at an election is by electoral pacts with other parties involving standing down candidates in seats so as to beat the distortion within the present system. The Alliance model that David Steel and Roy Jenkins favoured destroyed the SDP even though it took ten years to do it. Had the Alliance held after 1987, even though the reduced SDP would have had to concede many more seats at the next election to the newly formed Liberal Democrats, containing SDP members who had wished to merge, I believe John Major would not have had an outright majority in 1992 and the subsequent shape of British politics could have been very different.

Early in October 1982 Debbie and I had dinner with John Pardoe and his wife. It was a merry evening and we gossiped, with just a tinge of malice, about David Steel. John spent his whole time convincing me that life outside politics was much better than inside; not, at that stage, that I needed much convincing. Not only was he doing well in his business but also, as they both explained, the real delight was to have more evenings at home and time for all the things which politics had excluded. This upbeat view of non-political life was reinforced by a rather downbeat lunch with Lord Zuckerman a few days later at London Zoo. Solly, despite being a good friend of Roy Jenkins, was gloomy about the political situation. I was due to have lunch with Roy to talk about the deputy leadership and was by now in no mood for such a lunch. I needed cheering up. So I arranged to have lunch with Lord George Brown – if anyone knew anything about the perils of being deputy leader it was George. He gave a good analysis of the boundaries within which I could work in my relations with Roy. We both agreed that the prospects for the SDP looked pretty grim but that all I could do was to lie low. If I spoke out publicly the party's chances would be further damaged.

From 1982 onwards we were embarked on a very different struggle from that which many of us had begun in Limehouse in January 1981. Our struggle now was to survive and avoid being absorbed into the Liberal Party. In 1982 I said, 'Our epitaph might be that we had saved the Labour Party,' and added that 'there were worse fates than that'. After the tenth anniversary of the founding of the SDP a *Times* editorial on 27 March 1991, 'To the Four's credit', disinterred that quotation and concluded it was indeed our epitaph. Yet that editorial could not have been written immediately after the

1987 election. Then, it looked as if all the SDP might be remembered for was giving the Liberal Party a boost. For the Labour Party was still unreformed. By 1991, although the continuing SDP was dead its supporters could claim that Labour was reformed and by 1995 under Tony Blair that Labour was a social democratic party.

This was, however, as events turned out, too negative an interpretation of the SDP's contribution to British politics. By 2009, with New Labour in disarray, analysts were beginning to realise that a party without beliefs and principles but merely dedicated to doing 'what works' was bound to fail and that by contrast the SDP had been based on enduring principles, human rights, redistribution and the social market. Keeping the SDP an independent force after 1987, albeit one destined to be more a think tank than a party, was worthwhile. SDP ideas thereby flowed into the 1990s. SDP ideas may provide the basis for a rethink in the twenty-first century and could create the climate for coalition politics and reform involving Conservatives and Liberal Democrats. In ways as contributing fresh ideas to British politics after the ideological desert of the Third Way from 1997. It will only be historians who will be able to determine how successfully the SDP contributed to a change in political attitudes from 2010. But if fixed-term parliaments are introduced, a non-list-based proportional system elects a senate as a revising second chamber and radical politics ensue, that could prove to be a more lasting legacy than the SDP's considerable impact on reforming the Labour Party.

The extent to which Britain's electoral system militates against political parties whose support is evenly distributed has never been widely understood. In February 1974 the Liberals got 19.4 per cent of the vote but only 2 per cent of the seats. Despite the fact that this was a potent argument for reform, it was not in the SDP/Liberal Alliance's interests in the mid 1980s to point it out, for when people saw our opinion poll support at between 33 per cent and 34 per cent they thought we were level-pegging with the Conservatives and Labour. To disabuse them would have damaged our credibility and might have left people thinking we were a wasted vote. But in fact if the SDP/Liberal Alliance had got even one-third of the vote it would have won fewer than 100 seats and, because of the 1982 seat agreement, the overwhelming proportion of those seats would have gone to the Liberal Party. Only if we had gone over the 40 per cent level would the electoral system have started to work in our favour as, evenly spread, we would have then been overrewarded with seats.

At the start of 1983 the SDP/Liberal Alliance was sadly still stuck in the opinion polls. What rather unfortunately became known as the 'Alliance relaunch' was held in January. Originally envisaged as being in the Albert Hall, it took place more modestly in Central Hall, Westminster. Despite the splendid singing of the Aberystwyth Male Voice Choir we made little impression on the television news bulletins. The press gave us little coverage either for the London or the regional meetings. One opinion poll even put us down below 20 per cent, at 19 per cent.

Then fate served us a good turn. Bob Mellish, who had offered to make way for Shirley Williams earlier, resigned, creating the Bermondsey by-election. Bermondsey had been Labour for more than sixty years but now the Labour vote was split since a friend of Bob Mellish's ran independently from the official Labour candidate. Simon Hughes fought an excellent traditional Liberal community politics by-election campaign, but it was a campaign which was Labour's to lose and they lost it. Peter Tatchell, a Labour left-winger, was a totally unsuitable candidate, never likely to win the sympathy of Bermondsey council tenants. Simon Hughes won in February 1983 with a 44 per cent swing from Labour to the Liberal/SDP Alliance. It looked as if we might be back on the road to recovery when another by-election got underway at Darlington. Here the SDP was fighting the seat and had chosen a regional TV interviewer. Although our candidate was very well known, the campaign was not a success and we came third, Labour holding the seat. It was widely felt that if Labour had lost, Michael Foot would have resigned by the end of March and been replaced by Denis Healey, which would have meant a huge improvement in Labour's popularity at the general election.

With Michael Foot strengthened in office it was only the Alliance which still had a leadership question to answer. We had to decide when to announce that Roy was going to lead us or, as it was rather portentously and very revealingly expressed, become the Prime Minister designate. For months David Steel had delayed making the inevitable announcement and it was clear why. The Liberal MP

David Penhaligon, who understood polls, was incensed that there should be any question of endorsing Roy when there was such an obvious discrepancy in their respective appeal. A MORI poll in February had shown that 52 per cent of Alliance supporters wanted David Steel to lead and only 30 per cent Roy Jenkins. Among the whole electorate David had 46 per cent satisfied with his leadership whereas Roy had only 26 per cent. The most sensitive finding of all was that even SDP supporters had a higher regard for David Steel than Roy Jenkins in every respect other than experience. In March a MORI poll in the *Sunday Times* showed 52 per cent of voters preferring David Steel as Alliance leader while only 14 per cent preferred Roy. These findings sat very uncomfortably with David Steel's private agreement with Roy. Shirley was thought to have jumped the gun when she told the SDP Scottish conference at the end of February that Roy Jenkins would be Prime Minister if the Alliance won and that David Steel had accepted this; but she was only revealing what we all knew had already been agreed between the two of them.

The Liberals were not happy. David Penhaligon stated on television that he thought David Steel should be chosen to lead the Alliance and actually went to see Roy to persuade him to stand down. At the end of March a joint meeting of MPs agreed that an announcement about a single leader would not be made until the eve of a general election and in the meantime the joint leadership should be promoted. In the middle of April Brian Walden, writing in the *Standard*, 'Two heads are better than one', anticipated that David Steel would wait until the Prime Minister named the date of the general election and then, with all the insouciance he could muster, mention that Roy Jenkins was getting the job. With no time to debate the choice in the heat of battle, the Liberals would hopefully be too preoccupied to make much fuss.

There was also concern in the SDP. The trustees of the party, David Sainsbury and Sir Leslie Murphy, came to see me near the end of April to discuss how Roy could be moved aside. Both were convinced he was a disaster. I had to tell them that I was the last person who could do anything. David Sainsbury had voted for Roy but now regretted it. Leslie Murphy had voted for me.

As the election approached, the inevitable happened and Roy

became the Prime Minister designate with David Steel called 'leader of the campaign'. For parties which were by then facing a very difficult election, it was a dismal solution, but short of Roy Jenkins magnanimously standing down there was nothing any of us could do. Those who believed a single leader was essential had had their way, the breakthrough strategy was still being followed and we had handicapped ourselves before we started.

There was one bridgehead I would not ignore. Devonport had previously been marginal, but this election promised to be the toughest I had ever fought, for it had now become, as a result of boundary changes, on paper a safe Labour seat. I was determined to win and to demonstrate that the Labour voters who had supported me in past elections would stay with me as a Social Democrat. Up and down the country for the last two years Michael Foot had regularly promised his audience, to shouts of joy, that one thing he could assure them: I would lose in Devonport. Not only was I intent on proving him wrong, but I was determined not to be thrown on the defensive. I would campaign as a national leader and not hole up in my constituency. But I knew I would also cut myself loose from the attitudes of the Alliance and attack Labour's policies.

The Friday after Margaret Thatcher announced the election in May 1983 I went to Plymouth and started to plan my local campaign. This was quite unlike any other election I had ever fought. In the past I had been able to rely on the Labour Party machine, but in the last two years I had had to create my own. At the opening constituency press conference the press were like a pack of wolves. They had scented my political end. I decided that false confidence would be a mistake. The best strategy was to be perfectly frank, admit that I was lying third in a local opinion poll and put the issue straight to the electorate in Plymouth; they had my political life in their hands. Instead of trying to dismiss that poll as being of no significance, I promoted it, wanting people to know that I was facing the political battle of my life.

In my national campaign, I resolved I would present the electorate with the truth about Michael Foot's Labour Party and not make a foolish attempt to argue that Margaret Thatcher's party was just as bad. Fortunately, the Conservatives soon presented us with a theme enabling us to persuade fleeing Labour voters not to run into the arms of the Conservatives. It happened early in the campaign when I went on *Question Time* with Francis Pym and Roy Hattersley.

Pym, Foreign Secretary at the time, quietly interjected what was to prove, for him, a fatal phrase. 'Landslides,' he said, 'on the whole, do not produce successful governments.' Margaret Thatcher was furious at what she regarded as his impertinence. The next morning she said witheringly at her press conference, 'I think I can handle a landslide all right.' She had always disliked Pym and the feeling was mutual. She had only made him Foreign Secretary at the emotion-charged moment when Peter Carrington finally rejected all her entreaties to stay on after the invasion of the Falkland Islands. To him she was below the salt; to her he was a snob. His explanation for the Conservative troubles was 'we've got a corporal at the top, not a cavalry officer'. On the day after the election she summoned him to No. 10, saying, 'Francis, I want a new Foreign Secretary,' and peremptorily sacked him.

Often those present entirely miss the significance of political turning points. The prospect of a landslide provided the only serious anti-Conservative campaign issue. The advantage of a general election is that it often peels off the veneer. Seeing Margaret Thatcher chair the Conservative press conferences, journalists could feel that her Cabinet must be almost a session of the Spanish Inquisition. The way she humiliated, patronised and even bullied grown men at these conferences was all too revealing. I seemed almost the only politician who did not mind admitting that there was a danger of a Conservative landslide, so when I spoke I obtained a very receptive audience in the press.

Given the resonance of the landslide issue, I felt it was time to concentrate my attack on Margaret Thatcher and what I called 'rampant Thatcherism'. I likened her to a queen bee, unstoppable unless there was a strong opposition to curb her. I warned that the 'drones' were on the way out: 'Lord Carrington has been sacrificed, Mr Prior banished, Mr Walker bypassed, Mr Whitelaw put down and Mr Pym admonished.'

But the true issue was Labour. Next morning I flew in a small plane from Birmingham/Coventry airport to Plymouth, ready to take part in a down-the-line interview on the Jimmy Young show with Michael Heseltine and John Silkin. The internal Labour Party wrangle over nuclear defence was now in full spate. The previous day the headlines had been 'LABOUR TO DISPEL POLARIS CONFUSION' (*Guardian*) and 'FOOT FAILS TO HEAL RIFT WITH HEALEY OVER NUCLEAR POLICY' (*Times*). Now the headlines were 'LABOUR TOTTERS ON THE BRINK OVER NUCLEAR POLICY' (*Guardian*) and 'FOOT AND HEALEY IN BIG SPLIT OVER NUKES' (*Sun*). The *Times* had a particularly damaging story alleging that Denis Healey had vetoed any possibility of Michael Foot making a firm, unqualified pledge that Britain's Polaris nuclear deterrent would be phased out by a Labour government. John Silkin did his best to try and pretend that there was no difference between Denis Healey and Michael Foot. Everybody knew, however, that while Denis was trying to give the impression that Labour would negotiate, Michael would simply ban all nuclear weapons immediately. In some newspapers there was also a hint of even bigger trouble to come with the revelation that Jim Callaghan was due to speak on nuclear matters in Penarth that night. Neil Kinnock had also entered the controversy with an unequivocal statement supporting Michael Foot's line that Polaris would be scrapped.

I said, 'Labour's weasel words on the defence of Britain must stop.' I suppose that this was permissible humbug because of course I did not want the Labour row to stop at all. Nothing would do us more good in SDP seats than emphasis on this issue. It would help the Conservatives too, but the most important thing for us was that it was the best differentiating issue between Labour and the SDP. Michael Foot had trifled with Britain's national security, I claimed, and it was about time he levelled with the British people. 'Labour's defence policy began as an organised hypocrisy, now it has become a disorganised deception.' My boot was going in and starting to leave its mark.

That night in Penarth Jim Callaghan fully demonstrated why I had been right to leave the Labour Party in 1981. You can have private reservations about a manifesto but it is devastating if a prominent figure in a political party publicly disowns a major manifesto commitment during an election. It can be argued that if Jim Callaghan felt he had to act as he did then he really should not have stood as a Labour candidate at that election. As Ian Aitken described it in the *Guardian*, 'The former Labour Prime Minister took the unprecedented step of repudiating the defence policy of his own party in the middle of a general election campaign. He made it clear that he will have nothing to do with unilateral nuclear disarmament.' If I had fought as a Labour candidate in Plymouth in that election, as many people both before and since have argued that I should have done, I would have had to make the same speech as Jim Callaghan and, although it would not have had the same public impact, it too would have done considerable damage to Labour nationally. In Jim's case I believe he really had tried to be loyal but just could not keep quiet. I doubt he ever intended to speak out as he did when he decided to fight another election and be the Father of the House of Commons. But, quite apart from his own deep-seated patriotism, with his overseas friendships I suspect he could not have faced Gerald Ford, Helmut Schmidt and Valéry Giscard d'Estaing if he had said nothing. What is the honourable course? Shut up, put up, or get out! Certainly, the most prudent course when you disagree so fundamentally with central planks of policy that you cannot be silent is to leave. But Jim Callaghan wanted to stay, there being no question of him leaving Labour and, given his circumstances, the honourable course was to speak out when Michael Foot, who had been given every opportunity, still refused to give up his unilateralism.

Margaret Thatcher used to argue that the Gang of Four should have stayed supporting Labour and struggled from within. Nothing could have suited the Conservatives better than to have our voices destroying the credibility of the Labour Party while not challenging the Conservatives by being able to take their voters. I will always believe that the honourable course in my circumstances was to leave Labour. I personally felt far better and cleaner fighting Labour's defence and foreign policy openly in 1983 and 1987 from outside the party. I thereby avoided having to nominally fight to elect Labour as the government while at the same time desperately hoping it did not obtain the power to fulfil its election pledges.

The press had a field day with Jim Callaghan's speech. 'CALLAGHAN IN ARMS REVOLT' was the headline in the *Daily Mirror*, 'CALLAGHAN WRECKS POLARIS REPAIRS' (*Guardian*), 'CALLAGHAN'S BOMBSHELL' (*Daily Mail*) and 'CALLAGHAN'S BOMB SHOCK FOR LABOUR' (*Daily Star*). If the Labour Party had ever had a chance – which it did not –

this was a blow from which it could not recover. Michael Foot was bitter with Jim, but I reflected that in January 1981, Michael had tried to persuade me to stay in the Labour Party and told me I would be free to speak out. He had not answered when I had asked whether that included speaking out in a general election period.

I now became increasingly convinced that I could hold Plymouth Devonport by taking thousands of votes that had previously gone to Labour. I decided that I would help this along by choosing my moment and exposing Michael Foot's abdication from any involvement on nuclear matters when he and I were both Labour Cabinet ministers.

I met David Steel for a chat and a photocall outside the BBC studios in Plymouth. Pictures of him, Debbie and me smiling together made good television, but they were only a front for a deeply serious conversation. David told me that he had told Roy at the London press conference that morning that he thought there should be a change in the leadership of the Alliance. He had asked Roy to bow out, leaving David the Prime Minister designate. The opinion poll evidence supporting such a move had been building up. An Audience Selection poll for TV-am the day before, giving the Conservatives 45 per cent, Labour 32 per cent and the Alliance at 20 per cent, had shown that if David Steel were Prime Minister designate the Conservatives would have had 42 per cent, the Alliance would have moved to second place at 29 per cent and Labour third at 28 per cent. Our current level of support was alarming. If this evidence of the fillip we could get from making a change was even half right, then the leadership issue had to concern SDP as well as Liberal candidates. Apparently Roy had said he would think about the suggestion but had told David that I would object to any change on the grounds that it would damage the SDP. My response to David was what it had been for months. The question of a single leader was a matter between him and Roy and I would agree to whatever they settled between them. I told him that if, and I stressed that it was a very big if, Roy was prepared to step down then that was fine by me and I would do nothing to stop it. But I also warned against believing that it would, of itself, produce a dramatic turnaround in the opinion polls. I did not think we would in reality achieve anything as dramatic as a jump from 20 per cent to 29 per cent.

Nevertheless the addition of even 1 or 2 per cent was a bonus and might save some of the vulnerable SDP seats. There would, however, be no point in doing any switch if Roy was not prepared to sell it positively to the press. Roy refused to budge and foolishly David brought the issue up again at an Alliance leaders meeting in his house in the Scottish borders at a late stage in the campaign. It was humiliating for Roy to have the question openly discussed, but it was still rejected.

An opinion poll in the *Sun* showed us only 4 per cent behind Labour, with the Conservatives at 44 per cent, Labour 29 per cent and the Alliance 25 per cent. But there was better to come. The story of the day was Denis Healey's extraordinary outburst the previous evening that Margaret Thatcher after the Falklands was 'glorying in slaughter'. As Shirley Williams and I were driving to the BBC studios in Liverpool for me to go on *Today*, she used the word 'abattoir' about Denis's speech. I asked if she minded if I purloined it for my interview. She agreed, so I was able to produce probably the most quoted of all my remarks in the election: 'Mr Healey has moved from the politics of the gutter to the politics of the abattoir.'

I needed to concentrate on Plymouth now. I stepped up my efforts to convince reluctant Tories to switch to the Alliance, since the polls showed that a staggering 40 per cent of those planning to vote Conservative were doing so just out of fear of Labour. We needed to show that it was inconceivable that there could be a Labour government, and capitalise on their secondary fear – that of a Tory landslide. The problem was that this undermined the Steel–Jenkins strategy for it tacitly acknowledged that the Tories were going to win. The Alliance stance, forlornly pretending we could win, was pathetic. But despite these concerns, my confidence began to rise that we would win in Plymouth. That evening, at our traditional question-and-answer session organised by Devonport Methodists for all the candidates, I could sense the tide turning my way. My two opponents were both able people but they sounded as if they knew they were losing. Nationally, too, the *Sunday Mirror* had had a sensational poll showing that we had nosed ahead of Labour, with the Conservatives on 44 per cent, the Alliance on 27.5 per cent and Labour on 27 per cent.

I campaigned all day the following Monday and most of Tuesday in Plymouth. The dockyard 'mateys' would say spontaneously outside the main gate in the early morning, 'You're doing well, boy' or 'Good on you, David' and I knew I was home and dry when the bookies' odds moved heavily in my favour.

On the Tuesday evening I flew from Plymouth to Leeds for a television appearance. After my bumpy flight, I felt distinctly queasy when I arrived at Yorkshire TV studios. Edna and Denis Healey were both there and were incredibly kind. Given what I had said about Denis and the abattoir they would have been entitled to ostracise me but Edna was worrying about whether I could win in Plymouth. I took a healthy swig of medicinal brandy to settle my stomach and went in for the programme, which started at 10.40 p.m. We were well into the programme and as Geoffrey Howe answered a question I fell asleep. I woke up to see Jonathan Dimbleby looking straight at me, having clearly just asked me something. I mumbled vaguely that it was all very difficult and I was not sure I had any specific view on the matter! I felt a complete idiot for the rest of the programme but afterwards, when we were relaxing over drinks, no one remarked on it. When I asked my sister, who had accompanied me on the plane, and a few other people whether one of my answers had seemed slightly off the point, they said they had not noticed anything amiss.

I flew back next morning to Plymouth and concentrated on collecting the last few votes. My campaign team had done wonders in my absence and Debbie had as usual proved herself a formidable campaigner. It had been a difficult campaign at the start, with jeers and shouts of 'traitor'. But by the end even the most ardent Labour activist no longer had the gall to call me a traitor, not least because my response was so savage and full of contempt. I ended up with a majority of 4,936, the Conservatives had come second and Labour, despite having been the favourite after the boundary changes, were pushed into an ignominious third place.

I wish I could say that nationally we did ourselves justice. The BBC captured the essence of the campaign by asking the three party leaders, 'Would you push the nuclear button?' Roy Jenkins prevaricated: 'I find it difficult to believe the situation would arise.' Michael Foot was obdurate: 'It would be utter criminal insanity for anyone to say they would press the button.' Margaret Thatcher considered the alternative: 'If we don't say we will press the button the Russians would sweep over Europe and us with conventional forces.' In all the hours of debate, those words on this crucial defence issue clarified the attitudes of the parties more than anything else. I vowed that never again would I go through an election campaign with a defence policy so lacking in conviction. Nuclear defence had been the dominant issue in the view of most commentators.

The *Daily Mail* summed up the campaign as the measure of one woman's ascendancy and of one party's collapse. They were sympathetic to our attempt to fill the democratic vacuum between a Tory Prime Minister in her prime and socialism in decline. They said the voters wanted to believe in the Alliance but sensed 'that it is not enough in a rough world for those entrusted with government to be pleasant and accommodating. You need bottle.' They said, quite rightly, that we had fudged the Jenkins/Steel leadership, fudged the independent deterrent, fudged on private education, fudged on council house sales and on the central issue of the economy proposed a return to incomes policy and reflation. Ruefully I had to smile. I had left the Labour Party to finish with fudging and mudging.

Until we could sharpen our policies and develop a more populist appeal, the SDP/Liberal Alliance would neither bust nor deserve to bust the system, let alone break the mould. The more the SDP looked like the Liberals the better for both Labour and the Conservatives. The late surge in the opinion polls did much for our morale but not much for our eventual score of MPs. In the dying days of the campaign we were also helped by Neil Kinnock, who managed to put his foot in it. A member of a TV audience had shouted, 'At least Mrs Thatcher has got guts,' and Kinnock had replied, 'It is a pity that people had to leave theirs on the ground in Goose Green to prove it.' Once again the Falklands was back in the headlines, which could only help the Conservatives and hinder Labour. This also raised questions about Neil Kinnock's judgement under pressure.

The general election was won overwhelmingly by the Conservative Party with 397 seats. Labour had 209, the Liberals 17 and the SDP 6 MPs. For the Alliance as a whole the result was disappointing, though it represented a 6 per cent improvement for the Liberals on Jeremy Thorpe's February 1974 result. Because of the way the seats had been allocated, the SDP result was a predictable disaster. We had certainly not achieved the breakthrough, had not even, perhaps, established a bridgehead. Worse still, it was hard to imagine that we would ever again fight a Labour Party in quite such a dreadful state. Michael Foot had proved to be a worse leader even than the pacifist George Lansbury. For its 27.6 per cent of the vote Labour got 32 per cent of the seats. The Alliance, having 25.4 per cent of the vote, got only 3.5 per cent of the seats, 23 out of the 650 in the House of Commons. Our only new SDP MP was Charles Kennedy, who won Ross, Cromarty & Skye – a natural Liberal seat which Bob Maclennan had managed to squeeze out of the Liberals late in the Scottish seat negotiations. Charles came into the House of Commons at the age of twenty-three and went on to become Liberal Democrat leader.

Labour lost 120 deposits, showing how badly they had done in many parts of the country and how concentrated was their support in their safe seats. The SDP lost seven deposits. After many years of losing deposits in large numbers, the Liberals only lost five, the same number as the Conservative Party.

Some people believed that if the Alliance had managed to squeeze ahead of Labour in the popular vote it would have transformed the political situation. We would, these people argue, then have had greater legitimacy when we challenged the distorted representation of the first-past-the-post voting system. I disagree. Of course it would have been better to have beaten Labour in the popular vote but, after a few months, with Labour the official opposition in the House of Commons, we would have seen that nothing much had changed. With all the official opposition's frontbench speaking rights and their right to have their amendments called by the Speaker in preference to the other parties, I believe the old familiar pattern of British politics would have been re-established. In any case, the Conservatives, who under Baldwin had done so much to establish two-party politics in the 1920s and 1930s, would certainly have helped Labour reassert their position. Time and time again, the two old class-based parties came together in a conspiracy of interest to squeeze the Alliance as they had always squeezed the Liberals. But we in the SDP had helped them do so by looking so like the Liberals.

What the 1983 election should have achieved was an SDP

parliamentary party as big as, if not bigger than, the Liberal Party. It was our own fault that we did not ensure it. This had been the moment for the SDP to establish a bridgehead by smashing into the Labour Party and it was the SDP which should have won some of the most vulnerable Labour seats, not the Conservatives. It was a loss to politics that so many SDP MPs of courage and calibre had gone and what was even more tragic was that most, even the younger ones, would never return to the House of Commons.

# 5

# Leading the SDP

All of us in the Gang of Four had a heavy responsibility for the personal trauma that underlay the losses sustained in the 1983 general election. What had promised so much that day 2½ years before in Limehouse was unrecognisable now in the shadow of defeat. I knew in Plymouth on the day after the election following what the *Times* called a 'strong national campaign and outstanding personal victory', that the torch would fall to me and I feared that I might not be able to even keep it alight.

By the time Roy and I talked I already knew that the four other SDP MPs wanted a change of leader and wanted it immediately. Roy said that he favoured deferring his resignation until after the party conference. This would be too late, I told him, because it would cause uncertainty in the run-up to what would be a very important conference, so suggested that he consult the other MPs. I left him with the clear message that if he did not step down quickly an election was certain. Although under our rules – since he had not yet been leader for a period of twelve months – there could not be an election for a few more weeks I doubted whether he would want to tough it out. Sensing that I was not going to change my mind, Roy went ahead and issued a statement that he thought it was desirable that the SDP should immediately have a new leader for the next election and that fortunately, with my victory at Devonport, such a leader was available. He hoped I would be elected without a contest. He said he was not withdrawing from full political activity and that he would be 'particularly active in safeguarding the unity of the Alliance'. I tried to say nothing which would detract from his statement and the *Daily Telegraph* praised him for his dignity and generosity. Fortunately his resignation occurred without public bitterness. However, it is impossible to do things like this painlessly and the incident did leave its scars.

David Steel and I arranged to meet at Buttermere the following Saturday. Just before our meeting, Russell Johnston, the Liberal MP for Inverness, called for a merger before the next election. Perhaps this was fortunate for it meant that David and I could discuss the pressure for a merger quite frankly and I could make it clear that I would oppose it tooth and nail. I did, however, agree to limit what I said in public. I would say that merger was extremely unlikely but would not close the door to the possibility. In effect we ruled out merger before the next general election. I thought, wrongly as it turned out, that, in addition to accepting the formal position, he had accepted the rationale applying to our political situation. The SDP had to enhance its appeal to former Labour voters or at the very least retain that significant part of the Labour vote we had attracted at the election at the same time as aiming for more Conservative votes. We both knew that any new Labour leader would be better than Michael Foot.

The Labour Party, we agreed, could not be allowed to return to a position where it was seen by press and public as the sole challenger. I think we both managed to prevent this for the next four years. I told David that we had to go back to the original concept of the Alliance, with each party complementing the other's appeal, and counterbalancing strengths and weaknesses. In Scotland, for instance, and in some other parts of the country he and the Liberal Party would always be more popular than me and the SDP.

We also confronted the problem of two ambitious politicians of a similar age working so closely. Given the 'yo-yo' nature of politics there would be times when one of us was up or one of our parties was down and we would have to discipline ourselves not to exploit what would probably be only temporary changes in fortune. I considered myself bound by that conversation thereafter and never once tried to oust David Steel from our joint leadership. Much has been said and written about our relationship and most of it is false. For my part, I have no serious complaint about our partnership. Most of the tensions were predictable, arising from the necessity to safeguard the interests of our respective parties and reflect their concerns and their democratic decisions. Through all these moments of tension, our original agreement held. For instance, I resisted frequent incitements to push David aside when the SDP was in the ascendant. Shirley Williams, in particular, kept reiterating the argument for a single leader and her view that it should be me, but I always dismissed it as being impossible to achieve through agreement, which was the only option. I know that he had many similar representations made to him and that he too usually resisted them. I believed we had effectively bound ourselves to work an equal partnership until the next election and that we were two leaders of two parties, not two leaders of one. Moreover, if either of us had challenged the other seriously the resultant trauma would have been very damaging. Perhaps that was the real limiting factor, rather than personal obligation, but I suspect it was a mixture of both.

Of course we differed on the merger issue, but we were conscious of this from the outset. I am often described as being surprised and angry when David called for a merger on the Sunday after the 1987 election campaign. In fact I was neither surprised nor particularly angry. The timing and manner of his decision were more questionable, but whether or not we should merge was a legitimate question. David Steel believed afterwards that he should have pressed the case for a merger more thoroughly in 1983 and should not have allowed my objections to act as a veto. No doubt when he had dinner with Roy Jenkins after our meeting they discussed these issues and he could have reopened them if he had wished. However, he probably knew that I spoke for my party at that stage and that Roy could no longer deliver. So whatever his later thoughts, in practice pressing the issue would have been difficult then. In any case, he did not seek to reopen the matter, apart from in one letter prior to the Portsmouth South by-election in 1984. What he did for the next four years was what he had been doing for the last three, namely working for a merger while denying he was doing so. My attitude to this was, 'That's politics.' I never for one moment considered that David Steel was anything other than a believer in three parties, not four. From his own point of view that made good sense. There was never any danger after the seat allocation in September 1982 that the Liberal Party would lose its identity in a merger. Whereas in Parliament there had been a ratio of twenty-nine SDP MPs to fourteen Liberal MPs in May, in June there were seventeen Liberal MPs to six SDP MPs. Also since the Alliance was formed they had gained far more councillors than we had. With a merger they were on course for a takeover. The danger for the SDP was much greater – we could be snuffed out. In politics as in business true mergers are rare, takeovers, even if not always described as such, are common. In 1989 David Steel wrote of this period, 'Thus within days of the general election and thanks to our joint acquiescence, David Owen secured both the leadership of the SDP and a veto over merger of the two parties into one. It was a remarkably bloodless coup.'

Against this background the pattern of my leadership over the next four years emerged. First, I had to face the debate over merger which continued among the two parties' activists. A new term began to surface, 'organic merger'. It arose from a Liberal councillors' conference, soon after the election, which had envisaged local mergers taking place in piecemeal fashion. Their challenge was that no leader could oppose the democratic will of the local people. The enthusiasts for merger felt they could prove, at the grass roots, that the two parties' political interests were as one and that they could work better as an integrated operation. I realised that this organic merger was going to be helped along at our Salford conference in September by a concerted attempt to make the decision on whether the candidates should be chosen jointly a purely local one. What we were being offered was merger by stealth.

We could only counter this by convincing people that the fact that you could work together did not mean you had to merge. This involved familiarising people with the mechanics of the inter-party coalitions which operated in Europe. But the real task was to re-examine all policies and see whether we could start the serious work of producing social democratic ideas for the 1990s. Much would depend on the quality of these ideas. By August it was pretty clear that Neil Kinnock was going to become leader of the Labour Party as he was accumulating a substantial majority of votes over Roy Hattersley in the electoral college. The so-called dream ticket then emerged.

All new leaders have a honeymoon when their pronouncements are given much more attention than they deserve so I had to move quickly for public impact. Most people knew where I stood on foreign policy, so I needed to carve out a distinctive position on economic policy before Neil Kinnock was given the opportunity. I decided to return to the idea of the social market economy which I had tried to project in a Hoover lecture in 1981. The SDP had to break the stranglehold of the mixed economy. An understanding of the market economy was the first essential step towards the radical libertarian force I wanted to create. We needed, however, to make a splash, otherwise no one would notice the change in our economic outlook. My speech at the party conference would not be enough. I could flag the change there but then I would have to reinforce it with more detail. The Institute of Economic Affairs asked me to write an article for their journal, *Economic Affairs*, and this seemed the perfect forum. It would be a clear signal, for the IEA had established itself as the progenitor of Margaret Thatcher's emphasis on the market. The series of articles to which I would be contributing had been launched by Geoffrey Howe surveying his four years as Chancellor. My article would, like his, be assessed in print by four independent economists of the IEA's choice and I would then have a chance to reply in the same issue.

Incomes policy and government intervention in industry had permeated my political life up until then. I had grown used to thinking of them as an integral part of political activity and had been a supporter of many of the earlier failed initiatives. My personal revisionism had really started in 1978 when giving a Fabian lecture as Foreign Secretary, and progressed much further while writing *Face the Future*. The destructive nature and yo-yo effect of two-party politics could be easily summarised. When I was adopted as a candidate in 1962 the Conservative government, with Selwyn Lloyd as Chancellor, had created the National Incomes Commission. Labour had then replaced it in 1964 with the Prices and Incomes Board. The Heath government had abolished the PIB in 1970 but then set up the Price Commission in 1973, which was expanded by Labour in 1974 and abolished by Margaret Thatcher in 1979. The Labour government had set up the Industrial Reorganization Corporation in 1966 and later the Commission for Industrial Relations. Both were abolished by the new Conservative government in 1970, though they had created two new bodies, the Pay Board in 1970 and the National Industrial Relations Court in 1971. Both had been abolished by Labour in 1974, which then created the National Enterprise Board. This had been restructured in 1979 and then abolished. This record underpinned the failure of the British economy.

To align myself with Margaret Thatcher as a reformist had its political advantages, and being labelled 'sub-Thatcherite' by Roy Jenkins or, as Denis Healey so delicately put it, 'Mrs Thatcher in trousers' did not worry me. The public's impression was what mattered, not the pundits' or politicians'. Such abuse was a small price to pay to rid the SDP of the image of being stuck in the 1970s, promising in Ralf Dahrendorf's phrase 'a better yesterday'. I was determined to rediscover some of the *élan* with which we had launched ourselves and this could only come from new policy development, not another relaunch. Fortunately there was tremendous scope for developing our social policies in a more egalitarian and redistributive direction. If we could simultaneously break right on the market and left on social policy I believed we would find an electorally attractive political mix. If the social market were not to be a synonym for the mixed economy, our market policies and our social policies had to be hard edged, intellectually convincing and politically engaging. The SDP under my leadership would attempt, late in the day admittedly, to throw off the centrist 'splitting the difference' image with which we had been landed. We would fulfil our promise for a rebellion against the centre as well as the extremes. For the first time we would provide the British people with a party at once sensible, compassionate and unencumbered with the mistaken corporatism of the post-war era. It was worth a gamble. In addition, if I led with my chin on policy it would divert public attention from the internal debate about merger. Few things are more unattractive than political parties washing their dirty linen in public. We had to look outward to the electorate.

A considerable ally in this strategy was Michael Young and it was all the more significant that we had come to similar conclusions without consultation. Michael was chairman of the SDP's independent think tank, the Tawney Society, but was better known as the founder of the Consumers' Association. He saw the SDP as heir to the libertarian socialist tradition and feared that if we rushed into a new Alliance party we could never become that radical force. He knew the Labour Party well and he thought it possible then that it could contract still further to the size of the old Independent Labour Party. He stayed with the SDP after 1987, returning to Labour in 1989 after they made their big policy switches on the EEC, market economics and Trident. For people like Michael an emphasis on the market had to be linked to consumerism, while demonstrating that competitiveness need not be incompatible with compassion. I felt sure I could convince people that we were still a radical, redistributive party while embracing the market. There was a temptation to play down our market orientation until after the merger debate at our conference. But I was convinced that there was a window of opportunity at the SDP conference at Salford, and if I put my whole authority as new leader on the line I could get away with blocking the merger and turning to the market.

My main speech to the conference was much too wordy. Debbie made me promise that I would never again read a speech and with few exceptions I have followed her advice. It takes considerable skill to read a speech without putting a barrier between the speaker and the audience. The 'sincerity machines', introduced from America, where a speech is reflected up onto glass panels in front of you but which the audience and television cameras can look through, allow the speakers to keep their heads up and, if well used (President Reagan was a past master at it), can give the impression of spontaneity. I had tried them, but the real skill is not so much in the reading as in the writing. A written speech tends to be too dense to absorb. In a spontaneous one the arguments are looser and, although one does repeat oneself, it goes at a pace which people's brains can digest. Additionally there is an ease of expression and a genuine spontaneity which can be compelling to listen to. I know of no one who can hold the attention of the House of Commons while reading a speech, and most people find that having to keep to a text restricts their freedom to deal with interjections or to respond to their listeners. Nevertheless in its content my speech was probably one of the more important that I have given. Because I used a conversational tone, few in the hall, I think, fully realised quite how extensive a rethink of SDP policy I was envisaging. Though 'toughness and tenderness' was the theme of the speech it was also a synthesis of new policies.

It was the American philosopher William James who first formulated the concept 'The tough think of the tender as sentimentalists and softheads. The tender feel the tough to be unrefined, callous or brutal.' Yet the two characters are not incompatible and many people have elements of both. Why should not a political party be tough in pursuit of the market economy and sound defence and tender in supporting the NHS and fixing social security benefit levels? Combining virtues seemed good social democratic practice. This was not the same as the Third Way espoused by Tony Blair. They had significant points in common but my synthesis was not dominated by spin nor tailored to opinion polls; it strove for an inner intellectual coherence.

In the first week of October the Labour Party conference elected Neil Kinnock as leader, at the age of forty-one. He was Michael Foot's political heir and for many years Michael had supported and sponsored Neil, so on paper it was a victory for the left. But few of those close to Tony Benn rejoiced. They knew Neil Kinnock would eventually follow past heroes of the left along the well-trodden path towards the centre, impelled by electoral logic and the need to come nearer to the centre of gravity of the nation as a whole. For the moment, however, Neil Kinnock embodied every left-wing prejudice and passion. A longstanding CND supporter, he had also made speech after speech attacking our membership of the European Community, even being a member of the council of the 'Get Britain Out' campaign. It was unlikely that there would be any policy U-turns for a while, but a fresh face and a young image would, I knew, automatically boost Labour. It was bad luck for him that he slipped while walking along the beach with his wife on his first photocall and got his trousers wet in the surf. When he quipped, 'Bet it wouldn't happen to Maggie,' rather too many people agreed.

My *Economic Affairs* article, entitled 'Agenda for Competitiveness with Compassion', was published at the end of October. The *Financial Times* called it 'Thatcherism with a human face' and it was their correspondent Peter Riddell who really understood the true significance of my shift. I was not arguing, as we had done so far in classic centrist fashion, that we should freeze the frontier between the public and private sectors. I was welcoming change. Hitherto the SDP had been very cautious in talking about privatisation, never really supporting it and overstressing the value of stability on the frontier between public and private provision. I was now shifting our attack from opposition to all privatisation towards an objection in principle to all monopoly power, whether in private or public hands. Even a *Guardian* editorial, 'Embrace with proper caution', affirmed that there was much that was correct in my message, even if it was one which the present Prime Minister had seemed to make her own for the past five years. It pointed out, to the evident chagrin of some of the IEA's laissez-faire commentators, that my article was studded with useful reminders of how intervention in the market can both help in correcting problems of inequality which arise from its mechanisms and help the market itself to work better by reducing uncertainty. The article provoked considerable discussion and serious criticism, which in its turn helped me clarify my thinking and laid the basis for my next book, *A Future That Will Work*.

Establishing the SDP as a national party meant fighting hard for recognition at every level. It was never easy to judge when to make a stand but few issues were more delicate to handle than the question of an SDP wreath at the Cenotaph. The Armistice Day remembrance service is one occasion when the whole nation is as one and the two minutes' silence marks a precious moment which I had no wish to besmirch with partisan politics. Roy Jenkins had asked for us to be represented in 1982 but it had been turned down by the then Home Secretary. So in July 1983 I thought it best to put our case for representation privately to the Prime Minister. A convenient opportunity had arisen because the government Whips' Office had been in touch with me over the question of political honours. The practice had arisen of allocating opposition party leaders a certain number of peerages, knighthoods, CBEs, OBEs and MBEs each year virtually for their own personal patronage. This was undesirable for it extended and legitimised the government's political patronage system, which had been abused for decades. The SDP parliamentary committee had decided that, like the Labour Party, we would have nothing to do with this system until it was changed by all-party agreement.

My meeting with the Prime Minister in No. 10, our first formal one-on-one meeting, started in a friendly atmosphere. But when I raised the question of representation at the Cenotaph I was barely halfway through my case when she intervened to reject it, declaring that she was adamantly opposed to widening representation. Suddenly the atmosphere was heated. I told her bluntly that I could see absolutely no reason why a party that had attracted 3½ million voters should not be entitled to lay a wreath at the Cenotaph.

Eventually I rose to go and said that I hoped that, since the decision was formally the Home Secretary's, she would give the matter renewed thought, otherwise I would have to take my case before the bar of public opinion. She became incandescent, alternating between a prim 'How could you?' to a furious 'How dare you?' Clearly she had not been spoken to like this for years and I left uncertain if I should be forced to take issue with her in public. In October I had my answer. A formal letter came from Leon Brittan, rejecting our participation but promising an urgent review and admitting that the present arrangements had developed in a piecemeal way.

I decided to go public, in the uncertain hope of winning press support. My letter to the Prime Minister was outspoken: 'Many Conservative, Labour, Liberal and Social Democrat voters will see this as petty and partisan – the act of the leader of the Conservative Party and not the act of the Prime Minister of the whole nation.' The SDP had demonstrated its support for the armed services of the Crown 'not just in words but in action during the Falklands War, when we were steadfast in our backing of British interests'. Nevertheless we were totally opposed to making a demonstration, as some had suggested, for this would only have detracted from a sombre and moving ceremony of national unity. The *Daily Telegraph* reported that the issue had already sharply divided ministers, that many senior members of the government were unhappy and that one of the service chiefs had actually objected to our exclusion. In its editorial column the *Daily Telegraph* said that we should be permitted to lay a wreath next year, as did the *Evening Standard*, and many other newspapers up and down the country took our side. It was a good example of the basic fairness and decency of the British people asserting itself. The British Legion demonstrated its feelings by inviting Debbie and me to the Albert Hall and then to the dinner afterwards where Margaret Thatcher was the chief speaker. Symbolically we had to get up and leave in the middle of her speech, having ensured that everyone knew beforehand that we were doing so only in order to catch the midnight sleeper to Plymouth to lay a wreath on the war memorial on the Hoe next morning. The *coup de grâce* was when the television news bulletins that Sunday evening, after reporting the Cenotaph, had a shot of me laying a wreath in

Plymouth. Over the next few months much time was spent in Whitehall producing a formula to save the Prime Minister's face, it being agreed eventually that the leaders of parties with six or more MPs could lay a wreath and those with fewer would be invited to attend. In some ways it was a trivial issue, in others an important one. What the whole episode showed was that the Prime Minister, though still totally dominant, did not have an absolute hold on public opinion or newspaper editors. Even Rupert Murdoch, proprietor of the ever loyal *Sun*, *News of the World* and *Times*, was saying, 'She has run out of puff.'

By mid 1984 my relationship with David Steel was edgy but civil. A child's letter addressed to me and asking what I would do if I knew the world was going to end was erroneously delivered to David's office. He passed it on with a barbed note, which found its way into the press, suggesting that the end of the world was more my department. I replied to the press enquiry by saying that if I knew the world was going to end I would join the Liberal Party. About this time David wrote me a letter whose implications were all too clear: he would make a move to dominate the Alliance if we failed to win the Portsmouth South by-election, something he clearly expected to happen. It was like a black cone warning of a storm ahead.

The by-election in Portsmouth had been called by the Conservatives deliberately to coincide with voting in the European election on 14 June and stretch our resources. The SDP candidate was Mike Hancock, a young local councillor for the Fratton ward in the constituency, whom I had known in the Labour Party. He was an AEU shop steward and a character, with great charm, though with a common touch and streetwise. He had fought the seat in the general election for us and had been chosen to fight the by-election, amid some controversy, in preference to Bob Mitchell, the former SDP MP for Southampton Itchen. With its naval dockyard Portsmouth was seen to be perfect SDP territory and though it would be a surprise if we won, there could be no excuses if we had a bad result. I decided virtually to ignore the European election in terms of our headquarters staff and volunteer effort and concentrate all our staff and resources on Portsmouth. Mike Hancock proved to be a far better candidate than the Conservative import and his conscientious and sensitive handling of local council problems undoubtedly helped to take Labour votes.

We had a stunning victory. I knew then that the SDP would survive any attempt to rob it of its independence this side of the election. Mike Hancock polled 15,358 votes, the Conservatives 14,017 and Labour 10,846. We had vast publicity on the Friday and Saturday and this ensured that, when the European election results were announced on the Sunday, the relatively disappointing performance of the Alliance went largely unnoticed. The *Daily Mail* hailed our result as 'the Alliance victory that cannot be ignored'. The *Express* called it a 'famous victory' and the *Daily Mirror*, under the headline 'SUNK', said the Tories were left 'beached, battered and bewildered'. The *Guardian* called it 'a sharp kick on the lady's ankle'.

In March 1984, a national miners' strike had begun, led by Arthur Scargill and called without a ballot. Here was a litmus test issue for the Social Democrats. There was no dilemma for me – Arthur Scargill must be defeated. If he won, it would do irreparable damage to the market economy, to democracy and to the elected government's ability to govern. Once more the SDP had to show that it would not split the difference, would not call for compromise, would not show the loss of confidence that had characterised the centre too often. We had to back the government, and we did.

Until July there was no public difference between the Liberals and ourselves over the miners' strike, but in our inter-party discussions in Parliament we were aware that there were growing tensions within their ranks, a wish to hedge their bets and not give the appearance of being hostile to the miners. Early in July I went to a Liberal summer school and warned that if the government were defeated by the miners it could cause an avalanche of similar disputes with a general loss of confidence in government; this was one of the few industrial disputes which were 'clearly political and should be beaten in the name of economic and political sense'. Soon after this our unity broke. David Steel, who was coming under increasing criticism from within his own ranks for allowing me to dominate the Alliance, attacked me in thinly veiled terms, saying that it was foolish of the Prime Minister to talk in terms of victory and defeat. The press were briefed that it was not just the Prime Minister he had in mind and the headlines shouted 'STEEL ATTACKS OWEN LINE' and 'STEEL'S THATCHER REBUKE REBOUNDS

ON OWEN'. For David to have asserted himself on this issue seemed to me to be very bad politics. By then there were very few among the general public who wanted Arthur Scargill to win. They rightly saw this strike as a direct challenge to the rule of law and parliamentary democracy.

On the same day as these reports, I attacked Neil Kinnock in the *Sunday Express* for not speaking up for the moderate miners at the recent Durham miners' gala. Given that his father was a miner and that the Welsh miners were far from enthusiastic about Arthur Scargill's leadership, it amazed me that he had not stuck to his initial position and held fast to the need for a pit-head ballot. It would have given him a position of principle wholly in keeping with the miners' tradition.

By then I was getting worried about the mood for compromise that was developing. I genuinely did believe that Scargill had to be beaten and was horrified at any possibility of the government cobbling up some face-saving formula. The SDP MPs urged me to continue to make it quite clear publicly that we were not going to be diverted by Liberal criticism. With their backing I spoke in the adjournment debate before the House of Commons went down for the summer recess, demanding action on secondary picketing by miners, declaring that it was unacceptable that the law on the statute book had not been used after twenty weeks of the strike. Of course we wanted the dispute ended, but not at any price. The NUM should not be able to say which pits should or should not be closed. I ended by saying that 'Scargill's tactics of intimidation, violence, bullying and distortion are intolerable in this country'.

During the strike I established close contacts with the UDM, which had been set up by moderate miners, mainly in Nottinghamshire, seeing their leaders privately. They had no money at that time and I arranged with a friend for some financial support, although I chose not to have any publicity. Their cause was too important to be mixed with the party political debate. They needed to attract Labour moderates and being portrayed as an offshoot of the SDP would not help them. During the strike I deliberately went down a pit in Nottingham, ignoring the pickets. I was given a friendly welcome at the coal face. As I emerged from the shaft I was met by television cameras asking for a comment on the death of a taxi driver in south Wales as a result of a block of concrete being dropped on his car. It was a harsh reminder of the passions underlying the dispute and of the dangers.

Unfortunately it was all too typical of the Liberal Party that when the going got rough on a political issue they backed off. We had also been having trouble with them over renewing the prevention of terrorism legislation for Northern Ireland. Though David was being pressurised within his own party, on this issue the SDP's tougher stance was not damaging the Alliance and we were doing well in the opinion polls. We had also reached an agreement that our two policy committees would aim to have a draft general election manifesto ready by the summer of 1986. Yet Labour was in the lead in the polls, not so much because of positive support but because the Alliance was taking Conservative votes.

In August Ian Wrigglesworth, the SDP MP for Stockton South, publicly clashed with David Steel over the government's handling of the miners' strike. David was suggesting that Peter Walker, the Energy Secretary, should meet with the TUC leaders to try and resolve the strike. Ian flatly contradicted that view and said quite rightly that the one thing the government should not do was to be seen to intervene directly in the dispute. In effect the SDP backed Margaret Thatcher's stance throughout, rather as we had done during the Falklands War. We did, however, want more action on creating jobs in mining villages and argued that the National Coal Board should set up a company, as British Steel had done, to help revive communities likely to be severely hit by heavy redundancies.

When the pit deputies union, NACODS, threatened strike action at the end of October there had to be some flexibility in the coal board's position and it was ministers who leant on the NCB to give a little on the procedure for closing uneconomic pits. But it was a hostage to fortune and I was extremely worried that this could be used by Scargill as a face saver. Fortunately his Marxism came to the rescue and because he was not prepared to compromise at any stage he did not pick up the NACODS settlement and run with it as he could well have done. Not long after, I had the opportunity of a private talk with Margaret Thatcher. She seemed genuinely pleased to find that my worries about letting Arthur Scargill off the hook were exactly the same as hers. She made no attempt to conceal the fact that some of her colleagues wanted to settle but that she was adamantly against it. She was clear sighted about the danger of Scargill being able to claim a spurious victory.

In assessing Margaret Thatcher's leadership I believe the miners' dispute showed her at her best. She had cut her losses and settled when challenged by Joe Gormley in 1981 and had then planned ahead for the inevitable confrontation with Arthur Scargill. Some critics attacked her for having chosen Ian MacGregor as head of the NCB with allegations that he was personally provocative. Admittedly his public relations sense left much to be desired, but his management skills and rhinoceros hide were considerable assets. When I talked to him I found him cool and calculating. Few of our other leading industrialists would have had the nerve to hold as firm as he did. His experience in North America had taught him that managers have to be ready to withstand strikes. He did not hold with the fashionable assumption that a shift in the management's final offer is always inevitable. We were lucky to have him in that position.

The key to victory over the miners was keeping the government out of the firing line, at least in public, and letting MacGregor bear the brunt of the criticism. I advocated using the new picketing legislation, though I could see that there was some merit in demonstrating that Scargill could be defeated under the old legislation. The nature of the mass picketing at Orgreave damaged the reputation of the police. When the end came in March 1985, fifty-one weeks after the strike had started, it was the miners who disowned their leaders by streaming back to work with their funds running low and their self-respect in tatters. It was galling for Edward Heath to see 'that woman' defeat the very NUM which had so humiliated him and lost the Conservatives the 1974 election. But for the country as a whole it was essential for our self-confidence that intimidation and violence could be resisted without tear gas or mobilising the armed services. The police, with a few exceptions, did extremely well and showed that with good co-ordination between constabularies a national effort could be mobilised without the centralised danger of having to adopt a national police force.

In the early hours of 12 October 1984 I was telephoned for a comment on the IRA bomb explosion which had gutted part of the

Grand Hotel at Brighton and could well have destroyed the whole Cabinet. Margaret Thatcher had been very fortunate to escape and the IRA taunt, 'Today we were unlucky, but remember we have only to be lucky once', was revolting. But it was also a reminder of the constant threat with which she had to live. It was a numbing moment and I was very distressed for John Wakeham, who suffered appalling injuries himself and lost his wife, and for Anthony Berry's widow. Later I visited Norman Tebbit and his wife in Stoke Mandeville. He was very brave but his bounce had temporarily gone and she was showing the stoicism of a former nurse. Driving away from the hospital I felt all my medical cool, which had been on display, disappear and replaced by political anger. Debbie and I attended a special performance of Andrew Lloyd-Webber's *Requiem* in Westminster Abbey and felt the grieving of the whole Conservative Party. It was a terrible incident. When, much later, there was snide criticism of the security gates being put up at the Whitehall end of Downing Street, I was amazed at how short people's memories were. Can anyone believe that they would have been put up on any other grounds than that of security? Perhaps those critics felt some embarrassment when a mortar bomb nearly killed John Major and his colleagues in the Cabinet Room. There is very little anyone can do to stop a terrorist or fanatic who wants to kill a politician. I had long since resigned myself to that. Once in the Cambridge Union while Foreign Secretary, with six detectives present, someone stole in and dumped a bag of flour on my head while I was actually speaking.

In December I was elected Parliamentarian of the Year by the *Spectator*, sponsored by Highland Park whisky. It was the first year of their awards, which have now become a part of the parliamentary scene. The judges said that, though my aggressiveness was not to everyone's taste, I had employed it to great effect in the past year and had succeeded in putting down the hecklers on the bench on which we sat and in challenging the government, particularly the Prime Minister, with clear, simple, well-informed interventions. This was gratifying because I had gone out of my way to use the House of Commons as a forum for political argument, in effect as a bully pulpit for the SDP. My speech of acceptance, however, was so long that the judges must have regretted their choice. It was bad judgement: journalists are not the people to harangue on proportional representation; they are not receptive to concepts – they want hard news or witty asides.

I wrote to Jim Callaghan, who had been taken ill but was fortunately making a good recovery. In reply, while congratulating me on the parliamentarian award, he gently warned me not to acquire a right-wing image – and to remember my socialist origins, which went back a long way to when I first fought to enter Parliament and contained values worth advancing in today's society. He was correct, for the values of the best practitioners of the socialist vision do have an enduring relevance. It was like being back on a VC-10 flying to an international conference when a quiet word from Jim would flash a warning message. I took far more notice of his injunction than any jibe from my fellow Gang of Four members about being sub-Thatcherite. At various stages Jim gave an indication that it might be time for me to return to Labour, hardest to resist in the summer of 1996 when as the new chancellor of Liverpool University I gave him and Cyrus Vance an honorary degree.

Ever the contrarian, Alan Clark, a junior minister and my Conservative neighbour in Plymouth, was starting to persuade me to join the Conservatives, with which he persisted over the years. Though anonymous, those who knew him would not have found it hard to detect Alan's voice in this cavalier contribution reported in the press: 'The trouble is that he has landed himself with a real shower. The Liberals are useless and the SDP are a rabble. He is surrounded by pygmies and he is very uncomfortable company for them. They have become used to flabby chieftains.' Alan, the son of Kenneth Clark, who wrote the TV series *Civilization*, was himself an accomplished military historian and an original character. He relished being thought right-wing but in many areas was refreshingly radical. Few revelled in or generated more political gossip. I enjoyed his company, both the indiscretions and the insights. We lunched together from time to time and he had a novel way of introducing me to his friends: 'Have you met my doctor?' Our friendship started over the Falklands, when we were both desperately worried about the safety of our Plymouth constituents. He was close to Margaret Thatcher, but I was not sure how influential. I had to give up trying to stop him placing stories in the press about becoming a Conservative because he did it out of a mixture of affection and devilment. He knew perfectly well that I was never going to become a Conservative but gained raffish delight in perpetuating the myth that I would, particularly after I resigned as leader of the SDP in 1987.

I have never been able to decide whether those stories about me going to join the Conservatives did me and the SDP harm or not. But I had for some years refused to play the party game. David Steel used to make the odd jibe about it which never upset me much; like saying the Alliance would not succeed 'by presenting ourselves as crypto-Tories'. The reason this did not perturb me was that I wanted the Alliance to be seen as a potential coalition partner for whichever party – Conservative or Labour – that seemed at the time to be most likely to govern in sympathy with SDP policies. In the public mind I was inevitably associated with Labour because I had been Labour so to counterbalance this with talk of a Conservative future, as long as it did not get out of hand, might be beneficial. Nevertheless, in January 1985 I openly said, 'I would never join the Conservative Party.' Some people say that politicians should never say never. But I knew in my heart that it was true and saying so in such a public way gave me the freedom to support some Conservative policies while remaining firmly a Social Democrat. On that same occasion I was adamant that 'nothing that anyone says is going to change my fundamental position that when I think somebody is saying something right and in the country's interest I will support it, irrespective of which party they come from'.

Since 1982 I had been ready to negotiate a role in a coalition led by a Conservative Prime Minister if the circumstances were right for the SDP. Even if Labour had ever been ready to negotiate, it was not until 1989 that Labour's policies had sufficiently changed to be able to envisage the SDP being in a coalition led by a Labour Prime Minister. Coalition partners have no right to say who leads the larger party, which is why I have resisted saying that I would never serve under Margaret Thatcher or Neil Kinnock. Coalition politics needs to transcend personalities and focus on policies. For the SDP to be open to negotiation with either of the larger national parties was not being a political harlot. It simply meant being ready to practise the coalition politics which comes with proportional representation. I often tried, but singularly failed, to convince both David Steel and Roy Jenkins that this outlook has merit. Sadly the deep-seated nature of the party political battle in Britain made it very hard for some sensible people involved in the SDP and Liberal parties to think in these terms. Paddy Ashdown, when he dropped the strategy of being ready to coalesce with the Conservatives, gave Labour the upper hand in coalition negotiations, and it was no accident that Tony Blair led him into such a dance. Before 1997 Blair was trying to ensure, if there was no working majority for Labour, that he could rely on the Liberal Democrats. Once he had his landslide he slid out of all the prior agreements. A better and more principled approach is to follow the electorate's wishes and say you will talk first to the party with the largest number of MPs, Nick Clegg's position.

In February Roy Jenkins started likening me to the Javanese upas tree, poisoning all other life nearby. This was a charge soon to be repeated by Denis Healey. It was actually too delicate a barb for Denis to handle as well as Roy. He is a specialist in hyperbolic abuse. To be savaged by Denis Healey is a compliment to savour, spit out and return in kind. His best crack about me was that 'the good fairies gave the young doctor almost everything: thick dark locks, matinée idol features, a lightning intelligence – unfortunately the bad fairy also made him a shit'. That never made any difference to our friendship. Some people were surprised when in 1999 he joined me in creating New Europe, a pro-EU, anti-euro grouping. This had a profound influence with Business for Sterling in holding public opinion steady against euro entry and ensuring Tony Blair never dared put the issue to a referendum (see Chapter 8).

Towards the end of April 1985 the Labour Party completely lost its cool in the House of Commons and did itself a great deal of harm when its left wing attempted to prevent me opening a debate on trade union democracy. This was the first debate allocated to the SDP. The antics began with Labour MPs occupying the bench below the gangway when a division was called and we in the SDP had to vote. Labour MPs ran a shift system so that our bench was occupied throughout the vote and neither Ian Wrigglesworth nor I could get back onto our bench. Dennis Skinner then demanded of the deputy Speaker that we should speak from the Conservative benches, given our views on trade union ballots. By this time I was sitting in the gangway between the opposition front bench and the bench below the gangway which SDP and Labour MPs normally shared. I then moved to exercise my traditional right as a Privy Counsellor, which the Labour Party had forgotten about, to speak from the despatch box opposite the government. At this point I was elbowed away by John Prescott, the shadow Employment spokesman. I approached the despatch box again only to encounter legs stretched out and feet firmly planted on the table. Amid uproar the deputy Speaker was being continually asked whether I was entitled to speak from the despatch box. This continued for about forty-five minutes until finally a fifteen-minute suspension of the House of Commons was called, during which talks were held between us and the Conservative and Labour front bench. Labour finally agreed to vacate the bench below the gangway and I agreed to make my speech from there. It only served to make the Labour Party look loutish and draw attention to the SDP's popular policies on giving power to the individual trade unionist through postal ballots, a cause which had already been given a boost by the TGWU ballot-rigging rumpus then in the news – to which Ron Todd had responded by promising to hold another ballot.

In a Tawney Society lecture two weeks later Bill Rodgers issued what was described as a warning to me against going too far towards a market economy or in appealing to Conservative supporters. In this almost completely unreconstructed speech he made public what I had known for many months – that Bill, Shirley and Roy were going to challenge the policy direction in which I was leading the party more openly than hitherto. My reaction was to increase the pace of new thinking, propounding the theories of Professor Martin Weitzman on wider share ownership in a Gaitskell memorial lecture at Nottingham, and promoting the egalitarian concepts of Professor John Rawls, the Harvard University philosopher. I wanted privatisation of the big public monopolies like gas to be accompanied by a free distribution of shares to all gas consumers, an idea originally put forward by Samuel Brittan. But I was never able to carry the party with me on this because of the footling argument that some would cash in their shares. This did not worry me, they had the right to do what they liked with the distribution of their own asset; most would not do so and at least it would, like council house sales, spread wealth. It was better than just selling off assets to reduce the PSBR. Later that year Harold Macmillan, by now the Earl of Stockton, made a witty but wrong-handed swipe at the whole concept of privatisation: 'First of all the Georgian silver goes and then all the nice furniture that used to be in the saloon. Then the Canalettos go.' It was the paternalist voice of another era. Those who had shares for the first time in British Telecom, particularly the employees, were enjoying the increase in their value. They were not keen for Labour to renationalise these companies. There was a populist appeal in spreading shareholding, the making of mini-capitalists, that the Macmillan of the 1930s, writing *The Middle Way*, might have well understood. The real criticism of the government's privatisation programme was that it sold shares at too favourable a price insufficiently widely. Yet on the substance of the issue, the SDP supported almost all the privatisation sales, whether British Airways, Enterprise Oil, Sealink, Jaguar or Rolls-Royce. Our main criticism was over the sale of the regional water authorities, but as debate raged over pollution control of the rivers, the government conceded the National Rivers Authority and some potentially significant statutory minimum standards.

The polls were now showing Labour only marginally ahead of us with the Tories third. Neil Kinnock was getting rattled and provocatively described me as 'fat on arrogance and drunk on ambition'. My best tactic was of course not to reply in kind, saying rather prissily that I would avoid putting any emphasis on personalities. This was humbug, provoking the Labour Party to such an extent that Jack Straw wrote an article to prove, not without difficulty, that I had been just as tough on Neil Kinnock, quoting descriptions I had given of him as 'spineless' or 'the most vacuous leader in Labour's history' or 'in Arthur Scargill's pocket'. Throughout history politicians have abused each other when they think it is in their interests. It can go too far from time to time and then it backfires. But it does not usually cause a lot of ill feeling. Neil Kinnock and I found ourselves a few days later outside the House of Commons helping launch a campaign to mark the UN International Youth Year, and there were smiles on our faces, though we were not revealing what was in our hearts.

In the Brecon & Radnor by-election in July, despite a last-minute MORI poll in the *Daily Mirror* giving Labour the lead with 46 per cent and the Alliance second place with 28 per cent, the actual electors voted very differently. The Liberals won with 35.8 per cent of the vote, Labour came second with 34.4 per cent and the Tories third. It was a tremendous result for everyone, especially Richard Livsey, who went on to hold the seat at the general election. I was glad for David Steel. He had had a rough year and this result gave him great heart and balanced the SDP success in Portsmouth. If the partnership were to thrive, the more we could keep it in balance the better. We ended July with a joint conference of SDP/Liberal Alliance candidates in London where we both emphasised the dual leadership approach; a strategy meeting of Liberal MPs decided not to opt for one leader. It tends to be forgotten by those who wanted merger that we had had one leader during the 1983 election. It had not been such a great success that people could argue with conviction that a single leader was a crucial ingredient. What was crucial was to be seen as a credible governing force. If only the Alliance had spent more time achieving credibility and less on mechanistic mergers we would have been seen as a more cohesive political force.

The SDP conference started on 7 September in Torquay. It was to be the most successful in the party's history, helped by non-stop sunshine and having the conference hall and hotel on the same site, surrounded by a semi-tropical garden. In the run-up to the conference there had been a lot of tension in the air. Roy Jenkins had written an article about how, after Thatcher, the country would not want a 'sub-Thatcherite alternative', overt code for 'David Owen'. That was par for the course, but a more serious statement was his assertion that under no electoral system would there be room in the hearts of the British people for more than three mainstream political groups. Never before had he quite so clearly repudiated the four-party model on which the SDP had been launched.

Just before the conference, David Steel publicly argued for a freeze on the deployment of cruise missiles, presumably in an attempt to influence our debate, where the platform faced a challenge. Tom McNally had by then become obsessed with the belief that the freeze option was the way to defuse differences on defence between the two parties and was due to move an amendment to our SDP defence white paper. Roy Jenkins was involved in the freeze movement and it was soon to recruit Shirley Williams. The more serious challenge came in a motion from Stevenage which endorsed the SDP's maintaining many of the traditional values of the Labour Party. The wording looked fairly innocuous but it was being pushed as a proxy vote of opposition to purportedly sub-Thatcherite views.

As the conference gathered momentum it became clear that this was now a confident party, perfectly ready to sort out the wheat from the chaff, which is what it proceeded to do. Most unwisely Bill and Shirley had lined themselves up with the Stevenage motion, though it was noticeable that Roy had been a little more reluctant to do so, sensing that it was out of step with the mood of the party. The national committee, against Bill and Shirley's passionate argument, decided to oppose the Stevenage motion and some excellent speeches were made. Polly Toynbee, a member of the national committee, urged the party not to fall prey to middle-class guilt: 'Half of the Labour Party are Trotskyist Etonians, professional politicos and academic researchers assuming mock regional accents and calling each other "mate".' Sue Slipman, a former Communist, who replied on behalf of the national committee to the debate, said that emotionally and politically she was left of centre, a term which would not be rejected by most people in the SDP when used in the sense of supporting the have-nots rather than the haves. 'I am in this party not because I reneged on my loyalty to my class but because I maintain it and I want them to have the same privileges and opportunities I managed to get. I know this is the party that stands for that, not the Labour Party.'

A new young star appeared in the party's firmament. Danny Finkelstein, the chairman of the Young Social Democrats, argued that the strategy of the SDP should be based not on the old Labour Party but on the new politics of coalition. He borrowed the words of Monty Python: 'The old politics are dead. They have expired. They have ceased to be.' After the SDP collapsed Danny joined the Conservative Party and worked for John Major and then William Hague before becoming a senior journalist on the *Times*.

The social market was again resoundingly endorsed by the conference. Non-nuclear defence was once again rejected, with a replacement for Polaris specifically accepted. Most people wanted a series of hard-edged, coherent policies which were distinctive and uniquely SDP. In the words of Peter Riddell of the *Financial Times*:

> The Social Democratic Party has found itself at Torquay. After four years of introspection about whether it is a Labour Party Mark II or a centre group aiming at disillusioned Tories, the party's own activists have ended the debate. They have made it plain they dislike references to previous party labels and to the left–right spectrum. Instead, much to Dr David Owen's delight, the activists claim the party has its own social democratic values, combining in the market economy, and radical social priorities which cannot easily be labelled left or right.

The opinion polls were showing the Alliance in the lead, and one had us 9.5 per cent ahead of Labour, with the Conservatives third. Any poll euphoria was premature, for Neil Kinnock was preparing to take on Militant. At the Labour Party conference, in a most courageous speech with moments of great theatre, Neil Kinnock rounded on the militants. He singled out and savaged Derek Hatton, a key figure behind the total shambles in which the Liverpool Labour Party had landed the city. It was an electric performance and I watched spellbound. The public watching on television liked what they saw. As Labour's poll rating immediately rose our lead vanished overnight. Now we would be confronting an increasingly realistic Labour Party.

The Liberals held their conference in Dundee. I had to go and speak, which I dreaded. To Liberal activists, according to the *Daily Telegraph*, I was 'a cross between a serpent in the Garden of Eden and a walking threat to the eco-system, a sort of nuclear reactor on legs'. I escaped unscathed because their quarry was now Paddy Ashdown, who, having as they saw it sold the pass on Liberal unilateralism during our conference, was now referred to as 'Paddy Backdown' and had to suffer the ultimate indignity of lapel badges saying 'Ashdown has been doctored'.

After Dundee Roy sent me a card in which he was generous about my speech, saying he had watched it all on television, something he had not often done before, and commenting that though my method of speaking was obviously, and in his view rightly, very different from his own, he thought it was now more effective, particularly with the wider television audience. He went on to say that the impression of thinking as I went along came over very well and allowed me to relate general points to immediate events. He congratulated me on both Torquay and Dundee, which in general he felt went better than he had feared. This was a considerable gesture, particularly since he added, 'Incidentally, I don't think there are significant differences of policy between us now. I was slightly worried in 1983–4 but not now.'

I genuinely hoped this marked the end of our policy differences; obviously we would not agree on the merger issue but if Roy was happy with policy after Torquay I thought it meant he could now live with the social market economy and the replacement of Polaris, which made me very pleased. He even suggested that it was right to force the 'hung Parliament' issue onto the agenda, but had a point which he wanted to talk about. I am afraid this card lulled me into a false sense of security. I read it wrongly as the end of the sniping, that Roy, Bill and Shirley would now accept the new policies. Little did I realise that, through the Defence Commission, the three of them were within months going to launch the most direct policy challenge of my leadership.

On the evening of 3 December, more than fifteen million people stopped what they were doing and watched our party political broadcast. Apart from a James Bond movie and *EastEnders* it was the biggest TV audience that week. More than 5,000 people telephoned after the broadcast and over 2,000 wrote in to express their support. It started with John Cleese mid-yawn saying, 'I am sorry, but this is a party political broadcast and you know how boring they are. This one, I am afraid, promises to be outstandingly tedious.' He suggested switching over to snooker on the other side! His subject was proportional representation. He showed the grotesque unfairness of the British electoral system and lampooned the traditional argument that coalition governments are weak and indecisive. There were rollicking jokes about countries like poor, weak, old Germany and others with proportional representation whose standard of living far surpassed ours. For some time we had been breaking new ground in party political broadcasts thanks to party members freely giving their skills, but this was easily the best we had done and we achieved a good deal of favourable press coverage.

The year ended with the intergovernmental conference, under Article 236 of the Treaty of Rome, reaching agreement in Luxembourg. Here was Margaret Thatcher agreeing to majority voting on an extensive scale to introduce a single market by 1993. The powers of the European Parliament were increased to allow them to amend single-market decisions, there was an extension of Community competence, and political co-operation over foreign affairs was now formalised under the treaty. Margaret Thatcher then proceeded to carry this far-reaching legislation through the House of Commons with hardly any protest. This was an example of Margaret Thatcher the pragmatist. She wanted a single market and to achieve it she was ready to compromise on a specific issue with well-defined boundaries to it. Because of this readiness to grapple with Europe on a practical level there was no real political controversy over Europe prior to the 1987 election.

On the morning of 15 April 1986 I woke up to find that during the night the Americans had bombed terrorist targets in Libya using F-111 aircraft from bases in Britain. The Prime Minister was under immediate attack for authorising the airfields' use and I had to determine my attitude. Normally I would have supported action against terrorism, but this was illegal by any standard: the sort of retaliatory action which we had always condemned the Israelis for undertaking. For some weeks I had feared that this was going to happen, for the rhetoric and actions of the Reagan administration had shown they were increasingly cavalier about remaining within the limits of international law when dealing with terrorists. Washington was disillusioned with the pitiful response of the European Community to any suggestion of applying tough sanctions against Libya for harbouring terrorists and determined to act.

In a speech to US correspondents in London five days earlier I had gone out of my way to warn that, desirable though it was to take action to stop Colonel Gaddafi from harbouring and training terrorists, it was questionable whether any US action could be justified as being a proportionate use of force if it took the form of air strikes against Libya. Instead the US should ask the United Nations Security Council to impose a quarantine on Libya, stopping all movement of aircraft until Gaddafi ceased all terrorist and subversive activity.

Someone whose judgement I greatly valued took me to task on an article I wrote for the *Times* headed 'Bombing is not the answer'. He said bluntly that, from what he knew of me, if I had been Prime Minister I would have agreed to the American request to use British bases because to have refused would have very seriously undermined Anglo-American relations. His criticism struck a sensitive nerve for deep down I wondered whether he was right. I would have tried to steer the Americans much earlier towards an air and maybe even a maritime blockade of Libya. Yet though I believed passionately in respecting international law, I also knew that in government decisions have to be made where the choice is between two evils. The lesser evil in this case was to support President Reagan's request and try to pretend, as Margaret Thatcher had, that it was not retaliation but an act of self-defence, as covered under Article 51 of the UN Charter. Having been given crucial military support by President Reagan during the Falklands War, Margaret Thatcher knew that she owed him similar support. Given her personality, she would have found it impossible to refuse, and it is to her credit, in such trying circumstances, that she gave permission. She knew that Ronald Reagan had had doubts about the wisdom of her action in sending a task force to the South Atlantic, and that the Americans, under successive administrations, had never accepted our claim to the Falklands. Not only the President, but most of his advisers, believed the US's fragile relationship with Latin America would be gravely damaged by supporting us. Nevertheless Reagan agreed with his Defence Secretary, Caspar Weinberger, that the US could not refuse our request for help. Nor had the US ever made it a condition, as I was urging on the Prime Minister in the case of Libya, that their agreement should be subject to being involved in the operational decisions. They simply ensured that every request we made was delivered to our forces in the Southern Atlantic as soon as possible, sometimes accepting an operational penalty for their own forces. Weinberger richly deserved our thanks, as did the Pentagon for working round the clock, but none of this could have been done without Reagan's personal, private decision to help his friend Margaret and his favourite country, Britain, in their hour of need. Margaret Thatcher recognised all this and, in fulfilling her debt of honour, she offended some of her closest Cabinet colleagues like Norman Tebbit. She also went against the best Foreign Office legal advice. President Mitterrand refused President Reagan the right to overfly France and it can be argued that this did him no harm. But the Americans, and especially that President, were bound to expect different attitudes from Britain.

One of the hardest issues to settle between the Liberal Party and the SDP was differences over defence. In February I was alerted by David Dunn, one of our members on the Joint Alliance Defence Commission, that the commission was looking for a dangerous compromise on Polaris. On 25 February I wrote back to him:

> On the key question I do not think we should find a form of words on the Polaris replacement. The words will come unstuck if there is any equivocation. Politically we will not be able to carry cancelling Trident unless we can say clearly that we will replace Polaris; unless there is a miracle and *all* nuclear weapons are negotiated away. How we replace Polaris is better left open. I cannot understand why Paddy Ashdown is so upset about submarine-launched cruise, whether the US Tomahawk, or built by British Aerospace, or preferably the Europeans. But my main worry is this idea of trying to find a formula of words. We may have to do this for an election manifesto, but if the Liberals are not yet ready to say Britain should remain a nuclear weapon state, then I think it is better for the SDP at this stage to hold firm in a gentle non-aggressive way and wait for the arms control negotiations.

By the middle of April I had become uneasy about the Joint Commission, suspecting it was up to no good. When I enquired about progress on the all-important nuclear question, which they had wisely left to the end, I was met by evasion. I twice raised the issue of what was going to be said about the nuclear deterrent with Bill Rodgers, once on the telephone from Buttermere and once when he came into my office. On both occasions I suspected that Bill was dissembling. I also raised the issue directly with David Steel on a number of occasions and was told each time that he had no idea what was going to be in the report, but would look into it.

On the Friday morning I drove to Southport for a Council for Social Democracy (CSD) meeting, collecting Sue Robertson, our press officer, Alex de Mont, my economic adviser, and Sandra Jantuah, who dealt with all policy questions in my office. My draft speech dealt mainly with civil nuclear power, following the disaster at Chernobyl a fortnight before. As we drove up we were informed over the car telephone that the main front page article which had appeared in the *Scotsman* that morning carried the headline 'OWEN'S NUCLEAR HOPES DASHED. ALLIANCE REPORT REJECTS UK DETERRENT', and it went on to say, 'Dr David Owen's attempts to commit the Alliance to a policy of replacing Polaris with a new independent nuclear deterrent have been dashed by a joint SDP/Liberal policy commission'. It continued:

> The Alliance Commission on Defence has unanimously rejected his suggestion that Britain should purchase a new nuclear deterrent at the end of the Polaris lifespan in the 1990s. The unanimity of the finding by the commission, which is drawn equally from the SDP and the Liberals, means that the SDP leader's favourite policy has been rejected by the specialist nominees of his own party. The finding will strengthen the hand of Mr David Steel, the Liberal leader, in the difficult negotiations of ironing out the two parties' differences on nuclear defence policy.

The report was signed by Martin Dowle, the chief political correspondent, who, Sue Robertson knew, had recently talked to David Steel. We also knew that, the day before, a Liberal official, himself a unilateralist, had been briefing the press about the Joint Commission report along very similar lines. The *Guardian*, we thought, also had the story but surprisingly had not run anything that Friday. Sue Robertson, who was well respected among lobby correspondents and had carefully followed what was happening, was convinced that we were facing a systematic briefing by the Liberal Party about the commission's report. During the day we also heard that briefing had continued on the Friday for the Sunday newspapers.

David Steel admits in his own autobiography that he had lunch with Martin Dowle and that he had told him, foolishly but accurately, that the commission's report made no commitment to a replacement of Polaris. He makes no mention in his book, though, of the letter which was published in the *Scotsman* on 19 May in which he professed to be most surprised by their chief political correspondent's lead story. He wrote, 'I must make it clear, as I did to him, that I have yet to see any text or draft.' This denial of his involvement was too much for the *Scotsman* to stomach and underneath the letter was the following explanation: '(The story was based on unambiguous information given to our reporters – Ed.)' Much later I heard exactly what had gone on. There is no doubt that David leaked the report and then tried through the *Scotsman*'s letter column to pretend he had not done so.

The actual words of the final draft of the commission report showed that Bill Rodgers had taken no account of my anxieties, for the critical wording which I had objected to had not been changed. Nor, I knew, had he communicated my anxieties either to John Cartwright or Jim Wellbeloved, who both sat on the commission. On Trident, Bill had reverted to much the same position he had held in his paper in 1980 to members of the Labour shadow Cabinet. When we had all witnessed how dominant an electoral issue nuclear weapons had been in the 1983 election, to advance a formulation to delay a final decision on whether Britain should replace Polaris until after an election was amazing, particularly so coming from Bill. In the past he had been the strongest of the Gang of Four on nuclear questions.

The chairman of the Defence Commission was John Edmonds, formerly a diplomat in the Foreign Office, experienced in disarmament questions and someone I had suggested to David Steel. It was no criticism of the chairman that the commission had put forward this wording on nuclear weapons. He was there to try and broker an agreement and if the SDP members were not upholding SDP policy it was not his job to do it for them. In our discussions both before and after he became chairman he had always known that Polaris replacement was going to be the most delicate question for the commission. He had hoped, as I had, that David Steel and I would be able to sort it out through our intermediaries on the commission. But Bill had deliberately decided to go his own way.

The vast bulk of the commission's report was excellent, as one would expect given the quality of its members, but this nuclear question was so highly political that it was understandable that many of the specialist members were bound to leave it predominantly to the more senior political members.

It was vital for me to act urgently if the commission report was not to become Alliance policy. Once published, the Liberals would be bound to hold firmly to this quite unacceptable wording. I decided to spell out not just my views but the SDP position on both civil nuclear power and nuclear deterrence in my speech next day, and to do so in unequivocal terms. I judged it wiser not to refer directly to the commission's report. It was still a draft and I hoped that John Cartwright and Jim Wellbeloved, seeing the interpretation that the Liberals were putting on the form of words there, would realise it was not acceptable and insist on clarifying this question further before the report was finalised. There was no doubt in my mind that I was embarking on a very risky course. If I lost I would have to consider giving up the leadership of the SDP.

My speech in Southport was a marker for the future:

> Certainly you should know quite clearly that I definitely do not believe that I would carry any conviction whatever in the next election were I to answer – on your behalf – on the question of the replacement of Polaris, that that would have to depend on the circumstances of the time. That would get and would deserve a belly laugh from the British electorate. That sort of fudging and mudging was what I left behind in the Labour Party.

Not many people in the hall realised what I was doing, but both Bill and Shirley knew full well that I had decided to confront their challenge head on. They would now have to defeat me using the democratic procedures of the party if the commission's wording on nuclear weapons were to form the basis of any general election manifesto.

On 1 June I wrote an article in the *Observer* under the title 'Polaris must be replaced' and decided to follow it up with a detailed speech on defence in Bonn when I visited Germany four days later. My object was quite simply to ensure that when the commission's report was published it would already have been exposed as an unacceptable fudge.

In the *Guardian*, Hugo Young suggested that I was 'entering one of the disturbing phases he has experienced before, in which style and image become his obsessive preoccupations. In particular a style and image most closely emulating that of Mrs Thatcher.' He argued that a true coalitionist would find a way of moderating his convictions. He was confused, as one would not expect from a columnist of his calibre, about the meaning and the compatibility of words like 'conviction', 'consensus', 'compromise' and 'coalition' in politics. Compromise is the art of politics, but in order for democratic politics to retain any foundation in principle, its practitioners must not feel obliged to compromise their core convictions. A coalition is not a vehicle for consensus but a mechanism for compromise and for creating a climate in which it is easier to reach a consensus. Within a coalition there can and indeed must be respect for conviction and, when compromise is not possible, an open acknowledgement of differences. This is the difference between multi-party coalitions and internal party coalitions, where collective responsibility is normally the rule. A coalition government in European Community countries is not bound like a British Cabinet by the doctrine of collective responsibility. When policy differences between political parties cannot be resolved there is an open acknowledgment of them. The coalition partners fight the election on different platforms, even if they intend to resume the coalition after the election. This was the relationship I always sought between the SDP and the Liberals within the Alliance.

While it was better for us to agree policy in the Alliance, it could not be at any price, certainly not at the price of our country's security. Hugo Young and some like-minded people within the SDP seemed to believe that even differences over defence policy issues of fundamental importance for the country should be papered over. For them, coalition seemingly meant compromising on everything, never allowing conviction to threaten the consensus of a coalition. That was exactly the sort of thinking that had contributed to the mess the Labour Party was in. They had developed the broad church tradition so far that members and MPs were expected to accept conference decisions regardless of their convictions. The fact that a belief in nuclear deterrence was one of the reasons many of us had left the Labour Party was also being conveniently forgotten. It was inconceivable that on this of all issues I and many others in the SDP were going to abandon our convictions purely because the Liberals insisted on keeping their non-nuclear convictions. We would have to respect their convictions, but we would have to agree to differ.

David Watt now entered the field and his criticism or support really mattered to me. He was a personal friend of both myself and Bill Rodgers and I knew he would have pondered very hard on the issue, having heard both our arguments. He wrote on Friday 6 June in the *Times*, under the title 'When it's best to disagree', saying:

> An agreement at all costs suits the Liberal mergerites and those who want to cut Dr Owen down to size; an agreement to disagree is a visible endorsement of Owen's view that important principles still separate the two partners. But in the end these are side issues. The problem actually resides in the policy itself. Where nuclear weapons policy is concerned, a chasm exists in the Liberal/SDP Alliance as it does in the country as a whole.

He went on to describe those members of the commission who thought that Britain's nuclear status should be decided in the light of circumstances after the next election as being either terrified of the effect of disunity on the Alliance's electoral appeal or actually soft on the nuclear issue, or a combination of the two.

We were now back where we started in Llandudno in 1981, when within twenty-four hours the Liberals both endorsed the Alliance and voted to campaign against the deployment of cruise missiles. Roy Jenkins had spent those intervening years trying to pretend that there were no differences between the parties. Having sniffed the two parties as if they were bottles of claret, his nose, he kept telling us, was unable to detect a Liberal from a Social Democrat. This Olympian assessment owed too much to dining with Mark Bonham Carter and the type of old Asquithian Liberal who had little in common with the new community politicians and pavement politics. It meant conveniently ignoring not only repeated democratic votes in each of our parties, but also the realities among Liberal MPs and candidates. A very high percentage of Liberal parliamentary candidates were professed supporters of CND while in the SDP support for CND was a barrier even to being placed on the panel of candidates.

In Bonn I had a private chat with Chancellor Kohl and found him earthy and sensible. He had shown courage in going ahead with cruise deployment. I asked him, as I had asked Helmut Schmidt some years before: did he want Britain to remain a nuclear weapon state? The answer was an unequivocal 'yes'. By now the newspapers were inevitably giving the controversy considerable coverage. But since we were going to have to have a row, in my view it was better to have it now. The commission formula, which stated, 'No decision on whether, and if so how, British nuclear weapons should be maintained beyond Polaris can properly be made except in the light of...' was fraught with political danger. Yet the commission had listed four sensible criteria which should be the basis for such a decision and I could accept these criteria. My aim was to force the Liberal Party to answer those criteria now and make the decision on 'whether' to have the argument out during the summer, well before the election. Otherwise, the debate would take place during the campaign itself, when it would not be easy to duck an issue of that size, and there would be huge penalties for attempting to avoid the question of whether we should replace Polaris.

The series of rather unpleasant, but still vital, SDP meetings on defence came to its climax at the policy committee at the end of July. I had to use my casting vote to ensure that Bill Rodgers was not chosen to reply to the crucial defence debate due to take place at our September conference in Harrogate. The resolution which the policy committee was putting to the party formally welcomed the Joint Commission document, but we also deliberately reaffirmed SDP policy, so it would have been absurd for Bill, given what he had been saying, to speak on our behalf.

My public attitude to criticism that the Alliance was divided over defence was to admit it and not flannel around pretending otherwise. Sometimes in the past I had fallen into the trap of going too far in minimising the differences. But I was comfortable defending the Alliance as a new concept in British politics and was ready to ride out the fact that our differences were real and not just being played up in the press.

Understandably, now I had asserted my authority on defence, David felt he had to assert his own policies. The *Spitting Image* picture of him in my pocket was always a caricature. Fortunately we had different strengths and weaknesses. David took the opportunity of the tenth anniversary of his leadership of the Liberal Party to make it clear that he believed a formal union between the Liberal and the Social Democratic parties was almost inevitable. Stressing that he believed in union rather than merger he emphasised that a decision would depend on the parties' defining the constitutional shape of their common future after the general election, but that it would be wrong to press on against any substantial minority in either of the parties. I dearly wish that he had stuck by these words. I could take no exception to his speech, apart from wishing that we could get headlines on policy rather than on internal merger arguments. I conceded that merger was a legitimate subject for debate after the next election, though I was still personally opposed to it. I could already sense that there were many Social Democrats who would want to merge after the election. This was when I started to hope that if David really was prepared to accept that a minority could not be forced into a merger we might reach an agreement where some Social Democrats merged with the Liberals and others did not.

One symbol of the subterranean debate in the SDP came in a column by Hugo Young, who, clearly briefed by some of my party colleagues, returned to the attack on my personality in a piece published in the *Guardian* on 24 July: 'With brief lapses into collegiate mode he has become ever more dominant, ever more impatient and ever more convinced that hardly anyone else in the party is worth a row of beans.' According to him my motive was to ensure that if there were a hung Parliament I would be unencumbered by the Liberals.

> He has always found many of their attitudes uncongenial, and has the old Labour man's contempt for their nagging individualism. But far more important than that, in a certain configuration of seats, he would want to keep open the Tory option: to do a deal with a new Conservative leadership as the last hope of precluding what would be, for Owen personally, the ruin of his political life – the installation of Neil Kinnock in Downing Street.

By stressing personality Hugo's columns tended over the years to disparage the possibility that there might ever be principle behind any politician's stand. In as much as I would have expected SDP MPs in a hung Parliament to refuse to help install a government committed to unilateral nuclear disarmament, his surmise was quite correct. I was fearful that some Liberal MPs would be ready to install Neil Kinnock in Downing Street without safeguarding our national security. We had not created the SDP as a vehicle to let a Labour government in by the back door, committed to all the dangerous damaging nonsense that was then still part of their party policy.

On Wednesday 3 September David Steel and I visited NATO headquarters together with MP colleagues John Cartwright and Alan Beith. We met the American Supreme Allied Commander, who was extraordinarily frank about Anglo-French nuclear co-operation. Since François Mitterrand had taken office as President there had been clearly far more French nuclear co-operation with NATO than was generally known. We then went by train to Paris. This was the period of 'cohabitation' so it was natural to see key figures both on the right and on the left. We met the articulate young former socialist Prime Minister, Laurent Fabius. We also saw my friend Michel Rocard, who, though he had resigned from Mitterrand's Socialist government before they left office, was still a force to be reckoned with and was later to become Prime Minister. The Minister for Foreign Affairs was cautious, as befitted a professional diplomat appointed to serve the President without offending the Prime Minister, Jacques Chirac. We had lunch with the Minister of Defence, who was a Chirac appointment and very keen on Anglo-French nuclear co-operation. The meeting with President Mitterrand was extremely positive. Finally, we met Prime Minister Chirac, who was friendly about Margaret Thatcher but did not disguise his disappointment that she would only look to the United States over nuclear co-operation. Twelve years later Tony Blair tried to change that policy with the St Malo agreement in late 1998. Its intention, closer Franco-British co-operation, was sound but Chirac, by then President of France, was trying to build up EU defence at about the expense of NATO. When I spoke to Blair about this that December I did not think he understood the dangers of acquiescing in Chirac's design and undermining NATO.

In 1986 François Mitterrand was dominating continental Europe by then in a way which we in Britain had insufficiently realised. Everyone agreed that he was the great survivor of French politics. But there was less agreement on why he had survived so long. No one does so without having rare political skills, some of them born out of adversity. I had first met Mitterrand in *Gauche Européenne* meetings in Paris in the mid 1960s and had been deeply unimpressed. His appearance was then unappealing and he spoke unattractively. Yet even so, I had felt grudging respect, for he had recently pushed General de Gaulle into a second ballot in the presidential elections of December 1965 and demonstrated a formidable capacity to unify the vote of the left across what many thought was an unbridgeable chasm between the Socialist Party and the Communists. In May 1968, in the month of the barricades, Mitterrand, as the leader of the Federation of the Democratic and Socialist Left, challenged de Gaulle with virulent criticism. When de Gaulle resigned after the April 1969 referendum, Mitterrand declined to stand against Pompidou.

The French politician that I had known best over all those years was Michel Rocard, whom I had first met when he was in the Inspection des Finances. I had tended, therefore, to see Mitterrand from the perspective of Rocard and their antipathy was well known. Gradually, through the 1970s, I watched as Mitterrand's appearance and manner were changed. He began to cultivate an image of a man above the battle; a sage and seasoned politician. I met him when he came to the Labour Party conference in the late 1970s and I had heard him speak at meetings but I had not chatted to him in any depth for some years.

In the first round of the 1981 presidential elections in April, Mitterrand came a close second to Giscard d'Estaing, having squeezed the Communist vote down to 15 per cent, and voters felt safe in switching in the second ballot to Mitterrand. He became the first Socialist President in the twenty years of the Fifth Republic.

For the first two years, he governed as a socialist: cut working hours, increased holidays, enlarged social security, nationalised industries and abolished the guillotine. In the process he also smothered French communism. In an increasingly interdependent world economy, the French attempt at socialism in one country was a disaster. It ended in 1983 with a massive trade deficit, wage inflation and a gravely weakened franc. It was as bad as Wilson's period from 1964 to 1967, which started with hope and ended in devaluation. Yet whereas Wilson had to accept the IMF, Mitterrand was luckier: he could realign within the discipline of the EMS. He held to that discipline thereafter with tenacity. I was to work closely with him over Yugoslavia in 1992 until he finished as President in 1995 (see Chapter 7).

Seeing election defeat staring him in the face, Mitterrand switched to a proportional voting system for the National Assembly elections early in 1986. It was a move of the utmost cynicism which provoked Rocard to resign as Minister of Agriculture. However, when the Socialists lost in the assembly elections, Mitterrand could claim that they had not been wiped out as they would have been under the old voting system. Also the extreme right-wing party leader, Jean-Marie Le Pen, had reduced Chirac's majority. President Mitterrand had insisted on staying in office and when David Steel and I saw him he was intent on showing that cohabitation was feasible, whereby a President and Prime Minister from different parties could work together. It was always going to be the biggest test for de Gaulle's constitution and ironic that Mitterrand, the foremost critic of the Fifth Republic's constitution, made it work. That it survived cohabitation is a tribute not just to Mitterrand but also to Chirac. Cohabitation could, however, never have worked had it not been for the nature of Mitterrand's foreign policy. From the start it had been hard to criticise from the right. President Mitterrand had gone to the German Bundestag and used his socialist credentials to urge German Social Democrats, then in opposition, to support the deployment of cruise missiles and the modernisation of Pershing I missiles to counter the Soviet SS-20 missile deployment. In doing so he forged a close working relationship with the Christian Democrat Chancellor Kohl and the Republican President Reagan. Mitterrand had absolutely no sympathy with the prevalent mood of hostility to nuclear weapons among the socialists and social democrats of northern Europe. When we arrived in Paris, we did not expect to hear different notes on nuclear policy from Mitterrand and Chirac and nor did we. Mitterrand made it quite clear to us that France would remain a nuclear weapon state and that he wanted Britain to do the same.

So we had Mitterrand and Chirac going to great lengths to demonstrate to the accompanying British press and television cameras that they wanted to co-operate on nuclear defence with Britain and were irritated by the reluctance of Margaret Thatcher to envisage a nuclear relationship with anyone other than the Americans. The warmth of our reception surprised even the most cynical people in Britain. While we had gone as a way of helping the Alliance parties to get safely through a tricky defence debate at the Liberal Party conference, our trip had demonstrated, to some people's surprise, that Anglo-French nuclear co-operation was a real not imaginary prospect. By putting the red carpet down for us the French were signalling an important message to the British government. In the twenty-first century I hope that Anglo-French nuclear defence co-operation will continue. Both countries are committed with the Cold War over to the elimination of all nuclear weapons. To help alleviate that objective, the two countries could devise novel arrangements for developing together a strategy of minimum deterrence on behalf of Europe as a stage towards elimination with Conservative, Liberal Democrat and Labour support.

I watched with amazement as Mitterrand readily acquiesced in Chirac's reversal of the very proportional representation he had previously introduced, and later turned the tables by beating Chirac convincingly for a second presidential term in 1988. He did a tacit deal with Rocard that if Rocard supported him in the fight for the presidency he would appoint him Prime Minister. They then lived three years in an uneasy but successful partnership which ended only in 1991 when Mitterrand chose Edith Cresson to be France's first woman Prime Minister. In March 1993 Mitterrand had in *Le Figaro* contemptuously listed his chosen successors in order: Delors, Léotard, Barre, Giscard d'Estaing, Chirac, his dog, Rocard! Mitterrand deliberately and systematically destroyed all his likely Socialist successors, happily passing over in 1995 to a President from the right, Chirac.

Mitterrand was always ready to work with the Americans on defence provided they paid public lip service to his aspirations for French nuclear independence. During the build-up to the liberation of Kuwait, Mitterrand waited while his Defence Minister, Jean-Pierre Chevènement, went out on a limb, rejecting any French role in attacking Iraq, and kept France outside any US command structure. When public opinion shifted towards French involvement, he sacked Chevènement, ensuring that France, albeit with a modest role, got maximum credit from contributing to the allied effort, dropped its previous insistence on not attacking Iraq and de facto accepted US command and control.

By the time of our Harrogate conference on Saturday 13 September, I was pleased with the progress we had made on the defence issue. Even defence experts were taking the emerging Alliance policy seriously. But the merger question would not go away and the *Times*, in an editorial entitled 'Merger mania', said:

> Those in favour of merger tend to favour a deal with Labour, those against are in general more ready to deal with either Labour or the Conservatives. Much pro-merger fervour, of course, conceals simple envy and resentment of Dr Owen; many of his colleagues spend much of their time casting about for new engines to reinforce the long siege of their leader's independence . . . At its foundation, many of Dr Owen's present opponents regarded the party as a temporary vehicle to be led by Roy Jenkins into rapid merger with the Liberals. Mr Jenkins's dauphin, Mr David Steel, would then take over the combined entity and set out to replace the Labour Party as the principal opposition to Conservatism . . . Dr Owen has not yet proved that the Alliance is a plausible candidate for government. But as he faces today's defence debate, he can reflect that he has brought off two commendable successes. He has maintained a position on the British deterrent which is defensible in principle and he has, at least, helped minimise the danger of the early summer split growing wider.

When we came to the defence debate the policy committee's tough stance on defence was supported by a margin of four to one. John Cartwright put the issue very clearly to the party and, though Charles Kennedy, in winding up, made a speech with too many cheap jibes at the Americans, he was nevertheless firm on the main issue. I was able to tell the press at the end, 'I've got what I wanted – the freedom to go for the Labour Party's jugular on the crucial question of defence at the next election.' Unfortunately we did not get the same freedom from the Liberal conference at Eastbourne.

In many ways the most important SDP debate at Harrogate was on the policy document 'Merging Tax and Benefits'. We had published the proposals a fortnight before and they were given a rough ride. Removing the married man's tax allowance was correct, but it was difficult to do without making many middle-income couples worse off and we had not solved the phasing-out problems. It is interesting that in 1991, Norman Lamont decided to freeze this allowance as a first step towards phasing it out, and after 1997 Gordon Brown with his tax credits grappled with the same issues, albeit without total success. An editorial in the *Times* in 1986, 'Tax and displease', agreed that the logic of integrating the tax and benefits system was undeniable. It also commended us for not pretending, like the Labour Party, that it could all be paid for by taxing the rich. But it was correct in pointing out that the burden of our integration plans would fall on the middle class and we knew this would not go down well in every house in suburbia. The *Times* concluded that 'Dr Owen may find that proving he is not Mrs Thatcher is not wholly to his advantage'. David Steel expressed his anxiety that the proposals were a gift to Tory propagandists and we both agreed, having discussed it at Ettrick Bridge, that our presentation would have to be considerably improved. On the other hand, I was concerned that, whereas the toughness in SDP policy was always reported, the tenderness, which was less newsworthy, was too often ignored. A readiness to redistribute was essential to our claim to be social democrats and the conference, far from rejecting the package, gave Dick Taverne, its chief architect, a well-deserved standing ovation and strongly supported the policy. Dick and I did not agree on the merger question but this did not prevent us working closely on tax reform, where his experience was invaluable. Because of the defence row the wider public had been fed only the tough image of the SDP in recent months so I set out to offset this by emphasising the tender side in my final speech. I virtually ignored defence and tried to sell our tax reforms, not just for their redistrib-utive social justice but for the simplification and modernisation of the system. The *Guardian*, often critical of the SDP, concluded editorially that the net effect 'is of an SDP that, as well as challenging for votes from socially concerned Conservatives, is also now in a position to compete credibly and legitimately for votes on the left'.

Now in 2009, with the credit system failing to redistribute wealth and with very high administrative costs, the case for merging the tax and benefit systems is very strong. But it needs economic growth to be restored to soften some of the inevitable anomalies.

The mood of the Harrogate conference was not ebullient like Torquay. It was more workmanlike, even mundane. Quite a sizeable element in the conference were alarmed about confronting the Liberals on defence and anxious about the forthcoming election. The divisions in the Gang of Four were obvious in little jabs and coded phrases, but by the end we had achieved perhaps a better balance of SDP policy than in any other conference.

People often used to speculate on what the SDP membership was really like. I suppose inevitably I saw the grass-roots membership from my constituency vantage point. In our Plymouth SDP there were many former Labour members and council tenants. We were not wealthy nor even a predominantly middle-class group but a genuine mix. There was hardly a claret drinker among them. Try as I might, however, I never succeeded in ridding the national party of that claret image.

The Reykjavik summit in the middle of October 1986 had shown how dependent the domestic defence debate was on the shifting sands of international affairs. In his autobiography President Reagan describes how at Reykjavik his 'hopes for a nuclear-free world soared briefly, then fell during one of the longest, most disappointing – and ultimately angriest – days of my presidency'. Right at the end when Reagan thought they had negotiated the most massive weapons reductions in history, Gorbachev added, with a smile on his face, 'This all depends, of course, on you giving up SDI.' Rightly or wrongly Reagan had always attached immense importance to his Strategic Defense Initiative, better known as Star Wars. It was only because he had faith in this concept of an impenetrable shield that he, unlike most Western leaders, could envisage a non-nuclear world. To Reagan SDI was his insurance policy; it gave him confidence to argue with the American military that all ballistic missiles could go. Without it he would never have dreamt of taking on the fears of his top military advisers. Nevertheless the issue, once raised, was bound to return and in 2009 President Obama rightly put the weight of his office behind the quest for a world free of nuclear weapons.

In November I could at least start putting the knife into Labour's defence policy again. For the last six months I had operated under a self-imposed moratorium because it would have been ludicrous to rough Labour up while I had not won the battle within the SDP, let alone the Liberal Party. The fact that I was now able to do so was recognised in the *Mail on Sunday* of 14 December in an editorial entitled 'Dr Owen's vital decision to cut the Labour cord'. It concentrated on my recent statement that, as long as the Labour Party maintained its current defence policy, the Alliance would find it impossible, in the event of a hung Parliament, to throw their weight behind a Neil Kinnock attempt to form a government. 'Dr Owen, by finally cutting the umbilical cord with the Labour Party, is now firmly established as the leader of the real radical alternative to the Conservative Party.' Sadly, as events were to prove over the next six months, the umbilical cord linking David Steel's Liberal Party to the Labour Party had not been cut. Though we had a rational, firm defence policy, the Liberals were prepared neither to stand firmly behind it nor to abandon their traditional position of sitting even-handedly between the Labour and Conservative parties even when, as was the case on defence, Labour was still not fit to govern.

A Marplan poll in the middle of January 1987 showed the Conservatives ahead with 38 per cent, Labour second on 36 per cent and the Alliance on 23 per cent. The Labour Party was doing too well and we should have been cutting more deeply into their vote. In a perceptive article in the *Sunday Times*, Brian Walden attacked me for pursuing the wrong strategy: 'What Dr Owen needs is for the Labour Party to lose the election, preferably by many millions of votes. Dr Owen knows this, yet somehow his brain has severed communication with his tongue. Most of what he says indirectly helps Labour. He is lighting his own funeral pyre.' What he wanted me to do, and what I wanted to do myself, was to say that Labour was unfit to govern, that under no circumstances could we form a pact with them, and that the Conservatives would win the coming election. What was important was to build up the numbers of SDP and Liberal MPs so that we could become a more effective opposition. It was the old bridgehead-versus-breakthrough argument.

I agreed with Brian Walden that being anti–Labour was sellable to the electorate. It was not, however, sellable to the other members of the Gang of Four or a considerable part of the SDP, let alone to David Steel and the Liberal Party. I had after all tried and lost on this same argument within the SDP before the 1983 election, when the case for this strategy was even stronger. Then, after all, we were facing Michael Foot, a disastrous leader, and Margaret Thatcher, triumphant after the Falklands. Now with an election likely in the summer or autumn we faced not only a more voter-friendly Labour leader in Neil Kinnock but a Margaret Thatcher unleashing a consumer boom. It was still a credible strategy to rule out a coalition with Labour, but I knew it was impossible to make it the official Alliance line.

The best I could hope for was that the Alliance would do well enough in the polls for me to argue convincingly that we would hold the balance of power. Then, while nominally agreeing that we were prepared to form a coalition with either Labour or the Conservatives, I could point up the obstacles to doing so with the Labour Party in such a way that the electorate would know that we would not easily form a coalition with them. For the last three-and-a-half years I had been nudging, cajoling and positioning the Alliance to adopt something close to this strategy. It was endlessly discussed in the Joint Leaders Advisory Committee and I suspect most people present knew it was the logical course. But logic and politics do not always coincide. The strategy we finally adopted of pretending that the Labour and Conservative parties were equally acceptable coalition partners was not merely silly but, as Brian Walden with pardonable exaggeration said, quoting Mr Gladstone, touched the 'confines of lunacy'. Yet my experience of working within the Alliance meant that I was not convinced that I could hold even to my own compromise strategy of leaning towards the Conservatives as the favoured coalition partner. For now I had begun to doubt whether David Steel was personally capable of sustaining the impression that there were circumstances in which he might envisage working in a coalition under Margaret Thatcher. To say David hated her was hardly an exaggeration. At one stage he floated a suggestion of working in a coalition under Sir Geoffrey Howe, but that was predictably not only a trial balloon but a lead one. It is immensely difficult for the smaller grouping in a coalition to demand the head of the political leader of the larger party as their price. When that leader had twice been elected as Prime Minister and was in as dominant a position within the party as Margaret Thatcher, to pretend that we could shunt her out was just incredible.

I found it profoundly depressing that what seemed to me a commonsense electoral strategy was dismissed as crypto-Conservatism, in the same way as the social market had been. It ignored the electoral arithmetic and popular attitudes underpinning Margaret Thatcher's victories in 1979 and in 1983. To appeal to the people who had given her those majorities was not to be a Conservative. These people wanted what I wanted for Britain – a fairer society – but they would not vote Labour, which appeared dangerous and damaging to them. If the SDP had played its cards right in 1983 and 1987, worked as a new and separate party rather than as one merged electoral entity, and made some difficult choices, these people could have formed a permanent core vote for the SDP.

I understood David Steel's problem. In Scotland Margaret Thatcher was deeply unpopular, and almost all the Liberal activists throughout the UK loathed her. Within the SDP I had few such problems. The majority of the party did not like Margaret Thatcher but they had come into politics to co-operate, and possessed or had developed an instinctive understanding of coalition politics. They also had enough sense to see that she had some merits and that the Labour Party leadership was then far worse. We had, however, a minority, which included Roy Jenkins and Shirley Williams, who perhaps because of past slights and present aggravations over the European Community would not allow themselves to be seen to be even contemplating a coalition with Margaret Thatcher. Had we kept the SDP/Liberal Alliance going until 1992, with John Major rather than Margaret Thatcher, it would have been easier and we might have achieved a 'hung' Parliament.

The dilemma the Alliance faced in developing its strategy was well illustrated in the two by-elections which we were about to fight. In Truro David Penhaligon had died. His success as the Liberal MP had been virtually to dismantle the Labour Party vote. I well understood in the West Country how much he had done, for in the 1966 election Reg Scott, a Plymouth journalist and Labour councillor, whom I knew well and liked, had fought in Truro and had polled 17,093 votes, coming second to the Conservatives. To win the by-election in Truro the Liberals needed many Labour votes as well as those of the disillusioned Tories; they dared not offend Labour's natural constituency. They planned, therefore, to lay off Labour in public, putting the knife in only on the doorsteps where no one else could hear. In Greenwich the SDP, by contrast, did not have to worry about the sensibilities of Labour voters, many of whom were outraged both by Labour's policies and by the far-left candidate and were only too ready to vote SDP. Our problem was to convince Conservative voters to trust us and to believe that we had a chance to beat Labour.

Yet what I always tried to convince the Joint Leaders Advisory Committee was that if we wanted to play big league politics, we had to have a strategy which did not fundamentally differ whether we were fighting in Truro or Greenwich. The Alliance throughout its six-year life struggled to modify the old Liberal tactic of letting different constituencies have completely different strategies. Every party shifts the emphasis but serious parties do not switch the policies. The SDP as a partner with the Liberals did contribute more coherence in policy but the price was having to tone down policies that either SDP or Liberal activists wanted in full measure. Slowly, as we worked together and as those policies gelled, the parties might have come together. I was a sufficient realist by 1987 to know that the Alliance concept could not be unscrambled without paying a considerable price and that all we could hope was that what emerged had as much of the SDP in it as the voters wanted. In fairness to the Liberal Democrats under Paddy Ashdown, Charles Kennedy, Ming Campbell and most recently Nick Clegg, they have become more disciplined and less anarchic, reflected in a creditable increase in the number of MPs. A lot will depend for the intro-duction of proportional representation on how well the Liberal Democrats do in the next election, due before June 2010, and whether they can force a referendum.

Two by-election polls were conducted by BBC2's *Newsnight* pro-gramme at the start of February 1987. The poll in Greenwich gave Labour 48 per cent (up 10 per cent since 1983), the Conservatives 26 per cent (down 9 per cent) and the SDP 24 per cent (down 1 per cent). The one in Truro gave the Liberals 55 per cent (down 2 per cent since 1983), the Conservatives 32 per cent (down 6 per cent) and Labour 12 per cent (up 8 per cent). The tragic manner of David Penhaligon's death, in a road accident shortly before Christmas, meant that the sympathy vote would ensure that the Liberal candidate, Matthew Taylor, would hold Truro for the Alliance. If there was to be a surprise it could only be in Greenwich, where in Rosie Barnes we had chosen a charismatic, local and very determined campaigner. Building on John Cartwright's reputation in the neighbouring constituency, Woolwich, we had at last absolutely the right image for the SDP. John had represented Woolwich since 1974, when it was pronounced by Labour to be one of the safest seats in the country, winning by 12,425 votes. Self-taught after grammar school, he became leader of Greenwich Council and was agent to Christopher Mayhew, their former Labour MP, from whom he took over when Chris resigned to join the Liberal Party. John, an extremely tough political infighter, a fact belied by his rather slight, bespectacled appearance, had been on Labour's National Executive Committee for many years, standing for the Co-operative Party, and had been the scourge for years of Trotskyists and Labour infiltrators. He was an archetypal social democrat.

Rosie Barnes had never been a member of any other political party, though if anything she had been more sympathetic to Labour. She lived in the constituency and her children went to school there. Warm and friendly, it was not long before everyone was simply calling her Rosie. As a candidate her distinctive virtue was that at no time did she ever doubt that she was going to win, the advantage perhaps of being a political virgin but also the product of a self-assured, determined personality. We soon also found that Deirdre Wood's unpopularity locally was a key factor. Rosie's spectacular win was richly deserved. Not only did she have a majority of 6,500 but an exit poll had shown that she had a good chance of winning the seat in any subsequent general election. The SDP now had eight MPs.

By March, the Tories were moving ahead in the polls. Marplan still had the Alliance third but up at 27 per cent, with Labour slipping to 32 per cent and the Tories with an enhanced lead on 38 per cent. On 12 March, the Liberals held Truro with an increased majority.

Even their campaign managers had expected a slight dent in David Penhaligon's majority. With two victories the Alliance was feeling very confident.

So we proceeded in the build-up towards the general election, now only a matter of weeks away. My attention had been focusing on party political broadcasts for some time. We saw them as an important way of countering the BBC bias in reporting politics as if it were a mirror of the balance in the House of Commons. I had written one of my rare letters of actual complaint to Alistair Milne, the director general, when in January the BBC had given no coverage at all to our announcement of what was in effect an Alliance shadow Cabinet. The Alliance broadcast screened after our policy document launch in January had, I felt, been bland and boring, a real let-down since it was the first one done by our advertising agency. It was not even good technically, with very poor lighting. The agency had developed the theme of a seesaw to depict the Labour–Conservative alternation and the privatisation–nationalisation switchback, the classic plague-on-both-your-houses message. The SDP planned a controversial knocking piece against Labour. Unfortunately Labour got wind of what we were intending to say and we were taken to court in an attempt to stop our broadcast. On 1 April Mr Justice Drake decided that the SDP could go ahead with its party political broadcast. John Cleese's gag had pilloried Islington Council for accusing 'a five-year-old of reciting a racially offensive poem. You've got it – "Baa Baa, Black Sheep".' The council claimed in the High Court that it was not their policy to ban the rhyme, the teacher had only written that it had been identified as 'racially derogative' and was 'discouraged' by the council. The judge refused to grant an injunction banning the joke. He said there was evidence the SDP could justify its allegation. Nevertheless, because the child's mother specifically asked me not to broadcast that bit because she was unhappy about the effect of publicity on her child, I decided to cut it out, which angered the *Sun*. But the publicity certainly gave our party political broadcast a boost and served to remind people of how way out many Labour-controlled councils had become.

A general election is like a military campaign except that one knows in advance that after four weeks the exchanges will cease. It has a daily rhythm to it, actions are taken, reactions given, temporary advantages exploited and weaknesses buttressed. The leaders of the parties have to take the battle to the constituencies. This means criss-crossing the country to bolster the morale of the troops. Under the Representation of the People Act there is a statutory obligation on television and radio to be fair, and even the press feels obliged to project messages to the voters which their proprietors do not agree with. No party can buy TV advertising. Candidates can only spend up to a modest statutory limit in their constituencies and since 2000 there has been an overall limit on spending. Throughout the campaign almost every word a leader says is recorded and then examined; intonations, malapropisms, slips and mistakes are exploited and exaggerated. For a month a party leader lives like a goldfish in a bowl, with every movement watched, every statement weighed. Then suddenly, once the result is declared, the normal pattern of government and official opposition in the framework of the House of Commons returns, and the smaller parties are left sidelined and yet again subject to the distortion built into our first-past-the-post electoral system.

The Alliance was operating under severe constraints. All political parties fight elections under considerable constraints, but ours contributed to making us unelectable. The first constraint in 1987 was that the election had been called by the Conservatives at a point in their cynical pre-election economic boom when they were certain of victory. Inflation was down to 4 per cent. Interest rates were at 9 per cent and unemployment was falling. Nigel Lawson had matched the economic cycle to the electoral cycle with consummate skill. Voters, however, do not take kindly to Cassandra-like warnings. We found no resonance at all for arguments that the economic boom was not soundly based and that inflation would return. While the voters felt prosperous and wanted more prosperity, the Conservatives were bound to win. Yet the Alliance never felt able to admit that the Conservatives were going to win and that we were fighting at best for influence in a balanced Parliament. Instead we pretended that we were going to win.

The second constraint was that many felt we should give the illusion that our two parties were closer in policies and in attitudes than in fact they were; we never felt free to admit to policy differences and to present our Alliance only as a potential coalition. Instead we pretended we were already in effect a government with shared spokesmen and a single programme which just happened to have two leaders.

The third, totally self-imposed, constraint was that we were not free to say which party, Conservative or Labour, was our preferred coalition partner. We tried to hide the fact that the SDP would have preferred a coalition with the Conservatives, while the Liberals favoured Labour.

The fourth constraint reflected all the other constraints. Our manifesto in contriving to cover up all these differences was too bland. We could not openly endorse the social market, for Liberals felt that that positioned us too close to the Conservatives; we could not wholeheartedly support the British nuclear deterrent, for the Liberals were still deeply divided on this issue. Nor could we present Labour as totally unfit to govern, because that meant closing the option of being able to form a coalition with them. We could not choose because the Liberals did not want to choose. Yet most political parties fight elections under self-induced handicaps. Ours were just about manageable, but they contributed to making us unelectable. They were constraints that could be traced back to the Liberal assembly at Llandudno in 1981 and the flawed model for the Alliance that had been foisted on the SDP by an unelected steering committee and an unrepresentative political élite many of whom really wanted a single large third party from the outset. The grass-roots virgin politicians never had time to shape the party in ways they wanted.

On the Monday morning at our press conference in the basement of the National Liberal Club we launched our Alliance manifesto under the slogan 'Britain United'. It was well produced and aimed, as I explained in Cardiff that night, to 'reform, revive and rebuild a Britain efficient, caring, successful and united'. Good worthy stuff, but it was not dynamic or hard-hitting enough. It was the product of a committee. David and I had a photocall with our matching yellow campaign buses before leaving on the campaign trail. It all looked good, but that did not stop some of the press commenting that we were heading off in two different directions!

The press reporting for our manifesto was extensive. 'THE OTHER

VOICE OF RADICALISM' was the *Guardian* headline with 'RIGHT DOWN THE MIDDLE' in the *Financial Times* and 'LEAVING SOCIALISM?' in the *Times*. But some of our own confusions had been spotted. The *Guardian* concluded that 'the logic of the Alliance proposals is that they could more easily work with Labour than with the Conservatives. In German elections the Free Democrats always make a clear choice of this kind before the campaign rather than afterwards. The Alliance, too, should come off the fence.' Liberal Democrats need to reflect on this advice.

Our campaign was already far slicker and more professional than anything we had attempted in 1983. It needed to be, because the Labour campaign was transformed from Michael Foot's leadership days into one of the most polished campaigns ever waged by any party in Britain. Labour's problem was that their product did not have the necessary appeal, whatever the packaging. It was obvious that Labour were going to try and paint the Alliance, and me in particular, as Tories because we were ready to do a deal with Margaret Thatcher. For example, their attack on our manifesto focused on our readiness to privatise British Steel, a policy which immediately caused some Liberal candidates in Scotland to disavow our manifesto commitments. At the same time Norman Tebbit, in order to frighten off any weakly attached Conservatives from voting Alliance, bluntly ruled out negotiations after an election with any party and specifically with us. The Tory tactic was to present the Alliance as being as bad as Labour and, since they did not think this label would stick on me, to avoid criticising me unless I opened myself up for attack.

On Tuesday 19 May both the Conservative and Labour manifestos were published. The issue which seemed to me to offer the juiciest target was the Conservatives lumping the Alliance in with Labour, saying we favoured one-sided disarmament. They actually had the nerve to refer to us as taking the country 'down the same disastrous road as the Labour Party towards a frightened and fellow-travelling Britain'. 'Fellow-traveller' was a term that had gone rather out of fashion since Hugh Gaitskell had used it against people in the Labour Party who were far too close to the Communists, but its meaning was still clear enough. I denounced the Conservative manifesto for containing a 'foul smear' and wrote to Margaret Thatcher demanding a retraction, saying it brought dishonour on her office to campaign on such a deeply offensive charge. Raising defence at this point was not without calculation. It would be better for us to get our defence policy out of the way early for it was never going to be our best issue. From our own private information and contacts we knew the Tories intended to concentrate on Labour's defence policy towards the end. If we could establish an independent Alliance position early and dissuade the Conservatives from linking us with Labour, they might hesitate before pursuing this line later in the election. I hoped any fair-minded journalist would also see the Tory line as a smear, especially as the Tories proceeded to play the patriotic card again that night with a flag-waving election broadcast which virtually claimed that the country was only safe under Margaret Thatcher.

At our pre-press conference meeting on Wednesday none of the Liberals raised any objection to going for the Tories on defence and we agreed to devote Thursday's press conference to our own defence policy. At the press conference I said, 'It sticks in my gullet that there is this extraordinary belief that the Union Jack belongs to the Tory Party.' In London later that night I read our defence statement for the next day's press conference and it was excellent. But then, at the Thursday morning meeting before the conference, there was a Liberal outcry over the statement, with both Des Wilson and the Liberal national secretary in full cry. This was despite the fact that it had been agreed with Alan Beith. What they objected to was its detailed discussion of the possible options for replacing Polaris. As the argument went on and time was running out, I asked David Steel one simple question – could he live with it or not? He confessed worry, so we had no alternative. We could not issue it. Strangely those Liberals who were most anxious seemed quite happy for John Cartwright to speak the same words that were in the written statement. It was a sign of how divided we still really were on defence that they wanted nothing incriminating on paper, but nevertheless realised what was needed to satisfy the press. The press did not spot anything amiss and our attack on Margaret Thatcher was winning some plaudits. The *Independent* in an editorial, 'Nailing Mrs Thatcher's lie', said, 'For the Conservatives to attack an Alliance dominated by Dr David Owen as unilateralist is both inept and dishonest,' and went on to make the telling point that the Conservative Party ought not 'to declare itself in favour of One

Nation and then try to suggest that nobody but Conservatives can belong to that nation'. The press conference went well, John Cartwright being quite specific about possible nuclear replacements instead of Trident. I felt that now with a little luck we would not need to return to defence apart from swiping at the Labour Party. But the issue did not go away. That evening I did an interview for *This Week* in Liverpool and the Press Association report claimed that I had said that we would take advice from senior military figures about keeping a ballistic system, such as Trident. This was inaccurate. I had never used the words 'such as Trident', but that did not stop the BBC *Nine o'Clock News* repeating the words and suggesting that my readiness to keep Trident would divide our two parties. David flew back in my plane to London and when we were driving back into town in separate cars we were told by the campaign committee on our car radios that one of us should go on *Newsnight* to clear the matter up. We wound down our windows at the next lights and agreed that it would be better for David Steel to do it. It was a mischievous story which came back at our press conference on Friday. Fortunately I was able to show that I had not used the words on Trident and that we had actually referred to listening to advice on systems from the chiefs of staff in our defence statement published in November and again in January.

On the Friday morning there was an article by Matthew Symonds in the *Independent* following up their criticism of our manifesto as 'moderate *dirigisme*', under the headline 'Disappointing packaging buries the Alliance's ideals'. He said he could not find a single reference to the social market in the entire document. I did not fight to have the words 'social market' used in the document. It would have been pointless to try. We had decided to bring Roy Jenkins back as economics spokesman and to him the social market was a sub-Thatcherite term. Also, the Liberals saw the social market as Owenism. It was far wiser for Ian Wrigglesworth on the drafting committee to concentrate on establishing market principles and competition rather than forcing the term 'social market', which had become an anathema to Liberals. But the *Independent* was important to us in shaping the attitudes of what I called 'the thinking voter', and by being too bland we lost the chance to appeal to those who wanted a counter-revolution.

The following Tuesday David Steel and I had a live interview with Sir Robin Day on *Panorama* with an estimated audience of 4.7 million. No one watching could have failed to notice that we had very different attitudes to the Labour Party's defence policy: for me it was the disqualifying factor for being the government, for David it was one very good issue to measure Labour by, no more and no less. After the programme I took Polly Toynbee, Maggie Smart and Sue Robertson to dinner. Polly, her journalist's antennae ever alert, thought what I had said would be damaging and picked up in the press as a split. I was not so sure about the damage. I was more concerned about the millions watching than any press comment. The viewer knew and was meant to know that defence was my sticking point. It was neither a gaffe nor an indiscretion. My fear was that we would not gain the votes of disillusioned Conservatives if they felt that we in the Alliance did not have a sticking point on defence. And it was not just Conservatives either. The Liberals never understood how many working-class voters were antagonised by Labour's defence policy. They were hardly likely to turn to us if they did not perceive us as totally unequivocal. Watching *Panorama* were millions more people than would ever read what the press said next day. What was important was that they realised that voting Alliance was not letting Labour and unilateralism in by the back door.

In many ways the rest of the campaign hinged on this question of attitudes to the Conservatives and Labour. Since David Steel could not convincingly give the impression that he could work with a Thatcher-led government, he did not want to talk about a coalition. The journalists following us around, travelling in my bus and comparing notes on their mobile phones with colleagues in David's bus, were bound to exploit this. The truth is that David was fairly reflecting the views of his party and I of mine. Those who wanted us to say the same thing were not recognising that this was why we were two parties. It is like wanting the best of someone's personality while losing the worst parts. People are all of a piece and have to be taken with their strengths and their weaknesses. So are parties. When the Alliance tried to pretend we were one party it was presented as a fraud. When we were relaxed about being two parties and being honestly divided on some issues, it was a split. Selling the Alliance for what it was, a coalition, would have been a far better strategy.

The evidence was very clear in private and in publicised polls that if people believed that the Alliance would hold the balance they would vote for us in almost as many numbers as if they thought we could win. It was if they thought we would win only a few seats that our vote plummeted. Since 1983 the number of people believing we could hold the balance had increased and always more were prepared to believe we could hold the balance than said they would vote for us.

We held our last rally in Central Hall, Westminster on Tuesday evening. I stuck to my theme that people voted for the Conservatives out of fear, not out of enthusiasm. They were afraid of what Labour would do.

> Use your heads and your hearts; you can have the sound market economy, conventional and nuclear deterrence, the responsible trade unionism that your head tells you that Britain needs. You can have people back in work, with every pensioner enjoying a decent retirement, all our children fulfilling their potential, and with no one waiting years in pain for a routine operation, that your heart tells you Britain needs. You don't have to make the impossible choice. You don't have to cut yourself in two – half head, half heart.

Next morning we had our last press conference and I left for Plymouth. There had been a number of press articles writing my and the SDP's epitaph. Perhaps the most thoughtful was written by Matthew Symonds in the *Independent* under the title 'The political tragedy that may lie in wait for David Owen'. In it he said:

> The prospects for Dr Owen are really rather bleak. There will be renewed and possibly irresistible pressure on him to acquiesce in the merger of the SDP with the Liberals – an outcome which he has with good reason bitterly resisted hitherto. But infinitely more serious for Dr Owen is the likelihood that history and the course of events will no longer be seen to be on his side. If the Labour Party loses this election respectably (that means taking about a third of the popular vote and more than 250 seats) it is in business. During the next five years the purge of the hard left will continue, the policies – including defence – both fudged and brought up to date and the grip of the yuppie apparatchiks around the leader strengthened.

He went on to argue that old-style Liberal opportunism, which might result in the occasional by-election spectacular, was hardly mould-shattering and no strategy:

> A hand-to-mouth existence of this kind may not appal, may even appeal to, many Liberals, but to the SDP, and to Dr Owen in particular, it would be a kind of living death. The gamble, which began in 1981, would have failed. Under such circumstances Dr Owen may well not wish to stay in politics. The effort of leading a small, underresourced party in our political system is almost unimaginable.

I too was beginning to ponder what would happen after the election. I knew the merger battle would break out and that I would not wish to be part of a merged party. Nothing that had happened since 1981 nor in the month of this election campaign could convince me that I should try or could successfully live within a party made up predominantly of Liberals. Quite definitely, if elected as a Social Democrat for Devonport, I would stay for the lifetime of the next parliament. That was a judgement made not in anger or in frustration but from my heart. I was not and never have been a British Liberal. I had no serious complaints about David Steel or the Liberal Party's conduct in the campaign. They were what they were. Yes, there were differences but they were honourable, political differences and we had accommodated each other and each other's parties with a considerable amount of give and take. I had then and more than thirty years later have no wish now to make anyone a scapegoat for our election defeat.

The Conservatives won 372 seats, Labour 229; the SDP dropped from eight to five MPs. John Cartwright and Rosie Barnes had, to my immense relief, held their adjoining seats in Woolwich and Greenwich; Bob Maclennan and Charles Kennedy had, as I expected, held their adjoining seats in Caithness & Sutherland and Ross, Cromarty & Skye. Roy Jenkins had, as I feared, lost Glasgow Hillhead by 3,251 votes. Mike Hancock narrowly lost in Portsmouth South by 205 votes, Ian Wrigglesworth in Stockton South by 774 votes. Shirley Williams had predictably failed to win Cambridge and had lost by 5,060 votes. Also Bill Rodgers had failed to win Milton

Keynes by 13,701 votes. The Alliance's percentage share of the vote was down, but not by much: we had polled 25.4 per cent in 1983 and now in 1987 the figure was 22.6 per cent, higher than the Liberals had polled since the 1930s.

Like a general who has lost a battle, a political leader who has lost a general election either retires, is ousted or fights back. My firm belief was that, since Labour was still not fit to govern, the SDP still had a role to play. Only if Labour could become the government of the country without my losing sleep would I hang up my boots. Until that happened I would stay a Social Democrat, join no other party and fight for social democracy.

Up most of the night coping with the fallout of electoral defeat, I would have preferred to have had a few days' peace and quiet before considering what should be done about the Alliance. But there was no escaping the press – there they all were in the foyer of my Plymouth hotel on the morning of Friday 12 June waiting to pounce. We had travelled many miles together on the campaign and press relations had been excellent. I think they, like my team, had enjoyed the last month but they had a job to do and sympathy is not the journalist's stock in trade. So at the informal press conference the inevitable questions about merger began. Whether to merge, I said, was a 'legitimate question'. But within the SDP

> the endless examining of our own navels on whether or not we should exist is probably one of our greatest weaknesses. I have never doubted that we should exist. I know we needed a fourth party, and I think everything that has happened since then has justified the decision. I am sticking to what I have always said. The partnership is of two parties and two strands of British politics – social democracy and liberalism. I will stay as SDP leader as long as the SDP exists and they want me to stay as their leader.

I said the issue of merger, if people wished, would 'go to the membership, because we have within our constitution provision for a one member, one vote democracy'. It seemed to me that many in the SDP would wish to merge and I wanted them to do so with goodwill on all sides. I had no desire to prevent them, believing they had the right to unite with the Liberals if that was what they wanted. But, that morning on Plymouth Hoe, I never envisaged that any Social Democrat would try to stop me staying as the SDP MP for Devonport. I was soon to realise that was exactly what they were planning – it was not enough for them to join up with the Liberals themselves; they also wanted to liquidate the SDP and make any of us who wished to remain in it illegitimate and without a party. The enormity of the proposition that those of us who had been elected should be deprived of the right to continue as Social Democrats in the party we loved was never sufficiently appreciated by political commentators, nor initially by us.

My task as leader was to devise a mechanism, if possible, for everyone to respect the other's viewpoint. I was not going to use tricks to suppress open debate; this would be pointless. In the early years I felt it had been right to resist merger and I had succeeded in doing so. After two general elections and much experience of merged parties locally it was inevitable that those who wanted to 'unite' with the Liberals should be allowed to do so; equally that others should be free to continue with a Social Democratic Party. It was not 'losing' or 'winning' a merger ballot so much as upholding the rights of all individuals in the party that concerned me. I did not want to keep anyone in the SDP who wanted to join with the Liberals.

On Wednesday 17 June, after the House had met to elect a Speaker, the SDP parliamentary committee met for the first time since the election. All five MPs were present, as were Jack Diamond, leader of the SDP peers, Alastair Kilmarnock, chief whip in the Lords, and Sue Robertson, secretary to the committee. They unanimously re-elected me as leader. I then put to them a draft resolution for the national committee which I had considered from every possible angle. Having concluded reluctantly and sadly that there was no possible way of keeping the SDP together, I recommended to my parliamentary colleagues that we embark openly on an amicable divorce.

I had often observed that the most certain recipe for maximum ill will and minimum mutual respect when a marriage broke down was to bring in the lawyers. I felt we could use our one member, one vote ballot system to enable individual members to choose their own course and also allow for a collective negotiation with the Liberals on behalf of those who were certain that they wanted a merger. I suggested a way in which this could be done while keeping open every party member's option to make their own final choices when they saw the result of the negotiations with the Liberal Party. The assets of the party could then be split to reflect the balance of the members' choice. The key passages in my resolution were:

> Do you want your membership registration to remain with the SDP as a separate party?                                    YES / NO

> Do you want your membership registration to be transferred to an SDP group who will go into negotiation with the Liberal Party with the aim of forming a merged party?                          YES / NO

Unfortunately, at that meeting, I completely failed to convince any of my colleagues that a split in the SDP was inevitable. None of them showed any interest or put forward any arguments for merging, and they could not accept the inevitability of a split. I, who knew the party very well by virtue of being its leader and travelling more than anyone else, was convinced that the grass roots were deeply and irretrievably divided. Things could not stay as they were, a parting of ways was inevitable. But the parliamentarians just could not face that horror. No one, not even Charles Kennedy, expressed the slightest qualification about their opposition to merger and determination to remain members of the SDP. Jack Diamond, the oldest and most experienced person in the room, an old Treasury colleague of Roy Jenkins who had played a key role in the 1983 campaign, was resolutely opposed to a merger, but even he could not reconcile himself to a split. Bob Maclennan had not changed his mind in any way since we had met in Buttermere on Sunday and was still against a merger, but he thought I was overreacting and believed that a large majority of the party would want to stay separate but in a deeper Alliance. If anything, he was now even more determined and adamant that we should end the system of Alliance spokesmen. John Cartwright was not ready to accept a split either and all his old reflexes as a party agent were for a compromise solution to maintain the unity of the SDP. Rosie Barnes was for staying together within the SDP but felt we should concede a single leader for the Alliance before the next election.

They all felt I was being far too fatalistic about a split and they wanted to find a compromise along the lines of one of David Steel's options which he had already announced: the growing-together option, in effect a halfway house. Even when I pointed out that David was already showing every sign of going back on this option of growing together, they believed we could still persuade people that this was the wisest course. I tried to explain the passions and the jealousies that had been bottled up for years over this issue but they had not had the same experience of those tensions. They had not felt as I had the personal trauma surrounding the disintegration of the Gang of Four. Even these people, close to the top of the party as they were, did not understand the vehemence with which Roy Jenkins wanted to merge and how completely Bill and Shirley had now swung to his side.

I drew their attention to an article in the *Guardian* that morning by Richard Holme, whose views tended to be identical with David Steel's. It said that the options for the SDP and the Liberal Party were stark – to fight or unite. I failed to convince my parliamentary colleagues of the need for an amicable separation and agreed instead that Bob Maclennan should be charged with trying to produce a resolution for the national committee which would build on the option of growing together. My fellow parliamentarians had not convinced me that this was a viable option but since I had not convinced them either I felt I had no alternative but to go along with their views.

Among the activists in my own constituency there was no enthusiasm at all for becoming, effectively, Liberals and fury that our own victory should have been blighted within hours by a controversy which they saw as a supreme irrelevance. We had had less than a handful of Liberal councillors in Plymouth since the war. The Liberals had been a negligible force in the city, despite being reasonably strong in the West Country. Our SDP councillors did not believe they could win their seats if we were merged with the Liberals and many questioned whether I could hold my own seat if we lost our independence. As in other parts of the country, some started to drift away.

Time and time again, from those activists up and down the country who were closest to me came the comment 'If I had wanted to join the Liberals I would have done it in—' and then they would add the particular year when their frustration with the Labour or Conservative Party had come to a head, the moment when they had wanted an alternative but had not seen it in the Liberals. Some people's memories went back to 1959 and the Clause IV argument inside the Labour Party. Some went back to 1981 and their anger at massive and growing unemployment because of Conservative incompetence and insensitivity. For many people who had belonged to no other party the SDP had fulfilled their hopes, even their dreams. Their commitment was not transferable. They would refuse to follow me into the Liberal Party.

I had over the previous six days really tried to think afresh and consider whether it was not a moment to cut my losses and accept merger as inevitable. The pitfall I had to avoid was being stuck in a predestined groove, feeling that because I had been against merger from 1981 to 1987 I must inevitably continue to oppose it. I examined carefully whether it was possible for me to do a reverse takeover, to join a Liberal-dominated party and turn it into an SDP Mark II. But my power base was far weaker than in 1983. Then I had been the new leader coming in to replace the *ancien régime*, now I was associated with a disappointing election result. In addition, of course, I would be fighting all these battles without the help of some of those who had sustained me in the past and surrounded almost solely by those who had resisted every policy move I had made. No one can lead any organisation for long if he or she is too distant from its centre of gravity, and a merged party's centre of gravity would be far away from where my instincts lay. No doubt I could have initially held the line on policy, including the nuclear deterrent, but it would have been a constant battle, and again and again I asked myself: whom would I be able to rely on?

I do not believe that time has invalidated this analysis. It is true that under Paddy Ashdown and his successors the Liberal Democrats came to accept the nuclear deterrent. But it was only after Neil Kinnock changed Labour's policy that the Liberal Democrats shifted theirs and accepted while the Soviet Union/Russian Federation had nuclear weapons it was in the European interest for France and Britain to maintain a minimum nuclear deterrent. Another crucial issue was Europe. Those who argue that I should have fought to become leader of a merged party must consider what would have happened when the most important issue – moves towards European federalism – hit the headlines in 1991. The vast majority of Liberal Democrats have championed every step towards greater European integration since being formed in 1988. It would have been impossible for me to lead them away from federalism. I doubt it would have been right to even try, for it is a good thing that there is one party that is for a Federal Europe. They only accepted a referendum on the euro out of electoral expediency in 1999 and because Labour went along with the Conservatives. There were also problems over the Liberal Democrats' readiness to champion the market economy. This was not a pedantic matter of their refusal to use the term 'social market'. It was simply that they were not enthusiasts for the market idea and they sniped constantly at New Labour's enthusiasm for market solutions. Yet under Vince Cable Liberal Democrat economic policy became very much more realistic and he personally won a great deal of respect during the 2007 financial crisis. Nick Clegg and Chris Huhne are also realists about market economics.

My analysis of what the SDP was created for has never changed from 1981 to 2009: it remains that a soft liberal centre is insufficient to break through to proportional representation on its own; it needs to be broadened and strengthened by the development of a hard centre, and that this was easier to do in the 1980s and better maintained if one could form a centre coalition between two parties. The SDP was destined to be the hard centre. What of the Liberal Democrats? I believe that former SDP members have stiffened the policies of the Liberal Party and have widened its appeal. But it has taken time: one of today's stars of the Liberal Democrats, Vince Cable, came from Labour and then the SDP. A continuation of the SDP as a national party from 1987 to 1990, I believe, toughened the emerging policies of the Liberal Democrats and helped force the pace of Labour Party reforms. The question which may not be answered by the election due by June 2010 or for some years afterwards is whether the Liberal Democrats will become a party of government or slip back into being the predominantly soft centre party the Liberals had been since Lloyd George lost power in 1922.

Charles Kennedy showed courage in leading the Liberal Democrats in principle against the Iraq War and, although I personally did not agree with that stance, it was necessary for it to be represented sensibly in Parliament. Nick Clegg seems to have a greater understanding of the market economy than any Liberal leader since Jo Grimond and that is a huge advance. He also seems readier to contemplate dealing with the Conservatives than anyone since Grimond. I hope that the Liberal Democrats will by 2010 be part of the government of the country, what I hoped might have happened after the elections of 1992 and 2005, but it was not to be. To do so they must be prepared to negotiate with whichever party, Labour or Conservative, has the most MPs. In that way, as is proper in a democracy, the smaller party is seen to respect the choice of the voters. It does not exclude indicating a preference.

Some Liberal MPs in 1987 were very keen for me to be the leader of a merged party and came to persuade me. I could rely on the votes of many SDP members and, surprisingly, on a substantial number of Liberal activists. Possibly this would have been sufficient to make me leader, even against David Steel. But I also knew that too many of those people, particularly some who wrote in to urge me to head up the merger, would not stand firm in the policy disputes that take place in any party and would be inevitable in the merged party. Rightly or wrongly, I was by then a red rag to many active Liberals and some SDP members, particularly the London-based intelligentsia. Some of those urging me publicly to join and even saying they would vote for me as leader would, I knew, exact a price for their support. They wanted me leader for electoral reasons because they thought I would attract votes, but they would try to make me their prisoner on policy. I could see a miserable marriage ahead, flawed from the start and bound to end in tears. I had not left the Labour Party to end up in the Liberal Party. Nor had I lost hope that the Labour Party could be reformed. Ever since Neil Kinnock started to deal with Militant it was my belief he would eventually move on policy. Meanwhile people I respected and loved, such as my wife, like many in the SDP a party political virgin, were persuading me that the SDP must try and survive. As the Labour Party remained unfit to govern there was a case for keeping the SDP, as long as we were realistic about our own chances of surviving. But I knew that if Labour genuinely moved onto SDP ground we would die. Debbie and others close to me argued that it was my responsibility in this case to die with the SDP and that I was not entitled to pre-empt the outcome by upping sticks and leaving the party while many of its members were still ready to fight.

On Monday 29 June the *Independent*, which had become at times the house journal of the SDP, said in an editorial headlined 'In defence of the Doctor':

> It is fashionable to accuse the ambitious Dr Owen of attempting to rig the projected referendum, of trying to blackmail his colleagues, of demanding a veto over the policies of a democratic party and of acting as a little Napoleon on St Helena, divorced from all reality. He, it is said, has brought his party and the Alliance to an appalling pass. (These are only a few of the more printable remarks passed in public by those who fought the general election as Dr Owen's allies and apparent friends.) Such accusations are wrong.
>
> The immediate crisis in the Alliance was precipitated, quite deliberately, by David Steel in the immediate aftermath of the election. With the support of Roy Jenkins, he attempted to bounce the SDP when the younger party looked at its most vulnerable. They reckoned without the determination of Dr Owen and the unity of the other four SDP members of Parliament. These will, if pushed hard, declare UDI rather than be swallowed up by the Liberal Party.

Sadly this 'unity of the other four SDP members of Parliament' was to be shattered. In the national committee that same day Bob Maclennan had drafted a resolution for a 'federal solution' – a single leader, joint policy formation and some joint selection of candidates. Although the national committee voted by eighteen votes to thirteen in its favour, Charles Kennedy voted against the resolution, which he had helped to draft. Bob, who was closest to Charles, was apoplectic with rage and felt he had been betrayed, even saying 'Judas' to describe Charles's conduct. Oddly, as things turned out, John, Rosie and I were rather more understanding. Charles was young and had been showing signs of strain and, we later learned, was under great pressure from, among others, Roy Jenkins, with whom he had shared an office in the House of Commons for the last four years. The Ross, Cromarty & Skye constituency was essentially a Liberal one and many of the Liberals there felt it had been loaned to the SDP in 1983. He had already faced criticism from his Liberal activists, unhappy at the prospect of his staying in the SDP, and someone close to him told me it was a decision forced on him, not one he would have chosen. Though I was deeply disappointed and surprised, I did not feel bitter then, despite contrary reports, or since, about his change of mind. These were harsh choices for everyone. I did, however, realise that Charles's decision would do great damage to our chances of winning the membership ballot for the so-called federal solution, for now the parliamentary party was divided.

On 9 July David Sainsbury and Leslie Murphy, the two trustees of the party, wrote an article for the *Times*, explaining why they would not join a merged party, under the title 'This murder of ideals by merger':

> Political parties are not companies. They depend totally on the enthusiasm of their members, and their destinies cannot be settled, therefore, by simple majority votes. The merger should, therefore, take place only if there is an overwhelming vote in favour. It is nonsense for anyone to propose to have a ballot on a merger when the leader of the party, and majorities of the national committee and the MPs, have declared themselves against it. Unless, that is, they want to destroy the party.

These two most influential and independent members of the party, who had been towers of strength, then went on to say what should probably have been said to party members many years before. They exposed what Roy Jenkins had been up to:

> From the beginning the SDP was seen by some members of the Gang of Four as simply a device to get people out of the Labour Party. They thought, therefore, that as soon as possible it should be merged with the Liberal Party. This view, which was no doubt a careful political decision at the beginning, has become an article of faith, if not an obsession.

That obsession was now set not just to destroy the SDP and the Alliance but to do considerable damage to the Liberal Party itself. Everything I feared and anticipated in my original amicable separation resolution occurred. Civil war broke out. It was reminiscent of those internal battles of the Labour Party, which had occupied so many years of my life, and it was heart-rending to endure them in the SDP. Whether politics has some unique quality which fosters such behaviour I do not know; perhaps it is just that the clashes are more obvious because politicians are so exposed to scrutiny.

On 6 August the ballot showed that 25,897 votes (57.4 per cent) were in favour of opening negotiations to merge and those who voted not to merge and for the federal option numbered 19,229 (42.6 per cent). This meant that merger negotiations would be opened and that the results would be put first to next year's CSD in Sheffield and then to another members' ballot. Once through these hoops, merger would be complete. In honour I now had no option other than to resign. I could not remain leader for I had no intention of participating in the merged party, regardless of the outcome of the negotiations, and had decided, whatever happened, to continue as the Social Democratic Member of Parliament for Devonport, at least until the next general election.

When the ballot result was announced I took the result through to my office where other national committee members were waiting. After I had given them the news, I handed each a copy of my resignation statement. Rosie Barnes immediately wrung from me a pledge to speak at a fringe meeting at the forthcoming Portsmouth conference, where we had agreed we would launch the Campaign for Social Democracy. Since she was being so understanding about my resignation, I had little alternative but to agree. Until that moment I had made not the slightest personal commitment to a continuing SDP and I did not in my heart believe it was viable. But by agreeing to address this meeting, I left the door ajar and gave the grass-roots movement their opportunity, which they took, to push it open.

One thing I made quite clear was that I would not be party to any campaign if it sought to use the constitution, as it was still possible to do, to block those members of the party who wished to merge with the Liberals. As far as I was concerned I was not going to participate in anything to do with a merger, neither the negotiations nor the ballot after the negotiations. I wanted the merger to take place as soon as possible and, until then, I would take a back seat and enjoy myself, go to the theatre, read novels and poetry and see more of Debbie and the children. For fourteen years I had been working flat out full time in politics, since starting on the private member's Children's Bill in November 1973, through government and opposition, and now I felt like a break. If the grass-roots movement mobilised enough members for a continuing SDP I would consider that possibility and, if persuaded, campaign positively for it. I hoped we could restore a working relationship with the merged party, but blocking a merger was not for me. I held to that conviction with a tenacity that infuriated some of my closest friends. When the debacle over the Steel/Maclennan policy document took place in 1988, they begged me to mobilise against the merger and organise, as was certainly possible, for a third of the conference members at the Sheffield Council for Social Democracy to vote against the merger. This would have been enough to block it. But what would that have left us with? I felt that 1987 was the time to allow individuals to go their own way. I thereafter refused point blank to shift from what I considered was a principled position of non-participation.

'A defeat for the radical centre' was how the *Independent* in an editorial summed up the SDP ballot.

> The soft centre of British politics yesterday won a victory . . . Dr Owen's central insight is that policy matters. He is not good at building up a party organisation, it does not much interest him. Nor does he have the emollient manner which helps to smooth over differences of opinion among members of a party or coalition. He is not a diplomat, and his tactical judgement is questionable. But he has the ear of the House of Commons, which David Steel does not. Dr Owen's straightforward manner, his wide knowledge of government and his wry sense of humour also make him a formidable performer on television. Above all, he is deeply interested in what a political party says, not just how it looks.

The *Guardian* had a perceptive article by John Carvel, 'A journey into darkness', which posed the question of whether I would become the Enoch Powell of the 1990s. 'It is a common criticism of politicians that they are too ready to abandon principle to achieve compromise and maximise their power. Dr Owen shows what happens when people get the alternative sort of politician they ask for but may not actually want.'

The critics of my decision not to join the merged party have always had difficulty in squaring my alleged consuming ambition with my turning down the opportunity to lead the merged party. They find it very hard to understand that politics is not and never has been my whole life. I do not regard politics as a profession but as a transitory occupation. One can be voted in or out with no presumption that a political career is permanent. Perhaps this attitude was inculcated early because my Plymouth seat was so marginal at first, or because my victory in 1966 so surprised me. Maybe medicine remained my first love. Whatever the reason, I viewed the prospect of no longer being in politics with equanimity.

The Portsmouth conference followed soon afterwards. It was a sad affair. By agreement I spoke in the debate on the general election. The scene was described by Mark Lawson in the *Independent*:

> No doctor could close the gashes of the SDP but Dr Owen yesterday achieved something closer to faith healing than you could reasonably have expected.
>
> At 3.15 p.m., he sat slumped on the second row of the conference rostrum – the man now uniformly called tragic by ex-colleagues, a victim of political self-destruction. At 5.15 p.m., he was ducking under cheers, shutters clicking like crickets, even hands dabbing at eyes.
>
> What is to be made of these scenes? There was no hope of uniting the party but a different speech might have ignited the rankle and backstabbing.
>
> The best you could say by last night was that half the party was at peace with itself and so was the other half. Dr Owen had managed a significant amendment to the emotions of the conference.
>
> Its success was its unexpectedness. The media hordes had come to Portsmouth to watch the sensible party going barmy. In a tetchy conference, even conference chairperson Shirley Williams was moved to snap that 'even a confused mind could grasp that point'. It looked petty and messy, the dregs of social democracy. Delegates bickered that general election defeats end in the generals blaming their unelected troops.
>
> What could Dr Owen do? It was some minutes before he could

speak. 'This is one general who will not blame the poor bloody infantry,' he began.

He told them that, whatever happened now, the past six years had mattered; that social democracy was a child too young to die. Telling them what a swell party it had been touched something in both sects – whether sadness at their loss or a belief in his career to come.

A party alarmed by the prospect of a conference with no leader now had two on the platform. The real one had stood up and they returned the compliment. If he is headed for the wilderness he will hold there a searing memory of what could have been.

After my speech to the conference was over, in the privacy of my room my emotions got the better of me and for the first time I wept. The trigger was a chance remark recalling how Mary Lake with tears in her eyes, during our so-called victory celebration at Devonport, had said, 'How could they do this to us, David? How could Shirley, above everyone, do this?' Mary had been in the Labour Party with me, and had left with me. She had championed the SDP in the teeth of intense hostility from other members of the Labour Party in the early years on her council estate in St Budeaux. She had always adored Shirley Williams, in part because they were both Catholics, but in the main because she believed in her and thought Shirley shared her views about what the SDP was created to do. All she could repeat was, 'Why are they taking our party away from us?' Cynics may scoff, but these feelings are what drive a political party. Declaring oneself as a member of the SDP in a solid Labour ward in Devonport in the early years was not an easy thing to do. John Cartwright had experienced very much the same reaction among his party activists in Woolwich. They had put up with vilification and abuse for six years to find their own party about to be torn from them. It was significant that it was the three SDP MPs whose constituencies would normally be strongly Labour who were the ones who wanted to stay with the SDP. We were not political innocents. We knew exactly what we were doing, what risks we were taking and why we were undertaking them. If the Labour Party were to become a social democratic party then my mission would be complete, but until it did I felt happier remaining in the House of Commons as a Social Democrat, for the next four years at least. I also felt it would give me as good, if not a better, chance of being re-elected member of Parliament for Devonport if I remained a Social Democrat. One change of party had been enough for me, I did not want to join a new party. As John Cartwright expressed it to the conference, 'No ballot gives anybody the right to tell me which political party I should be a member of. Those who take my view are not just numbers on a computer. We are flesh and blood human beings and our position will not be altered by threats to run candidates against us.'

There was one headline I could have done without. 'From one-man band to megalomaniac' was the title over Peter Jenkins's column in the *Independent*. Peter was a longstanding friend and we had managed that difficult relationship between journalist and politician remarkably well. His problem and mine was that his wife, Polly Toynbee, had become increasingly committed to the SDP. While Polly was writing, mainly but not exclusively, on women's issues in the *Guardian*, she was not encroaching on Peter's political turf. But more recently her involvement had become a complicating factor, for Polly, with her outstanding ability, had become an influential voice on the SDP national committee. The problem came to a head with my invitation to her to serve on the Alliance Planning Group before and during the election. Then her identification with the 'Vote for the SDP' campaign had meant that Peter was in danger of being sucked into and identified with a cause to which he was profoundly opposed. In his column Peter said:

> Dr Owen has no title to the SDP. The result of the ballot cannot reasonably be construed as a vote for 'amicable separation'. SDP members were asked whether they favoured the idea of merger or not and a majority said they did. They were not asked if they would support Dr Owen splitting the party to set up one of his own.
>
> He hasn't a leg to stand on in his bunker. But there he is, surrounded by a last ditch entourage, inventing new schemes for the confounding of his enemies and moving imaginary armies on the map. The bitterness of defeat seems to have got the better of his judgement. The virtuoso one-man band performance which in the last parliament made him the most impressive politician in the country after Margaret Thatcher has degenerated into a display of megalomania.
>
> It happens that I agree with Dr Owen about nuclear weapons and

on other matters. I share his low opinion of the Liberal Party. But the politics of sectarian fantasy are even less attractive. There are – or rather, were – 23 per cent of the people who wish to vote for a third party. They should be allowed the best possible opportunity to do so.

Peter Jenkins had a powerful case and friendship should not have stopped him putting it. Yet in important respects he was wrong. Above all, it was not a 'third' party but an alliance of two parties for which that 23 per cent had voted. That is not a quibble or a pedantic point but a key fact. If David Steel had been leading the Liberal Party on its own in that election with no SDP I doubt if they would have polled as high as the 19 per cent they had achieved in February 1974. Polly knew better than most how little bitterness I felt at many going off to merge – resigned regret would be closer to my mood – and far from wanting to continue the SDP as a national party, I was one of its most reluctant recruits and even at this stage had not accepted it could be viable. As to Peter's motives, I knew he was finding that his journalistic access to leading figures in the pro-merger part of the SDP and in the Liberal Party was suffering. He was being seen, quite wrongly, as a partisan figure. Although he wished me well personally, his practical judgement was that the course I had chosen could not succeed. His own new paper, the *Independent*, was editorially against the merger and sympathetic to my plight. I could well understand how Peter began to feel fenced in and why he decided to establish his independence both from Polly and from me in such a dramatic way. It led to some stimulating encounters. On breakfast television Polly was asked how she could associate with the man her husband thought was a megalomaniac. She carried it off with a smile. I shrugged my shoulders and refused to be drawn when asked by Peter's fellow journalists what I thought. Inwardly I was of course hurt, but there has never been a friendship without pain. In generous letters we each moved towards the other's position. Fortunately, Polly was soon offered an excellent job as the social affairs editor for all BBC News programmes. This meant she had to give up party politics and made it much easier for both families to resume normal relations.

Although my decision not to join the new party was immutable, there still remained the question as to what I should do. There were many who argued that I should be an independent MP, a lone voice divorced from party, an Enoch warning in the wilderness. But for everyone who argued this course there were others warning against the danger of being without a party, however small; that the House of Commons eats up individuals but could not totally dismiss a party. I read everything I could about the life of David Lloyd George following his electoral defeat in 1922. I learnt about Winston Churchill's 'black dog' days when depression and despair blighted his life, how Baldwin had been able to dismiss him even in 1937 as a 'beached whale stranded on the shore'. John Grigg, Lloyd George's biographer, urged me to join and lead the merged party, and offered no comfort from Lloyd George's history. At the same time Julian Amery advised me of the vital need to secure funds and how Lloyd George's Fund had been the *sine qua non* of his influence in the 1920s and 1930s and how Joseph Chamberlain had needed the small party that he had.

Meanwhile all I could do was wait – wait until the negotiations were over, wait and see whether we could build up the Campaign for Social Democracy. We left Portsmouth bloodied but unbowed but the damaging Owenite label had been firmly fixed around our neck by the BBC and purportedly objective commentators, as well as by those who wished us ill. It was only a matter of weeks before Bill Rodgers quit party politics for a full-time job. Shirley Williams married an American professor and left Britain to live in the United States. She, however, generously invited all sides of the merger dispute to her wedding and it was an enjoyable occasion. But even Shirley's nearest and dearest were divided: her mother's old secretary, an active SDP supporter, decided to stick with us and refused to merge. It was like civil war – the merger divided families, damaged friendships, all in support of the politics of winner takes all, which we were supposed to despise. Negotiations then took place for some months among those who wanted to merge. I was not a participant in these negotiations.

The SDP ballot result was announced on 2 March 1988. Only 18,722 members had voted 'Yes', less than one-third of the SDP membership, which in July 1987 had been 58,357. The merger-or-bust campaign had alienated over two-thirds of the members. Despite our repeated urging of people intending to stay with the

SDP not to vote 'No' in the ballot, some had done so. It was hard to be sure what was the exact split in the 1987 membership. It had certainly gone three ways with the largest number, slightly more than one-third, being so disenchanted with the whole post-election fracas that they no longer wished to be involved. A little less than one-third had voted for the merger and are assumed to have joined the Social and Liberal Democrats, as the merged party was for a short time called. We were claiming at the time that the Campaign for Social Democracy had around 30,000 supporters and, allowing for 15 per cent slippage, that we could be sure of having 25,500 committed members. Some of those had joined without previously having been members of the SDP. Our claim was based on a computer printout which we invited the press to examine at our headquarters. Adam Raphael of BBC *Newsnight*, perhaps the most sceptical of our claim, had taken up our invitation and checked out some of the names, apparently discovering nothing wrong. His scepticism was correct, however, as we discovered a year later for we never had the numbers we thought we had.

So, the merger went ahead and the SDP was re-established on 8 March 1988 as Britain's fourth national political party. Three of the five SDP MPs elected in 1987 continued to take the party whip in the House of Commons, twenty-three out of forty SDP peers continued to take the whip in the House of Lords.

In July the new SDP managed to put in a reasonable effort in the Kensington by-election but we suffered from a shortage of canvassers and it was a struggle to match the effort put in by the Social and Liberal Democrats. Their candidate, William Goodhart QC, had previously fought the seat for the SDP in 1987 and had been a fellow member, with John Martin, our candidate, of the SDP area party. The Conservatives just scraped home with a much reduced majority of only 815 votes. We managed to save our deposit with 1,190 votes and the Social and Liberal Democrats came a poor third with 2,546 votes. Even the combined SLD–SDP vote at 16 per cent failed to match the 17 per cent William Goodhart had obtained for the Alliance in the 1987 election and few doubted that if the Alliance had still been in operation we would have polled substantially more than that although probably still coming third. All the signs were that we were now locked in an internecine war with the Social and Liberal Democrats. They for their part were about to embark on a dispute about their name with a strong groundswell for 'Liberal Democrats'. They were nevertheless doing quite well in local government and many former SDP councillors had joined them.

In early September 1988 I went to Moscow to attend a conference on human rights organised in association with the United Nations. It was a good opportunity to reassess Gorbachev's regime and I spoke to many people. I had never been convinced that he was ready to challenge the Leninist tradition of authoritarianism. He wanted a managed democracy and a managed economy. There were, however, signs that perestroika and glasnost in his hands were leading to an ever greater opening up of the USSR. But that individual republics such as Lithuania, Latvia and Estonia were going to have to struggle for their independence and talk of self-determination was for the UN not for the USSR. In a restaurant, the man at the next table was the nuclear physicist and Nobel Peace Prize winner Andrei Sakharov. We were introduced, and he thanked me for making representations on his behalf to Andrei Gromyko. It was a reminder of the extent of the changes, but in a short conversation he was scathingly critical of Gorbachev at the very time he was being lauded by the West.

The SDP conference in Torquay was a nerve-racking business. None of us really knew how many people would turn up. A little empty on Saturday, it filled up by Sunday and we were able to breathe more easily. The most important debate was that on the social market economy. It was based on a green paper whose principal author was Professor Robert Skidelsky, the definitive biographer of Keynes and a driving force in making the SDP rethink its economic policy from that adopted in the 1983 general election. We were at long last ready to abandon the ill-fated inflation tax, which had hung round our necks like an albatross since 1982. Our social market policy was based on five elements: support for the market as the main system for supplying goods and services; insuring the market's social accountability; recognising the limits of the market; compensating for market failure, and securing acceptable social conditions for buying and selling in the markets. The conference was a success. We had a good cricket match and morale was high, but we were a much smaller party and I could not be sure we could survive.

Peter Jenkins in the *Independent*, although still not reconciled to the SDP's survival, said I had made the speech of my political lifetime:

> The berries and locusts of the wilderness seem to have put fire into his belly. With nothing any more to lose, he did what a politician rarely does – he spoke all of his mind . . . Dr Owen envisaged the possibility of Labour returning to the social democratic fold. Who shall know whether he seriously believes this is likely or says it simply in order, as one Labour leader said, to 'shaft Ashdown'?

Yet after analysing what I had said he concluded, 'The wilderness is the natural habitat of the prophet.'

For the first time I had begun to sense that Labour was pulling back from its extremist years. Paddy Ashdown's belief that he could replace Labour as the main party in opposition was coming too late. In an interview with John Carvel of the *Guardian*, having first disposed of the fantasy that I was about to become a member of the Tory Party, I said:

> There is no question that I am wistful about Labour. If one of the penalties of the last year is that we can't make it, but that we make Labour a decent government again, that is not the end of the world. You needn't go to your grave regretting that. Whether or not I personally join the Labour Party is immaterial.

But when asked, 'But not inconceivable?' I replied:

> No, it is not inconceivable, it is the only other party I'd join . . . I have said I would never join the Tory Party, never. It is quite deliberate that I have not used the word 'never' about the Labour Party. Whether I would or not is a different question. But I could envisage circumstances when there were again two social democratic parties, the SDP and the Labour Party . . . At that juncture the SDP would have to consider what it wanted to do.

The reason I sensed a shift in the Labour Party's policy stance was that Jacques Delors, the former French Socialist Minister of Finance and now president of the European Commission, had given a fraternal address to the TUC conference, where his reception had been so warm and his exposition about the Social Charter so well received that it was apparent that Labour was in the process of abandoning its hostility to membership of the European Community. That process continued at the Labour Party conference with a series of policy papers, all moving closer to an acceptance of market economics. The old problem of the nuclear deterrent had not yet been resolved and Neil Kinnock's attempt to support unilateralism, bilateralism and multilateralism convinced no one, but it was nevertheless an indication that he personally was on the move, even though Ron Todd managed with the TGWU block vote to secure the passage of a hardline unilateralist resolution.

In December 1988 there was a by-election, this time in Epping Forest. Michael Pettman, a solicitor, had fought the seat for the SDP in the general election and was a local councillor. He had also been against the merger. If we felt we should fight, he was ready to put his name forward. Another by-election was also pending in Richmond, Yorkshire, for Leon Brittan, having been forced to resign over Westland, had accepted being a vice-president and Commissioner in Brussels. The Richmond seat had been fought previously for the SDP by Mike Potter, a local farmer and county councillor. He too had refused to join the merger and was an engaging and charismatic figure. We wanted to reach an agreement with the Social and Liberal Democrats that they would fight Epping and we would fight Richmond, but they rejected any and all co-operation at national level, referring every issue down to their local associations. So we raised it locally with the SLD in Epping and in Richmond. Michael Pettman had good personal relations with the probable candidate but unfortunately no deal emerged from the discussions. We could not forgo two consecutive by-elections so we decided that Michael Pettman should stand for the SDP. It was the fifteenth safest Conservative seat in the country and had a great history. There was a time when the words of the member of Parliament for Epping resonated around the world. Winston Churchill first won the seat in 1924, standing as a Constitutionalist on his way back to the

Conservative Party. He had a somewhat uneasy relationship with the constituency party, particularly over India and Munich, and in a speech on 14 March 1938 Churchill defended his right to speak unfettered by party restrictions. I recalled his words in the by-election in order to remind people of the virtues of independence in Parliament.

> What is the use of sending members to Parliament to say popular things of the moment, and saying things merely to give satisfaction to the government whips and by cheering loudly every ministerial platitude? What is the value of our parliamentary institutions, and how can our parliamentary doctrines survive if constituencies tried to return only tame, docile and subservient members and tried to stamp out every form of independent judgement?

I warned, as I had done often before, how Margaret Thatcher's power had increased as the power of the party whip grew, how patronage, which had expanded grotesquely, was used to put ever more subtle pressures on members of Parliament. I warned too how the status of members and of the House of Commons itself had been diminished because there was no credible official opposition and because the opposition within the party was wet both in name and nature.

The result was declared on Friday 16 December and had the Conservatives ahead on 13,183 but with their majority slashed from 17,009 to 4,504. The SLD candidate came a creditable second with 8,879, Labour third with 6,261 and Michael Pettman fourth with 4,077. Nobody had any doubt that if we or the Social and Liberal Democrats had stood down then the Conservatives would have been defeated.

At the end of January 1989 Paddy Ashdown, under pressure from David Alton and David Steel, made a rather confused speech about electoral pacts and said that if Labour's interest in proportional representation meant that the realignment of British politics was on its way then he had been mistaken in slamming the door so firmly. He also said that he had never meant what he had said in earlier speeches about destroying Labour in one go. Yet, despite this, and all other efforts, the SLD still refused to stand down in Richmond in the name of realignment, so battle commenced both there and in Pontypridd, where we had again failed to reach an agreement.

Our Richmond candidate, Mike Potter, fought a splendid campaign. Popular in the SDP, he attracted people from all over the country to help. For the first time since Rosie Barnes's victory in Greenwich, we were mounting a really effective by-election campaign with Chris Hopson's team having moved straight up from Epping with only a short break for Christmas. Though our resources were stretched, morale was high. Unfortunately there were no constituency polls until the last week of the campaign. On Tuesday 21 February a poll for Tyne Tees Television showed the Tory vote slashed, down to 40 per cent, with the SLD on 19.5 per cent and the SDP 19 per cent. Since in the last election the Liberal standing for the Alliance had polled 27 per cent it was already clear that our combined total was far greater, but it was not clear the way the voters would go. On Wednesday 22 February, the day before the vote, a poll for Yorkshire Television showed Mike Potter four points ahead of Barbara Pearce, the SLD candidate. We did our best to publicise this in a last-minute leaflet and it was carried by Yorkshire Television and the BBC. Unfortunately Tyne Tees ignored it despite the fact that they knew the findings. Next day when the ballot boxes were opened we did not appear to have done as well in the Tyne Tees area as in the Yorkshire TV area. We were agonisingly close but just unable to get our last-minute bandwagon rolling quickly enough. As it was, William Hague, who eight years later became leader of the Conservative Party, polled 19,543, Mike Potter came second with 16,909 votes and Barbara Pearce third with 11,589. Labour, who lost their deposit, were fourth with 2,591 votes. The 24 per cent drop in the Conservative vote was their worst performance since Margaret Thatcher became Prime Minister.

No one doubted that if the old Alliance had been fighting we would have had an easy victory to match the Liberals in Orpington or the SDP in Crosby. It was widely reported as a triumph for the SDP but also an example of the folly of our fighting each other. The *Evening Standard* headline was 'THE REAL WINNER – OWEN IS SO CLOSE TO BY-ELECTION SENSATION', the *Daily Express* 'DAVID OWEN RIDES AGAIN – ASHDOWN WOOS FLYING DOCTOR AS HE SHOCKS TORIES'. Some in the SDP believe that if we had won our survival would have been assured. I am not convinced. As at Warrington, the media awarded us a moral victory but there was no surge in applications for membership. And the underlying message lay in the Pontypridd result that same day: in many places both parties were now of marginal significance, the SLD candidate having polled 3.9 per cent and the SDP candidate 3.1 per cent of the votes. The seat was won by Labour despite the surge in support for Plaid Cymru.

The Richmond result added greatly to the deep feeling of betrayal among many voters who had voted Alliance in 1987. I believe it was the last opportunity for those of us who had once worked in alliance to hold these votes and to rebuild the 30 per cent and more levels of public support we had had from 1981 to 1987. I hoped that we would be able quietly to reach some form of understanding with the SLD. David Alton, the SLD MP who had developed into the most far-sighted and conciliatory of them all, and John Cartwright, the SDP's president, publicly renewed their call for an electoral pact, saying, 'A pointless competition for second and third places is about as rational and cost effective as subscribing to Conservative Party funds.' But Paddy Ashdown simply issued an immediate appeal for me to meet to discuss how the union of a single party could be achieved. Certainly I was ready to meet but obviously not on that basis.

Nevertheless David Sainsbury did arrange for a private dinner at his house with Paddy Ashdown and myself on 16 March. I hoped that we might be able to reach some understanding over the forthcoming Welsh by-election and the Euro-elections, but although it was a pleasant occasion there was no sign that Paddy Ashdown was personally ready to advocate any understanding over the Euro-elections. He took refuge in saying he would support any local arrangements but I was left with the impression that he would not encourage them. It was becoming painfully apparent that the SDP could not go on sustaining fights in every by-election, but if we did not stand we left the field open to the SLD and gave the impression that we were incapable of fighting as a national party. It gave more credence to the 'Owenite rump' label that was still disparagingly fixed on us by some of the commentators. When we eventually fought the Vale of Glamorgan by-election the level of activity was very poor in comparison to the SLD and it was left to a few of our people to work their hearts out. In the council elections due on 4 May, the same day as the Glamorgan by-election, the Green Party was fielding nearly double the number of candidates that we were and the SLD were fielding many more. This again emphasised how weak we were becoming on the ground.

In early April I flew to Karachi for a seminar to honour the memory of the former Prime Minister of Pakistan Zulfiqar Ali Bhutto. It had been planned for a long time and none of us could have anticipated that his daughter Benazir would be the elected Prime Minister when it was held. There was I, a former British Foreign Secretary, who had tried to prevent Bhutto's death, and Sardar Swaran Singh, a former Indian Foreign Minister, who had often negotiated on India–Pakistan problems with Mr Bhutto, speaking in the presence of his daughter as Prime Minister. Benazir's contribution to building a democracy in Pakistan over the next few years was formidable.

When I became Foreign Secretary Bhutto was the democratically elected leader of Pakistan. A general election was held on 7 March 1977, the first election to be called by a popularly elected government. But although Bhutto won there were strong allegations of ballot-rigging and considerable division within the country. It culminated in a military coup on 5 July 1977 and Bhutto's imprisonment.

A human rights task that I had undertaken as Foreign Secretary was to try and persuade General Zia to release Bhutto and allow free elections. I received a letter from a Dr Niazi, Bhutto's personal dentist, describing the appallingly squalid conditions in which Bhutto was being held. The Foreign Office had wisely ensured that I was shown the letter because it was so movingly written. It stimulated me to do everything in my power to get Bhutto out. Dr Niazi was himself put in prison for his outspokenness and it was Niazi's daughter who brought messages to and from the prison between Mr Bhutto and Benazir. In desperation towards the end Jim Callaghan wrote to General Zia reminding him of the old soldier's saying 'The grass grows swiftly over a battlefield but never over a scaffold'. Zia did not heed it and Bhutto was hanged.

So a scaffold hung hauntingly over our seminar; as stark, as sombre as when it was first erected. We hoped the seminar would be part of the process of healing, a kind of catharsis. Whatever the arguments about Bhutto's political legacy, and he was undoubtedly a controversial partisan leader, his overall record was one which deserved respect, and respect is the first step in reconciliation.

After the seminar we flew out to the Bhutto family home in the rural part of Sind province and, driving from the airport along narrow dusty roads, I saw people coming from all parts of Pakistan to mark the tenth anniversary of Bhutto's death and to visit the family mausoleum. Local buses were overflowing, peasants in their thousands could be seen walking across the fields, some of them having made a four- or five-day journey just to be there. It was a massive crowd. Benazir arrived by helicopter to address the large rally. Her car was mobbed and I feared for her life as the security completely broke down. One hears the expression 'being carried off one's feet', and this is literally what happened as I was squeezed tight by the vast crowd. Everyone seemed delighted to see a European face and I was eventually set down near the dais, where I sat on the floor listening to Benazir deliver an impassioned speech. Eventually we went back to the family house for lunch, after which I flew back with Benazir in her plane to Karachi.

Throughout the 1980s I had met Benazir at regular intervals and she had always come with a quietly spoken older man. I never realised he was the same Dr Niazi who had written to me, until he reminded me of his letter and my reply when he and his attractive daughter welcomed me on my arrival in Karachi. It was a moving visit to a country which had fascinated me in 1959 as a student. Benazir's assassination at the end of 2007 was for me a personal tragedy. By 2009, with her husband now President, Pakistan faced a horrendous task as the Taliban within the country fought the army and no one could be sure of the outcome.

Back in London I attended the speech delivered in Guildhall by Mikhail Gorbachev before flying to Stockholm for the final meeting of the Palme commission, named in honour of the late Swedish Prime Minister Olof Palme after his appalling assassination. Once again I was struck by how dramatic the changes had been since we started our work in 1980; now eastern Europe was on the threshold of freedom. It was both a sad and happy occasion. For nine years the members of this commission had worked together with remarkable

harmony on disarmament and security issues. Many lasting friendships were made and in particular I was pleased to have the
opportunity to work once more alongside Cyrus Vance. Olusegun
Obasanjo from Nigeria was also a member of the commission
together with Gro Harlem Brundtland, the Prime Minister of
Norway, Georgy Arbatov of the Soviet Union and Sonny Ramphal,
then the Commonwealth secretary general. Sonny chaired the final
meeting in Stockholm and we issued our final report, *A World at
Peace.*

When I look back at our despairing mood, and the fear that there
would be no dialogue between President Reagan and President
Brezhnev in the early 1980s, and contrast it with the relationship
which started between President Bush and President Gorbachev it
was as if we were in a different age. The INF Treaty was not only
signed and ratified but we witnessed the removal and destruction of
Soviet SS-20 missiles and American cruise missiles. At long last it
looked as if the United Nations might develop some of the 'sinews
of power' that Winston Churchill had called for in his 1947 Fulton
speech, best known for its description of the 'iron curtain' that
had fallen between East and West. The final Palme commission
report focused on reform of the United Nations and widened our
original concept to achieve common security through economic
development, social justice and protection of the planet. Our
detailed proposals for the UN Secretariat had the enhanced
authority of the involvement of Brian Urquhart, the most
distinguished of all UN peacekeepers, who had become a member
of our commission. The environmental aspects of our report were
also helped by the contribution of Gro Harlem Brundtland, who,
while being a member of the Palme commission, was also chairman
of the Independent Commission on Environmental Issues.

Meanwhile, as the battle of the mice was going on between us and
the Liberal Democrats, the Labour Party was making massive strides
towards the centre. A wholesale revisionist review had produced a set
of papers which were described by the *Independent* – in my
judgement accurately – as potentially as important as the decision
taken by the German Social Democratic Party at Bad Godesberg
some thirty years earlier to abandon its Marxist heritage. The review

not only recommended abandoning unilateral nuclear disarmament, but came out in favour of retaining three Trident submarines. The papers also advocated continued membership of the European Community. There was market socialism too and a recommendation for entry into the Exchange Rate Mechanism of the EMS. Within the year John Smith, their shadow Chancellor, had won acceptance for the ERM as a discipline against inflation. Labour became more enthusiastic for ERM than even the most ardent Conservative Europeans.

In the SDP we learnt in May 1989 that our membership figures had been badly wrong. We never had more than 18,000 supporters, let alone members. At my insistence we made a clean breast of this error as soon as it was discovered and admitted that our true membership by then was 11,000. Why this error was made we will never be totally sure. It was probably the result of an overzealous member of our staff exaggerating the figures so as to persuade John Cartwright and me to move from the Campaign for Social Democracy to re-establish the SDP. Everyone involved knew that we had made it crystal clear that without a certain minimum membership of the campaign we could not relaunch the SDP. At the end of January 1988, in an interview with the *Sunday Telegraph*, I had been feeling confident that we would in a few months' time relaunch the party and I said, 'I always thought 10,000 was a good campaign, 15,000 was halfway between a campaign and a party and 20,000 was a national party, although you have got to increase that.'

We now knew that the continuing SDP never had a viable membership. Those who called us 'an Owenite rump' could feel their jibe was justified. Even so, they underestimated the extent to which the continuing SDP was composed of people of independent mind, determined to keep it going and for whom my involvement was a bonus but not a prerequisite. One of the strengths of the SDP was its membership of political virgins, and it was these who were often the most adamant that the party should continue. Probably they were less aware of the difficulties of establishing a national party on a small membership. Their commitment to the SDP was uninhibited by the custom and practice of the old politics. Many of them, including my wife, thought John and I were far too cautious in insisting that we would not relaunch without the certainty of

20,000 members and the prospect of more to come. Yet for all their enthusiasm, had we then known the true figures we would not have relaunched the SDP.

Over the next few weeks I had extensive discussions with the trustees of the party, Eric Woolfson and David Sainsbury, both loyal to the end, about whether the SDP could survive. I believed that we were no longer viable and I was determined that David Sainsbury, whose generosity had continued, should be released from feeling any further financial commitment to the party and in particular from any commitment to help finance the elections for the European Parliament that were due in June. Most now believed that the SDP had to be allowed to die or live from now on within its own resources. This was put to an emergency meeting of the national committee on Saturday 13 May. In the midst of the meeting in St Ermin's Hotel we discovered a journalist from the *Mail on Sunday* with his ear against the door. Not knowing exactly what he had heard we decided that we had to go public ourselves on these decisions that afternoon. Next day, the *Mail on Sunday* and the *Sunday Times* led with the SDP story. The press generally wrote our obituary but in a fairly friendly fashion, using the words of one of our own members that our decision had been a 'rendezvous with reality'. The *Daily Mail* on Monday said it was a grisly end to a dream which had entranced millions of decent citizens.

The slow, painful death of the SDP continued. The only surprise of the 1989 conference season was that the SDP managed to pull off a successful conference in Scarborough. Morale was amazingly high and the press were glad to be back in the town. Surprised to be witnessing a political resurrection, they gave us more coverage than we probably deserved. In policy terms we accepted independent grant-aided schools, and developed the right of patients to be treated under an internal NHS market and if confronted by long waiting lists to go to another hospital. We built up the social market philosophy to stress competition and the breaking up of monopoly power. We were also the first political party to advocate independence for the Bank of England and simultaneously question the desirability of a single currency with fixed exchange rates for the European Community. We specifically decided at Scarborough that the SDP was not in favour of a United States of Europe, a rejection hitherto implicit but never explicit. The SDP had championed a broader-based counter-revolution than Margaret Thatcher, one which promoted social justice. It was the determination to continue market-led change, but in the shape of a social market economy, which raised the voice of the consumer, that was our distinctive contribution through the 1980s. We devised a radical way of merging the tax and benefit system to alleviate poverty and a 'Carers' Charter'. We advocated 'green growth', where the polluter pays, and that an investment in the environment is that of a repairing lease held in trust for future generations. We argued the case for cherishing and promoting the arts, and supported a National Lottery.

The conference ended with a bomb scare and we had to evacuate the conference hall just before I was due to make the leader's set speech to close the conference. When it became clear that we would not be able to go back in the hall for four or five hours and members had trains and buses to catch, I decided to speak from a makeshift loudspeaker outside. It became known as 'the Speech on the Beach' and we got far more publicity than we would have ever had inside. Speaking off the cuff, I let slip one Freudian passage which journalists seized on:

> Sometimes people think that we will not continue to exist. Sometimes people say that we have to continue to exist. Do not worship at the altar of party. I think it has always been a great mistake of the old parties to think that parties have to live forever. What has to live forever are values and ideas.

As I drove away from Scarborough I knew that it was just a question of time before the majority of our dwindling membership accepted that their dream was dying. As always the death throes are the most painful. People want to hear that all is well and listen only to siren voices telling them what they want to hear rather than what they should hear. Once I had persuaded David Sainsbury that we should live within the financial constraints imposed by a small membership, the members of the SDP slowly came to grips with reality. But even so the unreal voices were listened to more than they deserved. Good people were growing impatient, gradually doing less and less and drifting away.

Membership renewals in the first few months of 1990 slipped even further and I grew worried about the democratic base for the party. It was then argued that we should put a candidate up to fight the Bootle by-election. Our few local supporters were not keen. John Cartwright was opposed but I reluctantly went along with the decision, as if sensing that a final humiliation was necessary before the SDP could force itself to face reality. So it proved to be. Despite a brave personal fight by our candidate we not only lost our deposit but were beaten by Lord Sutch of the Monster Raving Loony Party. This was the end of the road for most people in the party and I knew we would now have to make the hard decision we had postponed last May. Twice during the campaign I visited Bootle and each time I was struck by seeing as many Labour posters on the council estates as there had been SDP posters for Shirley Williams in her by-election in 1981. The Labour Party had come back a long way in the last two years and the voters knew it. It was absurd for me to pretend otherwise and I was determined not to. Breakaway parties are too often unable to recognise any changes for the better in the party they left.

Over the Bank Holiday weekend I thought long and hard on what should be done about the SDP. I had known for some months that we were no longer viable as a democratic national party. After Bootle I believed that even the most committed of our activists would be ready to face the realities. At a meeting on Sunday 3 June the overwhelming majority of the national committee reluctantly agreed that we should close our headquarters and arrange generous redundancy terms for the small staff. Active local parties remained in different parts of the country but there was no pretence – we could no longer sustain a national party.

People around that table had dedicated the last nine years of their life to the SDP. For all of us it was a very painful decision but done with dignity. For our beloved SDP it had been a lingering death and not everyone even then was ready to accept that this was the end. Like other members in the country they were hoping against hope that a miracle would happen and the SDP would revive. For some the decision was a relief; for others the start of a grieving period that would last many months. Even when nearly 200 of us met together again for dinner in the House of Commons on the tenth anniversary of the SDP the following March there were a few who had not yet fully adjusted. We had not broken the mould of British politics, for our new party had not survived, but we had certainly shaken it enough to create more than a few cracks. Hopefully it would fracture. The carpenters would come into the House of Commons, as I once advocated, and build new benches across the floor facing the Speaker, demonstrating that the chamber was no longer just an adversarial one but one that could embrace a different style of debate and political dialogue.

Next morning the obituaries started. Most were kind and showed a genuine regret. No one sought to deny that the political scene was vastly different in 1990 to that in 1981 and that the SDP had had an influence in changing the scene. There were different interpretations as to the extent of the influence. Where I believe our influence was most profound was in taking Labour votes under the noses of their activists in such large numbers that they could no longer deny that Labour's policies were disastrous and had to be changed. If the Liberals or the Conservatives had been taking their votes there would have been the usual left-wing excuses. But for the SDP to do it was a humiliation they could not ignore. Even so it took three successive defeats for the Labour Party to transform itself. Between 1988 and 1991 the Labour Party reversed almost every policy that was losing it votes and it moved from a party wholly unfit to govern to a party that in a few years might well be trusted again to govern the country. By 1995 Tony Blair was determined to ditch Clause IV, the nationalising commitment in Labour's constitution, and rechristen the party New Labour, winning power 16 years after the SDP launch.

My main sadness looking back, and I take my share of responsibility for it, was that the Gang of Four never gave the SDP a chance to prove itself. Only for a few weeks were we the genuinely independent social democratic party that we had launched. By September 1982 I had written in my notebook that I feared that this was the moment when the historians would say we had lost our independence and I was unfortunately proven correct.

Most of my writing and speaking on international affairs at this time was focused on the Soviet Union and how we should respond to an empire in decline. For some years I had been speaking out against the naïve interpretation of what Mikhail Gorbachev was trying to achieve. I was not against Gorbachev personally, for he was by any standard a remarkable man and a deft political operator. What I was worried about was the wave of 'Gorbymania' that was then sweeping the West. We were underestimating his drive to retain power for himself and the elite around him. He had consciously abandoned the Soviet satellite nations in order to hold power and consolidate around the existing borders of the USSR. When the British Empire was declining and we gave independence to more and more nations previously under our rule, we did not admit that we were doing so out of economic weakness. We talked about democracy, freedom and independence to cloak our inability to retain our influence. Mikhail Gorbachev was paying us the compliment of using the same language, even talking at one stage of a Soviet Commonwealth. He was intent on covering a humiliating retreat, stimulated by profound economic weakness. Yet we were interpreting his motives along the propaganda lines set by the KGB.

Gorbachev was close to the same KGB-dominated elite that, over a decade previously, had begun to question the extended empire of satellite nations. They were masterminding retrenchment to the borders of the USSR. The process had been precipitate in 1989, and neither they nor we had anticipated the speed with which the satellite countries would crumble to the new forces of democracy, or how dependent they had been on the threat of Soviet invasion to keep them in line. It was essential, I felt, to recognise that the basic decision to retrench came in Andropov's time, and that it was not done for democratic libertarian reasons; it was done for the preservation of the USSR. The power elite had no intention of allowing that process to trigger the fragmentation of the USSR. They were always prepared to use force, as was Gorbachev in Georgia, Lithuania and Latvia.

I had fiercely criticised Gorbachev for clamping down on the Lithuanians in their capital, Vilnius. So I was especially pleased to visit for the first time Estonia, Latvia and Lithuania in a three-man, all-party, human rights delegation at the end of August 1990. I had become convinced that the vacillation of the Western democracies over the Baltic states had to end, and that it was essential to force Gorbachev to honour their right to self-determination and independence. If we could prise out of the USSR these three republics, which had been illegally occupied in 1940 as a result of the infamous Hitler–Stalin pact, we would not only redress a historic wrong but start an irreversible process by which Soviet communism would be transformed into a market economy and a genuine democracy. Once we had succeeded with Poland, Hungary, Czechoslovakia and the Baltic states, we could then edge in towards the big republics – the Russian Federation, Ukraine and Belorussia.

Nearly everyone in the Baltic capitals, Tallinn, Riga and Vilnius, was determined to win back their independence, but they were equally sure that Gorbachev would only concede their freedom under pressure from the Western democracies. It was fascinating to talk to people who were simultaneously negotiating with Mikhail Gorbachev and his ministers, dedicated to the maintenance of the USSR, and to Boris Yeltsin and his team from the Russian Federation. Whereas Yeltsin was surrounded by genuine market economists, and even budding democrats, they felt that Gorbachev's advisers were opposed to risking their hold on power to the ballot box. I believed that Gorbachev himself only believed in a managed democracy and a managed economy, but his views were evolving. No one was sure what either Yeltsin or Gorbachev would concede under the differing pressures ahead of them. But they felt there was everything to play for with Yeltsin, and that his thinking was more in flux. In as much as the two were interacting with each other, some hoped this process could provide the momentum for substantive and radical change inside the Soviet Union. The unanimous view was that Gorbachev should be pressurised and that we in the West should listen more to what the Soviet people felt about him and his policies. My fear that we were falling for KGB propaganda was strengthened by all I heard. The West's approach was so nuanced it was almost deferential. It needed to be more robust.

In early August Saddam Hussein invaded Kuwait. I had already crossed swords with Saddam's ugly Baathist regime in 1978 when, as Foreign Secretary, I decided to expel a group of Iraqi diplomats. My action had been provoked by the regime's campaign of violence against Iraqi residents in London and the gunning down of a former Iraqi Prime Minister in the street. I found no difficulty in fully supporting George Bush Senior's consummate handling of the West's response once the invasion of Kuwait had taken place, right up until the Iraqi troops had withdrawn. It was Bush who saw how vital it was to send troops early to Saudi Arabia and persuaded King Fahd that this was of crucial importance if sanctions were ever to bite. This was the all-important military decision for eventual success but it had profound political consequences. Without it Saddam Hussein would have threatened Saudi Arabia every time we turned the sanction screw and Arab solidarity would have collapsed. It was a considerable risk to deploy US troops without heavy armament or adequate air cover in the early period. If Saddam Hussein had pushed right down into Saudi Arabia these token American forces would have been initially defeated and George Bush humiliated. It might have been hard to hold US public opinion as the US forces regrouped and built up their strength to attack the Iraqis. The Saudis would by then have very likely settled on Saddam Hussein's terms.

The House of Commons was recalled on 6 September. I warned that it could be very difficult to make sanctions work and that Saddam Hussein would prefer to give up Kuwait as a result of a military battle, and I predicted that a battle would eventually be necessary. I went on to say that, if we maintained the consensus that had developed among the multinational force, 'there might be military action that would not last very long and would not involve a great deal of loss of life'.

The invasion of Kuwait injected a wholly new political factor into domestic politics. Though there were few parallels with the Falklands – since in this case Britain was not in the lead role – Margaret Thatcher must have seen the potential to stage a political comeback and she might well have done so had she not been forced out before the fighting commenced by her own MPs on the issue of Europe.

The autumn of 1990 meant that for the first time in thirty years I had no party conference to attend. I wrote an article in the *Mail on Sunday* on the eve of the Labour Party conference, warmer than for many years to Labour, entitled 'What the Labour Party must do to win power', in which I urged them to make a commitment to proportional representation to attract votes from the moderate centre. Labour, in policy terms, had transformed itself. It was now committed to the European Community and wanting to go into the ERM as an anti-inflationary discipline. It was ready to build three Trident submarines. It was rejecting state ownership of industry and talking at least some of the language of the private commercial marketplace. It was becoming hard to find areas in which it had not adopted SDP policy. And yet I had grave doubts that Neil Kinnock in particular could free himself in government from the influence of the public sector unions, which were still a powerful vested interest with real power at every level within the Labour Party. The electoral college with the trade union block vote remained in place, capable of being used to make or break a Prime Minister. Even so, deservedly, Labour was in a confident mood with its opinion poll lead building up. Yet, far from going out to widen its electoral appeal, it gratuitously slammed the door shut on any possible co-operation with us in the SDP. On 2 October – the very day, incidentally, that the two Germanys reunified in a spirit of reconciliation – it passed the following resolution:

> This conference resolves to oppose any rule changes on membership of the Labour Party, which can be construed as inducements for former members of the Social Democratic Party to rejoin the Labour Party. Specifically this motion notes the twelve-month membership qualification for party office and resolves to oppose any attempt by the national leadership to alter the aforementioned rule with a view to offering an accommodation to the three surviving SDP members of Parliament.

Up until this moment I had hoped that Labour would recognise that they would need every extra help that they could get to beat the Conservatives in an election due before July 1992. I was, however, too optimistic; Labour was not prepared to heal the breach between social democrats and democratic socialists in order to maximise their appeal. If Labour could have worked out a very small electoral arrangement with the SDP it would have underlined to many non-political people that it had really changed.

In October, during the weekend before the Conservative Party conference, John Major took Britain into the Exchange Rate Mechanism of the EMS. It was a feat of political adroitness that had eluded his predecessors, Geoffrey Howe and Nigel Lawson. I had talked to John Major that summer while we were both watching cricket at Lord's. It was striking how determined he was to get interest rates down before his party conference. He felt this was a political imperative as much as an economic one. Tying the cut in interest rates to ERM entry may have just tipped the balance in persuading Margaret Thatcher to enter the ERM, even though the linkage annoyed the governor of the Bank of England. I suspect that Margaret Thatcher agreed to enter the ERM, despite feeling it would restrict her freedom to cut interest rates in the run-up to a general election, because she knew she could not fight on two fronts. She decided, correctly, that the more important battle was to resist the Euro-federalist package which Jacques Delors was trying to push through so as to tie the hands of those on the intergovernmental conferences on political and economic union. By joining the ERM she hoped that some of the Conservative MPs who were strongly European would be able to live with her vetoing any irreversible move towards a United States of Europe. Nevertheless, for the first time in over a decade of watching Margaret Thatcher very closely, I felt that ERM entry represented a personal defeat for her. She had used every tactic to avoid it, she had delayed and delayed taking action, and yet now she had no alternative. I do not believe that she ever accepted the virtue of managed exchange rates within the ERM. She merely resigned herself to it.

At the European heads of government meeting, held in Rome at the end of October, it was clear that Giulio Andreotti, the Italian Prime Minister, had foolishly gone out of his way to isolate Margaret Thatcher. But what was alarming was that Whitehall had not picked up the mood about the coming ambush. Even people involved in the Community negotiations who were normally hostile to the Prime Minister were admitting that the Italian presidency had behaved pretty disgracefully. On Tuesday 30 October Margaret Thatcher came to the House of Commons to make a statement, and I helped wind her up by my question supporting the use of the veto. It was already clear from her Rome press conference, when she came out with her series of 'No, no, no' statements, that she was on an emotional high and the adrenalin was pumping round her system as she handbagged every federalist proposal. She was taking her stand on the single currency, and even beginning to backtrack from the agreed government position over the hard ECU. I watched Geoffrey Howe's face as she answered these questions; he looked miserable and unhappy, truly, I thought, a dead sheep. How wrong I proved to be.

On 1 November, the day Parliament prorogued, without any warning Geoffrey Howe resigned as deputy Prime Minister and Leader of the House. Margaret Thatcher's response to the Rome summit had been the final straw for him. He had suffered a humiliating cycle of events following his removal from the Foreign Office. Even before that his consistent support for ERM entry back in 1985 and again before the Madrid European summit in the summer of 1987 had antagonised Margaret Thatcher. When he became Leader of the House and foolishly insisted on being called deputy Prime Minister, the tension between them was there for all to see. A mild and decent man, he had been made to look ridiculous for too long. He was never a Tory wet and had made a quiet but distinguished contribution to the counter-revolution, though a less revolutionary figure would be hard to imagine.

At this crucial moment in domestic politics Thorvald Stoltenberg, the former Norwegian Foreign Minister who was the UN high commissioner for refugees, resigned in order to return to Oslo and join Gro Harlem Brundtland's new government. I was approached by some young activists within UNHCR in Geneva to ask if I would put my name forward. I rang Martin Morland, an old friend, who was the UK ambassador to the UN in Geneva, and found out some details about the job. I became sufficiently interested to let Douglas Hurd know and he agreed that private soundings should be taken in UN circles in New York and among a few governments. While it was apparent that Javier Pérez de Cuéllar, the UN secretary general, had in mind someone within his own secretariat it was also obvious that this did not command wide support. From the soundings that were made, it appeared that my candidature would have powerful support. I had to make up my mind quickly. At various times I had considered going back to medicine and not fighting a coming election, but I had never before contemplated resigning my seat.

Then to add to the complications, out of the blue on Thursday 8 November I was telephoned by Maurice Saatchi to say he had a proposition to put to me and to ask if I was free for lunch. We met that day at the Connaught Hotel. He came straight to the point, arguing that the Conservative Party under Margaret Thatcher had to change its image if it was to win the election and that there was an overwhelming mutual interest in me joining the Conservatives and taking a high-profile job in a Conservative Cabinet. Maurice's company had the Conservative Party account, handling their advertising, party political broadcasts, polling and public relations. So I was talking to a person who knew the Conservative Party inside out. With total frankness I went through with him all the obstacles to this course of action. I explained why I had said publicly over five years ago that I would never become a Conservative and had repeated it endlessly ever since. I had not said this lightly, and though of course I could in theory change my mind and put up with the jibes for doing so, in practice I did not want to. I was not and never would be a natural member of the Conservative Party. I reminded him of my opposition to Margaret Thatcher's basic attitude to the National Health Service, and that while I agreed with her on a number of very important foreign policy issues, not least the danger of sliding imperceptibly into a United States of Europe, I simply could not see myself becoming a Conservative. There were circumstances in which I would serve as a Social Democrat in either a Conservative or a Labour government. But I would need to feel I could carry some influence on the policies of any such government and have at least the power to argue for some of the constitutional changes I thought necessary. Maurice was adamant that his strategy would only work if I were a prominent Cabinet minister, for only that would give the necessary public profile to change people's perceptions.

It had been a fascinating lunch and Maurice Saatchi had handled his proposition with considerable skill. I gathered this was his own personal initiative and he never once gave any indication he had discussed it with any senior Conservative. Since his company would know all the private polling information, I asked whether he had the numbers to show I would have such a beneficial effect and he confirmed that he had. Given his own links with Conservative ministers, it would not have surprised me if he had consulted them, but as far as I was concerned it had been a private lunch and I told no one other than Debbie about it. Indeed I would not have disclosed it had it not been for the fact that the *Sunday Telegraph* on

10 February 1991 carried a detailed account of Maurice Saatchi's involvement with me under the headline 'THE TORIES GO OUT TO WOO DR OWEN'.

It was Margaret Thatcher in 10 Downing Street on 7 July 1988 who had last proposed quite directly to me that I should join the Conservatives. She had given a dinner for Lord Carrington to mark his retirement from the post of NATO secretary general and had quite deliberately taken both Debbie and me aside as we were leaving. In her blunt way she said to Debbie, 'Your husband has a big choice to make and it can no longer be avoided. There are only two serious parties in British politics and we women understand these things; it is time he made up his mind.' Debbie bridled and I politely refused to join the Conservative Party then, as I had refused Alan Clark and others who had raised the issue with me ever since the summer of 1983. It was a deliberate strategy of Margaret Thatcher's, which she had followed for a few years even before the SDP was formed, to attract the social democrats in the Labour Party to the Conservatives. Previously in interviews she had virtually invited me to join; this time it had been done in person. Her quoted remark that I 'would be the next non-Conservative Prime Minister' had also been often misreported, with the word 'non' removed, much to my embarrassment. I had also found out since then, interestingly in view of what was to transpire, that John Major shared her strategy. He had asked me, half-jokingly, while watching cricket that summer with David Frost, whether I would ever consider joining the Conservatives when Margaret Thatcher retired. I had explained that in some ways the opposite was the case; I was more attracted to her because she was not in my eyes a typical Conservative. The Conservative Party for me, I said, still stood for privilege. Yet by no stretch of the imagination despite her ruthless use of patronage could one identify Margaret Thatcher with privilege, and an instinctive wish to challenge vested interest wherever she encountered it was one of her most refreshing characteristics. He grinned and appeared to take the point, and we left the matter there.

As the hours ticked by I knew I had to make a decision about whether to go for the UNHCR job. That Saturday I attended Lucy's new school. Watching her excited and enthused, I shuddered at the idea of uprooting her, quite apart from asking Debbie to move to

Switzerland. Debbie's literary agency continued to give her great personal satisfaction and she felt that going to Geneva meant she could not continue, so I would be asking her to abandon the independence she had had since she had first gone out to work at the age of nineteen. So on Sunday, with some regrets but no reluctance, I let Douglas Hurd's office know that I did not want my name to go forward for consideration. For many years the whole family had sacrificed an immense amount for my career. It was not too much to ask me to do a little of the same for their happiness.

On Tuesday 13 November, Geoffrey Howe, annoyed by attempts to portray his resignation as an argument about style and not substance, used his right to make a personal statement in the House to considerable effect. I wish I had been there, but I was in Turkey. It was a full-frontal attack, the speech of an assassin, with every word sharpened to penetrate ever deeper: 'The time has come for others to consider their response to the tragic conflict of loyalty with which I have perhaps wrestled for far too long.' I returned to London to find Michael Heseltine's mind had been made up for him by that speech and he announced he would challenge Margaret Thatcher for the leadership of the Conservative Party.

I did not want Michael Heseltine to become Prime Minister. I had not been impressed by his judgement for some time, whether over the mace-waving incident in the House of Commons, wearing a flak jacket when he dealt with CND or flouncing out of the Cabinet while in full session. It was all too theatrical and revealed a pattern of impetuosity. I had also been appalled to read that Michael did not believe that the European Community should expand to include Poland, Hungary or Czechoslovakia as a high priority. Taken with my anxiety about his readiness to concede too much ground towards a United States of Europe, it was all a sufficient disincentive, despite his many good qualities, especially his views on race and the environment, to make me ready to put up with Margaret Thatcher for a little longer.

Yet I wondered what would be the views of Conservative MPs. It was easy for me as a Social Democrat to ruminate that she might step down if she were still unpopular next year. But with no objective signs of her being ready to do so, Conservative MPs had to worry about winning their seat and some were beginning to fear losing the election. Even those MPs still sympathetic must have feared that, if she stayed, by the summer Margaret Thatcher could have built up her public approval ratings on the back of a successful Gulf War sufficient to remain in power while still remaining an electoral liability. In this respect a vote for Michael Heseltine had its attractions, for he with no pretensions to the Thatcher legacy would have abolished the poll tax immediately and gone to the country straight after the Gulf War. At the inevitable jibes of a khaki election he would have comforted himself with the fact that his hero David Lloyd George had won the most famous khaki election.

On Monday 19 November, while Margaret Thatcher was in Paris attending the CSCE conference, the result of the first ballot was announced. She had failed by four votes to get the requisite majority. It was a sensational rebuff. Even though Michael Heseltine was fifty-two votes behind her, under the complex rules the contest automatically went to a second ballot unless she had a majority of fifty-six votes. In the House of Commons the following Tuesday, she had to report on the Paris meeting. There was a strange generosity about the House that day, as if most of us sensed her days were numbered. Unless you are a member of the party involved, you feel removed from these inner party elections, and yet they were choosing our Prime Minister, not just their party leader. It was hard not to see a certain poetic justice in that the worms had turned and the wets, after having been reviled over all those years, had had their revenge in the secrecy of the ballot box.

Margaret Thatcher's downfall was due to hubris. Her excessive self-confidence was by then being flaunted day by day in the face of friend and foe alike. The tragedy that the Greeks identified followed: nemesis. Watching her style of government from the outside, I had sensed in 1982 from the Franks report on the Falklands War that there was something seriously wrong. When a Foreign Secretary as formidable as Peter Carrington could be overridden on important issues by a mere prime ministerial memo, the system was not working properly. That he would not think it even worth putting his views to colleagues on the defence and overseas policy committee of the Cabinet was a sign of how dominating she had become. She had pitted herself against her own source of power, the Conservative MPs. She had reached a stage where she was not only not listening to her parliamentary colleagues but was contemptuous of their views. The Cabinet had been progressively reduced in stature and in quality. Majority opinion within it was frequently flouted or manipulated. People of substance, who well knew that Cabinet government was a great constitutional safeguard, had allowed this to develop over the years to the detriment of us all. It was not just because she was a woman that the Cabinet had been so supine but it was a material factor. With the Cabinet too weak to act, the Conservative MPs had shown their power.

So, with the country on the brink of the Gulf War, I had to watch while Conservative MPs chose our Prime Minister. Geoffrey Howe and Nigel Lawson were out of the running. Douglas Hurd was well up to the job but would be beaten by Michael Heseltine, while under John Major, he would definitely stay as Foreign Secretary and be influential. It seemed to me that John Major was a far better choice than Michael Heseltine. I believed he would be less flashy over the Gulf and show the necessary quiet determination in the European intergovernmental conferences, winning concessions that Michael Heseltine might not even demand. I sensed too that John Major would be far better in creating a climate of social cohesion. Among some of my friends who thought John Major was a conventional Thatcherite, that judgement was vigorously questioned. Yet I felt confident that he was the nearest of the Conservative leadership candidates to being a social democrat.

Nothing that happened in his premiership made me change that initial judgement. I had not met him socially until after the 1987 election, when Tristan Garel-Jones had invited John Cartwright and me to dinner at his home to talk to a number of Conservative MPs. Both Douglas Hurd and John Major had come and it had been a very friendly occasion. They had made no attempt to persuade us to become Conservatives – it was more of an occasion for gentle gossip and for them to question us about how we hoped to survive. They all appeared to have considerable sympathy with us for our refusal to merge with the Liberals. Of course they may have been feeling us out as to whether we would come over to the Conservatives, but nothing so indelicate was mooted. The government was then riding high in the opinion polls and it had no need of support from the three SDP MPs.

In numerous interviews on the day she announced she was going

I stressed both the achievements and the disappointments of Margaret Thatcher's period in office, while supporting John Major as the man best suited to make the good parts of her legacy stick and to achieve for these a deserved and necessary permanence. In the evening I went on a special BBC *Question Time* with Jim Callaghan, Enoch Powell and Simon Jenkins, the editor of the *Times*. We were all asked about who should be the next Conservative Prime Minister and while they hedged I plumped for John Major.

On 27 November John Major was elected the Conservative leader and next day, having been appointed by the Queen as Prime Minister, on the steps of No. 10 said that he wanted 'to see us build a country that is at ease with itself', a sentiment which then matched many people's mood but which by the 1997 general election was sadly far from reality.

As Margaret Thatcher drove away from 10 Downing Street, the iron will cracked and tears came to her eyes. I wrote to her and had a warm letter back, for both of us recognised similar instincts for what the British people wanted. All looked set for a far more dignified exit than ever seemed possible in the immediate aftermath of the first ballot. But she was bruised in the bone and those bruises last. At a private dinner some weeks afterwards, it was painfully apparent that her removal still rankled. Gradually she fell into the temptation to diminish John Major's efforts.

By this stage, with my parliamentary career coming to an end, I looked forward to the day, though I knew it might not come in my lifetime, when politicians of different parties would work together in and outside government. We did this on select committees to considerable effect and I felt that the sooner politicians widened their cross-party contacts and stopped the pretence of being poles apart on everything the better. I envisaged a time when no one would consider it odd for an MP of one party to serve in a Cabinet formed by another, and not necessarily because of the need for votes in the House of Commons. This change of climate, I hoped, would come when we had proportional representation, but there was no good reason why it should only be dependent on this. The reason US Presidents have people from the other party in their Cabinets is that it widens the base of government, improves the quality of decision-making and helps to widen their appeal.

Early in 1991 I was telephoned by a close friend of mine to pass on a conversation he had had with a person in regular contact with John Major. He had commented that the Prime Minister hoped for my endorsement at the next election, and did not even rule out standing down in the three SDP MPs' seats, although it would be very difficult to obtain agreement within the Conservative Party. I had no idea if this was a deliberately placed piece of information, but it was important intelligence from a valuable source and it meant that I began to approach a forthcoming lunch that Maurice Saatchi had arranged with Kenneth Baker in a far more thoughtful mood.

According to Frank Johnson, writing with wit but also with all the main facts in the *Sunday Telegraph* on 10 February, the lunch with Kenneth Baker, which he called a dinner, had come about as a result of a letter written to the Prime Minister by Maurice Saatchi.

> Mr Major consulted his soothsayers. It was agreed that at this stage there should be nothing so portentous as a meal involving the Prime Minister, Mr Saatchi and Dr Owen. So Mr Saatchi's information was discussed over a meal attended by Mr Chris Patten, the Conservative Party chairman, Mr Saatchi and Mr Michael Dobbs. It was still not thought time for serious eating between the Prime Minister and Dr Owen – serious being understood in politics as three courses plus closing Bendick's mints. So Mr Kenneth Baker, in his capacity as a former party chairman, was sent to raise the napkin on the prime ministerial behalf.

This only confirmed what I had suspected, that Kenneth Baker was not acting on his own but had been used as a conduit to discover my intentions.

The main difference between the previous lunch with Maurice Saatchi and the one with Kenneth Baker was that there was no longer any attempt to persuade me to join the Conservative Party. It was a sophisticated conversation in which the reality that I would not join was accepted and instead we explored all the possible permutations whereby I could co-operate as a Social Democrat. With goodwill we discussed the various options. For the Conservative Party it was clearly difficult, but not judged impossible, to persuade their people to stand down in our three SDP seats. It was understood that I was not prepared to do anything which would damage John Cartwright's and Rosie Barnes's chances of being re-elected. They did not deny my assertion that the Conservatives could not possibly win any of our three seats and that only Labour was the challenger. My contention was not challenged either – that if I endorsed the Conservative Party their local Conservative candidate and the Labour candidate would exploit the news against John and Rosie. We three, I explained, had stuck together since 1987 and I was not prepared to countenance any action which would harm them. Our independence was our best electoral asset, and not something to give up without a bankable return. Furthermore, we had an agreement with the Liberal Democrats covering their two seats, though I said I expected that they would use any electoral arrangement with the Conservatives as an excuse to break the agreement. If they were serious politicians, I hoped they should welcome an electoral arrangement as a precursor of things to come.

Although our lunch conversation was to say the least unusual in British politics over the previous forty years, it would be considered quite normal in other European countries. In 1951 Winston Churchill had offered Clement Davies, then the leader of the Liberal Party, a seat in his Cabinet, which, however, he turned down. Edward Heath had offered Jeremy Thorpe a seat in the Cabinet in February 1974. If in 1977 or 1978 Jim Callaghan had offered David Steel a seat in his Cabinet, I am sure David would have accepted. We now know that Paddy Ashdown expected after the 1997 election that Tony Blair would offer some electoral pact or inter-party agreement.

Before the Frank Johnson article appeared in the *Sunday Telegraph*, an approach was made to a friend of mine by a person near to Neil Kinnock, and they met shortly after the article had come out. This meeting was not leaked to the press and so I feel it must remain private. The underlying message was that Neil Kinnock was anxious to reduce the offputting effect of the conference resolution, although that was not specifically mentioned. There was no question of Labour withdrawing from the fight in our seats and they promised nothing, but I appreciated the attempt to bury the hatchet, albeit privately. They had correctly judged that I still felt a debt to the Labour Party. Without Labour I would never have even been an MP, let alone Foreign Secretary. As they shed their dangerous and damaging policy commitments, so I felt more inhibited in attacking Labour. My problem was that I liked John Major far more than the Conservative Party. I did not know Neil Kinnock, but while I thought he was courageous to abandon so many of his past political views I was worried about him becoming Prime Minister having held those views so recently.

To my immense surprise, a week or so later I was rung up by Kenneth Baker to ask if I would have dinner at his house with John Major and Chris Patten. I took this invitation to mean something serious was underway. For the first time I talked specifics rather than generalities with my two parliamentary colleagues, John and Rosie. I did not tell them who I was having dinner with, though I did say that it was being considered at a high level. Their attitude was that they enjoyed being independent and did not want to give that up. Nevertheless, it was important to them to use whatever influence we had to promote the ideas and philosophy of social democracy. We had always favoured cross-party agreements, and they were ready for me to negotiate.

At the dinner on Sunday 24 February 1991, before anything other than pleasantries had been exchanged, Chris Patten made it clear he did not think his people would stand down in our three SDP seats. Once that had been stated there was no point in discussing any of the various options and co-operative arrangements that I had previously talked through with Kenneth Baker. I replied that there had always been formidable difficulties and it was not surprising that it was impossible to deliver. The last time the Conservatives had done a seat deal was with the Liberal Party in the four constituencies in Huddersfield and Bolton in the 1951 and 1955 general elections, each party being given a clear run in two seats. Whether it was constituency resistance that was crucial I do not know to this day. It is fair to assume that they would not have arranged the dinner unless they thought there was a chance of standing down their local candidates. But they had probably tested the water since then in the three constituencies. The reaction of their MPs was also important, for it would not have been worth my while to have entered a Conservative Cabinet if I were only to be given sullen or half-hearted co-operation.

On the face of it an honest attempt had been made to break the convention that politicians of different parties cannot co-operate. We finished our dinner talking about the Gulf War, which we were in the midst of. I was disappointed that a seat deal had failed, but not because I was yearning to go back into government. I knew that would ignite all the old passions; I would be called a traitor by Labour and abused by Liberal Democrats and some Conservatives. Yet the aftermath of the Gulf War would have been a good time to establish a new approach. John Major was proving to be a welcome change from the stridency and partisanship of Margaret Thatcher.

In our political culture of hostility to any form of inter-party co-operation it is never the right time to co-operate. Tony Blair found that he could not deliver what I think he may have genuinely wanted with the Liberal Democrats after winning in 1997 by such a large margin. If you are ahead in the polls, those who are anti say: why do a deal? If you are behind, they say a deal will indicate you fear losing. The only way this sort of co-operation will come about is if politicians think voters will reward them because they feel it will provide better government. The opposition parties praised John Major for not exploiting the Gulf War. But no sooner was the war over than the politicians and the journalists heaved a sigh of relief and clambered back into the trenches to start firing political abuse. I do not believe the voters relish the nature of our political hostilities, and I am convinced they want a more civilised system. It is the tribalism of politics and politicians that ensures that while they try to reform every other aspect of British life they have not reformed the political system for more than a century. In 2009 after the scandal over MPs' expenses and allowances there was much talk of the mechanics of reform, but not enough thought about the attitudinal changes that are needed to underpin it.

The first Gulf War was broadly speaking a successful intervention. President Bush was the victorious and dominant figure. Not only was he determined to end the 'turkey shoot' on the road to Basra, but he was also adamant that he would not be sucked into street fighting in Baghdad. He was also obsessed with 'bringing the boys home' and haunted by Vietnam. I very much doubt whether Margaret Thatcher would have been able to do more for the Kurds than John Major did, and indeed she might not have been as ready to offend the Americans. The basic errors were in the military assessment that Saddam's Revolutionary Guard had been destroyed and also in the ceasefire arrangements negotiated between the generals which allowed the Iraqi forces to continue to use helicopters, supposedly for humanitarian reasons. When the Iraqis turned them into gunships the Allies' delay in responding was a disgrace. John Major's safe haven idea was then pushed through against American opposition in an exemplary manner, and with French support.

The big difference if Margaret Thatcher had been Prime Minister through the Gulf War is that she would have shown little wish to maintain the all-party consensus. When Labour did have its big policy wobble on 7 January and urged continuing sanctions on the eve of war, she would have tried to open their divisions up. I am sure she would not have acted as John Major did, to close them down. It was not as if Labour did not provide the political ammunition. It is hard to be charitable about Denis Healey's contribution to the Gulf War. For a former Secretary of State for Defence, knowing that British forces could be involved in battle within weeks, to say on BBC radio that fear of appearing a 'wimp' was driving President Bush to act as 'a sort of ersatz Rambo, pushing an unwilling world into disaster', was so far below the level of events that one wondered why he did it. It looked as if he was now trying to do the same for Neil Kinnock as he did for Michael Foot over the Falklands War, when Michael's initial response was to endorse the use of force and Denis Healey influenced him in favour of relying on sanctions. But Neil Kinnock, having put down Labour's marker in case anything went wrong, wisely supported our armed forces fully thereafter. To his eternal credit, John Major tried to minimise differences throughout the war and never exploited Labour's divisions. Some will say there are penalties for being too nice a Prime Minister; I would like to believe it has its reward. His conduct of the Gulf War deserves to be remembered, for it was a formidably testing time for an unproven leader. It helped him win the 1992 election against a difficult economic background. Historians will compare his conduct of the military intervention with that of Tony Blair in the second Gulf War of 2003 very favourably. Major practised honest, straightforward, collegiate Cabinet government.

A new phase in my political career was beginning. I was not going to fight the next election and for the first time since the Conservatives became the government I agreed with their handling of Europe. In particular I agreed with John Major's stance over a single currency within the European Economic and Monetary Union Treaty, which was well expressed in a speech in Swansea on Friday 14 June 1991. He said that 'any treaty would have to provide for the British government and the British Parliament to only move to a single currency if they took a further, separate and explicit decision to do so. Not just when to do so, but whether to do so at all.'

On Monday 17 June 1991, at a meeting of Foreign Ministers in Luxembourg, a paper was presented which, for the first time in the history of the European Community, made an explicit reference to the 'federal goal' of European union, and a further round of intergovernmental negotiations on a new federal constitution was proposed, to be held later in 1996. Douglas Hurd immediately rejected these words on behalf of the British government. The federalists had broken cover and sought to build in an explicit goal for what had hitherto been for them implicit in 'an ever closer union'. It was dismissed as only an aspiration. The background against which it was being put forward was one where already some of the Jacques Delors federalist proposals of the Rome summit had in part been turned back. Even so, committed journalists, diplomats and politicians tried unconvincingly to pretend that the word 'federalism' in this context only meant decentralisation. The controversy and argument over the word, however, would henceforth make it a little harder to argue that the Treaty of Rome had within it an inherent commitment to a federal United States of Europe. There then followed the negotiations over the Treaty of Maastricht.

# 6

# Second innings

When interviewing me on the publication of my autobiography in 1991, after I had announced that I was standing down at the next election, David Frost said he liked the title *Time to Declare* because, as a cricketing term, it allowed for a second innings!

I had decided that since it was clear that there was now no likelihood of arranging co-operation across political battle lines, it was time to declare my party political innings over. It was said that it was cussedness, megalomania, pride, arrogance, or any or all of these which made me stubbornly choose to stay a Social Democrat. It may have been inconvenient, but, like many others who supported the SDP, I knew I would remain a social democrat as a private citizen.

I had watched fading political idols haunt the corridors of power in the House of Commons and I had no wish to follow them. Knowing when to cease battling is as important as knowing when to fight. Most of the Labour policies I felt impelled to oppose in the 1980s had by 1992 been rejected. I believed that the counter-revolution would carry on, for if it did not our relative decline would continue. But I knew it was better to leave the House of Commons and not fight the 1992 general election.

Looking back on the big decisions I had taken in my more than quarter-century in the Commons, I had usually chosen them on the basis that I could make no other. That is not to say that all the decisions were judged correctly, but at least they were taken, with very few exceptions, on the basis of what I genuinely believed was in the best interests of the country. I did not worship as much as conventional politicians at the altar of party and I willingly paid a price for this disdain. I gave my all to the SDP for ten years and, though I believe it had a profound influence, I was sad that I could not ensure that it would remain a permanent feature of British politics. But the combination of policies and the philosophy which guided the SDP would, I believed, stay beyond our association with them in members of the Labour Party, Liberal Democrats and Conservatives.

The SDP had called for a classless society in the Limehouse Declaration and I watched with fascination as John Major developed his classless theme as Prime Minister. The political skill of Margaret Thatcher, by contrast, was her readiness, in a totally unabashed way, to mobilise the middle class. But it was a paradox of her stress on the individual that she was ready to assume greater powers for centralised government, in order, as she saw it, to protect the individual.

The antics of the Labour left in local government legitimised rate-capping. Then the poll tax had a corrosive effect on the standing and authority of local government. Margaret Thatcher's refusal to contemplate devolving power to a Scottish parliament and her dismissive attitude to constitutional change meant that, while she was condemning and exaggerating the centralising tendencies of the European Commission in Brussels she was herself presiding over the most centralised country in the European Community.

I saw then and still do today that an attractive feature of the social market is that it sees decentralisation as a natural development within a market economy. I had sought to develop this by establishing the Social Market Foundation (SMF), a charity devoted to promoting the concept of the social market economy in 1989. I could not as an active politician, with the Charity Commissioner zealously guarding the political neutrality of charities, be too heavily involved, though I was a trustee. Its executive director was Alastair Kilmarnock and its chairman was first Tom Chandos and then Robert Skidelsky, who was made a life peer by John Major at my request. Robert, who was professor of political economy at Warwick University, now as the biographer of John Maynard Keynes has a world audience in the light of the 2007 crisis. Both Tom and Robert remain close friends. The SMF celebrated its twentieth anniversary in 2009.

In Britain the role of the state was repeatedly extended through two world wars and consolidated in peacetime by Clement Attlee's Labour government. The Thatcher counter-revolution of the 1980s, part of which the SDP fully supported, was not just a wish to reverse those state powers, it went deeper than that – it sought to reassert a national self-confidence, to rediscover the commercial market-orientated prosperity of the Victorian era which had not just been the product of Empire but owed much to British invention, design, enterprise and industrial skill. But it did not initially draw enough on those other middle-class aspirations to serve the common good, to contribute to society as a whole; indeed at times the Thatcher counter-revolution quite unnecessarily upset those who held these values.

She also upset that broad group within her own party who thought of themselves as Europeans, starting with Harold Macmillan, who had believed in the early 1960s that Britain had to engage with the Common Market, as well as those who had firmly supported her government in its championing of the single market within the European Community in 1985 with extensive qualified majority voting. John Major's instinct was not to fall into the trap of sounding anti the whole European Community but to cut deals and negotiate toughly to protect British interests. Slowly over the winter of 1991 this is exactly what he did. The Maastricht Treaty imaginatively developed a so-called pillar structure. It had two supranational pillars, the Single Market and the Social Chapter, within which the European Commission would go on pushing the Council of Ministers to extend their coverage, and three intergovernmental pillars, Economic, Common Foreign and Security Policy and Justice and Home Affairs Policy. John Major, in my view unwisely, did not accept an extension of social policy through the new Social Chapter. He instead negotiated an opt-out from the chapter for the UK, which was then embraced by the incoming Labour government. While continuing within the Exchange Rate Mechanism Major sought to ring-fence the new European Monetary System by negotiating an opt-out for the UK. When those countries that were judged eligible to join had fulfilled the criteria, the UK and Denmark remained outside, retaining their own currency. Sweden later effectively stayed out of the euro despite not having negotiated a formal opt-out. A common, as distinct from a single, European foreign policy was established and despite arguments for voting by qualified majorities a system was negotiated where there could be no automatic majority voting and over defence issues at all times there had to be unanimity. Major was only able to secure these qualifications and opt-outs because of the understanding of the then German Chancellor, Helmut Kohl. Most Conservative

MPs were content to claim it as a negotiating triumph and in many ways it was. It added to Major's claim to competence that was first earned over the Gulf War. His personal handling of Europe proved a plus in the April 1992 election by the time the election was called in March. The Conservative Party looked very different by then from that hitherto identified with Margaret Thatcher. Chris Patten, the chairman of the party, was wisely talking about fixed-term parliaments and some interest was being shown in rediscovering Sir Alec Douglas-Home's blueprint for a Scottish assembly.

In the Dissolution Honours list I was awarded a life peerage. Membership of the House of Lords has been granted virtually automatically to every former Foreign Secretary that wanted it, so I did not feel that this was prime ministerial patronage. I decided I would be a crossbencher and sit as an independent Social Democrat. I had no wish, however, to continue as part of the legislative process. Having surpassed Nancy Astor's record as the longest-serving MP in Plymouth's history, more detailed involvement with legislation had no appeal.

I have been a long-time believer in electing a second chamber. I did not see legislation, other than suggesting revisions and preventing a parliament's life being extended beyond its five-year term, as being truly legitimate democratically. But I did want to talk from time to time on international affairs and I could not bear to lose access to Parliament's libraries, one of the best in the world in terms of quickly obtaining books on almost any subject.

The editor of the *Mail on Sunday*, an old friend, Stewart Steven, asked me to write three columns during the election campaign. The first, entitled 'Why I am still a floating voter', published on 22 March, claimed that former SDP voters had 'no natural home in any of the parties' but also argued, in relation to supporting the Liberal Democrats, that 'vindictiveness is always an unattractive characteristic, more so when it puts at risk one's political beliefs'. I stated, having highlighted some of the differences between Labour and Conservative policies, that 'if no party has an absolute majority, the calibre of the leader of the largest party, John Major or Neil Kinnock, will be crucial for us', that at this stage the election result was far from being set in concrete and that there was still all to play for in the next two and a half weeks.

On 29 March, in a reference to the disreputable way in which the NHS was being discussed, under the title 'Labour trump is a health hazard' I asked: will historians see the time a general election hinged on delays over inserting grommets for children with glue ear as being the moment Great Britain was relegated to the second division? I felt Labour was turning its back on essential reforms in health and in education. In a final column, headlined 'Keep Kinnock out of No. 10', I wrote about a dispiriting election. As a result I had found myself giving ever more weight to personality and a politician's actual record than to dubious promises and party posturing. I argued that voters should vote for Liberal Democrat MPs in their seats, for the two SDP MPs standing and for Liberal Democrats where there was a good chance of defeating the sitting Labour MP. But in Bath I said they should support Chris Patten, who would be a crucial influence in any hung Parliament, which would have happened if the SDP/Liberal Alliance still existed.

In the event, much to many people's surprise, John Major had a considerable personal success and the Conservatives won an overall majority of twenty-one seats. Surprisingly, Chris Patten lost in Bath and there was intense press speculation about him being offered the governorship of Hong Kong and that he had asked John Major for time to think it over. There was some speculation about whether I would be offered the governorship if he turned it down and decided to stay in British politics for a Cabinet position, either through fighting a by-election or going to the House of Lords. As fate would have it, the Owen and Patten families met in the lounge at Gatwick that weekend, both flying off with their daughters to France. It transpired that at that stage none of the daughters wished their respective fathers to go to Hong Kong! Debbie and I were very unsure that even if offered we would go. I had several irons in the fire for jobs in international business and was looking forward to no more politics, and when Chris decided to go to Hong Kong.

It transpired that on the afternoon of Wednesday 29 July 1992 I was just on the point of announcing a non-executive directorship of an international manufacturing company when the phone rang as I sat in my London office looking out across Birdcage Walk on St James's Park. It was a young researcher from the BBC radio programme *Today*, asking if I would come on the next morning to talk about the Serbian prison camps in Bosnia-Herzegovina. He was more persuasive than most but I was not keen. I had deliberately kept out of politics since leaving the House of Commons, to emphasise that I was not going back into party politics. I was already developing the work of a small charity, Humanitas, of which I was chairman. I had no wish, then, to be dragged in by the BBC to comment on the former Yugoslavia, an area of policy of which I had deliberately steered clear; but surprisingly I weakened slightly and suggested he might call after six that evening, when I would be back home.

The researcher had mentioned in particular the *Guardian* story on the camps in Bosnia-Herzegovina which I had read with shock that morning but had not fully absorbed. So that evening I read the *Guardian* exposé again with more attention. It was a horrifying tale and as I read it I became angry. I had been growing increasingly restless about the inaction of the Western democracies over Yugoslavia but wary of involving myself. The last serious discussion I had had on Yugoslavia had been with Douglas Hurd at the end of May at a mutual friend's house, sipping a pre-lunch drink on the grass, when he had asked me straight out if I would put British troops into Bosnia-Herzegovina; my reaction had been to say no – stay clear of becoming a combatant but bring EC diplomacy and UN peacekeeping together.

I asked myself that Wednesday evening two months later whether anything had changed. I was still against putting in troops on the ground, but the revelations coming in from the camps showed that we were witnessing grotesque abuses of humanitarian law and that the Bosnian Serb leadership was failing to act to curb them despite the clamour of world condemnation. Though the evidence was still patchy, all my instincts told me that what we were hearing and seeing was just the tip of an iceberg and I feared that, as over the humanitarian disaster that had faced the Kurds a year before, Western governments were deliberately shutting their eyes and blocking their ears. My role as chairman of Humanitas, which I had set up to build on the findings of the Independent Commission on International Humanitarian Issues, of which I was a member, was my one exception to withdrawal from political activity. I had been particularly interested in humanitarian intervention since Humanitas had sponsored a conference on the issue, focusing on the Kurds, so I was already mentally engaged in analysing what could be done in Bosnia.

The young man from the BBC rang back that evening, this time even more persuasive. Without much enthusiasm I agreed to be interviewed. So I pondered the whole issue afresh and turned my mind back to the history. I was no stranger to Yugoslavia, having travelled there more extensively than in any other country in Europe, except France. As a student I had read with fascination the writings of Milovan Djilas, the Partisan leader and erstwhile friend of Marshal Tito who had gone on to denounce communism in the 1950s. During my time as Foreign Secretary the main concern about Yugoslavia had been what would happen to the country when Tito died, which actually happened in 1980 – the year after I left office. Yet no one could forget that the First World War had been triggered in Sarajevo, and ominously the best of the futuristic scenarios on the start of a Third World War, by General Sir John Hackett, had taken Yugoslavia as its focus.

We all learnt at school that on 28 June 1914 the heir to the Habsburg throne, Archduke Franz Ferdinand, was assassinated while visiting Sarajevo. Yet I suspect I was not alone in never realising that the visit was made with deliberate Austrian provocation on Serbia's National Day, comparable – according to the historian A. J. P. Taylor – to sending a member of the British royal family to Dublin on St Patrick's Day at the height of the Troubles. On 23 July the Austrian government, knowing that the assassination had been done by a Bosnian Serb with the nationalist motive of achieving a greater Serbia, sent a threatening and humiliating ultimatum to the Serbian government. The British Foreign Secretary, Sir Edward Grey, offered to mediate and attempted to persuade the German government to restrain the incompetent militarists in Vienna. Despite the Serbian government accepting virtually every demand and satisfying Kaiser Wilhelm sufficient for him to comment that 'every reason for war disappears', on 28 July Vienna declared war and the Austro-Hungarian armies started to bombard Belgrade. Within six weeks Grey declared, 'The lamps are going out all over Europe,' and a war which claimed eight million lives in Europe had begun.

Serbia, Britain, France and Russia were now allies. The Croats and Bosnians were within the Austro-Hungarian Empire, whose army in

1915 pushed down to Istanbul, defeating the Serbs. The Serbian army retreated from Kosovo across the mountains to the Adriatic, where King Peter formed a government in exile on Corfu. A Yugoslav committee set up by exiled Habsburg Slavs in London campaigned for a united South Slav state to be founded after the war; and when the Austro-Hungarian Empire disintegrated, the political life of the Kingdom of Serbs, Croats and Slovenes began, on 1 December 1918. It was renamed Yugoslavia in 1929, as literally the country of the South Slavs. Yet in 1918 many of its inhabitants were not South Slavs but Germans, Hungarians, Albanians, Romanians, Turks and Greeks. There were three religious groups – Serbian Orthodox, Roman Catholic and Muslim; six customs areas, five currencies, four railway networks, three banking systems and for a time two governments, in Zagreb and Belgrade.

Even before the start of the Second World War Croat separatism had been fed and financed by Mussolini's fascist government. On 25 March 1941 an agreement was signed with Hitler in Vienna, linking Yugoslavia with the Tripartite Pact; two days later Prince Paul was deposed in a *coup d'état* by predominantly Serbian officers from the armed forces. The British Prime Minister, Winston Churchill, desperate for allies in the battle against Nazi Germany, appealed to the heart and to history in his broadcast to the people of Yugoslavia on 13 April: 'Serbs, we know you. You were our allies in the last war, and your arms are covered with glory. Croats and Slovenes, we know your military history. For centuries you were the bulwark of Christianity. Your fame as warriors spread far and wide on the Continent.'

In April 1941 Germany attacked Yugoslavia and the German Luftwaffe bombed Belgrade, killing between 5,000 and 17,000 civilians. Hitler proceeded rapidly to dismember Yugoslavia, giving parts of it to Nazi Germany's allies Hungary, Romania and Bulgaria. The Nazis also endorsed the creation of the Independent State of Croatia, which included Bosnia-Herzegovina, divided into German and Italian spheres of influence, with the Croat fascist Ante Pavelić as its puppet ruler. Over the next few years Pavelić and his armed Ustashas committed atrocities and massacres of an unspeakable kind. Later Nuremberg judged what happened to the Serbs at the hands of the Croats and the Germans as genocide. No one knows exactly how many Serbs were killed. The Serbs say three-quarters of a million; the Germans 350,000. Whatever the number, it is hard to deny that these killings are an essential part of the background to the wars of disintegration in the former Yugoslavia. A good short history of Yugoslavia says that the Croatian government attitude to the Bosnian Muslims in the early 1940s was ambivalent. Although there were cases of Ustasha atrocities against Muslims, there were also other incidents where Muslims were encouraged by the authorities to massacre Serbs. There were Muslim SS units but there were also Muslims who fought with Tito's Partisans.

The world has never recognised sufficiently clearly that a long and bloody civil war went on in Yugoslavia throughout the Second World War, and the reason for this ignorance is that the existence of that civil conflict was deliberately suppressed by Tito, both during and after the war. Tito wanted to concentrate on the Partisan victory over fascism and felt that to dwell on the Yugoslav civil war would detract from this victory and make it harder to weld the country together. It was Tito who after the war ordered the bulldozing of the Croat-run extermination camp at Jasenovac, near the river Sava, where hundreds of thousands of Serbs, Jews and Gypsies were murdered; and not until 1960 did he allow a museum and memorial centre to be built there. In total, of the 1.7 million Yugoslavs killed during the Second World War, about 1 million were slain by fellow Yugoslavs. For the Allies during the war the crucial question was to encourage the Yugoslavs to expend their energies not on fighting themselves but on fighting Hitler's and Mussolini's forces; hence they too somewhat glossed over the existence of the civil war. In 1942 Britain supported the Serbian nationalist resistance leader, Colonel Draža Mihailović, but by early 1943 it seemed the Allies had been backing, in war effort terms, the wrong horse and Churchill switched to Tito. At the Tehran conference of 28 November 1943 Churchill told Stalin and Roosevelt that Tito was doing 'much more' for the Allied cause than Mihailović and that the Balkan theatre was one of the areas 'where we could stretch the enemy to the utmost'.

Differences between the UK and US over Yugoslavia are not a new phenomenon. On 6 April 1944, learning that the Americans were about to send an intelligence mission to Mihailović at the very moment when Britain was withdrawing the last of its support,

Churchill cabled Cairo to delay 'by every reasonable means' any arrangements to fly the American mission into Yugoslavia, 'the greatest courtesy being used to our friends and Allies in every case, but no transportation'. Churchill also cabled Roosevelt that same day to warn that despatching an American mission 'will show throughout the Balkans a complete contrariety of action between Britain and the United States'.

There are many myths about Tito, one of which is that he was not a true communist. When Churchill met Tito on 12 August 1944 at Naples he told him he could not tolerate Allied war material being used against rival Yugoslavs. The records show that Tito reassured Churchill that 'he had no desire to introduce the communist system into Yugoslavia, if only for the reason that it was to be expected that most European countries after the war would be living under a democratic system from which Yugoslavia could not afford to differ'. Tito was, of course, lying.

Yugoslavia did not liberate itself to the extent that its propaganda and history books claim. The historian Michael Howard wrote, 'Though it is unfashionable to say so, it was liberated by Marshal Tolbukhin's Third Ukrainian Army, which by the end of 1944 occupied about one third of Yugoslav territory.'

It is another carefully fostered myth about Tito that he rebelled against Stalin. It was in fact Stalin who first isolated Yugoslavia because he felt it and Tito were getting above themselves. 'I will shake my finger and there will be no more Tito,' said Stalin. Moscow's decision came on 27 March 1948, in Tito's words 'as if a thunderbolt had struck me'. He thought of himself as a loyal Soviet communist. It was then that disillusionment, disengagement and non-alignment started.

Both the British Foreign Secretary, Ernest Bevin, and the US Truman administration decided in the autumn of 1948, at the start of the Cold War period, to keep Tito 'afloat' to weaken Moscow and show that a communist government could exist without Stalin's support. Britain again fostered the romantic image of Tito as Partisan leader. When as Foreign Secretary I met Tito in 1979, shortly before his death, Western democratic governments were still finding it convenient to take him at face value. Western aid and loans financed the absurdly large Yugoslav army long after any remote threat of

Soviet invasion had gone. We were, however, asking the question 'After Tito, what?', rather as we had asked 'After Kenyatta, what?'

Long before Tito died many had predicted division and disarray to follow; that it did not come as soon as forecast lulled people into believing that the old nationalisms had been forgotten. In truth, Croatian, Serbian and Slovenian nationalism was stirring in the 1980s though still suppressed. On Europe's television sets in 1989, when the Netherlands played a friendly football match against Yugoslavia in Zagreb, we saw how even sport could not keep a Yugoslav identity alive: the crowd turned their backs on the Yugoslav players, booed the Yugoslav national anthem and cheered for the Dutch team throughout the match. Serbian nationalism was in part assuaged by Serbian dominance in the higher ranks of the Yugoslav army and among the administrators in Belgrade. When in 1990 elections were held in all six republics – the first proper elections since 1927 – it was the nationalist parties that everywhere received the strongest support through the ballot box. In retrospect we in the West should then have recognised an inevitable trend and encouraged an ordered and negotiated path to nationhood for Slovenia and Croatia, with Serbia, Montenegro, Macedonia and Bosnia-Herzegovina perhaps emerging as a modern democratic Yugoslavia, for both Kiro Gligorov and Alija Izetbegović were content at one stage for a lesser degree of independence than Croatia and Slovenia. But the prevailing 'wisdom' in 1990 and 1991 was 'no fragmentation'. Mikhail Gorbachev was still striving to keep the Soviet Union together, and Yugoslavia was discouraged from splitting up its territory lest it encouraged a similar splitting in the USSR, a view which was maintained with the emergence of the Russian Federation under Boris Yeltsin.

Then, in 1992, the more I read and thought it all through the more I judged that John Major, as Prime Minister, should call for an international threat of air strikes in relation to the Serbs in a fashion not dissimilar to the 'safe haven' initiative which others including myself had urged him to take over the Kurds the previous year. I began to search for a limited form of military action which could make the Serbs stop practising ethnic cleansing in their war against the Muslims and force a military standstill. The prison camps were in western and northern Bosnia, not in the mountains that covered most of Bosnia-Herzegovina. The associated military installations could easily be reached from NATO airfields in surrounding countries and, given the flat terrain, action from the air against Serb military targets could in my view have been as surgical as in the desert flatness of Iraq. I had followed the arguments for and against military intervention in the former Yugoslavia with care and I genuinely felt that here, unlike in Sarajevo, there was an opportunity for limited action for a humanitarian purpose which did not set NATO on an automatic escalator to putting in ground troops. We had missed an earlier opportunity to intervene with naval forces when the Yugoslav navy shelled Dubrovnik. The UN was not yet involved on the ground in Bosnia-Herzegovina, except for a small contingent of 300 to keep Sarajevo airport open. They might have needed to be removed or reinforced before any strike action from the air, as also might UNHCR and other aid workers. The risk was that the Muslims in these camps, following air strikes, might have been massacred by undisciplined militia and vengeful local people; also, Sarajevo, already subject to a siege, might have been taken by the Serbs. These were genuine risks from military intervention from the air but from my limited knowledge it seemed feasible.

What I did not know is that on Sunday 26 July Governor Bill Clinton, campaigning in the US presidential election against the incumbent, George Bush, had authorised his campaign office in Little Rock, Arkansas, to issue a little-noticed policy statement on the fighting in Bosnia-Herzegovina, saying, 'The United States should take the lead in seeking United Nations Security Council authorisation for air strikes against those who are attacking the relief effort. The United States should be prepared to lend appropriate military support to that operation.' Looking back, Clinton's views then were identical to mine. He went on:

> We should make clear that the economic blockade against Serbia will be tightened, not only on weapons but also on oil and other supplies that sustain the renegade regime of Slobodan Milošević. European and US naval forces in the Adriatic should be given authority by the UN to stop and search ships that might be carrying contraband heading for Serbia and her ally, Montenegro.

Clinton also called for international action to charge people 'with crimes against humanity under international law – as we should have done long ago in the case of Iraq'.

For the White House press spokesman, Marlin Fitzwater, this was an opportunity for Bush to attack Clinton on an issue after Iraq on which the presidential team felt their candidate was strong. While Bush said nothing, Vice-President Dan Quayle began to point up Bush's experience in foreign policy and contrast it with Clinton's inexperience. Increasingly, Yugoslavia became a factor in the US election campaign. An old journalist friend of mine, Johnny Apple, wrote a detailed and perceptive analytical article in the 28 July edition of the *New York Times* entitled 'Campaign shifts to a new turf', which I read later, describing Clinton's foreign policy team as being divided along hawk-and-dove fault-lines that first emerged in the Vietnam War and as being fearful of seeming soft on communism and other foes of the United States. He reminded his readers that Clinton had spoken out on Bosnia, several times taking a more aggressive posture than Bush and cited an interview on 25 June in which he professed willingness to see US participation in a multilateral military force that would 'shoot its way into' Sarajevo airport, if necessary, to make it safe enough for a steady airlift of relief supplies. But on the evening of 29 July in London I was unaware of any of this and was only to discover it when I arrived in the United States a few days later.

It is not hard for me to see how these underlying attitudes coloured much of the policy ambivalence of President Clinton towards the Balkans over the next few years. We both started from the same basic position and in some ways we both trod the same painful learning curve, albeit at a different pace and along different paths. The biggest difference between us was that Clinton's foreign policy advisers took a long time to grasp the implications of the UN humanitarian intervention in Bosnia-Herzegovina after October 1992. Some of them did adjust, while others never appeared to accept that UN deployment in 1992 in vulnerable areas like Srebrenica, Žepa, Goražde and Bihać inhibited widespread intervention from the air and that these UN forces would have to leave these parts of Bosnia-Herzegovina before a lifting of the unanimously imposed arms embargo could be considered and supportive strikes started.

Leaving would then make it even harder to ensure that humanitarian convoys got through to isolated communities, mainly but not exclusively Muslim.

Next morning, 30 July, there was an emotive article in the *Daily Express* about the situation in the camps, drawing analogies with the Nazi concentration camps. In the BBC *Today* studio I called on John Major to act and to use NATO air power to impose a ceasefire. Immediately afterwards, I dictated a letter to John Major over the phone to my secretary, and sent the final version by fax direct to 10 Downing Street, the *Evening Standard* and the Press Association, all before nine o'clock in the morning. In it I said:

> The first essential step is to stop by threat of force the use or movement of any military aircraft, tanks, armoured vehicles or artillery in the former territory of Yugoslavia. It is perfectly within the power of NATO to enforce such an immediate ceasefire. Satellite and air reconnaissance could pinpoint any unauthorised military activity and retaliatory air strikes could be mounted from NATO airfields that ring Yugoslavia or by planes flying from aircraft carriers. This could be implemented within hours, not even days, once the requisite authority has been got from the UN Security Council.
>
> I believe that a few of the bigger cities currently under attack such as Sarajevo and Goražde should be reinforced by air with troops acting under the authority of the UN, if necessary initially para-chuting men and materials in to secure air communications. If these actions were taken within days then Bosnia would not be completely overrun by Serb and Croatian forces and a peace settlement could then be negotiated. If no action is taken now there will be virtually nothing left of Bosnia for the Muslim population to negotiate about.

Later that day Andrew Gimson, my godson, rang and said he was writing an article on Yugoslavia for the *Sunday Telegraph*, and we talked the subject through in some detail. He reminded me that the Balkans was the issue that had inspired Gladstone to return to the battleground of British politics, and how Disraeli, after the Congress of Berlin, had despaired of bringing order to Serbia, Bosnia and Herzegovina. I reiterated what was becoming a familiar mantra about not wanting to be sucked back into politics and preparing for an international business career. But Andrew also quoted with some passion Otto von Bismarck's saying that 'the Balkans were not worth the healthy bones of a single Pomeranian grenadier'. I was to discover that it was this view which was held by all the key governments when it came to committing troops on the ground in Bosnia-Herzegovina and which ensured that international diplomacy without military power was the hallmark of every attitude and action towards the former Yugoslavia.

On Monday morning I received John Major's reply to my letter. He wrote:

> We do not believe that this is the time to think in the terms you suggest of a military solution. We could not unite the international community behind such a policy. In practice we see real difficulties over proposals to use either air power or ground forces in the way you suggest. We have of course professionally studied the military implications which are more serious than you suggest. Air power would be unlikely to be enough. The numbers of forces involved, the likely length of operations and the level of casualties (civilian as well as military) would all be higher than you suggest. We are not dealing with an orthodox war, a single enemy, a front line, or clearly identifiable targets. Nor do I detect any support in Parliament or in public opinion for operations which would tie down large numbers of British forces in difficult and dangerous terrain for a long period.

On Wednesday 5 August, having flown to the United States the day before with my children, I woke up to a fine summer's day on Long Island at Debbie's family home. Yugoslavia was, however, not far away. In a back number of the *New York Times* I read for the first time the detail of Bill Clinton's stance. It was clear that the public mood in the US was responding to stories about the Serb detention camps more strongly than was the case in Britain. There was also in the newspapers the first hint of a State Department cover-up, with allegations that they had known much earlier about what was likely to be happening to Muslim prisoners. That day Governor Clinton, campaigning in Illinois, had said again, 'I would begin with air power against the Serbs to try to restore the basic conditions of humanity,' and on the same platform Senator Gore said, 'The Europeans have been a little timid about doing something to stop this mass murder,' a theme which he was to develop further.

On Thursday 6 August over lunch in New York I had a fascinating discussion on Yugoslavia with Cy Vance. We had remained friends since we had worked together in government from 1977 to 1979. He told me that Boutros Boutros-Ghali had asked him that morning to be his special representative for a new standing conference that was to be set up following the London conference. He asked me whether I felt he should accept. It was rather like when I saw him the day he resigned as US Secretary of State, just after he had been to see President Carter in the White House. He was questioning himself by asking me questions. Were the Europeans really committed to reversing ethnic cleansing? What did Douglas Hurd and John Major really think about the conference? I explained about the reaction to my letter calling for intervention from the air, and though Cy did not comment much on the substance he clearly believed that even such limited military action would not work. I advised him to accept the secretary general's request only if he was sure he would not be made a prisoner of policies that involved accepting the status quo, partitioning Bosnia-Herzegovina and acquiescing in a Greater Serbia. He was clearly adamant that ethnic cleansing had to be to a great extent reversed and that as far as possible no territory taken as a result of force should be conceded to the Serbs. It was almost certain from what Cy said that the standing conference would be a joint UN–EC venture. I already felt it was vital to involve the UN and that the EC had no longer much of a role on its own. Cy, in passing, mentioned that he was not sure how strongly Peter Carrington was committed to staying with the negotiations and how nice it would be if I could be involved, but I joked that I was *persona non grata* with the British government after my recent call for military action. As I left he said it would be pleasant for us to get together with Debbie and his own wife Gay, and I said there was a chance that we might be in New York on Tuesday evening before flying out to Salt Lake City on Wednesday morning. When I arrived back at the railway station that night, Debbie explained that Cy had rung and they had fixed dinner for Tuesday. Debbie's intuition was: 'He wants something, David. This is not just a social occasion.'

Over the weekend I read myself into American attitudes to the crisis in the former Yugoslavia. Leslie Gelb, who had been with Cy Vance at the State Department and whom I knew and respected, had written an article in the *New York Times* on Thursday 6 August entitled 'False Humanitarianism', which predicted future events:

> The Bush Administration seeks a much narrower focus for the London conference – to strengthen humanitarian relief efforts. Administration officials want to expand these efforts beyond Sarajevo. This will require land convoys, which in turn will require protection. The Administration will support giving UN relief units some firepower for self-protection. It will also grudgingly consider providing the convoys with air cover, but neither London nor Paris is enthusiastic about that.
>
> The effect of such an American focus on relief will be to preclude discussion of wider UN military action. And Washington is not alone in this stratagem. No UN Security Council member seems prepared to cross the line from humanitarian relief to combat. Russia even seems ready to veto proposals to do so.

At dinner with Gay, Debbie and me in the River Club that evening, Cy went straight to the point. He was flying to London by Concorde on Thursday for a meeting with Peter Carrington to plan the London conference. David Hannay, the UK permanent representative, would be there as well. Carrington had said on the telephone that he wanted to appoint an 'alternate' for himself as chairman, and had suggested another Conservative politician, whose name Cy had difficulty in recalling. Cy saw this as a sign that Carrington wanted out, and he even suspected that it was a device to get out since Carrington would expect him to refuse such an arrangement. Cy wanted to be in a position to suggest my name if this happened. Would I agree?

Over the weekend I had occasionally wondered what I would say to this question, so I had already weighed up the counter-argument about needing to gain experience of international business quickly and not waiting until I was too old to start a new career. But I never took the possibility very seriously because I thought my views on Yugoslavia would exclude me from consideration. I knew Cy did not share my opinions on using air power, but I suspected there was not a single European head of government who shared them either. The emphasis now being put on a humanitarian initiative by President Bush was itself a recognition that he was not ready to use US military power to dislodge the Serbs. The question was whether to go on being a voice in the wilderness over Yugoslavia or join in the quest for peace. Cy was a man I deeply respected, he shared all of my passion in wanting to reverse ethnic cleansing and it would be a delight to work with him again. My saying yes on the spot was not a snap answer but a considered judgement. All the same, I felt less certain than Cy that Peter Carrington would opt to go, and I gave a strong warning that Douglas Hurd might not want me to replace him if he did.

Early in the morning of Monday 17 August Cy rang me in Colorado, where I was about to spend a few days river-rafting, to say that he had heard from Peter Carrington that Douglas Hurd was keen for me to do the job. I told Cy what I had heard from Stephen Wall, my old private secretary in the Foreign Office who had dealt with Africa. He was now working in No. 10 and had told me about John Major's positive attitude to my appointment. It was now looking very likely that the UK, which held the EC presidency, would put me forward and the big question in my mind was whether the French would agree. I felt they might not like another British chairman. Peter Carrington had been offered the job by the Dutch when they held the EC presidency and there was no automatic right for the post to be filled by the UK. And although my strongest card was Cy Vance's support, this might be less of an advantage with the French, for they would be suspicious of anything that smacked of an Anglo-American axis.

On the Colorado River we stepped onto our rubber raft and pushed off for a memorable five days away from civilisation. I cannot say I had no cares in the world, and from time to time I mulled over the Yugoslavian situation and pondered: what if I was offered the job? Only international, not domestic, politics could have tempted me to give up being a private citizen. Objectively the prospect had moved from an unlikely possibility to a probability. On the raft, family and friends teased me about the way I pronounced 'Herzegovina', and indeed, so bad is my ear for pronunciation that it took all of that time to get it right.

On Friday 21 August we arrived at Lake Powell, feeling like astronauts: that part of America is like a moonscape and we had not heard a radio broadcast or seen a newspaper for five days. On the landing stage I called Stephen Wall to find out what had happened.

His news was that the Prime Minister and Douglas Hurd had agreed on my candidature and my name had gone forward to the EC. The response from the other European governments so far was very positive, though the French were grumbling that I was anti-Serb, so while it was not yet definite it was more likely than not that I would be appointed. Interestingly, and somewhat magnanimously, in view of my criticism of their premature recognition of Croatia, I was told the German government was in favour of my appointment.

Early on Monday 24 August we arrived back in London. Douglas Hurd rang me up and said he was delighted I had agreed to serve; he warned me that there were dangers ahead with the French, but thought it was likely they would be overcome.

On Tuesday 25 August I went into my office at the beginning of three difficult days when everyone was speculating almost to the point of assuming I was going to get the job, and yet I did not know for certain and heard little from anybody. It was hard to act normally. The French were in trouble with their public opinion over their referendum on the Maastricht Treaty, and François Mitterrand was allegedly inviting John Major to appear with him on a television programme; from that position it seemed hard for the French to say no to my appointment. Peter Carrington gave a press conference to confirm the BBC story in the *One o'Clock News* that he was going and said I was going to replace him. Douglas Hurd's private secretary confirmed that their intention was to announce my appointment on Thursday evening at the close of the London conference and Douglas rang to say we might need to discuss a form of words to cover my previous statements about use of air power, which still worried the French. In fact he never pushed a form of words which could have been impossible for me. On the BBC's *Newsnight* the leader of the Bosnian Serbs, Dr Radovan Karadžić, criticised my appointment as EC mediator, saying, 'It would not be right or advisable to nominate him to that job and I think that the Serbian side in Bosnia-Herzegovina would have a very hard time dealing with him.'

On Wednesday 26 August there was an excellent editorial in the *Guardian* entitled 'Carrot or stick needed for Serbia', saying, 'What is absolutely certain is that, unless Lord Carrington's successor can be delivered from the problem he faced, that of possessing neither stick nor carrot, we can expect no end to the tragedy of the South Slavs.'

On Thursday 27 August the Egyptian embassy rang to ask Debbie and me to a dinner that night for Boutros Boutros-Ghali. I accepted on the condition that my appointment had been announced by then. Shortly after 6.00 p.m. I heard that I had been appointed. Douglas Hurd rang with a quick confirmation of my appointment and invited me to the EC Foreign Ministers' informal weekend meeting at Brocket Hall on 12–13 September. Then the Foreign Office News Department rang to ask for a press statement. As I began to work through all the details the more dubious I became about accepting a salary from the British government, from whom it would have to come since they were holding the EC presidency. I had no wish to be seen as a British diplomat or civil servant and preferred not to accept the 'Queen's shilling'. Cy Vance had assured me that our task would only last for six months, and in the moral mess that was the former Yugoslavia it seemed better for me to be totally independent and not profiting in any way from the misery and despair of it all, so I refused a salary from the UK government.

When we arrived at the Egyptian embassy for dinner Boutros-Ghali and Cy Vance were still involved with John Major in a press conference and the French Minister of Defence, Pierre Joxe, was there waiting. We had a long chat on the use of air power, both of us being very worried about Serbian air activity, and he was far from ruling out enforcing a no-fly zone over Bosnia-Herzegovina. I was rather encouraged, because I wanted to persuade the French to put some steel behind our diplomacy. But Joxe's view was not that of President Mitterrand, as I discovered when I saw him in Paris a few days later. Mitterrand specifically warned me of the dangers of aggressive force against the Serbs and ruled out air strikes.

Eventually Cy and Boutros-Ghali arrived with their wives and we went in to dinner. Very astutely I was placed next to Cy. Whether he had asked or our hostess had guessed we would have much to talk about I do not know, but it was sophisticated diplomacy. He did not hide his utter delight that I was on the team and said he had not dared to telephone me but had just kept his fingers crossed while repeatedly asking whether there were any obstacles to my appointment. He wanted to start the Geneva conference in five days' time and was flying back to New York the next day. Boutros was very warm about my appointment and full of praise for John Major's chairmanship of the London conference. The Turkish Foreign Minister, who was also present, wanted NATO force to be used and was cogent as to why. The French Foreign Minister, Roland Dumas, came in late; he was very civil throughout our short conversation and I sensed no animosity over my appointment. The ambassador made a good speech and Cy replied gracefully. Many were clearly surprised to learn from his references to me how close we were. We agreed that I would come and meet Milan Panić, the Prime Minister of the Federal Republic of Yugoslavia (FRY), comprising Serbia and Montenegro, at his hotel the next morning.

# 7

# Balkan odyssey

I sensed that the Vance–Owen team was back in harness – fifteen years from when we had started developing Anglo-American policy towards southern Africa together, and thirteen years from when Cy had rung me on the Friday morning after Labour had lost the general election. Since then we had kept in constant touch, and had continued to work together on the Palme commission. We were a natural blend: he cautious, methodical, at times legalistic but brave and moral; I more innovative, mercurial, thinking more laterally but less experienced. After the post mortem on the 1987 general election and my period as joint party leader with David Steel I had begun almost to believe those who said that it was impossible for me or perhaps any two people to work in partnership in a political leadership role – and yet I knew it was not true. I felt the old compatibility and the added strength of two minds; and while Cy was older his vitality, far from being impaired, seemed even greater. Thereafter he kept up a cracking pace that at times left me reeling and many of the hard-working younger members of our team in Geneva exhausted.

Since 10 Downing Street was being painted I went to Admiralty House to see the Prime Minister, and we walked out into the courtyard for a photocall – which produced the front cover illustration for the satirical magazine *Private Eye*, as a mirror image of the picture with us shaking our left hands and speech bubbles from John Major's mouth saying 'I'm afraid it's a lost cause' and from mine replying 'I'm your man'. Most of the morning's press comment, while favourable to me personally, was not in the least optimistic about the task ahead. John Major and I had a good chat during which he pressed me quite hard to take a salary on the basis that he could not always appoint people of independent means like Peter Carrington, and I doubt he understood my somewhat confused objections. He made no attempt to hide the immense difficulties ahead. Then he asked me what I thought of Sir David Hannay, and since I knew of his recent clash with Boutros-Ghali I was conscious that I might lose him in New York if I said anything critical. I remembered David Hannay from when he dealt with energy in the Foreign Office – quick, bright, interested in detail; I was sure I could work with him and said so. He never gave me any cause to change that judgement. Exceptionally good at drafting and making sense of Security Council decisions, he and his French counterpart, Ambassador Mérimée, were able to check and counter most of the erratic and irresponsible actions contemplated in the Security Council.

I met Klaus Kinkel, the German Foreign Minister, whom I found friendly, informal and direct. Despite differences on policy I always enjoyed working with him. He was very conscious that since Germany was constitutionally prevented from deploying troops for the UN effort in Bosnia-Herzegovina he had to be very careful not to advocate policies that could lead to other countries' servicemen losing their lives. It was a sensitive stance to adopt and needed courage to maintain as the German press were strong advocates of a more aggressive policy. I found him at all times a man with genuinely liberal instincts, but he did not have the knowledge in foreign affairs, or authority within his party, of his predecessor, Hans-Dietrich Genscher. I decided then and there that I would not spend time on public finger-pointing about German support for premature recognition of Croatia and Bosnia or the rights and wrongs of EC policy hitherto. My task was to keep the twelve member states together, and the best way to do that was to look forward.

I adopted a somewhat similar attitude in public towards the causes of the wars in the former Yugoslavia. It was enough to deal with present outrages and future peace. What should have been done before the dissolution of Yugoslavia was an interesting but very divisive question. Also, the facts were not as I had first thought; while the terms 'aggressor' and 'victim' were being brandished as weapons in a propaganda war, the true situation was obviously far more complex than that dichotomy implied – and anyhow, they were terms better avoided publicly by a negotiator.

I saw Cy Vance again for a quick chat, while we appeared together for the cameras. Then I talked to Martti Ahtisaari, whom Cy had asked to come over. He was going back to Finland, where he was the diplomatic head of the Ministry of Foreign Affairs, to consult and give us an answer on whether or not he would join us in Geneva. Martti had successfully led the UN operation for Namibian independence, and we needed his experience badly; he became our anchorman in Geneva in negotiations with the parties in Bosnia-Herzegovina and made an invaluable contribution. He was elected as President of Finland in 1994 and played a role in presenting the Russian/US-brokered plan to end the war over Kosovo and then tried to resolve the questions over the recognition of Kosovo.

At the Foreign Office I saw Sir David Gillmore as arranged. With him was Jeremy Greenstock, the head of policy on the former Yugoslavia, who opened up immediately to say they had a problem over heavy weapons. Apparently Dr Karadžić had signed an agreement with Douglas Hogg accepting UN supervision and control of heavy weapons handed in by the Serbs. But the British government was embarrassed by Cabinet decisions which did not allow our troops assigned to the UN for humanitarian purposes to be tasked with supervising and controlling these heavy weapons. Cy had already told me that neither he nor Boutros was aware of the agreement before it had been signed and that they believed that it was a promise that Karadžić had no intention of fulfilling. Moreover, the UN believed the deal was quite unenforceable, for there were no troops mandated to do the job. I told them I would try to sort it out. So much for what the UK press was calling the main achievement of what was meant to be a joint UN–EC conference. Cy was clearly irritated and refused to give any clue or timetable in response to journalists' questions. He had earlier warned me to avoid using the word 'ceasefire' if at all possible, and we both stressed the hard road ahead. Cy was asked if he thought this more difficult than the Camp David negotiations on the Middle East and he replied with much emphasis, 'This is more difficult because the fighting is more severe, it is more brutal, the situation has been completely out of control. The ability to control the fighters is not in the hands of the government in the way it was at the time of the Middle East negotiations.'

On Sunday I saw Peter Carrington at his Buckinghamshire farm for tea. Peter was relaxed as ever, but as he talked about the way he had been treated by the European Foreign Ministers a hard edge came into his voice. There was no doubt he saw the EC recognition of Croatia in December 1991 as a betrayal, and as he chronicled the story I wondered aloud what they could do to me, only for him to chortle, 'Don't worry, there's nothing left for them to do.' His comments about the various Balkan leaders were unprintable but I was surprised that there was not much to choose between them on his scale of perfidy. He, even more than the press over the weekend, emphasised the scale of the problem facing me. Almost everyone believed that not much could be done to halt the fighting. The task was being labelled 'mission impossible'.

The International Conference on the Former Yugoslavia (ICFY) began in continuous session on the morning of Thursday 3 September 1992. Cy Vance had flown in from New York overnight and I had flown in from Rome; we met at the airport for an impromptu press conference. I had learnt much in my previous three days' travelling. I had been to Belgium (to see the European Commission), the Netherlands, Denmark, Portugal, France and Italy.

The Netherlands had held the EC presidency from the outbreak of the war in July until December 1991, and in consequence of my visit to The Hague I discovered that on 13 July 1991, when the Slovenian and Croatian declarations of independence were just eighteen days old, the Dutch government had suggested to the other EC member states that the option of agreed changes to some of the internal borders between the Yugoslav republics might be explored. Incomprehensibly, the proposal to redraw the republics' boundaries had been rejected by all eleven other EC countries. The first ground for objection was that it would open a Pandora's box. Secondly, it was considered out of date to draw state borders along ethnic lines. Thirdly, it was thought that republic boundaries could not be redrawn in view of the large numbers of separate 'pockets' where there were ethnic majorities not geographically connected. It is true that there could not have been a total accommodation of Serb demands; but to rule out any discussion or opportunity for compromise in order to head off war was an extraordinary decision. My view has always been that to have stuck unyieldingly to the internal boundaries of the six republics within the former Yugoslavia, namely Serbia, Croatia, Slovenia, Bosnia-Herzegovina, Montenegro and Macedonia, before there was any question of recognition of these republics, as being the boundaries for independent states was a folly far greater than that of premature recognition itself. The refusal to make these borders negotiable greatly hampered the EC's attempt at crisis management in July and August 1991 and subsequently put all peacemaking from September 1991 onwards within a straitjacket that greatly inhibited compromises between the parties in dispute. There are no easy parallels with other countries, but the Slovak–Czech division by agreement on 1 January 1993 shows that there is an alternative to staying locked in a loveless, even antagonistic, marriage.

Milovan Djilas, who during the Partisan war was given by Tito the main responsibility for designing the administrative boundaries of the republics and autonomous provinces within post-war Yugoslavia, never made any secret of the fact that sometimes they were made quickly 'during a march' without the fullest consideration, and were often arbitrary and driven by political expediency; and he confirmed to me personally that they were never meant to be international boundaries. Many Croats, not least President Franjo Tudjman, never in their hearts accepted the 1945 boundary between Croatia and Bosnia-Herzegovina, because the 1939 Cvetković–Maček agreement had given the Croatian nation control over substantial parts of Bosnia-Herzegovina. Similarly, the Serb-inhabited areas of northern Dalmatia, Lika, Kordun, Banja, Slavonia and Baranja, which together made up the Military Frontier territory, the Krajina, between the Habsburg and Ottoman empires, areas which had been ruled from Vienna but not from Zagreb, resisted incorporation into Croatia. This resistance was particularly strongly felt after 1945, for the inhabitants had been subjected to genocide by the Croat Ustashas during the Second World War. Very few commentators in 1995 understood or acknowledged that when the Croatian government attacked the Krajina they were not 'retaking' or 'reoccupying' this land, for the Serbs had inhabited it for more than three centuries. At most the Croats were reclaiming territory.

The Communist leaders did consider forming an autonomous province from these Serb areas in Croatia. According to Djilas the idea was rejected both because of the region's odd intestine-like shape and because of the number of Croats living there. To the Partisan leaders, nationalism was a product of capitalism. Croat and Serb national ambitions, Albanian and Hungarian minority feeling as well as Muslim identity would, they thought, weaken with the development of socialism; brotherhood and unity would weld a nation of Yugoslavs.

Milovan Djilas died in Belgrade in 1995. Fortunately for me, I had visited him at his home some months previously and we had discussed the present troubles. His writings were regularly reviewed during the late 1950s and 1960s in *Encounter*, a literary and political magazine which I read with delight every month to offset the diet of facts which is the least attractive part of being a medical student. To my generation in Britain the Yugoslav Partisans had an aura of glamour, conferred on them above all by Fitzroy Maclean through his book *Eastern Approaches*. Djilas's dissent had therefore a relevance to me personally and an air of dash and romance to it. I knew he was a tough Montenegrin but it did shock me when I discovered many years later that he had negotiated on behalf of Tito's Partisans with the German occupying forces – the very crime for which the royalist Serb Mihailović had been executed by the Partisans after the war.

While talking to Djilas, a vague memory had stirred of a short story of his which I had read. Going back through old copies of *Encounter*, I found it in the April 1962 edition. It was called 'War' and is about a peasant couple who tried to smuggle their sole surviving son out of the battle zone in a coffin; when discovered by soldiers he is summarily shot, still in the coffin, as a deserter. At the age of twenty-four I remember being shocked by the brutal nature of the writing but I now recognise that it represents many Yugoslavs' basic attitude to war. As Djilas writes:

> War has no mind, and it cannot tell what could or could not at any moment be of value to the opposing side; for this reason, the wisest course of action in war becomes the destruction of absolutely everything – houses and cultivated plots, bridges and museums, and naturally, first and foremost, human beings and their livelihood.

It is the frankness of Djilas's writing about his own past ideological commitments that is so refreshing. There is no trace of self-justification.

'One cannot be a Communist and preserve an iota of one's personal integrity,' he wrote in *Encounter* in December 1979 in 'A Conversation with Milovan Djilas'. If Djilas's advocacy of democracy had been given by Tito the hearing it deserved in the late 1950s and in the 1960s, the Serb–Croat, Serb–Muslim and Muslim–Croat wars could have been avoided. Although democracy puts a high value on self-determination, it also fosters a spirit of compromise and consensus. It was the absence of this spirit in Yugoslavia in the 1980s that made for the bitterness and bloody-minded intransigence that accompanied the state's disintegration. Democracies will defend the integrity of their country and use force to check secessionism; but consideration of when to fight, when to compromise, is the essence of democratic leadership. We saw this in the peaceful break-up of Czechoslovakia. If that negotiated 'velvet divorce' had occurred earlier, it could have influenced Yugoslavia and at least made the EC more open to boundary changes.

The calm of Geneva was shattered for us after we arrived on 3 September 1992 with the news that an Italian air force plane carrying humanitarian relief supplies into Sarajevo had been shot down over an area controlled by forces of the Bosnian Croat army. The territory contained some Bosnian government (mainly Muslim) forces, but the UN felt it most unlikely to have had any Bosnian Serb forces. Suspicion fell on the Croats, but what surprised me was that the senior people in UNHCR who controlled the flights and UNPROFOR's senior officers all refused to rule out the possibility that the very people who would gain most from the relief supplies, the Muslims, might be responsible for shooting down the plane. Up until then I had no idea that their past conduct had given grounds for any such suspicion. It was later thought that the Italian aircraft had been shot down by a Stinger hand-held ground-to-air missile, which had been used to considerable effect against Soviet forces in Afghanistan.

After the downing of the Italian plane all humanitarian flights into Sarajevo were immediately cancelled by UNHCR. This meant that the race against winter, already underway, suffered a major setback. UNHCR were saying that only 100 tonnes of flour and 90 tonnes of rice remained in its Sarajevo warehouses. UNHCR then had only 50 trucks and required 500. The impending crisis in having insufficient food to feed hundreds of thousands of people in Bosnia-Herzegovina was the dominating issue that confronted us over the weeks ahead in Geneva. The promised UN intervention force was still awaited and winter was approaching. As we grappled with the food problem we were hit by another humanitarian crisis that first weekend, setting a pattern of seven-day working that was to become the rule rather than the exception.

On 9 September I arrived for my first visit to the former Yugoslavia with Cy Vance, starting in Zagreb. We were met at the airport by the Indian UN general Satish Nambiar, with a copy of a letter which he had just sent to Bosnia's President Izetbegović about the most recent horror from Sarajevo.

> It is with a deep sense of outrage that I have to inform you that at approximately 1930 hours on 8 September 1992 troops under your command attacked an unarmed UNPROFOR logistical convoy at the entrance to the airport. This unprovoked attack in broad daylight, on an unmistakably UN humanitarian convoy, caused the death of two French soldiers, injury to three more, and the destruction or damage of four UN vehicles.

General Nambiar was a fine man, cool and courteous in all his dealings, but he was very angry when we talked to him about this premeditated ambush. A UN press release was also issued in the toughest terms. For me the incident was peculiarly devastating. Up until then I had, perhaps naïvely, seen the Bosnian Muslims as the decent, aggrieved party. Now I was having to accommodate the fact that, while behaving less badly than the Croats and nowhere near as badly as the Serbs, they too were capable of killing in cold blood UN troops in blue berets, the very people who had been sent to help feed and house their citizens. Now I began to understand why in the minds of UN officials the responsibility for shooting down the Italian plane could be Muslim as well as Croat.

What was the motivation for these and other provocative actions? Presumably, under the orders of someone in political authority, though not necessarily Izetbegović, the Bosnian Muslims were trying to plant the responsibility for their actions onto the Bosnian Serbs, thereby portraying the Serbs as even worse than they were in the eyes of world opinion. This behaviour they supposedly could justify if it brought the Americans and NATO into the war on the

Muslim side. It was the end justifying the means. Within a week of taking the position of co-chairman I had come to realise, and to say publicly, that there were no innocents among the political and military leaders in all three parties in Bosnia-Herzegovina. That is not to say that the leaders were all the same, and it is mere escapism to pretend that there was no difference between the parties. There was always a quantum difference between the horrors perpetrated by Bosnian Serb leaders and acts committed or authorised by the Bosnian Croat or Bosnian Muslim leaders.

In Zagreb President Tudjman told us about an Iranian cargo aircraft, a Boeing 747, that had landed on 4 September with a declaration that it was carrying relief supplies but was found also to hold significant quantities of various types of armaments. Tudjman's motivation in telling us was mixed, for this was not the first or by any means the last Iranian plane to land in Croatia with arms. Already the Croatian government had become skilled at evading the arms embargo which had been applied to them ever since 25 September 1991 by UN Security Council Resolution 713. They extracted a heavy price for being an arms conduit to Bosnia-Herzegovina, either in terms of money from the Bosnian government or by demanding 50 per cent or more of the arms for themselves; sometimes both. The landlocked Bosnian government forces, mainly Muslim, were dependent on the Croats. Yet when people talked of lifting the arms embargo for the Bosnian Muslim forces, they neglected to say that this could only happen with Zagreb's agreement, and that would mean lifting it for the Croats too. A selective lifting for the Bosnian Muslims was at that stage in the war totally impossible. Moreover, western European governments and the US tolerated and indeed in some cases condoned the Croatian government bringing arms and materials in, by road through Hungary and Slovenia and by air and sea in the early stages of the conflict. Nor did they do anything to stop the Croats transferring arms on into Bosnia-Herzegovina, for there were no UN or other monitors on the border with western Herzegovina or along the Sava. These rarely acknowledged facts put discussions surrounding the arms embargo in a better perspective. There was no effective restriction on Croatia building up effective armed forces, and it was Croatia which then dictated the quantity and quality of the arms that moved into Bosnia-Herzegovina, since it controlled all the border crossings that were not under Serb control. It was not ready to increase the effectiveness of the Bosnian Muslim forces.

Yet despite all that was happening around the arms embargo, the Security Council resolution that imposed it will go down in history as one of the most controversial of all those passed by the UN. But it was not seen as controversial when it was first suggested, and the motion was carried in September 1991 with virtually no dissent and with the US government in the lead. Why? In part because Yugoslavia was a major exporter of arms. Arms and ammunition factories existed all over the country and continued production during the war, even in Muslim-held Sarajevo, Zenica and Goražde. The initial effect of the embargo in 1991 was to hurt the Croatian forces, who had far fewer arms, tanks, armoured vehicles and planes than the opposing Yugoslav forces. Even so, UNSCR 713 has come to be seen by many as an example of religious discrimination and of the West's anti-Muslim bias; yet for the first six months of its operation it acted against the predominantly Roman Catholic Croats. Nor did the key members of the Security Council see fit even to consider lifting the ban when they recognised Croatia and Slovenia prior to recognising Bosnia-Herzegovina. In the case of Croatia the arguments for keeping the ban were quite straightforward and seen to be fair, namely that the UN forces were on the ground supposedly keeping the peace and for the UN officially to arm one side in the conflict while having its forces operating within both Croatian- and Serb-controlled territory was to put those personnel and equipment at even greater risk and call into question their impartiality. There was, however, a significant difference between the EC-led recognition of Croatia and that of Bosnia-Herzegovina. When the former was recognised by most countries there was a negotiated ceasefire in place between the combatants in the Serb–Croat civil war of 1991; when the latter was recognised in 1992 by most countries there were no UN troops on the ground. Recognition proved to be the start of a new war between the government of Bosnia-Herzegovina and the Serbs, whether the Serbs lived in Bosnia, Croatia or Serbia and Montenegro.

The recognition of Bosnia-Herzegovina was the trigger that many had predicted it would be to the formal outbreak of a war of aggression, on top of a civil war which was already simmering in the background before recognition. The critical mistake made by the EC as well as the US was to continue down the path towards recognising Bosnia-Herzegovina in the spring of 1992 when every single sign indicated that it would be like pouring petrol on a smouldering fire. Once they realised their mistake, to compound it by lifting the embargo and breaking co-operation with Russia inside the Security Council in 1992 was judged rightly as being far too inflammatory an action to take. There has been a tendency to blame the UN secretary general and Cyrus Vance for not coming to the Security Council with demands for a UN preventive force for Bosnia-Herzegovina early in 1992. Such a force should have been deployed but it is easy to forget the difficulty the Security Council was already facing in finding sufficient troops and deploying them quickly enough to maintain the 2 January ceasefire in Croatia.

On 10 September it was impossible for us to fly into Sarajevo since all flights were banned because of the loss of the Italian plane. Vance and I therefore decided to drive in from Split, leaving early in the morning. After a tortuous six-hour drive over roads that were literally being carved out of the hillside by UN engineers, and travelling with General Philippe Morillon, the French commander of UN forces in Bosnia-Herzegovina, we found a city that had been without water for eleven days and had had all its electricity cut off. Philippe Morillon was a considerable character, great fun to be with, normally informal and relaxed, but on this occasion he was sombre, truly grieving at the loss of the French soldiers. We met with President Izetbegović in the presidency building, to the accompaniment of shell and mortar fire, which, the cynics told us, was part of the normal accompaniment to such visits. In this case they were implying it was all laid on for us by government forces: thus another of my preconceptions of innocence fell by the wayside. We encountered much the same firepower on display when we crossed the airfield to meet with Dr Karadžić at Lukavica, this time presumably laid on by the Serbs. Karadžić told us that all their heavy weapons were now concentrated in eleven positions around Sarajevo and in five positions around another four towns. The UN commanders were adamant that he was 'lying through his teeth' – and indeed, we had driven past some tanks and artillery pieces en route to the meeting. It was one more example of things not being what they seemed.

Because of the delay in reaching Sarajevo we had to leave with General Morillon that same afternoon. Ours was the first plane to take off since the Italian aircraft was downed, and we flew out with the French soldiers who had been injured in the attack. I sat in the back of the pilot's cockpit and the tension could be sensed in the atmosphere as men intently watched their radar screens. When I asked Philippe Morillon what we could do if they picked up an incoming missile, he just gave a Gallic shrug: the answer was we had no defences, not even the capacity to put out diversionary material like aluminium chaff to attract any approaching missile. I felt too ashamed to show any apprehension, given the cool way in which Cy Vance and the others behaved.

From Zagreb we flew in a Russian Yak plane chartered by the UN on to Belgrade. The next day I met President Ćosić for the first time. Prime Minister Panić was with him, in his usual ebullient form and wanting to control the meeting. He nearly succeeded, but we sensed Ćosić wanted to be involved and with our encouragement he began to speak up, with good sense and dignity. The communiqué issued after the meeting, condemning ethnic cleansing and reporting on the whole visit, is described in the first of many official EU telegram or COREUs to the European Foreign Ministers. But what cannot easily be captured was the personal rapport we both started to establish with Ćosić. Steadily over the next few months the nationalistic posturing dropped away and he showed some of the qualities that have made and will in future make the Serbs a substantial people.

In Belgrade I met Slobodan Milošević, the President of Serbia, for the first time. Both Prime Minister Panić and President Ćosić had tried to persuade us not to see him, but Cy Vance was, rightly, firmly of the view that though his star was waning we must keep up a relationship with him. He was the man with whom Cy had negotiated the crucial ceasefire in Croatia at the end of 1991, and he suspected that Milošević was unlikely to remain on the sidelines for long. It was clear when we met that Milošević had a deep respect for Cyrus, as he always called him. I talked little in these early meetings, measuring up Milošević and trying slowly to build a relationship with him, knowing it would be a long time, if ever, before I could command the same authority with him as Cy did.

With President Ćosić, however, I had as good a relationship as Cy from the start. It was encouraging that Ćosić appeared to have distanced himself from Milošević and was ready to play an active role as President of the FRY and to give more support to Milan Panić. We encouraged him then and subsequently as the legitimate counterweight to Panić's flamboyance. We thought he might be ready to build a sufficient electoral power base to challenge Milošević in the elections for the Serbian presidency, and indeed for a short time in November it looked as if Ćosić might even beat Milošević.

On 30 September President Ćosić and President Tudjman signed a joint declaration in Geneva which built on our visit to Belgrade. The big breakthrough was the agreement that the Yugoslav army would leave Prevlaka on 20 October and security in the area would be resolved by demilitarisation and the deployment of UN monitors. In addition we achieved in the declaration what could have been an important warning, stating that 'the two Presidents declare their total condemnation of all practices related to "ethnic cleansing", and commit themselves to helping reverse that which has already happened. They also declare that all statements or commitments made under duress, particularly those relating to land and property, are wholly null and void.' All over Bosnia and in Croatia people were being coerced into signing away their property and rights of residence, and we hoped this declaration would have a positive effect; but it was totally ignored.

In the many letters of congratulations on my appointment there were some very useful nuggets of advice. In all wars the personalities of the leading figures do much to determine the character and the intensity of the conflict, and one letter from an old friend who knew how I liked to get into the minds of those with whom I was going to negotiate contained extracts from the writings of Presidents Ćosić, Izetbegović and Tudjman, which I read eagerly. We had now met all three.

Alija Izetbegović was born in 1925 and educated as a lawyer. He was one of the most enigmatic of all the political personalities in the former Yugoslavia. Of the six Presidents of the former Yugoslav republics, he was the only one who had never been a Communist, and it showed in the way he talked and thought. A question often asked was whether Izetbegović was an Islamic fundamentalist. The answer is difficult to give in terms of 'yes' or 'no'. He was, I am sure, a deeply religious man, which allowed him to take a long view of the war as a struggle for minds as well as territory; but as to whether he was a fundamentalist, very few knew for certain. If he was, he hid it behind a self-disciplined portrayal of himself as a secular politician, as any dissenter learnt to do in Tito's Yugoslavia. I found that Izetbegović's deepest feelings became apparent from time to time when he openly agonised – unlike some Muslim leaders – over whether to accept the compromises in various peace settlements. He had two loyalties, multi-ethnic Bosnia and his own Muslim party, but it was religion that gave him an inner certainty and composure. As with many people who spent time in prison for their beliefs, there was an inner toughness and a surrounding hard shell which was difficult to penetrate. In personal contact I always liked him and wanted to help him; as I got to know him I found him a perplexing personality: I would go out of my way to talk informally to him over a meal, but he kept himself to himself and was easiest to approach through his son or daughter, both delightful people who were part of his political entourage.

My favourable appraisal of Izetbegović was not shared by others who also spent long hours negotiating with him. Some felt he was the most difficult of all the people they had to deal with in the former Yugoslavia, manipulative and untrustworthy, and that his closest advisers were shadowy fundamentalists who played on his chronic indecisiveness and made him hold out against any compromise; and yet in fairness he had by far the most difficult position to defend and sustain. He built and rallied his much weaker army over three years and clung on to the legitimacy of his role as President of a country that had never known peace since being independent. At the same time he convinced the world that he spoke for the majority, not just for the largest group, namely the 44 per cent Bosnian Muslims, but for all those who had lived in what many believed was but a volcanic peace in Bosnia-Herzegovina even prior to the declaration of independence.

Europe has good reasons to honour and respect the Muslim religion and the many people who practise it and have done so over many centuries within our nation states. There are, however, mutual misunderstandings which I fear the war in Bosnia-Herzegovina did much to perpetuate. Sadly, in part it was a religious war, an aspect which was heightened as the war proceeded and the ideology of communism appeared ever more broken backed and its practitioners discredited.

Dobrica Ćosić had been put into the role of President of Serbia and Montenegro – the rump state of Yugoslavia – by Milošević in June 1992 in an attempt to regain the support of the intelligentsia, who had moved away from Milošević. Then seventy-two years old, he was Serbia's most famous living novelist, most of his works being a romantic retelling of Serbia's long history. In dwelling on the hardships and the subjugations of the Serbs he subtly reminds his readers that nationalism is a great calling for which sacrifices are an essential debt which each Serb owes to the nation and from which none should shrink. There is no invoking of ethnic cleansing or anything so crude as racism, rather a proud affirmation of national responsibility, and it was this aspect of his personality we tried to foster.

Both Ćosić and Izetbegović were dissenters under Tito. Ćosić actually protested publicly when Tito imprisoned Izetbegović for his political beliefs. As I grew to know them both I became more and more interested in gauging how their respective Orthodox and Muslim faiths influenced their political stance. The Serb Orthodox Church was important to Ćosić, but for its national identity; I never felt that he was a religious person. Visiting him in his house in Belgrade and having a meal with him and his wife, I felt Serbian history and heartbeat were more important than religion. For Izetbegović the reverse seemed to be the case: his religion was his life, and history did not intrude. There were no outward and visible signs that he was a Muslim. He, his son and his daughter dressed and acted as Europeans. He wanted to be President, by democratic decision, of a Muslim state accepting full multi-ethnic participation in that state. Yet he did not appear to comprehend how inflammatory it was to some Serbs and Croats for him to visit Libya in March 1991 to arrange a $50 million loan, and in July to ask that Bosnia-Herzegovina, while still part of Yugoslavia, should be an observer at the meetings of the Organisation of the Islamic Conference.

Franjo Tudjman was born in 1922 in Veliko Trgovišće in Croatia. He joined the Partisans in 1941, yet he was never very keen to talk about that period of his life. Having fought the fascist Pavelić and his Ustashas, by this time he depended on much of Pavelić's indigenous support. It was deeply provocative, even allowing for its historic links to the Serbs in Croatia, for his government to choose to adopt the symbol that Pavelić used, the red-and-white chequerboard, for the flag of an independent Croatia. But for Tudjman I suspect his Second World War years, when he fought Pavelić, represented the indiscretion of youth. Far from using his Partisan past to bind up the wounds between Croats and Serbs living in Croatia, he preferred to speak with pride of having been arrested and sentenced by Tito's regime to two years' imprisonment in the early 1970s, to play up his part in the 'Croatian Spring' unrest and his imprisonment for 'hostile propaganda' in 1981. His political development probably started while he was a senior figure in Yugoslav People's Army (JNA) intelligence, watching over the very Croatians living in exile who later became some of his most fervent supporters. He left the JNA with the rank of major general in 1960. As a civilian he worked as director of the Institute for the History of the Workers' Movement in Zagreb and served on the executive committee of Matica Hrvatska, the Croatian cultural society, where the Croatian intelligentsia had gathered until it was suppressed by Tito. In 1967 he published a 'Declaration on Croatian Literary Language' and then resigned from all his quasi-government posts and was expelled from the League of Communists of Yugoslavia. He was stripped of his military rank in 1981. Tudjman wore his nationalism openly on his sleeve. His soldiers knew that he was ready himself to fight for Croatia.

Ćosić, Izetbegović and Tudjman were all three nationalists if nationalism is defined as 'simply the determination of a people to cultivate its own soul, to follow the customs bequeathed to it by its ancestors, to develop its traditions according to its own instincts'. But was their nationalism a more malignant force than this? Serbian and Croatian nationalism, as it developed in the latter half of the nineteenth century, carries with it an inherent tendency to cross over into racial and religious discrimination and to ignite passions that feed on violence. Bosnian Muslim nationalism has historically been more benign, but the party Izetbegović led, the SDA, became ever more intolerant under the pressures of war. It was a reflection of Izetbegović's pre-war view that the state was a means to an end, not an end in itself, that he opposed the break-up of Yugoslavia, was reluctant to press for an independent Bosnia-Herzegovina and was against recognition being granted to Croatia and Slovenia. Once nationalism had found independent expression in Croatia and Slovenia, he felt he had to establish Bosnia's independence from Serbia. Izetbegović knew that this would lead to bloodshed. In his *Islamic Declaration* he warned that 'the Islamic renaissance cannot be imagined without people prepared for enormous personal and material sacrifice'.

I have often wondered whether Izetbegović might have found it easier to negotiate with the Serbs if he had not been a devout Muslim. An economic technocrat such as Kiro Gligorov, the leader from Macedonia, aroused less paranoia. Gligorov managed to negotiate the withdrawal of the JNA from its bases in Macedonia early in 1992 with all its arms and equipment and its dignity intact. Of course, there were fewer Serbs in the Former Yugoslav Republic of Macedonia and no Croats; and the Serbs were anxious to avoid having to fight on all their borders. But the absence of deeper religious conflict between the Macedonians and the Serbs was also a factor.

Nationalism, we all know, is a powerful force and when linked to religion it can gather even greater strength. It is, however, too simple to see nationalism as the fount of all evil. Fascism in 1940 was countered and fought by the UK when an international response was lacking, so national pride and independence cannot be lightly decried. The essential safeguard against the more extreme passions of nationalistic feeling is to set it on the bedrock of a true democracy. Yet nationalists often practise a manipulated democracy buttressed by highly selective referenda. Nationalism becomes authoritarian when people are not able to hold their leaders genuinely to account and to vote them out of as well as into office in fair and free elections. Nationalists who are in a minority within a multinational state need a fair measure of geographical or functional autonomy to express their nationhood in their day-to-day living and in familiar customs and traditions. Without that satisfaction nationalism finds its outlet in secessionism, and people are then prepared to fight for independence. It was clear that by 1992 the challenge facing us in the ICFY was to devise forms of decentralisation and autonomy in

Bosnia-Herzegovina, in Croatia and in Kosovo that would contain
the legitimate nationalism of Croatian and Bosnian Serbs, Bosnian
Croats, Bosnian Muslims and Kosovar Albanians, and ensure respect
for Albanians living in Macedonia.

On 16 September in the UK John Major faced the humiliation
of being forced out of the Exchange Rate Mechanism. The
importance of this was political because after Black Wednesday, as
it was called, Major lost authority nationally and internationally. In
fact the economic consequences of being able to devalue and
return to a more competitive exchange rate were hugely beneficial
and in retrospect the British economy, which had been in difficulties for a few years, began to grow; what followed was sustained
growth until the international banking crisis hit the UK in the
autumn of 2007. Far away in Yugoslavia my main concern was
seeing how the Conservative MPs who had come out of the closet
in objecting to the Maastricht Treaty after the election used the
political fallout to weaken John Major further and vigorously
oppose ratification of the treaty. From being one of the strongest
leaders in what was now the EU he became visibly weaker as the
internal battle within the Conservative Party impacted on his
authority and influence abroad.

Vance and I visited Banja Luka on 25 September, in response to
pleas from Red Cross and UNHCR officers on the ground who
were becoming ever more alarmed at the deteriorating situation for
the local Croat and Muslim population. We knew that mere
condemnation would not suffice and just hoped that our physical
presence might serve as a warning. Dr Karadžić insisted on being
present and met us at the UN Sava crossing point, from where we
drove past the Serb military airfield into Banja Luka. The city itself
was much as I remembered it as a student, but the menacing mood
that hung over our visit is hard to describe. A few weeks later on a
visit to Kosovo I felt something similar. We met the mayor of Banja
Luka and an extremely unpleasant General Ninković, commanding
the Bosnian Serb air force, who was adamant in rejecting a no-fly
zone. We saw a number of brave Muslim leaders in a hotel but they
were understandably frightened, having taken the risk of retribution
for even coming to see us. A few days afterwards one of them was
put in prison, though we later managed to have him released. He

then disappeared and both he and his family later emigrated to the US, aided by Serb friends.

We had one meeting which gave us a measure of hope, with the Roman Catholic Bishop, the Muslim Mufti and the Orthodox Bishop of Banja Luka. All three of them were unanimous in saying that totally unacceptable pressure was being put on both Muslims and Croats in villages around Banja Luka, particularly Prijedor.

At a meeting in Zagreb next day at UNPROFOR HQ we heard from an experienced UNHCR field worker of how he had come to the confrontation line between Banja Luka and Travnik and, from a small hill, had seen buses from Prijedor draw up off the road, a mile or more away. He watched as young and old were herded out and made to walk across 'no man's land' towards the waiting UNHCR vehicles. As they walked, weighed down by bags containing the few possessions that they had been able to gather up, the Serbs started to fire small arms over their heads and a few fell wounded or dying. Then, as they moved out of range, shell fire started and he watched as they struggled on stumbling and running as shells landed around them. Some were hit. He felt unable to do anything but stand transfixed by the horror of it all, suddenly realising that tears were streaming down his face. As he spoke there was not a dry eye in the room; military men and politicians alike were all at a loss for words. We shuffled on to other business, but I doubt that anyone who heard him will ever forget it. I retold that story a few days later on the BBC *Today* programme and received many letters.

If there had been any doubt in my mind as to the need for urgency it vanished that day. The pace of the conference, already that of a seven-day week, quickened as we all worked night and day to formulate our proposals. I wrote an account of all this to Douglas Hurd, as president of the Council of Foreign Ministers, asking for the deployment of UK forces for UNPROFOR to be accelerated and for some risks to be taken in resuming the humanitarian airlift to Sarajevo. We were by now acutely aware of the reluctance of Defence Ministers in all NATO capitals except Ankara to take on new commitments, and I knew that there was no support for suggestions that our troops should have their mandate extended beyond that of escorting convoys.

The pressure for the declaration of a no-fly zone (NFZ) was growing, not unreasonably, all through September. There was still anxiety about the idea in some European capitals and we gathered from newspaper reports that General Colin Powell, the chairman of the Joint Chiefs of Defence Staff in the US, was opposed. Douglas Hurd saw Vance and me in Geneva. We discussed an NFZ and he agreed that a Security Council resolution to press the Bosnian Serbs to accept monitors on their airfield was needed. I was very keen on the NFZ, though I remembered how firmly President Mitterrand had ruled out any use of air power in the former Yugoslavia when I saw him. Even Cy Vance initially had his doubts about the practicability of such a measure, but he was content to let me go on pressurising for a resolution, and UNSCR 781 was passed on 9 October. Another reason why I wanted an NFZ was that I was worried that we could have Iranian aircraft landing at Tuzla, which would so anger the Serbs that it would put all humanitarian efforts at risk, whether relief flights into Sarajevo or convoys throughout the country.

Our visit to Moscow on 10 October, where we met the Foreign Minister, Andrei Kozyrev, and his deputy, Vitaly Churkin, was worthwhile. They felt I was too sanguine over the chances of the Serbs moving on their two sacred cows – Kosovo and the Krajina – and also that if President Ćosić and Prime Minister Panić recognised Croatia they would be disowned in Belgrade and branded as national traitors. In truth, Vance was much more cautious than I over the Krajina and probably over autonomy for Kosovo as well, mainly because he knew the area better and, having spent months negotiating with Milošević, knew the limits to his flexibility. Our jointly agreed tactic was to push Ćosić and Panić towards Tudjman while trying to persuade Milošević not to block their agreements, in effect letting Ćosić take any political flak for decisions which Milošević knew he would have to take responsibility for if delayed until he replaced Ćosić.

On 13 October I met with Karadžić in Geneva, after President Bush had said he would enforce a no-fly zone, and virtually pinned him to the wall. At long last I had a stick to our diplomacy. Cy Vance's deputy, Herb Okun, wearing his American hat, described in vivid terms the consequences if flights continued and Karadžić folded.

Karadžić seemed attracted to the offer that all Bosnian Serb combat aircraft could fly to UN monitored airfields in the FRY, from where they could take part in strictly limited training flights; but, ominously as it turned out, his air force officers preferred to keep their aircraft in Banja Luka.

I did not attend the European Council meeting in Birmingham on 16 October because I had my own little humanitarian crisis. I had been suffering from progressively worse sciatica with pains down my leg as I sat for hour after hour in the negotiations, but foolishly ignored all the clear neurological signs that this was serious and continued with meetings until I found my foot catching on the pavement and realised there was a muscle weakness that was giving me foot drop. This was a dangerous sign that the nerve was becoming permanently damaged, and I was told by a Swiss physician and then by a Swiss neurosurgeon that same day in Geneva that I needed an immediate operation to remove a disc. I should either fly straight back to London or come into the public hospital on Monday. I decided to stay in Geneva that weekend, in the flat I had taken in the old part of the city on the Place du Bourg de Four above a restaurant called Mortimers. Debbie flew over and I went into hospital and straight into the operating theatre on Monday morning. I was up walking that evening, left hospital the following afternoon and spent all the next day, Wednesday, sitting at my desk in the Palais des Nations. The surgeon had used microsurgical techniques to remove a lumbar disc, avoiding any weakening of the vertebral column, and by thus keeping the skeletal system totally intact enabled me to avoid the weeks and months of convalescence that previously used to follow such an operation.

In Sarajevo it became ever clearer that there were in fact two sieges of the city: one by the Bosnian Serb army, with shells, sniper fire and blockades, and the other by the Bosnian government army, with internal blockades and red tape bureaucracy which kept their own people from leaving. In a radio broadcast the army – not the government – said that able-bodied men aged 18–65 years and women aged 18–60 years were forbidden to leave because they were needed for the city's defence; but their main reason was different. In the propaganda war the Serbian siege aroused the sympathy of the world, and for this they needed the elderly and the children to stay.

It was their most emotive propaganda weapon for bringing the Americans in to fight the war, and they never wanted to lose it by allowing family members to escort them out.

On 29 October Cyrus Vance and I flew down to Pristina in Kosovo, which the Serbs consider the cradle of their civilisation, on what was one of the more extraordinary visits that I have ever been involved in. Prime Minister Panić was to accompany us, which was nothing if not brave; some would say foolhardy. In November he said to Simone Veil in the European Parliament, 'The less I know about the history of the Balkans the better I feel.' Rather stuffily in retrospect, we declined to fly in his plane, but on arrival we were obliged to go into the small office at the airport and meet with the local Serb officials. We had already indicated that we had no wish to do this, but Panić explained it was vital we did, both as a courtesy and to maintain his own authority. We separated from Panić, who was going to talk to the Serb local authority representatives, and went to see the Albanian nationalist leader, Ibrahim Rugova. As we approached Pristina in the car a deep sense of gloom descended on me. Everything looked depressingly drab, the worst of communist architecture, and there was no sense of a proud history, no ancient monuments being visible, just dirt, grime and a foreboding of doom. Rugova was in a 'shanty town' office and to walk in you had to jump across large puddles of water. Inside, however, the welcome was warm and we eventually agreed that Rugova would come with us to meet Panić in the official City Hall building; but he was firmly against meeting the representatives of the local Serb authorities. We did not press him at that stage. When we arrived we saw Panić, who was adamant that we should meet the Serbs with or without Rugova. So, leaving Rugova in an anteroom, we went into a meeting which can only be described as bedlam to find Panić berating the local Serbs with gusto and clearly enjoying himself.

Panić was a 63-year-old Californian who spoke English with a Serb accent and Serbo-Croat with an American accent. He had defected from Yugoslavia in 1955 during an international bicycle race when he had been a successful racer. He always claimed that 'I bicycled to freedom' and arrived in the US with two suitcases and twenty dollars, from which he soon became a millionaire. His pharmaceutical company was worth half a billion dollars. He described the talks as 'rough but constructive'. We felt for a moment that we were making headway in persuading them to negotiate over the return of the Albanian schoolchildren who were being taught in their homes to their primary schools. But even that was too much for the local Serbs to concede to Panić, who would then have exploited his success against Milošević, something they were not prepared to countenance. As we flew away I was appalled by what we had seen and felt there was no immediate prospect of even minimal autonomy being granted to the Albanians, let alone a reversion to the very considerable degree of autonomy which had operated under Tito.

There is no gainsaying that at this key moment in the formulation of a peace plan for Bosnia-Herzegovina we were all reluctantly but realistically facing the fact that we would never have substantial UN forces for implementation. Doubling the 7,000 humanitarian intervention force was the most we thought we could rely on from the Security Council, and a UN force of 15,000 was what Generals Nambiar and Morillon took as their target figure in working on their plans for implementing our peace plan with the demilitarisation of Sarajevo, the withdrawal of heavy weapons and the withdrawal of armed forces to agreed peace settlement lines.

On 4 October Vance and I had received from Martti Ahtisaari an important paper giving five constitutional options, setting out the pros and cons of each. We chose the second option, a centralised federal state with significant functions carried out by between four and ten regions, as the basis for what became known as the Vance–Owen Peace Plan – the VOPP. It seemed the best compromise among the widely differing positions of the three parties and promised the most stable governmental form for the whole of Bosnia-Herzegovina, since much of the predicted intercommunal friction could be kept from the central government by giving the provinces competence over the most divisive issues, e.g. police, education, health and culture, while depriving them of the right to be a state within a state. It fulfilled the London declaration of principles, which enjoined us as negotiators to try and keep the citizens of this newly recognised country together in one state.

The daunting challenge for the ICFY in November 1992 was whether, armed only with moral authority and weak economic sanctions, and with no credible threat of selective counterforce, we could roll back the Serb confrontation lines and create a new map for Bosnia-Herzegovina. We took it as our mandate that we would have to ensure that the three constituent peoples lived within Bosnia-Herzegovina's internationally recognised boundaries. Our task was to devise a structure whereby Serbs could retain control of those aspects of daily life that preserved and safeguarded their national identity. We could not, however, accept a state within a state and therefore had to avoid, which we did, a geographical continuity of provinces likely to be governed by a Serb majority.

In New York Cy Vance and Herb Okun had a meeting in Cy's flat with Anthony Lake after Clinton's defeat of Bush in the presidential election. Lake had been in the State Department as head of the Policy Planning Staff under Cy and was now due to become the new National Security Adviser. Apparently the issue he raised repeatedly with them was the moral case for lifting the arms embargo, but Cy and Herb never gave me any impression that we were likely to have the difficulties ahead with the new administration that we were soon to encounter. Later in December they went down to Washington to talk to President Bush. When they called in at the Democrats' Transitional Office and spoke to two of the incoming Clinton administration's National Security officials, they found them not only going on about the arms embargo but also querying whether we were accepting too much ethnic cleansing. I did not know at the time that at Washington dinner parties aspiring candidates for the new administration were apparently criticising Cy Vance on Yugoslavia as being ready to negotiate until the last man remained alive. In retrospect, our antennae in Geneva should have been more focused on Washington and on picking up the signs of a build-up in negative perceptions of the Geneva-based ICFY.

On 18 November I was sufficiently worried that the military attitude of the Bosnian Serb military commander general, Ratko Mladić, might destabilise the constitutional talks to send a personal telegram to Douglas Hurd in his capacity as president of the Council of Foreign Ministers to ask for enforcement of the no-fly zone under Chapter VII of the UN Charter. This telegram revealed my private thoughts, which I could not always express publicly. I wanted 'no-fly' enforcement as a sign to the Serbs that we meant business, but as

France, Britain and most other EC countries were against this, I could not say so in public, where I had to voice the EC consensus. Also, as a negotiator, I had to be sparing in my references to military pressure on the Serbs if I did not have EC support. The Serbs for their part still felt that I was more anti-Serb than Vance and far readier to bomb them into submission.

Vance and I visited the four UN protected areas (UNPAs) in Croatia between 19 and 20 November. It was becoming clear that the Vance plan was not being implemented and we needed to find out if anything could be done to recover lost momentum. In Knin we had a dreadful meeting with the Croatian Serbs, who refused to countenance anything but secession and pretended they were an independent government with their own Foreign Minister. I was adamant that we would make it clear that we considered we were in Croatia, a fact the UN tended to walk around with semantic blurring. My definition provoked a rant about how this was an independent Serb republic. I was called by one Serb leader on their local radio a rogue and a Serb hater, whereas Vance was described as 'tolerant'. Driving into the northern UNPA that same evening it was noticeable that very few houses had any electric light, and the battle-scarred villages we drove through appeared deserted.

President Tudjman was understandably determined from the start to avoid a repeat of what had happened in Cyprus, with the UN presence entrenching the de facto partition of the island, and so he never abided by the ceasefire, which ensured that eventually, in 1995, he got back all the UNPAs and won the war. That fundamental and unavoidable tension kept an incipient Serb–Croat war simmering in the background, always dangerous and providing the fuel for an increasing disillusionment of the Croatian people and government with the UN, seen as responsible for the status quo. As memories of how awful the war had been faded, so more Croats began to be readier to risk another war, particularly as the Croatian forces were becoming ever better equipped. By late 1992 the arms embargo was barely touching Croatia, and soon the Croatian army was being equipped with planes, tanks and heavy artillery. As this was happening in full view of the Serbs it was not hard to see why they resisted demilitarisation and refused to demobilise. The Croatian Serbs were the consolidators and the Croatian government the destabilisers. The Croatian government needed to convince the Croatian Serbs that they had nothing to fear in living under their rule if there was to be peace, but they believed this would only encourage the Serb leaders to remain independent. It was a Catch-22 situation. Tudjman's style was diplomacy by histrionics, but nevertheless, from the Croat point of view, it was effective. The Croatian government-controlled press constantly identified UN peacekeepers as failing to allow Croats to return to their homes, and at times came close to depicting them as the enemies of the state, an attitude reflected in the vulgar V-signs flashed at passing white UN vehicles on the roads.

I was beginning to despair as to how we could settle these conflicting aims. This mood was further deepened when I discovered that, far from Croats returning to their homes, Serbs in increasing numbers were arriving from other parts of former Yugoslavia, particularly Bosnia-Herzegovina, and were being relocated in Sector East. This was ethnic accretion, understandably seen by the Croats as an attempt to change the demographics of the area by creating a permanent Serbian majority where before the 1991 war there had been a Croatian one. The large influx of Serb refugees was also leading to Serb-on-Serb violence with gang activity, extortion and protection rackets. All this was happening under the nose of the UN civilian police, who saw their role passively, as was explained to us, 'to observe and report on the activities of local police and authorities and to cultivate good relationships with all residents'. Given the circumstances in Croatia at that time, and particularly after the war in Bosnia-Herzegovina started, which changed the priority that the UN could give to the Vance plan, it was impossible to see how the UN could become anything other than the butt of everyone in Croatia, unloved and unappreciated. Unable to bring refugees back until the Serb militia were disarmed, the UN lacked the resolve, and arguably also the power, to disarm the Serbs forcibly. Deadlock continued over the next 2½ years, until in January 1995 President Tudjman deliberately tried to bring all his people's dissatisfactions to a head by unilaterally declaring that the UN mandate would end on 31 March 1995. Our visit was a sad occasion for Cy Vance, but he took the criticism of his plan from the UN people we met in the eastern UNPA on the chin with no attempt to cover up its deficiencies, which were laid before us with painful clarity at our briefings. The alternative, however, as had been the case in 1991, was full-out war.

A key country in the region was Greece. When Prime Minister Mitsotakis met Vance and myself on 23 November in Geneva he said that he was ready to visit Belgrade and meet Milošević if we and the British Prime Minister thought it useful. Panić had raised this question at a meeting with us on 25 November and he and his advisers expressed strong opposition on the grounds that such a visit would only strengthen Milošević's position. Panić felt Greece was Milošević's only friend in the EC, and that Milošević would use his control of the media to portray the visit to his advantage. I advised London, as the EC presidency, that on balance such a visit would not be useful since I suspected that it would give the appearance of Mitsotakis's being an envoy from the EC, with the personal endorsement of the British Prime Minister as president of the EC, whereas if he did go I thought it would be better for him to do so on his own initiative. But it was important that Greece, which supported our constitutional proposals, should exert influence on all the political factions in Belgrade and I urged Mitsotakis to do so. Later, over the VOPP, he was consistently helpful. A tall, commanding figure from Crete, his shrewdness and influence on Milošević were certainly beneficial.

Then President Tudjman invited Cy and Gay Vance, Debbie and me to come to the beautiful island of Brioni for a social weekend. It had been Tito's favourite place to stay and I hoped we would have time to discuss some of the more challenging concepts that I had in mind about how to break out of the rigid box which the world had made for both Croats and Serbs at the time of recognition. Could we break the deadlock by means of a comprehensive settlement? This was a delicate area for me, since the EC countries had rejected this in July 1991 and some were very sensitive at any hint of border changes. But my job was to think the unthinkable and to challenge conventional attitudes.

My ambitions for confederal links and border adjustments became more modest as I walked around Brioni with Tudjman and his Defence Minister, Gojkov Sušak. Without giving much away, they made their underlying views pretty clear: they saw Knin as a crucial communication link and they would not give control of it to the Serbs under any circumstances. Even autonomy for the Krajina was highly suspect, and confederal linkage was going far too far.

After the Brioni weekend Vance and I flew to Jeddah for the summit meeting of the Organisation of the Islamic Conference. The Saudis treated us with immense courtesy and we were allowed to speak and put our case for a negotiated settlement and advise against lifting the arms embargo. I also had a meeting with the Iranian Foreign Minister, Ali-Akbar Velayati, who had been a paediatrician. We got on remarkably well, and though he refused to see Cy Vance, Cy and I felt we should try to involve Iran on the ICFY steering committee; but within the EC I could not assemble a consensus for them to be invited.

When I first met General Mladić I sought to persuade him not to take Travnik, the capital of the Ottoman province of Bosnia, for this would have had disastrous humanitarian consequences. Thereafter, whenever we met, he referred to his promise not to do so – initially as emblematic of his keeping his word, and later on as a manifestation of one of his biggest mistakes, for he said he had come to believe he had underestimated the strategic significance of Travnik to the Serbs. Despite his protestations to the contrary, all that I know of General Mladić convinces me that he would have taken Travnik had he thought it was in the Serb interest to do so. General Mladić, having emerged as the dominant military figure in the region, signalled his authority by openly declaring that might made right when he addressed a joint session of the Bosnian Serb and Croatian Serb assemblies in Prijedor, itself the hub of ethnic cleansing and the administrative centre for a network of Serb detention camps including Omarska and Trnopolje. According then to Mladić,

> the existence of the Serb Republic may be disputed in the world, but the existence of its army is indisputable. The Serb Republic exists because we have our territory, our people, our authority and all the attributes of a state. Whether they want to recognise it or not is their affair. The army is a fact.

I found Mladić to be a racist in conversation and in action, as well as being ruthless and brutal. He was not just thumbing his nose at the international community but signalling loud and clear that for him Greater Serbia had been achieved; 'roll it back if you dare' was his challenge, and he never believed that the international community would dare. What is more, until the end of August 1995 he was right: the international community did not dare to take military action. Neither Mladić nor any of his officers considered that there was an international boundary between Knin and Banja Luka. To Mladić, Serb forces were entitled to move as freely in the former Yugoslavia as they did before 1991. Indeed, for Mladić, and for many of his kind in the military, for most purposes Yugoslavia still existed. 'Safe areas' were all right as a place to 'dump' Muslims, but if they became the focus of Muslim military activity they just became another target, as he was to show over Srebrenica, first in spring 1993 and fatefully in the summer of 1995.

A major new, and for me highly desirable, development was the involvement of NATO. On 4 December I flew from Geneva to Brussels to speak to an informal gathering of NATO ambassadors. This was an important meeting as it was the first time I could speak frankly, knowing my views would not reach the newspapers but would go to capitals and in particular Washington. I took the opportunity to give a stark warning of the risk of explosion in Kosovo and signal my continued faith in the possibility of a negotiated settlement after the Serbian election. Cy was initially dubious about involving NATO too closely with the UN, arguing that the cultures of the two organisations were very different. He feared that NATO and the UN were an oil-and-water mix; and so at times it seemed. The strains and stresses that emerged within UN–NATO relations during the next three years were very considerable. But against that, what was the alternative? Allow the Bosnian Serb air force to again start strafing Bosnian Muslim forces and military targets from the air, or, far worse, to bomb and rocket civilian hospitals, schools and churches? Vance and I decided to write a joint letter to Boutros-Ghali to encourage him to approach NATO.

The London conference on the former Yugoslavia had invited Cyrus Vance and myself to recommend how the international community should deal with people who might have committed war crimes in the various wars that had engulfed the former Yugoslavia since 1991. We recommended establishing an ad hoc tribunal specifically to deal with crimes committed in the territory of the former Yugoslavia. We believed it essential that any tribunal should be free-standing, independent and not connected in any way with the ICFY, thereby consciously divorcing its decisions from the peacemaking or peacekeeping process.

The recommendation that it should be established under the authority of Chapter VII of the UN Charter was made because this route would be faster than establishment by a treaty and we felt the tribunal would be able to draw on the enforcement power of the Security Council to bring people to justice and comply with a warrant of arrest, in effect to extradite. Any political judgements as to the duration of the tribunal's jurisdiction would be taken by the Security Council. In this way we hoped the issue would not be subject to bargaining between the leaders of the countries involved in the war, some of whose leaders might themselves be issued with arrest warrants to bring them to trial. I gave evidence not for the prosecution but as a witness of the court in Milošević's trial in The Hague in 2003. Unfortunately he died in 2005, I personally suspect by suicide. It was diagnosed, however, as a heart attack after a post mortem, before he could be sentenced. Again as a witness of the court I have been willing to give evidence in Karadžić's trial in 2010, but the Court want me to be a Prosecution witness.

Genocide is a crime against the whole of humanity. The UN Convention on Genocide defines it as certain 'acts committed with intent to destroy in whole or in part a national, ethnical, racial or religious group, as such'. It is a highly specific crime to eliminate a definable group from this planet. Genocide was committed against the Serbs by the Croat Ustasha in the Second World War. The specific problem is to distinguish between genocide and ethnic cleansing. News organisations and specialists, after three years of war, talked of 200,000–250,000. The Bosnian government in April 1995 lowered its previous estimate to just over 145,000, about 3 per cent of the pre-war population. But George Kenney, who resigned from the State Department in 1992 to protest at the failure of US policy to do more for the Muslims, puts the figure between 25,000 and 60,000. He argues:

> Bosnia is not the Holocaust or Rwanda; it's Lebanon. A relatively
> large number of white people have been killed in a gruesome fashion

in the first European blow-up since World War II. In response the United Nations has set up the first international war crimes trials since Nuremberg. But that does not mean the Bosnian Serbs' often brutal treatment of the Bosnian Muslims is a unique genocide.

There have been many estimates of the overall death rate; probably it is something over 100,000 but the exact figure is hard to establish.

In mid December I spent some time in Sarajevo, to try to get to know the key figures and to feel what it was like to live under constant shelling in a state of siege. In those days I got a taste of the atmosphere. No tap water or flushing lavatories. No lights in the streets at night. Shots ringing out and intermittent explosions. Trees all disappearing for firewood. Football pitches converted to graveyards. The grotesqueness of modern buildings with holes right through them somehow seemed more disturbing than the older buildings being knocked about. Each morning before most people were out of bed I would walk the city streets as an almost childish act of defiance against the Serb snipers looking down on me from the surrounding hills. On the first day I wore a blue helmet and flak jacket, but felt so foolish that I gave up wearing them, believing there was a slighter risk of being shot at in normal clothes. One morning I bumped into the local head of UNHCR, a young Englishman, Jeremy Brade, outside Philippe Morillon's house and he asked if he could show me the city in his UNHCR Land Rover. I went everywhere in the inner city with him, going to places I had last seen as a student. It was also refreshing to see him and Larry Hollingworth, a bearded UNHCR worker often on television talking concerned common sense, dining in the UN officers' mess with Morillon as part of the team. Today Larry runs a very successful one-month humanitarian diploma course which I helped start in New York, Geneva and Nairobi under the responsibility of the Center for International Humanitarian Cooperation.

One important visit I made, completely impromptu, was to the Kosevo hospital early one morning, where I was shown the cold operating theatre and a modern intensive care unit yet with no electricity to run the sophisticated machinery. Two large shell holes in the wall of the recovery room were a reminder of the constant danger under which the staff worked. The contrast of having all the most modern complicated electronic monitoring equipment yet having no heat and few medicines was a stark reminder of the vulnerability of modern life to war. It left a deep impression and I felt driven over the next few days to at least negotiate the delivery of an oil supply to heat the hospital for Christmas. Each day Morillon and I shuttled to and fro between the Bosnian Serbs on the Serbian side of the airport at Lukavica and the Bosnian presidency.

On the morning of Saturday 19 December I met General Mladić for the second time and this was when he first reminded me he had not taken Travnik. That evening together with the young leader of the Bosnian forces, General Halilović, I visited the 1st Motor-Rifle Brigade in Sarajevo and took Graham Messervy-Whiting, my military adviser, with me. A young photographer from Agence France-Presse acted as interpreter when I answered searching questions from the men. To my surprise there was no publicity. I was woken that night as I slept on a canvas portable bed in General Morillon's HQ by a particularly loud noise. We discovered next day it was the heavy-calibre end-of-trajectory ricochet from an unusual direct-fire heavy weapon which gave small explosions with no shrapnel and which turned out to be an anti-aircraft gun now directed at buildings. It was a very personal reminder of the real horror that the citizens of Sarajevo faced with such immense fortitude and self-discipline. Over Vukovar, in what is now Croatia, the Serb army appeared to learn the lesson that capturing urban areas in modern warfare extracts a terrible price, something the Russians forgot when they fought for Grozny. So instead, the Serbs rediscovered the medieval siege, putting citizens under barrage and psychological pressure but not launching a frontal attack. The Bosnian Serbs did their cause immense harm by their brutal tactics over Sarajevo and would have been wiser to have pushed for UN administration from the outset. Their problem was the personal affinity with Sarajevo felt by their three political leaders, Karadžić, Momčilo Krajišnik and Nikola Koljević.

Through intensive personal contacts with the most senior political and military leadership of all parties in Sarajevo during the next four days Morillon and I attempted to break the vicious circle which up until then had prevented progress on the demilitarisation of Sarajevo contributing to a genuine cessation of hostilities throughout Bosnia-

Herzegovina. No party had been willing to make real concessions, fearing that others could take advantage of them; but at the same time each party had insisted that the others make the first concession. I had tried to get the British government to move to Sarajevo their Warrior vehicles which were in the Croat areas but they were not ready to become so exposed, but we needed their capability so as to convince the Serbs that they would not be overrun by larger numbers of Bosnian government troops in the city.

I left Sarajevo worried, for I had detected that the strongest resistance to our agreement was coming not from the Bosnian Serbs but from Ejup Ganić, the Vice-President of Bosnia-Herzegovina. Demilitarisation in Sarajevo would remove the most powerful weapon in his propaganda armoury for involving the US. A quiet Sarajevo was, he almost admitted, not in his interests, and he preferred a continuation of the siege. Also, in fairness, he genuinely feared that demilitarisation could lead to a freezing of the confrontation line dividing the city. Philippe Morillon shared all my concerns. He had been amazingly tolerant in allowing me to intrude into his area of responsibility in our joint negotiations. We had travelled everywhere together, as the itinerary shows, in a spirit of shared endeavour. He had panache and courage; but even so, as I left him we had the hardest problem still to resolve, namely convincing the Muslim leaders that our plan was in their interest. Sadly Ganić appeared to block a settlement. Oil went to the Kosevo hospital for a few days to cover the immediate Christmas period, but then was diverted for military use. The military talks became bogged down in minor differences and momentum was lost. The breakdown left the Serbs disillusioned and the moment for a negotiating breakthrough temporarily disappeared.

On the election in Serbia our predictions proved correct and on 20 December, with a 69 per cent turnout, despite an excellent campaign by Prime Minister Panić given where he was coming from, Milošević gained 56 per cent of the votes and Panić 34 per cent. Some calculated that Panić lost votes from the intervention of Lawrence Eagleburger, the US Secretary of State, when he called Milošević a war criminal, but even if he did, which I doubt, it was not enough to have changed the result.

Exhausted after non-stop activity and travel, Christmas at home was a time for thinking and recharging batteries. Now all hinged on the VOPP negotiations due to start early in January and whether or not the parties would at long last negotiate together around the same table. After 3½ months of kaleidoscopic activity and hectic travel, working eighteen to twenty hours a day, seven days a week, I was far more knowledgeable on the Balkans and far more sceptical about the personalities and the peoples that made up the former Yugoslavia. The problems were even more daunting than I had imagined and the urgency for a peace settlement within Bosnia-Herzegovina even greater than Cy Vance had impressed upon me in August in New York. For every week and month that went by without a settlement, ethnic cleansing was going to be harder to reverse, and the polarisation and divisions would partition not just the country territorially but the minds of its people. We had reached the stage when we knew that as co-chairmen we would have to put down as the judgement of Solomon a map for the provinces, and then fight for it and stick to it with all the tenacity we could muster. We had built in those last few months in Geneva a remarkable team whose biggest test lay ahead. There were few illusions left about the parties. They were all masters of disinformation, propaganda and deceit. So far the countries that made up the conference had given us all the support we could have asked for. Cyrus Vance had just returned from a visit to Washington, where he had seen President Bush; he was not at this stage aware of the threat to our plans ticking away in the transitional team that was preparing for President Clinton's inauguration on 20 January 1993.

As I left for Geneva after lunch at Chequers on 1 January 1993 John Major asked me what the chances were of obtaining an agreement. I put them at fifty-fifty. The next day at 11.00 a.m. the first plenary session of the Bosnian parties convened by the ICFY took place. The meeting was attended by five delegations, headed for the Bosnian Croats by Mate Boban, for the Bosnian government by President Izetbegović and for the Bosnian Serbs by Dr Karadžić, as well as by President Tudjman for Croatia and President Ćosić for the FRY. They were all sitting around the same table for the first time since the London conference in August, and used the opening session to let off steam.

Cy Vance explained that the work would continue in two

working groups: one chaired by Martti Ahtisaari, which would deal with constitutional issues, including the proposed provincial map for the administrative boundaries within Bosnia-Herzegovina, and the other presided over by the UNPROFOR commander, General Nambiar, on military issues.

In my statement, carefully prepared with Cy Vance, I introduced our own peace plan, a three-part package comprising ten constitutional principles, a detailed cessation-of-hostilities agreement and a map. We were careful not to label any provinces Serb, Croat or Muslim, contrary to the impression given by some newspapers and commentators, putting only numbers and place names on the map.

At the close of the meeting on 4 January the Bosnian Croats accepted our three-part package in full: the constitutional principles, the cessation-of-hostilities agreement and the map. For the Bosnian Serbs, Karadžić said the map was 'acceptable as a basis for starting negotiations'. He rejected Constitutional Principles 1 and 2, which precluded a state within a state, and generally kept all the cessation-of-hostilities options open. It was obvious that the Bosnian Serbs would never accept the map unless and until they were totally isolated. Meanwhile, we were contemplating asking Ćosić if he would consider it appropriate to include Milošević in his delegation next time. We thought that after the election result Milošević would be readier to put pressure on Karadžić – and more effective in doing so – than Ćosić, and so later it proved.

The key to immediate progress lay with President Izetbegović. He accepted the ten constitutional principles and also at that time the detailed proposals for a cessation of hostilities, but said the map was 'not acceptable'. Izetbegović also commented that the two co-chairmen's efforts were not unprincipled. We understood his reservations, and in an ideal world a case could be made for many of his wishes; but in the mess that was then Bosnia-Herzegovina his objections, if maintained, represented a totally non-negotiable position. What was more serious was that he probably knew that if he persisted he would destroy the VOPP. We had to convince those governments that could influence Izetbegović, particularly the US, that his objections were unsustainable and that he should accept the package 'warts and all'. We then intended to turn the world's frustration and anger onto the Bosnian Serbs and pressurise them to accept the package, which meant giving up their claim for a state within a state. We invited all the parties to return to Geneva on Sunday 10 January for another round of negotiations.

Meanwhile Izetbegović said to the press in Geneva that our map ratified and legitimised the fruits of 'ethnic cleansing' and effectively prevented the return of refugees. When Vance and I tackled Izetbegović personally he backed off immediately, but the damage was done and from then on any quite legitimate pressure on the Bosnian Muslims to compromise was all too often depicted as unfair bullying. Some in the US State Department were encouraging Izetbegović to seek changes in the map which we knew were not negotiable and in all probability they too knew were not negotiable. For some time in Geneva, Vance and Okun had been complaining of US misrepresentation both of our intentions and of the details of the plan in reporting back to the State Department. We needed to go direct to the White House, so I talked to Stephen Wall in 10 Downing Street and he offered to speak to Brent Scowcroft, the National Security Adviser, to see if he could convince him. Scowcroft was not persuaded by all our arguments on the map but he did admit that he did not believe that Izetbegović would get a better deal and said he would tell him so in very firm terms and that he should accept what was on offer. My explanation of Scowcroft's position cheered Vance up enormously, for he was angry at the drip of criticism coming from across the Atlantic.

Key decision makers in the US administration had now said categorically that they had no problem with the VOPP and that if they did, they would have told us; if the US mission in New York had implied otherwise, they were talking out of turn. With the Bush administration being generally supportive of the VOPP in Washington and in New York, in Geneva we were watching apprehensively for signs of what we could expect from the Clinton administration. In an interview for the *New York Times* from Little Rock on 13 January the President-elect had said he supported the peace talks now taking place in Geneva. But we knew that some of his advisers had said privately in recent days that the conference was a sham that only confirmed Serbia's takeover of certain areas of Bosnia-Herzegovina. Clinton also said that if Geneva did not lead to an end to ethnic cleansing then he would be prepared to be more assertive than the Bush administration, and he did not want to rule out something short of the introduction of a large ground force that would change the dynamics. For his first 2½ years in office that was never offered.

By 19 January we achieved, on the three documents before the conference, six of the nine signatures we needed. The Croats had signed the constitutional principles, the map and the cessation-of-hostilities agreement. The Muslims had signed the constitutional principles and the cessation of hostilities. The Serbs had signed the cessation of hostilities.

The inauguration of President Clinton was due on 20 January. A week earlier I had received a reassuring message from Washington that Tony Lake, who was going to be the new National Security Adviser, had given an explicit commitment that the new administration would support the VOPP and that the Bosnians should be urged to accept. But still we heard in Geneva contrary views from people in Washington who were either going to be in or were close to the Clinton administration. And in the US media the VOPP was coming under further ill-informed attack. *Time* magazine printed a big piece with the sub-headline 'Milošević should be pleased. The West's plan will reward his aggression by giving him almost everything he wants'. Disgracefully, the accompanying map bore so little relation to ours that it was unrecognisable. I tried to counter these stories and there was a question-and-answer piece in *Newsweek*, but the formidable disinformation machine that was operating in the US swamped our small press office in Geneva and we began on public relations grounds alone to think we would do better if we were physically in New York.

Zbigniew Brzezinski, appearing still to nurse a grudge from his clashes with Vance in the Carter administration, leapt into the fray with alacrity in the *Washington Post*. He called us

> negotiators whose basic concept of dealing with thugs is to talk endlessly while assuring the aggressors that their use of force will not be matched by a counterforce. Not surprisingly, the result has been that mass murders have been propitiated and 'ethnic cleansing', not to speak of mass rapes, tolerated.

Vance hit back, calling the charges 'hogwash' and saying, 'If we refuse to talk, on so-called moral grounds, to all parties to a conflict, how could we ever settle any problem?' He was reported as saying in clipped tones, hammering the table with the tip of his pen in a rare moment of indignation and anger:

> Frankly, I am getting fed up with this mindless criticism that doesn't face up to a central fact. In Bosnia there is no viable alternative to a negotiated settlement. There could well be war criminals among the people we are dealing with, but I'll leave that to the courts to decide. David and I have been working round the clock to stop the slaughter of innocent civilians and keep alive the humanitarian effort. It's nonsense to say we are appeasers for talking to the people who can make a difference in our pursuit of a lasting settlement.

But there was worse to come. On 21 January the new Secretary of State, Warren Christopher, through his spokesman Richard Boucher, said that although the Clinton administration supported the negotiations, he 'expressed doubts about whether it can realistically be achieved, whether they can, in fact, find an agreement'. Then, to rub salt into the wound, Mr Boucher declined to say whether the Clinton administration believed the Vance–Owen plan ratified ethnic cleansing. Cy Vance tried to downplay the situation by saying that Boucher was a holdover from the Bush administration, but I pointed out that this meant that he would be doubly careful to ensure he was accurately reflecting Warren Christopher's views. It seemed to us to be an amazing turnaround, given Tony Lake's reassurance of only a week before.

Vance and I decided to stand our ground and give no quarter to our US critics. We were confident that we had the support of the EC and Russia, so we decided to go to New York and put the fate of the VOPP in the hands of the fifteen members of the Security Council. It was a high-risk strategy but if we wanted to keep the VOPP alive there was no alternative. A few European diplomatic voices could be heard from Washington arguing that the administration needed time and they could be won around, but against that was the firm belief of many Americans whom Vance and I knew in Washington that delay meant death for the VOPP. We were hearing that key members of the administration were already privately saying that the VOPP would be dead in a week, smothered in diplomatic verbiage and in press criticism, for the *Washington Post*'s editorial pages were not being helpful to us either, although they were not as mindlessly negative as those of the *New York Times*.

John Major invited me to attend a seminar on Yugoslavia at No. 10 on 22 January and after a little thought I felt it did not compromise my EC status to accept. I welcomed the opportunity for an exchange of views, particularly with Robin Renwick, our ambassador to the US, flying in from Washington, on what was really happening in the Clinton administration, and with key British military figures serving in the UN flying in from Split. I sent in a memorandum of my own because I wanted to put the case on the table for using selective air power to impose a specific peace settlement and to have it discussed. It was odd to be back around the Cabinet table, and the mixed representation of the meeting reminded me of 1977 when Jim Callaghan had convened a meeting with service chiefs to draw up rules of engagement for the naval ships and submarine we were despatching to the Falkland Islands.

Malcolm Rifkind, the Defence Secretary, intelligent and sharp, was totally opposed to any imposition of a settlement and managed rather effectively to lampoon my proposal for using air power. I did not engage in a debate with him as I was not part of the UK collective decision-making body assembled around the table, but it was confirmation – not that I needed it – that there was no support in the UK government for any more military intervention than the humanitarian support which was currently being undertaken by UNPROFOR.

John Major's handling of the meeting interested me. His style was more reminiscent of Jim Callaghan than of Harold Wilson, encouraging everyone to speak and marshalling the crucial questions well, at the end painstakingly summing up our con-clusions in a way which made the Cabinet secretary's task rather redundant. Over all the time that I was co-chairman of the ICFY, he gave me personally every support. But he would not be edged over into a combatant role under any circumstances. He was on guard against an apparently innocent decision whose military implications had not been sufficiently thought through and which had the potential for creeping the UK commitment forward into uncharted territory.

Douglas Hurd's emphasis was slightly different. He became less certain of the value of UNPROFOR as the years went by. His attitude to the use of force was inextricably linked to whether the US would participate with troops on the ground. Despite being a strong believer in the European Union, he fretted as the strains developed in the Atlantic relationship and did everything he could to alleviate these, keeping in constant touch with Warren Christopher. No one could have tried harder to bridge the differences. He agonised in a thoughtful and concerned way about the turn of events in Bosnia-Herzegovina, and though I did not agree with him on all issues I always had a courteous and serious hearing for my suggestions.

Over the next few months with other governments I tried to argue the case for imposing a settlement, but it never won support. All countries preferred to shield themselves behind the ideal of a negotiated settlement agreed to by all the parties, failing in that posture to acknowledge that this gave a veto power to any one of the parties, which of course they exercised, not just the Bosnian Serbs but also the Bosnian Muslims. Henry Kissinger, writing in the *New York Post* on 23 February, put his finger on the issue, arguing that 'if a Bosnian settlement is to be just it will have to be imposed', and dismissing as an illusion Warren Christopher's condition that the parties would 'voluntarily embrace' anything meaningfully. But he wanted any US participation in enforcement confined to aerial measures, since this 'will reduce the danger of American forces becoming hostages'. He did not add, but of course it was implicit, that there were already forces on the ground who ran a real risk of becoming hostages. That was the perpetual military dilemma which was rarely faced up to in either the Pentagon or the White House: if widespread air strikes were to be used it was essential that UNPROFOR be removed first, at the very least from vulnerable areas where they could be shot at or captured.

After more than a dozen lengthy bilateral and trilateral meetings, at the final plenary session of the conference Cy Vance said these had reinforced our view that the map submitted by us was just and equitable, based on the fundamental premise that Bosnia-Herzegovina would remain a sovereign, independent, multi-ethnic state. The map did not accept the results of ethnic cleansing but was on the contrary designed to reverse them, and it struck a fair balance in the allocation of land and natural and industrial resources. In my speech I said that we were taking the dispute in effect to the world's parliament and we hoped they would all come to New York and put their case to the members of the Security Council. All three parties signed the constitutional principles; the Bosnian Croats and, somewhat to our surprise, the Bosnian Serbs signed the agreement on the cessation of hostilities. President Izetbegović, for the Bosnian government, having previously agreed, now said his reservations on heavy weapons precluded him from signing. On the map Karadžić got far closer to signing than we had anticipated, and I am convinced he would have signed if Izetbegović had signed.

Both Vance and I thought Karadžić had been told by Milošević to settle. Evidence to support this was visible in Karadžić's presenting the talks as 'a great success' and briefing positively about going to New York. Karadžić said he could agree to most of the map but wanted areas under dispute to be put to a plebiscite, which we had earlier ruled out. We were certainly closer to an agreement than any of us could have imagined a week earlier. Why did Izetbegović not sign? In essence because he sensed that Karadžić might sign if he did and he felt encouraged by US attitudes to hold out for a better deal.

The most flagrant and best-documented episode of Muslim army units provoking the Serbs to fire on their fellow Muslims occurred when a United Nations Military Observer (UNMO) team near Kosevo hospital in Sarajevo had witnessed a Bosnian government mortar crew set up in the grounds of the hospital and fire over the hospital into a Serb area. They had quickly packed up and gone, only for the UNMOs to see a television crew arrive and then record the retaliatory Serb shelling of the hospital. It was the very hospital that I had visited the month before and which had so shocked me with its shell holes in the recovery room. I asked General Morillon why the UN had not made it public. He wanted the truth out but said, 'We've got to live here.' It was uncomfortable for the UN in Sarajevo, but if they had been bolder on the few agent provocateur incidents they could have been more forthright on the many Serb outrages and avoided appearing to equate the two sides. I was aware that this type of action tended to occur in civil wars. But I found this particular

Muslim provocation, involving the very hospital about the shelling of which I had personally protested strongly to General Mladić a few weeks before, especially troubling. Even at that time there was a feeling among some in UNPROFOR that an element, albeit only small, in the continuous sniping in the central part of Muslim-held Sarajevo was being undertaken by Muslim units firing on their own people. Those suspicions were never confirmed until August 1995, when a French UN team pinpointed some of the sniping to a building which they knew was controlled by the Bosnian government forces.

Vance and I were due to meet Warren Christopher on 1 February. We subsequently came to know a little about how he prepared for our meeting from an account of a meeting he had with Warren Zimmermann, the last US ambassador to Yugoslavia, who in 1996 wrote about it in his book *Origins of Catastrophe*:

> Warren Christopher invited me to participate in an informal discussion of Bosnian policy. Christopher asked our small group for views on the Vance–Owen plan, which provided for a primarily ethnic division of Bosnia but contained some benefits for the Muslims. It held the Serbs to 43 per cent of the territory of Bosnia, divided the country into ten provinces . . . provided for multi-ethnic provinces, and preserved at least nominally the sovereignty of Bosnia. The secretary had not yet discussed the plan with Vance, whose deputy he had been in the Carter administration. I said I thought it was an acceptable compromise in the circumstances, since the Serbs had by then consolidated their hold on more than two-thirds of Bosnia.
>
> Christopher said he was concerned that the Muslims would reject the plan. I told him I had a piece of accidental inside knowledge on that. I had been in Vance's office in Geneva a few weeks before, when Vance and Owen received the Bosnian government's reaction to the plan. It was not only positive, but enthusiastic; the Muslims said they were ready to announce support immediately. Vance urged them to delay; he was afraid a quick Muslim acceptance would cause the Serbs to raise the price. With that background, I gave Christopher my view that any current Muslim objections were likely to be tactical and that in the end they would probably accept the plan. Unfortunately, the administration delayed in its support for the plan, thus missing a chance to get it launched.
>
> The conversation turned to policy options. Bob Galluci, then in charge of political-military affairs, and I argued that air strikes had to

be a serious option; we both felt they would be necessary. Others in the room were more cautious. Tarnoff [Peter Tarnoff, Under-Secretary of State for Political Affairs] drew up an inventory of possible steps that could be taken short of force. They included such things as breaking diplomatic relations with Milošević's rump Yugoslavia and tightening the economic embargo. Perhaps unwisely, I said that nothing on that list would deter Milošević; the language of force was the only language he understood. Christopher said with a smile that this was a pretty gloomy way to end a meeting. He added that he would convene the same group often for further discussions. But we were never called again.

Our meeting with Christopher in the US mission to the UN in New York was disillusioning, not so much for what was said but for what was unsaid and for what was apparently unknown. I had last met Christopher over a breakfast meeting at Carlton Gardens, the Foreign Secretary's residence, in 1978 when he came to tell us that President Carter had decided not to go ahead with the neutron bomb. Cy Vance was suffering from a flu-like illness, but he marshalled the arguments for our plan, which covered seventy pages of typescript, with considerable skill. Yet, as the questioning went on it became painfully apparent that the Secretary of State knew very little about the detail of our plan. Particularly surprising, in view of the administration's public criticism, was that he had not been briefed on all the human rights provisions and safeguards that we had built in with the express purpose of reversing ethnic cleansing. For Cy Vance, who knew from personal experience the pressures that weigh on any new Secretary of State, it was a severe disappointment, for Warren Christopher appeared as if he had not had time to read even a short factual information sheet on the essence of our plan. I was baffled as to how Christopher could come so badly briefed to meet his old boss, Cy, who was under virulent public attack for a plan which his critics claimed favoured ethnic cleansing. This very criticism was one on which Christopher himself had been dismayingly equivocal, and yet on our actual proposals he had clearly not even paid Vance the courtesy of having done his homework, thereby showing that he had made no real attempt to understand what it was that Cy was being criticised for. Herb Okun was very surprised by this aspect. Not that the atmosphere of the meeting was unpleasant; quite the contrary, but he was embarrassed that his old department could have so badly informed the new Secretary of State. Being charitable, perhaps the problem was Christopher's continued involvement throughout the transition period in Little Rock, at Clinton's request, in the selection of administration members. Whereas in the past, incoming Secretaries of State used the months of the transitional period to become well briefed and versed in all aspects of the current foreign policy agenda, Christopher had had, through no fault of his, no such opportunity. We thought during the meeting that we had enlightened him and cleared up some of his misapprehensions about the plan, and that the dialogue would continue. Christopher told us:

> This meeting has been illuminating to me . . . We hope the process can be kept going, and we will look for ways to help it . . . I want to work with you, to move forward together . . . I will say we had a good meeting. It explained a lot I hadn't heard before. It was a candid discussion of hard issues. You've impressed us with the urgency. We hope the parties will continue to negotiate. There is a strong case that this plan, while not perfect, is the best available.

We left with Vance saying very little to the television cameras on the sidewalk, as we had agreed, and all went back to my room in the UN Plaza Hotel for a drink. Then I switched on CNN and we watched Warren Christopher a few hundred yards down the street speak to the same television cameras. Again it was not what he said but his manner and the omissions which conveyed a clear message. None of us after hearing what he had said could question the *New York Times* headline next day, 'US DECLINES TO BACK PEACE PLAN AS THE BALKAN TALKS SHIFT TO UN', nor the reporting that Warren Christopher was 'setting the stage for a possible confrontation between the mediators and the Clinton administration'. The report also had a senior UN official saying that at a lunch given by the secretary general, Boutros Boutros-Ghali, Christopher had 'expressed his "ambivalence" about the Vance–Owen plan. Mr Christopher added that he had problems "with the map included in the plan".' The account that we had of that lunch meeting was even more disappointing than our own meeting.

The new Clinton administration had already made up their mind and were intent on killing off the VOPP. Behind the scenes, while giving the appearance to the European governments of still being open minded and of considering the plan carefully, the administration had already abandoned it. That night Johnny Apple, the chief of the *New York Times* Washington bureau, told me what was really being said on a non-attributable basis in Washington, namely that Cy Vance was an 'old-style Democrat' and just what Clinton's 'new Democrats' wanted to put behind them. Johnny told me that he had seen this clash developing and on the day after Clinton's inauguration he had personally decided to give more prominence in the paper to what was said on 21 January by Richard Boucher. He warned me that the Vice-President, Al Gore, felt very strongly that the Muslims had to be helped and he confirmed that Boucher was a professional and would never have spoken as he had for a new administration without being absolutely sure of his ground.

Turning around a new President was going to be a formidable task, for every US President takes office with a groundswell of goodwill from political opponents as well as political friends. Americans vest in their new President a respect for the office akin to the feeling most Europeans give to their monarchs. Also, the moral strand of US foreign policy exemplified by Woodrow Wilson lent itself to support for the Bosnian Muslims, who were widely, and not unreasonably, seen as the victims. One strategy was to play a waiting game and hope that slowly the administration would come round to the European's position of support for the VOPP. But we came to the conclusion that it was full-frontal assault or failure, for I could not expect to keep the present level of support from the European countries if they sensed that Vance and I were not in American parlance 'hanging in there'. This would particularly apply to the French, who were in turn crucial in holding the Germans to the VOPP. If Paris saw me adopting the usual British posture of bending the knee to US objections then Mitterrand would go off on his own with a purely French initiative.

Also, it would be a sign of European Community weakness were the EC to back off from its considered judgement of what could bring peace to Bosnia-Herzegovina because, as it seemed from Europe, a new US administration was unwilling even to consult on a campaigning position adopted in the summer of 1992. There had been a transformation of the air strike option since the autumn 1992 decision to mount a UN humanitarian intervention, but the administration's failure to recognise the change in circumstances that occurred between July and September 1992 was to bedevil the US–EU dialogue over Bosnia-Herzegovina. I decided that night that I had not been appointed as the EC negotiator to behave like an ambassador. Mine had been a political appointment, and I would go for the jugular vein of US policy, namely their refusal to put troops on the ground in Bosnia. I would simply urge the Clinton administration to do so in every interview, with the implicit message that only then would they have the right to veto or subvert the VOPP. In the process I was bound to make myself unpopular in Washington, but I did not want another international job after this one and I had no need to ensure their patronage.

Vance and I gave a joint press conference that Tuesday in an attempt to put our case and when Vance was asked whether he was appeasing Serbian aggression he replied, 'This is hogwash. It makes me pretty damned angry.' Privately his language was even stronger and amazed those of us who knew him, for even under intense provocation he was normally the most restrained person. A few days before in Geneva we had discussed how to handle the media and Cy Vance had made it quite clear that he wanted me to put our case powerfully and rebut forcefully the charge that we were ratifying ethnic cleansing. I fully understood that it was impossible for him to criticise Warren Christopher publicly, given the history of their relationship, and that Americans would expect Vance to give his former deputy, within days of taking office, proper respect and a fair wind. Fred Eckhard, our joint press spokesman, who was doing a brilliant job for us both, recalls my warning Vance that 'some blood will be spilt on the carpet' and Cy shrugging his shoulders and saying, 'So be it.' Few ever realised how passionate a man underneath his constrained exterior Vance really was. We both felt throughout a deep sense of outrage at the behaviour of many Serbs and it hurt to be accused of favouring ethnic cleansing. We knew that in the final analysis only peace would stop ethnic cleansing and that every month of war that went by only served to set ethnic divisions harder in concrete and make them near impossible to reverse.

As I had predicted, blood was spilt the next day. The *New York Times* of 3 February carried prominently on the front page a story from R. W. Apple Jr, headlined 'Mediator is upset at US reluctance over Bosnia talks – says Muslims await move – "Only act in town" Owen says after he and Vance fail to persuade Christopher'. In the text, which was a mixture of what I had said at the press conference and to Johnny Apple himself over dinner, I was described as complaining that the Clinton administration's reluctance to back the effort threatened to 'scuttle chances of ending the war':

> Against all the odds, even against my own expectations, we have more or less got a settlement but we have a problem. We can't get the Muslims on board. And that's largely the fault of the Americans, because the Muslims won't budge while they think Washington may come into it on their side any day now. What do they want down there, a war that goes on and on? This isn't just the best act in town, it's the only act in town. It's the best settlement you can get, and it's a bitter irony to see the Clinton people block it.

I had talked too freely over dinner with Johnny, at his invitation, letting my frustration bubble over about Warren Christopher, saying that he 'didn't really take in what I was saying' and recalling that President Clinton had promised bolder action in Bosnia in his election campaign, 'and because they've had to pull back on so much already, they're afraid to do so on this too; eventually they'll get it and help us'. This went too far when seen in newsprint. For a fleeting moment – which was entirely my fault – I had forgotten that Johnny was not just a friend but one of the best journalists in America. There was no misunderstanding between us: his notebook was open in front of me and he was taking notes throughout dinner. I should not have risked making such comments and I regretted it deeply. I suspect this, more than the substance of the VOPP, permanently damaged my relationship with Warren Christopher.

To fight for the VOPP was always going to be traumatic. The US is the most powerful country in the world and is used to having its way in foreign policy. The diplomatic world is normally characterised by those whose priority is to avoid confrontation, for whom splitting the difference is second nature and for whom ensuring that policy remains within the middle of the pack is an art form. It was, therefore, all the more surprising that the EC countries who had so far all stayed loyal to the VOPP continued to do so. Klaus Kinkel was coming to Washington in a few days' time, and when he did he supported the plan; but he ran into criticism from within the ranks of his coalition partners the CDU and CSU for doing so. The German press and public wanted more positive action to help the Muslims and were pressing for the lifting of the arms embargo. It was my responsibility to keep the EC together, but I was now attempting to do so on a high-risk policy, with no country in Europe really wanting to damage relations with the new US administration. I knew that I risked being disowned by the EC, but felt there was no alternative if we were to achieve a decent peace settlement.

Yet I have little doubt that had we not fought our corner the VOPP would have been dead in the water by the middle of February and we would have never reached the stage of having it approved in Athens by all of the parties three months later. On the MacNeil–Lehrer current affairs television show a Democrat Congressman, Frank McCloskey from Indiana, who had earlier referred to our 'appeasement strategy', launched into an emotive string of soundbites to which I finally retorted, 'Congressman, that is not a policy, that is a rant.' This exchange encapsulated the essence of the problem. Vance and I certainly had the same deep emotional feelings as our critics, and so did European intellectuals and politicians, but emotion is not of itself a policy. The UN Security Council, with a nasty, brutal war on its hands, had for months confined itself to rhetoric in its many resolutions. Now, in fairness, many countries in the Security Council knew that there was an urgent need for solutions. There was no sign, however, that the Clinton administration had done any new thinking during the transition period between one President and another. They promised to come up with an alternative policy over the next few weeks, but in the meantime seemed intent on killing off a detailed plan backed by all their allies and close to being agreed by the parties. It was by any standard of international diplomacy outrageous conduct.

But it was not all criticism. Under an ironic headline in the *New York Times*, 'The crime of Vance and Owen', A. M. Rosenthal wrote:

> When everybody is screaming nobody is listening. Rarely have so many American commentators, editorial writers and think tankers

screamed so loud and bitterly at any Western diplomats as they are
doing . . . villains, Vance, Owen, villains . . . The truth is that the Vance–
Owen plan is trying to create Bosnia, not to destroy it – a fact that the
screamers cannot hear over themselves . . . The Clinton administration
is doing something more dangerous for a great power than screaming
– mumbling. The mumblemouths say Washington does not oppose
the plan but will not ask the parties to accept it – death through
lockjaw . . . If Vance–Owen is rejected, the war will go on, Bosnia will
probably disappear in Serbian–Croatian partition . . . More likely
somebody will get a bright idea – that's enough killing, let's tell these
people they have to live together in a decentralised state in which
they share power. And somebody else will wonder it out loud – say,
whatever happened to those fellows, you know, the quiet American
and the other one, the kind of crabby Englishman?

My brief foray into US domestic politics was nearly over – apart
from a blast at the East Coast liberals at a Foreign Affairs Council
lunch meeting in New York for not defending Cy Vance enough. I
knew it was time now to let the internal debate we had triggered
take its course, and go back to quiet diplomacy. The European
Community countries had made it clear that they stood by the
VOPP. We now had to rely on that innate decency which char-
acterises most American attitudes, albeit sometimes overlaid by a
vulgarity and loudness that do not truly reflect the inner voice of a
fine democracy. I felt confident even in the midst of all this
controversy that there was no new or different policy for the Clinton
administration to discover and that this truth would now come to
the surface far sooner than would have otherwise been the case. The
key question was whether this would happen in time for the VOPP
to be rescued and put back on the negotiating table. President Özal
of Turkey came to Washington and advocated force as the only thing
the Serbs would ever understand, which did not help; the Prime
Minister of Canada, Brian Mulroney, visited Washington and
emphasised that a lot of constructive work had been done on the
VOPP and that any inadequacies in it could be fixed with some
amendments and greater American involvement, which did help.
Not for the first or last time, the Canadian voice in the crisis of
former Yugoslavia was that of common sense stemming from a

readiness to share the UN military burden and a depth of understanding of what the UN could and should be able to achieve.

In Washington on 10 February Christopher announced the new
policy of the US administration. It had been extensively leaked in
advance, and the London *Times* on 9 February had a story headlined
'American bluster marks qualified approval for peace plan'. 'It is
becoming plain', the article remarked, 'that the Clinton administration cannot have a policy in the Balkans without committing
ground troops.' Since they had no intention of committing troops,
we hoped they would develop a more supportive and coherent
policy. Warren Christopher's statement was far better than either
Vance or I had hoped for in relation to the VOPP. Cy felt
comfortable with it and told me that it totally justified us putting
them under so much public pressure. The *New York Times* headline
the next day was for once a joy to read – 'US BACKS BOSNIAN PEACE
PLAN' – and the paper said that the administration had abandoned
the tough campaign talk and embraced an international peace
process.

The British position throughout my open battle with the US
administration had been totally supportive, largely due to John
Major, but also to consistent backing from Sir David Hannay, our
representative at the UN in New York. His nerve and backbone had
been decisive in countering the wobbles from our embassy in
Washington, which had wanted to be onside with the new
administration. As the flak began to fly, the Foreign Office in
London, under the then political director, Len Appleyard, also held
steady. Douglas Hurd, after a little understandable anxiety, reflected
in a telephone conversation we had, rallied to my support when I
admitted the Johnny Apple interview had come out badly and had
been my mistake. The British press were split between those who
wanted me to stand up to the US and those who preferred the
traditional diplomatic posture of at least publicly pretending to be in
total accord. The EC presidency had by now passed from Britain to
Denmark and the Danish Foreign Ministers, first Uffe Ellemann-
Jensen and then Niels Helveg Petersen, both very committed
Europeans, were firm throughout in their belief that we had an
agreed EC policy and that we should uphold it, even if that meant
upsetting the Americans. On 16 February Helveg Petersen, speaking

for the EC presidency in Washington, said that the EC had arrived at a clear position of support for the VOPP and that he could see no reason to trim. At one time reports out of Washington tried to imply that my personal position with Cy Vance was under strain at this period and that Cy would soon bow out, but that story did not run since Vance made it utterly clear to everyone, from Warren Christopher downwards, that he stood by me and what I was saying. All this time, too, Boutros Boutros-Ghali was firm in standing by us both, helped by his longstanding friendship with Cy Vance. Our negotiating team, though now divided between Geneva and New York, was totally united and there were none of the self-serving leaks about unnamed individuals having their own personal reservations that can be so debilitating and which the parties would have exploited.

A UNHCR report released on 3 March made a devastating contrast to the complacency of the politicians, describing the situation on the ground in eastern Bosnia as 'total domination of war logic over humanitarian concerns'. While the UNHCR's cancellation of the convoys had impacted internationally, the situation on the ground had reached an 'unspeakable state'. This situation we tried to highlight in a press statement drawing attention to the heavy fighting around Srebrenica, where the Serbs were continuing to impede access. The Serbs' linkage of humanitarian access to political and military conditions was deplorable; but even as one's tongue formed words of condemnation one knew the international community would accept and even tolerate it. This was the daily discomfort that we lived with – my weapon was words and beyond them there was no prospect of international power being exercised. Here we were in New York talking to the Security Council at the apex of international power, and yet these humanitarian horrors might have been happening on another planet for all the deterrent response they elicited. My powerlessness was uncomfortable for me, but for the UNHCR worker in Sarajevo or Srebrenica the situation was a living nightmare.

The slow soft shuffle of the Clinton administration towards supporting our peace plan was under way but nothing was going to happen quickly, particularly while the Muslim politicians from Sarajevo were not evincing the need for speed. I suppose because of my medical training I could never accept this disconnection between war and peace: for me, the more serious the symptoms the greater the need for early treatment. As negotiators, we had to be optimistic and buoyant in order to create and foster an atmosphere of hope. A negotiator in a time of war has this constant problem of how to build and sustain momentum when the parties to a negotiation, particularly their politicians not directly involved on the battlefield, often have a vested interest in appearing pessimistic and downbeat and want to give the impression that their negotiations are getting nowhere in order to justify and give heart to those condemned to fight on the home front and in the battle lines. Negotiating during a war can only be compared with negotiating during a strike, but at least in a strike those whose services are being disrupted raise their voices in favour of resolving the dispute. In a war the civilians facing hardship cannot easily demand peace without being accused of undermining the morale of the fighters at the front. The saddest feature of the war in Bosnia-Herzegovina was that the voice of its people was but rarely heard. We tried to raise the profile of the multi-ethnic civic groups, decent people wanting to live together as before the war, but their voice, while championed by a few abroad, was drowned out by the propaganda of war. We knew the urge for peace was there but it manifested itself only in little things, like the tears in the eyes of the mainly female interpreters brought out from Sarajevo as they realised that we had reached deadlock, or in their pleading to us to carry on negotiating into the night – even when they personally were obviously tired out, for interpreting can be hard work. Sometimes, when there was a real interchange and the negotiation moved beyond set speeches, we could sense the relief and hope in the interpreters. This small number of ordinary people, sometimes mothers with children, were far more important than they probably realised in keeping up our flagging spirits and in making us sit for so many long hours searching for a settlement. By contrast the Bosnian politicians, whether Serb, Muslim or Croat, were almost without exception impossibly negative.

On 9 March it was announced from Paris that Vance and I had asked President Mitterrand to invite President Milošević to Paris for talks with the co-chairmen, which while 'under the auspices of

France is a working session between negotiators'. We met at the
Elysée Palace on 11 March in the late afternoon. Mitterrand had a
preliminary tête-à-tête with Milošević. During the five hours of
meetings that followed, the greater part of which he attended,
Mitterrand was in top form, despite the fact that the world now
knew he had prostate cancer, which he had concealed for eleven
years of his presidency: he was well briefed and his interventions
were timely and frequently delivered with great emotion. He
allowed Vance and me to take the lead for much of the time and
reinforced our arguments where appropriate to great effect. Looking
to us for guidance in his response, and making clear his full support
for our proposals, he described the plan at one stage as a baby more
beautiful than its parents believed. I was greatly struck by the verve
and stamina he showed, in marked contrast to his performance when
I had last met him in December.

Mitterrand used all forms of persuasion and argument when
dealing with Milošević. France, he said, was one of Serbia's historical
friends, and did not want to see Serbia isolated or unfairly punished;
but Milošević had to face the realities of the current situation and
the international climate. If the war continued there would be little
even Serbia's oldest friends and allies could do to prevent its further
isolation. Even Russia was unlikely to step out of line if the
international community called for tighter sanctions. It was
imperative to get an agreement in the coming days. Milošević was
faced with a historic choice. No one was claiming he could twist the
Bosnian Serbs around his little finger, but they looked to him as their
'big brother': he had real authority. Either 'the war continues, the
tragedy gets worse, sanctions get tougher', or it is halted, enabling
Serbia to rebuild its economy and play its rightful role in Europe.
Coming on the heels of President Mitterrand's visit to Washington
and immediately before his visit to Moscow, the meeting was all the
more timely.

When Mitterrand rejoined the meeting in the evening, he had
clearly thought long and hard about the importance Milošević
attached to economic arguments, and in particular the question of
lifting sanctions. He had obviously decided that if progress was to be
made with Milošević, this bullet had to be bitten, and he set out
France's position in dramatic and unambiguous terms. If the map

was accepted, 'then sanctions must and should be lifted as soon as technically feasible'. He admitted that this stance would no doubt be opposed in some quarters, but he would put his full weight behind getting others such as Chancellor Kohl to support it. France would 'fight and win the battle to lift sanctions'. He left Milošević in no doubt about what was on offer, but also made it clear that there was a real danger of losing this opportunity. The time for taking a decision was very short: in three weeks he would have lost his majority in the French National Assembly, and his power would be only some 60 per cent of what it was now. Thereafter it would be much more difficult for him to deliver.

I detected a marked change in Milošević's attitude as he realised the opportunities Mitterrand was offering if there were a peaceful settlement. We rose from dinner well content with what Mitterrand had achieved. Now we had to tighten sanctions but give a little time before they came into effect to act as an incentive for Milošević to deliver.

Another aspect of winning support for the VOPP was to have in position a credible implementation force. The Europeans, including the French, believed that our original proposal for a purely UN implementation force was now insufficient and were adamant that the US had to be involved. But the US had their bottom line defined with some exactness by the chairman of the Joint Chiefs of Staff, General Colin Powell. In his autobiography Powell describes how the early meetings of the administration on Bosnia were full of 'belligerent rhetoric' and how the 'debate exploded at one session when Madeleine Albright, our ambassador to the UN, asked me in frustration, "What's the point of having this superb military that you're always talking about if we can't use it?" I thought I would have an aneurysm!' Powell then explained to her that tough political goals had to be established first. For him it had to be a NATO operation under UN authority with adequate command and control arrangements, and he would not countenance the French sidelining NATO's Supreme Allied Commander.

Never far from our minds was the deteriorating humanitarian situation. Sir Donald Acheson, whom I knew and thoroughly respected, was the WHO special representative and was keeping me in regular touch with what was happening on the ground. On 16

March he sent me a copy of his fourteenth and final report in his period in office, after having travelled widely in Bosnia in an attempt to make a general assessment of the health of the people for his successor. His most striking conclusion was that although the degree of suffering varied, the nature of the misery was similar everywhere: insufficient food, both in quantity and quality; interrupted electricity supplies; compromised water supplies; inadequate collection of rubbish; large numbers of refugees and displaced persons with varying degrees of malnutrition; and often a high prevalence of lice and scabies – all in the midst of economic collapse. In Sarajevo, in addition to these problems, there was destruction of the utilities and serious damage to the sewage system. He concluded that, having survived the winter, the people of Bosnia, many of whom had reduced resistance to infection due to malnutrition, now faced the equally threatening problems of warm weather with its attendant hazards of illnesses due to microbial and rodent multiplication. It was impossible for me to forget my medical training and to ignore the existence of this physical misery, quite apart from the shelling and shooting. I knew by now that serious outside military intervention was completely out of the question and that the US, despite sometimes giving an impression that it was under consideration, were really grandstanding with an even greater reluctance than hitherto to committing forces on the ground. It was therefore imperative that we implemented the VOPP and pressed for peace.

It took until 25 March, more than three months of negotiating, to obtain the Bosnian government's agreement to the VOPP package and the delay had been very damaging. We now had the hardest task of all still left: to get the Bosnian Serbs to sign. I knew that only Milošević could deliver the Bosnian Serbs and that he was vulnerable in one area: financial sanctions. The Security Council had to squeeze his assets. This time the US were strong and correct, and the UK position was weak and obtuse. We had to tighten every area of sanctions, for there was much economic intelligence showing that Milošević was becoming really worried about the Serbian economy.

The UN financial sanctions resolution went through in New York late on Saturday 17 April and I heard about it driving into the BBC studios for a David Frost interview on breakfast television the following day. The French had been adamant that there had to be a vote that day, whereas the US and the UK had been ready to give Moscow another day. The Russian ambassador consulted Moscow and eventually got Yeltsin's agreement to abstain on the vote; so UNSCR 820, introducing financial sanctions, was then adopted just before midnight on Saturday, with thirteen votes in favour and Russia and China abstaining. In the Frost interview I talked of the need to interdict the Bosnian Serb supply lines by air until they agreed the VOPP. My military adviser, Brigadier Messervy-Whiting, had sent me a well-thought-through options paper concluding that interdiction warranted further study inside NATO. He wrote of the Serbs' long and vulnerable lines of communication, which could probably be taken on most effectively east of the Posavina corridor and in the Bijeljina region, and that there were three railway lines we could interdict as well as the road from Zvornik to Pale, which if interdicted would undoubtedly affect the Bosnian Serb army's offensive capability in this area.

I could never get any major government interested in developing a sound military counter-force strategy of a sort that might have carried the Russians with it and really made General Mladić pause. In Washington, where there was considerable anger at the deteriorating humanitarian situation in Srebrenica, there was some apparent sympathy for my call for air intervention to cut Bosnian Serb supply lines, though also a recognition of UK and French concerns that this could lead to retaliation against the weak and overstretched UN forces. Some were arguing that if air strikes were not agreed then lifting the arms embargo was the only way forward. They were forgetting that whereas Belgrade might see well-judged interdiction as not necessitating their further involvement, 'lift and strike' would be far more likely to stimulate public demands for their overt intervention. Washington never understood at that stage that splitting the Serbs was a delicate matter requiring some finesse, in part because some of them were obsessed with 'getting Milošević' rather than using his influence for our purposes.

The Serbs now had nine days before financial sanctions would take effect, and this meant that during my visit to Belgrade I was going to be able to put them under the maximum pressure. I went on BBC radio and deliberately toughened my stance another few notches:

> At the moment the Serbs are still taking territory and they are not
> being checked. So it's up to the governments of the world – are they
> going to be rolled over by the Serbs? I would counsel governments
> against ruling out military pressure. In a war situation to rule out
> military pressure is very dangerous.

The EC Foreign Ministers, although they publicly acknowledged
that the behaviour of the Bosnian Serbs around Srebrenica obliged
them to do something, and although they left open the option of air
strikes, were all hesitant to take up my suggestion to threaten to
interdict the Bosnian Serb supply lines from the air.

We were now looking to turn sanctions into a blockade. In the
Adriatic from 26 April we were empowered to prohibit all
commercial and maritime traffic from entering the territorial waters
of the FRY. On the Danube, an active supply route, there were plans
for a lead monitoring flotilla from the Western European Union, an
organisation unconnected to the EU which dealt with defence
matters, and for more effective co-ordination between the riparian
states to close existing loopholes. There could now be a closure of all
land freight crossing points, with only limited exceptions, and there
would be more sanctions assistance missions to help the customs
authorities of the neighbouring states. Also, action could now be
taken against all of the FRY financial assets. If complied with, this
was going to be a formidable package and would, I hoped, give
Milošević pause for thought.

What of Slobodan Milošević the man? He was the son of a
Serbian Orthodox clergyman of Montenegrin origin. His parents
separated when he was young and both later committed suicide. A
crucial figure in his life was Mirjana Marković, his wife, for they
were extremely close personally and politically. He joined the
League of Communists in 1959 and graduated from Belgrade
University's Law Faculty in 1964. He was involved in ideological and
political activities with the League of Communists, was economic
adviser to the mayor of Belgrade and worked in the Information
Department, where he learnt his formidable media skills. Above all
he understood the power of television. He was director general of
the enterprise Tehnogas from 1970 to 1978 and then president of a
Belgrade bank from 1978 to 1982, a period during which he

travelled to America and elsewhere, acquiring fluent English. Thereafter he became head of the Communist Party organisation in Belgrade in 1984–6 and party chief for the entire republic from 1986 to 1989.

Milošević's public profile was suddenly raised in April 1987 when he twice visited the Serbian community in Kosovo, who were complaining about their plight as a minority and about being beaten up by the local Albanian police. On his second visit Milošević became uncharacteristically emotional, proclaiming, 'No one will be allowed to beat you! No one will be allowed to beat you!' He then, with manipulative skill, set about getting Serbian politicians thought to be soft on the Albanian question voted out of their positions. Riding the wave of nationalism, he overturned the provincial Communist leadership and insisted that Belgrade must be able to exercise effective control over Serbia's two autonomous provinces of Kosovo and Vojvodina. As a popular hero, 'Slobo', he began to draw large audiences and in November 1988 he addressed a Belgrade rally of around a million people. By this time he was speaking for most Serbs, and he had a knack of poking fun affectionately at Tito. 'Even before his death the system didn't function, Tito functioned. After his death nothing has functioned.'

There was a ruthlessness and a pursuit of power for its own sake about Milošević that underpinned the pragmatism that otherwise seemed so neatly to characterise Milošević's political personality. The private man was not a racist, nor was he paranoid about the rest of the world. Only once over the years did he make an aside which offended me on racial grounds, and he checked himself as he said it. Proud of Serbia, he gave vent to a paranoia about the international community in public almost as an obligatory jibe, but even so not to an excessive degree. Milošević carried his nationalism lightly and it did not intrude in an offensive manner in conversations with foreigners. He used nationalism for the purpose of gaining and holding power but his economic attitudes were those of a man fully conscious of international realities. He knew America well and talked knowledgeably about Democrat and Republican politics.

One aspect of Milošević's character was his readiness to regard individuals as disposable: to use them and then discard them. He had risen within the Communist Party on the back of his friendship with Ivan Stambolić, then brushed him aside and later had him killed.

On almost every occasion that we met I would at some stage raise Kosovo, and when I did I knew I was striking a jarring note. Over Kosovo the polite mask sometimes broke and we would be into an ugly confrontation. It was as if he knew this was the area of his most indefensible behaviour on which he was personally vulnerable, and he would sometimes turn snarling on me or anyone who raised it. I suspect none of those close to him ever did confront him. Yet once we had confronted each other he would soon return to a courteous dialogue, almost as if he welcomed someone standing up to him. It was on Kosovo that Milošević had risen to power and in the process had spoken for almost all Serbs, who genuinely believed Tito had sacrificed their interests for the sake of keeping the Albanians quiet. I often likened him to someone who jumped on to the tiger of nationalism and found it difficult to get off again without the tiger eating him. In Paris in 1995 he got off at least that portion of the tiger's anatomy marked Bosnia-Herzegovina, in front of Clinton, Chirac and Major, and in fairness he stayed true to that strand of policy from then onwards. Predictably his undoing was Kosovo, which led to the NATO bombing, his defeat in the election in Serbia and his transfer for his trial to The Hague.

On Saturday 24 April, after meetings in Belgrade with Milošević and Mladić, I put together a long message to the EC Foreign Ministers, who were attending an informal meeting at Hindsgav Castle in Denmark. The memo ran to twenty-five paragraphs, and two crucial paragraphs read:

> But if we do not lift the arms embargo, we have to be ready to take further action within the UN to tilt the military balance against the Serbs. We have done this since October when under President Bush's threat of enforcement I was able to negotiate with Dr Karadžić the grounding of all combat aircraft. We have taken a symbolic further step by enforcing the no-fly zone. It is a perfectly logical next step to ask the Security Council, if sanctions fail to dissuade the Belgrade Serbs from supplying the Bosnian Serb army, for authorisation to take the necessary measures to interdict the supply lines from the air. Of course this action would not of itself defeat the Bosnian Serbs, but it would tilt the balance in favour of the two armies that have signed up

for the peace plan. It would be difficult for the Russians to accept such action, but it is far more likely that they would accept this limited peacekeeping action than authorise offensive air-to-ground attacks on military targets. Any of these military actions would almost certainly lead to the withdrawal of UNPROFOR troops and affect the humanitarian effort, but with the winter over it is easier to give the highest priority to ending the war.

My own advice is to do everything to contain the fighting to Bosnia-Herzegovina: and facing down the Bosnian Serbs' direct challenge to the authority of the Security Council now is, for all its problems, a far better option than trying to halt a Serb–Croat war, or increased Serbian oppression in Kosovo.

I left for Belgrade once more on Sunday morning well aware that it was crucial to persuade Milošević that this was his last chance to avoid the new sanctions package. We had one message: if the Bosnian Serbs signed up for the VOPP before Monday's deadline on UNSCR 820, new sanctions would not start. Milošević, who had mastered all the detail in the documents, then said that with these changes he would recommend Karadžić to accept the VOPP, and summoned Karadžić and his political partner Momčilo Krajišnik to the meeting. They both had to delay their departure by road to Bijeljina, where the Assembly was due to meet. I again explained our position in painstaking detail, for they had not anywhere near the same knowledge of our actual proposals as Milošević. Eventually they left us, now seemingly ready to accept the VOPP, a decision both Ćosić and Montenegro's President Bulatović had been strongly urging them to take. In Belgrade over a late lunch Milošević was in an expansive mood and said, stretching his arms above his head, that he felt comfortable with the decision. He knew there would be a lot of criticism, but the plan was fair and it was time for peace. He showed no signs of being in any doubt as to the outcome in the Bosnian Serb Assembly.

The relief that we had seemingly broken through left us all a little light headed and, as it turned out, overconfident. I had no doubt then, and have never doubted since, that it was the prospect of financial sanctions which Milošević most feared: the chance of avoiding any further economic misery was too attractive domestically for him to go on humouring Karadžić as he obstructed virtually any deal.

Apparently late that evening Milošević was alerted that all was not going well in the Bosnian Serb Assembly discussion in Bijeljina. A somewhat peremptory letter from the three Presidents, Ćosić, Milošević and Bulatović, was drafted sometime after midnight when it became clear that the mood of the Assembly was moving against signature to the VOPP. In their letter the three Presidents urged the Assembly to accept the VOPP, as developed and amended in talks over the weekend with our team. But shortly before 6.00 a.m. local time, the Bosnian Serb Assembly decided unanimously that it was unable to take a final decision on the VOPP, and that the question would be put to the people in a referendum. This was interpreted in the domestic and international press as a rejection of the VOPP, though no text issued from Bijeljina stated this in as many words. Karadžić said only that there had been no final decision and that this would have to be taken in a referendum in about three weeks' time, around 15–16 May.

Radovan Karadžić, having been captured on a bus in Belgrade disguised with a long grey beard, now shaven off, is due to be tried in the Hague starting in early 2010. He was born on 19 June 1944 in the village of Petnjica on Mount Durmitor, Montenegro. He lived in Sarajevo from the age of fifteen and enrolled at the Medical Secondary School, later graduating from the Medical Faculty in the city and specialising in psychiatry. He completed part of his education in the US. His main activity had been in the state hospital in Sarajevo. Before the war he was a reasonably well-known psychiatrist. He spent eleven months in investigative detention in 1987 and was discharged as innocent – a fairly unusual finding in the Yugoslav republic of Bosnia-Herzegovina – since it was never proved that he had built his summerhouse in Pale with embezzled money. Krajišnik was also jailed and charged for involvement in the same case, and this is where their relationship was forged in an atmosphere of adversity.

In 1968 Karadžić made an emotional Serb nationalist speech from the roof of the Faculty of Philosophy in Sarajevo, after which he claimed he was put under constant surveillance by the Yugoslav secret police. In 1989 he was chosen as president of the Serbian Democratic Party (SDS) – as he tells people, because nobody else wished to take on the job. At the founding congress of the SDS, Izetbegović was guest of honour and received the longest applause.

In the summer of 1990 Karadžić and Izetbegović went to a memorial meeting for Serb and Muslim Second World War victims on the bridge over the river Drina in Foča, and both said that 'blood must never flow down the Drina river ever again'. At the time, Karadžić was reported as saying, 'Our Muslims are much closer to us [Bosnian Serbs] than many Christian peoples in Europe'. I watched as, hour by hour, that relationship deteriorated. At times one saw a flicker of the old relationship and Karadžić would call Izetbegović 'Alija', but Izetbegović never referred to the other man in my hearing as 'Radovan'. They talked together eventually without our presence, but it was a guarded and at times hostile relationship.

Karadžić's especial skill, and it is a considerable one, is to deflect and defuse a hostile question with an innocent facial expression and apparent concern in his voice. When asked, 'Why are you shelling Sarajevo?', he replied, 'We're not, it's the Muslims. We're not attacking, just protecting our homes in and around Sarajevo.' He claims, 'Muslims were never our enemies. Only the Ustashas are our natural enemies. Serbs and Muslims have never clashed, and history proves this, unless a third party was involved.' Again and again I heard him claiming, 'Serbs and Croats were never enemies before 1918, when they entered a joint state. Serbs and Croats will never be enemies once they separate their states.' He once said, 'Serbs cannot live together with Muslims and Croats. I told Owen not to dump us into the same sack like cats and dogs.'

Perhaps because we have both trained as physicians I found it hard to believe that he could be a practitioner of ethnic cleansing and espouse such an odious philosophy, so totally at odds with the Hippocratic oath. I initially hoped that there was more respect within the inner man for human life and dignity, but I was doomed to disillusion. He is a poet and has written four books, but despite my own love of poetry, I never talked of it to him. I suppose it says something that I have never wanted to talk about medicine with him either, even when we were discussing inconsequential matters. We had to socialise over meals while we negotiated but I never wanted a relationship with him of any degree of intimacy. The longer the war went on the more debauched, dishonest and brutal he became. He has a lot to answer for.

In London on 29 April a young man tragically set himself alight in Parliament Square as a protest against the war in Bosnia-Herzegovina. The same day in the House of Commons the Prime Minister said air strikes were not ruled out, while officials were reported as saying limited air strikes might succeed in pressurising the Serbs to accept the VOPP. The former Conservative Prime Minister Sir Edward Heath called on me to resign because it was no use having a peace negotiator who was advocating war.

In New York on the same day we announced that all three parties, as well as the Presidents of Croatia, the FRY, Serbia and Montenegro, had agreed to meet in Athens on Saturday 1 May. Boutros Boutros-Ghali decided to delay the moment that Cy Vance would step down as co-chairman until Monday 3 May and Thorvald Stoltenberg, whose appointment as Vance's successor had been announced on 2 April, was to attend as co-chairman designate.

In Athens on a fine Saturday afternoon in a hotel complex by the sea the participants began to arrive. I said that 'peace was within our grasp' and that we hoped to sign all the parties up to the VOPP. Prime Minister Mitsotakis opened the evening session with an appeal for boldness and courage; Cy Vance then spoke, saying that what was urgently needed to bring the plan into force was for Dr Karadžić to sign the provisional provincial map and the agreement on interim arrangements. I then introduced a carefully worded document which was designed to win over Dr Karadžić but also, just as importantly, to avoid objections from President Izetbegović, and this was given to all parties to scrutinise. I hoped that it would now be possible for the Bosnian Serb delegation to agree to sign the two outstanding documents. Vance then quickly closed the formal conference down for the night, and the real work began. Churkin, the Russian negotiator, Mitsotakis and Milošević argued with Karadžić into the small hours of the night and started again early next morning. Mid-morning Vance and I were invited by Mitsotakis into his room in the hotel to be told Karadžić would sign subject to a caveat about having to get the agreement of the Assembly of the Republika Srpska at a meeting which was eventually fixed for 8 May in Pale. Milošević was so convinced that Karadžić might change his mind between the room and the plenary meeting place that he wanted us to sign the two documents then and there, but we agreed only to witness his caveat statement there and insisted on him signing openly in front of

Izetbegović, Tudjman and Boban. We then all as quickly as possible assembled in plenary session. Vance made his statement, followed by an apprehensive hush as Karadžić signed the two documents. I immediately brought the proceedings to an end without any further discussion. Karadžić was in a state of high emotion, clearly having been bullied all night into submission. Mitsotakis had agreed to go to Pale with Milošević to help Karadžić persuade his Assembly, and most of us felt that this would be sufficient.

I went on various countries' television shows and the sunshine and the lifting of the strain of four months' intensive negotiations since we had begun to win acceptance of the VOPP in Geneva at the start of the New Year encouraged me to lower my guard and talk of a 'bright day' for the Balkans – for so it seemed. Implementation, we knew, would be difficult, but I really felt we had won the peace that Sunday. As I said goodbye to catch my afternoon flight back to London I looked back and there, sitting in swimming trunks by the hotel pool, was Cy Vance in his last day as co-chairman, looking like a man with a load off his shoulders. I thought what a wonderful retirement present it was for him and so richly deserved. I knew I would miss him greatly in the months ahead, for it had been a joy to work together, while Athens appeared to be an excellent starting point for Thorvald Stoltenberg. Flying over the Acropolis I could barely believe it, but it seemed the bloody Bosnian war was over at last.

On Sunday 2 May, while we were prematurely celebrating in Athens, Warren Christopher took off from Washington for Britain. The problem facing him was that after much agonising President Clinton had decided on a policy of 'lift and strike', which Christopher was meant to champion, but from the moment his plane touched down in Britain he faced a different problem, namely that the new post-Athens situation demanded immediate pressure on the Serbs to keep to the Athens agreement. The very last thing that was needed was advocacy of a policy bound to split NATO members.

Meanwhile in the *New York Times*, A. M. Rosenthal, in a piece entitled 'Tell Vance and Owen you're sorry', wrote:

> Apology is due to these two honourable men from all the columnists,
> editorial writers, politicians and academics who vilified them while

they fought for a political basis for peace. I have been in rooms where journalists treated them as prisoners in the dock. In print they were accused of being Chamberlains, of creating a new Munich, of selling out freedom and human rights by outlining a political settlement. Americans, private and journalistic, sent hate mail and spiced dinner table nastiness.

He then analysed the last few months and ended on a handsome note, saying that since we were unlikely to get our apology here was one of his own: 'In one column I referred to Lord Owen as a rather crabby Englishman. He corrected me, Welshman, he said, Welshman.'

In France, Alain Juppé warned on the Sunday, 'There is a division of tasks that I don't think is acceptable – that of some flying in planes and dropping bombs, and others, the Europeans, especially the French, on the ground.' France and the US were still at odds over the role of NATO's Supreme Allied Commander, Europe (SACEUR) in any implementation of a settlement after Christopher's visit to Paris. On Wednesday 5 May I visited NATO and found out that the French were sending in a team to NATO the next day in an attempt to resolve the differences over command and control. In order to tighten up co-ordination between the co-chairmen and both NATO and the UN, I arranged for my own military adviser, Brigadier Messervy-Whiting, to remain at NATO HQ for the next couple of weeks and Stoltenberg's military adviser from UNPROFOR, an Australian, Brigadier John Wilson, went to UN headquarters in New York for the same purpose, which was greatly welcomed.

That same day Christopher met with Yeltsin and Kozyrev in Moscow. The day before, visiting US senators led by Sam Nunn and Richard Lugar had been told by the Russian military that the conditions in the Yugoslav theatre made air strikes both dangerous and useless, but Yeltsin avoided commenting on what would happen if the Bosnian Serbs did not sign up and instead wanted only to commit to supply Soviet forces to help with implementation.

Shortly before 5.00 a.m. local time on 6 May, after a sixteen-hour session, the Bosnian Serb Assembly in Pale voted fifty-one to two, with twelve abstentions, against ratification of the Vance–Owen plan and for the holding of the referendum, previously agreed, on 15–16 May.

Milošević left the session through a side door, without speaking to the press. Ćosić accused the Bosnian Serb Assembly of taking the 'worst and most fatal' decision: political sense had been defeated; the country and the people now faced great uncertainty and there was no knowing what the coming days and nights would bring.

Milošević rang me that morning in London, having driven back to Belgrade. He had been up all night and was angry, fed up and tired. He was vitriolic about Krajišnik for delaying the vote when he was afraid it would have been won and said that Mladić had intervened in the small hours against acceptance of the plan to considerable effect. We agreed to meet when we had both had time to reassess the situation, but he said he would take measures to make the Bosnian Serbs aware of their responsibilities, which I took to mean some form of sanctions. I learnt that Ćosić too was 'tired and angry' and had apparently described the deputies, privately, as a band of ignorant peasants, military fanatics and war profiteers. He very much doubted whether many of them had even read the Vance–Owen plan. He had also been horrified by some of the scenes of devastation he had driven through on his way to Pale. As far as Ćosić was concerned, Karadžić had been a disaster. Instead of coming out firmly for the plan, he had been more interested in sitting on the fence and preserving his political skin. Ćosić considered Krajišnik to have been the villain of the piece, closely followed by Mladić.

In Belgrade we were given information that the Serbian leadership's dominant concern would now be to persuade the international community not to channel its military efforts into punitive military strikes and other measures, such as lifting the arms embargo, which would make it impossible for them to continue to support the VOPP. Senior advisers to the leadership were, however, prepared to consider favourably military imposition of the VOPP and I summarised their suggestions as follows:

1. The rules of engagement of a UN implementation force should be not to shoot first, but to respond with force when attacked. The act of firing on the UN force should be declared by the FRY as a crime against humanity.

2. The FRY leadership, on the basis of such a threat, would gain acceptance in the FRY and then in Bosnia for the concept of an implementation force as an occupying force rather than as

a hostile attacking aggressor force: moreover, the Serb population in Bosnia could be persuaded that neither they nor the army should ever fire on the troops of countries who had been their allies in two World Wars. Therefore the predominant nationalities in the UN force would have to be British, French, American and Russian.

3. The UN should issue an ultimatum as soon as they were ready, giving the Serbian forces surrounding the Muslim enclaves in eastern Bosnia a period of, say, three days during which they should withdraw their troops to a perimeter line and their heavy weapons to a position 30 kilometres behind that, after which the UN would move in to establish demilitarised zones. A similar 'ultimatum' approach should be used to 'occupy' the areas outside designated Croatian and Muslim provinces currently under Serbian control.

4. Yugoslav Army liaison officers should be attached to UN forces in Serb populated areas. This would ostensibly be on the basis of offering guarantees to the local population, but they would equally serve as a 'protective shield' for the UN. Similarly, JA liaison officers should be attached to UN humanitarian aid convoys to provide them with an additional 'protective shield' during the initial period of VOPP implementation.

5. The Geneva negotiations should not give up their search for additional guarantees that could be offered to the Bosnian Serbs.

It was a position of far greater realism than we had yet heard from the Belgrade Serbs and something that needed to be followed up immediately, for it offered an immense opportunity to bring the war to a speedy end on a viable basis.

The VOPP should then have been imposed, taking some account of Serbian sensitivities in Belgrade, by NATO. President Clinton should have approached President Yeltsin, urging him to join in NATO's initiative, as eventually happened at the end of 1995 after the Dayton accords. Instead, the US were still hooked on 'lift and strike', a policy which the Russians and their main European allies rejected and which bore no immediate relation to a settlement but on the contrary would, at least initially, ignite the war. It was a reminder of how fateful and mistaken had been Warren Christopher's 10 February undertaking never to impose a settlement. Specifically the US policy makers advocated 'lift and strike' with UNPROFOR in situ, although differently configured, but with UNHCR convoys stopping. They did not know how long air strikes would have to continue while humanitarian supplies ran short. There was no obvious sign of any thought having been given to what might be an acceptable new peace settlement. It was no wonder that US policy started to be derided as 'lift and pray'. It was inconceivable that even America's closest European allies would say 'yes' to Warren Christopher in his consultation, because there was no thought-out package to say 'yes' to.

In the meantime, while Europe pondered this US initiative, President Clinton was having second thoughts about 'lift and strike'. According to one account Les Aspin, then Defence Secretary, returned to the Pentagon after a talk with Clinton in the White House and rang Peter Tarnoff at the State Department and Tony Lake, the National Security Adviser, to say, 'Guys, he's going south on this policy. His heart isn't in it.' Warren Christopher, still in Europe, was immediately told about this shift in the President's position. Soon after he returned to Washington it became clear that 'lift and strike' was dead, killed appropriately by the very person who would have had to carry the responsibility for it – the US President.

The fact that the President had developed cold feet mid-consultation seemed to stimulate many people connected with the administration to try to put the blame on the Europeans. The tactic of scapegoating, at which the Clinton administration was becoming a past master, was once more swinging into operation. A new policy had begun to emerge under the rubric of 'containment': damp down the conflict, take Bosnia off the front pages, send some troops to join the UN effort in Macedonia to quieten the 'do something' lobby and above all avoid getting any US troops on the ground in Bosnia-Herzegovina; also ensure that the VOPP was killed off at the same time as 'lift and strike'.

Stoltenberg and I then flew to Moscow and met Kozyrev on 16 May to discuss the next steps, particularly how to pressurise Milošević on border monitors and to pursue our ideas for progressive implementation of the VOPP. But as we were doing this the US was starting to set the stage for killing off the VOPP and, in marked contrast to the last three months of US criticisms based on the VOPP not being sufficiently generous to the Muslims, there began to be hints of the view now being taken that the VOPP was too hard on the Serbs. In Moscow, Kozyrev stated his intention to table a framework resolution for Security Council decision at a ministerial-level meeting on Friday 21 May.

Meanwhile the new US policy of 'containment' for Bosnia-Herzegovina was spelt out by Warren Christopher on 18 May before the House Foreign Affairs Committee, a testimony he concluded by saying, 'At heart, this is a European problem.' Critics of the VOPP still had nothing positive to put in its place except the so-called 'safe areas' policy, so often discussed and just as frequently – and wisely, without sufficient resources – rejected. This time France was advocating a 'safe areas' resolution and Russia wanted a Security Council debate, which the US was blocking. There were the makings of a deal around perhaps the phased, as distinct from progressive, implementation of the VOPP and that is what we thought was going to develop.

NATO generals presented a very detailed implementation plan to Stoltenberg and me in Naples on 19 May involving some 50,000 people. From this it was clear the VOPP was capable of full implementation – all that was needed was for the US government to endorse their own SACEUR General Shalikashvili's plan.

It was clear that the Russian proposal for a ministerial Security Council meeting over the implementation of the VOPP was likely to be postponed as a result of the American refusal to attend. Back in London on 21 May I found in my pile of telegrams from the Foreign Office one from Washington about a new diplomatic initiative involving the US, France, the UK and Russia. I had just finished reading it when my assistant, Maggie Smart, was rung up to say that it had been sent to me in error – which meant that, for the first time I was aware of since I had been appointed co-chairman, I was being deliberately kept in the dark by the British government on a substantive question. In fairness to them, I served the European Community, and in this case the British and French governments were embarking on a diplomatic initiative in an attempt to heal the Atlantic rift, knowing this was contrary to EC policy. Douglas Hurd and Alain Juppé were entitled to try to do this, and to involve me would have presented me with conflicting loyalties – particularly since the presidency was held by the Danes, for if I had known this was going on I would have had to warn the Danish presidency.

It was obvious from the telegram that Washington, London and Paris had been in communication for four to five days on the substance as well as on the form of the initiative. Christopher and Kozyrev had now agreed a text, after negotiating for most of 20 May, and this was being passed to the French. The two of them had apparently agreed to say nothing to the press about the statement and the US had asked the British to hold it very close. Nevertheless, CNN had already got wind of its existence and some of the details. Douglas Hurd had flown out to the US by Concorde to arrive in time for meetings that morning, and Alain Juppé was coming to Washington for a meeting on the following Saturday. Assuming that neither had difficulties with the draft an announcement was planned for that day, 22 May.

The problem with this tidy arrangement was the whole story was in the 21 May edition of the *New York Times* under the headline 'US AND RUSSIA AGREE ON STRATEGY ACCEPTING SERBIAN GAINS FOR NOW'. Douglas Hurd rang me from the US to explain, unaware that I had the actual text of the US–Russian draft in front of me. There was a certain negative humour to the whole conversation. I was hearing the death knell of the VOPP wrapped up in diplomatic language. Douglas kept stressing how he was trying to get adjustments made towards acknowledging the VOPP while I kept coming back to the *New York Times* story, pointing out that his intentions had been completely overtaken by events. The whole package was bound to be seen for what it was – depressingly from the European Community viewpoint, jubilantly from Pale, despairingly from Sarajevo and cynically from Belgrade. We were back with the basic incoherence of the 10 February US position. Nothing should be imposed, and yet without the threat of imposition why should the Bosnian Serbs withdraw? To be credible, implementation had to have an element of imposition or there would be no Serb withdrawal from the really sensitive territory which their forces currently occupied. It was bizarre and, for me personally, exasperating that the US, who had been against the VOPP map for favouring ethnic cleansing, were now advocating a map that allowed the Serbs to keep more territory. Nor could I see any evidence that they were facing up to the inevitable consequence, namely the partition, not the unification, of Bosnia-Herzegovina. Allowing the Serbs more territory might enable any peace plan to be monitored – not implemented – by a smaller UN force, but it also meant partition, and the death of most of the London principles.

I kept stressing to Douglas Hurd on the telephone that since it was the State Department who had given authority to the political story in the *New York Times*, he and Juppé had to dissociate themselves from the story or the VOPP was dead. Datelined Washington, May 20, the story read:

> The United States and Russia agreed today to forge a common strategy with other European nations that accepts, at least for the moment, the territorial gains made by the Serbs in Bosnia.
>
> The goal would no longer be to roll back any of the gains achieved by the Bosnian Serbs in 14 months of fighting, but rather, in the words of a senior administration official, 'to contain and stabilise the situation and to put the brakes on the killing'.
>
> When asked whether this approach appeared to reward the 'ethnic cleansing' campaign by the Bosnian Serbs, the official replied, 'First things first.'
>
> Vance–Owen Plan Put Off
>
> The new strategy, which was discussed by Secretary of State Warren Christopher and Foreign Minister Andrei V. Kozyrev of Russia at the State Department today, would essentially set aside for now the over-arching goal of the Vance–Owen peace plan, which would require the Bosnian Serbs to withdraw from about half of the territory they hold.

I gathered from Douglas that the problem facing the French, British and Russians in Washington for the drafting of an agreed text was the deep American pessimism, verging on hostility, towards the Vance–Owen peace plan. He confirmed that the US argument had changed completely in recent days: whereas they had originally argued that the VOPP was too generous to the Serbs, they were now saying it was unrealistic to expect the Serbs to give up so much territory.

Although I went through the motions of keeping open the European Community position on the VOPP for the next few days I knew that the plan had now been effectively ditched by the Americans and could never be got back on the road. The only way to revive it would have been for the Europeans to say that they would implement the VOPP through the Western European Union and hive off from NATO the command and control structures to do so, a very difficult task. Then they would have to rally sufficient troop numbers from non-EU countries like Russia, the Ukraine, Poland, the Czech Republic and Slovakia to give the implementation force credibility. The truth was that there was not the political or military will in Europe without France and Britain to do this and in my heart I knew neither Paris nor London was prepared to act without the Americans. From then on I knew that some form of partition would be the miserable outcome of any diplomacy.

As to the Joint Action Programme (JAP) of the US, the UK, France, Russia and Spain, which was now on the Security Council agenda, it was destined to fail. The US military, who were more clear headed than their political leaders, did not pretend that the immediate objective of the JAP, while introducing 'safe areas', was to stop the killing, for to do that effectively there needed to be a clear reinforcement plan that had not even been worked out for the safe areas. The UN had done work on increased force numbers, but many of us felt it needed rules of engagement and command and control procedures for peace enforcement, not peacekeeping, if the areas were to be kept safe. The US were adamant about not committing their own troops and their military saw great difficulty in the so-called 'oil slick' approach of trying to use force to gradually enlarge the 'safe areas'. One redeeming feature of the JAP was the commitment to establish the Yugoslav War Crimes Tribunal; but that apart, it was in effect an inaction programme.

Izetbegović, in a statement from Sarajevo on 23 May, derisively rejected the JAP. Referring to what the 'great four' had to say, he claimed that the programme would allow the Serbs to retain territory taken by force, prevent displaced populations from returning to their homes, and turn safe areas into reservations. It was therefore absolutely unacceptable. Signature of the VOPP had been the Bosnian government's final word. It was the minimum they could accept and they would not waste their time any longer in futile negotiations. Izetbegović called upon all those citizens who loved Bosnia to unite and defend, with all permissible means, its integrity and freedom. I agreed with every word and I felt very sorry for the predicament in which Izetbegović now found himself. The US had totally let him down.

I was only glad that Cy Vance had been able to leave Athens on such a high note and did not have to face the personal anguish which now engulfed me: should I resign or battle on? I had said nothing over the weekend and when I flew in to Geneva all I would say was, 'I am facing a new situation following the Washington meeting and I want to talk to a number of my colleagues in Europe. My role as a negotiator stems from the European Community and I want to talk to them.' Thorvald Stoltenberg called the Joint Action Programme a 'very real basis for progressive implementation of the Vance–Owen plan'. I wished I could agree with him but I held my tongue. On reflection it is the only time that I can recollect when we ever disagreed on a major issue, though he was trying to keep the show on the road. For Thorvald the next few days must have been very trying. I was clearly on the point of resigning, while he was very keen I should stay. Yet I was well aware that Thorvald had only been in the job a few weeks and, just as Cy had carried me for my first months in post with his knowledge and experience of the key players, so Thorvald needed my help for at least a few more months. At the specific request of the UK, France and various other EU governments, those few months went on for two years.

I was no stranger to resigning on policy questions. I had given up being a Labour frontbench spokesman on defence in 1972 because of Harold Wilson's about-turn over membership of the European Community. I had resigned from the Shadow Cabinet when Michael Foot was elected Labour leader in November 1980 because of his opposition to the EC and his belief in unilateral nuclear disarmament. I had resigned from the Labour Party in February 1981 after Labour's special conference had rejected one member, one vote to elect its leader. I had also resigned as leader of the SDP after the members' ballot decision to negotiate to join up with the Liberal Party. Each of these four resignations had a purpose behind it; each was part of a strategy for challenging and changing policies with which I profoundly disagreed. But a resignation over the VOPP would not bring it back to life or change US policy (if one could dignify it with such a name). Also, my differences were with the US administration, not the European Community, the bulk of whose member states had given Vance and me their full backing for many months. This was borne out in a cable I saw from New York reporting how delighted someone in the US mission to the UN was that the press out of Geneva were predicting that I would soon resign. If anything that comment inclined me to think that perhaps I should stay and live with the partition that was inevitably now going to be part of any peace settlement, in order to rescue as much as I could from the VOPP. Vance was advising me to quit, but I felt that to down tools now might look like pique. I had deliberately kept Cy Vance's advice very private, but his judgement was troubling me and I found it hard to determine what was the best course of action.

Nothing is simple in the Balkans. History pervades everything and the complexities confound even the most careful study. Never in over thirty years of public life had I had to operate in such a climate of dishonour, propaganda and dissembling. Many of the people with whom I was having to deal in the former Yugoslavia were literally strangers to the truth.

My vantage point was that of a negotiator who became involved in the autumn of 1992, after the war in Bosnia-Herzegovina had already taken a very heavy toll, with Serbs occupying more than 70 per cent of the territory. A negotiator inevitably starts with an inbuilt bias towards achievable solutions. I tried to be impartial; I was not neutral, nor did I pretend to be, about ethnic cleansing, crimes against humanity, racial prejudice or religious intolerance. Our task as co-chairmen of the ICFY steering committee was to search at all times for a just and peaceful settlement. Not a just settlement alone, for sadly every year of war in the former Yugoslavia made that harder to achieve, but at least a settlement which would roll back much of the Serb territorial advance in Bosnia-Herzegovina and allow many of those ethnically cleansed in Croatia as well as Bosnia-Herzegovina to return to their homes. The more speedily a settlement was reached, the greater the chance would be of reversing ethnic cleansing. The killing and maiming made it impossible to justify waiting until the fighting petered out into an exhausted peace. The penalties for delay – permanent ethnic division, lives lost and a population disabled in body and spirit with fewer and fewer displaced people and refugees ready to return to their homes – always had to be costed against the price of an unfair peace.

War is often a proving ground of personality; for good or ill, it highlights the underlying nature of individuals and groups, and it is in that sense all-revealing. In Yugoslavia, the most distinctive feature of the fighting was its callousness, evident in one episode after another: the three-month pulverising of Vukovar and the wanton shelling of Dubrovnik by the Yugoslav army and navy; the Serb militias; the selective destruction of houses on ethnic grounds, predominantly by Serbs but also by Croats and Muslims; the long Serb siege of Sarajevo; the destruction by Croat forces of the historic bridge in Mostar, perhaps the greatest architectural monument in the former Yugoslavia; the conditions in some prison camps; the widespread raping of women and the peculiar defiling of the bodies of the dead. Physical callousness of action, moreover, was only one side of the coin; leaders who had had no experience of democracy also displayed a callousness of mind in which the people's view never seemed to come anywhere near the conference table, despite much consulting of assemblies and the holding of referenda in circumstances of dubious democratic validity.

History points to a tradition in the Balkans of a readiness to solve disputes by the taking up of arms and acceptance of the forceful or even negotiated movement of people as the consequence of war. It points to a culture of violence within a crossroad civilisation where three religions, Orthodox Christianity, Islam and Roman Catholicism, have divided communities and on occasions become the marks of identification in a dark and virulent nationalism. All wars bring evil to the surface, but the peculiar ferocity of civil wars is well chronicled throughout history. The fact that the wars in the former Yugoslavia contained elements both of a war of secession and of civil war only added to the difficulty of forming objective judgements and is part of the legacy we still face in 2009.

On 26 May I had dinner with Javier Solana, the Spanish Foreign Minister, at the Spanish embassy in Geneva. He had flown in on his way back from Turkey especially so that we could talk together personally on my predicament and he left later that night for Madrid. We had known each other since I had invited Felipe González to London for a semi-official visit in 1979 when he was in opposition and I was in government. It was a generous gesture to stop off in

Geneva, and his entreaty to stay and hammer out a new policy with him and others on the EC Foreign Affairs Council was very hard to resist, for unlike Peter Carrington I had no complaints about European political support, just their inability to mobilise military support. I suspect that this was the moment that I really decided to stay. But I left my options open for one further meeting. I wanted to know what President Izetbegović wanted me to do. So, when I saw him in Sarajevo on 4 June I asked him in front of Thorvald Stoltenberg whether I should stay: he made it crystal clear that he wanted me to do so and that it would be damaging to the Bosnian government's interests if I left. That was the clinching argument, which helped counter the humiliation of my meeting in Pale with Dr Karadžić, who was revelling in my discomfort and savouring every moment of his victory in holding on to more Serb land and seeing off the VOPP. What seemed, in part, to be behind US thinking over the VOPP was a resentment at the structure of the ICFY. The incoming US administration had been surprised that, for instance, Lawrence Eagleburger, then the Republican Secretary of State, had been prepared to come to the ministerial meeting of the ICFY and sit in a room under the chairmanship of Cy Vance, for the UN, and myself, for the EU. Warren Christopher was never ready to accept that format, nor did he appear to like the political authority which the conference had built up, and he revealed his desire for the US to take power back from the ICFY in congressional hearings before taking office. In addition, it was always difficult to determine how large an element of US attitudes to the VOPP stemmed from Christopher's personal relations with Vance. Superficially correct and controlled as their relationship was, it was obvious that there was always a tension between them that, I suspected, had its origins in the time that Christopher had been Vance's deputy, particularly in the failed attempt in 1979 to airlift the hostages out of the US embassy in Tehran. Whatever the truth of the relationship in the past, I had little doubt that Christopher did not find it pleasant to have Vance so visible in such a prominent foreign policy role for his first few months as Secretary of State. As soon as Vance left the co-chairmanship of the ICFY in Athens, Christopher tried to abolish the conference and took the opportunity to dump the VOPP.

I soldiered on as the EU negotiator for another two difficult and depressing years with dwindling authority, waiting for one thing, an intervention from NATO to enforce a settlement. Sometimes in international politics one has to be patient and simply wait for the doctrine of ripe time to assert itself. Often it is the UN that takes the rap for these periods of indecision from the permanent members of the UN Security Council. In this case the EU's authority was also diminished, helped along by the Americans. The plan that gave the Bosnian Muslims most territory was the EU Action Plan developed on HMS *Invincible* in the international waters of the Adriatic on 20 September. The plan split Bosnia into a Union of Three Republics. President Izetbegovic and Prime Minister Siladjic told Stoltenberg and me while flying back in a UN plane back to Zagreb that they would try and win support for the Plan in Sarajevo. But Izetbegović's acceptance was undermined by Warren Christopher telling him that there would be no US troops on the ground to help safeguard their new Republic. By 20 December it proved impossible to get the Bosnian Serbs to increase the Bosnian Republic beyond 33.5% with the Croat Republic at 17.5% and the Republika Srpska at 49%. The Contact Group of the US, Russia, UK, France and Germany in the summer of 1994 proposed a two-way split of 51% for the Bosnia-Croat Federation and 49% for the Republika Srpska. I suggested the Contact Group mechanism, which Vance and I had used over Namibia in 1978 involving Germany, France and Canada. It was impossible for the EC to propose it but it was the only way to involve the US and we were getting nowhere with them sidelining themselves. With French and British support and the tacit acceptance of the Danish presidency I just announced it as a fait accompli. This meant less work for me, with Thorvald also now working for the UN in Zagreb. Later with the German presidency's permission I joined the board of Coats Viyella, an international textile company, towards the end of my term in 1994.

I consoled myself as we waited with how long it had taken to move from the Anglo-American plan for Zimbabwe in 1977 to independence in 1980, how the UN resolution for Namibia that we had hammered out with the South Africans was only implemented twelve years later with Namibian independence. Negotiators are not decision makers; we provide a framework for peace but only governments wield power. Patience and persistence had not hitherto been hallmarks of my character. It surprised many that on this task I was ready to stay and sit it out, in all for nearly three years.

It was on 4 June 1993 that UNSCR 836 on 'safe areas' had passed, which referred to Chapter VII without any qualification for the first time, and the Security Council embarked on the path of enforcement with no intention of backing it with the necessary resources, the most irresponsible decision taken during my time as co-chairman and taken by four of the permanent members of the Security Council as part of their Joint Action Plan. It was just a matter of time before a so-called safe haven was overrun by the Serbs with the UN being incapable of stopping it. The inevitable happened in Srebrenica in July 1995 with the genocidal massacre of 8,000 Bosnian Muslim males. I had stepped down from being negotiator by then, but I was ashamed that all of us had not done more to ensure that it could not happen. General Mladić must be brought to trial at the International Criminal Tribunal for the Former Yugoslavia at The Hague, but regrettably he had still not been captured by the summer of 2009. Until he is brought to trial there will be no final reconciliation for the Muslims, for there is no doubt that Mladić was the person above all responsible for the massacre in Srebrenica.

Ratko Mladić was born on 12 March 1943 in Bosnia at Božinovići, some 50 kilometres south of Sarajevo, and both his parents had fought with the Partisans. His father was killed by Croatian Ustasha fighters in a raid on Bradina, the home of the Ustasha leader, Ante Pavelić, when Mladić was only two years old. Much has been written about how this experience made him nurse a grievance and gave him a permanent hatred of the Croats, but I found no evidence that he was particularly anti-Croat. He joined the League of Communists in 1965 after attending the Military Academy, and in the 1991 census chose as his nationality to be classified as a Yugoslav. In conversation he would step back from politics, usually with a wry smile and a remark about 'being a simple general and not a politician'. The one thing he is not is a simple general. He has had a brilliant military career and emerged from the Command Staff Academy in 1978 as an officer marked for the highest commands. Given the traditions of the JNA at that time he would not have progressed as a battalion and brigade commander so quickly if there had been any hint of his being a rabid Serb nationalist. When the Serb–Croat war started in June 1991 he was chief of staff of the 9th Army Corps, based in Knin. Like many other corps it was disintegrating as officers and men started identifying themselves as Croat or Slovene and began to leave the JNA, either to join up with their national forces or to quit military service and in some cases leave the country. Those, mainly Serbs, who remained with the JNA did not have it all their own way and many were humiliatingly blockaded into their barracks by surrounding Croatian forces – one reason why the JNA responded so massively in places like Vukovar. By that stage a classic civil war had developed, with the army splitting up and brother officers breaking friendships and leaving to fight each other. The atmosphere at this time is well caught in Misha Glenny's *Fall of Yugoslavia*. Mladić was widely judged to have fought with considerable skill in the Knin; but he also developed a reputation as a braggart.

In ditching the VOPP, along with the Russian, French and British governments, the Clinton administration were abandoning their attempt to claim the moral high ground of keeping Bosnia-Herzegovina together as a unified state. They had decided that the price for putting US troops on the ground in order to reverse ethnic cleansing was too high. By 1995, when they were ready to pay that price, it was too late to enforce a unified country. The US and the EU were not ready to stand up militarily to the Bosnian Serb leaders in May 1993 despite the full support of the FRY, the Serbian and Montenegrin Presidents, the Greek Prime Minister and Russia, but preferred to back down and offer Karadžić and Mladić the opportunity to remain on more territory than was ever envisaged on the VOPP map namely 49% rather than 43%.

The land distribution of 49% for the Serbs in December 1993 was the settlement brokered by the US through the Dayton accords in the winter of 1995. The consequences were to be challenging to the authority of the US and the EU as well as for the cause of a just peace and the rule of international law. It is rare for history to demonstrate within a few years the folly of governments' decisions. A chronicle of those two years can be found if anyone wishes in my book *Balkan Odyssey*, and in many other books and articles, not least in the successful negotiator Richard Holbrooke's book, *To End a War*.

Richard Holbrooke deserved much credit for the diplomatic breakthrough, and American political muscle and ability to fine-tune

NATO's air strikes had been crucial. We were at an end to the wars in the former Yugoslavia. I felt personally an immense sense of relief, for even though I had announced my departure in May for the next few months I was never able to put what was happening in the region out of my mind. Now, with Milošević and Tudjman firmly anchored into the diplomacy, I hoped that all the elements of a settlement were in place. My personal odyssey was over.

Yet the tragedy of Bosnia continues to this day. It was good to see Barack Obama's Vice-President, Joe Biden, visit Sarajevo in May 2009 and warn all the politicians in strong language about their prospects if naked nationalism continues and to spell it out in their own parliament. It is hard to be optimistic about a quick resolution of their deep-seated problems.

The harsh reality is that the US and the EU will have to think afresh in the Balkans. An article entitled 'The Balkan mess redux' in the global edition of the *New York Times* on 3 June 2009 by William Montgomery, for more than 15 years involved in the region and US ambassador to Bulgaria, Croatia and Serbia/Montenegro, spelt it out. 'We want to believe we can bring peace to the Balkans without changing borders. We can't.' He argues that 'The end result is continued tension between the two Bosnian entities, a dysfunctional country and the prospect of many more years of efforts by Western politicians – like Vice-President Joe Biden.' In going on to mention the unmentionable he writes, 'In Kosovo, this probably means some form of partition between the Albanians and the Serbs,' and suggests a probable solution 'permitting the Republika Srpska, the Serbian portion of the divided country, to hold a referendum on independence'. It is hard to see the international community being ready to eat so many of their own refusals from 1990 onwards to look at boundaries which they fixed, but it is also hard to contemplate continuing with the present deeply unsatisfactory status quo. We are some way from ensuring peace in the Balkans, I fear.

On 19 June 2009 Valentin Inzka, an Austrian diplomat appointed in March as Bosnia's High Representative, invoked again the extraordinary legal powers agreed in Bonn in December 1997, allowing him to issue decrees, to impose laws and remove officials. This was done in reaction to the Prime Minister Milorad Dodik's challenges to the integrity of the Bosnian state from the Republika

Srpska's national assembly in 63 areas. Inzka was supported by the US and UK. But Javier Solana, the EU's High Representative for Common Foreign and Security Policy, was opposed to using the Bonn powers, believing a political solution was still possible.

EU membership for Bosnia-Herzegovina is once again stalled. International recognition for Kosovo is still blocked. The legacy of not giving President Yeltsin and Russia sufficient credit for the diplomatic settlement of NATO's war in Kosovo still lingers. Russia's recognition of South Ossetia and Akhazia in Georgia has won much less international acceptance than Kosovo. I suspect that realpolitik will confirm mutual recognition in all three areas as a way out of these crises rather than changes in existing boundaries to either Kosovo or Bosnia-Herzegovina. But it is a demonstration that abandoning the UN Charter on recognition of states is a hazardous course on which to embark, whether you are the US, EU or the Russian Federation.

# 8

# Yes to the EU – No to the euro

On 21 January 1999, despite personal representations against my doing so by the then Prime Minister, Tony Blair, a month before, I outlined the case as to why the UK should be a fully committed member of the EU, but stay out of the single currency. I had chosen Manchester as the venue for this speech deliberately; historically it has been one of the great radical outposts and at no time more so than at the time of the Anti-Corn Law League. What we needed was a somewhat similar grass-roots campaign in the provinces, not just in London. For six years around the country I spoke more on this issue than any other.

The arguments I had been developing for some years, including in an article in the *Economist* the previous year, were that the progressive enlargement of the EU to twenty-six or more nations opened the prospect of such a different EU that it would not be an exaggeration to call it a new EU. Hence the title of our campaigning organisation, 'New Europe'. Hitherto, the evolution of the Common Market to the European Community had been an inclusive development across the territory of democratic countries in what was then called western Europe. The new European Union would represent Europe as a whole, including many parts of eastern Europe. It would extend from Estonia to Romania, and probably Ukraine. I believed, too optimistically, it turned out, that it might eventually include both Turkey and Russia. Germany and France now openly oppose Turkish entry, and Russia has made it abundantly clear under Presidents Putin and Medvedev that it does not wish to join.

Within what will still be an all-embracing Europe there would be a single market. Also an important grouping of countries – perhaps more than half – would operate a single currency. As part of sustaining that currency I believed, along with many others, that these eurozone countries could be driven to develop most of the characteristics of a single state. Those nations which did not want to participate in the single currency or were economically unable to participate would nevertheless remain full members of the EU and would not as members of European Monetary Union (EMU) lose their option to join the single currency.

The variable-geometry model of a multifaceted Europe, I believed, had now replaced the fully integrated multi-speed Europe. The Exchange Rate Mechanism (ERM) within the European Monetary System had first established this variegated pattern. EMU with the option of not participating in its single currency had confirmed the trend.

For many continental European politicians a single currency was above all a political, not an economic, issue, a return in history to the empire of Charlemagne from 768 to 814, which stretched from the Atlantic to the Danube, from the Mediterranean to the North Sea. It had a central silver coinage and some historians have termed it the 'first Europe' with its own international executive class. By the sixteenth century there had emerged another trans-Elbean 'second Europe', which lasted until 1918 when it was broken up after the First World War but then revived again by Hitler. Flitting in and out, often in the wings, has been a Muscovy 'candidate Europe'. In the nineteenth century there were three failed attempts in parts of Europe to create monetary unions. The German monetary union was fully fledged by the 1870s but it began some forty years before, initially with a customs union. The Prussian thaler, as the currency was called, held sway while Bismarck dominated Europe. The French attempt at a Latin monetary union started in 1865 and included Belgium, Italy, Greece and Switzerland; at the time Walter Bagehot warned that if Britain did nothing we would be 'left out in the cold'. We in Britain wisely declined to join all of these experiments and never regretted it. In 1873 Sweden, Denmark and Norway started a monetary union which was dissolved in 1924. The lesson of all this seemed to be that monetary unions fail after a period of time unless they are underpinned by political union.

Since the Second World War there had been a less dramatic but determined drive to build on the back of the European Coal and Steel Community a democratic or 'third Europe'. This deliberately concentrated on a continental Common Market core of six nations. Winston Churchill advocated it for the Continent but not for the UK. General de Gaulle openly opposed widening it to include the UK but did talk of a Europe from the Atlantic to the Urals. By 1973, under President Pompidou, the Channel had been crossed and the UK was included in an enlargement to nine. This 'third Europe' has amongst its leaders people who aspire, often only in private, to a United States of Europe. They see the USA as a most successful continental-size federation and they want to achieve over time the same degree of integration. This is a legitimate objective, even though I believe it is profoundly misguided. But it is only honourable if it is openly and democratically espoused. Unfortunately in some countries, and for the most part in the UK, those who want such an outcome operate by stealth, denying that it is their ambition while edging constantly towards it. Also even to state one's concern about such a federalist Europe is to risk being categorised as a Eurosceptic, implying that one is not just questioning ever greater integration but has a hostility to even the concept of European unity.

The 'third Europe' has had its successes – best illustrated economically by the Single Market and politically by continued enlargement. It still has its extravagances – demonstrated by the Common Agricultural Policy, which pays farmers not to grow crops and costs around half of the European Union's budget. There have also been failures, particularly when attempting to realise the ambitions of its federalists. The most ambitious federalist project was the Pleven plan for creating a European defence community, but this was eventually rejected by the French National Assembly in August 1954. In the late 1960s and early 1970s the federalists made their first attempt at monetary union with the Werner plan. This was for 'the total and irreversible convertibility of currencies, the elimination of margins of fluctuations in exchange rates, the irrevocable fixing of parity rates and the complete liberation of movements of capital'. The Werner plan for the Common Market was to include all members and was supported by Edward Heath's government but never put to the test in the British Parliament. Britain's entry into the so-called 'snake in the tunnel' was ended after six weeks following the oil price shock of 1973. It is salutary to reflect that had it still been in operation it would have been blown to smithereens by the after-effects of the Arab–Israeli War.

The old arguments about deepening or widening as the best way of developing the European Union have produced a creative tension that has never been resolved. In reality, with every EU enlargement the integrationists have had to accept some changes and delays to their original model. Their hope remains that at the start of the twenty-first century they can build political union through monetary union by establishing what they call an 'inner core' of countries operating a single currency within a wider Europe. Common sense tells us that the eurozone is unlikely to work unless those countries who join it forge a political union in all but name. We know from the Marjohn report of 1975 that the underlying aim was for a monetary union where 'national governments put at the disposal of common institutions the use of all the instruments of monetary policy and of economic policy whose action should be exercised for the Community as a whole'. That has both logic and sense behind it, yet so far the political will is lacking if for no other reason than that the people of Europe obstinately refuse to give up their own national identity. The elite, nevertheless, continue to press for it despite public opinion in their countries.

The challenge for us all now in the EU during the twenty-first century is to build a new Europe, in effect a 'fourth Europe'. I believe we are already moving towards such a union, which would not be as prescriptive as the 'third Europe'. It would be designed so that individual states can group on some issues and not on others, thereby reflecting the natural diversity between states of a larger Europe. Such variable geometry for the European Union appears to be what most British people want. The design should not be too rigid and it must be adaptable enough to allow different countries within the EU to choose greater or lesser integration on certain issues. This design was followed when some countries signed the 1985 Schengen agreement to open their frontiers. This was initially outside the EU treaties and then came within EU rules, with Britain, Ireland and Denmark, which were not prepared to do away with their border controls, choosing to opt out. Many UK Euro-enthusiasts criticised the British position that free movement in the 1987 treaty only applied to EU nationals but, given the panic in the Schengen countries when in 1998 there was movement of Kurds from Turkey and Iraq, the British position that freedom of movement only applies to EU nationals seems fully justified and likely to remain.

After the Maastricht Treaty and after the Amsterdam Treaty the third intergovernmental pillar, Justice and Home Affairs, was partially taken over by the European Commission and policy on visas, asylum, immigration and other policies related to the free movement of persons would now come under Community law unless five years after ratification of this treaty the member states voted against the trigger clause. In any circumstances Britain had the right if it wished to stay outside. Most of these changes were being justified by practical arguments that intergovernmentalism in this area of policy was thought not to be working effectively.

The differential approach to the design of the new EU was inherent in the UK's Maastricht opt-out provision for the euro and the Amsterdam opt-out from open frontiers. The Maastricht Treaty and the Amsterdam negotiations, far from being the most massive step towards the integrative 'third Europe' model that the anti-Europeans and sceptics in Britain claimed, might, I hoped, have proved to be its high-water mark. But the Treaty of Nice then followed, which showed that the integrationists wanted still more integration and not just in the obvious areas, such as the environment.

This was then followed by the start of negotiations over a new EU constitution. As is usual with Community developments, some dismissed it as of little relevance, a mere tidying-up exercise – although it was to prove far more than that. Meanwhile in the UK some of us began to argue 'Yes' to Europe but 'No' to federalism. We accepted we were inextricably involved in the EU and must not act as a distant offshore island. But we did have a choice as to whether we joined the single currency. We wanted to define our own destiny case by case, joining in some new activities while declining others. In this process one had to ask: was it our destiny to lead the EU? Or was our destiny instead to fully involve ourselves in the EU? The two were not quite the same. Leadership rhetoric sounds good but coming from the UK it challenges the ethos of a community founded on the Franco-German alliance. It also belies the UK's true role. We can be and have been instigators in the EU, problem solvers and good Europeans, but we are also the grit in a soggy consensus. It is important that we carry clout within the EU councils but our destiny is also to retain close relations with the United States – not as the apologist for or the defender of US policy but as a constant European friend through good times and bad. Standing up to the US when they are wrong, as we did over the Balkans in 1993; supporting them over Iraq from 1990 to 1998, when they were right. This, I believe, is Britain's role, not always uniquely ours but a role which, by the very nature of their joint relationship, neither France nor Germany can always fill. This was borne out before and during the second Iraq War of 2003, when the EU was deeply divided. This brought a little more realism into the soft language of European unity.

The political origin of the euro was that after the fall of the Berlin Wall in November 1989 a pact was formed initially between the Chancellor of West Germany and the President of France early in 1990, well before the formal reunification of Germany on 3 October 1990. The motivation of Helmut Kohl was to demonstrate to his friend François Mitterrand that France had nothing to fear from a much larger Germany for they would put their Deutschmark with the French franc into a single currency to forge out of the 'third Europe' the historic 'first Europe'. The Maastricht Treaty of 1992 was the manifestation of that Franco-German political deal but its detail had within it compromises of a deeper significance. For while the Ministry of Finance in France conceded to the Bundesbank on the design of an independent European Central Bank, so Germany conceded to the Elysée and the Quai d'Orsay on the crucial three intergovernmental pillars, all of which were written into the treaty. Thereby, Maastricht, for the first time, put treaty parameters to the extent of European integration. In Britain the treaty was, in my judgement wrongly, disliked for being too federalist; in continental Europe many federalists disliked the pillared structure and were determined to knock the pillars down. Because the motivation for a single currency was political the criteria for entry spelt out in the Maastricht Treaty were stretched for those political leaders who had vested much of their own personal credibility in the 1999 start date. This was particularly the case for Italy and Greece. In doing so the founders of the euro were taking an immense risk with the political, as well as the economic, stability of Europe. Hence the predictable problems in 2009 that face Italy, Greece, Spain, Portugal and Ireland inside the eurozone and which could lead to one or more countries having to leave in order to devalue.

The Benelux countries had already developed a co-ordinated currency link built around the Deutschmark which France wanted to join, but France needed a new structure to justify joining. This became the European Monetary System (EMS) and its origins are described earlier. The UK had in 1979 decided to join the EMS but would not participate in the substantive part, the actual Exchange Rate Mechanism. Entry at that time into the ERM certainly did not suit our economy. Nevertheless the enthusiasts for all things European in Britain advocated immediate entry regardless of economic concerns because for them it was a political project. By the mid 1980s the Labour Party, the SDP and the Liberals thought that ERM entry would be advantageous. Margaret Thatcher did not allow the then Conservative government to join but acquiesced in Nigel Lawson shadowing the Deutschmark. This went on for far too long, and the government failed to introduce higher interest rates to cool the ensuing economic boom. Margaret Thatcher's government then compounded this error by entering the ERM at a too high a rate. It fell to John Major's government in 1992 to defend the pound at an absurd cost inside the ERM because the French in the run-up to their referendum on Maastricht asked the Germans not to make any currency readjustment in the ERM, although such a readjustment was allowed under the rules. The ERM was by design a flexible system for stabilising rates, very different to the next development, the euro. As often before, when in a situation of managed exchange rates, the politicians began to see keeping the rate unchanged as a virility symbol. That same vice was followed by British governments, Labour and Conservative, after the Second World War under the Bretton Woods fixed-rate system, most damagingly by Labour before the devaluation of 1949 and again in 1967. Although this rigidity towards exchange rate policy was deeply unfortunate at least we were able from time to time to adjust the value of the pound. Belatedly, but eventually successfully, we devalued by leaving the ERM in 1992, albeit in some disarray. To give up the pound and to join the euro now, in 2009, would mean that there was no way we could depreciate short of breaking out of the EMU and recreating our own currency. Fortunately we have been able to depreciate during the crisis since 2007.

I was a believer in the UK Treasury's wish for a parallel currency of a hard ecu in the late 1980s but that policy came too late and was seen as a disruptive tactic which failed to carry our EU partners. It was inevitable that some countries within the ERM would want to go to the next stage and align their currencies in a monetary union. Once the EMU was proposed it was, nevertheless, correct for the UK, while staying out of the euro, to ensure that any monetary union affecting a significant number of member states was developed within the broad framework of the rules of the EU. For that reason successive UK governments have ensured we remained, in effect, part of the EMU structure even while not participating in the single currency.

Underpinning economic concerns about the euro is the gut instinct of the British people, who will not allow their government to give up the pound to join a single European currency if they sense that to do so will be to forgo some of the essential sinews of nationhood they still feel are well worth preserving in the twenty-first century. But even in 1999 with a strong economy we could not be sure that Britain would be sufficiently successful economically, or self-confident politically, in the long term to stand aside from a single currency. New Europe said that no British government was ever likely to say 'never' but there was no obligation to say when. The single currency, therefore, was for pragmatists an issue best left open with no timetable for a referendum on it, which had been promised by all parties in the 1997 election, and no assumptions that there would ever need to be a referendum. The serious economic arguments against the UK joining the single currency do not weaken my support for the EU, nor do they make me against the option of a single currency for those member states who want to develop some of the characteristics of a single state. Democracy does not sit easily in a rigid box and a flexible EU is far more likely to survive the passage of time.

It has always been an important downside, however, that without considerable internal discipline a country in the single currency can face a political crisis because of high unemployment and falling living standards with no currency of its own to adjust, no interest rates of its own to change. Inside the euro there is literally no safety valve. Many independent economists never believed that the necessary economic convergence in Italy, Spain or Portugal existed for stable membership of the euro. The years 2010–12 will test whether convergence can be increased; in 2009 the verdict is uncertain. Germany has found it hard enough to cope with the fiscal transfers needed for absorbing the east of their own country and France has problems of its own before paying out to weaker eurozone countries. The Dutch had wanted to start with a smaller group of nations whose economies were on a definite convergent course and all the signs are that they were correct.

In 1977 the MacDougal Group of economists reported to the UK government that a budget for the then Community of nine of 5–7 per cent of their total GDP would be needed for redistribution across those nine countries to bring about the convergence of their economies sufficient to have a successful monetary union. There was no chance of assembling the necessary political commitment then to earmark such resources across the Community and there is little sign of such a commitment now. What is more, after the European elections of 2009 it is clear that there is still not the public support for the dream of the European elite. There is still little passion for this degree of European economic redistribution on the scale needed. The European project of economic convergence can probably continue but it will take a long time. Voter turnout across the EU falling to only 43 per cent, a new low, is hardly a sign of great enthusiasm.

The countries operating a single currency have agreed to accept the discipline imposed by the European Central Bank, which settles their interest rate. Yet a major unresolved issue lies between those countries, such as France, who want a political forum to inject social and other considerations into the bank's decision-making and those, such as Germany, who wanted, and still want, Bundesbank disciplines for the European Central Bank and for its management to be totally independent. Obviously those countries which have adopted a single currency must have the right to consult and cooperate together on detailed aspects of the management of their currency. But the framework of a single currency must lie within the EU and that is why EMU operates as part of the EU treaties. Therefore all the EU Finance Ministers, whether or not from participating countries, must determine the rules of the EMU even though only its participants are bound by those EU rules. This is a vital issue in the arguments about what can legitimately be done by the informal grouping of member states within the eurozone to enable them to discuss management questions about the single currency. Those who are part of the euro also know they need to adopt self-discipline on some major economic harmonisation issues to ensure the success of the currency, for, if it is to survive, it is not just interest rates that have to be the same. Much of the anxiety about the sustainability of the single currency relates to these inner tensions, as we have been seeing since the world economic crisis of 2007.

A key question and one very hard to predict is when, if ever, the euro might take over the dollar's status as the world's reserve currency. The dollar in the 1930s quickly replaced sterling because its transaction costs became lower as it was used more. The US will act to maintain the dollar's pre-eminence, although it might be that China will develop a strong enough economy to challenge the status quo and insist that the world's reserve currency be composed of a basket of currencies. Bankers wanted the European Central Bank to establish the euro as a hard currency and the ECB wanted as many central banks around the world as possible to transfer much of their reserves into euros as well as public and private institutions.

Tony Blair's decision as Prime Minister – after coming into office in 1997 – that Britain should plan on the basis that the euro would not replace the pound in the lifetime of that parliament, which in fact lasted to 2001, was well judged. That decision was supported by Gordon Brown. But it was not clear later how much Brown's opposition on the euro owed to his wish to assert his authority over economic questions and his refusal to accept the normal influence that had traditionally come from No. 10. It was fortunate that Blair and Brown did not succumb to the blandishments of those in all three parties, such as Roy Jenkins and Ken Clarke, who wanted Labour to use their initial parliamentary majority and public popularity to push through a referendum perhaps endorsing entry into the eurozone at some unspecified date after six months of pro-Europe publicity orchestrated as part of the British presidency. Opinion polls showed, however, an anti-euro feeling of 2:1 in the autumn of 1997. Also Blair might have been warned off an immediate euro referendum by the difficulty he experienced in shifting entrenched public opinion during the September 1997 referendum on Welsh devolution. My anxiety was that Blair would commit to joining the euro in the 2001 election manifesto, ditching the commitment to a referendum. Fortunately he looked at the poll figures and once again ducked the challenge.

It was in the interests of a sensible UK debate about the euro that the public recognised that from 1999 it would start to impact on our country even though we would not ourselves be giving up the pound. The euro has, in fact, become as much a part of the City of London's financial and trading life as the dollar or the yen. The City is a global, not a European, financial centre, where the pound has for many years been less important than the dollar. Those big multinational firms which used to advocate the euro for Britain were always perfectly free to introduce it into every nook and cranny of their own business in the UK if their customers were content for this to be done. There is no aspect of the euro as a global currency to which Britain needs to be hostile. Indeed it is in the UK's interests to be euro friendly. The appearance of the euro in Britain did not influence unduly our own debate over whether we should give up the pound and adopt the euro as our currency.

I became the chairman of New Europe in February 1999. To be effective it had to embrace all three of the main political parties and I was determined that it should carry the active support of a younger generation. Janet Bush, economic editor of the *Times*, came to be the executive head and she proved to be an excellent choice – a Labour supporter but nevertheless independent minded and quite content to tilt against Blair or Brown. She had good friends like Larry Elliott of the *Guardian*, one of the few journalists to predict the 2007 financial crisis. For six years we tried to provide both intellectual ammunition against the euro but also the emotional appeal of sticking to the pound. On that appeal few were more important than Trevor Kavanagh of the *Sun*.

I had warned Blair in December 1998 that in the battle for opinion we would confound him and that is what we did. The parliamentary battle on this question was a relative sideshow. What Janet and her team did brilliantly was to build up the feeling in the country that common sense inside all the main political parties was on the side of sticking with the pound. We formed a steering group around Christopher Smallwood, who had been the first policy director of the SDP under its then leader, Roy Jenkins; John

Wakefield, formerly secretary of the Labour Party Manifesto Group in 1978 and later director of *Weekend World*; Mary Ann Sieghart, assistant editor of the *Times*; and Christopher Leaver, who acted as the treasurer. There were many economic and political heavyweights on our advisory council, most of whom were very active, coming to regular meetings over dinners; they included Jim Prior, Denis Healey, John Sainsbury – who had been joint honorary treasurer of the European Movement from 1972 to 1975, during the time of the referendum campaign on keeping Britain in the European Community – Nigel Lawson, John Burnett and David Howell. There was also a cross-party group formed in the House of Commons by Frank Field and Ian Davidson, which George Osborne later joined, as did John Cruddas. No one could claim that this grouping, which included my old private secretary in the Foreign Office, Sir Ewen Fergusson, and two former heads of the Diplomatic Service, Sir Antony Acland and Sir John Coles, were closet 'outers' who really wanted Britain to withdraw from the EU. We later joined up with Rodney Leach and leading business people in Business for Sterling, who had their own highly effective campaign and who had raised serious money for a very effective joint campaign on the slogan 'Yes to Europe, no to the euro'. This campaign even included a short film, shown in cinemas, which was aimed at people in their twenties and thirties and featured stars likely to appeal to them.

Though the Prime Minister constitutionally had the right to use any general election so as to seek a mandate to join the euro and thus avoid a referendum he never did so, and the Chancellor of the Exchequer, Gordon Brown, had in practice closed the manifesto option by saying in the House of Commons, 'Under this government there will be a referendum. Government, Parliament and the people must all agree.' Some have argued that this wording still left open the possibility of combining a referendum with a general election but by 2005 this looked like casuistry. The purpose of a referendum commitment was to enable the public to focus their minds on one major issue and not subsume it in numerous others in an election linked to party political positions. Juxtaposing the general election with a euro referendum would be seen, I argued then, as a cynical device and deeply resented as such. But it cannot be excluded that at some future date it will be tried. We began to see how referendum commitments could be cynically discarded with Blair's promise in 2005 to hold a referendum on the EU constitution, whatever the result in the promised French and Dutch referenda. When these two countries, surprisingly to some but predictably to others, voted no, Blair went back on his pledge to have our own referendum. Instead the Constitutional Treaty was replaced by the Lisbon Treaty. At least President Sarkozy won his election with a promise to ratify this time only through the French National Assembly. In the UK ratification was forced through both Houses of Parliament through whipped party votes under the convention that international treaties were not amendable. No wonder public disillusionment started to grow with Labour. In fairness Brown inherited Blair's position, but apart from a rather silly attempt to avoid signing the Lisbon Treaty, which ended up with his doing it alone in a blaze of publicity, he followed the Blair line and it was an early sign that he was going to act no differently from Blair on many issues. I have no doubt that his Lisbon Treaty stance dented his popularity.

Tony Blair's stance over these years was one of wanting to be seen to be leading opinion on the single currency and yet finding this sat uneasily with his 1997 and 2001 electoral stance of appealing to readers of the *Sun* and its proprietor, Rupert Murdoch. By adopting a calculated degree of ambivalence, to put it kindly, in public and in private to the euro he contributed to the public view that the UK should stay out. Public ambivalence from Prime Ministers on European issues was, however, not new. Edward Heath, while Prime Minister from 1970 to 1974, denied at all times supporting the Euro-federalism that he later openly espoused. Harold Wilson never made it publicly clear for three years which way he would come out on the promised EEC referendum, from 1972 until just before it was called in 1975, though in private he was clearly in favour. The appearance at least that he and Jim Callaghan had only made up their minds just prior to the referendum campaign ensured that their opinion carried far more weight than the already well-known views of the pro and anti campaigners. It is also worth recalling that Margaret Thatcher took office in 1979 on a platform of being more positive about Europe than the outgoing Labour administration, which irked me, having been grappling with the issues in government. Her 'No! No!

No!' stance in 1990 came after many years during which she, surprisingly, had played a positive role in creating the Single Market and accepted a significant extension of majority voting. John Major's achievement was to negotiate the British opt-outs in the Maastricht Treaty, for which he received little credit from his party, despite winning the election. One reason for this was the venom which developed over the issue of Europe within the Conservative Party, connected in the minds of many to what they thought had been the assassination of Margaret Thatcher. Neither the Europhiles nor the Eurosceptics, as old warriors, were prepared to recognise that the EU itself was significantly changed for the better by Maastricht. They debated the issue as if we were still in the old integrative model where all states had to accept the same obligations.

At the 2005 election euro entry was not an issue; indeed it was hard to find any MP, even among the Liberal Democrats, who would put their head above the parapet and demand it. We decided, therefore, after the 2005 election to wind up New Europe. It had been highly successful but no pressure group remains vigorous and coherent when its arguments have won the day. Also soon afterwards the *Financial Times* wisely, under its new editor, pulled back from being the constant advocate of early entry. 'Wait and see' is not a weak position for Britain to adopt on the euro, provided that it is not a cover for a decision to 'wait and join', and provided that we act constructively and produce our own forward thinking in these areas of currency management. The UK will need to play a full part in setting fresh limits to the EU, after the election which has to be held before June 2010, by the force of its ideas and to set those ideas in the context of practical European unity in the twenty-first century. Britain did this in the creation of the Single Market. We must now make a reality of the variable geometry in the new EU, not just with rhetoric but with resources.

In this David Cameron and William Hague are likely to be the leading players. Much will depend in the European Parliament on whether the Conservatives can build up the new fourth grouping of 55 MEPs dedicated to setting limits to future integration, but it is clear: setting limits will never come from the three existing major groupings, for all are dominated by the federalist dream. Hopefully a European group of non-federalist MEPs on the left will emerge.

Never underestimate, however, the extent to which the integrationists keep coming back to their own agenda. For them bringing the UK into the euro is a major target. As long as the UK stays out then the EU cannot move inextricably to a single European state. I have little doubt that around 2011 some Liberal Democrats and Labour MPs will start pressing the case for the euro when the immediate financial crisis is hopefully receding and we will hear arguments such as are already current in Iceland and Ireland that membership offers a safety net. Membership of the eurozone did not protect Ireland from a savage downturn and there are respectable grounds for arguing that it made it worse. If Iceland comes into the EU and the euro, its entry negotiations would open up the Common Fisheries Policy (CFP) and it might even be possible to persuade the Norwegians to think again about EU membership. Since the CFP is a total disaster, with fishing stocks being depleted in the waters of most member states at a horrifying rate, new negotiations over the entire policy are greatly needed. This is an issue which might be resolved before any UK referendum on the Lisbon Treaty held before a 2014 general election.

The UK has demonstrated that even in the world economic crisis of 2007 we were not 'out in the cold' by not having participated in the single currency. We were able to exercise a far greater degree of democratic accountability of our government and even of the governor of the Bank of England than was exercised by the euro grouping of Finance Ministers with regard to the European Central Bank. For that democracy and independence, however, there is a price. The eurozone countries will on monetary matters have far more influence than ECOFIN. We need to be realistic therefore; UK influence on the eurozone is limited. How effective we are outside the eurozone depends on the strength of our own economy. This is what went wrong in the first decade of the twenty-first century. For a man who prided himself on his prudence, Gordon Brown after 2002 became too profligate with public expenditure, in part to maintain his popularity inside the Labour Party and prevent Tony Blair from moving him away from the Treasury. Yet as the advocate of not entering the euro he should have known that that required us to be particularly careful not to run up sizeable fiscal deficits which would have to be funded by government gilt sales, in part to foreigners. This message that Britain can champion a new Europe and end its hesitant approach to the EU, which has characterised the last twenty-five years, only if its economy recovers more quickly and deeply than the eurozone cannot be downplayed. We have depreciated our currency, so economic recovery can still happen, if we are ready to make substantial reductions in the public expenditure levels which marked the latter years of the Blair–Brown presidency.

Most people in Britain have recognised that it would be foolish if we were to cast ourselves as the adversary of monetary union and seek to destroy the euro. The hallmark of the City of London is that it provides a global service handling all currencies for all comers. Nevertheless practically no one of any political significance believed that the 2007 crisis meant that Britain should have become part of the eurozone. Most people thanked their lucky stars that sterling had been able to lose value; indeed that was the view of Vince Cable, the popular Treasury spokesman for the Liberal Democrats, previously a Labour and SDP member.

What now needs to be clearly established in 2009 is: what are the limits to European integration? Those in Brussels who argue for harmonising many taxes amongst member states will not just use the single currency to make their case, instead they will cite any economic provision that can remotely bear on the working of the single market. There are also those who want to harmonise welfare and social benefits, their aim being gradually to leave very few areas in which a Finance Minister can act independently. We are seeing that same agenda coming up in the EU proposals for financial regulation singling out hedge funds, which had little responsibility for the economic crisis, and restricting the appeal of the City of London with regulations which will help alternative centres of finance such as New York, Zurich and Dubai.

Much will depend on the current debate about the value of a flexible labour market, identified with previous US and UK economic success but called into question by some during the financial crisis of 2007–9. It is true that the single market cannot operate fairly if big inter-state differences in financial, social and environmental costs persist over time. The question is, therefore, one of achieving a broad balance across member states of what contributes to unit costs rather than prescribing from the Commission uniform policies for all the elements which contribute to unit costs. This particularly applies to wage levels. For countries operating a single currency, differential wages will be one of the main ways of adjusting their relative economic performance when interest rates can no longer be varied except across all the participating states.

Enlargement of the EU will probably slow down in part as a consequence of the crisis of 2007. To be effective it has to be financially backed by the EU and to carry conviction Germany, Britain and France must be generous. Hopefully, however, we will maintain the commitment to bring into the EU all the countries in the Balkans. The EU went too fast over Romania and Bulgaria and must not make the same mistake again. The decision in Berlin to introduce a balanced-budget law in the German constitution, no more than 0.35% by 2016 and 0% by 2020, will not help.

Britain also needs to restrict the operations of the External Action Service so that it does not become the in-house champion of a single foreign and security policy. Yet in doing this the UK must also demonstrate that we are ready to become a key player within the EU. France wants Britain to be more forthcoming over European defence and France is undoubtedly more pragmatic over NATO, as witnessed by President Sarkozy's welcome decision in 2009 to rejoin the integrated command structure. Britain's defence partnership on the ground with France from 1992 onwards in Bosnia, as I witnessed, has left both armed forces with considerable mutual respect. The far closer working relationship between the Foreign Office and the Quai d'Orsay, also established with the break-up of Yugoslavia, has meant that the old scars from the failed collaboration over Suez in 1956 have healed. Paris noted with both surprise and appreciation London's readiness to openly differ from the Washington line over Yugoslavia. It is essential for Britain that we build on this relationship with France, which also has at all stages to involve Germany. Just as the UN has the veto mechanism of the permanent members of the Security Council, which though disliked exists as a matter of realpolitik, so in an EU of thirty-plus there is a strong case for an informal directoire of three in the Common Foreign and Security Policy. But for this to have any chance of working these three countries must not attempt to hold the key positions, namely the president of the Commission and the high representative of the

CFSP. The UN permanent five works because they accept they will never put up candidates for the secretary general.

The time for general criticism and rhetorical flourishes about the EU are over. All of our economies are in serious trouble. In the UK we have now to grapple with a public opinion that is hostile to much that stems from the EU. The Lisbon Treaty is already virtually sealed and its substance may only be changed by detailed checks and balances in relation to its often very loose wording that have their origin and their legitimacy within the British parliamentary and legal system. The Lisbon Treaty has been ratified by the UK Parliament. That ratification can be withdrawn by an incoming government provided the treaty is still open to ratification by one or more member states. Otherwise it will come into force when ratified by all member states. The German Constitutional Court in its ruling of 30 June 2009 made ratification subject to strict legal limits according to *Die Spiegel* for future decisions regarding the EU, which if breached means that 'future EU law will be declared inapplicable in Germany'. *Handesblatt* noted 'for the Court there is only one real basis for democracy in the EU: the national parliaments'. The UK needs its own Constitutional Court.

If the Conservative Party wins the next election, after the Lisbon Treaty has been ratified, and have a working majority they will need a credible policy to make the treaty and the EU more acceptable to the British people and win that acceptance in a referendum. If Labour is the largest party as a result of that election they will go along with the Lisbon Treaty. If the Conservative Party is the largest party and yet has not got an overall majority, the Liberal Democrats would be wise, on democratic grounds, to try to draw up a programme for government with them including how to deal with the Lisbon Treaty. But the highest priority, whoever forms the next UK government, will be economic and some highly unpopular curbs on expenditure and the raising of taxes will be inevitable if the UK is to finance its fiscal deficit. For the Conservatives, with or without an outright majority, how to work within the Lisbon Treaty is, therefore, an important, but not an immediate, issue. It would be sensible for the Conservatives, if they win outright or if they need to talk to the Liberal Democrats, to approach the treaties in much the same way as Harold Wilson did in 1974. Having listened to the hostility to the EU expressed in the 2009 European election, having seen the strength of the UK Independence Party and having started a new grouping in the European Parliament not committed to ever greater integration, the Conservatives will not be ready to accept the status quo and nor should they. But they will want a negotiable position facing a situation in which it will not be possible under international law to ignore the Treaty of Lisbon. I can personally attest to the value of having the country become united behind a European policy for this is what happened after the 1975 referendum. That unity was broadly maintained until the parliamentary ratification process of the Maastricht Treaty in the autumn of 1992. After the next general election any British government must restore that unity and a referendum can be the mechanism to do it, provided that the negotiations prior to that referendum are grounded in the realities of European politics. It is in the interests of the Liberal Democrats, the most European of all the parties, to help achieve it if they hold the balance of power, but they too know, at least the realists among them, that they are currently dangerously out of touch with public opinion on this issue of Europe.

It should be possible to clarify and constrict the implications of the Lisbon Treaty and to agree a fresh interpretation of some of its provisions before putting the future options to the British people in a referendum. One sensible idea, which has already been suggested by the Liberal Democrats, is to have a referendum containing two questions. The first could be: 'Should the United Kingdom remain within the European Union?' The second question could be seen as fulfilling the 2005 general election manifesto commitment given by the Labour, Conservative and Liberal Democrat parties: 'On the assumption that the United Kingdom remains a member of the European Union, do you accept the clarifications of the Lisbon Treaty and renegotiated EU?'

If there were two questions, this would reduce the risk that the answer to any question on the Lisbon Treaty would be treated as an answer to the question of continued membership of the European Union. It has long been the objective of those who want Britain out of the EU that the two issues should be conflated in public debate and voting. By having two separate questions, the issues could be separated in a referendum before a 2014 general election.

The Lisbon Treaty does ring-fence the CFSP. There is also more scope in terms of protecting the UK from encroachment by what is called the 'Union method' or by the European Court of Justice (ECJ) than is sometimes realised. Yet those UK citizens opposed to the Lisbon Treaty, on the principled ground that it dismantles the inter-governmental pillars which were the foundation of the Maastricht Treaty, will need more comfort in this area. This is not nitpicking, but of vital importance.

'Primacy' under the Lisbon Treaty is confined to codifying the case law of the ECJ, which does not extend to foreign and security policy. There are also fairly clear guarantees of the continuation of the specific character of the CFSP. One declaration underlines that the new provisions 'do not affect the responsibilities of the Member States, as they currently exist, for the formulation and conduct of their foreign policy nor of their nationals' representation in third countries and international organisations', while another emphasises that the provisions on the CFSP will not affect the legal basis, powers and responsibilities of each member state in relation to the formulation and conduct of its foreign policy, its national diplomatic service, relations with third countries and participation in international organisations, including the UN Security Council. All of these clarifications need to be entrenched in UK legislation. Arguments that the ECJ will be constricted by these declarations are not convincing in view of past judgments.

There are also unresolved contradictions on common defence in the wording of the treaty, where Article 10(c), paragraph 1, reads 'the progressive framing of a common defence policy that *might* lead to a common defence [emphasis added]'. Yet Article 28(a), paragraph 2, reads: 'The common security and defence policy shall include the progressive framing of a common Union defence policy. This *will* lead to a common defence, when the European Council, acting unanimously, so decides [emphasis added].' The use of 'might' and 'will' can only lead to obfuscation. So again it is important for these words and meaning to be clarified in UK legislation so as to mean 'might lead'.

A major criticism which has not been met concerns problems that may arise over the dual mandate of the high representative of the CFSP, with loyalties divided between the Commission, of which he or she is a member, and the Council, which is in effect his or her boss. It needs to be made clear that the high representative is to carry out the CFSP 'as mandated by the Council' and enshrine that in UK legislation.

The provision which gives the Charter on Fundamental Rights equal legal status with the various treaties and the attached protocol is legally unsatisfactory and not watertight. From the point of view of the United Kingdom we need to have our own legal inter-pretation of this relationship.

On the president of the Council, the wording allows the appoint-ment of someone who is not a head of government. Nevertheless it also allows the Council to elect one of its own heads of government, which is, at present, done under rotation. I do not believe that the experiment of introducing someone from outside to be president of the Council will work well. An incoming UK government could make it clear that in future they will vote and campaign for other member states in the European Council to vote for one of their own practising heads of government for all future appointments. It is almost beyond belief that President Sarkozy for months advocated Tony Blair as the first president of the Council, to take office on 1 January 2010, less than six months before there has to be a general election in the UK. It is a travesty of democracy to choose a former Prime Minister who was pushed out of office earlier than he wished by his own party's MPs. For two years Tony Blair might be the president of a Council containing a Conservative Prime Minister whose party everyone knows has been opposed root and branch to his appointment. Hopefully the German Chancellor, Angela Merkel, who has already raised questions about the wisdom of this appointment, will in effect veto it. Also perhaps it is too much to hope that Tony Blair will see the folly of continuing to campaign for this post and quietly concede that it is not an appropriate position for him to occupy, defying the views of British voters in polling research and when Labour has done so badly in the 2009 European elections.

But the most serious objection to the wording of the Lisbon Treaty is that it allows for the post of president of the Council to be double hatted so that he or she can also be the president of the Commission, and this decision can be made by a qualified majority vote. Potentially, if that one single decision were to be taken, the EU would in effect come very close to unifying itself into a nation state. On this issue the current Labour government claims that it cannot legally happen. It may or may not be right, but we cannot leave this to chance. To make sure, it is perfectly reasonable to enshrine all pledges that it has been given on the interpretation of the words into UK legislation. The Dutch government, for example, has held a very different interpretation. It wrote to the Dutch parliament on 31 March 2004, 'The government also shares the opinion that the possibility should be kept that in future the president of the Commission can also be the president of the European Council. The texts before us leave this possibility open.' Article 9(b) of the treaty requires that 'the president of the European Council shall not hold a national office' but does not expressly exclude the concurrent holding of another European office.

In Peter Norman's book *The Accidental Constitution*, there is a good account of what happened behind the scenes and of the perception behind the drafting of these words. The author describes how the Praesidium, chaired by Valéry Giscard d'Estaing, which was responsible for the initial European constitution, 'also agreed the European Council President could hold office in another EU institution'. As influential a figure as the former Italian Prime Minister Giulio Amato is described as having the view that the 'Union must come at some time to having a joint President of the Commission and the European Council'. The United Kingdom government can, therefore, by enacting the pledges given in its own legislation, warn in the clearest possible terms that any attempt to do this would be considered a fundamental breach of trust within the EU and would invoke the Luxembourg compromise, a procedure upheld by the French government in the French National Assembly vote on the Maastricht Treaty in 1992.

Never since 1957 have there been reservations added, post-negotiation, to any Community or Union treaty. In the case of the Lisbon Treaty, once ratified, any UK amendments not a matter of a negotiated opt-out clause would have to be accepted as legally valid in a new treaty, which will be needed for the next enlargement covering Croatia. It is in this treaty that the Irish government will try to place all the verbal guarantees that they were given prior to the second referendum in October 2009.

All of these suggestions for UK legislation, however, need buttressing further by a new reform. The time has come for the UK Parliament to create a constitutional court around the new Supreme Court, mirroring the German Constitutional Court. This would immediately give substance and teeth to UK legislation relating to European legislation. It would not bind the ECJ but it would know that if it made a contrary interpretation UK citizens, not just governments, would have the right to bring such a matter through the lower courts to the Supreme Court. In legislating for this safeguard, Parliament would do much to protect the UK from further encroachment under the Lisbon Treaty. At present the newly established Supreme Court is one in name but not really in fact. Giving this court, in addition to its other powers, the power of a constitutional court and modelling those powers on the German Constitutional Court would be a potent way of limiting EU power. This is a big political issue for it is a step towards a written constitution. Hopefully it will be flagged up as an intention in the manifesto of one, or preferably more than one, political party at the next general election. It is a key part of a suggested reform package which I detail at the end of this book.

Legislation can also be introduced in the UK to ensure a parliamentary braking mechanism so that all further integration will require primary legislative approval in the UK. The European Assembly (Elections) Act 1978, for whose passage through the House of Commons I was in part responsible, established this precedent. Its provisions are incorporated in the Lisbon Treaty through the European Parliamentary Elections Act 2002. What Parliament did in 1978 was to ensure that in future no British minister could in any European forum commit to enhancing the powers of the then Assembly, now Parliament, without prior primary legislation in the Westminster Parliament. That parliamentary braking mechanism should now be systematically introduced over the Lisbon Treaty to cover the most sensitive political questions that concern the British people. The British Parliament should legislate for this additional safeguard in UK legislation concerning the following four areas of controversy, which would entail proper consideration in both Houses of Parliament and going through all the safeguards of first and second readings, the committee and report stages and third reading:

1. The supremacy of European Community law given effect in the UK by the 1972 Act never covered the three intergovernmental pillars in previous treaties. It is argued that the CFSP retains its separate legal character in the Lisbon Treaty. The declaration affecting 'primacy' is considered a legally binding addition to the Lisbon Treaty since it reflects existing case law. This means that the ECJ cannot extend its powers to cover the CFSP. Therefore no British minister should be able to accept any new authority for the ECJ over the CFSP without prior specific UK primary legislation.

2. The flexible framework in the treaty allowing for the dynamic development of EU law, what is often referred to as 'living law', is a potentially dangerous provision. It is within the UK's constitutional rights to subject any further changes in these areas, however modest they might appear, to UK primary legislation. This particularly applies to the article extending qualified majority voting. No British minister should be able to accept any of these extensions without prior specific UK primary legislation.

3. The application of the Community method to common justice and home affairs is from now on to be across the board, replacing an intergovernmental approach to these sensitive issues. The present position is that there is a UK opt-out. This too should be subject to a parliamentary brake so only if there has been prior specific UK primary legislative approval can any UK minister agree to it being given up.

4. The House of Commons European Scrutiny Committee believes that the protocol on the Charter of Fundamental Rights will not prevent EU labour laws taking force in Britain. It should be made clear that the whole Charter of Fundamental Rights will be acceptable and justiciable in the UK only after specific authorisation under UK primary legislation.

The major negotiating lever capable of impacting helpfully in the 'trade off' negotiations on all these issues, which any government taking office in 2010 will have at its disposal, is that agreement on a new EU budget is needed by 2013. A new government determined to keep what is left of the 'Thatcher rebate', after Tony Blair's totally irresponsible and economically unsound concession when the UK last held the presidency (absent: real CAP reform) will be in a very strong position to hold out, in a minority of one if necessary. This is another reason why it would be wise to postpone a referendum on the clarifications of the Treaty of Lisbon and negotiations on the EU until this critical negotiation has been resolved, which must take place well before a general election in 2014 under any legislation for a fixed-term parliament of four years.

Membership of the EU is a continuous negotiation and in that process there is considerable room for political manoeuvre on almost all aspects of the Treaties. In retrospect, despite the prediction that it would be impossible to negotiate, it was that room for manoeuvre which Harold Wilson and Jim Callaghan exploited from 1974 until the 1975 referendum. A new government in 2010 will have a two-year window in which it would be feasible to achieve much of the EU reform agenda outlined in this chapter. This will be much easier to negotiate following the decision in June 2009 of the German Constitutional Court. Wolfgang Munchau, having read the entire 147-page ruling, explained in the *Financial Times* on 13 July what it means. The Court has ruled that all sovereignty in the EU is national and while powers may be shared within the EU sovereignty cannot be shared. The Court has also seen through the nature of the European Parliament, in that it has no government and opposition within its midst, and as a consequence it does not control considerable powers of the EU executive, whichever body - Commission or European Council - exercises them. We can expect continuing argument about the changes that will now be necessary in German domestic law. On past precedent the Court may not hold up ratification if faced by what they regard as unsatisfactory and incomplete legislative response but the Court has ruled in a way that will establish limits for the future. Military operations; the police and criminal law; fiscal and social policy; education, media, culture and aspects of religion are all areas in which they argue Member States have full sovereignty.

As a result of the decision of the German Constitutional Court no one can seriously argue that the proposals spelt out in this chapter are anti-EU. As the Chairman of the German Bundeslander said in July 2009 'the times when a German government takes decisions in backrooms in Brussels are finally over'. Even if the legislation in Germany is not as stringent as advocated here, the legitimacy of the UK acting in this way cannot be credibly questioned by other EU Member States; nor can it be depicted as a hostile act were the UK to give its new Supreme Court the same powers over EU legislation as is already given to the German Constitutional Court.

In short, we do not need to use the term renegotiation, but we can negotiate for a New Europe model within the EU. What is more, public opinion in almost all the countries of Europe is aligned with UK public opinion in wanting substantial change and reform, only the elite cling to the ever greater integration of the old Europe model.

# 9

# The second Iraq War of 2003

I first met Tony Blair for a serious conversation on 15 July 1996 at his home, when he was Leader of the Opposition and the issue was whether I was ready to publicly support New Labour. I decided not to, mainly because I disagreed with his wish for the UK to join the eurozone as soon as he became Prime Minister. I could not rejoin Labour, given my record of dissent, and then start to disagree soon after. Also I had built a sound working relationship over Yugoslavia with John Major and as it was clear he was going to lose the next election there was no need for me to campaign against him. I had no reason either to re-enter party politics, particularly as I knew that former SDP members liked me remaining unaligned, whether they were members of other parties or had stayed out of politics. I was very comfortable where I was but, I admit, from time to time tempted to return if I really ever felt confident Labour was a genuine social democratic party. Sadly that has never been a correct description of New Labour though I hoped it might become so.

I first discussed Iraq with Blair on 2 March 1998 in Downing Street and, as a sign of my depth of feeling about Saddam Hussein's regime, gave him a book about the Kurds written by Jonathan Randal, an experienced war correspondent with the *Washington Post*. This brilliant book posed many questions for the future. For example, it discussed how the aftermath of the Iraqi forces' defeat in 1991 had been handled in a way that left much to be desired. Randal wrote:

> The American planning was a hodgepodge of naivety and *realpolitik*, more tactics than strategy, seemingly consistent only if its peculiar assumptions were correct. No-one should have been surprised by anything that happened from 2 August 1990 when Iraq invaded and

occupied Kuwait to the end of the following March, when Saddam Hussein crushed the Shia and Kurdish uprisings.

For some years I had been ever more troubled by what was happening in and around Iraq. In November 1995 the US armed forces' continued presence in Saudi Arabia was highlighted when al-Qaeda killed five American members of a joint military training team. This was followed by the Iranian-backed Hezbollah attacking a residential block outside Riyadh with a suicide truck bomb, killing nineteen Americans. Then a fatwa calling on all Muslims to take part in a jihad to force all US forces to leave Saudi Arabia was announced by Osama bin Laden. On 7 August 1998 truck bomb attacks organised by al-Qaeda on the American embassies in Nairobi and Dar es Salaam had a horrific impact, to which President Clinton responded with Tomahawk missile attacks in Afghanistan and Sudan. This was followed by a telephone call from a laughing Mullah Omar, the leader of the then Taleban government in Afghanistan, to a senior official in the US State Department. No one should ever argue against that background that Iraq was contained and that Saddam Hussein's continuation in office was not part of the regional disarray, since it was because of him that the Americans correctly continued to maintain troops on the ground in Saudi Arabia.

I followed up the concerns I had expressed at my meeting with Blair in a letter on 12 November, arguing that there had to be a political strategy involving the Kurds to help topple Saddam Hussein. Blair replied, 'We are not working to bring down Saddam Hussein and his regime. It is not for us to say who should be President of Iraq, however much we might prefer to see a different government in Baghdad.' This exchange encapsulated the UK's particular problem: successive British governments have felt legally bound to use wording on regime change based on a particularly inflexible interpretation of the United Nations Charter.

Following the withdrawal of UN inspectors from Iraq in December 1998 in response to Saddam's non-co-operation, the United States and Britain launched a four-day bombing campaign against Iraqi targets. The military operation was undertaken, as in 1993 and 1996, and again in 2002 and 2003, with the US and the UK claiming the authority of the UN resolutions passed in 1990 and

1991 and UN Security Council Resolution 1205, passed in 1998.

Blair had asked me to dinner at 10 Downing Street on 18 December 1998, the third evening of the bombing blitz. The main reason for the invitation was Blair's wish to dissuade me from establishing New Europe. But we also discussed Iraq at some length. After dinner with our wives I found him relaxed, almost laid back. He had started well as Prime Minister, particularly in handling Northern Ireland, and it looked as if he was set to be a successful premier. There was no undue hyperactivity. He did not excuse himself to get an update on the attacks that had been launched and I found him cool, rational and anything but hubristic. He was ready to discuss the complexity of the relations between the Shiite majority and the Kurds and Sunnis in Iraq in some detail but he was not very knowledgeable about them and he had obviously not yet read Randal's book. We agreed that the situation which allowed Saddam to stay in power was totally unsatisfactory and shared frustration at UN limitations within which he, Blair, felt formally he had to operate. The United States' congressional resolution for regime change, called the Iraq Liberation Act, had meanwhile been passed by an overwhelming majority, which President Clinton did not veto. The challenge was Saddam's continuation in power, not WMD, which were only briefly mentioned though we both believed they were still present in Iraq.

The US and the UK dropped more than 600 bombs and launched 415 cruise missiles against Iraqi targets during this action, killing an estimated 1,400 members of Iraq's Republican Guard. The action, which had been targeted on some nuclear facilities, was later assessed as having set back Saddam's nuclear weapons programme by two years. Clinton, though committed to the congressional resolution calling for regime change in Iraq, was never likely to authorise the full military invasion necessary to achieve this. American public opinion was not ready for military re-engagement on the ground in Iraq. Clinton's failed impeachment over Monica Lewinsky in February 1999 had weakened his authority to go to the American people and demand action and this may have been a factor also when deciding what to do with the growing threat to the United States of Osama bin Laden and al-Qaeda. The priority issue for military action for NATO, in the year ahead, was Kosovo.

My next conversation with Blair was during the Kosovo crisis when NATO was engaging in air attacks on Serbia. On 16 April 1999, the Prime Minister unexpectedly rang me wanting a long and detailed talk about his anxieties over the deteriorating situation. The Serb military were still largely unaffected by the NATO bombing and he wanted to discuss my publicly stated views that we should from the outset have been prepared to use NATO ground forces. Somewhat unconventionally, I had been attacked by name for these views, along with Henry Kissinger, in an article by General Charles Guthrie, then the UK chief of the Defence Staff. This was a small but significant sign of an undue politicisation of the chiefs of staff. Clinton's advisers had apparently told the President that Slobodan Milošević would fold if threatened and, when he did not, that bombing would do the trick in forty-eight, then seventy-two, hours. It took eventually seventy-eight days of bombing and, even more importantly, a powerful intervention from Boris Yeltsin for Milošević to agree to withdraw the Serbian armed forces and police. They left reluctantly, never conceding military defeat.

I mentioned to Blair at an early stage that I was speaking from Berlin on an open line. He laughed and said he wanted anyone listening to know about his anxieties. Blair was surprisingly frank and we had an animated discussion. I sensed, however, for the first time a note of exaltation in his voice. Soon afterwards real tension developed between Blair and Clinton about the need to prepare to send in ground forces and on 21 April Blair told Parliament that ground troops were an option.

The following day Blair made a speech in Chicago, in which he tried to identify the circumstances in which Britain 'should get actively involved in other people's conflicts' in defence of our values. Whatever its rights and wrongs, and in large part I agreed with it, what was extraordinary for such an important speech was how little examination of its implications took place in Whitehall. It was drafted by a professor of war studies, Lawrence Freedman, who was himself surprised that Blair made very few changes to his proposed text. The input from the Foreign Office and the Ministry of Defence was minimal.

One damaging side effect of Kosovo, in retrospect, was the mood of self-confidence and personal dominance that began to appear in

Blair's handling of foreign affairs. Kosovo was Blair's first test in a big international crisis and unmistakable signs of hubristic attitudes were beginning to emerge. Visiting refugee camps he was hailed as a hero. At one stage, Clinton angrily told Blair to 'pull himself together' and halt 'domestic grandstanding'. He was starting to display excessive pride in his own judgements. Clinton's aides mocked Blair's 'Churchillian tone'. One official who frequently saw him said, 'Tony is doing too much, he's overdoing it and he's overplaying his hand.' One of Clinton's aides suggested Blair 'was sprinkling too much adrenalin on his cornflakes'.

It is worth noting how often this hormone is referred to when people discuss manic or hubristic behaviour. But if there is any linkage it is a complex one embraced within the two-factor theory of emotion, where the adrenalin may produce a physiological arousal but there also needs to be a thought process or cognition to interpret the meaning of this arousal.

After my telephone conversation with Blair, I was beginning to appreciate how personalised and very different his style of leadership was from the measured and structured style I had watched James Callaghan adopt as Prime Minister. Blair liked to claim he was following Margaret Thatcher's style of leadership, but this claim was false in many respects, particularly with regard to her precise handling of the Falklands War. Unlike him, she had a formidable commitment to a political philosophy and she was renowned for her close attention to detail. But most of all, she was already experienced when she became Prime Minister, having served for many years in governments led by Harold Macmillan and Edward Heath. On taking office Blair was the most inexperienced British Prime Minister since Ramsay MacDonald in 1924, neither having held any ministerial office before entering No. 10. That lack of experience in retrospect was to prove more damaging to Blair's record than I initially thought it would.

Furthermore, Blair had had no formal training or experience in management. He tried to make up for this by talking to management thinkers and seemed, according to an article in *Management Today*, to want to act like a chief executive: 'fast on his feet, flexible in his thinking and able to make quick decisions, often taken on the hoof, in shirtsleeves, on the sofa, coffee latte in one hand, mobile phone in the other, running Great Britain plc as if it were a City investment company'. But the role of Prime Minister is not that of a chief executive and the UK government is not a company making profits for shareholders.

Like Blair, Thatcher had sought to accrete more power in No. 10 but she had worked within the existing Cabinet structures to do so. Even though Thatcher made considerable use of a personal foreign affairs adviser, Charles Powell, then a serving diplomat, the Cabinet Secretary remained a powerful independent figure. By contrast, Blair chose a formalised and progressive destruction of the Cabinet system. He started by appointing a political chief of staff, Jonathan Powell, the brother of Charles. He, however, along with Blair's press secretary, Alastair Campbell, was exceptionally given the powers of a civil servant. This progressively undermined the authority of the Cabinet Secretary. Also collective Cabinet discussion and responsibility were substantially reduced. Later, in 2001, and in the flush of victory after winning a second general election, Blair, with no parliamentary scrutiny, was to change the whole basis of Cabinet government as it related to foreign and defence matters. A system which had evolved during the First World War was swept aside without a single serious objective study. This was not modernisation but hubristic vandalism, for which, as Prime Minister, Blair alone bore responsibility.

The new structure was deliberately designed by Blair to ensure he could exercise over international policy much the same powers as a US President. The Cabinet Office method of handling foreign and security matters had, until then, been designed to service the Cabinet as a whole. From the summer of 2001 onwards, the key officials and their staff on foreign affairs, defence and the European Union were brought into the political hothouse atmosphere of 10 Downing Street in two new secretariats. The No. 10 secretariats were intended to service the Prime Minister alone, politically and strategically. Blair was to do much the same to the Joint Intelligence Committee (JIC), in terms of its working arrangements if not of its formal structure. This new structure in No. 10 was designed to cause the progressive downgrading of the Foreign Office and the Ministry of Defence and their respective secretaries of state. Inexplicably, it was virtually ignored by the press, who had become enamoured of the aura which Blair began to project of a successful Prime Minister. A few months after the two secretariats were in place in No. 10 the new structure provided the means to project Blair's very personalised response to the 9/11 attacks in New York and Washington.

A warning sign of Blair's developing hubris was the astonishing speech that he gave to the Labour Party conference immediately after 9/11, when he promised the American people, 'We were with you at the first, we will stay with you to the last.' The consequence of Blair's exclusive dependence on his new No. 10 secretariats was the lack of objectivity, probity and collectivity which were to become the hallmarks of his misjudgements and incompetence in handling the aftermaths of the 2001 invasion of Afghanistan and the 2003 invasion of Iraq. The Labour peer and historian Lord Morgan described Blair's speech thus:

> Blair seemed a political colossus, half-Caesar, half-Messiah. Equally, as times became tough following the Iraq *imbroglio*, he became an exposed solitary victim, personally stigmatised as in the 'cash for peerages' affair. Blair discovered, like Lloyd George and Thatcher before him, that British politics do not take easily to the Napoleonic style.

President Bush chose, first, to take action militarily against Afghanistan and its Taleban government, who had been sheltering al-Qaeda. Even though the invasion of Afghanistan was justified, worrying signs of a developing hubris within Bush emerged from the start of the campaign. For example, the longer-term problems of controlling the country after the invasion had been achieved were grossly underestimated from the outset.

There have, of course, been incompetent Presidents and Prime Ministers before but Blair's incompetence was to be of a very particular sort, and it was largely shared by Bush. It was triggered by three characteristic symptoms of hubris: excessive self-confidence, restlessness and inattention to detail. A self-confidence that exclusively reserves decision-making to itself, does not seek advice and fails to listen to or is contemptuous of the wisdom of others, particularly if it conflicts with the leader's own viewpoint, is hubristic. If this is combined with an energy that is restless for action

THE SECOND IRAQ WAR OF 2003    573

and is ready to intervene on the basis of a loose sense of the broader picture rather than the detailed study of all the relevant information, then serious mistakes are almost inevitable. Such was to be the case in Bush and Blair's handling of affairs after 9/11.

Bush and Blair liked to pride themselves on being 'big picture' politicians who had the insight to realise that the whole world, not just Afghanistan and Iraq, must now be seen anew and in fundamentally different terms after 2001. In fact, the world, as looked at from the perspective of many centuries, did not change fundamentally on 11 September 2001. There was, however, more irrationality and less predictability. Islamic fundamentalists were ready to sacrifice their lives as part of committing an act of terrorism, which made bomb-carrying more deadly and a primitive nuclear device in a suitcase conceivable. It took some years for the rhetoric to cool and only in April 2007 did the British government announce formally that it was stopping using the term 'war on terror'.

Blair had appeared to have an excellent relationship with Clinton when President, but he later said to one of his aides, 'Clinton messes you around but when Bush promises something, he means it.' Experienced officials, however, have questioned whether Blair was deluding himself about his relationship with Bush. They worried about the lack of substance in the Bush–Blair dialogue and about the extent of the mutual posturing. They noted how Margaret Thatcher had nailed Ronald Reagan down in a way that Blair never did with Bush, or how John Major, though only having a short time before the 1991 Gulf War period, afterwards built a relationship of some depth with Bush's father.

Blair's own particular form of hubris was his obsession with presentation and his need to put himself visibly at the centre of events. This had already become evident when a private memo he wrote to his staff in 2000 was leaked. In it he urged them to search around for 'two or three eye-catching initiatives . . . I should be personally associated with as much of this as possible'. David Marquand, the biographer of another Labour Prime Minister, Ramsay MacDonald, wrote of Blair's ten years in office:

> The true origin of his tragedy lies in an intellectual deformation that is becoming more and more prevalent in our increasingly paltry

public culture. The best word for it is 'presentism' . . . His fascination with fashionable glitz, his crass talk of a 'New Britain' and a 'Young Country' and his disdain for the wisdom of experts who had learned the lessons of the past better than he had were all part of the deadly syndrome.

The world after 9/11 provided Blair with endless opportunities for such eye-catching initiatives and he indulged in considerable posturing. Following 9/11 he pursued a frenetic schedule. He held fifty-four meetings with foreign leaders, and travelled more than 40,000 miles on some thirty-one separate flights.

The British press were encouraged by No. 10, with its new foreign affairs and defence secretariats, to exaggerate to the British people the extent of the UK's early involvement in Afghanistan, beyond the UK launching some cruise missiles and a contribution from the SAS. The invasion was, first and foremost, an American operation: in all its major parameters it was led by the CIA, who used dollars to build up the Northern Alliance, and by the Pentagon, using its special forces and air power to tilt the balance of fighting in favour of those Afghan leaders ready to take on the Taleban. But to reinforce the impression of his own central role, Blair flew into Kabul in early January 2002, just eight weeks after the Taleban-controlled capital had fallen to the Northern Alliance. He was chronically short of sleep and despite a recent holiday in Egypt was exhausted, mentally and physically.

Blair tried to keep up the same pace through 2002 and much of 2003. His determination to be at the centre of everything was designed for and highlighted by the British press. US public opinion, however, liked Blair's easy style, and admired his verbal felicity and presentational skills. It therefore suited Bush to build up Blair's importance over Iraq. By now there was little pretence but that British foreign policy was being run from 10 Downing Street, with the Foreign Office being increasingly sidelined. The British ambassador in Washington recorded this: 'Between 9/11 and the day I retired at the end of February 2003, I had not a single substantive policy discussion on the secure phone with the Foreign Office. This was in contrast to many contacts and discussion with No. 10.'

Debbie and I met Tony and Cherie Blair again for dinner at

No. 10 on 24 July 2002. It became very clear to me that Blair was going to commit Britain to Bush's Iraq policy and I agreed with him. What was especially noticeable was that, while he had been ready at the dinner in 1998 to explore the complex internal politics of Iraq, Blair was now, in marked contrast, totally unwilling to have any detailed discussion about the consequences of invading. I felt that the political difficulties certain to be encountered in the aftermath of replacing Saddam and Sunni dominance needed to be explored dispassionately. So I tried to do so in a 'Devil's advocate' manner, but Blair was wholly dismissive. There were no problems, he seemed to believe, that could not be solved and were not being solved. I mistakenly took this reluctance to discuss as a sign that he considered all this information highly classified, as indeed in a way it should have been, but it was very different from his readiness to discuss sensitive military matters with regard to Kosovo.

Blair's purpose in talking to me about Iraq that evening was evidently not to consult me but to brief me about what he was going to do and to bring me into the personal 'big tent' of supporters which he liked to create around any controversial new policy. It became utterly clear to me that he had made up his mind on Iraq, and that if Bush later authorised an invasion, Blair would ensure that Britain was there with him. I realised that Blair intended me to report from that meeting to my own contacts in the press, on an unattributable basis, that Britain was definitely going to go to war. This I did as, no doubt, did others. Later, when this readiness to plan for war was eventually confirmed in leaked documents, many people were outraged. But in all fairness, neither Bush nor Blair could have done much more to indicate their intentions than by such selective background briefing. It was still months before any invasion could take place. Wars and even the realistic threat of going to war have to be planned for with some secrecy. It takes time, as in the build-up to the Iraq war in 1990–1, to deploy significant armed forces, particularly tanks and heavy weapons.

But my concern about Tony Blair from that meeting was not his support for an invasion, which I shared, nor his wish to get the message out indirectly, which I understood, but the closed nature of his mind. I regret this did not sufficiently alarm me at the time but I was left with the strong impression that Blair was a very different man from the one I had met over dinner 3½ years earlier. Besides the firm belief in his purpose, which I discussed afterwards driving home with Debbie, there was a total confidence in himself and as a new feature a restless, hyperactive manner. His brushing aside of the difficulties that circumstance was likely to throw in his way meant to me that the die was cast in his own mind over forcing regime change. As before, WMD were not a major topic in Blair's conversation; he was focused quite simply on getting rid of Saddam for moral and geopolitical reasons, all of which I supported. But, as Debbie said afterwards, he was messianic.

The opportunity to exercise decisive and controversial leadership is one of the strengths of representative democracy and there is a need from time to time for a certain boldness. But representative democracy also demands that leaders' decision-making be open to democratic scrutiny, that they tell the truth and that after making the key decisions they should be held accountable and, if found wanting, be ready to resign from office.

It subsequently became clear from a leaked memo that by the end of July 2002, the Whitehall machine seemed to be assuming that a protracted and costly nation-building option was likely to be forced on them in Iraq, but, along with the intelligence services, the military were deeply alarmed by the lack of any post-invasion planning in Washington. Yet Blair appeared to ignore the warnings his own people were giving him, and in that dinner conversation with me he was trying to give me the impression that it was all being dealt with. This was not ordinary incompetence, it was hubristic incompetence. He was becoming immune to all arguments about the practical difficulties that might ensue, which many people were putting to him. A senior official recalls that when advising Blair about the difficulties ahead, Blair said in a perfectly friendly way, 'You are Neville Chamberlain, I am Winston Churchill and Saddam is Hitler.' It is difficult to conduct a serious dialogue with a leader thinking in this emotional and simplistic manner.

This was also Blair's frame of mind when dealing with outside advisers. Charles Tripp, an academic expert on Middle East politics, was called in along with other experts to give advice. Some months later he wrote an account of his meeting:

At a Downing Street meeting in November 2002 attended by Blair, Straw [Jack Straw, the Foreign Secretary] and six academics familiar with Iraq and the Middle East, two things became clear. The first was that Straw thought post-Saddam Iraq would be much like post-Soviet Russia and could thus be easily pigeon-holed as that strange creature, a 'transitional society'. Either he had been persuaded of this by the recycled Cold Warriors clustering round the Bush administration, or they had failed to inform their 'key ally' of their determination to dismantle Iraq's state and security structures. More ominously, Blair seemed wholly uninterested in Iraq as a complex and puzzling political society, wanting confirmation merely that deposing Saddam would remove 'evil' from the country.

That Blair should be interested only in being reassured that he was fighting evil can be equated with Bush's simple talk of his crusade to rid the world of 'evil doers'.

Apologists for the British policy and for Blair personally over Iraq tend to put all the blame for the admitted incompetence on the Americans. This is to underestimate British knowledge of the region. Britain, unlike America, had been involved in Iraq through most of the twentieth century. By 1918 David Lloyd George had sent more than a million British and Commonwealth troops into Ottoman territory to impose a post-war settlement. Britain had administered Iraq, albeit not very successfully, under a League of Nations mandate from 1920 until 1932, and had remained close to King Faisal and Nuri al-Said, who dominated the country for the next two decades. The British Foreign Office and Ministry of Defence had knowledge and experience and some well-formulated views on the best way of handling the aftermath of any invasion, especially in the light of the mistakes of 1991. But Blair never utilised this expertise. A Foreign Office strategy paper, which the State Department was hoping would arrive, their own having been ignored by the Pentagon, never came. The then British ambassador to Washington has written about the 'titanic struggle' for six months to keep Britain 'onside for war' and how 'there was little energy left in No. 10 to think about the aftermath. Since Downing Street drove Iraq policy, efforts made by the Foreign Office to engage with the Americans on the aftermath came to nothing.'

We now know that Blair was told in early March by Major General Tim Cross that the post-war planning was completely incoherent. 'The plan was, we do not need a plan' was Cross's summary view of what had been going on in Washington and in Iraq, where he was working with the Americans on this very issue. Cross revealed in a *Sunday Times* interview on 21 October 2007, 'As we teased out the issues, Blair listened and questioned. None of it seemed to come as much of a surprise. Indeed it seemed to reinforce what he was starting to pick up from elsewhere.' Cross remembers telling Blair, 'We want to be jolly careful that we don't start this war until we know how we are going to finish it. And I, for one, am far from clear on how we are going to do that.' Cross left Downing Street thinking that Blair 'didn't seem to have the instinct for or understand the scope and complexity of what was going to be needed in the aftermath of an invasion. I don't think he understood what the possible consequences could be.' For Cross the story was a failure of leadership. 'We got it wrong. We underestimated the resources we would need to see the campaign through. We under-estimated the time we would need.'

Politicians down the ages have presented their side of any case in the best possible light, focusing on what is positive and ignoring the negative. Political spin, as it is called, did not start with Bush and Blair. What was new about them was their readiness to spin intelligence matters. Their 'spinmasters', in the shape of Karl Rove and Alastair Campbell, were not only more powerful than similar figures in the past but they were uniquely deeply involved in the domestic debate about Iraq and themselves briefed on intelligence matters. In Blair's case, Campbell was involved in the publication of two dossiers purportedly outlining the threat posed by Saddam. One of them, which came to be known as 'the dodgy dossier', was dismissed by Jack Straw as a 'Horlicks' and was withdrawn by the government itself; the other was widely believed to have used tentative intelligence assessments in order to make a compelling propaganda case in favour of war. One Cabinet minister, the former Foreign Secretary Robin Cook, questioned the validity of the interpretation being put on intelligence information and wisely asked for – and received – a personal briefing from MI6. He then resigned and voted against the invasion of Iraq, saying in the House of Commons that he did not believe the intelligence justified it. Also Charles Kennedy, then leader of the Liberal Democrat Party, came out against the whole venture. The vote in Parliament supported the government and Labour MPs' votes on their own gave Blair a majority. But it was gained at a bitter price.

Blair had had trust from all sides of the political spectrum in Parliament until this point, but his manipulation of the facts that day in retrospect gravely damaged that trust. It may have left lasting damage to the very concept of bipartisanship over foreign and security policy. As the facts became better known, Blair's name began to be defaced to 'Bliar' and he could no longer rely on the automatic support that the British Parliament and people traditionally give to a Prime Minister in a time of war. Matthew Parris, commenting on Tony Blair's mental state in the *Times*, referred to him as 'unhinged', in the serious sense of the word, as early as 29 March 2003 and went on to cite a throwaway remark in Parliament that he would ignore Security Council vetos which were 'capricious' or 'unreasonable'.

Revealingly, an American book on the Iraq War was simply called *Hubris*. On 1 May 2003, George W. Bush, dressed like a Hollywood actor in flying gear, flew onto the aircraft carrier *Abraham Lincoln* off the coast of California and stood on the flight deck to celebrate victory in Iraq, the ship's control tower emblazoned with the slogan 'Mission Accomplished'. It was a hubristic act of a very high order. It was also a contemptuous, if unintended, insult to the troops in the field, who knew all too well the slogan's patent absurdity. Donald Rumsfeld had the sense to dissuade Bush from actually using the phrase in his speech but even so Bush did say, 'In the battle for Iraq, the United States and our allies have prevailed.'

Blair never went so far but his early rhetoric was also much too triumphant. In his case, the reality of the invasion's aftermath, and the absence of post-conflict planning, in which he had taken so little serious interest beforehand, was made clear to him on 11 May 2003, only ten days later. Then John Sawers, the British ambassador to Egypt, who had previously worked in No. 10 and the new head of MI6 was sent into Iraq by Blair. He wrote a memo entitled 'Iraq: What's Going Wrong', a summary of the Americans' aftermath team under General Jay Garner was succinct: 'No leadership, no strategy, no coordination, no structure and inaccessible to ordinary Iraqis.' Sawers's clear view was that more troops were needed and he suggested that 'an operational UK presence in Baghdad is worth considering, despite the obvious political problem ... one battalion with a mandate to deploy into the streets could still make an impact.' Sawers's view about the need for more troops was backed up by Major General Albert Whitley, the most senior British officer with the US land forces, serving in the US headquarters of Lieutenant General David McKiernan. The issue was whether to bring the British 16 Air Assault Brigade, in Iraq but due to return home, to Baghdad. The Sawers memo could hardly have been a more serious communication to a Prime Minister with thousands of troops at risk in Basra, for what affected Baghdad was soon bound to affect Basra too. But what then happened in Downing Street to the Sawers memo?

According to Anthony Seldon, 'When Blair heard of the plan, he gave his full backing.' But why did nothing happen? It ran, according to Seldon's informants, into the implacable opposition of General Sir Michael Walker, who had succeeded Admiral Sir Michael Boyce as chief of the Defence Staff. Yet Blair and the War Cabinet could have decided to redeploy these troops, and if they had done so, it would have been impossible for Bush to refuse to do so as well. Donald Rumsfeld would not have been allowed to 'offramp' the 16,000 soldiers of the 1st Cavalry Division. This was a classic case of how the UK can have a powerful influence on the US if it is ready to act independently and decisively. The opportunities do not come often, but when they do the best of our Prime Ministers seize the opportunity. This episode should be one which the privy councillors' inquiry to be established in the summer of 2009 devotes particular energy to, along with the incompetent handling of the so-called second resolution in the Security Council prior to the invasion, which the French found so provocative and rightly predicted could not be won.

By 2004 I had become convinced that Blair had permanently lost authority and credibility and should choose an early moment to step down and take another job. I wrote an article in the *Sunday Times* on 4 January entitled 'Self-rule by Blair gives him a Suez crisis'. While still believing that toppling Saddam Hussein was a legitimate policy, I suggested that Blair should step down as Prime Minister no later than the expected 2005 general election. I wrote:

> Blair's authority has been severely, probably irreparably, damaged over Iraq, not just in his party but within the country ... A well-conducted exit would make it more likely that Blair's prime ministership would be well regarded by history. There are other opportunities that lie ahead for Blair, not least perhaps as the next head of the World Bank.

I have had no substantial discussions with him since.

We now know that from Easter 2004 Blair was under considerable stress, but it was from a matter unrelated to Iraq or his duties as Prime Minister, and over which the press collectively showed great restraint, not reporting on what they rightly considered to be a genuinely private, family matter. Blair had actually decided to step down as Prime Minister around late May/early June 2004. Whether this was because he had simply recognised that his failure meant it was time to resign, because he was depressed or because he was very stressed we do not know; probably it was a combination of all three. Some friends claim he was despondent and that explained his wobbling. He had also suddenly announced after Easter without any Cabinet consultation that there would be a referendum on the Lisbon Treaty, after being urged to do so by Jack Straw. Blair was dissuaded from resigning by some of his loyal friends in the Cabinet.

On 14 July 2004 the so-called Butler report, on failures of intelligence prior to the invasion of Iraq, was published. Blair was apparently surprised that it was not more damaging, but it was he who had deliberately circumscribed its terms of reference. When a former Cabinet Secretary such as Lord Butler is asked to conduct an inquiry on the committee of which the Prime Minister places a loyal former Cabinet colleague, that Prime Minister knows that criticism will have to be deftly drafted so as to reflect a consensus and thereby fall well short of any call to resign. Nevertheless the Butler report had, unusually, gone beyond its remit into intelligence failings before the war and commented on the nature of Blair's decision-making process, singling out for criticism his personalised sofa-style way of making key decisions: 'We are concerned that the informality and circumscribed character of the government's procedures . . . risks reducing the scope for informed collective political judgement.' Deftly drafted and in Whitehall language deeply damaging. But the Blair spin machine defused the potential fallout.

In a devastating intervention in the House of Lords, on 22 February 2007, Butler spoke for the first time as an individual, not as the chairman of the inquiry. He accused Blair of being 'disingenuous' about the intelligence, a word that only just avoids the parliamentary ban on saying that someone has lied:

> Here was the rub: neither the United Kingdom nor the United States had the intelligence that proved conclusively that Iraq had those weapons. The Prime Minister was disingenuous about that. The United Kingdom intelligence community told him on 23 August 2002 that we 'know little about Iraq's chemical and biological weapons work since late 1988'. The Prime Minister did not tell us that. Indeed, he told Parliament only just over a month later that the picture painted by our intelligence services was 'extensive, detailed and authoritative'. Those words could simply not have been justified by the material that the intelligence community provided to him.

In the 2005 general election, Blair tried initially to campaign on his own, downplaying the electoral role and importance of Gordon Brown. This strategy was clearly failing in terms of public opinion, particularly with Labour Party supporters, and Brown was quickly brought back with a central role in the campaign. Much to my surprise, two days before polling day, I received a telephone message from a senior Cabinet minister. I suspected he wanted me to publicly endorse Labour and was worried about the Liberal Democrat vote and thinking perhaps an endorsement of Labour from me might check this. Next day, on Wednesday 4 July, visiting the Temple of Apollo in the Peloponnese, where the concept of hubris had deep roots, I telephoned back and found that was exactly what was wanted. After a chat I declined to make the endorsement. I did not want a Conservative government, but wanted the Liberal Democrats to do sufficiently well to ensure a greatly reduced Labour majority. I also hoped that such a result might convince Blair to step down as Prime Minister soon thereafter, if need be by invoking his health (of which more later) for the political purpose of explaining his departure so soon after the general election. I discovered later the very same day, on the eve of polling, when it had been proposed I should declare for Labour, a tawdry interview had appeared in the

*Sun* newspaper with Tony and Cherie Blair boasting about his sexual prowess. Increased sexual drive is associated with manic behaviour but in this case the interview had every appearance of being carefully staged and timed to come out on the last day of the campaign, with no scope for a critical backlash. Blair's conduct in his high office was now well below an acceptable standard.

Labour won that general election, albeit with a greatly reduced majority and with only 36 per cent of the vote. Blair and Brown still had power but, with only 9.6 million votes, down from 10.7 million in 2001 and 13.5 million in 1997. Blair privately recognised that it was virtually a defeat and said it was his fault because of Iraq. But he still clung onto office and, despite a massive reduction in the number of votes and seats, his self-confidence soon returned. He never understood why the country would not 'move on' over Iraq. His hubris revived in 2005, though never becoming as marked as in 2001–3. His obsession about his legacy dominated decisions over the date of his promised resignation. He conveyed the impression that he and he alone, with a unit in No. 10, could put into effect the programme of change his government had embarked upon for education and health, but, as over military matters, his constant intervention and 'presentism' destabilised these services, demoralised the professional staff and had the effect of reducing the benefits of the substantially increased funds being allocated. 'Deliverology' as developed by Blair had one all-pervasive weakness, the wish to exercise central control from No. 10 of services that should be decentralised and are decentralised in every other large nation in the world.

An example of the contempt which often comes with hubris that Blair developed and displayed comes from the account leaked from Downing Street of a conversation between him and Jack Straw after the result of the French referendum which rejected the EU constitution. Straw, who campaigned for a 'No' vote in the UK's 1975 referendum on remaining in the EEC, wisely welcomed the French result and it was reported, after their conversation, that privately Blair turned to an aide and contemptuously remarked, 'Tart!' This remark, made within Blair's closed circle, was given much publicity and, though formally denied, the story was never quashed. Somewhat undiplomatically, Straw also described any military pre-emptive attack on Iranian nuclear installations as 'nuts'. This appeared quite deliberate, as if he feared that Bush and Blair might use the existence of any threat, as part of a negotiating stance over the Iran nuclear enrichment programme, to legitimise their acting pre-emptively. Straw was demoted by Blair in May 2006 and replaced for a short time as Foreign Secretary by Margaret Beckett, someone with no experience of foreign affairs.

By the time of the Lebanon crisis in July–August 2006, with two new and inexperienced secretaries of state in the Foreign Office and the Ministry of Defence, there was no one with sufficient experience to challenge Blair's refusal, along with Bush, to publicly endorse a ceasefire. It was an extraordinary omission. Even in Israel there was, and after the eventual ceasefire continued to be, detailed criticism of the nature of the Israeli air attacks on Hezbollah targets in Lebanon. Not only did they destroy a large part of Lebanon's infrastructure but they had little impact on Hezbollah's capacity to launch missile attacks. Bush and Blair were both party to the well-judged G8 summit communiqué from St Petersburg calling for a rapid deployment of a multilateral force. Had they made an immediate contribution to the deployment of a rapid reaction force to Lebanon it would have ensured an early ceasefire. In a swaggering display at a press conference in Washington on 28 July, they both refused to put the weight of their diplomacy behind such a ceasefire. Almost alone among world leaders, they seemed to believe that repeated Israeli attacks from the air on targets in Lebanon, including houses and apartments in urban areas, would destroy Hezbollah. The informed criticism of Israeli strategy from inside Israel made their high-flown rhetoric about values appear totally cynical. Both the senior diplomats initially put in charge by Blair of his secretariats disowned the policy, Sir Stephen Wall, who had retired, publicly and Sir David Manning, ambassador in Washington, privately. Blair's stance was morally indefensible and also one that was doomed militarily. Blair then spoke in Los Angeles about an 'arc of extremism now stretching across the Middle East', totally ignoring that it was his and Bush's failure to make a success of the Iraq invasion which had made by far the largest contribution to setting the region aflame. Strangely, it was Lebanon, not Iraq, that triggered the moderate centre ground of Labour MPs at last to say that 'enough was enough'.

They forced Blair to recognise that he had to say publicly in September 2006 that this would be his last party conference.

In trying to assess why Blair made such a mess of the Iraq War it is reasonable to consider any personality traits which might incline him towards hubris. Several in Blair stand out very obviously. Firstly, as all his biographers make clear, his early passion was not politics but performing: both at school and at Oxford his interest was on the stage, as an actor or a member of a rock band. It appears that he was not led into politics by ideological conviction – he was, at school, a Conservative and he has always struggled to articulate a political philosophy that would root him in the Labour Party – but politics offered him a very large stage on which to perform. The brilliance and range of Blair's acting repertoire as a politician has been much noted. Politicians, particularly when they are not interested in detail, appear susceptible to narcissism but actor-politicians tend to be especially narcissistic – their political vision tends to have themselves at its centre, commanding the stage with all eyes upon them. Blair prefers to have information on one or, at most, two pieces of paper; he often does not read background material. It is hardly surprising that presentation and spin become so important for such politicians. But such narcissism in actor-politicians makes the hero role almost irresistible. The potential is, therefore, present for this to induce hubris.

A second trait of Blair's personality concerns his view of himself, in that he thinks he is always good. The journalist and author Geoffrey Wheatcroft has argued that this is so strong in Blair that he is a latter-day antinomian – the name given to the sixteenth-century heretics who believed that 'to the pure all things are pure', meaning that whatever they did was, by definition, pure. Someone who believes they cannot act badly lacks the constraint on behaviour which the fear that they might would otherwise impose on them. They believe, particularly, that they cannot lie, so shading the truth can easily become a habit. Again, the link to hubris is obvious: to believe that you are always good removes an impediment to behaving hubristically. In 2003, Blair grandiosely boasted that he personally had 'got rid of four dictators in Kosovo, Sierra Leone, Afghanistan and Iraq'. But the Kosovo operation in 1999 was a NATO operation, reinforced by Russian diplomacy; in Sierra Leone in 2000 Blair did have a personal success with the UK keeping control of its forces, albeit while working closely with UN forces; Afghanistan was initially in 2001 a CIA operation, with US Special Forces; in Iraq there was US domination and, despite the UK being the largest coalition partner, Blair did not confront Bush, instead while talking tough always backing down. Few saw more of Blair's relationship with Bush than Colin Powell, but he told Blair's sympathetic biographer, Anthony Seldon:

> In the end Blair would always support the President. I found this very surprising. I never really understood why Blair seemed to be in such harmony with Bush. I thought, well, the Brits haven't been attacked on 9/11. How did he reach the point that he sees Saddam as such a threat? Blair would express his concerns, but he would never lie down on the railroad tracks. Jack [Straw] and I would get him all pumped up about an issue. And he'd be ready to say, 'Look here, George.' But as soon as he saw the President he would lose his steam.

This can be read as weakness, but more likely it represents the missionary zeal of two people bound together by a project of transcending importance for each of them and blind to its complexities.

Linked to this is the nature of Blair's religious beliefs and the particular way he sees his relationship with God. Blair is a very convinced Christian whose Anglo-Catholic faith mattered deeply to him when in office. He tended to keep quiet about it publicly since in Britain a politician playing on their religion is definitely not an electoral asset, as it sometimes appears to be in the United States. However, in a television interview on 4 March 2006, and perhaps because he knew he was committed to stepping down as Prime Minister before another general election, Blair abandoned his reservations in talking about his religion and said, in relation to Iraq, 'If you have faith about these things then you realise that judgement is made by other people. If you believe in God, it's made by God as well.' The implication is that the accountability that really mattered to Blair as Prime Minister was not to the electorate but to God. If, however, he was already convinced of his own goodness, that accountability was not constraining as it would be to the believer aware of his own capacity to sin. The belief in God becomes a spur to hubris rather than a constraint on it. After he ceased to be Prime Minister Blair announced he had become a Catholic and then lectured at an American university on his faith and established the Tony Blair Faith Foundation. After a fund-raising event for this an American priest who I had known over the years and who had attended to assess the appeal on behalf of a rich friend, summed up the appeal up by saying, 'In my experience, those who start believing they can bring the great religions of the world together end up inventing their own religion.'

Another area to consider in assessing Blair's conduct of the war in Iraq relates to his health. On Sunday 19 October 2003 it was leaked to the press that Blair had attended Stoke Mandeville Hospital, near to Chequers, his official country home. Only later was this news officially confirmed by 10 Downing Street. Blair was then transferred to west London's Hammersmith Hospital to be treated, allegedly, for only a commonplace increase in his heartbeat. Later that night, when Blair returned to No. 10, it was stated that he had never suffered from heart problems before. But it was also announced that at Hammersmith Hospital he had had cardiac shock treatment, or cardioversion. In as much as a medical condition was named at all, it was referred to as a 'supra-ventricular tachycardia', a term which in this context was ambiguous. It meant either a relatively benign arrhythmia (an abnormality of the heartbeat), or something from a range of arrhythmias not so benign such as atrial fibrillation and atrial flutter, caused when the arrhythmia has its origins above the ventricles.

Some cardiologists were surprised that the Prime Minister had had cardioversion for what was an apparently benign condition and felt his real condition was likely to be atrial flutter. The suspicion that there might be something more serious about Blair's medical state was strengthened by Bill Clinton blurting out, 'As soon as I heard what happened I called to check he was OK. We had a talk and he sounded in good shape ... I've known about this for a long time. He told me about it quite a few years ago.' In a later TV documentary, Tina Weaver, editor of the *Sunday Mirror*, described 'being at a restaurant in Barcelona, days after the Prime Minister's heart scare last October', when Clinton arrived. She said:

I told him who I was and asked if he had heard if the Prime Minister had had a heart scare. He was very relaxed about it and said, yes, he had and indeed had spoken to him. Then he went on to say he wasn't surprised, it was a condition he knew about and in fact the Prime Minister had told him that he suffered from this condition some years earlier and it was brought on by a combination of too little sleep and too much caffeine.

On 27 October a statement was issued from No. 10 to deal with Clinton's claim: 'The Prime Minister did not have, and had never had, a heart condition, nor had he had this complaint before.' Clinton's claim was also flatly contradicted by Blair on BBC Radio 2. Asked whether he had told Clinton that he had a heart condition, Blair said, 'No, this is the first time this has ever happened to me. I'm told it is a relatively common thing to have happen to you and it is a relatively minor treatment.' We now know from the diary of a senior Cabinet minister, David Blunkett, that two days after treatment, 'Tony told me when I spoke to him on the telephone that he had had the heart problem, on and off, for fifteen years, but this time he had to go into hospital, which was why it became public knowledge'.

On 4 November 2003 I talked to Blair at a diplomatic reception. I noted down afterwards that he was clearly very worried and that he had aged very much, deep in his face, the contours of which seemed to have changed. He also appeared to have lost weight. The suspicion that Blair was covering up a longstanding heart condition also increased when a journalist working undercover, as a footman, in Buckingham Palace wrote in the *Daily Mirror* on 20 November that the Queen had asked a page to delay dinner until she had heard that the Prime Minister's treatment was successful. She was purported to have said to the page, 'He's told me he's had similar complications in the past,' reinforcing Clinton's claim. Downing Street responded to this by repeating, 'The Prime Minister does not have, and never has had, a heart condition.' But one book has claimed that a previous episode had transpired as early as 1997. This may have stemmed from the report in the *Guardian* on 21 November 2003 that 'a well-placed source from the Prime Minister's Sedgefield constituency claimed that the Labour leader suffered palpitations or a similar condition before the 1997 election and had sought medical treatment in north-east England for a heart ailment when Labour was still in opposition though he believed the problem was not serious'.

It was then suddenly announced, on 1 October 2004, that Blair had been taken back to Hammersmith Hospital for a catheter ablation, as a daytime procedure. Blair's doctor described the condition only as an 'irregular heartbeat' but the hospital called it atrial flutter. The likelihood is that the ablation, involving a radio frequency burn in a localised part of the heart, has been completely successful.

There has been speculation that for some years Blair had been on beta-blocking drugs for his heart arrhythmia. I asked a scientist with long experience of these drugs whether he knew of any long-term side effects that might predispose Blair to hubris in that the normal alerting mechanism in the body to strain and stress was being damped down. He claimed to have had a similar request from the Foreign Office about Saddam Hussein! His answer was that he could not find anyone who has reported studies on the long-term psychological effects of beta blockers, nor any on their acute psychological effects, but there were plenty of anecdotes. One of his favourites came from a professional concert pianist, who told him how emotionally unbalanced his performances used to be before and after the interval, prior to taking beta blockers. Before beta blockers he would play the first half with such passion that, by the interval, he was emotionally exhausted. Going into the second half after a shower and a quick change, he felt emotionally flat. After taking the beta blocker propranolol he found that he could play the first half in better intellectual control; he no longer felt emotionally drained, giving, for him, a more satisfying second half. The result was a more even performance intellectually. He wasn't sure which experience he preferred or whether the audience noticed!

One doctor wrote to me speculating on the medication Blair might have been taking, that having watched him on television for many years, he had noticed how his receding hairline had moved forward and then, after his announcement of his treatment for tachycardia, had moved back again. The doctor wondered whether Blair might have been taking Regaine for hair growth, which has a recorded side effect of triggering tachycardias. He postulated that when the doctors realised he was on Regaine, they told him to stop using it. Whatever the truth, the likelihood is that it is Blair's personality rather than his heart condition that has contributed to him developing what I have called 'hubris syndrome', a condition which I explain in more detail in Chapter 11.

It had become ever more obvious that Blair covered up the true nature of his illness and misled the electorate as to its seriousness. One investigative journalist, Peter Oborne, labelled it deceit. Blair was not the first and will probably not be the last head of government to do this. It was, however, emblematic of his tenure at No. 10 and compatible with hubris that he should have embarked on a course of deception.

Meanwhile for Blair, nemesis in 2007 could not be avoided. The Parliamentary Labour Party had under Gordon Brown's guidance pushed him out of office at least a year earlier than he had expected or planned for. The man who had won power in 1997 with a landslide majority of 179 seats was leaving after bequeathing his party appalling results in the May 2007 national elections in Scotland and Wales and local elections in England. While such mid-term election results have often been turned around in the UK, Blair's self-indulgent long goodbye, in search of a legacy, damaged all around him. Never before had any British Prime Minister started so well and yet ended so badly. Blair eventually stepped down on 27 June 2007. His successor, Gordon Brown, had an impressive honeymoon and was tempted to call an early election in September. But within two months the country faced the economic legacy of the Blair/Brown years under the umbrella of the international banking crisis and the credit crunch.

Its particular UK component had its origins in the public expenditure levels from 2002 until 2007. In the *Financial Times* of 1 July 2009, in an article entitled 'Britain has sunk itself deep into a fiscal black hole', John Kay argued 'even if there were a rapid economic recovery there would still be a large deficit. At least half of the current deficit will need to be eliminated by cuts in public expenditure and increases in tax rates. These will have to be very substantial.'

My fear is that the British people are being misled, in the run-up to the general election, as to the depth of the fiscal deficit, likely to be more than 12% of national income. After that election there will be the days of reckoning and I believe whichever party forms the government, even if they have a majority of MPs, they would be wise to try and enlist the support of other parties so that the government can speak with the authority of having the support of over 50% of the electorate.

# 10

# The financial and economic crisis of 2007 onwards

On 20 June 2007 Gordon Brown, after ten years as Chancellor of the Exchequer and seven days from becoming Prime Minister, made remarks that were very revealing. He talked of 'the beginning of a new golden age for the City of London'. Having boasted for some time of ending 'boom and bust', in this speech he claimed that during the first decade of the twenty-first century, out of 'the greatest restructuring of the global economy, perhaps even greater than the Industrial Revolution, a new world order was created'. Within months banks were being nationalised or bailed out and the world was facing its worst economic crisis for more than seventy years. Soon over half of British banks were either nationalised or had the government as their largest shareholder.

Yet despite that hubristic quotation I do not think that, unlike Tony Blair, he has hubris syndrome nor that hubris is the biggest problem Brown faces as Prime Minister. There is too much inner tension brought out from self-doubt in his personality. He finds it difficult to admit mistakes, not because he is super-confident but because there is an underlying lack of confidence. One senses he knows when he has made mistakes and regrets them, but he believes as a tribal politician and a practitioner of the black arts of politics, mistakenly, that the admission of error is a demonstration of weakness, so any apology has to be dragged out of him. His bitten-down nails reflect an inner anxiety and his mood changes, which make him difficult to work with, are compensated by real knowledge and a dedicated work ethic. He is a very complex and at times charming man, eaten into by ambition.

To Brown's credit, he had always recognised as Chancellor that joining the eurozone was not in British interests and that we needed to have a flexible exchange rate. The ability to depreciate by something between 25 per cent and 30 per cent during the current crisis has been one of the advantages the UK has within the EU. It means our economic crisis is more manageable than our fiscal crisis, which promises to remain dire for some years ahead. Brown's replacement as Chancellor, Alistair Darling, had the courage to warn in a deliberately frank interview early on that we were arguably facing the worst crisis in sixty years and then, when criticised by briefings from No. 10, compounded his offence by saying the worst in 100 years. He showed himself to be cool under fire. His and Brown's problem was that when the banks ran out of money for the second time they took on vast liabilities through the so-called Asset Protection Scheme. The UK from then on had to maintain international confidence in the manner and the timing of large public spending cutbacks and raised taxes so that it could fund its fiscal deficit, otherwise it risked its AAA credit rating and being forced to the IMF.

My contacts with Gordon Brown over the years have been minimal. But he did ask to see me on Wednesday 12 September 2007 in 10 Downing Street, the day before, with great publicity, he saw Margaret Thatcher. By Friday evening, while travelling between Chicago and Athens, I was being inundated with telephone calls from Sunday newspaper journalists who had been variously briefed by No. 10 that we had talked and that I was returning to the Labour Party. I had to correct this impression, which was untrue, while indicating that I wished Gordon Brown well personally.

In our long conversation it became pretty clear that Brown wanted me to advise him on the NHS, in effect as part of his GOAT – government of all the talents – initiative. For many good reasons it was not something that I was ready to undertake. Devoted though I am to the NHS, I doubted I would have had real influence, and I was out of date. Three years' virtual absence over Yugoslavia meant that my knowledge of the NHS was much less than it had been. Also Labour seemed to have moved too far from the internal market I had espoused in the 1980s to an external market in the NHS. In any case there was part of me that was disillusioned with Labour and wanted to remain independent. I had thought that New Labour might carry the flag for what the SDP would have been. But on that score Blair's record left me totally despairing. Furthermore, too many of my good friends had long been very critical of Gordon Brown and believed that he was not going to be a good Prime Minister. Strangely, I did not share their views and hoped he would return New Labour to social democracy. They said that I was too optimistic about his personality, his style of working and his readiness to return to Cabinet government, that he was too embroiled in the presidential model after having, in effect, operated a joint presidency, at the expense of the Cabinet, with Tony Blair. At times during the banking crisis the UK seemed to be benefiting from Brown's long Treasury experience and he gathered around him a good team for the G20 summit in London. He wisely used Mark Malloch Brown, an experienced UN diplomat and former SDP candidate. He was a successful part of GOAT initiative, as was Ara Darzi, a distinguished surgeon, who added valuable expertise. The concept should be maintained.

Sadly my friends' fears have been shown to be more justified than my optimism. Ironically Brown appeared to try to be the 'heir to Blair' at the very time when David Cameron was wisely moving steadily away from that absurd mantra, which he unwisely embraced on becoming Conservative leader. By 2009 even Polly Toynbee, whose important contribution within the SDP is described in this book, had also changed her mind about Gordon Brown. Polly, who never wanted to merge with the Liberals after 1987 and went to work for the BBC before returning to the *Guardian*, had become the best and most committed advocate for New Labour throughout its existence. She also, while becoming disappointed with Blair, had been very hopeful about Brown, extolling SureStart and believing that his social policy was redistributing income. She undoubtedly influenced my views of him. Yet on 12 May 2009 she wrote, devastatingly:

> Politics tests character, often to destruction. The character of some ministers, their shadows and MPs of all parties has been wrecked by exposure of their expenses. How can those caught pilfering from the public purse denounce benefit fraud? How can those with state-purchased silk cushions support the cash-limited social fund that denies beds and blankets to families sleeping on bare boards? MPs with fingers in the till will blush to justify paying the unemployed £60.50 a week to live on. Nor can they rant convincingly at City greed or tax-dodgers fleeing to Guernsey.

The one character who has been tested to final destruction is Gordon Brown. The music stopped on his watch, first for the economy and now MPs' sleaze, for which the government of the day takes most blame. Labour used to lay claim to higher moral ground, while the right always said greed was the motor of growth. When he first talked of his moral compass, Brown should have cleaned up party funding, MPs' expenses and honours – and linked these reforms with curbs on the power that money breathes over the nation's affairs. The expenses mess would not be fatal if the Prime Minister were upright and strong. But Labour is already dangling over a cliff, and this affair prises its fingers off the edge.

It's all over for Brown and Labour. The abyss awaits.

In that same article Polly called for Labour to change its leader before the election. This was, I thought, a very dubious tactic, and I had expressed that view in the summer of 2008 at the Edinburgh Book Festival. Parties cannot change their leaders so as to have three Prime Ministers in one parliament without losing their credibility with the electorate. Brown was entitled to fight to survive.

As the country looked over the abyss it was not just the Labour Party but the whole body politic which was being called into question. The British people were angry. We suddenly found ourselves with a dysfunctional government and Parliament. Even at the depths of my disillusionment with party politics in 1981, when I broke away from the Labour Party to help create the SDP, I did not doubt, however much I disagreed with some aspects of their policy, that the then Conservative government, in the midst of an economic crisis, could function effectively. In many ways the Falklands War came to the rescue of Margaret Thatcher. It gave her opportunity to demonstrate, after the mistakes that brought about the invasion, that she was a highly effective leader. It looked at one stage in June 2009 as though Gordon Brown would be thrown out, but the Cabinet with one exception looked after their own careers. Fear of losing an autumn general election, after performing worse than UKIP in the European elections with only 16 per cent and losing control of all its remaining county councils in England, meant that Brown hung onto power by his bitten-down fingernails. The country needed a general election in late October or early November 2009. But it looked likely that Labour would carry on until near the latest possible date in June

2010. A wise Prime Minister would have called an election after the various MPs who needed to be held to account for the mishandling of their expenses and allowances had either resigned or been deselected by their own constituency parties. Once done, an October election would have served the best interests of fiscal and economic management, but also, I suspect, the Labour Party. For the alternative, postponing by-elections at all costs in Labour MPs' seats where they should have been kicked out, would only compound public anger. Whatever happens, the Blair/Brown presidential period, sadly, for it promised well, will have turned out to contain fatal flaws of both personality and politics, and thirteen years looks likely to be more than enough for the electorate. Predicting elections months ahead is a mug's game but I began to want a balanced Parliament just as I had in 1992 with the SDP holding the balance. The question mark hung over whether the Liberal Democrats would be up to the challenge.

All one can hope is that the next government, even if it is a Conservative one with a working majority, is capable of re-establishing trust and that the years of spin and sleaze, hubristic incompetence and a culture where our own British politicians have become strangers to the truth are speedily brought to an end. We need procedures to ensure that the next government, whatever its composition, has the length of time and the stability to come up with the hard-headed decisions necessary to restore confidence in the economy, fund the fiscal crisis that will haunt any new administration and restore the authority of Cabinet government within a parliamentary democracy. I elaborate on such a reform programme later but before I do this I would like to analyse the deeper questions raised about our leaders, whether in banking, business, finance or politics.

Since leaving active international politics in 1995 I have spent most of my working time in business, initially as a non-executive director at Coats Viyella plc, and also as chairman of Yukos International, the offshoot of what was a major Russian oil company. Since 1996 I have been a director of Abbott Laboratories, a very large healthcare company in Chicago, and associated with the same Russian steel company and iron ore mine in which the British company which I chaired, Middlesex Holdings plc, was an investor. I was also on the advisory board of the private equity firm Terra Firma for five years. This has given me a fascinating new international career. I have experienced how US business adapted to the Enron scandal and in its aftermath introduced new regulatory procedures for audit committees and main company boards in the Sarbanes–Oxley legislation. During all this time I have become well aware that hubris is a problem not just for political leaders but for banking and business as well. It is a condition that does not pick its professions. And just as the effects of it can prove deeply damaging to good government and public welfare, so too can it have devastating consequences for companies and for the wider economy. I believe that for all the money and time business spends on risk management, building complex models and using quantitative statistical methods, it needs to devote as much effort to human resources, personality and behavioural assessment. In March 2009 Stefan Stern in the *Financial Times* reviewed a lucid and technical analysis of risk management in the *Harvard Business Review* by Professor Rene Stulz. He added his own comment: 'True understanding of risk also requires a maturity of outlook, an ability to see the big picture, and deep experience. This last is a rare commodity; impossible to fake and acquired only over time.'

I have never doubted that the hubris which I have described developing in Tony Blair at the time of the Iraq War develops also in some business leaders. In the light of the financial cataclysm which has wreaked such havoc in the world since 2007 and whose full economic consequences have still not been uncovered, it is abundantly clear that some of the leaders in the world of finance and banking have succumbed to hubris and will do so again in the next economic cycle unless we deal with the problem at its root.

A study on General Motors published in 1991 spoke of business leaders who deceive themselves and distance themselves from reality. And it said, 'The Greeks called this hubris and they knew that the gods, whom we might refer to as reality, do not stand for it. They demand humility.' The issue for those who are interested in human risk management is: how can you identify these people in time to mentor them and constrain any propensity they may have? And how do you get rid of them from their position as president, chairman or chief executive if there is no chance of constraining their hubris? In my experience the non-executive board members see this as one of their major responsibilities, for in many respects only they have both the authority and the knowledge to act. As well summarised by David Brooks in an article in the global *New York Times* on 20 May 2009, wise non-executives are well aware that research shows that the 'CEOs that are most likely to succeed are humble, diffident, relentless and a bit unidimensional. They are often not the most exciting people to be around.' The market seems to want a CEO 'to be resolute, even at the cost of some flexibility' with a relentless commitment to incremental efficiency gains. Quoting a study by Steven Kaplan and others, 'Which CEO Characteristics and Abilities Matter?', Brooks identified the traits that correlated most powerfully with success as being attention to detail, persistence, efficiency, analytic thoroughness and the ability to work long hours. In his article, entitled 'Dullness Wins', Brooks warns against fame, recognition and awards.

The American psychologist Robert Hare, who has done more than anyone to bring rigour to the study of psychopathy, a condition related to recognised disorders such as anti-social personality disorder and involving severe emotional detachment and consequent moral emptiness, has written, alarmingly, that business is the most agreeable vocation for psychopaths. In his book *Snakes in Suits: When Psychopaths Go to Work*, Hare and his co-author, Paul Babiak, point out how difficult it is to spot the psychopath coming. They argue that some core psychopathic personality traits may seem initially attractive to recruiting employers. Charm is one. Another is that 'some hiring managers may mistakenly attribute "leadership" labels to what are, in actuality, psychopathic behaviours'. Furthermore, the tendency of many businesses to abandon the old, massive, bureaucratic organisa-tional structures in which people got on by not rocking the boat, in favour of what has been called a 'transitional' organisational style – one that has fewer layers, simpler systems and controls and more freedom to make decisions – encourages the recruitment of people who can 'shake trees'. As Hare and Babiak put it, in this changed business climate 'egocentricity, callousness, and insensitivity suddenly became acceptable trade-offs in order to get the talents and skills needed to survive in an accelerated, dispassionate business world'. Concomitantly, individuals who like to break rules and enjoy manipulation – that is to say, a group that includes psychopaths – are attracted to such work.

It would be a lot easier if there were as simple a test for psychopathy as may well be developing for assessing more beneficial traits in potential executives, such as levels of confidence and the propensity to take risk, both vital elements in any successful business leader. These qualities are, in part, related to levels of testosterone and it is claimed that the levels in any individual are determined by the degree of exposure to it in the womb. What is extraordinary is that this itself is detectable in what is known as the 2D:4D ratio – the relative length of the index finger to the fourth finger. Research on this has been conducted by John Coates, a former Wall Street trader interested in the boundaries between economics and neurology, together with Mark Gurnell, an endocrinologist, and Aldo Rustichini, an economist. They claim in *Proceedings of the National Academy of Sciences* that the advantage gained by those with a low 2D:4D score (and so high testosterone) derives from two things. First, high pre-natal testosterone shapes brains with quicker reactions and a greater ability to concentrate; and it amplifies what they call 'rutting stag' behaviour, which perhaps does not need defining. It would be very convenient if personality disorders, let alone hubris syndrome, could be detected simply by measuring the relative length of fingers or some such unequivocal measure. But it is most unlikely such a simple test will ever be devised. Nonetheless, there are tests which can alert companies in some cases to the possibility that young executives may suffer from most orthodox personality disorders that could later wreak havoc in the company if the sufferers were allowed to exercise greater power.

But there is another difficulty which business has in relation to hubris which in my experience the political world to some extent escapes. Both attract people with a propensity to hubris and who already may exhibit hubristic traits. But the modern commercial world is *collectively* more susceptible to hubris, making it harder to single out *individuals* who are especially hubristic. As Andrew Jackson, professor of economics at the University of Warwick, wrote in a letter to the *Financial Times* in March 2009, about herd behaviour:

> Herding happens when *relative* position matters. Think of sheep in a field or fish in a pool. They cluster together because safety from outside predators comes from being on the inside of the group.

Although most do not recognise it in themselves, human beings are like other animals . . . Homebuyers paid extraordinarily high prices for houses, even though not justified by fundamentals, because they felt they were trailing behind the Joneses. Brokers sold unsound mortgages not because they were convinced of the absolute merits of those products but because they had to keep up with rival brokers. Most economists kept quiet about the house price bubble; they were frightened of speaking up.

This collective susceptibility operates at two levels. It operates globally within economies as a whole. What else is a bubble? Indeed one might say that the expression 'boom and bust', which Gordon Brown believed he had permanently overcome, embodies the ineradicable condition of capitalist economies. It is merely a modern way of talking about hubris and nemesis in business.

But collective hubris can operate also at the company level. Collective hubris at both levels provides camouflage to individuals working within the business world who may, in addition, be susceptible to the syndrome themselves. The reason why the business world is vulnerable to collective hubris is clear enough. The goals of business, unlike the goals of politics, are defined almost exclusively in terms of growth. Economic growth and profit are reflected in bonuses to employees and in dividends to shareholders, increased share price, increased salaries for those who work in the enterprise and beneficially in some companies in increased investment in corporate social responsibility.

Expanding the business and taking risks to achieve higher profits motivates business people. Of course there are politicians who are drawn to similarly expansive goals and evince the same willingness to take risks to achieve them; but what politicians primarily seek is re-election and that may often lead them to put aside such goals and to eschew risk-taking. Doing little or even on rare occasions nothing is sometimes a wise course in politics in a way that is rarely the case in business. Consequently hubristic leaders incapable of being cautious tend to stand out in politics and in many instances that brings, at least initially, success, whereas they can be camouflaged in business.

A good example of collective hubris operating at company level is the case of Enron. It was among the first and certainly the highest profile of the large diversified companies to emerge in the era of deregulation in the 1980s. Being a new sort of animal it was able to develop its own culture. And it is clear from the testimony of many who worked within it – testimony forthcoming at the trials of its leaders after the company's collapse in 2001 – that it was a highly hubristic culture. In America some of the most spectacular collapses from 2007 onwards are likely to be openly examined in the courts when people, such as the key decision maker in Lehman Brothers, may turn out to be charged for specific offences. In the UK, in my view mistakenly, the law looks like being sidelined by a belief that we should turn the page and not look back.

An interesting new book is *Think Again: Why Good Leaders Make Bad Decisions and How to Keep It from Happening to You*, in which the authors identify four common sources of error: misleading experiences, misleading prejudgements, inappropriate self-interest and inappropriate attachments. In the case of Sir Fred Goodwin, chief executive of the Royal Bank of Scotland, we saw how past experiences might give misleading guidance in making decisions: Goodwin's success in the NatWest takeover appears to have encouraged him and the RBS chairman to make the reckless decision on ABN Amro. With regard to misleading prejudgements – that is to say, fallibility in recognising patterns – at HBOS Peter Cummings, the head of corporate lending, was apparently unable to 'read' the situation and went on lending even after the world had started to fall in and Lord Stevenson, the chairman, and Andy Hornby, the chief executive, failed to rein him in.

With reference to inappropriate self-interest one needs in general to refer only to the levels of business leaders' remuneration, especially the method behind bonus payments where the link to personal performance is weak. But for those with hubris syndrome it amounts to very much more. Their identification of themselves with the organisations they run, one of the fourteen identifiable symptoms of hubris syndrome detailed in the next chapter, means that they see no difference between their own self-interest and the interests of their own organisations, a truly frightening condition with obviously potentially ruinous consequences for the organisations they lead. In relation to inappropriate attachments, Andrew Fastow, who became Enron's chief financial officer in 1998, developed an excessive attachment to the company, whereby he saw himself as a 'hero' to Enron, and this led him to take decisions which helped cause the downfall of his company and sent him to prison.

Contempt of court is very serious because it undermines an essential safeguard in our democracy, namely that the truth and only the truth is told in court. Even if it involves only a relatively small point it should always, in my view, be pursued in the courts as a deterrent. This is particularly important where it involves high-profile leaders. Contemptuous behaviour often goes with hubris and was something the Greeks focused attention on. Contempt is hubristic because the risks entailed in lying suggest the recklessness of someone who has lost touch with reality and the dangers that lie ahead, such as being found out by a court. That loss of touch with reality is itself one of the symptoms of someone in thrall to hubris. The penalty for such loss of touch with reality can be nemesis.

Lord Browne, the former chief executive of BP, discovered this when he invoked the power of a court of law. In this case Mr Justice Eady referred to Browne's 'willingness to tell a deliberate lie to the court'. He said of the lie that 'it may be that it should be addressed as contempt or as some other form of criminal offence', although he added that he had decided not to refer the case to the Attorney General for possible prosecution. He did say, however, 'I am not prepared to make allowances for a "white lie" told to the court in circumstances such as these – especially by a man who prays in aid his reputation and distinction, and refers to the various honours he has received under the present government, when asking the court to prefer his account of what took place.' When Browne's attempts to overthrow this ruling were rejected by the House of Lords, and the injunction was lifted, he resigned at once from BP on 2 May 2007.

Yet in Browne's case, as in the case of President Clinton, lying about sexual risk-taking is often judged as falling into a separate category. A majority of the public seem to understand this and judge a leader's competence and claims to stay in office as a somewhat separate issue. To some extent they accept that lying over sexual activity, even in court, is different. This was evident during Clinton's impeachment procedures. Action under impeachment was the only sanction available; not to have invoked it risked condoning the offence but, in my view wisely, the politicians invoked the impeachment procedure but, as they were entitled to do, used their common sense in reflecting the American people's toleration of Clinton's false responses in his deposition. At the end of Clinton's period in office he accepted a two-year suspension of his law licence in Arkansas and a $25,000 fine.

Although I have no further evidence to corroborate the point, it is at least possible that it may have been the detection of hubristic traits in Lord Browne, even before the legal case, that brought Peter Sutherland, as BP's chairman, to argue against extending Browne's term of office. If that was so, the outcome of the law case retrospectively justified Sutherland's determination. According to the *Guardian* of 9 March 2009, Sutherland cited the relative recovery in the fortunes and reputation of BP since Browne's departure as a reason for making performance-related share issues to his successor and snubbed Browne by excluding him from the incentive payment for which he was eligible for 2006. Browne, nevertheless, it is claimed, has an annual pension of just over £1 million.

The BP example also raises questions about the value of separating the roles of chief executive and chairman, common in the UK but rare in the US. In the US more weight is given to the role of the senior non-executive and to boards meeting from time to time without the company's fully employed directors being present. Both systems have merits in my experience as a board member in the US and the UK. What is vital is that boards monitor very closely their chief executive and such other executives that operate with independent authority so that they can pick up hubristic traits and the signs and symptoms of gathering hubris. Alertness is particularly important when the company is seemingly doing well, because it is much easier to relax and miss signs which are more likely to be picked up if business is poor.

In the UK there are no grounds for general optimism about the vigilance of chairmen and directors. The RBS experience shows that Peter Sutherland, on the board of that company, seems to have played a less activist role as a non-executive. Also a recent survey of 375 company chairmen and non-executive directors, conducted by the remuneration consultants MM&K and the headhunters Hanson Green, revealed that a quarter of non-executives said they were unsure they could control chairmen and chief executives and a further 10 per cent said they knew they could not. Shareholders and the wider public cannot therefore rely on non-executives unless there are significant changes in the balance of power within the company.

The first and probably the biggest step in solving any problem is to recognise the nature of the problem. In her book *Fool's Gold: How Unrestrained Greed Corrupted a Dream, Shattered Global Markets and Unleashed a Catastrophe* Gillian Tett writes:

> I am still trying to make sense of the last decade of grotesque financial mistakes. I have found myself drawing on my training as a social anthropologist before I became a journalist . . . What social anthropology teaches is that nothing in society ever exists in a vacuum or in isolation . . . In recent years regulators, bankers, politicians, investors and journalists have all failed to employ truly holistic thought – to our collective cost. Bankers have treated their mathematical models as if they were an infallible guide to the future, failing to see that those models were based on a ridiculously limited set of data. A 'silo' mentality has come to rule inside banks, leaving different departments competing for resources, with shockingly little wider vision or oversight. The regulators who were supposed to oversee the banks have mirrored that silo pattern too, in their own fragmented practices. Most pernicious of all, financiers have come to regard banking as a silo in its own right, detached from the rest of society.

This acute analysis demonstrates how the recent banking and business crisis has many deeply rooted factors which have contributed to its emergence.

Politicians together with the Federal Reserve and the Bank of England curbed business excess and personal recklessness and exuberance after the economic troubles of the late 1920s and early 1930s with new regulations. Politicians in the US and the UK, urged by business, removed some of these curbs in the 1980s and 1990s. We are having to learn again from these mistakes but also from a culture that derided mutualism, friendly societies and co-operatives. One of my quirks is that I enjoy displaying my debit card to New Labour friends when paying for a meal, which reveals that my personal bank account has remained with the Co-operative Bank. All through the present financial crisis I never doubted the safety of my Co-op account but my wife's and our joint accounts with the Royal Bank of Scotland were for months in grave doubt.

The recent massive global financial bubble, from the bursting of which we are now all suffering, is a clear case of collective hubris. When I asked a banker friend why no one had been able to blow the whistle on what was going on his answer was simple. He said that anyone in banking who had had the temerity to argue that his bank was following the wrong course would simply have lost his job and there is some evidence that this did happen to a few whistleblowers. What makes the recent collective hubris so alarming is that it was also so blind. Those participating at high levels in the financial bubble now confess, as, before, many of them admitted privately, that they simply did not understand the game that they were playing. The complexity of the securitised financial world, collateral debt obligations, credit default swaps, was beyond many people's comprehension.

Yet not all bankers were blind. I asked the former chairman and chief executive of Standard Chartered Bank, Lord Davies of Abersoch, now a government minister, and still giving, I am sure, wise advice, whether I should become involved with a hedge fund. 'Do you understand it?' was the answer. Since I did not, I declined to get involved and now thank my lucky stars.

Businessmen become susceptible collectively to what Keynes called 'animal spirits'. Alan Greenspan, the former chairman of the US Federal Reserve Board, called it 'irrational exuberance' – note the word 'irrational' – and has had the grace to apologise for his own excess, not something we have yet heard from many politicians. Yet booms and busts go with the territory of risk-taking capitalism: sweep it all aside and you are left merely with a bureaucracy.

Complacency and specific mistakes of policy and regulation are being glossed over in global reports. We already have the IMF's views in their published discussion papers that 'at the root of market failure was optimism bred by a long period of high growth, low real interest rates and volatility'. The lesson the IMF wants world leaders to learn is that 'flawed incentives and interconnections in modern financial systems can have huge macroeconomic consequences'. These are, however, mere generalisations. What is needed are specific solutions and sanctions, otherwise we can be certain that the 'animal spirits' will return. Greed, hubris and exuberance are kept in check – we know from experience – by the fear of disgrace, bankruptcy, prison and penury. Such sanctions are national, not global. They bite, the rest is talk. The Americans understand this better than the British.

It is very, very depressing to see the politicians who presided over this bubble, Presidents Clinton and George W. Bush and Prime Ministers Blair and Brown, pass the buck to the bankers and hide their responsibility for the 'light touch' regulation of the Anglo-Saxon financial service model behind the constant stress on a global crisis. Independence for the Bank of England in fixing interest rates had considerable merit. But the former governor of the Bank, Eddie George, was right to tell Gordon Brown and Tony Blair that their decision in 1997 to also deprive the Bank of its regulatory role was wrong. In retrospect, if George had followed his initial instinct and resigned over the issue of regulation it probably would not have been introduced. If the Bank of England had kept its regulatory function we would never have had the FSA with its damaging and inexperienced regulation. Canada was the exception in still retaining old banking legislation and traditional banking attitudes on the American continent over the last decade, demonstrating that not everything or everyone went global.

Both collective hubris and groupthink influenced politicians in their support for the heady economics of the booming mid to late 1980s through to the first seven years of the twenty-first century.

# 11

# The intoxication of power

The Pulitzer Prize-winning historian Barbara Tuchman wrote about power in *The March of Folly: From Troy to Vietnam*:

> We are less aware that it breeds folly; that the power to command frequently causes failure to think; that the responsibility of power often fades as its exercise augments. The overall responsibility of power is to govern as reasonably as possible in the interest of the state and its citizens. A duty in that process is to keep well-informed, to heed information, to keep mind and judgement open and to resist the insidious spell of wooden-headedness. If the mind is open enough to perceive that a given policy is harming rather than serving self-interest, and self-confident enough to acknowledge it, and wise enough to reverse it, that is a summit in the art of government.

The extent to which illness can affect the processes of government and the decision-making of heads of government, engendering folly, in the sense of foolishness, stupidity or rashness, was an issue I faced quite directly on a number of occasions once I became Foreign Secretary and it has interested me ever since. I was also fascinated by those leaders who were not ill and whose cognitive faculties functioned well but who appeared to develop a distinct condition, something that I have come to describe as 'hubris syndrome'. The behaviour of Tony Blair and George W. Bush described in Chapter 9 is not exceptional; acts of hubris are much more common in heads of government, whether democratic or not, than is often realised and hubris is a major contributor to Tuchman's definition of folly: 'a perverse persistence in a policy demonstrably unworkable or counter-productive'. She continued: 'Wooden-headedness, the source of self-deception is a factor that plays a remarkably large role in government. It consists in assessing a situation in terms of preconceived fixed notions while ignoring or rejecting any contrary signs . . . also the refusal to benefit from experience.' A characteristic of hubris is the inability to change direction because this involves admitting that one has made a mistake.

Bertrand Russell once wrote: 'The concept of "truth" as something dependent upon facts largely outside human control has been one of the ways in which philosophy hitherto has inculcated the necessary element of humility. When this check upon pride is removed, a further step is taken on the road towards a certain kind of madness – the intoxication of power.' Leaders intoxicated with pride and power are often described by laymen as having become 'unhinged', 'barmy', even 'mad', though these are not terms the medical profession would use about them. Democratic societies, especially those which have evolved out of absolute monarchies, have developed systems of checks and balances to try to protect themselves from such leaders. But these mechanisms – Cabinet, Parliament and the media – are not always effective. Under despotic leaders, where there are no democratic controls and few internal mechanisms, short of a coup, to remove them, there is often little that can be done. External condemnation and international sanctions have so far proved of only limited value while external military force has had questionable success.

Public discussion of illness in political leaders is reasonably straightforward when the illness is described as physical but is less so when it is described as mental. This is because, regarding mental illness, the general public and professional practitioners do not speak such a shared language as they do when talking about ordinary physical illness. There is also a mismatch between what the press and public talk about as mental illness and what the medical profession are ready to diagnose as mental illness. When the press and public use terms such as 'madness', 'lunacy', 'psychopath', 'megalomania' or 'hubris' – some or all of which have been used about despots as diverse as Adolf Hitler, Idi Amin, Mao Zedong, Slobodan Milošević, Robert Mugabe and Saddam Hussein on one hand and democratic leaders as different as Theodore Roosevelt, Lyndon Johnson, Richard Nixon, Margaret Thatcher, Tony Blair and George W. Bush on the other – they are using words which the medical profession has either long abandoned, redefined or severely restricted. Madness and lunacy for doctors are terms which have been totally replaced by whether a defined mental disorder is present. Psychopathic behaviour has been narrowed into specific personality disorders and megalomania to delusions of grandeur. Usually heads of government who are popularly dubbed as in some sense mad are not considered to have any mental illness by the medical profession.

It may be that people expect, even want, their leaders to be different from the norm, to display more energy, work longer hours, appear exhilarated by what they are doing and full of self-confidence – in short, to behave in ways that, taken beyond a certain point, a professional would mark down as manic. So long as those leaders are attempting to achieve what the public wishes them to achieve, it does not want to be told that they are mentally ill. But when those leaders lose the support of their public, it becomes a very different matter. Then the public is ready to use words long discarded by the profession to describe mental illness, as a means of expressing its objection to the way its leaders are behaving.

One such traditional term, no longer part of the professional lexicon but, it seems to me, a wholly legitimate word for the public to use, is 'megalomania'. I have described in Chapter 5 how I was myself charged with 'a display of megalomania', by Peter Jenkins in the *Guardian* in the summer of 1987. By using the term he was saying not simply that he thought what I was doing was wrong (in resisting the merger of the SDP with the Liberal Party) but that it was the consequence of a mental state I had got myself into at a time, after I had resigned as leader, when the SDP was breaking up. The medical profession may not use the term 'megalomania', but that does not mean that no one else should. Megalomania can be an occupational hazard for politicians, and its manifestation in a developed form, hubris, is a legitimate topic of study for the medical profession.

In February 2009, together with Jonathan Davidson, the emeritus professor of psychiatry at Duke University, North Carolina, I wrote an article for the journal *Brain* entitled 'Hubris Syndrome: An Acquired Personality Disorder?' Professor Davidson was the lead author of a study entitled 'Mental Illness in US Presidents between 1778 and 1974: A Review of Biographical Sources'. In our article Professor Davidson and I proposed fourteen potential symptoms which might trigger a diagnosis of hubris syndrome. These symptoms typically grow in strength the longer a political or business leader remains in post. Lists can be tedious, yet it is worth detailing what these fourteen potential symptoms are, not least because I suspect that some of them may well ring bells in others' minds, recalling powerful leaders they have had experience of themselves. Many overlap with well-recognised personality disorders, but we labelled some unique as being particular to hubris syndrome (HS).

1. A narcissistic propensity to see the world in which the leader operates primarily as an arena in which to exercise power and seek glory.
2. A predisposition to take actions which seem likely to cast the individual in a good light – i.e. in order to enhance their image.
3. A disproportionate concern with image and presentation.
4. A messianic manner of talking about current activities and a tendency to exaltation.
5. An identification with the nation or organisation which the individual leads to the extent that he or she regards his or her outlook and interests as identical with it (unique to HS).
6. A tendency to speak of himself or herself in the third person or to use the royal 'we' (unique to HS).
7. Excessive confidence in his or her own judgement and contempt for the advice or criticism of others.
8. An exaggerated self-belief, bordering on a sense of omnipotence, in what personally he or she can achieve.
9. A belief that rather than being accountable to the mundane court of colleagues or public opinion, he or she answers to a far grander court – History or God.
10. An unshakeable belief that in that court he or she will be vindicated (unique to HS).
11. A loss of contact with reality, often associated with progressive isolation.
12. Restlessness, recklessness and impulsiveness (unique to HS).
13. A tendency to allow his or her 'broad vision' of the moral rectitude of a proposed course to obviate the need to consider practicality, cost or outcomes (unique to HS).

14. 'Hubristic incompetence': not the ordinary incompetence where things go wrong because a faulty judgement or a miscalculation has been made, but where the incompetence is due to too much self-confidence that has led the leader not to worry about the nuts and bolts of a decision.

Very rarely in medicine has one patient all the possible symptoms or signs of a syndrome. In the case of hubris syndrome we believe the diagnosis can be made if three or more of these symptoms are manifest, and provided they include at least one of the five symptoms we classify as unique.

In our article, Professor Davidson and I depict hubris syndrome as developing only after power has been held for a period of time and in this sense it is acquired and follows a tradition which acknowledges the existence of pathological personality change, such as the enduring personality change after trauma called traumatic stress disorder. The nature of leaders who have the syndrome is that they are resistant to the very idea that they can be ill, for this is a sign of weakness. They are likely to be amongst the first to use the new category of so-called cognition enhancers. *Nature*, in an informal survey of its mainly scientific readers, found that one in five of 1,400 respondents were taking stimulants and wake-promoting agents such as methylphenidate and modafinil, or beta blockers for non-medical reasons. To the extent that hubris syndrome shares common elements with narcissistic and sociopathic disorders, such as impaired decision-making, poor impulse control, poor modulation of aggression and lack of appropriate empathy, the findings of altered dopaminergic, noradrenergic and serotonergic function in the brain in these conditions could all be relevant.

'Hubris' is not yet a medical term. As mentioned briefly in Chapter 10, the most basic meaning developed in ancient Greece, simply as a description of an act: a hubristic act was one in which a powerful figure, puffed up with overweening pride and self-confidence, treated others with insolence and contempt. He seemed to get kicks from using his power to treat others in this way, but such dishonouring behaviour was strongly condemned in ancient Greece. In a famous passage from Plato's *Phaedrus*, a predisposition to hubris is defined: 'But when desire irrationally drags us toward pleasures and rules within us, its rule is called excess [*hubris*].' Plato saw this 'rule of desire' as something irrational that drags men into doing the wrong thing through acts of hubris. In his *Rhetoric*, Aristotle picks up the element of desire Plato identifies in hubris and argues that the pleasure someone seeks from an act of hubris lies in showing himself as superior. 'That is why the young and the wealthy are given to insults [*hubristai*, i.e. being hubristic]; for they think that, in committing them [acts of hubris], they are showing superiority.'

But it was in drama rather than philosophy that the notion was developed further to explore the patterns of hubristic behaviour, its causes and consequences. A hubristic career proceeded along something like the following course. The hero wins glory and acclamation by achieving unwonted success against the odds. The experience then goes to his head: he begins to treat others, mere ordinary mortals, with contempt and disdain and he develops such confidence in his own ability that he begins to think himself capable of anything. This excessive self-confidence leads him into misinterpreting the reality around him and into making mistakes. Eventually he gets his comeuppance and meets his nemesis, which destroys him. Nemesis is the name of the goddess of retribution, and often in Greek drama the gods arrange nemesis because a hubristic act is seen as one in which the perpetrator tries to defy the reality ordained by them. The hero committing the hubristic act seeks to transgress the human condition, imagining himself to be superior and to have powers more like those of the gods. But the gods will have none of that: so it is they who destroy him. The moral is that we should beware of allowing power and success to go to our heads, making us too big for our boots.

Power is a heady drug which not every political leader has the necessary rooted character to handle: a combination of common sense, humour, decency, scepticism and even cynicism that treats power for what it is, a privileged opportunity to serve and to influence – and sometimes determine – the turn of events. The havoc which hubristic leaders can wreak is usually suffered by the people in whose name they govern. The virtues of a representative democracy lie in the scope it gives elected leaders to exercise real leadership and to show the decisiveness most voters prefer to hesitation, doubt and vacillation. But the exercise of that leadership needs to carry the trust of the electorate, which is usually lost when the leader crosses the line between competent decision-making and hubristic incompetence.

Curbing political leaders' hubristic behaviour has to rely on strengthening national democratic checks and balances. These have been built up over the years in both the US and the UK. The most important is vigilance and scrutiny by the Cabinet, for it comprises the people who see the most of their head of government's true conduct in office. The readiness of Cabinet ministers to resign on principle is very important. Elliot Richardson resigned as US Attorney General rather than sack Archibald Cox, the special prosecutor, as ordered by President Nixon. Secretary of State Cyrus Vance resigned when President Carter against his advice ordered helicopters into Iran in a botched attempt to extract American hostages. As leader of the House of Commons Robin Cook resigned in 2003 over the invasion of Iraq. Had Colin Powell or Jack Straw resigned before the Iraq War the effect might have been considerable. Elections offered the general public a chance to remove Bush and Blair from office in 2004 and 2005 respectively, but both men through their parties won re-election. Even so, in mid-term elections in 2006 and 2007 there was considerable dissatisfaction recorded with each leader.

Press criticism was muted in both countries before the war in Iraq and for a while afterwards, either because the newspapers agreed with the decision to go to war or because they were embarrassed, having predicted a much more difficult military operation for the invasion than proved to be the case. Also it was very difficult to predict the insurgency without knowing more about the paucity of aftermath planning. There should have been more investigative journalism on both sides of the Atlantic and greater scrutiny by Congress and Parliament of aftermath planning.

In a democracy nothing can replace knowing more about the true nature and character of the person we vote in to become head of our government. The press have a key role to play in this. The importance of character is made clear in the work of the Jungian analyst James Hillman. In his book *The Force of Character*, he writes, 'The limiting effect of one's innate image prevents that inflation, that trespassing or hubris that the classical world considered the worst of human errors. In this way character acts as a guiding force.' We need more clues, or alerting information, as to why some leaders may develop hubris when in office. The good sense of the people in a democracy is then more likely to ensure that those chosen have qualities in their character which are less likely to succumb to the intoxication of power.

The decisive leaders who are most likely to avoid hubris are usually those who are careful to retain a personal modesty as they stay in power, to keep as far as possible their previous lifestyle, to listen to those close to them – spouses, family and friends – and to eschew the trappings of power. These leaders try to consult carefully even if that process may not alter their opinions. They make errors of judgement but they are not often errors born of ignorance or stemming from contempt for the views of others. Above all, in a democracy, they accept that the inbuilt institutional checks and balances should be scrupulously respected and they make little or no attempt to circumvent them, whether in Cabinet or Parliament.

One of the best modern historians, David Reynolds, describes the hubris of leaders for whom their own personality is the key to their whole approach while writing about Neville Chamberlain:

> A well-intentioned leader convinced of his rightness, whose confidence in his powers of persuasion bordered on hubris. Who squeezed out critical professional advice, controlling policy and information from an inner circle, and who played his best hands too early at the conference table. A leader whose rhetoric became increasingly extravagant and deceptive, yet whose apparent naivety may have been the outward face of a man who knew he had gone too far to turn back. Who does all this remind us of? For all their differences, Tony Blair's approach to summitry had a good deal in common with that of Neville Chamberlain.

Other democratic heads of government who suffered from hubris syndrome in the last century, apart from Chamberlain and Blair (and George W. Bush), are David Lloyd George and Margaret Thatcher. Theodore Roosevelt and Lyndon Johnson were hubristic but have been diagnosed as having had bipolar disorder. Woodrow Wilson was hubristic but he suffered from arteriosclerosis, repeated strokes and dementia. Franklin Roosevelt looked as if he might be taken over by hubris when, in 1937, he fought and lost a battle with Congress over the Judicial Branch Reorganization Plan, affecting the nomination of justices to the Supreme Court. But, fortunately, he had a sense of humour and a certain cynicism, which meant he never lost his moorings in the democratic system. From 1941 to 1945 his personal determination, and his qualities of ruthlessness, guile and optimism, in part the product of his illnesses, gave him the political authority to mobilise his country for war and to win that war in the interests of the whole world. I do not believe Franklin Roosevelt developed hubris syndrome; nor did Winston Churchill.

One of the simplest and best safeguards against hubris syndrome developing while in office would be if more democracies would enact legislation to ensure that no head of government could remain in office for longer than a set number of years. After Franklin Roosevelt was elected for a fourth term it was widely felt in the United States that there should be legislation to limit a President's tenure in office. Accordingly, a law was passed limiting any President to two elected terms, meaning a maximum of eight years. In Britain, there is no legislative limit on how long a Prime Minister can serve. There is also no fixed term for a parliament, although no parliament can remain for longer than five years without a general election unless an extension is authorised by both the House of Commons and the House of Lords. Britain should legislate for fixed terms and to limit the number of years anyone can hold the office of Prime Minister to eight years of service, continuous or broken. Harold Wilson gave eight years' broken service. Margaret Thatcher, had she stepped down after eight years in May 1987, would have gone with her reputation very high and far better placed to be judged by history than after being removed by Conservative MPs in 1990. An eight-year limit would have meant that Tony Blair had to step down no later than May 2005, rather than being removed by MPs in 2007.

The environment of power that surrounds most leaders has considerable impact on even the most stable personality. They are sustained by an executive service, and have large numbers of advisers, chauffeur-driven cars, often with police outriders, and personal aircraft. This gives a standard of living that only a few very rich people in the world can match. But more importantly it creates an isolation which is now buttressed by a far greater personal security apparatus. When I first became an MP in 1966 I could walk along Downing Street without showing any pass, nod to the policeman on the door and enter No. 10 to be met inside by an attendant. At that time, only three Cabinet ministers had personal protection: the Prime Minister, the Foreign Secretary and the Home Secretary had one or sometimes two security officers at any public occasion. Now many more politicians have personal protection and the number of police involved has expanded greatly. Today Downing Street is closed to the public, and barriers are raised and lowered in the road to admit cars. To watch the arrival of a US President at No. 10 is to witness a military operation. Also the comings and goings of the Prime Minister involve a major display of police, arms and vehicles. We have, sadly but for the most part necessarily, come a long way in Britain since 1945, when Violet Attlee drove her husband in their own car to Buckingham Palace to receive the seal of office as Prime Minister from George VI.

There is a yet more insidious isolation and that is the hierarchical structure, the deference within government which bolsters the Prime Minister so that he or she can easily come to believe that they are not as other men and women. There is, therefore, a much greater need for vigorous checks and balances on every head of government, to check their perks and the extent of the cocoon that surrounds them. The necessity for periodic endorsement by the electorate with the risk of defeat used to be one of democracy's most salutary experiences. Sadly, the beneficial effect of campaigning, with its levelling down, bringing the leader nearer to the life of the normal citizen, has not lasted. The trappings of power, particularly personal security, now stay with a head of government during an election, and this has meant they are shielded from normal electioneering. Ticket-only meetings stacked with party activists mean that old-style husting meetings have gone. John Major, as Prime Minister, mounting his 'soap box' to campaign in the 1992 general election already seems a distant memory.

I conclude by quoting Lord Acton's famous dictum, 'All power tends to corrupt and absolute power corrupts absolutely.' But it needs to be remembered that Acton preceded that dictum with a plea to judge those who hold power by a higher standard than those who do not: 'I cannot accept your canon that we are to judge Pope and King unlike other men, with a favourable presumption that they did no wrong. If there is any presumption it is the other way against the holders of power.'

# 12

# A timetable for reform

We have lived through, over the last sixteen years, an unprecedented period of sleaze and corruption in Westminster politics. Cash for votes in the House of Commons in the 1990s and the more recent involvement of peers in the House of Lords, the cash-for-honours scandal, general abuse of prime ministerial patronage in the Lords, and to cap it all public outrage over the system of MPs' allowances and pensions. This culminating crisis shows every sign of diminishing the standing of politics, not just politicians. Already the politicians are trying to control and manipulate a new reform agenda to ensure that their party will gain at the expense of another.

We must be careful how we proceed. The British National Party now has two seats in the European Parliament and UKIP's stance in the 2009 European election was not just to come out of the EU but to highlight immigration into the UK and put an EU label on it. This demonstrates that there are still ugly moods that can be exploited in the British electorate. In March 2009 John Cruddas, the Labour MP for Dagenham, one of the voices who deserves and will in my view achieve far greater influence, argued in the *Guardian* for proportional representation 'not as a preserve of the liberal metropolitan intelligentsia but as a core mechanism with which to combat a sense of working-class alienation'. He said, 'People are worried and unless they live in one of the fifty "super-marginal" seats, then under the first-past-the-post system it doesn't really matter who they vote for.' This exclusion from the democratic process is a debilitating aspect of the current political malaise. Cruddas has done much to focus concern on the rise of the BNP. It will not be defeated by throwing eggs at its leaders; that only encourages them. Yet many decent people feel that proportional representation will bring on the BNP, and discussion of this topic often turns to Germany and proportional representation helping to bring about the Third Reich.

I believe there are many mistaken interpretations of what happened at that time. The world depression which had begun in 1929 in the United States hit Germany very hard, particularly in 1931. In the harsh economic climate of the time, Hitler saw the political opportunities that reparation payments, foolishly still insisted upon by the Allies, gave him, and he moved with consummate skill to exploit them. Alan Bullock, in a biography of Hitler, wrote, 'In 1930 the mood of a large section of the German nation was one of resentment. Hitler, with an almost inexhaustible fund of resentment in his own character to draw from, offered them a series of objects on which to lavish all the blame for their misfortunes.' The list was a long one, mainly focused on the Allies (especially the French), reparations, the Weimar Republic, financial speculators, big business, communists and above all Jews. Hatred of the Treaty of Versailles was widespread in Germany and under its terms three million Germans still lived in Poland, Czechoslovakia and Austria while Austria could not unite with Germany.

Hitler calculated that his best route to power lay in keeping the country's ageing and infirm President, Paul von Hindenburg, in office, while he could exploit the bad constitution, which gave Hindenburg considerable power, to use the armed forces to clamp down on opposition and to suspend the constitution itself. Hitler's strategy was to make use of Hindenburg's power over the German army to keep it onside during a legal handover of power from the President to himself.

By late 1932 Hindenburg was coming under pressure from industrialists and bankers to let Hitler become Chancellor. On Monday 30 January 1933 he asked Hitler to form a government. Again, with calculating shrewdness, Hitler put only three Nazi Party members into the government. Then the Reichstag was dissolved and elections were called. Now the Nazi stormtroopers came out on the streets with a vengeance. The Communists split the Social Democratic vote and the Nazi Party won the election with 43.9 per cent of the votes, giving them a bare majority in the Reichstag. The subsequent proscription of the Communist deputies allowed an enabling law which gave Hitler unbridled power to be passed by the necessary two-thirds majority.

Before the vote on 21 March the Nazis and the army were reconciled at a dramatic formal ceremony in the Potsdam Garrison Church to mark the opening of the Reichstag session. The visibly ageing President Hindenburg and the young Chancellor walked down the aisle together. Hitler in his speech lauded the Field Marshal President, then walked over and, bending low, grasped the old man's hand. In this gesture Hitler dramatised the reality: he had secured the army, was legally the head of government and on course to hold absolute power.

On 21 June 1934 a crisis developed and Hitler went to see Hindenburg, now virtually senile and very sick. He was told that the President was about to declare martial law and hand power to the army unless something was done to curb the power of the two million-strong SA, the Nazis' stormtroopers. Hitler and Hermann Goering, fearing that even on his sickbed Hindenburg might declare martial law, moved quickly. On the night of 29 June they arrested and killed Ernst Röhm, the leader of the SA, and many others. Hindenburg, in as much as he knew what was happening, and above all his supporters in the military, were delighted.

Hindenburg died on 2 August and it was announced immediately that the offices of President and Chancellor would be merged and that Hitler would become head of state as well as supreme commander of the armed forces of the Reich. That same day the officers and men of the German army took the oath of allegiance, not to the state or the constitution but to the Führer of the German Reich and People, Adolf Hitler. In a plebiscite on 19 August, the German people endorsed the change to Führer and Reich Chancellor by an overwhelming majority – 89.93 per cent of the 95.7 per cent of the electoral roll who voted, or 86.06 per cent of the entire electorate. This was helped by publication of President Hindenburg's Political Testament, endorsing Hitler but without his personal reference where he stated his wish for the restoration of the monarchy. Hitler waited a long time – until 4 February 1938. Then at the last Cabinet meeting of the Third Reich, he assumed Blomberg's title and office as commander in chief of the armed forces in addition to his own title of supreme commander and got rid of the post of War Minister. The once all-powerful German army was now totally subjugated to the will of Hitler in form as well as substance. Slowly, relentlessly, once Hindenburg had died, Hitler began to dismantle Cabinet government and it ceased to exist after the successful occupation of the Sudetenland in October 1938.

After the World War a new German constitution and voting system were heavily influenced by the British. We would never, with all that history so recently in our memory, have advocated a constitution, with a proportional system of voting, a fixed term parliament, a constitutional court and federal decentralised government, without the most careful thought. The fact it has worked so well in Germany is something we in the UK should reflect on very deeply. Proportional representation could well be one of the mechanisms carefully introduced to check the growth of extremism. Trying to strangle extremism by excluding or ignoring it rarely works: its appeal has to be exposed to democratic scrutiny, not allowed to fester.

A YouGov poll showed that in the 2009 European election 57 per cent were influenced by Britain's relationship with the EU and 51 per cent by the economy, jobs and their standard of living. Forty per cent named the conduct of MPs and 35 per cent said immigration. All other issues were much lower on the scale of influence: 14 per cent mentioned the environment, 12 per cent the NHS, 12 per cent crime and 7 per cent education. It is very clear from this that the political elite can no longer sensibly scoff at public anxieties over the EU and immigration, for along with the economy they are core concerns. The far right nostrums, once exposed, will be no match for the more balanced solutions But will a new House of Commons mobilise Conservative and dissident Labour votes to address growing public concern over the European Union?

Over forty-three years within Parliament I have watched many metamorphose from backbencher to powerful Cabinet ministers and the emergence of seven Prime Ministers. I have become convinced that character and personality are the essential elements underpinning successful leadership. That is why I have written about the deeper questions of leadership and the corrupting influence of power, whether in politics or business. True reform is about changing attitudes and values, and ensuring wiser decisions. Mechanisms can make changes in these areas easier to achieve but they are a means to an end, not an end in themselves. Westminster is proud of the fact that as a nation we have not needed a written constitution and that our system of government has grown up naturally with public support. Our concept of parliamentary democracy has been underwritten by the assumption that we have Cabinet government, which has been tested and which served the country well in two World Wars. Yet Westminster over the last twenty-five years has allowed for a steady erosion of the power of the Cabinet and an accretion of power to Prime Ministers in No. 10. This reached its apotheosis from 1997 to 2007, when we saw the virtual abolition of Cabinet government as we knew it since 1916. Furthermore, there was an imposition of a double presidency, with power shared by private agreement between Tony Blair and Gordon Brown, and an unprecedented politicisation of the Civil Service. This continued with a lesser form of presidential government under Gordon Brown. At no stage have these new procedures been supported by parliamentary authority, legislation or public support.

It is essential now to understand that this whole system has failed and the next Prime Minister must take office pledging to restore the Cabinet as the main decision-making body. To buttress such a pledge we need to legislate firstly that no Prime Minister in future should hold office whether for continuous or broken service for longer than eight years. Secondly, there should be a fixed term for the Westminster Parliament for four years with safeguards to ensure this cannot be broken under anything other than exceptional circumstances, provisions which successfully operate in Germany. There is no reason to believe that these two reforms could not be agreed between the parties and enacted quickly at the start of a new parliament, whether one party had an outright majority or not.

It is also of critical importance to ensure that constitutional legislation, as judged to be so by the Speaker of the House of Commons, can only be introduced following the prior endorsement of a referendum. We already live under all parties' manifesto commitments to a referendum before any constitutional change can be made in Northern Ireland and before the United Kingdom could adopt the euro. The reason for not relying on manifesto commitments is that twice on constitutional issues the Blair–Brown government reneged and did not carry out its manifesto commitment: for a referendum on electoral reform and a referendum on the EU constitution, which was introduced under another name in the Lisbon Treaty.

The cumulative effect of the EU Treaties and the European Convention on Human Rights becoming justiciable in the UK has meant we have developed a written constitution. Commitments undertaken in the EU under international treaty are binding in international law on successor governments and we are finding that intergovernmental promises made about such legislation are not always fulfilled and the interpretation of the wording of such treaties not always upheld because of the judgements from the European Court of Justice. Recently a new UK Supreme Court has been established. That court is already involved in constitutional issues but should be given in relation to EU legislation the powers of a constitutional court similar to that which exists in Germany. A Conservative manifesto commitment on this, even if they did not have an overall majority, might well be supported by a significant number of Labour MPs.

It has been the boast of many inside Westminster that it is the mother of parliaments and the envy of the world. That has become a sick joke. The House of Commons needs root and branch reform. Some of that reform must come from the political parties themselves. The conduct of intra-party elections cannot be imposed by legislation, nor can a decision to move towards primaries in the selection of candidates and deselection procedures; such an acutely sensitive issue must be left to the good sense of party members. Yet it is right that there should be parliamentary legislation to reduce the number of MPs. The Conservatives are proposing to bring it down to 600; I would be bolder than this and fix the total at 400. Whatever figure is arrived at, it will need to be done quickly since it will take time to draw up new boundaries through the independent Boundary Commission. Only when that has been done does it make sense to have a referendum on whether or not we should continue with the first-past-the-post system of electing MPs. Such a referendum should take place after the third year of the next parliament, which would allow for a general election within the fourth year of the Parliament on a new system or the old one, as chosen by the electorate. The argument that you can rush in with a referendum on proportional representation to coincide with the next election, as Labour's Home

Secretary suggested in 2009, is manipulative politics. It should be opposed by the Electoral Commission and the Lords. These issues cannot be rushed. They have to be considered as a whole and timetabled very carefully. It is easy for precipitate changes to distort further, not strengthen, our existing democracy.

We have seen with the reform of the House of Lords how easy it is to botch the process. Some want to give further Lords reform a low priority but I believe it cannot continue in its present deeply unsatisfactory state. The House of Lords should become a directly elected Senate. It must not, however, become a staging post to membership of the House of Commons. Senators should not be eligible under the age of forty-five and they should not be able to sit beyond the age of seventy-five. If the political parties cannot agree to have a 100 per cent elected senate and stick to their last vote for 80 per cent elected and 20 per cent appointed, those 20 per cent who are appointed should become crossbenchers. There is much to be said for reconsidering the concept discussed a hundred years ago of having these crossbench senators speaking but not normally voting. They could vote in committees but not the floor of the senate except when the Speaker judges the issue suitable for a free vote of the senate as a whole. Senators should be elected under proportional representation but the closed list system used for the European elections would not be acceptable. The voting system would have to allow people to choose on the voting paper for individual members of different parties and also for independents. That points to using the single transferable vote system, which is already used in the United Kingdom for local government elections in Northern Ireland and Scotland, for European parliamentary elections in Northern Ireland and in choosing the Northern Ireland Assembly. In my view this is the next logical step towards proportional representation. If the next parliament has no overall majority then a referendum on proportional representation for the House of Commons is a legitimate demand for Liberal Democrat MPs to make on a Conservative minority government early in the fourth year although it is probable that the Conservatives would argue against such a change in a referendum. As to a Labour minority government they may well concede proportional representation and a referendum would be supported by them and so it would not be so divisive to hold it earlier and they would not be cutting the number of MPs requiring a Boundary Commission. But some Labour MPs are strongly opposed to proportional representation, preferring the Alternative Vote which is not guaranteed to produce a fair result and is not therefore proportional representation. The mathematics of fair voting is not easily understood but an excellent summary appeared in *The Week* on 20 June 2009:

> There are many ways of achieving proportional representation, and they're all complicated – not for the individual voter (he just turns up and places his crosses as instructed), but for anyone wanting to grasp how the votes are aggregated. The Single Transferable Vote system, the purists' favourite, is a case in point. It's damn hard to explain, but here goes.
>
> Let's assume, first of all, that we have a constituency in which three candidates are to be returned. Under STV, each will need to secure 25% of the vote to get elected. Turn now to the voters: when they fill out their ballots, they can put an X against as many candidates as they like, but in doing so must indicate their order of preference – 1,2,3 and so on. Any candidate who gets 25% of the first preference votes – let's say just one of them, for the sake of argument – is immediately elected. At this point all the votes he receives above the crucial 25% are 'transferred' – meaning that whichever candidates are ranked second on those surplus ballots can now add these votes to their first preference total. Meanwhile the same process is at work from the bottom up: if your first choice gets the fewest votes, your ballot is added to the pile of your second-choice candidate. And so it goes until there are three who score 25%.

The ever growing gulf between Westminster and the rest of the country must also be addressed, for it is a source of growing discontent and indeed anger. For example, Parliament intervenes or legislates for tax, regulation and procedures which affect the boards of public companies with independent directors. Parliament tries to ensure that key decision makers, such as chairmen and chief executives, are controlled and curbed in how they conduct their business. These light-touch or heavy-handed regulations and procedures have been exposed during the banking crisis to be woefully insufficient. Yet Parliament's authority to criticise the bonus culture of banks has been savagely reduced by the revelations of its conduct in relation to its own members' pay, allowances and expenses.

Parliament regulates and restricts national pension provision and there is an increasing economic necessity to peg back some of the inflation-proof pensions in the public sector. Yet pension provision for MPs and Prime Ministers has few precedents in its generosity. This will have to be brought into line with the rest of the country with legislation as soon as possible. MPs insist on compulsory retirement for key decision makers in many walks of life, yet they refuse to impose a retirement limit on themselves. These and many other mismatches between the way MPs, ministers and Prime Ministers live their lives in comparison with others must be changed if trust between Parliament and the people is to be restored.

Over the last three general elections the number of MPs from parties other than Conservative and Labour has increased steadily, particularly for the Liberal Democrats. It is now obvious that after the next general election, whichever party or parties form the government will face unparalleled problems in dealing with our economy. There will be very painful decisions that will have to be taken urgently. We have experienced the drift of governments formed without working majorities in difficult economic circumstances before, most recently in 1964–66 and 1974–79, and many of the problems that faced those governments are chronicled in this book. If a small party is to join in some way with a large party and take some responsibility for decisions which may well be unpopular in the short term, they have to be assured that the Prime Minister, who will inevitably come from the large party, cannot at a time convenient to themselves ask the Queen for a dissolution and call a second election which could disadvantage the small party. The case for a fixed term stands on its merits in general. In the particular situation that realistically we might well face, of a hung Parliament at the next general election, we, the people, must insist that no such government is formed without immediate legislation for a minimum term of four years.

In this situation it is necessary to protect the small parties from an early dissolution of Parliament being granted by the Queen at the request of the Prime Minister. It should be stipulated in this legislation that no dissolution can occur within four years, unless sufficient number of MPs who voted for the last Queen's Speech to sustain a minority government or coalition vote for a specific motion to ask the Monarch to grant a dissolution of that Parliament.

There are former members of the SDP who today play a prominent part in almost all of the political parties represented in the House of Commons. There are a few million former SDP voters who will be voting at the next election. They have long wanted to break the mould of British politics. We have had commissions and select committees producing a forest of reports on political reform. Normally implementation would depend on the policies of the parties at the next election. This will happen if either the Conservatives or Labour have an overall majority.

In my experience voters, having watched the downturn in British politics over the last two decades, are ready to support a balanced substantive reform programme such as I have suggested. There is a widespread feeling in the country that we cannot continue with the status quo in Westminster. But people know, having watched the decline in political coherence, that reform has to be measured, that there is no quick fix in any of these issues and that they all hang together and the more controversial of them must be underpinned by referenda.

The vital question is how can this be achieved. Much depends on how the Liberal Democrat leaders, Nick Clegg and his deputy, Vincent Cable, conduct themselves over the next few months. They have first to convince the electorate that they are ready to take the tough decisions to ensure the UK's massive fiscal deficit is dealt with in a determined way and are ready to risk the unpopularity of supporting necessary public expenditure cuts and tax rises. Only after this will the electorate be ready to listen carefully to their views on a political reform package and become convinced that such reforms would be best introduced by a government of national unity. The definition of national unity would be a government where those MPs who supported Queen's Speeches over a four-year fixed term can claim to have the support of 50% of the voters. This allows for either a minority government supported by smaller parties or a coalition government. Polling evidence from the past suggests the electorate will support the Liberal Democrats, almost as much, if they believe they can hold the balance, as be the government of the country. As yet the electorate are not convinced that there will, or even should, be a government of national unity and in the opinion polls appear to prefer a Conservative majority government.

My political innings is coming to an end. I believe that an effective government of national unity in 2010 is in the national interest. But that has not yet emerged as a credible alternative. I hope it will. All I know is that with my eyes open I have chosen the least trodden path.

> Two roads diverged in a wood, and I –
> I took the one less travelled by,
> And that has made all the difference.
>                 Robert Frost*

---

\* Quoted from 'The Road Not Taken', *Seven Ages, Poetry for a Lifetime* chosen by David Owen, initially published by Michael Joseph and Penguin. Now a Gardners print on demand book, £15, with proceeds continuing to go to the Hospital for Sick Children at Great Ormond Street, London. *The Poetry of Robert Frost, Henry Holt & Co,* New York, OWL Book edition 1979.

# Index